Crillon Tours s.a.
Bolivia

Titicaca Hydrofoils

INCA UTAMA HOTEL & SPA
★★★★★

LA POSADA DEL INCA
SUN ISLAND

ANDEAN ROOTS
CULTURAL COMPLEX

BOLIVIA: Crillon Tours P. O. Box 4785 • Av. Camacho No. 1223 • E-mail: titicaca@wara.bolnet.bo
• Phone 374566/7 - 350363 • Fax (591-2) 391039 • La Paz
• Inca Utama Hotel en Huatajata • Phone/Fax: 591-811-5050

USA: 1450 South Bayshore Dr. Suite 815, Miami, Fl. 33131 • Toll Free 1888 TITICACA
• E-mail:darius@titicaca.com • Internet Web Site: http://www.titicaca.com
• Phones (305) 358-5353 • Fax (305) 372-0054

Bolivia Handbook

South American Handbook, the longest running
guidebook in the English language, has provided
generations of travellers with comprehensive coverage
of the entire continent. This Handbook is in
Footprint's series of new guides to the individual
countries of Latin America. The first to be published
are Handbooks to Peru, Chile, Ecuador & Galápagos
and Bolivia. These will be followed by guides to Brazil,
Colombia, Argentina, Venezuela and Cuba.

Bolivia
Handbook

Alan Murphy

Latin America series editor: Ben Box

Footprint Handbooks

Clear as crystal, motionless as a sheet of glass, green
as the edge of an iceberg, it stretched in front of us
under its leafy archway, every stroke of our paddles
sending a thousand ripples across its shining surface.
It was a fitting avenue to a land of wonders.

Sir Arthur Conan Doyle, *The Lost World*

Footprint Handbooks

®

6 Riverside Court, Lower Bristol Road
Bath BA2 3DZ England
T 01225 469141 F 01225 469461
E mail handbooks@footprint.cix.co.uk

ISBN 1 900949 09 1 ISSN 1368-4264
CIP DATA: A catalogue record for this book is
available from the British Library

In North America, published by

PASSPORT BOOKS
NTC/Contemporary Publishing Company

4255 West Touhy Avenue, Lincolnwood
(Chicago), Illinois 60646-1975, USA
T 847 679 5500 F 847 679 24941
E mail NTCPUB2@AOL.COM

ISBN 0-8442-4923-8
Library of Congress Catalog Card
Number: 97-68360
Passport Books and colophon are registered
trademarks of NTC Publishing group

©Footprint Handbooks Limited
1st Edition
October 1997

® Footprint Handbooks and the Footprint mark
are a trademark of Footprint Handbooks Ltd

**Every effort has been made to ensure that
the facts in this Handbook are accurate.
However travellers should still obtain
advice from consulates, airlines etc about
current travel and visa requirements and
conditions before travelling. The editors
and publishers cannot accept responsibilty
for any loss, injury or inconvenience,
however caused.**

**Maps - the black and white text maps are
not intended to have any political
significance.**

Cover design by Newell and Sorrell;
photography by South American Pictures and
Robert Harding Picture Library

Production: Design by Mytton Williams;
Secretarial assistance Rhoda Williams;
Typesetting by Jo Morgan and Ann Griffiths;
Maps by Sebastian Ballard, Kevin Feeney and
Aldous George; Proofread by Rod Gray.

Printed and bound in Great Britain by
Clays Ltd., Bungay, Suffolk

Contents

We try as hard as we can to make each Footprint Handbook as up-to-date and accurate as possible but, of course, things always change. Many people write to us with new information, amendments or simply comments. Please do get in touch. In return we will send you details of our special guidebook offer. See page 353 for more information

The editors

Ben Box

A doctorate in medieval Spanish and Portugese studies provided very few job prospects for Ben Box, but a fascination for all things Latin. While studying for his degree, Ben travelled extensively in Spain and Portugal. He turned his attention to contemporary Iberian and Latin American affairs in 1980, beginning a career as a freelance writer at that time. He contributed regularly to national newspapers and learned tomes, and after increasing involvement with the *South American Handbook*, became its editor in 1989. Although he has travelled from the US/Mexico border to southern Chile (including a very memorable trip to Bolivia with James Dawson, publisher of Footprint Handbooks) and in the Caribbean, Ben recognises that there are always more places to explore. He also edits jointly the *Mexico and Central American Handbook* and the *Caribbean Islands Handbook* with Sarah Cameron and is series editor of Footprint Handbook's South American series. To seek diversion from a household immersed in Latin America, he plays village cricket in summer and cycles the lanes of Suffolk.

Alan Murphy

In true Butch and Sundance style, Alan Murphy abandoned his freeloading playboy lifestyle in Scotland and escaped to the relative obscurity of Bolivia. There, on the tranquil shores of Lake Titicaca, he settled down with his own Etta Place to breed guinea pigs for the discerning Bolivian palate.

But the bright lights of the big city beckoned and, after a brief but near-fatal stint as a professional llama wrestler in Potosí, he set off for La Paz. Together with 'Etta', he taught English, worked with orphans and street children and, in between times, helped establish a local English newspaper.

Suddenly, it all ended and Alan disappeared. Several unsubstantiated reports of his whereabouts circulated, one of which had him performing the role of a condor on the streets of Oruro during Carnival.

Many months later, he turned up in London, where fate played her propitious hand and introduced him to the Editor of the famous *South American Handbook*. The rest, as they say, is history. Now Alan has the opportunity to share his deep love and knowledge of Bolivia and its people with the adventurous traveller.

The team

Editorial team

For substantial contributions to the text the Editor would like to thank:

Yossi Brain, a climbing guide in La Paz and regional correspondent for the *South American Handbook*. Yossi researched and wrote the adventure tourism section, as well as all the treks covered in the La Paz and North of La Paz sections. Yossi also researched the updates on La Paz, Sorata, the Cordillera Apolobamba, Oruro, Potosí, Uyuni and the Salar de Uyuni and Lagunas Colorada and Verde, as well as providing general information on visas, bus and rail travel and many maps.

Geoffrey Groesbeck Thanks also to Geoffrey Groesbeck who lives in the USA but spends much of his time travelling and working in Bolivia and contributes to several publications on the subject. He researched and wrote the sections on national parks, Amboró and tours from Rurrenabaque and researched and updated Rurrenabaque, Cobija, Tarija and San José de Chiquitos as well as providing several maps.

Specialist contributors

Peter Pollard for geology and landscape; Nigel Dunstone (University of Durham) for flora and fauna; Dr Valerie Fraser (University of Essex) for painting and sculpture; Sarah Cameron for the economy; Gavin Clark for literature; Keith Richards (University of Leeds) for cinema; Mark Eckstein for responsible tourism; Dr David Snashall for health; Richard Robinson for world wide radio; Ashley Rawlings for motorcycling; Hallam Murray for cycling; Lucy Davies and Mo Fini (Tumi) for arts and crafts; Dan Buck for information on Che Guevara and Butch Cassidy and the Sundance Kid.

Acknowledgements

Much additional help has been received during the preparation of this edition. All contributions have been tremendously helpful and are duly acknowledged on page 329.

Section 1

Bolivia

JUST OVER A CENTURY AGO a diplomatic crisis was brewing in La Paz over a glass of chicha. The new British ambassador to Bolivia had made the mistake of sneering at this local drink when served it by the incumbent dictator. As a punishment, he was forced to drink a barrelful of chocolate and be led through the streets of the capital strapped to a donkey. When news reached London, Queen Victoria was not amused. She demanded a map of South America, drew a cross through the country and declared, "Bolivia does not exist!"

Relations between the two countries have improved since then. But for the majority of foreign tourists, Bolivia might as well not exist. It remains one of the least known of all South American countries – and one of the least visited.

Those who do know about Bolivia will tell you that this land-locked country in the heart of the continent is a place of natural highs. It boasts the world's highest capital city, the highest navigable lake, the highest ski-run, the highest golf course and the highest number of military coups during its turbulent post-independence history – more than your average Mexican has had hot dinners.

On arrival at La Paz's airport, yet another high will spring to mind. This is the world's highest commercial airport – at 4,000m above sea level. The pilot has to ascend to land. Well, nearly. The sight of Bolivia's capital 500m below at the bottom of a deep canyon will take your breath away – literally – for at this altitude breathing can be a problem.

Exploring the capital is an adventure in itself. Aymara women in traditional bowler hats and brightly-coloured voluminous skirts will sell you absolutely everything you could possibly need at one of the myriad markets – from a pair of cheap Levi jeans to a dried llama foetus. These grotesque objects can be found in the Witches' Market; great piles of them, like a scene from the latest David Cronenberg movie. The foetuses are burned and used along with incense, bits of wool, grease and coca leaves in white magic ceremonies and to rid houses of evil spirits.

If you soon get the feeling that La Paz is no ordinary city, a trip into the hinterland will lead to the conclusion that Bolivia is like no other country. Less than two hours away you can ski at 5,000m. Only 70 km to the north you can go sailing at almost 4,000m on the sapphire waters of Lake Titicaca. Four hours northeast is the original Garden of Eden – or so the local people believe. In the southwest of the country you can drive 200 km across the world's largest salt lake then through a surreal Salvador Dalí landscape to a bright red lake filled with flamingoes.

If all this sounds just a bit too bizarre then remember that part of Bolivia was the inspiration for Conan Doyle's Lost World. Here, in the Amazonian lowlands, the romantic image of the jungle found on the glossy pages of National Geographic is alive and well. A vast, unexplored green carpet stretches east from the Andes and, though you probably won't find any dinosaurs roaming around, you could easily discover a new species or two. People eulogise a place like Costa Rica, which has nine life zones, but that's kid's stuff. Bolivia has no fewer than thirteen. It has been estimated that parts of tropical Bolivia contain more species of insect, bird, flora and fauna per hectare than anywhere else on earth.

A final word about those dinosaurs. Though none have actually been spotted, their tracks have been discovered. But then, Bolivia is such a weird and unexpected place that seeing a prehistoric creature sitting on a bus beside you would probably come as no surprise.

Alan Murphy

Where to go

Bolivia's major attraction for tourists is probably its wild natural beauty. Much of the country lies off the beaten track, a vast wilderness waiting to be explored and appreciated. This isolation, of course, brings attendant problems. Many parts of the country are remote and can be reached only with a lot of time and effort.

The trouble is Bolivia's road network – or lack of one. Only 4% of the nation's roads are paved and in many of those cases the term can be used loosely. Furthermore, a mere 20% of roads can be used all year round. The rest are often impassable in the rainy season due to landslides or being washed away.

The only roads that will not present any problems all year round are the ones heading north from La Paz to Lake Titicaca, west to Tiahuanaco, south to Oruro, the new lowland route from La Paz to Cochabamba and the stretch of road between Potosí and Sucre. Other than those routes, travelling can be difficult during the November-March wet season, especially in the tropical lowlands. During the rest of the year, you can pretty much go wherever you want, given enough time, patience and stamina.

The only real alternative to road travel is flying. Rail travel in Bolivia is in a fairly perilous state and the future of the rail network is uncertain as it is currently in the throes of privatization, or capitalization as the Bolivian government euphemistically calls it. The only reliable rail route in the country is the one east from Santa Cruz to the Brazilian border at Puerto Quijarro.

Flying, though is a relatively cheap and efficient way to see the country. Two companies, Lloyd Aéreo Boliviano and Aero Sur, are the main airlines and both offer a fairly reliable service with not much to choose between them. They fly to all the main cities and also to many of the smaller lowland towns. For more details, see under the relevant destination in the main text. Flying is also a great way to appreciate the unique geography of this amazing country. A flight from the lowlands over the Andes to La Paz is an unforgettable experience.

PLACES TO VISIT

As you can probably gather, seeing a lot of Bolivia by bus in the space of a few weeks is a forlorn hope. If you do have limited time, then you really will need to fly in order to see more than the capital and its immediate surroundings. In saying that, however, there is enough to see and do within a few hours' drive from La Paz to satisfy even the hungriest tourist appetites.

AROUND LA PAZ

The capital is a fairly small and manageable city and easy to explore on foot in a couple of days. There are several worthwhile museums to visit and the warren of streets running west uphill off the Prado – the city's main thoroughfare – lead you into a fascinating and completely alien world.

Several interesting trips can be made from the capital, including the ruins of the great pre-Incan city of Tiahuanaco. Further north takes you to the shores of Lake Titicaca. From the attractive little town of Copacabana you can visit the beautiful Isla del Sol (Island of the Sun), site of the Inca creation legend. Three hours away on a spectacular and terrifying road is Coroico, a sub-tropical idyll in the Yungas and the perfect place to escape the Andean chill. Four hours away is the mountain paradise of Sorata. La Paz is also the jumping-off point for some of Bolivia's best treks, taking you over the cordillera and down to the warm Yungas valleys.

SOUTH OF LA PAZ

Spending more than a few weeks in the country will give you to time to visit the Southern Altiplano, one of the most remote corners of Bolivia and also one of the most fascinating. Potosí is probably the most interesting of all Bolivia's cities and a visit to its former silver mines is a must. Nearby is the country's official capital, Sucre, a real gem of colonial architecture. Southwest from Potosí is Uyuni, the starting point for a trip to the Salar de Uyuni, a vast, blinding-white salt lake which really should not be missed. From Uyuni you can also cross into neighbouring Chile. A week would allow just enough time to appreciate Potosí and then take a trip to the Salar, while a long weekend would allow time to visit Sucre and its environs.

For those with more time, there are many other attractions in the south to suit all tastes. You could visit the vineyards of Tarija, the graveyards of dinosaurs and the graves of Wild West outlaws, Butch Cassidy and The Sundance Kid. You could easily spend a week just exploring the many weaving villages around Sucre and Potosí. Climbers have the added attractions of Sajama National Park, which includes Bolivia's highest peak, and the wildly remote Cordillera Quimsa Cruz, just to the south of La Paz (see **Adventure tourism** below).

EAST OF LA PAZ

This part of Bolivia is probably the least visited, except by those heading east to Brazil. Cochabamba, 7 hours by bus east of La Paz, offers a pleasant respite from the cold Altiplano nights and hot, humid lowland days. Further east (around 10 hours by bus) the relatively prosperous city of Santa Cruz serves as a base for one of Bolivia's many beautiful national parks – and perhaps its finest – Amboró, or a tour of the incredibly beautiful Jesuit mission towns to the northeast. You would need a week at the very least to do justice to both of these. Further east, on the border with Brazil, the Bolivian Pantanal is now opening up to tourism and offers great wildlife-watching, as does the stunning but difficult to reach Noell Kempff Mercado National Park further north. Both these would require at least another 2 weeks to visit.

Santa Cruz also serves as an alternative point of entry to Bolivia's Amazon Basin via the city of Trinidad, capital of the Beni department and reachable by a good road (in the dry season) or by air from Santa Cruz.

THE AMAZON BASIN

Those visiting Bolivia during the dry season – April to October – and with at least 3 weeks to spare, would be strongly advised not to miss a trip to Rurrenabaque, from where you can take a jungle or pampas tour and experience this country's amazing diversity of wildlife.

Rurrenabaque is a gruelling 18-hour bus journey from La Paz, or a short flight. Those braving the bus trip can break the journey at Coroico in the Yungas.

The more adventurous travellers for whom time is not an issue could venture further north to Riberalta and Guayaramerín on the Brazilian border. This is a part of Bolivia which sees virtually no tourism and is therefore almost completely lacking any infrastructure.

ADVENTURE TOURISM

Adventure tourism in Bolivia may be at a relatively primitive stage of development, but the potential for eager thrill-seekers is limitless. Not for nothing is Bolivia known as the Tibet of South America. It certainly matches anything the Himalayas have to offer in the way of climbing and trekking and has the added benefit of not appearing like Piccadilly Circus on a hot summer weekend. Those prepared to rough it a bit will pretty much have the place to themselves, for much of Bolivia remains pioneer country.

MOUNTAINEERING

Bolivia has getting on for 1,000 peaks over 5,000m (12 at or above 6,000m) in four cordilleras: the Real (the main area for mountaineering), Apolobamba to the northwest, Quimza Cruz to the southeast and the volcanic Occidental near the border with Chile.

The Bolivian climbing season runs from May to September. The weather June-August is better and more stable than in any other major mountaineering area in the world. This is just as well as there is no rescue service in the country.

Access is easy from the flat Altiplano, but public transport is not always possible. Proper technical equipment, experience and/or a competent guide are essential to cross glaciers and climb snow and ice safely. A number of summits are achievable by acclimatized beginners with a competent guide and the correct high altitude climbing equipment.

Most equipment is available for hire in La Paz but if your feet are smaller than size 38 or larger than 44 it could be difficult or impossible to hire plastic boots.

All mountaineering agencies have some equipment for hire, though Colibrí has the biggest selection. Remember to take 100% ultraviolet-proof glacier glasses as snowblindness is a real danger and counts as a permanent eye injury.

If you are interested in climbing, check out possibilities for Pequeño Alpamayo 5,370m (3 days), Huayna Potosí 6,088m (2 days), Illimani 6,439m (4 days) and Bolivia's highest mountain, Sajama 6,542m (4-5 days). Other peaks of 6,000m or over: Ancohuma 6,427m, Illampu 6,368m, Chearoco 6,104m, Chachacomani 6,000m.

NB None of these climbs should be attempted without first spending at least a week at the height of La Paz or equivalent owing to the danger of potentially fatal altitude sickness.

Huayna Potosí
This is the most popular peak, normally climbed in 2 days, including one night camped on a glacier at 5,600m. Climbing Huayna Potosí requires climbing experience for ice and crevasses on the way to the top. However, bad weather, apart from mist, is rare.

To get to the start of the normal route take transport to the Zongo Pass (see page 111). The Refugio Huayna Potosí organizes regular transport plus guides and porters: contact Dr Hugo Berrios (fluent English and French) at *Hotel Continental*, Calle Illampu 626, T 323584/795936, Casilla 731, La Paz. The luxury refuge has bedrooms, a kitchen, electric light, food and water and sleeps ten; it costs US$10 per night, food is extra. Do not camp in the Zongo Pass area as there is a major theft problem.

Illimani
This beautiful five-peaked mountain overlooks La Paz and the normal route is not technically challenging, but difficult because of the altitude. Public transport is difficult and irregular to *Estancia Una* (mules and porters available for US$6; Antonio Limachi is recommended) where most people start the 4-hour walk-in to

first camp at Puente Roto. The only reliable way to avoid paying the US$150 jeep fare (one way) is to get a bus going to Tres Ríos or further (see **Takesi trek** page 119), get off at Paso Pacuani and follow a disused mining road to Puente Roto in 4-6 hours (carry your kit – there are no mules or porters). Day 2 is spent moving up a rock ridge to high camp at Nido de Cóndores where there is no water; take extra fuel for snow melting. A 0300 start to day three should see you to the summit, down to Nido de Cóndores and on down to Puente Roto for running water. Day four is basically a walk back to where you find transport.

Condoriri
This is a group of thirteen mountains, 5,100-5,700m, including Pequeño Alpamayo, which is beautiful and not technically difficult. Non-climbers can go up to the Mirador for fantastic views of the surrounding peaks and Huayna Potosí. There is no public transport; take a jeep to Tuni dam (US$70 one way) and then it's a 3-hour walk-in to base camp (mules available).

There are alternatives, but we don't recommend them: one is to take public transport to Milluni (see **Zongo Valley** page 111) and then walk for 24 km to Tuni; another is to take a bus/truck/minibus heading north from La Paz (eg to Lake Titicaca, Huarina or Achacachi) to Patamanta (garage on the left) and then walk 20 km or more to Tuni. There's an established tent guarding system at base camp which costs from US$1 per tent per day.

Quimza Cruz
This very beautiful range of mountains is still considered the future of Bolivian mountaineering because it is difficult to reach and few people make the effort to get there. The northern part, the Araca, offers good rock climbing on peaks up to 5,300m; eg near Mocaya, 6 km after Viloco. The southern part offers easy ice climbs up to 5,700m. There are beautiful lakeside campsites and trekking possibilities, eg Viloco to Mina Caracoles in 2-3 days. It takes a day to get in and another to get out. The whole region is virtually unexplored,

Travel is not only moving from place to place. More than that, it is finding a haven for the spirit, nurturing the soul and learning anew.

Ortega y Gasset

Genesis de la Cultura Andina ®

Flotel Reina de Enin
Motorboat expeditions, Jungle Lodge

Tours for people who don't like tours

Fremen Tours
ANDES & AMAZONIA
SINCE 1985

LA PAZ
Pedro Salazar 537 (Plaza Avaroa).
Tel. (591.2) 416336. Fax (591.2) 417327

E-mail: **vtfremen@caoba.entelnet.bo**
Web: **http://www.andes-amazonia.com**

Offices in the main cities, including Cochabamba, Santa Cruz, Trinidad.

so you pretty much have to find your own way.

● **Accommodation** The only place to stay is in Araca at *Hacienda Tenería*, a Swiss-style chalet, US$5 per person, hot showers, sauna, spectacular views of Illimani, camping possible. The German owner, Hans Hesse, can take his jeep to Mocoya, from where it's a 4-hour hike to base camp for the climbs.

● **Transport** A jeep can do the drive in under 7 hours for about US$300 but make sure the driver knows where to go. One driver who does is Vitaliano Ramos (T La Paz 416013).

If you have a jeep, there are two routes. The best is to go to **Konani** (Km 149), 20 km north of Oruro on the road to La Paz (there's a garage here – check everything and fill up tank plus extra containers with petrol). Turn left, then take the **Quime** road to **Caxata** (55 km); 3 km after Caxata turn left to **Rodeo** which is 30 km further on. From here the road to **Viloco** (50 km) is very poor but spectacular, often passing the foot of glaciers. Some of the southern peaks can be reached in a day from the road. There are buses and trucks as far as Viloco, a poor mining village with no accommodation. From there, with luck, you can catch a truck to cover the last 15 km to **Araca**, but it is better from **Talla-pata**, a village 2 km away, where there is a small shop that sells gasoline and basic foodstuffs (bring anything else from La Paz). The driver will let you off at *Haci-enda Tenería*.

The other route is shorter but very difficult and there's no public transport. It's only 150 km but can take up to 3 days. Follow the road south past Valle del la Luna until **Tawapalca**. The road climbs steeply past **Cohoni** to Mina Uranai (4,200m) at the foot of Illimani, then de-scends again to cross Río La Paz (1,700m), then it climbs up to **Araca**. The road is very scenic but also prone to landslides. It was badly damaged by rains in 1996. It's cut deep into mountains slopes and crosses fast rivers.

For the **Western Cordillera** with the peaks of Sajama, Parinacota and Pom-erape, see page 186.

The **Cordillera Apolobamba**, the north-ern extension of the Cordillera Real, with many 5,000m-plus peaks, can be reached by public transport from La Paz, the main starting out points being Charazani and Pelechuco. See **North of La Paz**, page 158.

EQUIPMENT

The best selections in La Paz are *Condoriri*, Local 8, Galería Sagárnaga, Calle Sagár-naga 339 (T/F 319369) opposite *Hotel Alem*, open Monday to Friday 0930-1300, 1430-2000, Saturday 0930-1200. They also do an excellent repair service and rent equipment. *Andean Summits*, Calle Sagár-naga 189, T/F 317497, Casilla 6976, have a good selection of new camping and climbing gear. Best hire selection is at *Colibrí*, Calle Sagárnaga 309, T 371936, F 355043, Casilla 7456. The cheapest way to buy kit is from outgoing climbers. *Club Andino Boliviano* (see below) has a notice board where you can advertise your wares for sale. Also many adventure travel agen-cies, including those mentioned above, will buy second-hand kit. **NB** If you are offered builders' helmets instead of UIAA-approved climbing helmets, refuse them. They are not up to the job and don't have chin straps.

CLIMBING CLUBS

It's not worth getting involved unless you are going to be around for a few months. *Club Andino Boliviano*, Calle México 1638, La Paz, T/F 324682, the national moun-taineering club has a staffed office where some climbing information is available but the club is mainly into skiing and runs the Chacaltaya facilities.

Club de Excursionismo, Andinismo y Camping (CEAC to its friends), Calle Goi-tia 155, contact through *Condoriri* (ad-dress above), friendly, organizes regular climbing, hiking and camping trips, pro-duces a magazine about once a year.

GUIDES

Guides must be hired through a tour com-pany. *Club Andino Boliviano*, Calle México 1638, T 324682, Casilla 5879 (closed Saturday) can provide a list of guides. Dr Hugo Berrios (see above for contact) is an excellent guide, he is recommended for Huayna Potosí. *Ozono*, Edificio Labtec, planta baja, Avenida Ballivián y C14, Calacoto, La Paz, Casilla 5258, T 791786, F 722240, e-mail: bolivia@ozono.bo, Casilla 5258, British-Bolivian owned agency specializing in mountaineering, trekking, rock climbing and other types of adventure tourism, including skiing, can also organize radio cover. *Colibrí* (address above), specialize in climbing, with up-to-date information, trips arranged for all levels of experience and adventure tourism in all parts of Bolivia. They are very helpful, recommended and have a full range of equipment hire.

Colonial Tours, next to *Hostal Austria*, provide information and advice on routes and organize transport. Iván Blanco Alba, *Asociación de Guías de Montaña y Trekking*, Calle Chaco 1063, Casilla 1579, La Paz, T 350334, has been recommended. *Trek Bolivia*, Calle Sagárnaga 392, T/F 317106, organizes expeditions in the Cordillera as well as trips to Peru. Also recommended are Ricardo Albert at *Inca Travel*, Avenida Arce 2116, Edificio Santa Teresa; and Dr Juan Pablo Ando, Casilla 6210, T 783495, trained in Chamonix, for mountaineering, rock climbing, trekking and ecological tours.

In Europe the following have been recommended for group tours: *Aventura Ultimos*, Arzgruben weg 1, 8102 Mittenwald, Germany, and Dr Erich Galt, A-6020 Innsbruck, Amraser Strasse 110a, Austria.

The *Club de Excursionismo, Andinismo y Camping*, CEAC, helps people find the cheapest way to go climbing, trekking, etc; foreigners may join local groups, T 783795, Casilla 8365, La Paz, or ask at the University or for Catherina Ibáñez at *Plaza Tours*, Avenida 16 de Julio 1789, T 378322, F 343301 (she has an information service for CEAC). Each week there is a meeting and slide show. See also the list of La Paz Tour companies & travel agents on page 105.

TREKKING

Bolivia is endowed with numerous excellent treks, some of them on existing Inca roads. Most of the popular treks begin around La Paz and cross the Cordillera Real, finishing in the sub-tropical Yungas, but many other parts of the country also offer excellent possibilities. The intrepid hiker could find him/herself in glorious isolation for days on end with only the occasional llama for company, passing through tiny campesino villages, where the inhabitants may never have set eyes on a fleece jacket or pair of hiking boots.

The best known treks are covered under the relevant country section in the main text, with maps and detailed route descriptions. These are: **Choro** (see page 123); **Takesi** (see page 119); **Yunga Cruz** (see page 125); **Mapiri** (see page 153); **Camino de Oro** or Gold Diggers' Trail (see page 156); **Illampu Circuit** (see page 149); **Apolobamba** (see page 158).

SKIING

90 minutes by car from La Paz (36 km) is **Chacaltaya**, the highest ski run in the world at 5,345m and the first ski lift in South America, opened in 1940. Unfortunately there has been little development in the last 50 years. A 2-litre car engine welded to the floor of the hut pulls a frayed steel cable which skiers have to attach themselves to using a bent piece of metal, 2m of static cord and a piece of wood. This is as dangerous as it sounds. As the Warren Miller video "Endless Winter" commented, the only blue run in the world with a black ski lift. Basically, you sidle up to the cable, put one ski across the slope, the other straight up, place the hook over the cable and then pull it. The hook shoots off, at the same time you hold on with all your might, move the first ski so it is pointing uphill and at the same time get the piece of wood between your legs so you can pretend to sit on it.

Out of season the lift only goes if there are five or more people. Ski equipment is very limited and of poor quality. It's best to queue at once, or better still, take your own. A good tip is to share equipment since, at that altitude, you will need a long break between activities.

The second major problem with Chacaltaya is that the glacier is receding at 6-10m a year. If this continues there will be nothing left in 30 years. A sad state of affairs, especially when you remember that the first president of the Club Andino was killed in an avalanche at Chacaltaya in 1943.

However, you don't have to risk life, limb and clothing to make a trip to Chacaltaya worthwhile. It is a fantastic viewpoint from where it is possible to look down on La Paz, El Alto and Lago Titicaca and across to Huayna Potosí, Illimani and, on clear days, Sajama, Bolivia's highest peak. Laguna de Milluni, near Chacaltaya, is a beautiful lake to visit, but do not drink its heavily contaminated water. A vehicle will get you to the car park in 1½ hours from central La Paz leaving only 45m of ascent for you to claim you have climbed a 5,000m + peak.

The ski season is February-May depending on snow coverage. Equipment hire costs US$10. When there is a lot of snow giving the best conditions the road becomes impassable. There are plans to asphalt it, but don't hold your breath. The best time for views is May to September.

The *Club Andino*, Calle México 1638, T/F 324682, runs the refuge (entrance US$2 if you don't go with their bus) which serves drinks and snacks (check prices before ordering). The Club also organizes the cheapest regular transport to Chacaltaya; US$10 per person for the 2½ hour bus journey, leaving La Paz at 0800 on Saturday and Sunday, and returning about 1530.

NB Do not go to Chacaltaya without first spending at least a week at the height of La Paz or equivalent due to the danger of potentially fatal altitude sickness. When you get there, move slowly and drink plenty of clear liquids. Take 100% ultraviolet-proof sunglasses. Emergency services are non-existent. (Chacaltaya skiing is described in Bradt's *South America Ski Guide*.)

• **Accommodation** For the really hardy, accommodation at the Chacaltaya ski station is free, but take very warm clothes, sleeping bag and bed roll, food and water, as there is no heating, or bedding. Meals are available at the hut at weekends.

• **Transport** Taxi or minibus costs US$30 (whole car) for a ½-day trip. Hiring a jeep and driver for the trip costs US$70. The trip can be hair-raising as buses carry no chains. Often the buses and tours only go half way. Many agencies do day trips for US$12.50, often combined with Valle de la Luna.

MAPS AND GUIDEBOOKS

Trekking in Bolivia, Yossi Brain (The Mountaineers, 1997); *Bolivia – a climbing guide*, Yossi Brain (The Mountaineers, Seattle, 1998). A paperback reprint of *La Cordillera Real de los Andes, Bolivia*, by Alain Mesili (Los Amigos del Libro, La Paz, 1984) is available in Spanish. Serious trekkers should look at *Backpacking and Trekking in Peru and Bolivia* (6th edition) by Hilary Bradt, Jonathan Derkson and Petra Schepens.

Liam O'Brien covers the whole of the Cordillera Real at 1:135,000 in *A New Map of the Cordillera Real*. This is a full colour, shaded relief topographic map of the Cordillera Real, covering all treks; US$10 per copy, from 28 Turner Terrace, Newtonville, MA02160, USA (add US$2 for shipping), or from map distributors (Bradt, Stanfords, etc). Bigger scale sheets are listed with each mountain. Takesi, Choro and Yunga Cruz are covered by the Walter Córdova 1:50,000 map, which is available from bookshops in La Paz. There are also the IGM 1:50,000 sheets: Takesi Chojlla 6044 IV; Choro Milluni 5945 II, 6045 III and Coroico; Yunga Cruz Lambate 6044 II and 6044. The German Alpine Club (Deutscher Alpenverien) produces two good maps of Cordillera Real North and South; these are best bought before arrival. (See also La Paz section under Maps, page 103.)

How to go

WHEN TO GO

The main consideration for travellers regarding the weather is how it affects the condition of Bolivia's notoriously poor roads. The rainy season is November-March and some roads into the tropical lowlands may be impassable at this time. These are also the months when mosquitos and other biting insects are at their worst, so this is not a good time to visit the jungle.

As for the rest of the country, the Altiplano does not receive much rain, so timing is not so crucial here, although hiking trails can get very muddy during the wet season. During the winter months of June and July, nights tend to be clearer but even colder than at other times. These are the best months to visit the Salar de Uyuni, as the salt lake is even more impressive under the clear blue skies.

June-August, while offering the best weather conditions, are also the busiest months. At this time some of the better hotels will be full and tour prices will be higher. Furthermore, many of the best festivals happen during the rainy season, such as Carnival and Holy Week.

Trekkers and climbers should, of course, pay closer attention to local weather conditions and those are given above under **Adventure tourism**.

HOW TO GET THERE

There are no direct flights from Europe to La Paz. Those wishing to fly to Bolivia from Europe have to go to Lima, São Paulo, Rio de Janeiro, Buenos Aires or Miami for connections to La Paz. Flights from Miami also go to Santa Cruz. Those flying with Lloyd Aéreo Boliviano (LAB) can buy a 4 week air pass (see **Information for travellers**).

La Paz is the best place to start your visit. This is where you will find all the tourist information, travel agencies and the widest range of hotels and eating places.

Few nationalities require more than a valid passport to visit Bolivia. On entry, you will be given a tourist card entitling you to 90 days stay in the country. If, for any reason, you are only given 30 days (and this is not unheard of) you can easily extend to 90 days at immigration in La Paz.

PRACTICALITIES

MONEY

The currency is the boliviano and the exchange rate has been relatively stable in recent years. Changing US dollars (cash, travellers' cheques or with a credit card) presents no problems. Cash can be withdrawn from ATMs in most major towns where you see the 'Enlace' sign. Make sure you shop around for the best rates and only take dollars.

COMMUNICATIONS

Communications into and out of Bolivia are generally good. International calls by phone and fax can be made in all major towns and cities and communication via the Internet is expanding.

The official language is Spanish,

though many in the countryside may only speak their native Aymara and Quechua languages, or a confusing mix of the two. Outside La Paz and the main tourist centres, travelling without some knowledge of Spanish would be a hindrance.

ONCE YOU ARE THERE

Bolivia is generally a safe country and free from many of the problems that beset its larger neighbours. However, crime is not unknown to the country and travellers should take the same precautions that they would anywhere else, especially around markets and bus terminals.

People in the highlands may not be the friendliest and most open people in the world, but they are polite and courteous. A smile, a greeting and a few friendly words in Spanish will go a long way to endearing you to the local people, and generally making your trip easier and more enjoyable.

Your greatest enemies in Bolivia will be altitude sickness and diarrhoea (see below) and frustration. The latter may result from not being understood or not being able to understand, in which case, make sure you take at least a basic knowledge of Spanish. Another cause of frustration is pressure of time. As already mentioned, Bolivia is not designed for a whistle-stop tour by bus. Make sure you don't try to do too much, especially at altitude, always allow for delays when travelling and try not to book flights etc too much in advance, unless you really have to. Above all, be patient and remember that this is not only a Third World country, but the poorest in South America.

Tourists from Europe and North America, and indeed from many other South American countries, will find Bolivia a relatively cheap country to visit. Though not quite as low budget as Ecuador, it is certainly better value than its neighbours, in particular Brazil and Argentina. Buses, accommodation and eating out are all cheap and two people could travel around the country on US$25 per day without having to endure any hardship.

ACCOMMODATION AND RESTAURANTS

There are hotels to suit every budget and in many places there are establishments which offer excellent value, particularly places which are popular with foreign visitors or which have been opened by foreigners. The same applies with restaurants.

Away from the main cities, high-class hotels are few and far between. Getting off the beaten track really does mean sacrificing creature comforts, but not necessarily standards of hygiene. Many of the hotels we recommend are not luxurious but conform to certain basic standards of cleanliness and are popular with travellers, which is often the best sign of an establishment's pedigree.

As mentioned above, prices are comparatively low in Bolivia, but not uniformly so. The eastern part of the country tends to be a bit more expensive, especially the city of Santa Cruz, which is geared more towards commerce than tourism and therefore has few good budget places to stay. Smaller places which see a lot of tourists, such as Coroico, Rurrenabaque, Sorata or Copacabana, on the other hand, are full of good value budget accommodation.

Eating out in Bolivia can be hazardous, and this is one area where travellers should not over-economize. The satisfaction accrued from saving the odd dollar here and there by eating in the markets will be soon be heavily outweighed by the trauma of spending your entire trip on the toilet. That's not to say that market food is unhygienic, just that you need to be careful, especially until your stomach has had time to adjust.

La Paz and most other major cities offer a wide variety of eating places, some of which are of very high standard. Away from the main centres, however, your chances of suffering from "Atahuallpa's revenge" are increased.

GETTING AROUND

"The rich fly, a tiny minority own cars, and the rest of Bolivia jostles at mega bus terminals. A huge network of risk-taking, enterprising, endlessly ingenious bus operators, whose achievement should rank among the legends of transport history, grapple with washed-out roads and icy Andean passes to keep those who must, moving between cities". So wrote Matthew Parris in *The Times* on 17 January 1994. Going by bus in Bolivia may be the cheapest way to get around but it is also dirty, uncomfortable, extremely time-consuming and, at times, downright scary.

Actually catching a bus can present serious problems. La Paz and the other major cities have central bus terminals, but not all buses leave from them and finding out where and where the others leave from can take as long as the journey. On top of this, bus times are regularly changed to take account of local, regional and national festivals, elections and soccer matches. During the wet season journey times can be increased by hours, even days, as roads get washed out and vehicles get stuck in the mud. Only 5% of Bolivia's roads are paved and only 20% can be used all year, due mainly to landslides and sections being washed away during the rainy season.

Bolivian road warning signs take the shape of crosses, which line the side of the road to indicate where vehicles have gone over the edge. Most of the crosses appear on particularly dangerous bends and

many drivers, being devout Catholics, will cross themselves on seeing one. This, of course means that many of the sharpest bends on the road are negotiated with one hand on the steering wheel.

Similarly, many of the buses do little to inspire confidence. For a start, they are usually packed to suffocation point with people, luggage and livestock. Overcrowded, it seems, is not a word familiar to Bolivian bus company employees. And secondly, they tend to break down a lot. But don't worry – seemingly anything can be repaired at the side of the road, given time. The driver and his *ayudante* (helper) will disappear under, or into, the engine, hit things, tie bits together with wire and probably pray a lot. Magically, the bus starts and the journey continues.

Probably the worst bus journey in all of Bolivia is the trip from La Paz to Pelechuco in the Cordillera Apolobamba – 18-24 hours of dust-filled torture crossing the Altiplano in some battered old hulk that should have been consigned to the scrapheap years ago. Anyone over 172 cm will spend the entire trip smashing their kneecaps into the back of the seat in front and arrive in need of major surgery and a good night's rest. The pain, cold and tedium is only alleviated by the need to get out and push the bus every so often. All males of working age get off and push with all their might until it becomes obvious that the combined weight of the female passengers still on board is preventing any significant movement. So, off

they get and the bus can then be pushed out of the mud/sand/hole.

But it's not all discomfort and near-death experiences. There's no better way to see the country, meet the people, sit on their chickens, sleep on their sheep, or be kept awake all night by their screaming children. Just look on it as cultural interaction.

HEALTH

For anyone travelling overseas health is a key consideration. With sensible precautions the visitor to Bolivia should remain as healthy as at home. There are general rules to follow which should keep you in good health when travelling in Latin America. These are dealt with in the full health section on pages 338-348.

KEEPING HEALTHY IN BOLIVIA

Before you travel make sure the medical insurance you take out is adequate. Have a check-up with your doctor, if necessary, and arrange your immunisations well in advance. Try ringing a specialist travel clinic if your own doctor is unfamiliar with health in Latin America. You would do well to be protected by immunisation against typhoid, polio, tetanus and hepatitis A. Yellow fever vaccination with a certificate is only required if you are coming from infected areas of the world or, for your own protection, if you are going to be roughing it in the Bolivian jungles. Check malaria prophylaxis for all lowlands rural areas to be visited, particularly the Beni region and along the borders with Peru and Brazil. Vaccination against cholera is not necessary.

WHILE YOU ARE TRAVELLING

The commonest affliction of visitors to Bolivia is probably traveller's diarrhoea. Shellfish are always a risk and so is ceviche (raw fish marinated in lime), which has recently become popular in La Paz. They are delicious, however, and should be safe in well-run hygienic establishments.

Fruit is plentiful and excellent, but ensure it is washed or peel it yourself. Avoid raw food, undercooked food (including eggs) and reheated food. Food that is cooked in front of you and offered hot all through is generally safe.

Tap water in Bolivia is unsafe to drink. The better hotels have their own purification systems and in many restaurants you can get boiled water, water that has been filtered or, more popular these days, commercially bottled water. There are good doctors and reasonable hospitals in the major Bolivian cities, but don't expect good facilities away from the major centres.

ALTITUDE AND CLIMATE

Altitude is such a feature of travel in Bolivia that a place like Cochabamba, at over 2,500m, feels like sea level. Nearly everybody arrives at the capital La Paz which is at 3,600m and its airport at over 4,000m. At this height, acute mountain sickness (soroche) is a real possibility. It by no means effects everybody but in any event the first thing you need to do upon arrival is to slow down to the appropriate pace. Rushing around at this altitude will leave you gasping for oxygen, so take a hint from the locals and walk slowly. Respect the altitude and follow the advice in the main health section.

You will not be surprised to read that Bolivia, considering its latitude, is extremely hot in the lowland regions. Keep up your fluid intake. It is also extremely cold at high altitude, so take appropriate clothing and do not forget about sun protection at altitude, where the ultraviolet rays are particularly strong.

RETURNING HOME

Report any symptoms to your doctor and say exactly where you have been. Keep taking anti-malarial tablets for 6 weeks after leaving the malarial area.

Section 2

Horizons

GEOLOGY AND LANDSCAPE

Bolivia is the 5th largest of the 13 South American countries in size (just over 1 million square km) and the 8th largest in population (just under 7.6 million people in 1996). That makes it about the same size as France and Spain together but with only 7.6% of their population. This low population density – the lowest in the continent except for the Guianas – is explained by the high altitude and aridity of much of the terrain in the west and south, and the remoteness of the wetter, forested areas of the northeast.

Bolivia is bounded by Chile and Peru to the west, Brazil to the north and east, and Argentina and Paraguay to the south. It is, like Paraguay, landlocked, although the latter has access to the sea via the Paraná. Bolivia had a Pacific coastline until 1880 when it was lost to Chile in the War of the Pacific, 1879-1884. Since then its principal surface link to the rest of the world has been the railway and road to Arica built by the Chileans. The road linking the capital, La Paz, and Arica was brought up to modern standards only in 1996.

Bolivia also lost territory to Brazil (Acre was lost under the treaty of Petrópolis in 1903), and to Argentina and Paraguay, notably in the Chaco War, 1932-35. The country lies wholly between the Tropic of Capricorn and the Equator.

Structure
The Andes are at their widest in Bolivia. They are formed of two main ranges (*cordilleras*), of which the most westerly is the frontier with Chile, and stretch for 250 km across Bolivia. The formation of the Andes began at the end of the Cretaceous geological period about 80 million years ago and has continued to the present day. To the east are much older structures of granite and crystalline rocks belonging to the South American Plate which comes to the surface further east in Brazil.

In Bolivia, however, these rocks are overlain with thick, geologically recent, deposits of alluvium brought down from the mountains by rivers and glaciers over millions of years of widely differing climates. During the most recent ice age (Pleistocene), a continuous ice-cap extended from the Antarctic to southern Bolivia, with a much lower snow line on the mountains to the north. With heavy precipitation and vast quantities of meltwater, the deep valleys were gouged out to the east and vast lakes were formed on the plateau, the most notable of which remains today as Lake Titicaca.

The Altiplano
The Altiplano is one of the largest interior basins in the world extending from northern Argentina some 900 km into southern Peru, and is nearly 10% of Bolivia. It is between 100 and 200 km wide throughout its length. The high Andes rise on either side of the Altiplano, the Cordillera Occidental to the west which includes the highest mountain in Bolivia, Nevado Sajama, 6,542m, and the Cordillera Oriental to the

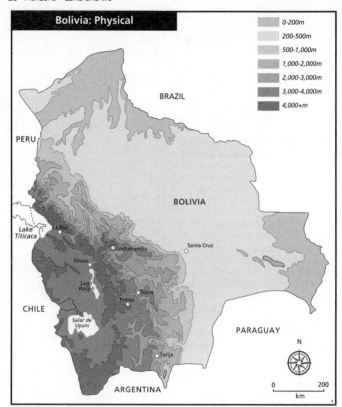

east, whose highest point is Nevado de Illampu, 6,485m. There are many peaks, mostly volcanic in origin, in both these ranges, between 5,000m and 6,500m, all with permanent snow caps.

The Altiplano itself lies at around 3,500-4,000m, and being in the rain shadow from both east and west, has very little direct precipitation. It is a bleak, almost treeless area – just a few eucalyptus in sheltered spots in the north near villages – the southern part is practically uninhabited desert. The winds can be strong and are often violent, stirring up dust clouds and compounding the discomforts of the cold dry climate. Much of the time, however, the air

is unbelievably clear and the whole plateau is a bowl of luminous light.

There are no passes out of the Altiplano below 4,000m. The easiest exit, ie the least mountainous, is to the southeast, across the plateau and the salt desert to Argentina through Villazón. To the southwest is a remote area of volcanic activity which gives rise to some unusual saline lakes where specialized algae create the colourful Laguna Colorada, (bright red) and Laguna Verde (green).

In spite of this hostile environment, almost 70% of the population of the country live on the Altiplano, one of the highest inhabited areas of the world. Half are in the mining towns and the city of La Paz, and the other half live in the north on or near the shores of Lake Titicaca.

Lake Titicaca

This is the largest lake in South America (ignoring Lake Maracaibo in Venezuela which is linked to the sea) and at 3,812m is the highest regularly navigated body of water in the world. It covers about 8,300 square km, running a maximum of 190 km from northwest to southeast and 80 km across. The average depth is over 100m with the deepest point recorded at 281m. The border with Peru passes north-south through the lake and about half is in each country.

Over 25 rivers, most from Peru, flow into the lake and a small outlet leaves the lake at Desaguadero on the Bolivia-Peru border. This takes no more than 5% of the inflow, the rest is lost through evaporation and hence the waters of the lake are slightly brackish, producing the totora reeds used to make the mats and balsa boats for which the lakedwellers are famed.

The lake level fluctuates seasonally, normally rising from December to March and receding for the rest of the year but extremes of 5m between high and low levels have been recorded. This can cause problems and high levels in the late 1980s disrupted transport links near the shoreline. The night temperature occasionally falls as low as -25°C but high daytime temperatures ensure the surface average is about 14°C which in turn modifies the extremes of winter and night temperatures of the surrounding land. One of the reasons for the relatively high population round the lake are the rich volcanic soils of which good use is made where water is available.

The outflow from the lake, called the Río Desaguadero, continues intermittently for 250 km to Lake Uru Uru, and Lake Poopó, which has no surface outlet and indeed often dries up in the summer.

Titicaca, Uru Uru, Poopó and other intermittent lakes are the remnants of a vast area of water formed in the last Ice Age known as Lake Ballivián. This extended at least 600 km south from Lake Titicaca and included Lake Poopó and the salt flats of Salar de Coipasa and Salar de Uyuni. Its surface was estimated to have been over 100m above the present Lake Titicaca level and 225m above Poopó.

The Yungas and the Puna

La Paz is built in several layers, starting on the Altiplano and going east down a steep, narrow valley which may have been one of the Ice Age exits of Lake Ballivián. Northeast from La Paz, the road to Coroico goes through a section of the Eastern Andes chain called the Cordillera Real. Immediately after the pass at La Cumbre (4,725m), the descent towards the interior plains begins. This area of precipitous valleys and mountain spurs is called the Yungas, has considerable rainfall and is heavily forested.

The escarpment stretches northeast to the frontier with Peru, and in spite of the difficulty of the terrain, is the most fertile part of the country. South from this point, the escarpment, now facing east, falls less steeply towards the interior of the continent, backed by a plateau at around 4,000m, called the Puna, whose western edge also overlooks the Antiplano between the high peaks of the Cordillera Oriental. The eastern slopes become drier to the south, but are still important crop growing areas. The name Yungas is used for all the semi-tropical mountain valleys. Most of this sector drains into the Madeira river system and thence to the Amazon, but from 20° south to the border with Argentina, the rivers flow into the Paraná basin.

The Oriente

Beyond the Yungas and the Puna are the lowlands that stretch northwards and eastwards to Brazil and Paraguay and represent almost 70% of the territory of Bolivia. Similar to Peru and Colombia that also have extensive provinces east of the Andes, Bolivia's Oriente is remote, sparsely inhabited and poorly served by roads and other communications. In the northeast of this region there is dense tropical forest and wetlands. In the extreme east, the border runs close to the Río Paraguay and the Pantanal of Brazil. In the centre, the land is drier, more open with rough pasture and scrub, while in the south close to the Argentine frontier, there is still less rain and there is little more than arid savannah.

In the 18th century, much of this area was prosperous, guided by the Jesuit missions. However, when they were expelled the whole area fell into decay. In the recent past a revival has begun. In the 1950s, the Brazilians completed the railway from Santa Cruz crossing the Oriente to Brazil and all weather roads are being built to service this potentially productive part of the country. Santa Cruz itself has become a large agricultural centre and is now the second city of Bolivia.

CLIMATE

The main factors controlling the climate of Bolivia are the trade wind systems and the Andes. The rising of the hot air in the tropical centre of the continent draws in the southeast Trade Winds from the south Atlantic, which are not significantly impeded by the eastern highlands of Brazil. As these moist winds rise up the lower slopes of the Andes, the rain falls. Humidity is high and temperatures high also, but not excessive, 27°C on the lower slopes, 19°C in the upper valleys of the Yungas. Rainfall is higher in the summer (November-March) as the Trades are less active in the winter months. Nevertheless, there is some precipitation all year round in the north of the country as far west as Titicaca.

In the Andes and the Altiplano, different conditions prevail. By the time the Trades have crossed the Cordillera Oriental, they have lost almost all their moisture. On the Pacific side, air is also drawn inwards over the Cordillera Occidental. However, because of the cold Humboldt current off the west coast, the air does not absorb moisture from the sea and is dry when it rises over the land. There is therefore no regular source of rain for this region. Violent local storms do produce snowfalls on the highest peaks and rain lower down from time to time.

Temperature in the Altiplano is a function of altitude, both in average levels and daily ranges. The average of 10°C at 4,000m can be 20°C at midday often falling to -15°C at night. Arctic conditions prevail at 6,000m. Although there can be considerable day to day fluctuations in climatic conditions, there are no noticeable seasonal changes apart from the tendency for rain to fall in the summer months.

There is one other factor which affects the south of the country. Winds originating in the south of the continent blow up the eastern side of the Andes across Argentina and push the southeast Trades northwards. This reduces the rainfall in the south of Bolivia particularly in the Altiplano resulting in near desert conditions. On the eastern slopes too, the land gets progressively drier to the south to become the semi arid scrubland of the Chaco.

FLORA AND FAUNA

Bolivia is a land of superlatives. It contains the most extensive tropical rainforest in the world; the Amazon has by far the largest volume of any river in the world and the Andes are the longest uninterrupted mountain chain. The fauna and flora are to a large extent determined by the influence of those mountains and the great rivers, particularly the Amazon. In Bolivia there are vast forests carpetting the lowlands and ascending the slopes of the Andes. Equally spectacular are the huge expanses of open, tree-covered savannahs and dry deserts of the Altiplano. It is this immense range of habitats which makes Bolivia one of the world's greatest regions of biological diversity.

This diversity arises not only from the wide range of habitats available, but also

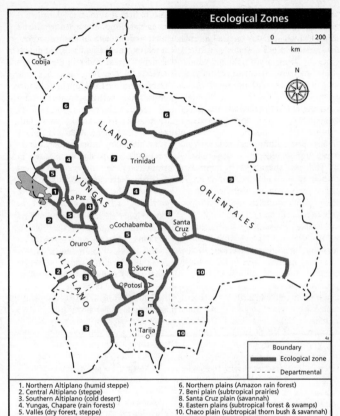

Ecological Zones

0 — 200 km

N

Cobija

LLANOS

Trinidad

YUNGAS

ORIENTALES

La Paz

Cochabamba

Santa Cruz

Oruro

ALTIPLANO

Sucre

Potosí

VALLES

Tarija

4a

Boundary	
▬▬▬	Ecological zone
– – –	Departmental

1. Northern Altiplano (humid steppe)
2. Central Altiplano (steppe)
3. Southern Altiplano (cold desert)
4. Yungas, Chapare (rain forests)
5. Valles (dry forest, steppe)
6. Northern plains (Amazon rain forest)
7. Beni plain (subtropical prairies)
8. Santa Cruz plain (savannah)
9. Eastern plains (subtropical forest & swamps)
10. Chaco plain (subtropical thorn bush & savannah)

from the history of the continent. South America has essentially been an island for some 70 million years joined only by a narrow isthmus to Central and North America. Land passage played a significant role in the gradual colonization of South America by species from the north. When the land-link closed these colonists evolved to a wide variety of forms free from the competitive pressures that prevailed elsewhere. When the land-bridge was re-established some four million years ago a new invasion of species took place from North America, adding to the diversity but also leading to numerous extinctions. Comparative stability has ensued since then and has guaranteed the survival of many primitive groups like the opossums.

Bolivia is a complex mosaic of more than forty well defined ecological regions and the transition zones between them. Each has its own characteristic geology, soil, flora and fauna. There are seven major habitats worth considering here: descending from the Puna and the high Andes there are the narrow sub-tropical valleys or Yungas, the interandean valleys, the dry chaco, semi-humid woodlands, savannahs and lowland rainforest.

The Lowland Forests

Situated between latitudes 10° and 15° south and below 250m altitude the great lowland forests of Bolivia encompass the entire department of Pando and parts of those of La Paz, Beni, Cochabamba and Santa Cruz. Bisected by the great tributary rivers of the Amazon – the Madeira, Mamoré, Madre de Dios, Manuripi and Beni – the area appears at first sight to be in pristine condition. But the past activities of timber operators extracting mahogany and South American cedar, latex tappers, Brazil nut gatherers, and present day mineral extraction have had a major impact on the larger species of mammals. These were extensively hunted and the result is an impoverished fauna in many areas.

Notable exceptions are the 1.8 million hectare Manuripi-Heath National Reserve in central Pando and the Noel Kempff Mercado National Park. Here in the relatively constant climatic conditions animal and plant life has evolved to an amazing diversity over the millennia. It has been estimated that 2 square kilometres of lowland rainforest can harbour some 1,200 species of vascular plants, 600 species of tree, and 120 species of woody plants.

In the lowland forests, many of the trees are buttress rooted, with flanges extending 3 to 4m up the trunk of the tree. Among the smaller trees stilt-like prop roots are also common. Frequently flowers are not well developed, and some emerge directly from the branches and even the trunk. This is possibly an adaptation for pollination by the profusion of bats, giving easier access than if they were obscured by leaves. Lianas are plentiful, especially where there are natural clearings resulting from the death of old trees. These woody vines reach the tops of all but the tallest trees, tying them together and competing with them for space and light. Included here are the strangler figs. These start life as epiphytes, their seeds germinating after deposition by birds. Aerial roots develop which quickly grow down to the ground. These later envelop the trunk, killing the host and leaving the hollow 'trunk' of the strangler.

In the canopy epiphytes are also common and include bromeliads, orchids, ferns, mosses and lichens. Their nutrition is derived from mineral nutrients in the water and organic debris they collect often in specialized pitcher-like structures. Animals of the canopy have developed striking adaptations to enable them to exist in this green wilderness, for example, the prehensile tails of the opossums and many of the monkeys, and the peculiar development of the claws of the sloth.

Many of the bird species which creep around in the understorey are drab coloured, eg tinamou and cotingas, but have loud, clear calls. Scuttling around on the ground are the elusive armadillos, their presence marked by burrows. Pockmarked areas may be indicative of the foraging activities of pacas or peccaries, where their populations have not been exploited by over-hunting.

The forest is at its densest along the river margins; here the diffused light reduces the density of the understorey plant community. The variety of trees is amazing, there are no pure stands. The forest giants are the kapok and the Brazil nut or *castanheiro*. These river corridors are often the best places to observe wildlife. Caiman and turtles are commonly seen basking on the river banks. Neotropical cormorants, Roseate spoonbills and Jabiru storks are commonly observed fishing in the shallow waters. The swollen rivers of the lowland forest are home to perhaps 2,000 species of fish including piranha, sting ray and electric eel. Many species provide an important source of protein for the native communities, for example, giant catfish. River dolphins also frequent these torpid waters.

The vast river basin of the Amazon is home to an immense variety of species. The environment has largely dictated the lifestyle. Life in or around rivers, lakes, swamps and forest depends on the ability to swim and climb; amphibious and tree-dwelling animals are common. Once the entire Amazon basin was a great inland sea and the river still contains mammals more typical of the coast, eg manatees and dolphins.

The best way to see the wildlife is to get above the canopy. Ridges provide elevated view points from which excellent views over the forest are obtained. From here, it is possible to look across the lowland flood plain to the very foothills of the Andes, possibly some 200 km away. Flocks of parrots and macaws can be seen commuting between fruiting trees and noisy troupes of squirrel monkeys and brown capuchins come tantalisingly close.

The Savannah

The savannah habitat comprises grass and low shrub criss-crossed with rivers and contrasts greatly with the lowland rain forest. It is more obviously seasonal, dry in August and verdant with profuse new growth in December. Small palm groves are characteristic and provide nesting opportunities for macaws.

In the Beni region the savannahs are seasonally flooded, and the mammal fauna then has to congregate on high ground. Impressive aggregations of birds flock to feed on the fish stranded in the withering pools. Large anacondas and caiman abound and herds of russet coloured capybara and swamp deer are commonly seen from roads that intersect the area. Small isolated fragments of dry deciduous forest are found interspersed among the flooded plains, and these hold a characteristic fauna in refuges from the ingress of cattle ranching and the burning of grassland associated with it.

In the northwestern part of the Beni region and southeastern Santa Cruz there are also permanently flooded savannahs which are swampy and have characteristic floating mats of vegetation (some with trees), that are shifted around by the wind.

The well-drained soils and moderate climate of the region of Santa Cruz provide conditions for the growth of semi-humid forests from about 300m to 1,200m above sea level. The altitudinal and climatic range experienced provides for a wealth of flora and fauna which has been exploited by man.

The Chaco

This is a dry region with an annual precipitation of usually less than 300 mm and an average temperature of 26°C, but characterized by cold fronts that on occasion kill new growth in the forest leaving bare trunks. Somewhat surprisingly many species of larger mammals are found here including tapir, jaguar, brocket deer and peccary.

The chaco consists of a variety of habitat types ranging from a mixture of thorny chapparal, with natural grasslands, palms and dry deciduous forests. Due to exposure to heat and intense insulation most of the animals are nocturnal, giving the impression of a low density of mammals. The Bolivian chaco is perhaps the last refuge for the Chacoan peccary and guanacos. The saó dwarf palm used in the manufacture of the traditional straw hats from Santa Cruz is found here also.

Some of the drier valleys have a mesothermic vegetation (eg cactuses) as they are in the rain shadow of the surrounding mountains. The valleys have a very rich bird fauna, to which the military and golden macaw are unique. Rare mammals such as the spectacled bear, *taruca* (a deer), and the *pacarana* (a large rodent) are found here. At higher altitudes the cloud forests contain tree ferns and epiphyte clad trees, including birch (*aliso*) and podocarpus.

The Yungas

The Yungas comprise a belt of very humid forests at altitudes ranging up to 3,600m. The headwaters of many of Bolivia's major rivers rise here and flow as clear, rapid streams through deep canyons. The vegetation ranges from that typical of lowland forest through to cloud forest and, at the tree, line elfin forest with ferns and bamboo. The great diversity of habitats has led to a great diversity of fauna, likely to be the richest in the country. The spectacled bear, and exotic birds such as the Andean cock of the rock and the horned currasow are denizens of this habitat.

The Highlands

Life is rare in the puna and high mountains. The climate is dry and cold, particularly in the Altiplano where there is little or no vegetation except for a few shrubs, cacti and dry grass. The vast climatic range, from 15°C during the day to a minus 25°C during the night, impose severe limits on life. An exception to this concerns the Laguna Colorada where a vast lake warmed by fumaroles is home to thousands of flamingos and other water birds. Vicuñas, vizcachas, rheas and Andean wild cats survive in a delicate balance within this fragile environment.

The Pantanal

The Bolivian pantanal is an ecologically diverse zone continuous with that in Brazil. When flooded from December to March, it creates the largest area of wetlands in the world. In addition it includes dry savannahs or *cerrado*, chaco scrublands as well as gallery rainforest. The area is very flat and flooded by the rising rivers leaving isolated islands (*cordilheiras*) between vast lakes (*bahais*) which become saline as the waters evaporate.

This mixed ecosystem supports a highly diverse fauna characteristic of the constituent habitat types which includes 200 species of mammal. Capybara, tapir and peccaries are common along the water's edge, as are marsh deer. Jaguar, more commonly associated with the forest, prey on these herbivores and the cattle and feral pigs which graze here. Spectacular numbers of wading birds – egrets, Jabiru storks, ibises, spoonbills and herons – prey on the abundant invertebrate and fish fauna. Anacondas and caiman are still common, although the black caiman has been hunted out.

History

PRE-CONQUEST HISTORY

The barren, windswept Altiplano, the highest plateau in Latin America, has been home to various indigenous cultures from the earliest times. Artefacts found on the Altiplano date the first human occupation at around 7000-8000 BC. Early man followed a seasonal cycle of hunting and gathering around the shores of Lake Titicaca, travelling as far as the eastern valleys and the desert coast of southern Peru and northern Chile.

One of the most important developments of life on the Altiplano was the domestication of the llama and alpaca, which centred around Lake Titicaca and developed in conjunction with arable farming. The llama was of crucial importance to the Altiplano people. It provided protein to supplement their basic diet as well as wool for weaving and was also a beast of burden. The combination of the domestication of camelids and the development of arable farming helped give rise to the great Andean civilizations.

Tiahuanaco

The greatest of the pre-Inca civilizations is at Tiahuanaco, or Tiwanaku (see page 112). Most visitors are aware of this mysterious site just south of Lake Titicaca but few people understand the extent of this culture's influence throughout the South Central Andes and the reason for its sudden demise. The remains of Tiahuanaco culture show that the inhabitants reached a high degree of development and organization. Remains of a huge ceremonial and urban centre with palaces, temples and

Bolivia: Departmental

Not to scale

pyramids, elaborate textiles and beautiful pottery suggest a sophisticated culture.

Sustained by forms of intensive arable farming, the Tiahuanaco region became one of the most densely populated areas of the Altiplano. The influence of the culture gradually spread to other areas, through military conquest or trade. After around AD 500 its influence was felt in almost all parts of Bolivia, southern Peru, northern Chile and northwest Argentina. Civilization reached its high point here around AD 1000, after which a period of decline set in, leading to its complete collapse around AD 1100-1200. The cause of its sudden demise remains a mystery.

After Tiahuanaco

After the fall of Tiahuanaco a proliferation of distinct political groups evolved to control the vast territory formerly under the influence of the great empire. These independent Aymara kingdoms, which shared a common language and many cultural patterns, played a leading role on the Altiplano for 300 years until the arrival of the Spaniards. Each kingdom boasted a powerful organization based on a collective and military model.

At the centre of Aymara society were the *ayllus*, groups based on kinship which owned and worked the land collectively (see also page 64). The Aymaras cultivated potatoes and cereal crops and kept llamas and alpacas for meat, milk and wool and used them as pack-animals. Indeed, the wealth of the kingdoms was measured in the number of alpacas and llamas. Like the Tiahuanaco empire before them, the Aymaras maintained important connections with communities in the eastern valleys and on the Pacific coast. They exchanged potatoes, meat and wool from the cold, barren plateau for fruit, vegetables, maize and coca from the sub-tropical valleys.

The most powerful kingdoms were the Lupaca, based at Chuquito, southwest of Lake Titicaca, and the Colla, with their capital at Huatuncolla, near present-day Puno. These two kingdoms were in constant warfare until around 1430, when the Lupaca conquered the Colla.

The Incas

While the Aymara were fighting among themselves to establish their territorial rights to lands around the Titicaca basin, the Quechua-speaking Incas from Cusco were preparing to invade the kingdoms and incorporate them into their expanding empire. Despite the fact that they were divided, the Aymaras resisted obstinately and were not finally conquered until the latter part of the 15th century in the reign of Inca Túpac Yupangi (1471-93).

The origins of the Inca Dynasty are shrouded in mythology and shaky evidence. The best known story reported by the Spanish chroniclers talks about Manco Capac and his sister rising out of Lake Titicaca, created by the Sun as divine founders of a chosen race. This was in approximately AD 1200. Over the next 300 years the small tribe grew to supremacy as leaders of the largest empire ever known in the Americas, the four territories of Tawantinsuyo, united by Cusco as the umbilicus of the Universe. The four quarters of Tawantinsuyo, all radiating out from Cusco, were: 1 – Chinchaysuyo, including northern Peru and Ecuador; 2 – Cuntisuyo, including the coastal lands; 3 – Collasuyo, southern Peru, Bolivia and Chile; 4 – Antisuyo, the eastern highlands of Peru.

At its peak, just before the Spanish Conquest, the Inca Empire stretched from the Río Maule in central Chile, north to the present Ecuador-Colombia border, containing most of Ecuador, Peru, western Bolivia, northern Chile and northwest Argentina. The area was roughly equivalent to France, Belgium, Holland, Luxembourg, Italy and Switzerland combined, a total of 980,000 square kilometres.

The first Inca ruler, Manco Capac, moved to the fertile Cusco region, and established Cusco as his capital. Successive generations of rulers were fully occupied with local conquests of rivals, such as the Colla and Lupaca to the south, and the Chanca to the northwest. At the end of Manco Capac's reign the hated Chanca were finally defeated, largely thanks to the heroism of one of his sons, Pachacuti Inca Yupangui, who was subsequently crowned as the new ruler.

From the start of Pachacuti's own reign in 1438, imperial expansion grew in earnest. With the help of his son and heir, Topa Inca, territory was conquered from the Titicaca basin south into Chile, and all the north and central coast of Peru. Typical of the Inca method of government was to assimilate the skills of their defeated enemies into their own political and administrative system.

Though the Incas respected the languages and cultures of the subjugated peoples and only insisted on imposing their religion, a certain amount of Quechuanization did occur. Around Lake Titicaca Aymara language and culture remained practically intact but the cultural and linguistic traditions of other peoples of the Altiplano were almost completely displaced, especially as groups of Quechua-speaking Incas were brought from Peru to live and work in Collasuyo. But Inca culture was tied to the highlands and they never succeeded in annexing all of the peoples of Bolivia. Their powerful armies could not defeat the semi-nomadic peoples in the lower-lying Valles (valleys) and the eastern plains, such as the Guaraníes.

Although the Incas left a great impression on the country in the shape of an extensive road system, architecture, ceramics and metal artefacts and established their own language in many parts, the duration of their stay in Bolivia was no more than 80 years.

CONQUEST AND AFTER

The end of the Inca empire was signalled by the landing of Francisco Pizarro in Peru in 1532. The political capital, Cusco, fell in 1535 and soon afterwards the Spanish began the conquest of Bolivia. Diego de Almagro travelled south with an army of Spanish and native forces through Bolivia to the Chilean coast and in 1542 the entire area was annexed as the Audencia of Charcas of the Viceroyalty of Peru.

During the Spanish colonization, towns were founded and grew rapidly. In 1538 La Plata, now Sucre, was founded and, in 1559 became capital of the Audiencia of Charcas (it is still the official capital of Bolivia). Another administrative centre, La Paz, was founded in 1548. In the eastern lowlands the colonization process was rather different. Like the Incas before them, the Spaniards experienced enormous difficulties in conquering the native peoples of this region. Apart from a number of Jesuit mission settlements (see page 271), the Spanish presence here remained limited to the town of Santa Cruz.

At first the Spanish left the existing socio-economic structure more or less intact. They also adopted the system of compulsory labour (*mita*) which the Incas had imposed, though much more forcefully. Over time Spanish rule became more aggressive and motivated solely by greed. The barter economy and communal working of the land were replaced by a society based on the extraction and exportation of wealth through the ownership of large estates (*haciendas*) and mining.

Bolivia's destiny was shaped in 1545 with the discovery of silver at Cerro Rico (Rich Mountain) in Potosí (see page 204).

Charcas became one of the most important centres of the Spanish colonial economy, sending a constant supply of silver to Spain. The mining town of Potosí grew rapidly and by 1610 had a population of over 160,000, making it for a long time by far the largest city in Latin America. Potosí's opulent extravagance became legendary and for decades a favourite Spanish description for untold wealth was 'vale un Potosí' (worth a Potosí).

Together with precious metals from smaller mining centres such as Oruro, silver from Cerro Rico was crucial to the maintenance of the Spanish empire and financed their wars in Europe. Many hundreds of thousands of Indians were forced to work in the mines as miners, in the workshops of the crown mint or on the *haciendas*.

The Spaniards regarded the indigenous peoples as inferior and cared little for their welfare. The suppression of indigenous culture went as far as making it compulsory to wear Spanish-style dress. According to popular belief this is the origin of many of Bolivia's distinctive hats and the chola's skirts (see page 66). The mortality rate among the Indians was high, because of appalling working conditions in the mines and the import of European diseases, against which the indigenous population had little resistance. By the mid 17th century the Indian population had been almost halved.

During the 18th century many of Potosí's rich silver veins became exhausted and the colony of Alto Perú (as Bolivia was known), lost much of its influence.

INDEPENDENCE

Resistance to Spanish colonial rule had been less intense in Bolivia than neighbouring Peru. The most notable uprisings took place between 1780 and 1782, led by Túpac Katari, and were eventually crushed. But inspired by the French and American revolutions at the end of the 18th century, the *criollos*, descendants of Spaniards born in Latin America, became

War of the Pacific

One of the major international wars in Latin America since independence, this conflict has its roots in a long-running dispute between Chile and Bolivia over the ill-defined frontier in the Atacama desert.

There had already been one conflict, in 1836-1839, when Chile defeated Peru and Bolivia, putting an end to a confederation of the two states. The discovery of nitrates in the Atacama complicated relations. In the Bolivian Atacama province of Antofagasta nitrates were exploited by Anglo-Chilean companies.

In 1878 the Bolivian government, short of revenue, attempted to tax the Chilean-owned Antofagasta Railroad and Nitrate Company. When the company refused to pay, the Bolivians seized the company's assets. The Chilean government claimed that the Bolivian action broke an 1874 agreement between the two states. When Peru announced that it would honour a secret alliance with Bolivia by supporting her, the Chilean president, Aníbal Pinto, declared war on both states.

Despite several naval defeats and the loss of its capital, Peru did not sue for peace, although Bolivia had already signed a ceasefire as early as 1880, giving up its coastal province. Under the 1883 peace settlement Peru gave up Tarapacá to Chile. Although the provinces of Tacna and Arica were to be occupied by Chile for 10 years, it was not until 1929 that an agreement was reached under which Tacna was returned to Peru, while Chile kept Arica. Apart from souring relations between Chile and her two northern neighbours to this day, the War gave Chile a monopoly over the world's supply of nitrates and enabled her to dominate the southern Pacific coast.

With the loss of its Litoral province, Bolivia had lost its access to the sea. Many Bolivians still blame their country's underdevelopment on this event and since 1880 it has played an important part in foreign policy. During the dictatorship of Hugo Banzer (1971-78) the issue of Bolivia's access to the sea flared up, allowing the general to divert attention from domestic problems. In 1976 there was even talk of war.

Since then there have been continual negotiations between Chile and Peru over Bolivia's rights to the coast. In 1992 President Paz Zamora succeeded in agreeing a treaty with Peru giving Bolivia a zona franca (free zone) along the road from La Paz to the southern Peruvian port of Ilo. For the first time since 1880 goods could be transported free of duty to and from Bolivia via the Pacific coast.

increasingly frustrated by trade restrictions and high taxes imposed by the Spanish bureaucracy in the interests of Spain.

While Spain was occupied defending its borders against Napoleon's armies between 1808 and 1810, the University of San Francisco Xavier, at Sucre, called for the independence of all Spain's American colonies. When Spain tried to restore its rule in the following years the *criollo* commercial elites rebelled and took up arms against the Spanish authorities, under the leadership of the Venezuelan Simón Bolívar. On 9 December 1824 Simón Bolívar's general, General Antonio José de Sucre, won the decisive battle of Ayacucho in Peru and invaded Alto Perú, defeating the Spaniards finally at the battle of Tumusla on 2 April 1825.

On 9 February 1825, when he first entered La Paz, Sucre had already promulgated the decree of independence, but his second in command, Santa Cruz, was for retaining links with Peru. Bolívar was in two minds, but Sucre had his way and Bolivia was declared independent on 6 August in Sucre. In honour of its liberator, the country was named República de Bolívar, soon to be changed to Bolivia. La Plata became the capital and Sucre became the first president.

POST-INDEPENDENCE

For most of the period since independence, three main features have dominated Bolivian history: the importance of mining; the loss of territory through disputes and wars with neighbouring countries; and chronic political instability.

The noble principles of revolution were soon forgotten as the *caudillos* (military 'strongman' leaders) revealed themselves as defenders of the political and economic status quo. Although in the nineteenth century the army was very small, officers were key figures in power-struggles, often backing different factions of the *criollo* landowning elite, whose interests had replaced those of the former colonial rulers. At the end of the 19th century the political elite ended the existence of the *ayllus*, the Indian communal lands, which were simply swallowed up into the huge ranches (*latifundios*) of the landowners. The Indians, who had previously suffered under the *mita*, the system of compulsory labour, now became serfs, as their lives and labour were effectively owned by the estate owners.

Although silver had been so important in the colonial period, the Bolivian economy has depended for much of this century on exports of tin. The construction of railways and the demand for tin in Europe and the USA (particularly in wartime) led to a mining boom after 1900. In 1902 tin's export earnings exceeded those of silver for the first time. By the 1920s the industry was dominated by three entrepreneurs, Simón Patiño, Mauricio Hochschild and the Aramayo family, who exercised great influence over national politics.

POLITICAL INSTABILITY

Bolivian politics have been even more turbulent than elsewhere in Latin America. When the governing class was not engaged in conflicts with neighbouring countries, internal power struggles consumed all its energies. Between 1825 and 1982 there were no fewer than 188 coups d'état, earning the country a place in the Guinness Book of Records. The longest lasting government of the nineteenth century was that of Andrés Santa Cruz (1829-1839), but when he tried to unite Bolivia with Peru in 1836, Chile and Argentina intervened to overthrow him.

After the War of the Pacific (1879-1883) there was greater stability, but opposition to the political dominance of the city of Sucre culminated in a revolt in 1899 led by business groups from La Paz and the tin-mining areas, as a result of which La Paz became the centre of government.

Since independence Bolivia has suffered continual losses of territory, partly because of communications difficulties and the central government's inability to control distant provinces. One of the most politically damaging of these losses came as a consequence of a long-running dispute with Paraguay over the Chaco which erupted into war in 1932 and ended in ignominious defeat in 1935 and the loss of three quarters of the Chaco.

The Chaco War

In the 1920s the US Standard Oil Company was drilling for oil in the Bolivian Chaco. The company and the Bolivian government had designs on the Río Pilcomayo to transport the oil to the coast. It also seemed likely that there were further reserves in other parts of the inaccessible wilderness of the Chaco plain.

The problem was, however, that the Bolivian frontier with Paraguay had never been precisely defined. From 1928 there were border clashes with Paraguayan army patrols and in 1932 the Chaco War broke out. The Paragauyan forces knew the terrain much better than the Bolivian soldiers, who were mostly from the Andes and unused to the intense heat and humidity. By 1935 Bolivia had lost the war, practically the whole of the Chaco and 55,000 lives, but it did keep the oil-fields. Paraguay, though, won no more than a symbolic victory as no oil has ever been found in the Chaco.

MODERN BOLIVIA

The Chaco War was a turning point in Bolivian history. The political influence of the army increased and in 1936 it seized power for the first time since the War of the Pacific. Defeat in the Chaco War bred nationalist resentment among junior army officers who had served in the Chaco and among the Indians who had been used as cannon-fodder. After demobilization thousands of Indians refused to return to serfdom. Instead they settled in towns where they played a significant part in the political radicalization of the population, particularly the peasants and miners.

This growing national malaise among different sectors of society led to a group of young intellectuals setting up a nationalist party, the Movimiento Nacional Revolucionario (MNR) headed by Víctor Paz Estenssoro, Hernán Siles Zuazo, Walter Guevara Arce and Juan Lechín Oquendo. Their anger was directed against the mine owners and the leaders who had controlled Bolivian politics and they claimed to stand for the emancipation of the poor masses.

In 1944 Víctor Paz Estenssoro, a key party leader, succeeded in taking the MNR into the radical government of young army officers led by Major Gualberto Villaroel. However, in 1946 Villaroel was overthrown and publicly lynched and Paz Estenssoro had to flee to Argentina.

NATIONAL REVOLUTION

The 1951 elections were won by Víctor Paz, the MNR candidate. However, the incumbent government refused to recognize the result and transferred power to a military junta. The organized and radicalized miners reacted immediately and revolution broke out on 9 April 1952, backed by sections of the police as well as the campesinos, urban factory workers and the lower middle classes. Two days later the army surrendered to the MNR's militias and the National Revolution was a fact.

Paz Estenssoro became president and his MNR government nationalized the mines, introduced universal suffrage and began the break-up and redistribution of large estates under the Agrarian Reform programme of 1953 which ended the feudal economic conditions of rural Bolivia.

A shrinking nation

By the 1935, just over one hundred years after its proud declaration of independence, Bolivia had lost more than half of its original territory. Between 1835 and 1841 two wars were needed to determine the border with Peru, who, along with Brazil and Argentina, were determined that Bolivia should not become too powerful.

In 1867, Brazil seized a large portion of the Bolivian Amazon region and a part of the eastern Llanos, the Mato Grosso. Argentina had already occupied the central Chaco and then proceeded to help itself to another share of Bolivian territory, acquiring the Puna de Atacama. Following its rapid defeat at the hands of Chile in the War of the Pacific Bolivia lost its coastal provinces. As compensation Chile later agreed to build the railway between Arica and La Paz.

Railways traded for valuable territory has been Bolivia's fate. A railway to Yacuiba was Argentina's return for annexing some of the Chaco. During the first decade of the 20th century Bolivia lost the greater part of its northern territories. In 1903 Bolivia recognized Brazilian sovereignty over the rich Acre region in exchange for yet another railway, which was to create a passage to the Atlantic along navigable rivers. But this Madeira-Mamoré line never reached its destination, Riberalta, and proved of little use, eventually being closed in 1972.

There was not even an unbuilt railway to compensate Bolivia for its next loss, a huge part of the Chaco, in the southeast of the country.

In the aftermath of the revolution, the COB (Bolivian Workers Central), under the leadership of Juan Lechín Oquendo, became a major political force in the country. The giant mineral barons, Simón Patiño, Hochschild and Aramayo lost their massive political and economic influence and a new leadership class developed that would dominate Bolivia's political life for almost the next 40 years.

POST REVOLUTION

As the Bolivian constitution does not permit a second successive term of office, Paz Estenssoro stood down in 1956 in favour of the more pragmatic Vice-President Siles Zuazo. Faced with a drastic fall in the price of tin, Bolivia's main source of foreign income, and galloping inflation, Siles Zuazo accepted a 'stabilization' plan designed by the International Monetary Fund (IMF). Hardest hit by the policy of freezing wages and scrapping basic food subsidies were the working class and the MNR became increasingly distanced from its original power base. The rank and file of the MNR split into peasants on the one side and miners and the urban proletariat on the other.

Víctor Paz, who had now become leader of the centre-right faction within the MNR, was re-elected president in 1960, with Juan Lechín Oquendo as Vice-President. Growing ideological divides were tearing the party apart and by 1964 it disintegrated into factional warfare. The constitution had to be changed to allow Paz Estenssoro to stand again, which he did with the support of the charismatic General René Barrientos. Shortly afterwards, however, Víctor Paz was overthrown by his Vice-President, who relied on the support of the army and the peasants to defeat the miners.

MILITARY COUPS

As in many other Latin American countries, the 1960s and 1970s were dominated in Bolivia by coups d'état and military governments. The many military dictatorships of this period were very different in nature. Some were authoritarian and repressive while others were more populist. Under the Barrientos regime (1964-69) political opponents and trade union activists were brutally persecuted and miners' rebellions were put down violently, just as they had been before the Revolution. The death of Barrientos in a mysterious air crash in 1969 was followed by three brief military governments. The third, led by General Juan José Torres, pursued left-wing policies which alarmed many army officers and business leaders.

In August 1971 Torres was overthrown by the right-wing General Hugo Banzer, whose rule lasted until 1978. During those years tens of thousands of Bolivians were imprisoned or exiled for political reasons. Apart from the Bolivian Socialist Falange (FSB) and the MNR, which shared government with the military for the first three years, all political parties and trade unions were banned. The state universities were subject to military supervision and there was strict censorship. In 1974 the MNR left the government and Paz Estenssoro, who had returned in 1971, went back into exile. The new Banzer regime continued to rule in an even more authoritarian manner, though mild by comparison with contemporary regimes in Argentina and Chile. In 1978 Banzer was forced to call elections, partly as a result of the pressure which US President Jimmy Carter exerted on the military government because of its human rights abuses.

There followed another period of chronic instability, political unrest and military violence between 1978 and 1982, with three presidential elections and five coups. Civilian rule returned on 10 October 1982 when Hernán Siles Zuazo once again took office, but not before the notoriously brutal military coup led by General García Meza (1980-1981). In August 1982 the military returned to barracks and Siles Zuazo assumed the presidency in a leftist coalition government with support from the communists and trade unions. Under this regime inflation spiralled out of control.

The Cocaine President

In the elections of June 1980, Hernán Siles Zuazo managed to gain a decisive lead over his opponents but yet again a military coup d'état was to prevent the country from having its elected civilian president when the army commander Luís García Meza seized power.

A period of brutal repression began in which human rights abuses were more widespread than ever before. The regime's involvement with notorious Nazis such as Klaus Barbie and neo-fascists from Argentina and elsewhere was an open secret. Paramilitary groups made frequent night raids on political opponents, dragging them from their beds and subjecting them to torture. Following Pinochet's example in Chile, the sports stadium in La Paz was used as a prison camp. Other subversive elements were imprisoned in concentration camps in the Oriente.

García Meza's government was the most corrupt Bolivia has ever known. The dictator and his partners-in-crime amassed huge fortunes through their close involvement with the national and international drug mafia. As a result the US and most other states would not recognize the regime and Bolivia became an outcast. The end of the cocaine regime came in August 1981 when García Meza was replaced by a military junta angered that his corrupt administration had brought the armed forces into disrepute.

Despite the innumerable human rights violations and his involvement in cocaine trafficking, García Meza did not face trial until 1993, when he was sentenced to 30 years in prison. Although several of his accomplices were imprisoned at the same time on human rights charges, García Meza himself managed to escape during the much-publicized trial. He was captured in Brazil in early 1994 and held there by the military until February 1995, when he was extradited to Bolivia. He is now held in solitary confinement in a prison outside La Paz.

TOWARDS DEMOCRACY

The elections of 14 July 1985 were won again by Víctor Paz Estenssoro, but only by forming a coalition with Jaime Paz Zamora of the Movimiento de la Izquierda Revolucionaria (MIR). In order to save the economy, Víctor Paz enlisted the help of Dr Jeffrey Sachs, a Harvard professor who imposed a radical programme of structural adjustment, known as the New Economic Policy (NEP).

No one could have predicted it would be so tough. One of its main thrusts was the radical dismantling of the state sector which Víctor Paz had himself set up 30 years before. Under Professor Sach's neo-liberal economic model the first sacrificial targets were the by-now outdated mines of the state-owned Comibol. By the end of 1985, 23,000 miners lost their jobs. Some remained to form their own co-operatives but most left in search of new livelihoods in the coca regions of the Oriente, or in the larger cities.

In the elections of 7 May 1989 a new character appeared on the political stage, Gonzalo Sánchez de Lozada of the MNR, chief architect of the stabilization programme. Sánchez de Lozada, or 'Goni', won most votes but the result was so close that Congress had to choose a president from the three leading contenders. Paz Zamora, who came third in the elections, was inaugurated as President on 6 August 1989 after having made an unlikely alliance with the former military dictator, the retired General Hugo Banzer of Acción Democrática Nacionalista (ADN), in return for certain cabinet posts.

The presidential election of 6 June 1993 was fought between Acuerdo Patriótico, led by Hugo Banzer, a coalition of MIR, Banzer's own ADN and two other parties, Gonzalo Sánchez de Lozada of the MNR, Unidad Cívica Solidaridad (UCS), led by the brewery owner Max Fernández, and the populist Conciencia de Patria (Condepa) of Carlos Palenque. Gonzalo Sánchez de Lozada won the greater number of votes but failed to gain the required 51% majority to win the presidency outright.

Shortly afterwards, however, the other candidates recognized Sánchez de Lozada's victory and withdrew from the contest. In a shrewd move to gain the support of the Indian population, Goni formed an alliance with Víctor Hugo Cárdenas, leader of the Movimiento Revolucionario Túpac Katari de Liberación (MRTKL), one of Bolivia's two small indigenist parties which aim to promote the emancipation of the Indian population.

The 1997 presidential elections were won by former dictator General Hugo Banzer (1971-78) with 23% of the vote. Former president Jaime Paz Zamora (1989-93), whose US visa was withdrawn in 1996 for alleged drug money links, came second with the next three parties all polling 15-17% of the vote. A coalition of four of the five leading parties secured Banzer a working majority and Banzer and his advisers immediately took a flight to Washington DC to secure approval from the US. Interestingly, it was former US president Jimmy Carter's decision to stop funding Third World regimes with human rights problems which helped lead to Banzer's downfall in 1978.

Economically, Banzer's party, Acción Democrática Nacionalista, supported the previous government's privatization programme (called capitalization in Bolivia), which saw the sale of major state-owned companies, and major changes are therefore not expected. Bolivia is the largest recipient of foreign aid in South America and so major economic policies must meet with World Bank and International Monetary Fund approval. Banzer's first presidential decree was one promising continued support for the neo-liberal regime that has been forced on the country since 1985 when inflation hit 24,000%.

Economy

STRUCTURE OF PRODUCTION

Bolivia suffers from a rugged terrain, which makes communications difficult, while its landlocked position hinders export development. A history of dictatorships and coup d'états did nothing to improve the living standards of the mostly Indian population, who eked out a living with subsistence farming on the altiplano or down the mines. The restoration of democracy in the 1980s is having a gradual beneficial effect and redistribution of income is a long term goal.

Agriculture is an important sector of the economy, contributing 16% of gdp and employing over a third of the population. Small scale farming of traditional products is in the highlands, where excess produce is sold in local markets. In the east, however, there is very fertile land. The most productive area is in the province of Santa Cruz, where the fluvial plains are extremely rich in nutrients. Here the tropical climate allows two crops a year of soya beans and farmers achieve yields of around 3 tonnes a hectare, compared with 1.5-2 tonnes in neighbouring countries. Bolivian and foreign investors have bought large estates to grow soya and other crops, such as cotton, sunflower and sugar, and agroindustry is booming as processing plants are built. The tropical lowlands of the Chapare region are where some 25,000 families grow the coca leaf on about 50,000 hectares. Although growing and chewing coca leaf is legal in Bolivia, almost all the Chapare coca is illegally refined into cocaine and exported. US-funded eradication programmes have been largely

Bolivia: fact file

Geographic

Land area	1,098,581 sq km
forested	53.5%
pastures	24.4%
cultivated	2.2%

Demographic

Population (1996)	7,592,000
annual growth rate (1991-96)	2.4%
urban	57.7%
rural	42.3%
density	6.2 per sq km

Education and Health

Life expectancy at birth,	
male	60.9 years
female	65.9 years
Infant mortality rate	
per 1,000 live births (1990-95)	75.1
Calorie intake as %	
of FAO requirement	88%
Population age 25 and over	
with no formal schooling	23.3%
Literate males (over 15)	87.7%
Literate females (over 15)	71.8%

Economic and Employment

GNP (1994 market prices)	US$5,601mn
GNP per capita	US$770
Public external debt (1994)	US$4,113mn
Tourism receipts (1994)	US$135mn
Inflation (annual av 1990-95)	11.9%
Population economically active (1992)	
	2,530,409
Unemployment rate	2.5%
Military forces	33,500

Source *Encyclopaedia Britannica*

unsuccessful. It is believed that about US$350 million a year comes back into the economy from drugs trafficking.

Mining contributes only 10% to gdp, but it is an area of considerable investment and growth. Bolivia is a major producer of tin, antimony, wolfram, bismuth, silver, lead, zinc and gold, while there are large reserves of iron, lithium and potassium. The state mining company, Comibol,

closed most of its operations during the recession of the 1980s, forcing unemployment for 23,000 miners. In the mid-1990s all Comibol's deposits, mines, smelters and refineries were put up for sale. Comibol remained as a small operation to administer leasing and joint venture contracts. The 1991 Mining Code allows equal treatment for foreign and national companies and free remittances of profits abroad. Foreigners in joint ventures with Bolivians may now explore and develop the previously prohibited zones within 50 km of borders. Investor interest is considerable, particularly in gold. The Kori Kollo gold mine, near Oruro, is the second largest in Latin America. Total gold output is about 14 tonnes a year, making it a leading export earner. Although Bolivia is one of the largest producers of tin in the world, low prices in the 1980s and 1990s have reduced export income. The Cordillera Real is the traditional mining zone for silver and tin, but companies are now looking in the W Cordillera and E towards the Brazilian border where mineral deposits are unexploited. There are iron reserves at El Mutun in Busch province on the border with Brazil, believed to be 40,000 tonnes with 30-50% iron, making it one of the world's largest deposits.

The oil and gas industry traditionally provided the Government with its largest single source of income. The state oil and gas company, Yacimientos Petrolíferos Fiscales Bolivianos (YPFB), was the largest company in Bolivia in 1994 with a workforce of 14,900. YPFB was partly 'capitalized' (see below) in 1996. Bolivia exports natural gas to Argentina worth US$120 million a year, and a joint project with Brazil to build a pipeline to transport initially 8 million cubic feet a day of natural gas from the Santa Cruz area to São Paulo will become an even bigger source of foreign exchange in 1998. An agreement has also been signed with Paraguay for a gas pipeline to Asunción. In 1995 proven reserves of gas were 4,500 billion cubic feet, but exploration in progress is expected to triple those reserves.

RECENT TRENDS

The recession which afflicted most Latin American countries from 1980 hit Bolivia with six consecutive years of contraction of gdp, accompanied by accelerating inflation, massive and frequent devaluations of the currency and social unrest. Government spending to support key export sectors was hampered by massive public sector deficits and external indebtedness. Economic problems were compounded in 1983 by a severe drought in the Altiplano and floods in the eastern lowlands, which devastated farming. The resulting food shortages exacerbated existing inflationary pressures and led to hyperinflation with annual rates reaching over 20,000%.

In the mid-1980s the Government introduced severe austerity measures to stabilize the economy, in which price controls were lifted, subsidies removed, public sector wages frozen and a new currency was created, the boliviano, linked to the US dollar in a controlled float. Tax reform was passed, the first of many IMF credits was negotiated, bilateral and multilateral lending began to flow again and steps were taken to buy back at a discount the external commercial bank debt. Inflation came down to 10-20% a year, although unemployment continued to rise and living standards to fall. Nevertheless, by the 1990s growth and employment were recovering.

In 1994 the Government began an ambitious reform programme encompassing fiscal decentralization (Popular Participation Programme), education reform and removing the state from the means of production, aiming to increase investment and savings. The Bolivian divestment scheme, known as 'capitalization', brought no direct revenue to the state. Investors agreed to inject fresh capital into a state-owned company in return for a 50% controlling stake. The other 50% of the shares were distributed to all Bolivians over 18 via a private pension fund scheme, an ambitious proposal in a country where only 5% of the population had bank accounts and savings were negligible. Five state companies, accounting for about 12.5% of gdp, were chosen for capitalization in 1995-96: electricity, telecommunications, air transport, railways and several sectors of YPFB.

By the time President Banzer took office in mid-1997, gdp growth had been averaging 4.2% a year for 4 years, inflation was in single figures, exports had grown by 25% a year and net international reserves stood at US$1 billion, all of which put the economy on a sound footing for the new government to concentrate on combating poverty.

Culture

ARTS AND CRAFTS

The Incas inherited many centuries of skills and traditions from the peoples they incorporated into their empire. All of these played important roles in political, social and religious ceremonies. Though much of this artistic heritage was destroyed by the Spanish conquest, the traditions adapted and evolved in numerous ways, absorbing new methods, concepts and materials from Europe while maintaining ancient techniques and symbols.

TEXTILES AND COSTUMES

Some of the most beautifully woven and dyed textiles to be found anywhere were produced by the Aymara Indians of the Bolivian Altiplano up until the late 19th century. These reflect the incredibly rich textile tradition which flourished in the Lake Titicaca basin since ancient times.

History

Originally, textile production arose out of the simple need for clothing. Gradually, though, more complicated techniques and designs evolved. Far from being merely of utilitarian purpose, Andean textiles played major political, social and religious roles. Woven cloth was the most highly-prized possession and sought after trading commodity in the Andes in precolumbian times and was used to establish and strengthen social and political relationships. It also played an essential role in all phases of the life cycle.

The Incas inherited this rich weaving tradition from the Aymaras and forced them to work in *mitas* or textile workshops. The largest quantities of the finest textiles were made specifically to be burned as ritual offerings – a tradition which still survives. The Spanish, too, exploited this wealth and skill by using the *mitas* and exporting the cloth to Europe.

Spanish chroniclers reported that, upon retreating from battle, Inca soldiers sometimes left behind thousands of llamas and prisoners, and even gold and silver, but chose to burn entire warehouses filled with cloth rather than leave them for the conquistadores. Indeed, in the Quipus, the string knot recording system of the Incas, only people and camelids ranked above textiles.

It is, therefore, not surprising that ancient weaving traditions survived the conquest while other social and cultural traditions disappeared. Textiles continue to play an important part in society in many parts of Bolivia. They are still handed down from one generation to the next and used specifically for ritual ceremonies. As a result, the finest textiles have survived until today. However, the influence of modern technology has reached even remote highland areas. Rural people have begun to wear machine-made clothes and many aspects of the ancient art of weaving are now lost.

Costumes

Prior to Inca rule Aymara men wore a tunic (*llahua*) and a mantle (*llacata*) and carried a bag for coca leaves (*huallquepo*). The women wore a wrapped dress (*urku*) and mantle (*iscayo*) and a belt (*huaka*); their coca bag was called an *istalla*. The *urku* was fastened at shoulder level with a pair of metal *tupu*, the traditional Andean dress-pins.

Probably in imitation of the Aymara, the Inca men had tunics (*unkus*) and a bag for coca leaves called a *ch'uspa*. The women wore a blouse (*huguna*), skirts (*aksu*) and belts (*chumpis*), and carried foodstuffs in large, rectangular cloths called *llicllas*, which were fastened at the chest with a single pin or a smaller clasp called a *ttipqui*.

In isolated Andean villages and communities women still wear the traditional *aksu*, a skirt over two pieces of cloth overlapping at the sides and held up by a belt. The women of Tarabuco and Potolo, near Sucre, for example, commonly wear *aksus*, while Tarabuco men wear red and orange striped ponchos, and hats similar to crash helmets, possibly inspired by the Spanish army helmets. Tarabuco women's hats are small white *monteras* decorated with sequins. One item of costume which plays a particularly important role in the lives of the native population is the belt. The Aymara devote much of their lives to making belts for different occasions.

During the post-conquest period native dress was modified to satisfy Spanish ideas of propriety. Spanish policy concerning dress demanded that the Indian population should be fully and properly dressed at all times and that each person must be dressed according to his/her class. Spanish dress was restricted to the upper-class Indian.

The last century of the colonial period was disturbed by numerous Indian uprisings. The Spanish rulers believed that by restricting the natives' traditional clothing it could diminish their identification with their ancestors and that discontent would, therefore, be reduced. Thus the native male costume became pants, jacket, vest and poncho. In the less accessible parts, people were able to preserve their customs to a certain extent. While the Spanish influence is still evident in much of the Indians' dress, indigenous garments are also worn, forming a costume that is distinctly Andean.

Textile materials and techniques

The Andean people used mainly alpaca or llama wool. The former can be spun into fine, shining yarn when woven and has a lustre similar to that of silk, though sheep's wool came to be widely used following the Spanish conquest.

A commonly used technique is the drop spindle. A stick is weighted with a wooden wheel and the raw material is fed through one hand. A sudden twist and drop in the spindle spins the yarn. This very sensitive art can be seen practised by women while herding animals in the fields.

Spinning wheels were introduced by Europeans and are now prevalent due to increased demand. Precolombian looms were often portable and those in use today are generally similar. A woman will herd her animals while making a piece of costume, perhaps on a backstrap loom, or waist loom, so-called because the weaver controls the tension on one side with her waist with the other side tied to an upright or tree. These looms can't be used on the treeless Altiplano so the Aymara people use four sticks set in the ground to hold the loom in place. The precolumbian looms are usually used for personal costume while the treadle loom is used for more commercial pieces in textile centres such as Villa Ribera, near Cochabamba, as it provides greater efficiency and flexibility.

Most weaving occurs during the winter season, after the harvest and before the next year's planting. The women spend much of their day at the loom while also looking after the children and carrying out other daily chores. A complex piece of textile can take up to several months to complete and, because of the time taken, is built to last many years.

Today, there is increasing pressure on indigenous people to desert their homes and join the white and mestizo people in the cities. Furthermore, Indians in native costume are often looked down on and considered uncivilized. There is a danger of the traditional textiles of the Andes becoming museum pieces rather than articles of daily use and wear. In some areas foreign aid and leadership of experts is proving effective. In Sucre, for example, a group of anthropologists has successfully brought about the revival of traditional village weaving (see page 220).

Knitting has a relatively short history in the Andes. Fibres commonly used are alpaca, llama and sheep's wool. During the past two decades though, much of the alpaca and llama wool has been bought by larger companies for export. Today, much of the wool for knitting is bought ready-spun from factories.

Outside the towns the majority of knitting is still done by hand. Traditionally many of the *chullos*, knitted hats with ear flaps worn on the Altiplano, are knitted with four small hooked needles. In the Andes the more traditional pieces still have patterns with llamas, mountains and other scenic and geometric designs.

The skills of dyeing were still practised virtually unchanged even after the arrival of the Spaniards. Nowadays, the word *makhnu* refers to any natural dye, but originally was the name for cochineal, an insect which lives on the leaves of the nopal cactus. These dyes were used widely by precolumbian weavers. Vegetable dyes are also used, made from the leaves, fruit and seeds of shrubs and flowers and from lichen, tree bark and roots. Although the high price for cochineal in the use of food colouring has discouraged its use for textiles, it is still widely combined with man-made dyes in textile centres such as Villa Ribera and around Lake Titicaca.

Symbolism

Symbolism plays an important role in weaving. Traditionally every piece of textile from a particular community had identical symbols and colours which were a source of identity as well as carrying specific symbols and telling a story. In the Andean world the planet Venus (*Chaska*) played an important role in mythology and in the agricultural pattern. Its appearance was used to forecast the coming year's rainfall. This symbol and that of the Sun (*Inti*) predominated in textile decoration and were universal to the *ayllus*, the self-sufficient and self-governing communities. The Jalq'a people of Sucre weave bizarre animal motifs on their *aksus*, or overskirts. These symbols perhaps represent *chulpas*, creatures that inhabited the Earth before the birth of the Sun.

The arrival of the Spaniards in the 16th century initiated a new era of symbolism as old and new elements appeared side by side. Symbols such as *Inti* may be found together with a horse figure introduced after the conquest. Sometimes the meanings of motifs have multiplied or been superseded. The cross, for example, in prehispanic times signified the constellation of Cruz del Sur, the Southern Cross, or Cruz de la Siembra, guardian of the fields. Both have been eclipsed by the Christian symbol.

Buying textiles

Bolivia is an excellent source of textiles, which vary greatly from region to region in style, technique and use. For mantas the best place is in the shops behind San Francisco church in La Paz (see page 102). Prices are lower if you buy direct from the Tarabuco Indians who carry their loads of textiles up and down the steep streets. Other good places to find textiles are the market in Tarabuco and at ASUR, a textile project based in Sucre which works closely with rural communities (see page 222).

Among the many villages dotted throughout the Andes, the following produce textiles which are particularly sought after and, therefore, more expensive: **Calcha**, in southern Potosí; **Tarabuco**, near Sucre; **Charazani**, in the Apolobamba mountains in the north of La Paz department; **Sica Sica**, between La Paz and Oruro; **Calamarca**, south of La Paz on the road to Oruro; **Challa**, halfway between Oruro and Cochabamba. In the northern part of the Potosí department, southeast from Oruro and northwest of Sucre, are the villages of **Llallagua**, **Sacaca**, **Bolívar** and **Macha**. Here, traditional weaving is maintained more than in any other part of Bolivia and the textiles are the most widely sold, especially in La Paz.

If you are asked to pay US$200-300 for a manta, which usually takes around 2 months to weave, this a more realistic price than US$10-20. If a manta has old stains on it, it may be better to leave them, as cleaning it may damage the textile. In general, though, Andean weavings are tough and can cope with washing, though at cool temperatures. If buying a newly-woven piece, check that the dyes are properly fixed before washing. Wet a small part then wipe it on white paper to see if any of the colours appear.

HATS

Hats were an important element of much prehispanic costume and Bolivia has perhaps a greater variety of styles than any other region in South America. According to Peter McFarren (*An Insider's Guide to Bolivia*) there are over 100 styles of hat. One reason hats are so important in Bolivia is the high altitude of the Andes, where the sun's rays are more intense, making hats a necessity. Another is the survival of traditional costume among the country's Indian majority. The hat is the most important piece of the Indian's outfit and accompanies the wearer everywhere. The reason it is so important is because it is worn on the head, the most sacred part of the body and spirit.

One of the most familiar features of La Paz are the Aymara women with their brown or grey bowler, or derby hats, locally called a *bombín*. While the vast majority of the hats are made of felt, some are still made from rabbit hair, as they all were originally. Among the many styles is the 'JR Dallas', a Stetson named after JR Ewing, a character from the hit TV show, 'Dallas'. Another style, worn by the residents of Tarija, near the Argentine border, is based on those worn by their colonial ancestors from Andalucia. In Potosí, the women's hat is like a 'stove-pipe'.

In Cochabamba, Quechua women wear a white top hat of ripolined straw, decorated with a black ribbon. According to legend, a young unmarried Quechua woman in the city was reprimanded by a Roman Catholic priest for living with her boyfriend, a practice common among Indian couples intending to marry. As a punishment, she was made to wear a black ribbon around the base of the hat. The next day at Mass, much to the priest's chagrin, all the women were wearing the black ribbon and the style stuck.

POTTERY

In all their variety the prehispanic ceramics found in burial sites across the Americas have emphasized the extent to which the precolumbian potters imbued their work with religious or magical symbolism. The potter's skill was not merely required to produce utilitarian objects necessary for daily life but was evidently a specialized, sometimes sanctified, art which required more than technical expertise.

Inca ceramic decoration consists mainly of small-scale geometric and usually symmetrical designs. One distinctive form of vessel which continues to be made and used is the *arybola*. This pot is designed to carry liquid, especially chicha, and is secured with a rope on the bearer's back. It is believed that *arybolas* were used mainly by the governing Inca élite and became important status symbols.

With the Spanish invasion many indigenous communities lost their artistic traditions, others remained relatively untouched, while others still combined hispanic and indigenous traditions and techniques. The Spanish brought three innovations: the potter's wheel, which gave greater speed and uniformity; knowledge of the enclosed kiln; and the technique of lead glazes. The enclosed kiln made temperature regulation easier and allowed higher temperatures to be maintained, producing stronger pieces. Today, many communities continue to apply pre-hispanic techniques, while others use more modern processes.

JEWELLERY AND METALWORK

The Incas associated gold with the Sun. However, very few examples of their fine goldwork remain as the Spaniards melted down their amassed gold and silver objects and then went on to extract more precious metals from the ground. The surviving Indians were forced to work in barbaric conditions in gold and silver mines, where the death toll was horrifically high, most notoriously at Potosí.

During the colonial period gold and silver pieces were made to decorate the altars of churches and houses of the élite. Metalworkers came from Spain and Italy to develop the industry. The Spanish preferred silver and strongly influenced the evolution of silverwork during the colonial period. A style known as Andean baroque developed embracing both indigenous and European elements. Silver bowls in this style – *cochas* – are still used in Andean ceremonies.

Part of the Inca female costume was a large silver pin with a decorative head, the *tupu*, worn at the neck of the cloak, or *lliclla*, to hold it in place. Today, it continues to be made and used by the majority of Quechua-speaking people in Bolivia, though its form has changed over the centuries. In Inca times the decorative head was usually disc or fan-shaped, thought to derive from the tumi knife, which was used for surgery. During colonial times Western emblems superseded the Inca forms. When in the 19th century uprisings caused native costume to be strictly regulated by the authorities, the *tupu* developed an oval, spoon-shaped head, sometimes incised, and had decorative charms suspended on silver chains.

In the Amazon basin seeds, flowers and feathers continue to be used as jewellery by many peoples. The western fashion for natural or ethnic jewellery has encouraged production, using brightly-coloured feathers, fish bones, seeds or animal teeth.

WOODCARVING

Carved religious figures, usually made from hardwoods, were a central influence in the development of woodcarving. In Eastern Bolivia, as in Paraguay, the tradition of carving and painting religious figures originates with the Jesuits, whose missions, or *reducciones*, gathered the indigenous people into settlements (see also page 271). They were set to work to build churches and produce handicrafts, such as earthenware pots, paintings and wood-carvings to adorn the churches. After the Jesuits' expulsion the Indians were left to fend for themselves. They kept their techniques and traditions that had been passed on to them and from these evolved the style of woodcarving today.

In La Paz and Cochabamba good examples of indigenous woodcarving can be found. Images of Indians, mountains, condors and Tiahuanaco are carved on wooden plaques. In La Paz, carvers specialize in male and female Indian heads.

MUSIC AND DANCE

When people talk of Bolivian music they are almost certainly referring to the music of the Quechua- and Aymara-speaking Indians of the high Altiplano which provides the most distinctive Bolivian sound. The music of the Andes has become very well known throughout Europe and North America ever since the Bolivian song 'El Cóndor Pasa' was recorded with English lyrics by Simon & Garfunkel and became an international hit. Now the distinctive sound of the Andes can be heard echoing around shopping malls and pedestrian precincts from London to Los Angeles.

THE ORIGINS

The music of Bolivia can be described as the very heartbeat of the country. Each region has its own distinctive music that reflects its particular lifestyle, its mood and its physical surroundings. The music of the Altiplano, for example, is played in a minor key and tends to be sad and mournful, while the music of the lowlands is more up-tempo and generally happier.

Precolumbian music, which is still played today on towns and villages throughout the Andes, sounds very different from the music normally associated with that region now. The original uninfluenced music can sound unusual and even unpleasant to western ears with its shrillness and use of scales and notes to which we are unaccustomed. Precolumbian music consisted of a 5-note (pentatonic) scale, supposedly based on the 5 notes ancient people discovered in the wind. With the arrival of the Spaniards Andean music changed and took on western forms, notably the 7-note scale. As more notes became available, so more varied themes could be played and the music we understand today as being Andean began to evolve.

MUSICAL INSTRUMENTS

Before the arrival of the Spaniards in Latin America, over 400 years ago, the only instruments were wind and percussion. Although it is a popular misconception that Andean music is based on the panpipes, guitar and *charango*, anyone who travels through the Andes will realize that these instruments only represent a small aspect of Andean music. Bolivian music itself has more Amerindian style and content than that of any other country in South America. It is rare to find an indigenous Bolivian who cannot play an instrument and it is these instruments, both wind and percussion, that are quintessentially Bolivian.

The *quena* is a flute, usually made of reed, characterized by not having a mouthpiece to blow through. As with all Andean instruments, there is a family of *quenas* varying in length from around 15 cm to 50 cm. The *siku* is the Aymara name for the *zampoña*, or panpipes. It is the most important prehispanic Andean instrument, formed by several reed tubes of different sizes held together by knotted string. Traditionally they are played singly, one person having one row of pipes. *Tarkas* are a type of flute made from the wood of the taco tree, from which their name derives. They are used a lot in festivals and have a shrill sound. *Pinquillos* are bamboo flutes with three octaves manufactured in Patacamaya, between Oruro and La Paz, and *moseños* are long, thick bamboo instruments played from the side.

Phututos were prehispanic trumpets originally made from sea shells, wood or ceramics. Now the horn of a bull is used to produce the low, deep sound used by rural communities to call meetings. In Tarija, bull's horns are also used to make *erkes*, which are very similar to *phututos* but are tied to long reeds, some as long as 4m, and played collectively.

Amongst the percussion instruments are the *bombo*, a drum of various sizes, originally made from a hollowed-out tree trunk with the skins of llama or goat. *Chaj'chas* are made from sheep's hooves, dried in the sun, oiled and sewn onto a wrist cloth. Virtually the only instrument of European origin is the *charango*, which is traditionally made in the village of Aiquile, near Cochabamba. When stringed instruments were first introduced by the Spanish, the indigenous people liked them but wanted something that was their own and so the *charango* was born. Originally, they were made of clay, condor skeletons and armadillo or tortoise shells. Now, though, they are almost always made from wood. One of the main production centres is Oruro. In the Chuquisaca region, a group of players of three or even four sizes of *charango* with different voices is traditional.

Where to hear music

Every town in Bolivia has its own *peña*, where you can hear popular Bolivian folk music. Some of the top hotels also present shows.

During periods of military dictatorship many folk musicians used their performances in *peñas* to register their opposition to repression and censorship in protest songs. *Peñas* became a focus of resistance to military rule. In recent years, though, with the return to democracy and the rise of more contemporary varieties of youth culture, *peñas* have been losing their attraction. Today, *peñas* are more likely to attract tourists than native young Bolivians.

Bolivia's many festivals are also good places to hear traditional music. For example, La Fiesta del Gran Poder in La Paz (see page 87), the Carnival in Oruro, or the Luzmilla Patiño festival in Cochabamba. The Fiesta de la Cruz takes place all over the Andes on 3 May, when thousands of musicians come together to play all shapes and sizes of instruments, including the *toyos*, which are huge pan-pipes over 1m long and hail from the Titicaca region.

The region of Tarija near the Argentine border has a distinctive musical tradition of its own, based on religious processions that culminate with that of San Roque on the first Sunday in September. The influence is Spanish and the musical instruments are the *caña*, *erke* and *violin chapaco*. The first named is an immensely long bamboo tube with a horn at the end.

There are many professional folk groups on record. The most popular, Los Kjarkas, actually wrote the original song *Llorando se fue*, but the hit version was recorder by a French group under the now-famous title *Lambada*. Other well-known folk groups are Wara, Los Masis, Los Quipus and Rumillajta who have built up a considerable following in Europe. The greatest exponent of the charango is the legendary Ernesto Cavour, who can be heard at some of the best-known *peñas* in La Paz (see page 99).

DANCE

Just as music is the heartbeat of the country, so dance conveys the rich and ancient heritage that typifies much of the national spirit. Bolivians are tireless dancers and dancing is the most popular form of entertainment. Unsuspecting travellers should note that once they make that first wavering step there will be no respite until they collapse from exhaustion.

Organized group dances

Comparsas are organized groups of dancers who perform for spectators dances following a set pattern of movements to a particular musical accompaniment, wearing a specific costume. These dances have a long tradition, having mostly originated from certain contexts and circumstances and some of them still parody the ex-Spanish colonial masters. The most famous *comparsas* are those from the Oruro Carnival (see page 182).

Another notable *comparsa* is the comical *Auqui Auqui* (auqui is Aymara for old man). The dance satirizes the solemnity and pomposity of Spanish gentlemen from the colonial period. Because of their dignified dress and manners they could appear old, and a humped back is added to the dancers to emphasize age. These little old men have long pointed noses, flowing beards and carry crooked walking sticks. They dance stooped, regularly pausing to complain and rub aching backs, at times even stumbling and falling, to the accompaniment of *pinquillos*.

A number of dances replicate hunting scenes, the origins of which are thought to lie in the *chacu*, the great annual Inca hunt which involved 20,000-30,000 people forming a huge circle and then closing in until the animals could be caught by hand. The main protagonist in most of the hunting dances is the *K'usillu*, a mischievous character, half monkey half devil. He wears a bright costume, a horned crown and carries a whip, tambourine or pinquillo. The *Liphi* dance, or vicuña hunt, often involves the *K'usillu* carrying a stuffed vicuña while being chased by an old man representing the *achachila* or spirit of the mountains. When the *K'usillu* is caught, an old woman, the spirit of the earth, beheads the vicuña and the body is then carried off by a condor.

In the *Wititis* the *K'usillu* carries a live partridge, singing out in imitation of the bird. He is accompanied by men dressed as young women and condors. Other dancers try to lasso the fleeing partridge but often hook the young women instead. In the *Chokelas*, or fox hunt, the *K'usillu* carries a stuffed fox and chases the women relentlessly, mimicking the Spaniards' pursuit of native women.

Dances for everyone

Many dances for couples and/or groups are danced spontaneously at fiestas throughout Bolivia. These include indigenous dances which have originated in a specific region and ballroom dances that reflect the Spanish influence.

One of the most popular of the indigenous dances is the *Huayño* which originated on the Altiplano but is now danced throughout the country. It involves numerous couples, who whirl around or advance down the street, arm-in-arm, in a '*Pandilla*'. During fiestas, and especially after a few drinks, this can develop into a kind of uncontrolled frenzy.

Similar to the *Huayño* is the *Chovena* from the Beni and Santa Cruz regions. The *Chovena* originated from tribal dances, as did the *Machetero*, another folkloric dance from the lowlands. The *Chapaqueada* is a dance from Tarija which is performed at religious festivals such as Christmas and Easter. The name derives from the word Chapaco, a person from Tarija. The dance is accompanied by typical Tarijan instruments (see above). There are countless other indigenous dances, far too many to list here.

Of the ballroom dances, the *Cueca* is perhaps the best known. The Bolivian *Cueca* is a close relative of the Chilean national dance of the same name and they share a mutual origin in the *Zamacueca*, itself derived from the Spanish *Fandango*. Today the *Cueca* is very representative of Bolivia, as typical of this country as the Tango is of Argentina. Similar to the *Cueca* is the *Bailecito Chuquisaqueño*, though it is more delicate without the emphasis on provocative mannerisms. Other regional dances include the *Khaluyo Cochabambino* and *Rueda Tarijeña* from the southeast and *Carnavalito Cruceño* and *Taquirari Beniano* from the tropical lowlands.

Outside of the fiestas, the most popular dances are not of Bolivian origin: *Salsa*, *Merengue*, Brazilian *Soca* and *Samba* and Colombian *Cumbia*. *Salsa* dancing should probably not be attempted by anyone unfamiliar with the basic steps or unable to wiggle their hips in time to the beat. If you really must attempt this, then make sure enough alcohol has been consumed to render you unaware of the fact that you are the laughing stock of the dance floor. *Merengue*, *Soca* and *Samba* are just about viable, given a crowded dance floor and very understanding partner.

Cumbia, on the other hand, is a cinch. It was originally invented by black slaves as a means of moving more easily while shackled together. All you need to do is shuffle around a bit, dragging one leg behind the other, occasionally performing a clumsy spin, rather in the manner of a drunken sales rep at a Friday night disco.

FESTIVALS

Fiestas are a fundamental part of life for most Bolivians, taking place up and down the length and breadth of the country and with such frequency that it would be hard to miss one, even during the briefest of stays. This is fortunate, because arriving in any town or village during these inevitably frenetic celebrations is one of the great Bolivian experiences.

Bolivian fiestas range from the elaborately choreographed processions of Oruro to a simple llama sacrifice in a tiny

Eat, drink and be merry

One of the most prominent figures in Andean fiestas is the *Danzanti*, a character of Spanish origin but fully adopted by the Bolivian Indians. The dancer wears a huge, green and red mask with bulging eyes and large protruding ears, decorated with mirrors and feathers.

Traditionally, the man chosen to become the *Danzanti* would be in his prime and strong both morally and physically. For several days before the festival nothing was denied him. He gorged himself on the finest food and drink and could indulge himself on the most beautiful young virgins. The *Danzanti* was then expected to dance continually for 3 days and nights until exhaustion, or even death. His death was seen as a sacrifice of the best that can be offered and ensured the safety of the community from plague and drought.

rural community. Some are highly Catholicized, particularly in the more Spanish dominated towns of Tarija and Santa Cruz, while others incorporate Spanish Colonial themes into predominantly ancient pagan rituals.

Invariably, fiestas involve drinking – lots and lots of it. There's also non-stop dancing, which can sometimes verge on an organized brawl. What this means is that, at some point, you will fall over, through inebriation or exhaustion, or both. After several days of this, you will awake with a hangover the size of the Amazon rainforest and probably have no recollection of what you did with your backpack.

Fiestas also involve much throwing of water, paint, oil – anything, in fact, that people can get their hands on. The more paranoid travellers may assume that they are being picked on, but to someone from the Altiplano, a six-foot tall, blond-haired gringo makes an easier target. So, arm yourself with a waterproof jacket, plenty water bombs, a good sense of fun and have a great time.

The meaning of fiestas

It is only when they don their extravagant costumes and masks and drink, eat and dance to excess that the Bolivian Indians show their true character. The rest of the time they hide behind a metaphorical mask of stony indifference as a form of protection against the alien reality in which they are forced to live. When they consume alcohol and coca and start dancing, the pride in their origins resurfaces. The incessant drinking and dancing allows them to forget the reality of poverty, unemployment and oppression and reaffirms their will to live as well as their unity with the world around them.

The object of the fiesta is a practical one, such as the success of the coming harvest or the fertility of animals. Thus the constant eating, drinking and dancing serves the purpose of giving thanks for the sun and rain that make things grow and for the fertility of the soil and

livestock, gifts from Pachamama, or Mother Earth, the most sacred of all gods. So, when you see the Aymara spill a little chicha (maize beer) every time they refill, it's not because they're sloppy but because they're offering a *ch'alla* (sacrifice) to Pachamama.

The participants in the dances that are the central part of the fiesta are dressed in garish, outlandish costumes and elaborate masks, each one depicting a character from popular myth. Some of these originate in the colonial period, others survive from the Inca empire or even further back to the Tiahuanaco cultures. Often the costumes caricature the Spaniards. In this way, the indigenous people mock those who erased their heritage.

Over time, new details have been introduced to reflect the changing reality of Bolivian life, so that the precise origins of the dances become more blurred. For example, in the most famous fiesta of them all, the Carnival of Oruro (see page 182) the traditional main characters such as monkeys, bears and condors have become peripheral players in colonial dances such as La Diablada (Devil's Dance) and La Morenada (Dance of the Black Slaves).

Who pays?

A lot a careful organization and preparation goes into a community's fiesta, and a lot of expense. The brass bands, the food, the beer, the pipe bands, the decorations, are all laid on free for the participants, and someone has to foot the bill.

Every fiesta needs a patron, or a sponsor. It's an honour to bear the *cargo* (cost) of a fiesta. So great is the prestige that it's impossible to rise in the community without sponsoring fiestas.

But how does a patron pay for it all? There are two ways: one is to save, the other is to get help from friends. They will lend the money on the understanding that when they have a *cargo* the favour will be returned. This bond of mutual assistance is known as an *ayni*. A man may spend lots of money on other people's

Hidden behind the mask

One of the most striking features of the Bolivian fiesta is the fantastic variety of wildly imaginative masks worn by the dancers.

The indigenous peoples of the Andes believe that masks transform individuals – not only into characters from popular folklore but also into spirits of another time and place and defenders of a sacred knowledge.

This can be explained by the legend of the *amaut'as*, or wisemen. The *amaut'as* are the keepers of the wisdom and values of the Andean civilization. They are said to personify the indigenous cultural identity and reaffirm its rebellion against foreign domination. Upon hearing of the death of the last Inca, Atahuallpa, the *amaut'as* were so horrified that, instead of rebelling, they retreated into themselves and stoically endured the injustices of a world that had ceased to be theirs.

In the same way, the Indians adapted to the oppression of daily life under a mask of submission and indifference. It is only during ceremonies of rebellion and remembrance that the Indians come back to life. Crucial to the success of such ceremonies – fiestas in other words – is the excessive consumption of alcohol, food and coca as well as repetitive, incessant dancing. This collective altered state draws the community together until the individual members are indistinguishable from one another. In this way, the community communes with itself and with its surroundings, thus affirming its will to live.

So, when the indigenous people put on their masks and costumes they cover their psychological masks of obstinate passivity, which allows them to show their true faces. Only by covering themselves up can the indigenous people uncover their repressed energies and desires and hidden resentments. These pent-up emotions overflow during the wild, excessive and colourful celebrations of the fiesta; the awakening of a sleeping culture.

---

fiestas before he can even sponsor one himself. But the more *ayni* bonds he can accrue by helping others, the more money he'll be able to raise when it's his turn. Thus, the principle of the *cargo* is that the more you do for the community, the more it'll do for you. Lay on a good fiesta and you'll rise in the hierarchy.

FESTIVAL CALENDAR

Here is a list of Bolivia's main festival dates. For a more detailed list of each region's festivals and a description of the activities, see under the relevant section in the main travelling text. Note that dates may change slightly from year to year.

● **1 January** Año Nuevo: rural communities on the Altiplano, in Cochabamba and in the Chiquitano area of Santa Cruz hold a celebration to thanks the outgoing civil authorities and welcome the incoming officials.

● **6 January** Reyes Magos: a celebration of the arrival of the Three Kings in various provinces of the Beni, also in Oruro, Sucre and Tarija. In the rural communities of Cochabamba and Potosí there are traditional ceremonies for the changing authorities.

● **24 January** Alasitas: festival of Ekeko, the God of Plenty, celebrated over 6 days in La Paz.

● **2 February** Virgen de la Candelaria: one of the most important festivals, celebrated in Copacabana, Samaipata, Aiquile and Colomi in Cochabamba, Tarija and Challapampa near Oruro.

● **February/March**: many of the towns and rural communities have their Carnival at this time, though there are no fixed dates. The most elaborate is at Oruro, though there are worthwhile celebrations in the cities of Sucre, Tarija and Santa Cruz and in the outlying villages.

● **8 March** San Juan de Dios: in Tarija; also around this time is the Celebration of the Grape.

● **Second Sunday in March**: Phujllay in

Tarabuco near Sucre. One of the largest fiestas in Bolivia.

● **19 March** San José: the patron saint of carpenters is honoured in Cochabamba and Potosí. In Oruro at this time is San José.

● **March/April** Semana Santa: Easter is celebrated nationally but varies according to location. In the Jesuit missions near Santa Cruz festivities are solemn, while in Tarija celebrations are more enthusiastic. On **15-16 April** Tarija also goes wild during its anniversary celebrations.

● **3 May** Fiesta de la Cruz: celebrated throughout the country. In the Andean rural communities they are more precolumbian than Christian. In Potosí the ritual Tinkus are carried out (see page 207).

● **13 June** San Antonio de Padua: celebrated in small towns in the departments of La Paz, Santa Cruz, Cochabamba and Tarija.

● **24 June** San Juan: celebrations take place in rural provinces throughout Bolivia and in the cities of Tarija and Santa Cruz. Also at this time is the traditional burning of woods and fields.

● **29 June** San Pedro and San Pablo: fiestas are held throughout the country.

● **June**: Santísima Trinidad is the most important festival in the Beni; there's no fixed date but it's usually around the start of the month. Similarly Corpus Cristi in Potosí, Sucre and Copacabana. Gran Poder is La Paz's biggest party, held also at the beginning of June.

● **First Sunday in July** Pentecost: in the Cochabamba countryside offerings are made to Pachamama.

● **16 July** Virgen del Carmen: takes place in La Paz, Oruro, Cochabamba, the Yungas and Sucre.

● **25 July** Apostle Santiago: held throughout the Andes and in Tarija, which has Santiago as its patron saint.

● **31 July** San Ignacio de Moxos: one of the most important festivals in the Beni.

● **2 August**: Dia del Indio in Iturralde province in La Paz; **5 August** La Virgen de las Nieves in Italque and Copacabana; **6 August** San Salvador in Oruro; **10 August** San Lorenzo in Tarija and Santa Cruz.

● **15 August** Virgen de Urkupiña: the greatest religious celebration in Cochabamba department is held in Quillacollo. Hundreds of other festivals are held across the country on the same day, for example in Tarija, La Paz, Sucre and Oruro.

● **24 August** San Bartolomé de Huayco: also known as the festival of the Chutillos, held in Potosí.

● **28 August** San Agustín: an 8-day festival in Toledo, 40 km from Oruro.

● **First Sunday in September** San Roque: a major 8-day party in Tarija.

● **8 September** Virgen de Guadalupe: in Santa Cruz and Sucre. Also the Fiesta of Viacha near La Paz.

● **14 September** Lord of the Exhaltation: celebrated in Potosí, Cochabamba and over a marathon 15 days in Oruro. There is also a festival in Sorata.

● **21 September** Spring Equinox: celebrated at Tiahuanaco.

● **29 September** San Miguel: held in Potosí and featuring Tinkus.

● **1-2 October** Virgen de La Merced and Virgen del Rosario: a sacred procession in Potosí.

● **7 October** Virgen del Rosario: held in Oruro (where it is known as Huayllas), Warnes in Santa Cruz, Sucre and Cochabamba. Also in Cochabamba is the Luzmilla Patiño Folklore Festival, held every 2 years (next in 1998).

● **First Sunday in October** Virgen de Guadalupe: held in Entre Ríos in Tarija. On the **Second Sunday** it is held in the city of Tarija.

● **24 October** San Rafael: a popular 4-day festival in Santa Fe, near Oruro.

● **1-2 November** Todos Santos and Difuntos: All Saints and Day of the Dead, celebrated in cemeteries throughout the Andean world; particularly interesting in Potosí.

● **First Sunday in November** Virgen de Socavón: the first training parade for the Oruro Carnival 3 months later. Also in Oruro, on the **10th**, is Santo Domingo.

● **18 November**: Anniversary of the foundation of Beni Department. Festivities in Trinidad are recommended.

● **30 November** San Andrés: celebrations in Santa Cruz and Taquiri in Cochabamba.

● **3 December** San Francisco Javier: celebrated in the various Jesuit mission towns in Santa Cruz.

- **8 December** Dia de la Inmaculada Concepción: held in towns in Santa Cruz and Cochabamba departments.

- **14 December** Santa Bárbara: 7-day festival in Oruro. On **21 December** in Oruro is the Virgin of Lourdes.

- **24 December** Navidad: celebrated throughout Bolivia. Some of the best are Villa Serrano (Chuquisaca), Vallegrande (Santa Cruz), San Ignacio de Moxos (Beni) and Tarija where celebrations continue until the end of January.

FOOD AND DRINK

FOOD

Bolivian cuisine can be divided into three distinct regional varieties: the Altiplano; the Valleys; and the Tropics.

The Altiplano

The high plateau produces mostly grains and potatoes. Quinoa is a grain unique to this area. It has an exceptionally high protein content and is the basis of the Altiplano diet.

There are literally hundreds of varieties of potatoes, more than you could shake a knife and fork at. Some of the most commonly used in cooking are the *oca*, which is sweet, and *chuño*, which is a kind of freeze dried potato.

Bolivian highland cooking is usually very tasty and often cooked in *ají*, a very piquant chili-like plant. You won't fail to notice the *salteña*, a meat or chicken pastry which is sold absolutely everywhere. These originate from Salta in Argentina, but are popular throughout the Andean countries. *Salteñas* are eaten regularly by Bolivians, especially in the morning, and accompanied by a cold drink. The trick is to eat them without spilling copious quantities of gravy all over yourself (not very easy, particularly on buses). Some are *muy picante* (very hot), but for lesser mortals (wimps, in other words) *medio picante* and *poco picante* are available.

Other local specialities include *chairo*, a soup from La Paz made of meat, vegetables, *chuño* and *ají* (hot pepper) to which the locals like to add *llajua* or *halpahuayca* (hot sauces always set on restaurant tables) to make it even more *picante*. *Fricasé* is a traditional hangover cure, which I would not recommend unless you are within groping distance of a toilet bowl. It is another soup made with pork, *chuño*, *ají* and God knows what else. *Anticuchos* are small slices of beef heart and a boiled potato on a skewer cooked over an open grill. *Thimpu* is a popular lamb dish served as a kind of soup and usually found on more native restaurant menus. *Plato paceño*, as the name suggests, is a native La Paz dish, made from cheese fried and served with potato, broad beans, corn on the cob and the very piquant sauce called *llajua*.

A *picante* is a meat cooked in an *ají* sauce and served with boiled potato and *chuño*. Among the most popular *picante* dishes are: *sajta de pollo*, hot spicy chicken with onion, fresh potatoes and *chuño*, *saice* (chopped beef), *ají de lengua*, ox-tongue with chilis, potatoes and *chuño* or *tunta* (another kind of dehydrated potato), and *ranga ranga* (tripe).

Those with strong stomachs could try a local Oruro favourite, *rostro asado*, which is baked lamb's head. A speciality in Potosí is *fritanga*, which is *fricasé* without the broth, made with red *ají*.

The Valleys

The departments of Cochabamba, Chuquisaca and Tarija produce some of Bolivia's finest cooking. Tarija is the wine and singani capital, while Cochabamba is the agricultural and dairy centre.

Among the typical dishes from Cochabamba, two stand out: *silpancho* is fried breaded meat with eggs, rice and bananas, and *pique a lo macho* is a delicious, and massive, dish of roast meat, sausage, chips, onion and pepper. *Chicharrón* is pork cooked in its own fat and is an ingredient in other dishes, such as *chairo*. In Cochabamba it is served with *quesillo* or fresh cheese. Sucre is famous for its *chorizos* and also claims to have the best *salteñas* in the country. Tarija, being so close to Argentina, is, of course, a carnivore's paradise. Restaurant menus here basically consist of meat, meat and more meat. *Parrillada* is a Bolivian kind of mixed grill.

The Tropics

The staple foods produced in the tropics are yucca, rice, bananas, tropical fruits, soy and beef. Consequently, dishes tend to feature these heavily.

A favourite dish in the tropics is *locro*, a rice soup made with beef jerky or chicken, bananas, potato and egg. Another is *masaco*, fried jerky and banana. *Pollo broaster* is chicken with rice, chips, yucca and fried banana.

Note that many types of wild meat are served in tourist restaurants and on jungle tours. Bear in mind that turtles whose eggs are eaten are endangered and that other species not endangered soon will be if they stay on the tourist menu.

The bread in this region is often sweet with cheese on top, and the rice bread is also unusual. Among the pastries produced are *cuñapes*, made with yucca flour and cheese, *biscochos*, which are corn biscuits; also *empanadas* (cheese pasties) and *humitas* (maize pies). The latter two are also popular throughout the country. Before trying some of these pastries it should be noted that a method of preserving them in the humid climate is to dry them in the oven until they become very hard.

In the *pensiones* and cheaper restaurants a basic lunch (*almuerzo* – usually finished by 1300) and dinner (*cena*) are normally available. The *comida del día* is the best value, in any class of restaurant. Good cheap and clean breakfasts are served in the markets in most towns (most restaurants do not open very early in the morning). Lunch can also be obtained in many of the modern market buildings in the main towns; eat only what is cooked in front of you. Dishes cooked in the street are not safe. Llama meat contains parasites (similar to those in pork), so make sure it has been cooked for a long time and is hot when you eat it. Be very careful of salads; they may carry a multitude of amoebic life as well as vile green bacteria.

DRINK

The several makes of local beer, lager-type, are recommendable, though trying to pour a beer in La Paz without ending up with a glass of froth is an art in itself. El Inca is a dark beer, sweet, like a stout. Singani, a brandy distilled from grapes, is quite cheap and drinkable. Chuflay is singani and 7 Up or Canada Dry (or whatever carbonated drink is available). The best wines are produced in Tarija and many of them are very recommendable, eg La Concepción (see Southern Highlands, page 234).

Chicha is a traditional Andean drink made from fermented corn in the valleys around Cochabamba, where it is sold in *chicherías*, which are small places without a sign or a name. They can be found by looking out for a little white flag on a pole in front of the house. *Chicha* is also served in *chicharronerías*, where it is drunk to accompany a dish of *chicharrón* cooked in huge vats.

The hot maize drink, *api* (with cloves, cinnamon, lemon and sugar), is good for breakfast, especially on the freezing cold Altiplano. *Tostada* is a cold drink made by boiling toasted corn and barley with honey, cinnamon, cloves and fennel. In Tarija it is called *aloja*. In the tropics fruit juices are delicious; tamarindo, carambola and guapurú are particularly good.

Bottled water, Viscachani, is easily available but make sure the seal is unbroken (rain water is sometimes offered as an alternative). There are also several brands of flavoured mineral water, Cayacayani, La Cabaña and Mineragua. Naturagua is purified water. The local tap water should not be drunk without first being sterilized. Local water purifier is 'Lugol Fuerte Solución', an iodine-based product, US$1.75/small bottle; also *iodo* from *farmacias*, US$0.50. For milk, try sachets of Leche Pil (plain, chocolate or strawberry-flavoured), at US$0.25 each.

LITERATURE

Pre-independence

The absence of a written language in pre-Hispanic Bolivia means that there is no recorded literature from this period, though there was an oral tradition of storytelling which still survives today. The primary function of early Spanish literature in Bolivia, then known as Alto Perú, was to spread Catholicism through the newly-conquered empire. One of the earliest known of these works was the *Crónica de Perú*, by Pedro Cieza de León (1518-60). The Spaniards' fear of the unknown culture of the indigenous people meant that these early chronicles lacked much local detail, focusing more on the religion and the activities of the conquerors themselves. Even the early texts by native Bolivian authors showed the extent of their indoctrination with colonial ideas.

The only area in which the Indians were allowed to maintain their own culture was in theatre and poetry. One of the few texts to survive, *La Tragedia de Atahuallpa*, indicates that plays were passed orally from generation to generation. Poetry in the Quechua and Aymara languages also continued to flourish, again orally, throughout the colonial era. Not until the early 18th century does a text appear which takes the religious chronicle into the realms of literature: Bartolomé Arzán's *Historia de la Villa Imperial de Potosí*, written between 1700 and 1736, is an epic account of most of the colonial period. Unlike any other text produced until then, it mixes fact and fantasy, the author even immersing himself in a fictional context into phases of history hundreds of years earlier. It is a remarkable Baroque example of what later came to be known as *Lo real maravilloso*.

The transformation of Bolivia into a republic is recorded by a native of La Paz, Vicente Pazos Kauki (1779-1853) in *Memorias Histórico-políticas*, in which he defends the notion of Latin American independence from the Spanish. Again, the literary qualities of this work bring the skill of fictional narrative to the sections based on historical fact.

Post-independence

The birth of Bolivia as an independent nation in 1825 coincided with the beginning of Romanticism in Latin America. European Romantic fiction was widely read and local authors developed a similar style of writing to create tales of contemporary life in Bolivia. The sentimental novel was popularized primarily by Vicente Ballivián (1816-91) with *Recreos juveniles* in 1834. Julio Lucas Jaimes, a Bolivian Romantic writing in the mid-19th century, gained the admiration of the well-known Nicaraguan writer, Rubén Darío, who dedicated part of his *Prosas profanas* to him.

European-influenced Romanticism came to an end with the birth of Latin American Modernism at the turn of the century. Ricardo Jaimes Freyre was one of the forerunners of the movement. His *La Villa Imperial de Potosí*, published in 1905, examined the pervading mood in Latin America and sought inspiration from past events, such as the French Revolution of 1789, which he saw as an example of positive rational action distinctly lacking in his homeland. Jaimes Freyre went on to found an important literary review in Buenos Aires with Rubén Darío and gained an international reputation with his poetry, plays, novels and critical essays.

Nataniel Aguirre's 1885 *Juan de la Rosa* was another landmark literary work. In this highly original novel, he subverts the whole concept of the 19th century novel by placing the narrative in the hands, or voice, of one of his characters, thus relinquishing the privileged position of the author/narrator.

A major contribution to Feminism was made by the modernist poet Adela Zamudio (1854-1928). She formed a Latin American triad of Romantic-Modernist poets with José Martí in Cuba and Manuel González Prada in Peru, all of whom used their innate spirit of rebellion as an inspiration for their poetry. Zamudio dedicated her life and work to the struggle against the oppression of women.

The Bolivian Modernist movement

continued to flourish with the publication of *Odas* in 1898 by Franz Tamayo (1880-1956). His analysis of post-colonial Latin America saw the huge divide between the ruling minority and the anonymous, voiceless majority. He was nominated president of the Republic in 1935, but was prevented from assuming the post by a military coup.

Early 20th century prose reflected the injustices of the *latifundista* system. Alcides Arguedas (1879-1946) began his fictional account of the inequality of Bolivian society with *Wata Wara*, which he later incorporated in his 1919 *Raza de bronce*. This is one of the major novels in Bolivian letters, examining the life of the Indian in a society dominated by a white ruling class. Jaime Mendoza's (1874-1939) novels also denounced the exploitation of the Indians, in particular their conditions in the tin mines and rubber plantations. His best known work is *En las tierras de Potosí* (1911). The extreme politicisation of his work has led some critics to refer to him as the Bolivian Gorky.

The literature of the Chaco War (1932-35) was mainly by those who had fought in it, documenting a national sense of despair at having been forced to fight a protracted and futile war. Augusto Céspedes (1904-1997) was one of the key figures of this era, both in politics and literature. He had already founded the Nationalist Party of Bolivia by the time he published his account of the Chaco War, *Sangre de mestizos*, in 1936. This collection of short stories saw that for the first time whites and Indians had shared the same plight, fighting alongside each other and united in bitter disappointment at the outcome. This book is now considered a classic and Céspedes went on to become a major literary and political figure until his recent death at the age of 94.

The revolution of 1952 did not produce any significant literature, but this can be explained by the fact that a revolutionary consciousness had already been established by writers and intellectuals in the 20 years after the Chaco War. The pressing issues of exploitation of the Indians and conditions in the tin mines, criticized in fiction since the early 1930s, had finally been addressed by the revolution. Some writers also gave up their craft to work in politics. The few novels that did emerge just after the revolution, such as *Cerco de penumbras* by Oscar Cerruto (1912-81) and *Los deshabitados* by Macelo Quiroga (1931-80), broke with the tradition of social realism and began experimenting with a more abstract, existential kind of work, mirrored by the dark poetry of Jaime Sáenz and Gonzalo Vázquez Méndez.

The next significant change in Bolivia to be marked by literature was the guerrilla uprising led by Che Guevara, and his subsequent execution in 1967. The key novel in this new subversive literature was *Los fundadores del alba*, by Renato Prado de Oropeza, which won the coveted Cuban Casa de las Américas prize in 1969. Many poets from this period, the most important being Pedro Shimose (born 1940), denounced the violence that was then shaping society in all of Latin America.

Literature in the 1970s and 1980s continued to criticise Bolivian society, though the presence of various military dictatorships restricted the writers' freedom to chronicle the injustices around them with such blatant acrimony as before. However, an important collection of short stories *Antología del terror político* was published in 1979, combining the work of established figures like Raul Leyton with younger writers like René Bascope and Roberto Laserna. All the stories are concerned with the restrictions placed on all levels of life by dictatorship. Other writers of the same period avoided social realism altogether, turning to experimentation and poetic writing. The fantasies and myths of indigenous culture have also been a source of inspiration for many contemporary writers, reflecting a common trend throughout Latin American literature in general.

PAINTING AND SCULPTURE

Before independence

As a result of the discovery of the fabulously rich silver mines of Potosí in 1544 Bolivia, then part of the Viceroyalty of Peru, was one of the major commercial and cultural centres of colonial Spanish America. Artists and craftsmen followed the merchants, churchmen, colonial administrators and adventurers along the trade route from the Viceregal capital of Lima to Potosí via Cusco, La Paz and Sucre. The demand for paintings, sculptures and altarpieces was met first by Europeans such as the itinerant Italian Jesuit **Bernardo Bitti** (1548-1610?), who after a spell in Lima moved on to Lake Titicaca, La Paz, Sucre and Potosí, and the influence of his delicate mannerist style can be traced through several subsequent generations. Another mobile and important Jesuit painter but in this case of Flemish origin was **Diego de la Puente** (1586-1663) who worked in towns and cities throughout the Viceroyalty. His paintings were often based on engravings after works by Rubens, an influence that was to persist in Bolivian painting until late in the 18th century. The work of **Gregorio Gamarra**, active 1601-1630, is typical of the first generation of Bolivian-born artists in combining elements of the Italianate style of Bitti and the Flemish tradition of Puente, as in his 'Adoration of the Kings' in the Museo Nacional de Arte in La Paz.

Colonial sculpture, however, has its stylistic roots in Spain. Andalusian sculptors were attracted by lucrative commissions for altarpieces and choirstalls. Several workshops were established in highland Bolivia by the 1570s, and Spanish-born craftsmen continued to be influential into the 17th century. The Sevillian **Gaspar de la Cueva** (active 1613-1640) settled in Potosí where many of his best works are still preserved in the churches for which they were made. His 'Christ at the Column' in the church of San Lorenzo, for example, is elegantly dignified despite the numerous bleeding lacerations on his white skin. This powerful colonial tradition of silent suffering in the face of physical abuse continues to reverberate in Bolivian art.

The work of painter **Melchor Pérez Holguín** (1660?-1733) combines Flemish, Spanish and Andean elements, and is typical of the cultural heterogeneity of later colonial painting. The composition of his 'Rest on the Flight into Egypt' in the Museo Nacional de Arte in La Paz is based on a Flemish engraving; the style, however, is reminiscent of Zurbarán, while the anecdotal detail owes much to Andean traditions. While the infant Jesus sleeps, the Virgin, dressed in a manta and travelling hat, washes nappies in a portable wooden basin. This 'Americanization' of subject matter owes much to the Cusco school of painting and although Holguín largely resisted the typical Cusco hallmark of applying gold to the painted surface, the next generation of Bolivian artists did not. The painting of San Francisco de Paula (Museo Nacional de Arte, La Paz) by Holguín's follower **Manuel de Córdoba** (active 1758-1787) is a striking example of the resulting tension between the real and the divine. The saint's hands and face are painted with close attention to every vein, tendon and wrinkle in the tradition of Caravaggio and Ribera while his habit is overlaid with a flat wallpaper pattern in gold. The effect is simultaneously to emphasize and deny the figure's corporeality. Another follower of Holguín, **Gaspar Miguel de Berrio** (active 1706-1762) uses gold to emphasize the divinity of the principal figures in his impressive 'Coronation of the Virgin' (Museo Nacional de Arte, La Paz). He is also remembered for his detailed documentary view of Potosí (c 1760, Museo Charcas, Sucre) which shows the distinctive triangular mountain, the colonial city below it, and in the surrounding hills the elaborate system of dams and canals which channelled water to the mine-workings.

Initially European craftsmen worked mainly for the creole elite while indigenous workshops developed to meet the needs of the newly-Christianized Indians, often with remarkable results. In 1582 **Francisco Tito Yupanqui**, a native of Copacabana who claimed descent from the Incas, wanted to make an image of the Virgin for his parish church and travelled to Potosí to learn to carve. The fame of the resulting sculpture derives from the tradition that after two years' work and still unable to finish the piece to his own satisfaction, Yupanqui appealed to the Virgin for help whereupon she kindly obliged. Once installed in Copacabana the miraculously-completed statue quickly became the focus of a popular cult, so perpetuating the sacred significance Lake Titicaca had had under the Incas. Native Andean beliefs include the veneration of important geographical features, and the rigid triangular representations of the Virgin can often be related to mountain peaks. The Virgin of Sabaya (Museo de la Moneda, Potosí) by the Indian **Luis Niño** (18th century) is associated with the Sabaya volcano in Oruro, while in the anonymous painting of the Virgin of Potosí in the same museum the Virgin's body is the mountain: her head and hands, radiating silvery light, are superimposed on the landscape making her the Christian embodiment of Pachamama, the Andean earth mother goddess. Other indigenous divinities reappeared in Christian garb in the 18th century, most famously the forces of nature. These were transformed by Andean artists into richly-dressed archangels with arquebuses: powerful, unpredictable intermediaries between celestial and earthly realms. Examples can be seen in many rural churches as well as in the major museums.

After independence

In the years following independence in 1825 itinerant artists of diverse origins played an important role, as they had in the early colonial period. The Peruvian **José Gil de Castro** (died 1841), the Ecuadorean **Manuel Ugalde** (1817-1881) and the Austrian **Francisco Martín Drexel** (1792-1863) helped to meet the new demand for portraits of military leaders and society hostesses. Bolivian-born **Antonio Villavicencio** (born 1822) trained in a conventional academic manner in Paris before returning in 1858 to head the Escuela de Dibujo in La Paz. It must be said that the interest of the works of this period, including Villavicencio's monumental series of presidential portraits in the Museo Charcas, Sucre, lies less in their artistic merit than in the historical personalities they represent.

Portraiture was the dominant form of artistic expression. 19th century political nationalism was not paralleled by a strong school of landscape painting although **Zenón Iturralde** (born 1838) and **Melchor María Mercado** (19th century), both self-taught, painted interesting topographical scenes. **José García Mesa** (1851-1905), despite extensive studies in Europe, returned to paint city views which sometimes seem closer to the colonial topographical tradition of, for example, Berrio's Potosí, than to the Impressionism of his French contemporaries (eg 'Plaza de Cochabamba', 1889, Casa de Cultura, Cochabamba).

Popular religious artistic expression was largely unaffected by the political changes. In the later colonial period many rural churches had been decorated with brightly-coloured and often iconographically complex murals, a practice which persisted throughout the 19th century, and artists such as **Juan de la Cruz Tapia** (1830?-1892), a sculptor as well as a painter, continued to produce devotional images in the tradition of Holguín.

20th century art

Art in Bolivia during the first decades of the 20th century, dominated by figurative styles and local subject matter, is scarcely touched by developments in Europe. **Cecilio Guzmán de Rojas** (1900-1950) presents himself in his precocious self-portrait of 1919 as a bohemian dandy (Museo de la Moneda, Potosí) but although he spent the 1920s in Europe the modern movements passed him by. While in Madrid he painted sentimental visions of the Andes using naked or semi-naked Indian figures in questionable taste (eg 'The Idol's Kiss/El Beso del Idolo', 1926, Museo de la Moneda, Potosí). On his return to Bolivia in 1930 he saw his country afresh and adopted a more sensitive if politically anodyne indigenist mode, but his real importance lies in the way in which, as Director of the Escuela de Bellas Artes of La Paz, he was in a position to promote the land, landscape and peoples of Bolivia as serious subjects for painters and sculptors. Other practitioners include **Juan Rimsa** (c 1898-c 1975), **Gil Coimbra** (1908-1976) and **Jorge de la Reza** (1901-1958).

The success of the revolution of 1952 inspired artists of the younger generation of '52' to add a much-needed social and political dimension to Bolivian art. As in Mexico, murals offered a way of reaching a wide audience and during the 1950s the government sponsored numerous narrative and allegorical works in schools, hospitals and the offices of nationalized companies. Two major exponents were **Miguel Alandia Pantoja** (1914-1975) several of whose works survive in La Paz (eg in the auditorium of the Hospital Obrera in La Paz) and **Walter Solón Romero** (born 1925) who executed murals and stained glass windows for the Catholic University in Sucre. The euphoria was short-lived and after the military coup of 1964 artists had to find alternative means of expression. The Indians **Gil Imana** (born 1933) paints in the 1970s are no longer folkloric and rural, as in the generation of Guzmán de Rojas, nor inspired by Marxist optimism, but simply hungry and oppressed. **Enrique Arnal** (born 1932) paints faceless Indian porters in ragged western clothes; they inhabit not a traditional picturesque landscape but an abstract, lonely no-man's land of blank planes.

The two best-known artists of 20th century Bolivia are both women, the painter, **María Luisa Pacheco** (1919-1974), and the sculptor **Marina Núñez del Prado** (1910-1996). Both worked in a predominantly abstract mode, but with a distinctively Bolivian flavour. In her mixed-media canvases Pacheco used a cubist vocabulary and coarsely-textured surface to evoke to the peaks, crags and sharply-faceted rocks of the Andean landscape. Núñez del Prado, by contrast, carved iron-hard native wood and stone into softly curving, often feminine forms.

In recent decades Bolivia has seen the growth of numerous different artistic tendencies, dominated by a continued preoccupation with figuration. The Museo Nacional de Arte in La Paz has a very good collection of contemporary art and there are several new commercial galleries. Look out for **Gaston Ugalde** (born 1946), **Edgar Arandia** (born 1951) and particularly **Roberto Valcarcel** (born 1951) who produced powerful indictments of political repression in the 1970s and has gone on to explore different aspects of Bolivian iconography including a fascinating recent series in which he dissects and reworks the colonial image of the archangel.

CINEMA

The Bolivian film industry has usually been known for its strength and courage in producing films against the opposing forces of repressive political regimes. However, since 1994, the industry has undergone something of a renaissance, concentrated particularly in five new feature films. Though by no means similar, the five films share a common departure from Bolivian cinema's confrontational stance, while retaining an underlying awareness of social issues.

La oscuridad radiante, based on the novel by Oscar Uzín, is about a rebel fighter who becomes a priest. He is sent by the church to a remote village near a border. When a group of rebels arrive seeking protection and help in crossing the border, the priest's former loyalties are put to a severe test.

Sayari, by Mela Márquez, is the first Bolivian feature film directed by a woman. It is about a Quechua-speaking community struggling for land rights and cultural survival. Another landmark feature of this film is the fact that the entire cast are indigenous people.

Jonas y la ballena rosada is set in Santa Cruz in the Bolivian Oriente, marking a cinematic shift in geographical emphasis. Nearly all Bolivian films have up till now been set in La Paz or the Altiplano area. Both the oil and cocaine industries have increased the political and cultural diversity of Santa Cruz and *Jonas y la ballena rosada*, directed by Carlos Valdivia, deals with the encroaching economic and social power of the *narcotraficantes* in the Santa Cruz area.

Director Jorge Sajinés has been a leading figure in Bolivian cinema since the sixties. His most recent film *Para recibir el canto de los pájaros*, uses the film-within-a-film format to look at the effect of the arrival of a film crew in a remote Andean village. The villagers' idea of the conquest is explored in their re-enactment of it during the film. The title refers to episodes of ritual dialogue between musicians and birds.

Cuestión de fe has broken all box-office records in Bolivia. It is the story of three marginalized urbanites trying to transport a figure of the Virgin Mary from La Paz to the Yungas in the north, an area now opening up to the drugs trade. One of the protagonists is a *santero* who performs ancient rituals before the journey. The film explores the cultural diversity of mestizos' faith through a subtle use of music and colour. Director Marcos Loayza has portrayed a society sufficiently at ease with itself to have accepted this picaresque and parodic self-portrait.

Travellers wishing to see any of these important Bolivian films should check out the Cinemateca Boliviana in La Paz (see page 99).

People

Bolivia is a culturally diverse country. Its population can be roughly divided into three distinct ethnic groupings: about 60% are of pure indigenous stock; about one third are mestizos (people of mixed European and Indian ancestry); and the remainder are of European origin. The racial composition varies from place to place: indigenous around Lake Titicaca; more than half indigenous in La Paz; three-quarters mestizo or European in the Yungas, Cochabamba, Santa Cruz and Tarija, the most European of all.

The Highland Indians are composed of two groups: those in the north of the Altiplano who speak the guttural Aymara (an estimated 1 million), and those elsewhere, who speak Quechua, the Inca tongue (3 million). Both cultures were dominated by the Incas but the Aymara were allowed to keep their own language. Both have kept their languages and cultures distinct. Outside the big cities many of them speak no Spanish, but knowledge of Spanish is increasing. About 70% of Bolivians are Aymara, Quechua or Tupi-Guaraní speakers. The first two are regarded as national languages, but were not, until very recently, taught in schools, a source of some resentment.

THE AYMARA PEOPLE

The Aymaras, who populate the Titicaca region, are descendants of the ancient Tiahuanaco people. They are a squat and powerfully built race who have developed huge chests and lungs to cope with the rarefied air of the Altiplano. Since the agrarian revolution of 1952 the Aymara campesinos own the land on which they live, but still live in extreme poverty.

Though introduced to Catholicism by the Spaniards, the Aymara remain grudging converts. They are a deeply religious people who may observe Christian rituals but also continue to worship the ancient animist spirits and celebrate rituals which date from the Tiahuanaco period. Aymara culture is permeated with the idea of the sacred. They believe that God, the Supreme Being, gives them security in their daily lives and this God of Life manifests him/herself through the deities, such as those of the mountains, the water, the wind, the sun, the moon and the wa'qas (sacred places).

As a sign of gratitude, the Aymara give wax'ta (offerings), wilancha (llama sacrifices) and ch'alla (sprinkling alcohol on the ground) to the achachilas (the protecting spirits of the family and community), the Pachamama (Mother Earth), Kuntur Mamani and Uywiri (protecting spirits of the home).

The remote mountains of the bleak Altiplano are of particular importance for the Aymara. The most sacred places are these high mountains, far from human problems. It is here that the people have built their altars to offer worship, to communicate with their God and ask forgiveness. The community is also held important in the lives of the Aymara. The achachila is the great-great grandfather of the family as well as the protector of the community, and as such is God's representative on earth.

The offerings to the sacred mountains take place for the most part in August and are community celebrations. Many different rituals are celebrated: there are

Things go better with Coke

Coca was first cultivated in the warm valleys (Yungas) of the eastern Andes by the Aymara Indians many, many centuries ago. Awareness of coca in the First World is rather more recent, however. In 1862 German chemists had taken coca leaves brought by an Austrian scientific expedition from Peru and isolated an alkaloid, or nitrogen-based compound which they labelled cocain. By around 1880, it was being tried as a cure for opium addiction and alcoholism. The young Dr Sigmund Freud, reading of its effect on tired soldiers, took some himself and pronounced it a "magical substance", which was "wonderfully stimulating".

Today, there is a huge demand for this drug from the millions of North Americans and Europeans who snort, smoke or inject it. Supply on this scale is not a problem. Making cocaine hydrochloride is as easy as baking bread. The leaves go into a plastic pit with a solution of water and a little sulphuric acid where they are left to soak for a few days. Then follows a succession of mixing and stirring with more chemicals until the liquid turns milky-white and then curdles, leaving tiny, ivory-coloured granules. This cocaine base is then transported to Colombia, where it is refined into the familiar white powder, before being shipped abroad. The costs involved to produce a kilo of the stuff are around US$5,000. The return on this investment can be as much as US$50,000.

Cocaine also has its legal uses. Patent medicines containing cocaine were popular – for hay fever, sinusitis and as a general tonic. Today, it is still used in hospitals world-wide as a local anaesthetic. Another legal use of cocaine is in soft drinks. The most famous soft drink in the world doesn't actually contain cocaine, but has something from the coca plant in it. Coca leaves from Peru and Bolivia are shipped to the USA where cocaine is extracted for medical use. From what's left comes a flavouring agent which goes into Coca-Cola, enjoyed in practically every country around the globe.

those within the family; in the mountains; for the planting and the harvest; rites to ask for rain or to ask for protection against hailstorms and frosts; and ceremonies for Mother Earth.

All such rituals are led by Aymara *Yatiris*, who are male or female priests. The *Yatiri* is a wise person – someone who knows – and the community's spiritual and moral guide. Through a method of divination that involves the reading of coca leaves, they guide individuals in their personal decision-making.

THE QUECHUA PEOPLE

The Quechua language was imposed by the Incas on several culturally and linguistically divergent groups and, to this day, many of these groups have maintained separate social identities.

The Quechua language, much more than the Aymara, is divided by many variations in regional dialect. Geographically, they are more varied, too. There are Quechua speakers in the fertile valleys of Cochabamba, on the high plateaus of Potosí, in Chuquisaca and parts of Oruro.

Some Quechua communities have lived free from outside influence for centuries. Others, such as those of the Cochabamba valley, have long been in close contact with *cholos*, a term used to describe indigenous people who have abandoned the traditional rural way of life and moved to the towns (see also page 78). These people have always been bilingual and have adapted easily to the *cholo* way of life, thus weakening their own ethnic distinctiveness. Their religious life lacks the specialized rituals of the Aymara and the music and dance also shows considerable *cholo* influence. The Quechua youth of the Cochabamba valley are becoming fluent and literate in Spanish.

OTHER ETHNIC GROUPS

There are also other smaller ethnic groups, such as the Uru and the Chipaya of the Altiplano. The Chipaya, who inhabit the inhospitable Carangas region of the western Oruro Department and speak their own language, are now so small numerically that they are in danger of disappearing. A similar fate could befall the Uru, a fishing and herding people who live in the swamps of the Río Desaguadero on the fringes of Lake Titicaca.

In the lowlands are some 150,000 people in 30 groups, including the Guaraní (numbering about 20,000), Ayoreo, Chiquitano (about 15,000), Chiriguano, Guaravo (about 15,000), Chimane and Mojo. Each group has its own language and, though the Jesuits settled missions in some of these remote areas over 300 years ago, have only recently been assimilated into Bolivian culture. There are also about 17,000 blacks, descendents of slaves brought from Peru and Buenos Aires in 16th century, who now live in the Yungas.

RELIGION, CUSTOMS AND BELIEFS

Although some 97% of the population ostensibly belong to the Roman Catholic religion, in reality religious life for the majority of Bolivians is a mix of Catholic beliefs imported from Europe and indigenous traditions based on animism, the worship of deities from the natural world, such as mountains, animals and plants.

PACHAMAMA

Ecotourism is the current trendy buzzword on the lips of all self-respecting travellers and tour operators. But though ecology may be a relatively new concept here in the West, to the people of the bleak northern Bolivian Altiplano, this idea is absolutely fundamental to their very culture and almost as old as the land itself.

Pachamama, or Mother Earth, occupies a very privileged place in indigenous culture because she is the generative source of life. The Aymara believe that Man was created from the land, and thus he is fraternally tied to all the living beings that share the earth. According to them, the earth is our mother, and it is on the basis of this understanding that all of human society is organized, always maintaining the cosmic norms and laws.

Women's and men's relationship with nature is what the Aymara call ecology, harmony and equilibrium.

The Aymara furthermore believe that private land ownership is a social sin because the land is for everyone. It is meant to be shared and not used only for the benefit of a few.

Vicenta Mamani Bernabé of the Andean Regional Superior Institute of Theological Studies states: "Land is life because it produces all that we need to live. Water emanates from the land as if from the veins of a human body, there is also the natural wealth of minerals, and pasture grows from it to feed the animals. Therefore, for the Aymaras, the *Pachamama* is sacred and since we are her children, we are also sacred. No one can replace the earth, she is not meant to be exploited, or to be converted into merchandise. Our duty is to respect and care for the earth. This is what white people today are just beginning to realize, and it is called ecology. Respect for the *Pachamama* is respect for ourselves as she is life. Today, she is threatened with death and must be liberated for the sake of her children's liberation."

DAY OF THE DEAD

One of the most important dates in the indigenous people's calendar is the 2nd of November, the 'Day of the Dead'. This tradition has been practised since time immemorial. In the Inca calendar, November was the eighth month and meant *Ayamarca*, or land of the dead. The celebration of Day of the Dead, or 'All Saints' as it is also known, is just one example of religious adaptation in which the ancient beliefs of ethnic cultures are mixed with the rites of the Catholic Church.

According to Aymara belief, the spirit (*athun ajayu*) visits its relatives at this time of the year and is fed in order to continue its journey before its reincarnation. The relatives of the dead prepare for the arrival of the spirit days in advance. Among the many items necessary for

Hair today

One of the many customs initiated by the Incas which is still practised is the hair-cutting ritual, *ruthuchiku*. The Inca custom was to hold a fiesta lasting several days when the child reached the age of two. This was accompanied by the hair-cutting ceremony in which the child's head was completely shaved. At the same time the name given to the child at birth was substituted by a new, permanent one.

Today, when a child's head is shaved, the celebration may last one day and gifts of money are given. So, if you happen to be staying with an indigenous family, you'll know what to do if you're presented with a pair of scissors and a squirming child.

these meticulous preparations are little bread dolls, each one of which has a particular significance. A ladder is needed for the spirit to descend from the other world to the terrestrial one. There are other figures which represent the grandparents, great grandparents and loved ones of the person who has 'passed into a better life'. Horse-shaped breads are prepared that will serve as a means of transport for the soul in order to avoid fatigue.

Inside the home, the relatives construct a tomb supported by boxes over which is laid a black cloth. Here they put the bread, along with sweets, flowers, onions and sugar cane. This last item is an indispensable part of the table as it symbolizes the invigorating element which prevents the spirit from becoming tired on its journey towards the Earth. The union of the flowers with the onion is called *tojoro* and is a vital part of the preparations. It ensures that the dead one does not become disoriented and arrives in the correct house.

The tomb is also adorned with the dead relative's favourite food and drink, not forgetting the all-important glass of beer as, according to popular tradition, this is the first nourishment taken by the souls when they arrive at their houses. Once the spirit has arrived and feasted with his/her living relatives, the entire ceremony is then transported to the graveside in the local cemetery, where it is carried out again, together with the many other mourning families.

This meeting of the living and their dead relatives is re-enacted the following year, though less ostentatiously, and again for the final time in the third year, the year of the farewell. It does not continue after this, which is just as well as the costs can be crippling for the family concerned.

ECONOMIC LIFE

As well as being culturally diverse, Bolivia is also a very poor country, the poorest in South America, and one which has, for centuries, neglected its indigenous majority. Since 1985 successive governments have embraced the free-market model and there has been an explosion of jobs in the 'informal sector', in street trade, personal services and small workshops. Because of a shortage of real jobs, poorer families have created their own work in order to survive, often demonstrating remarkable inventiveness and making use of family networks and contacts.

Economic necessity has led to the growth in the number of working women and also the numbers of children working, which in turn has increased the level of drop-outs from school: under 40% of children of school age attend school even though it is theoretically compulsory between seven and fourteen. This explosion is most obvious in the towns with the swelling ranks of shoe-shiners (*lustrabotas*), lottery ticket sellers, beggars, cigarette and sweet vendors and street musicians.

But it is the rural population which has been hit hardest by the pursuit of economic stability. Bolivia has the highest percentage of rural poverty in the world.

97% of the rural population has an income below the poverty level, according to the UN International Fund for Agricultural Development. This can be seen most clearly on the Altiplano, where 70% of the rural population lives. Scenes of llamas grazing on the shores of Lake Titicaca under the snow-capped Mount Illimani are misleadingly idyllic. Here, average life expectancy is 46 years, infant mortality is 172 per 1,000 live births and family incomes average US$11.50 a month. A former World Health Organization representative in Africa has stated that poverty in Bolivia is worse than in Ethiopia.

MIGRATION

The departments of Bolivia show remarkable differences in patterns of population growth, caused mainly by migration from the countryside to the large towns and cities. Apart from the urban centres, the newly-colonized regions in the Llanos and in the Yungas also attracted migrants. The Department of Santa Cruz, for example, has grown twice as fast as the national average in recent decades. The Altiplano, in particular, has been rapidly depopulated since the collapse of tin mining.

As in the rest of Latin America, urbanization is increasing rapidly. In 1992, 57% of Bolivians lived in towns, compared with 42% in 1976, meaning that Bolivia has now changed from a predominantly rural society to an urban one.

The political and cultural position of Bolivia's indigenous peoples has been improved significantly since the 1952 revolution, but the economic neglect of Indian communities continues. This is partly due to the fact that rural Bolivia is at a huge disadvantage in terms of education, healthcare, employment opportunity and government service. About two-thirds of the population lives in adobe huts, and medical services are sketchy outside the towns and mining camps. Epidemics are comparatively rare on the Altiplano, but malaria and yellow fever are still problems in the Oriente and Santa Cruz, and hepatitis and Chagas disease (see page 338) are endemic in the warmer parts of the country.

But not all Bolivia's Indians are 'poor'. There is a very large community of urban Indians, or *cholos*, who are, on the whole, much better off than rural Indians and who make a decent income from the wholesale or retail trade.

REGIONAL DIFFERENCES

Before the arrival of the Spaniards, most of Bolivia's population lived on the Altiplano and in the higher-lying basins of the Valles. This is still the case today. The highest population densities are in the central and northern Altiplano, while the Llanos remain very thinly populated. But the rural population of the Altiplano, especially in the Departments of Oruro and Potosí, are now departing for the big towns and more economically-viable lower-lying areas.

In the Valles the population is actually growing. Most people are moving to Cochabamba and the smaller surrounding towns. This is a direct result of the process of agrarian colonization which began after the 1952 Revolution. Campesinos were encouraged to move to lower-lying regions in order to increase agricultural productivity and reduce demographic pressure on the densely-populated highlands. However, colonization has proceeded on a much larger scale than planned, creating an enormous strain on land and infrastructure. While many migrants earn a reasonable living from coca, rice, citrus fruits and coffee, others live in rural depression.

Since 1952 successive governments have favoured the Department of Santa Cruz in terms of capital investment. This has resulted in a thriving large-scale agricultural industry. The eastern regions of Bolivia have thus become the driving force of the economy. This has, of course, led to a massive influx of people. The city of Santa Cruz has grown much more rapidly than any other Bolivian city; from well below 100,000 in 1950, the city's population has passed 700,000 and could reach one million by the turn of the century. As a result of growing prosperity in the Oriente at the expense of the highlands, regional tensions between the *collas* (altiplano dwellers) and the *cambas* (lowlanders) have become more marked in recent decades.

Responsible Tourism

Much has been written about the adverse impacts of tourism on the environment and local communities. It is usually assumed that this only applies to the more excessive end of the travel industry such as the Spanish Costas and Bali. However it now seems that travellers can have an impact at almost any density and this is especially true in areas 'off the beaten track' where local people may not be used to western conventions and lifestyles, and natural environments may be very sensitive.

Of course, tourism can have a beneficial impact and this is something to which every traveller can contribute. Many National Parks are part funded by receipts from people who travel to see exotic plants and animals. Similarly, travellers can promote patronage and protection of valuable archaeological sites and heritages through their interest and entrance fees.

However, where visitor pressure is high and/or poorly regulated, damage can occur. It is also unfortunately true that many of the most popular destinations are in ecologically sensitive areas easily disturbed by extra human pressures. This is particularly significant because the desire to visit sites and communities that are off the beaten track is a driving force for many travellers. Eventually the very features that tourists travel so far to see may become degraded and so we seek out new sites, discarding the old, and leaving someone else to deal with the plight of local communities and the damaged environment.

Fortunately, there are signs of a new awareness of the responsibilities that the travel industry and its clients need to endorse. For example, some tour operators fund local conservation projects and travellers are now more aware of the impact they may have on host cultures and environments. We can all contribute to the success of what is variously described as responsible, green or alternative tourism. All that is required is a little forethought and consideration.

It would be impossible to identify all the possible impacts that might need to be addressed by travellers, but it is worthwhile noting the major areas in which we can all take a more responsible attitude in the countries we visit. These include, changes to natural ecosystems (air, water, land, ecology and wildlife), cultural values (beliefs and behaviour) and the built environment (sites of antiquity and archaeological significance). At an individual level, travellers can reduce their impact if greater consideration is given to their activities. Canoe trips up the headwaters of obscure rivers make for great stories, but how do local communities cope with the sudden invasive interest in their lives? Will the availability of easy tourist money and gauche behaviour affect them for the worse, possibly diluting and trivialising the significance of culture and customs? Similarly, have the environmental implications of increased visitor pressure been considered? Where does the fresh fish that feeds the trip come from? Hand caught by line is fine, but is dynamite fishing really necessary, given the scale of damage and waste that results?

Some of these impacts are caused by factors beyond the direct control of travellers, such as the management and operation of a hotel chain. However, even here it is possible to voice concern about damaging activities and an increasing number of hotels and travel operators are taking 'green concerns' seriously, even if it is only to protect their share of the market.

Environmental Legislation is increasingly being enacted to control damage to the environment, and in some cases this can have a bearing on travellers. The establishment of National Parks may involve rules and guidelines for visitors and these should always be followed. In addition there may be local or national laws controlling behaviour and use of natural resources (especially wildlife) that are being increasingly enforced. If in doubt, ask. Finally, international legislation, principally the Convention on International Trade in Endangered Species of Wild Fauna and Flora (CITES), may affect travellers.

CITES aims to control the trade in live specimens of endangered plants and animals and also 'recognizable parts or derivatives' of protected species. Sale of Black Coral, Turtle shells, protected Orchids and other wildlife is strictly controlled by signatories of the convention. The full list of protected wildlife varies, so if you feel the need to purchase souvenirs and trinkets derived from wildlife, it would be prudent to check whether they are protected. Bolivia is a signatory of CITES, in addition, most European countries, the USA and Canada are all signatories. Importation of CITES protected species into these countries can lead to heavy fines, confiscation of goods and even imprisonment. Information on the status of legislation and protective measures can be obtained from Traffic International, UK office T (01223) 277427, F (01223) 277237, e-mail: traffic@wcmc.org.uk.

Green Travel Companies and Information The increasing awareness of the environmental impact of travel and tourism has led to a range of advice and information services as well as spawning specialist travel companies who claim to provide 'responsible travel' for clients. This is an expanding field and the veracity of claims needs to be substantiated in some cases. The following organizations and publications can provide useful information for those with an interest in pursuing responsible travel opportunities.

Organizations Green Flag International Aims to work with travel industry and conservation bodies to improve environments at travel destinations and also to promote conservation programmes at resort destinations. It provides a travellers' guide for 'green' tourism as well as advice on destinations, T (UK 01223) 890250. **Tourism Concern** aims to promote a greater understanding of the impact of tourism on host communities and environments; Stapleton House, 277-281 Holloway Road, London N7 8HN, T UK (0171) 753-3330, F UK (0171) 753 3331, e-mail: tourconcern@gn.apc.org. **Centre for Responsible Tourism (CRT)** coordinates a North American network and advises on North American sources of information on responsible tourism. CRT, PO Box 827, San Anselmo, California 94979, USA. **Centre for the Advancement of Responsive Travel (CART)** has a range of publications available as well as information on alternative holiday destinations; T (UK – 01732) 352757.

NATIONAL PARKS OF BOLIVIA

Bolivia boasts a number of National Parks, departmental parks, wildlife reserves, recreation areas and other sanctuaries designed to protect and preserve its astonishing (and in many cases unique) ecosystems and wilderness lands, as well as the often endangered animal and plant life that inhabit them. In fact, on paper, Bolivia has a vast amount of land under government supervision – more than any other Latin American country except Costa Rica, and possibly Chile.

As a signatory to many of the world's envirnomental-impact treaties and bans, and as a long-time member of the Amazon Basin Pact, Bolivia also participates on a global level where such matters are concerned. Bolivia was also the world's first nation to reduce its foreign debt under a highly successful debt swap arrangement through the World Bank, whereby creditors forgave a portion of the country's bilateral debt in exchange for

Bolivia's promise to create and maintain sustainable development initiatives and promote responsible, environmentally friendly progress, especially in the north and east. Recently, the country has been at the forefront of developing an ambitious but viable ecotourism programme, although the infrastructure for managing it is still a long way from completed.

Although some of these initiatives have succeeded, much more remains to be done before Bolivia can lay claim to having a responsible national programme for the environment, much less one for its many parks. Some, such as Parque Nacional Amboró, are bona fide world-class, unique wilderness areas that are well on the way to achieving a full or partial working infrastructure to allow camping, tours and the like, supervised or otherwise. Others, such as Parque Nacional Noell Kempff Mercado or Parque Nacional Isiboro-Securé are either too remote or potentially dangerous to support a viable ecotourism regime. Still others, including the once-pioneering Reserva de Fauna Andina Eduardo Avaroa, are embroiled in political or legal controversy and suffer from a lack of funds for any initiatives at all.

Still, as any traveller to these areas will vouch, all of Bolivia's protected areas, regardless of the state of their infrastructure or tourism development, have much to offer the visitor, whether interested in camping, hiking, birdwatching or botany. Virtually all of the parks will allow the traveller an opportunity to see first-hand many rare species of flora and fauna in their natural habitat, along with the chance to observe how these fragile environmental microcosms survive in an increasingly threatened world.

Bolivia's parks are found in virtually every department, incorporate all major ecosystems, and offer everything from the chance to scale unmapped mountains, to unearthing dinosaur bones or discovering new animal or plant species. For the careful and observant visitor, a trip to any of these parks will be an unforgettable experience.

The true number of Bolivia's designated national parks is expected to increase dramatically within the next decade. No less than ten new parks have been proposed by congress, the majority of them within the Amazon basin. At present, there are at least ten fully-fledged national parks and six reserves; three are wildlife reserves, two forestry reserves and the other a biosphere reserve.

SANTA CRUZ DEPARTMENT

Easily the best known is **Parque Nacional y Area de Uso Multiple Amboró** in the far west of Santa Cruz Department. Even at 430,000 hectares, it is only Bolivia's fifth largest protected area, but it is best-known thanks to its relative ease of access and rudimentary tourism infrastructure. It also contains three distinct ecosystems and an amazing array of wildlife, particularly birds (see page 268).

Another national park that could give Amboró a run for its money, were it not so remote, is **Parque Nacional Noell Kempff Mercado** (see page 286), located along the border with Brazil at the far northeast of Santa Cruz department and covering 1,600,000 hectares. Created in 1979, its name was changed in 1988 in honour of the Bolivian biologist who was killed there. At US$30 per head, it is Bolivia's most expensive park, and finding it is an adventure in itself. By road, it is an arduous 200-km journey on mostly unpaved roads due north from the provincial capital of San Ignacio. At La Florida, 25 km west of the park's sole vehicular entrance, a dirt road veers right and enters the park at a guard station, Los Fierros, which also serves as the park's official headquarters. There are also an increasing number of air taxi services to the area, most of which land along the banks of the Río Guaporé, which forms the park's (and Bolivia's) eastern border with Brazil. Services at Mercado are marginal, except at Los Fierros and Flor de

Oro, which is along the western reaches of the river. Several tour operators also offer 3-7 day guided tours of the park. Recent studies have shown that Mercado may even surpass Amboró in terms of both numbers and diversity of wildlife. Its chief attraction is the stunning Catarata el Encanto, a 150m waterfall about 20 km in from Los Fierros.

Also in Santa Cruz department is the 1,400,000 hectares **Reserva de Vida Silvestre Ríos Blanco y Negro**. The country's second largest preserve is also one of its newest, having been created only in 1990. It sits at the extreme northwest of the department and spills over into adjacent Beni department. At roughly 310 km north of Santa Cruz, and accessible only

by air, and with only one settlement in the area, the reserve is the most isolated in the country. This has proven to be a blessing in disguise, as it has enabled the area to retain its rare species, particularly its plant life, as well as several rare animals, including capuchin and squirrel monkeys, jaguars, tapirs and even wild dogs. Tours may be arranged in Santa Cruz. A solo visit is ill-advised due to the lack of essential facilities.

Santa Cruz department is also home to the brand-new **Parque Nacional y Area Natural Gran Chaco Kaa-Iya**, the largest park in the country (and second largest in the entire continent) at 3,440,000 hectares. The park alone covers 4% of the department. Home to a unique dry forest

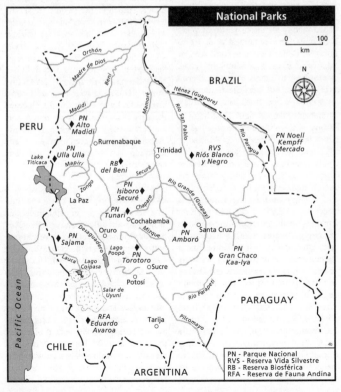

National Parks

0   100
km

BRAZIL

N

PERU

PN Alto Madidi

Rurrenabaque

Lake Titicaca

PN Ulla Ulla

Madidi

Orthón

Madre de Dios

Beni

Mamoré

Iténez (Guaporé)

Río San Pablo

Trinidad

RVS Ríos Blanco y Negro

Río Paraguá

PN Noell Kempff Mercado

Mapirí

RB del Beni

Securé

Zongo

PN Isiboro Securé

Chaparé

Río Grande (Guapay)

La Paz

PN Tunari

Cochabamba

Desaguadero

Oruro

Mizque

PN Amboró

Santa Cruz

PN Sajama

Lauca

Lago Poopó

PN Torotoro

PN Gran Chaco Kaa-Iya

Lago Coipasa

Sucre

Salar de Uyuní

Potosí

Río Parapetí

PARAGUAY

Pacific Ocean

RFA Eduardo Avaroa

Tarija

Pilcomayo

CHILE

ARGENTINA

4b

PN - Parque Nacional
RVS - Reserva Vida Silvestre
RB - Reserva Biosférica
RFA - Reserva de Fauna Andina

ecosystem, Kaa-Iya is the only park in the western hemisphere administered by its indigenous people, in this case the Kaa-Iya tribe of Guaraníes. At present, access is either by train from Santa Cruz or the road that parallels it. No facilities exist as yet, though both USAID and several Bolivian conservation groups have invested more than US$4 million in infrastructure development, which began in May, 1997.

COCHABAMBA DEPARTMENT

West of Santa Cruz Department lies Cochabamba Department, home to the small (14,000 hectares) but pleasant **Parque Nacional Tunari** (see page 248). Bolivia's most accessible park, it lies at the foothills of the mountains just outside the city of Cochabamba. One of the country's oldest parks, established in 1962, it is now visited mainly for the magnificent views of the area from its highest peak, Cerro Tunari. It is also a starting point for 1 or 2-day hikes in the local mountain range. Its proximity to the city means there is no infrastructure, but there are a number of campsites (all free) along its main trails.

Cochabamba Department is also home to **Parque Isiboro-Securé** (see page 293), a 1,200,000 hectares reserve established in 1965 in the northwest of the department. Unfortunately, the surrounding area – the Chapare – is Bolivia's main cocaine-producing area, with all its attendant dangers, and the park is a very dangerous place, especially for the independent traveller. North Americans in particular are warned against visiting because of their government's Drug Enforcement Agency presence in the region. Still, the park is lovely and is easily travelled by the many rivers that intersect it. There are a handful of tour agencies that organize trips to the park, usually from Cochabamba or Trinidad, but proper documentation is a must. Access is via the Cochabamba-Santa Cruz highway at Villa Tunari and then along private roads, but getting there is considered very dangerous.

POTOSI DEPARTMENT

Parque Nacional Torotoro was set up in 1988 in neighbouring Potosí Department (see page 250). Roughly 200 km south of Cochabamba, it lies well off the Sucré-Oruro road and access is impossible without a 4WD vehicle. Travel by air to the staging town of Torotoro is a better option. Trips can be organized with Cochabamba tour agencies (see page 247). Apart from dinosaur tracks and fossils, Torotoro offers Inca ruins, cave paintings and several underground waterfalls and lakes with a strange collection of creatures, including a blind catfish.

Also in Potosí Department is **Parque Nacional Sajama** (see page 186), which borders Chile's well-known Parque Nacional Lauca. Although the poorer cousin in terms of infrastructure, Sajama contains within its 80,000 hectares the world's highest forest and Bolivia's highest peak, Volcán Sajama (also known as Nevado Sajama), at 6,542m. It is also Bolivia's oldest national park, created in 1945. Entrance is US$1 and access is made by any bus on the La Paz-Arica route. Once in the park itself, the trails are reduced to footpaths. The park is especially recommended for experienced climbers. Treks to Volcán Sajama and nearby peaks are organized out of La Paz by numerous tour agencies (see page 104).

BENI DEPARTMENT

The Beni has few preservation areas yet, although plans call for several to be established in the next decade or so. Perhaps its best-known reserve is the 334,200 hectares **Reserva Biosférica del Beni**, created in 1982. At US$5 per person, the entrance fee is a bargain. All manner of Amazonian wildlife, including tapirs, peccaries and caimans are easily seen and most of the reserve is largely flat terrain. Local guides are available in El Porvenir, the nearest town. Access is 180 km west of Trinidad via the main road running east from San Borja to San Ignacio de Moxos (see page 306).

Literally next door to the Biosphere is the **Reserva Forestal Chimane**, a 1,150,000 hectares restricted use forest. By law, only the 1,000 or so remaining Chimane Indians can live in and use the forest. Also established in 1986, the experiment worked well for 4 or 5 years, but by 1991, outside interests – mostly loggers – had encroached on the land and only a spirited campaign by the Chimane to attract international attention led to the preserve keeping its protected status. Fortunately, many species of wild game survive here, several of which are unique to the area. 'Responsible' visitors are allowed access, though prior permission from both the government and the Chimane people is required.

LA PAZ DEPARTMENT

In La Paz Department is the **Parque Nacional Alto Madidi**, founded in 1995 with more than 200,00 hectares of mostly virgin forest. No infrastructure exists as yet, but the Bolivian government has high hopes for making it – along with Amboró – the centrepiece of its ecotourism efforts. The park encompasses several different ecosystems, ranging from tropical lowlands and jungles to the Altiplano and everything in between. At present, the area is virtually intact, although logging companies are attempting to exploit it. Like many of Bolivia's parks, Madidi allows indigenous peoples the right to live and hunt within the territory, and here the programme seems to be working well, as evidenced by a special citation received from UNESCO in 1996. Some estimates place the park's diversity of birdlife as the world's highest; with more than 1,000 types of birds. It may contain more than 10% of all known species!

Also in La Paz Department is **Parque Nacional Ulla Ulla** (see page 164), a 200,000 hectares wildlife reserve established in 1972 along the Peruvian border about 115 km northwest of La Paz. It is reached by bus or 4WD from the towns of Ulla Ulla in the south or Pelechuco to the east. Ulla Ulla contains the largest vicuña and condor populations in Bolivia, huge numbers of flamingos and other waterfowl. Trekking throughout the park is possible and affords amazingly beautiful views in every direction. Entry to Ulla Ulla is free, though there is no accommodation outside the access towns.

ORURO DEPARTMENT

Oruro Department contains the **Reserva de Fauna Andina Eduardo Avaroa** (see page 192), a small wildlife sanctuary established in 1974 along the border with Chile. Home to the rare llama-like guanaco and vicuña, Avaroa is also noted for its desert beauty. It is reached from the town of Avaroa, best approached by train from Uyuni, 125 km to the northeast.

Section 3

La Paz

FEW CITIES can boast such an impressive setting as La Paz. The view is staggering as you drop down from the Altiplano towards the highest capital city in the world, lying huddled at the bottom of a huge canyon with the triple-peaked Illimani providing a dramatic backdrop. It's a sight that leaves most visitors breathless – literally – for La Paz stands at 3,100m-4,100m depending on where you are, and the centre, officially Plaza Murillo, is at 3,600m, so altitude sickness is a real problem.

Apart from the geography of the place the other striking feature immediately noticeable to the visitor is the high proportion of people wearing traditional dress. Bolivia is the most indigenous of the Andean countries and one of the most familiar sights in the capital is the *chola* – a woman wearing bowler hat, twin plaits, voluminous skirts and often carrying on her back babies, animals or the shopping in a multicoloured blanket called an *ahuayo*. She wears traditional dress that has not changed since independence from the Spanish. Other dress styles from other parts of the country are also visible. Many lemon sellers come from the Potosí area and men from the Tarabuco area come to sell weavings on Calle Sagárnaga.

La Chola Pacena

The traveller arriving in La Paz will be struck by the distinctive dress of the *chola paceña*, a woman born in La Paz who wears full skirts and a derby, or bowler, hat.

Chola Paceña from 1910

There is some disagreement as to the origin of the term *cholo*, which is used to refer to Indians who have abandoned the traditional rural life and moved to the towns. One version is that the word comes from the Aymara word *chhulu*, which means *mestizo* in Castilian Spanish. Another is that the term derives from the Spanish word *chulo*, still used to refer to people from the lower class areas of Madrid. At the time of the conquest, the Spaniards referred to the *mestizos* (children born of native and Spanish parents) as *cholos*.

It is said that the style of dress of the *chola paceña* was influenced by the women of 17th century Toledo. The most distinctive garment of the *chola* is the voluminous skirt known as the *pollera*. This comes from the Spanish word *pollo* (chicken), so *pollera* translates as some kind of cage for chickens. Up until 1920 *polleras* were made of silk, velvet, taffeta and brocade in bright colours. Today, for practical as well as economic reasons, polyester and other acrylic fabrics are used.

The long-fringed *manta* (shawl) has not changed in shape since originally worn by the *cholas* in the 16th century. It is similar to that worn by the women of Salamanca in Spain, the only difference being that the *chola* wears it folded in a rectangular shape, in keeping with the tradition of the *llijlla*, which was worn by the *ñustas*, the princesses of the Inca empire (see page 46).

The hat of the *chola paceña* has changed in shape and in the materials used since its original design. The felt hat of today appeared only after 1925. Its origin is something of a mystery, though one theory is that a merchant mistakenly imported this derby hat. Not knowing what to do with them, he passed them off as ladies' hats, which turned out to be a very lucrative move. In the 1930s the Italian firm of Borsalino began to mass produce the derby hat for export to Bolivia.

The future of the distinctive style of the *chola paceña* would appear to be in some doubt. One of the reasons is that women want their daughters to adopt a European style in order to better their chances in society. Another reason is a simple economic one, since the purchase of a *pollera* alone represents 1 month's salary (about US$95), not to mention the cost of the derby hat and *manta*.

La Paz (*Population* 713,000; *Altitude* 3,600m; *Phone code* 02) is probably the safest city in Latin America, but that isn't to say that crime doesn't exist. Your biggest problem, though, will be the effects of *soroche* (altitude sickness). Anyone arriving straight in La Paz from sea level should rest for the first day or so and drink plenty of clear liquids (excluding alcohol). Take it easy and move slowly. **NB** There is no medical evidence that Sorojchi pills on sale in pharmacies and given out by some hotels work.

Climate

La Paz might be in the tropics but often it doesn't feel like it owing to the altitude. In the strong sunshine shorts and t-shirt would feel good, but go inside a building or into shadow and you need long trousers and a jumper. Nights are cold.

During the austral summer (December to March) when air temperatures are higher, it rains most afternoons making it feel colder than it actually is. The average temperature is 10°C, annual rainfall 600 mm. The difference between day and night length is less than 3 hours through the year.

HISTORY

La Paz was originally founded on the Altiplano in what is now Laja, a small town with an old church 30 km west of La Paz on the way to Desaguadero on the route to

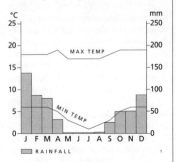

Climate: La Paz

Lima. The Spaniards soon had enough of the cold plateau. In 1548 they moved down to the valley of the Río Choqueyapu to escape from the cold winds and the city of Nuestra Señora de La Paz was founded. Another factor was the alluvial gold in the river whose name in Aymara means 'God of Gold', though 'Lifeless God of Heavy Metal and Major Pollutants' would be more accurate today. Silver had been discovered in Potosí 3 years earlier and La Paz was on the route between the mines and Lima, initially the main Spanish city.

Unlike, the rest of Bolivia's cities, La Paz has grown steadily since its foundation and has not fluctuated with the prosperity (or not) of mining. This is due to its role as the commercial centre of the northern Altiplano and its links with the Yungas to the east.

The official capital of Bolivia is technically Sucre, a pleasant colonial town in the southeast of the country, but La Paz has been the country's biggest city since the decline of Potosí in the 17th century. While the supreme court is still based in Sucre, government has been based in La Paz since a short civil war in 1899. La Paz's economic superiority is coming under threat from the continuing agriculture-fuelled growth of Santa Cruz.

MODERN LA PAZ

The centre of La Paz has always been around Plaza Murillo and the cathedral. The first real suburb was Sopocachi which boasts mature trees, cobbled streets and some fine buildings. The spread down to what is now Obrajes happened during the early 20th century while the development of the Zona Sur has been going on for 30 years. During this time working class areas have spread out farther and farther from the centre including Villa Fátima and anything with Alto in its name; Alto Obrajes, Alto Seguencoma, Alto Sopocachi.

There are relatively few surviving examples of colonial architecture in La Paz (see page 84).

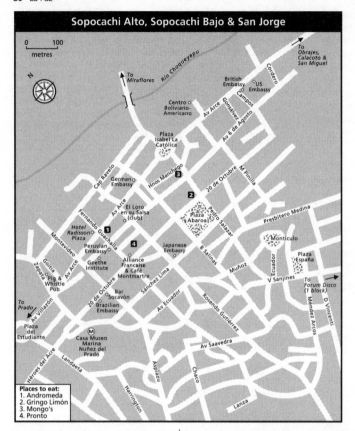

Sopocachi Alto, Sopocachi Bajo & San Jorge

Places to eat:
1. Andromeda
2. Gringo Limón
3. Mongo's
4. Pronto

The centre

Orientation around the centre is relatively simple. Running along the bottom of the canyon is the broad main street called El Prado (though it has four official names, starting in the north: Avenida Montes, Avenida Mariscal Santa Cruz, Avenida 16 de Julio and Avenida Villazón). All streets go uphill from the Prado. On Sunday it is often closed to traffic while various displays and events take place and toddlers ride their tricycles up and down. It is also the centrepoint for any demonstration in the city, which causes traffic chaos.

El Prado runs southeast from Plaza San Francisco down to the Plaza del Estudiante. The business quarter, government offices, university and many of the main hotels and restaurants are situated in this area. On the hills above Plaza Mendoza are the poorer parts of the city. **Sopocachi**, through which runs Avenida 6 de Agosto, has many restaurants, discos and bars, and the Mercado Sopocachi, on F Guachalla, is good but not cheap (a bimonthly *Sopocachi* magazine of cultural events, with map, is sold at newsstands). When giving directions in La Paz, you are often asked "¿Qué altura?" ("What altitude?"). This is not a test of your altimeter but merely asking for the street that crosses the one you are going up.

The Zona Sur

From the Plaza del Estudiante, Avenida Villazón and its extensions lead further southeast towards the wealthier residential districts, which run from Sopocachi to the bed of the valley at Obrajes, 5 km from the centre and 500m lower than Plaza Murillo. Beyond Obrajes are the upper-class districts of Calacoto and La Florida. The main sports and social clubs are in these districts.

These southern suburbs are lower and warmer and there's more space to build. Some of the houses in areas such as Los Pinos have to be seen to be believed; Swiss chalets (though somewhat larger than the originals), mosque-style domes, gothic structures or mock-Tudor.

EL ALTO

(*Population* 406,000; *Altitude* 4,058m; *Phone code* 02) Apart from the airport, there was nothing on the bleak Altiplano surrounding the canyon of La Paz until the 1960s. Since then the relatively poor district of El Alto

has sprung up. With a population of officially 406,000 but at least 50% higher, El Alto is now a city in its own right. Apart from the district known as Ciudad Satelite, it is almost 100% indigenous.

El Alto presently holds the record for the fastest growing city in South America; it is growing at 10% per year, compared with 4% growth in the wealthier districts of La Paz. Immigrants from the countryside seeking their fortune, or at least integration into the monetarized economy, steadily arrive. They build adobe brick huts and after a whole suburb has developed, roads are put in followed by electricity and finally water. The flat land means there are no physical obstacles to growth and the people are used to the temperatures in the 4,000m range. However, it freezes virtually every night from the start of June to the end of August and drunks who do not make it home die of hypothermia.

Costs are much lower than in La Paz, but construction and infrastructure are much more basic. There is a market on Thursday and Sunday in Avenida Alfonso Ugarte, more interesting for its size than the items for sale. El Alto is connected to

Cholita in El Alto

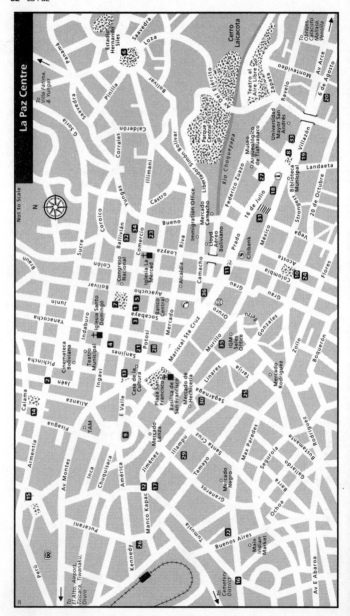

La Paz Centre

Not to Scale

La Paz by motorway (toll US$0.50, cycles free). Buses from Plaza Eguino and Pérez Velasco leave regularly for Plaza 16 de Julio in El Alto.

PLACES OF INTEREST

The best way to explore the city is on foot and at a leisurely pace. Just take the time to investigate its many nooks and crannies and you'll be rewarded with some unforgettable sights.

Markets

After a few days wandering around La Paz you may come to the conclusion that it's one great street market, and you wouldn't be far wrong. Everywhere you'll find Aymara women in traditional dress squatted on haunches selling fruit and vegetables, razor blades, camera film, Vicks Vaporub, Snickers bars, dried llama foetuses – anything, in fact, you'd find in the local supermarket. The llama foetuses are used to protect a dwelling from evil spirits and you can find great piles of them, like extras from a horror movie, in the **Witches' Market** (*Mercado de Hechicería*) on Calle Linares between Calle Sagárnaga and Santa Cruz, where charms and herbs are also sold.

Behind the San Francisco church a network of narrow cobbled streets rises steeply. Much of this area is a permanent street market. The lower part of Calle Sagárnaga, from Plaza San Francisco to Calle Illampu, is lined with shops and stalls selling handicrafts, clothes, guitar covers, silver and leatherware. So informal is the retail trade here that stall holders go for lunch leaving their stall with a piece of plastic or blanket over it to show it is shut.

Further up Sagárnaga turn left on Max Paredes. Where it meets Calle Rodríguez and becomes Calle Zoilo Flores is the **Mercado Rodríguez**, a blaze of colour, fruit, vegetables, identifiable and unidentifiable parts of animals. Main market days are Saturday and Sunday mornings but there are stalls every day.

Turning right on Max Paredes, heading west, between Santa Cruz and Graneros, is the **Mercado Negro**, a bewildering labyrinth of stalls where you can pick up a cheap pair of Levi jeans, or almost anything else.

Continuing west towards the cemetery district, Max Paredes meets **Avenida Buenos Aires**, one of the liveliest streets in the indigenous quarter, where small workshops turn out the costumes and masks for the Gran Poder festival (see **Local festivals**, page 87). The streets are crammed with stalls selling every imaginable item, household goods, clothing, hats, food, festive goods. Transport converges on the cemetery district (for more information see **Buses** page 107). Do not expect to go anywhere in a hurry in this part of the city; just enjoy the atmosphere and the marvellous views of Illimani.

On Avenida Libertador Simón Bolívar (to which Mount Illimani provides a backdrop), is the Central Market, called **Mercado Camacho**. It's a colourful and raucous affair with the ubiquitous *cholas* haranguing passers-by with their cries of "¡Cómprame! ¡Cómprame!" as they preside over their stalls. Further east is the residential district of Miraflores. Another good view of Illimani can be had from the top of the rise on Calle Illimani.

La Paz: Key to map
1. Cathedral; 2. Museo Costumbrista, Museo Casa Murillo, Museo de Metales Preciosos and Museo del Litoral Boliviano; 3. Museo Nacional de Arte; 4. Museo Nacional de Etnografía y Folklore; 5. Palacio Quemado; 6. Parque Prehistórico Tiahuanaco (Museo Semisubterráneo). **Parks and squares:** 7. Plaza Murillo; 8. Plaza del Estudiante/Franz Tamayo; 9. Plaza Mendoza; 10. Plaza Sucre/San Pedro; 11. Plaza Venezuela; 12. Plaza Vicente Eguino; 13. Plaza Velasco; 14. Plaza Riosinio; 15. Plaza Antofagasta; 16. Garita de Lima. **Hotels:** 17. *Continental*; 18. *El Dorado*; 19. *Copacabana*; 20. *España*; 21. *Gloria*; 22. *La Joya*; 23. *Libertador*; 24. *Max Inn*; 25. *Milton*; 26. *Panamericano*; 27. *Plaza*; 28. *Presidente*; 29. *Res Rosario*; 30. *Sagárnaga* and *Alem*; 31. *Sucre Palace*; 32. *Viena*; 33. *Hostal Claudia*; 34. *Hostal República*. **Restaurants/Peña:** 35. Casa del Corregidor; 36. Los Escudos.

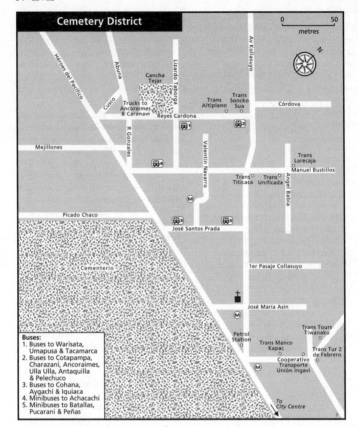

Cemetery District

There are few colonial buildings left in La Paz. Probably the best examples are in **Calle Jaén** and **Calle Murillo**. Late 19th/early 20th century architecture, often displaying heavy European influence, can be found in the streets around Plaza Murillo, but much of La Paz is modern.

Emilio Villanueva added local features to European styles, eg the Tiwanaku-style decorations on the University building, but much 20th-century architecture was influenced by Frank Lloyd Wright, eg the new *Correo*.

The **Plaza del Estudiante** (Plaza Franz Tamayo), or a bit above it, marks a contrast between old and new styles, between the traditional commercial and the more elegant. The Prado itself is lined with high-rise blocks dating from the 1960s and 1970s.

Plaza Murillo, three blocks north of the Prado, is the traditional centre. Facing its formal gardens are the huge, modern, but very graceful **Cathedral** and the **Palacio Presidencial**. The latter, usually known as the Palacio Quemado (burnt palace), is in Italian renaissance style and has twice been gutted by fire in its stormy 130-year history. On the east side of Plaza Murillo is the **Congreso Nacional**.

In front of the Palacio Quemado is a statue of former President Gualberto Villarroel who was dragged into the plaza by an angry mob and hanged in 1946. Across from the Cathedral on Calle Socabaya is the **Palacio de los Condes de Arana**, dating from 1775, now the **Museo Nacional del Arte**. Calle Comercio, running east-west across the Plaza, has most of the stores and shops.

A worthwhile walk is to **Mirador Laicacota** on Avenida del Ejército, where you can enjoy one of the delights of La Paz – the change from day to night, when all the lights begin to twinkle on the surrounding hillsides.

Churches

At the upper end of Avenida Mariscal Santa Cruz is the Plaza San Francisco with the church and monastery of **San Francisco**, dating from 1549. This is one of the finest examples of colonial religious architecture in South America and is well worth seeing. The church is richly decorated using native religious themes; the mestizo baroque façade clearly displays how the traditional baroque vine motif is transformed into an array of animals, birds, fruits and plants. The interior contains huge, square columns and gilt altars on which stand many saints. Local indigenous weddings can be seen on Sats 1000-1200; otherwise the church opens at 1600.

Other churches of more than passing interest are **Santo Domingo** (originally the cathedral) on the corner of Calles Ingavi and Yanacocha, with its 18th-century façade. Next door is the Universidad Pacensis Divi-Andreae, 1826, and the distinctive pink Colegio Nacional San Simón de Ayacucho.

Also of note are **La Merced**, on a plazuela at Calles Colón and Comercio, and **San Juan de Dios**, on Loayza between Merced and Camacho, with a carved portico, circular paintings of the life of Christ and, above the altar, figures holding lighted (electric) candles around a statue of the Virgin. **San Sebastián**, the first church to be built in La Paz, is on

San Francisco Church

Plaza Alonso de Mendoza (named after the church's builder). On the pleasant Plaza Sucre is **San Pedro** church, Avenida 20 de Octubre y Colombia, built in 1720. It boasts large paintings of the life of Christ along the nave, a huge chandelier below the dome and a gilt altar.

Also on Plaza Sucre is one of the city's less well-known tourist attractions, **San Pedro Prison**. This may not be everyone's idea of a pleasant outing, but it does offer a truly surreal, if slightly disturbing, experience. Many of the 1,500 mostly violent criminals will talk freely and openly about the bizarre goings-on in an open complex where new inmates buy their accommodation from paroled prisoners. These range from luxury penthouse apartments complete with jacuzzi costing US$5,000 to a more modest US$20 for a cramped space under the stairs. The poorest prisoners have to work in the kitchens and, worse still, eat what comes out of them.

Many inmates even share their accommodation with wives and children.

Visits can be made on Thursday and Sunday, 0800-1500, and last 1 hour; take passport. Ask the police for Freddy who'll show you around for US$4.

MUSEUMS

Museo Nacional de Arte, across from the Cathedral at Calle Socabaya 432, housed in the 18th century baroque palace of the Condes de Arana, with beautiful exterior and patio. It has a fine collection of colonial paintings including many works by Melchor Pérez Holguín, considered one of the masters of Andean colonial art, and also exhibits the works of contemporary local artists. Open Tuesday-Friday 0900-1230, 1500-1900, US$0.25, Saturday 1000-1300, entry US$0.50, students US$0.25.

Museo Tiahuanaco (Tiwanaku), or Museo Nacional de Arqueología, easily reached by going down the flight of stairs by María Auxili church on the Prado. This modern building, simulating the Tiahuanaco style, contains good collections of the arts and crafts of ancient Tiahuanaco and items from the eastern jungles. It also has a two-room exhibition of gold statuettes and objects found in Lake Titicaca. Open Tuesday-Friday 0900-1230, 1500-1900, Saturday 1000-1230, 1500-1830, Sunday 1000-1300; entry US$1.20, includes a good video show.

Museo Semisubterráneo, or Templo del Estadio, is in front of the National Stadium, with restored statues and other artefacts from Tiahuanaco. It's in a sunken garden and much can be seen from street level. No explanations are given and the statues are being badly eroded by pollution.

Museo Nacional de Etnografía y Folklore, on Calle Ingavi 916, is housed in the palace of the Marqueses de Villaverde, with exhibits on the Chipaya and Ayoreo Indians. It's worth a visit and has quite a good library adjoining. Open Monday-Friday 0830-1200, 1430-1830.

The following four museums, all on Calle Jaén, are included on a single ticket, which costs US$0.75 (free on Saturday), from Museo Costumbrista. All are open Tuesday-Friday 1030-1300, 1600-2030, Saturday and Sunday 1030-1300, and all are well worth seeing, with well-displayed items in colonial buildings. Calle Jaén, a picturesque colonial street with many craft shops, is worth seeing in itself.

Museo Costumbrista is near Plaza Riosinio, at the top of Jaén, T 378478. Miniature displays depict incidents in the history of La Paz and well-known Paceños. Also has miniature replicas of reed rafts used by Norwegian, Thor Heyerdahl and Spaniard, Kitin Muñoz, to prove their theories of ancient migrations.

Museo Casa Murillo, on Jaén, T 375273, was originally the home of Pedro Domingo Murillo, one of the martyrs of the abortive La Paz independence movement of 16 July 1809. This colonial house has been carefully restored and has a good collection of paintings, furniture and national costumes of the period. There is also a special room dedicated to herbal medicine and magic (Kallawaya) along with two rooms of paintings.

Museo de Metales Preciosos, Jaén 777, T 371470. Well set out with Inca gold artefacts in basement vaults, also ceramics and archaeological exhibits.

Museo del Litoral Boliviano, Jaén 789, with artefacts of the War of the Pacific, and an interesting selection of old maps.

Casa Museo Marina Núñez del Prado, Ecuador 2034, open Monday-Friday, 1000-1300, 1500-1900, Saturday, 1000-1300; excellent collection of her sculptures housed in the family mansion.

Museo Tambo Quirquincho, Calle Evaristo Valle, near Plaza Mendoza, open Tuesday-Friday, 1030-1300, 1600-2030, Saturday-Sunday, 1030-1300, US$0.50, Saturday free. Housed in a restored colonial building, displaying modern painting and sculpture, carnival masks, silver, early 20th century photography and city plans. A visit is highly recommended.

Museo de Historia Natural, Calle 26, Cota Cota, 30 minutes from centre by micro-bus marked 'Cota Cota' from Plaza San Francisco; open Tuesday-Sunday 1000-1700, entry US$0.60.

LOCAL FESTIVALS

Particularly impressive is the **Alasitas Fair** held from the last week of January to the first week of February, in Parque Central up from Avenida del Ejército, also in Plaza Sucre/San Pedro.

At the end of May/early June is **Festividad de Nuestro Señor Jesús del Gran Poder**, the most important festival of the year, with a huge procession of costumed and masked dancers. Among the many dances on display is the *Waka Thokoris*, which derives from the disdain and reproach for the Spanish bullfight. The *Morenada* and *Diablada* are also featured. These two are more commonly associated with the Oruro carnival (see page 182). *Los Caporales* originates in the Afro-Caribbean cultural tradition of the Yungas and is a burlesque of the African slave bosses. This dance is a recent addition to *Gran Poder* and has spread to other parts of the country.

Other festivals: **Corpus Cristi**, at the beginning of June. **San Juan**, on 21 June, is based on the Aymara New Year. People used to mark the passing of the old year by burning all their rubbish in the streets, especially old tyres; now it is mainly an excuse to let off fireworks. **Fiestas de Julio** is a month of concerts and performances at the Teatro Municipal and offers a wide variety of music, including the **University Folkloric**

Plenty to cheer about

One of the most intriguing items for sale in Andean markets is *Ekeko*, the god of good fortune and plenty and one of the most enduring and endearing of the Aymara gods and folk legends.

He is a cheery, avuncular little chap, with a happy face to make children laugh, a pot belly due to his predilection for food and short legs so he can't run away. His image, usually in plaster of paris, is laden with various household items, as well as sweets, confetti and streamers, food, and with a cigarette dangling from his lower lip. Believers say that these statues only bring luck if they are received as gifts, and not purchased.

The *Ekeko* occupies a central position in the festival of *Alasitas*, the Feast of Plenty, which takes place in La Paz every January. Everything under the sun can be bought in miniature: houses, trucks, buses, tools, building materials, dollar bills, suitcases, university diplomas, you name it, you can find it here. The idea is to have your mini-purchase blessed by a *Yatiri* (an Aymara priest) and the real thing will be yours within the year.

Ekeko at Alasitas Fair

Fiesta del Gran Poder

In 1939 one of the most important folkloric festivals of La Paz began its life. This has come to be known as *Festividad de Nuestro Señor Jesús del Gran Poder*. The name derives from a sacred painting of Jesus which was moved around various neighbourhoods in the city as a symbol of Christian faith until, after a long pilgrimage, it came to rest in a house in Chijini. Years later, a temple was built and that particular *barrio*, or neighbourhood, came to be known as Gran Poder.

Many of the inhabitants of this part of La Paz were originally migrants from the Altiplano, working their way up the social ladder as traders, drivers or craftsmen to achieve the level of *cholos*, who as part of the lower middle class have reached positions which earn them respect and status. As in the rural villages, the many patronal festivals in the towns offer people an opportunity to enhance their status by means of generous *prestes* or financial contributions towards the huge costs involved. And *Gran Poder* is such a festival. The various traders and dealers make their presence felt by sponsoring groups in the procession. While the extravagantly costumed and masked dance groups compete for honour and status, *los señores del Gran Poder*, the rich and powerful of La Paz, compete for bigger stakes with ever larger *prestes*.

Over the years *Gran Poder* has developed into a massive carnival in which tens of thousands participate. A far cry from its humble beginnings when local people and those from further afield would come on pilgrimages to the temple of Gran Poder and burn candles as an act of devotion and to ask for celestial favours. Now, this custom has diminished and the festival has become music-based, attracting numerous groups of dancers and musicians, some even from the famed Oruro Carnival. The festival has also spread out from its own *barrio* and now takes over completely the modern centre of La Paz.

(From *Bolivia in Focus*, by Paul Van Lindert and Otto Verkoren, Latin American Bureau, 1994).

Caporales dancers during Gran Poder

Festival. Independence Day, on 6 August, is marked by a very loud gun salute at 0630 which can be heard all over the centre of the city. On 8 December a festival is held around **Plaza España**. It's not very large, but very colourful and noisy. On **New Year's Eve** fireworks are let off and make a spectacular sight, and a din; best viewed from higher up.

For a fuller description of festivals and a list of those outside the capital see page 55.

LOCAL INFORMATION

Try to arrive in La Paz early in the day as accommodation, especially at the cheaper end of the market, can be hard to find. Major hotels quote their prices in dollars. Bills can be paid with dollars or bolivianos at the day's rate. Prices include tax and service charge (20% in all).

● **Accommodation**

Hotel prices			
L1	over US$200	**L2**	US$151-200
L3	US$101-150	**A1**	US$81-100
A2	US$61-80	**A3**	US$46-60
B	US$31-45	**C**	US$21-30
D	US$12-20	**E**	US$7-11
F	US$4-6	**G**	up to US$3

Expensive hotels: **L3** *Radisson Plaza*, formerly *Hotel La Paz* (still referred to as *Sheraton*), Avenida Arce 2177, T 316163, F 343391, good five-star hotel with all facilities; **L3** *Plaza*, Avenida 16 de Julio 1789, T 378317, F 343391, excellent, good value restaurant (see under **Places to eat**), peña show on Friday; **L3** *Presidente*, Potosí 920 y Sanjines, near Plaza San Francisco, T 368601, F 354013, including breakfast, 'the highest five-star in the world' with great views from the top floor, pool, gymnasium and sauna all open to non-residents, bar, disco, excellent service, comfortable, good food, recommended; **L3** *Ritz Apart Hotel*, Plaza Isabel La Católica 2478, T 433131, F 433080, five-star self-catering apartments, including breakfast; **L3** *Europa*, 64 Tiahuanacu Street, T 315656, E-mail: europa@wara.bolnet.bo, has all the usual five-star facilities.

A1 *El Rey Palace*, Avenida 20 de Octubre 1947, T 393016, F 367769, including breakfast, large suites, excellent restaurant, stylish and modern; **A1** *Gran Hotel París*, Plaza Murillo

esq Bolívar, T 319170, F 372547, including breakfast, English spoken, elegant restaurant.

A2 *Camino Real*, Ravelo 2123, T 314542, F 335575, self-catering apartments, including breakfast, TV, parking.

A3 *Gloria*, Potosí 909, T 370010/18, F 391489, opposite *Presidente*, 2 restaurants, one is on the top floor with good views, the other is vegetarian, excellent food and service (see under **Places to eat**), recommended; **A3** *Libertador*, Obispo Cárdenas 1421, T 351792, F 391225, very good value, colour TV, good cheap restaurant, helpful (baggage stored), highly recommended.

B *Eldorado*, Avenida Villazón, T 363355, F 391438, including breakfast, may be able to bargain for longer stays, safe luggage deposit, secure parking nearby; **B** *Max Inn*, Plaza Sucre 1494, T 374391, F 341720, small but clean rooms with bath, heating, TV, nicely furnished but poor service; **B** *Nikkei Plaza*, Calle México 1555, T/F 326341, half a block from the Prado, opened in 1997, sauna, pool, international restaurant, including continental breakfast, good value; **B** *Sucre Palace*, Avenida 16 de Julio 1636, T 363453, F 392052, hot water a problem, overpriced, *Karin* snack bar on ground floor is excellent though expensive, there's also a disappointing restaurant on the first floor.

Medium-priced hotels: **C** *Continental*, Illampu 626, T 378226, with bath, hot water, cheaper rooms available if you ask, clean, friendly, limited book exchange, has its own travel agency, nice bar downstairs; **C** *Copacabana*, Avenida 16 de Julio 1802, T 352244, with bath, restaurant and grill room (lunch only at latter), good service, safe deposit, rooms a bit small but otherwise good; **C** *Hostería Blanquita*, Santa Cruz 242, T 352933, described as 'baroque', including breakfast, hot showers, comfortable; **C** *Hostal Embajador*, Juan de la Riva 1438, T 392079, with bath, TV, heating, breakfast included, German spoken, helpful; **C-D** *Hostal República*, Comercio 1455, T 357966, with bath, **E** without, breakfast extra, beautiful old house of former president, nice patio, very clean, warm water, inadequate shared bathrooms, luggage stored, helpful, laundry service, very popular with cyclists, usually full, recommended, there is also a separate house available which sleeps six, with all facilities, US$25 a night; **C** *La Joya*, Max Paredes 541, near Buenos Aires, T 324346, F 350959, in the heart of the market

district, with bath and TV, phone, **E** without bath or TV, breakfast included, clean, modern and comfortable, laundry, free pickup from town centre, mixed reports on standard of service, but still recommended; **C** *Neumann*, Loayza 442, T 325445, with bath, **D** without bath, bargaining is possible for students; **C** *Residencial Copacabana*, Illampu 734, T 367896/375378, hot water, **D** without bath, including breakfast, changes travellers' cheques; **C** *Residencial Rosario*, Illampu 704, T 326531/316156, F 375532, a steep 15-minute walk uphill from Plaza San Francisco, a very attractive and modern colonial-style hotel, has Turisbus travel agency downstairs (see under **Travel agents**), with bath and good electric shower, cheaper without bath, the most popular mid to top-range hotel with foreigners, avoid the noisier rooms near the foyer, sauna, laundry, excellent restaurant (see under **Places to eat**), stores luggage, friendly and helpful staff, highly recommended; **C** *Sagárnaga*, Sagárnaga 326, T 350252, F 360831, basic breakfast included, with bath, **D** without, English spoken, mixed reports about service, no heating, good location near Plaza San Francisco, laundry; **C** *Viena*, Loayza 420, T 323572, with bath, **E** without, a beautiful old building with elegant entrance and patio but the rooms are gloomy, good lunch in restaurant, friendly, clean, arrive early as it is often full, has its own Vicuña Tours agency, generally good.

D-E *Andes*, Avenida Manco Kapac 364, T 323461, near railway station, with bath, soap and towels provided, good breakfast included, clean, hot water 24 hours a day, motorcycle parking, **F** per person in single room without bath and including breakfast, discount for IYHA card holders, safe deposit box, stores luggage

for US$0.20 per day, good restaurant, very good value, recommended; **D-E** *Dinastía*, Calle Illampu 684 esq Graneros, T 379096/390568, Casilla 11171, cheaper without bath, very clean, friendly, English-speaking owner, rooms on street can be noisy, good value; **D** *El Alem*, Sagárnaga 334, T 367400, hot water, **F** per person without private bath, breakfast included, clean, helpful, secure, same day laundry service US$1.50 per kilogram, has helpful travel agency; **D** *España*, Avenida 6 de Agosto 2074, T 354643, good location near Plaza del Estudiante, rooms with shared bath, hot water, TV, quiet, friendly, restaurant, quite good value; **D-C** *Hostal Claudia*, Avenida Villazón 1965, T 372917, with bath, **E** without, breakfast extra, clean, secure, friendly, recommended; **D** *Latino*, Perú 171, T 358341, near the bus terminal, with bath, **E** without; **D** *Milton*, Illampu y Calderón 1124, T 368003/353511, F 365849 (PO Box 5118), in the market district, with bath, hot water, breakfast included, laundry, safe parking around the corner, popular with travellers, will store luggage, excellent views from roof, good restaurant, very friendly and clean, secure, rooms at the back are quieter, recommended; **D** *Residencial La Estancia*, Mexico 1559, T 324308, with bath and breakfast, helpful, good restaurant; **D** *Residencial Sucre*, Colombia 340, on Plaza San Pedro, T 328414, F355506, cheaper without bath, quiet area, warm water, big rooms set around a courtyard with a beautiful garden, clean, luggage stored, friendly and helpful, recommended; **D** *Tambo de Oro*, Armentia 367, T 322763, near the bus station, hot showers, clean, friendly, helpful and safe for luggage.

Budget hotels: **E** *Alojamiento Illimani*, Avenida Illimani 1817, T 325948, hot water,

Hotel "Sagárnaga"

Calle Sagárnaga No. 326 - Teléfonos 350252-340356-375374-
P O Box 3049 - Fax 00-591-02-360831 LA PAZ, BOLIVIA

Sagárnaga Hotel is located in the very centre of La Paz. We are one block away from San Francisco. Staying a night in our hotel is like staying near very well known folkloric peñas, great restaurants, handicrafts and the very well known art market "Mercado de los Brujos".

This enterprise is very well known because of its experience and tradition with tourism. We wish to offer you the following service: Beautiful rooms with 120 beds available, good view with private bathroom and hot showers with a solar energy system, telephone and television, as well as international telephones and fax, we also offer a service of a Direct International Calling Telephone Cabinet throughout a system of cards, laundry service and good security. We also offer certain rooms with common bathrooms at low prices. "Diego's Restaurant" for your continental breakfast, international and national food as well as cable television.

If you wish to visit La Paz, Bolivia, do not think twice, come and stay at Sagárnaga Hotel.

Salon "Cesis"

A Salon Auditorium of 70 square metres with a capacity of 70 people, also you can enjoy our Peña-Show with folkloric music and dances, every Wednesday and Sunday from hours: 20:00 to 22:00.

Diana Tours Agencia de Viajes Y Turismo

- Copacabana - Puno -
  Directly connected to:
  Cuzco-Machu Picchu
  Arequipa-Lima and other countries
- *Daily excursions to:*
  Tiwanaku/Chacaltaya/Coroico/City Tours/MoonValley/Yungas/ Island of the Sun/Titicaca Lake/Suriqui Island

- Adventure Tours
- Different kinds of excursions in Bolivia
- Reservations of hotels in Bolivia
- Reservations of hotels in Peru
- Issue and reconfirmation of air tickets

Our services include the latest tourist buses, multi-lingual guides, and the most important, the best prices on the market. Remember, when you are here, in La Paz, Bolivia, your preference is the best incentive for you.

We are in the most important touristic place of La Paz, Sagarnaga Street 328 where 70% of your time is spent in this street, our telephone numbers are 375374 - 340356 - 350252. P O Box 3049 Fax 00-591-02-360831 La Paz, Bolivia.

DISCOUNTS FOR GROUPS AVAILABLE.

friendly, clean, quiet and safe, uncomfortable beds, laundry facilities, often full; **E Austria**, Yanacocha 531, T 351140, without bath, **F** per person in shared room, clean, hot water, but insufficient showers, safe deposit, very cosy, good for longer stays, use of kitchen, laundry, TV, friendly and helpful staff, very popular so arrive early or book in advance, repeatedly recommended; opposite is **E Hostal Yanacocha**, large clean rooms, dirty bathrooms, warm water, secure; **E Bolivia**, Manco Kapac 287, T 375030, opposite the railway station, clean, shared tepid showers, good views from rear upper rooms, very noisy; **E Hostal Ingavi**, Ingavi 727, T323645/355178, nice rooms, not much hot water, poor service, good value; **E Hostal Latino**, Junín near Sucre, clean, hot water, motorcycle parking, luggage stored, helpful; **E La Paz**, Acosta 487, near Plaza Sucre, hot showers, very clean, friendly, quiet, stores luggage, secure; **E Residencial Plaza**, Plaza Pérez Velasco 785, T 322157, nice old building, clean, hot water, **F** without bath, washing and luggage storage facilities, helpful; **E Scala**, Calle Unión 425 entre Avenida América y Chuquisaca, T 350725, very clean, good hot showers, nice rooms with window, a bit noisy at weekends, family-run, luggage stored, secure, friendly, 'the cheapest good hotel', excellent value, highly recommended; **E Torino**, Socabaya 457, T 341487, near Plaza Murillo, hot water on request, shared bath, formerly the most popular gringo hotel but increasing reports that it is dirty, noisy and run down with poor beds, rooms on third floor warmer and quieter, disco at weekends till 0300, 2400 curfew, has noticeboard, stores luggage, book exchange, bar, good restaurant with set lunch for US$3.

F Alojamiento Universo, Inca 575, **G** pp in dormitories, clean, friendly, stores luggage, laundry, very popular, usually hot water, motorcycle parking, basic but good; **F** pp **Hostal Duendes**, Avenida Uruguay 470, T 351125, Casilla 8765, breakfast included, cheaper without, great showers, a nice place to stay, discount for IYHA card holders; **F Max Paredes**, Max Paredes 660, T 362726, with bath, cheaper without, modern, clean; **G** pp **Posada El Carretero**, Catacora 1056 entre Pichincha y Sanjinés, T 322233, possibly the cheapest in town, five beds to a room, helpful, pleasant, hot shower extra, not much hot water, can use kitchen for breakfast, great value; **F-G** pp **Residencial Belzur**, Plaza Belzur 256, in San Pedro district, T 330119, with hot shower, luggage stored, large clean rooms, good views, recommended; **F Residencial Imperial**, Pando, esq Incachaca, clean, friendly, hot water 24 hours, stores luggage, cheap laundry, recommended.

Youth Hostel association, **Asociacón Boliviana de Albergues Juveniles**, ABAJ, Edificio Alborada piso 1, of 105, Calle Juan de la Riva 1406 y Loayza, T 361076/321597, has hostels at *Hostal Duendes* and *Hotel Andes* (see above). Other hostels around the country are given in the text. To use hostels you must have a Bolivian YHA card, US$2, two photos needed, available from ABAJ, which also sells international cards, US$20.

For people staying several weeks, often looking for permanent lodging, boarding houses (*pensiones*) are popular, eg Illimeier, Calle Resequin 1978 in Sopocachi, **D** with breakfast, English and German spoken.

● **Camping**
There is no organized site, but the Municipal Park at Mallasa, at Valencia and Palca below the suburb of La Florida, has been recommended. It is unmarked; turn left at Aldeas Infantiles SOS. Club Andino Boliviano rents equipment (see page 18). For camping equipment and camping gas try *Caza y Pesca*, Edificio Handal Center, Avenida Mariscal Santa Cruz y Socabaya; *Sajama*, Sagárnaga 177, 2° piso; or *Epcot*, Avenida 6 de Agosto 2190, local 9, T 342424. Kerosene for pressure stoves is available from a pump in Plaza Alexander. Public showers are at Duchas La Paz, 20 de Octubre 1677.

● **Places to eat**
In La Paz these can be roughly divided into two categories: either they serve international cuisine and are expensive or they serve local dishes and are fairly cheap. The restaurants with international cuisine are to be found mainly on three streets; Avenida 16 de Julio (the Prado), Avenida 6 de Agosto and Avenida 20 de Octubre. Service charges and tax of up to 23% are usually included on the bill but it is customary to leave a tip of 10% anyway. Always check prices before ordering, and then your bill and change.

Few places accept credit cards even when they display the signs; check first. If they do, they probably add at least 7% to the bill. There are very few places open on Sunday nights and Saturday is none too popular either. Recommended places open on Sunday are *Mongo's* and *Eli's*, which is open most national holidays (see below).

On Avenida 16 de Julio (Prado) (street numbers given in brackets): there are many snack bars, including *Confitería Eli's* (1497), with good plate lunches, excellent soups, breakfast of waffles, pancakes and French toast, you pay extra for coffee refills and pastries, not cheap; on the same block is *Eli's Pizza Express*, English spoken, US$1.50 for a slice of

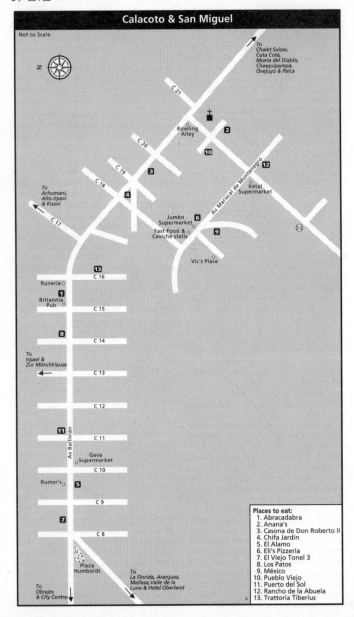

Calacoto & San Miguel

Not to Scale

N

To
Chalet Suisse,
Cota Cota,
Muela del Diablo,
Chasquipampa,
Ovejuyo & Palca

C 21

Bowling
Alley

2

10

C 20

3

C 19

C 18

4

Av Mariscal de Montenegro

Ketal
Supermarket

12

To
Achumani,
Alto Irpavi
& Koani

C 17

Jumbo
Supermarket

6

Fast Food &
Ceviche stalls

9

Vic's Place

13

C 16

Ronería

1

Britannia
Pub

C 15

8

C 14

To
Irpavi &
Zur Mönchklause

C 13

C 12

11

C 11

Av Ballivián

Gava
Supermarket

C 10

Rumor's

5

C 9

7

C 8

Plaza
Humboldt

To
La Florida, Aranjuez,
Mallasa, Valle de la
Luna & Hotel Oberland

To
Obrajes
& City Centre

Places to eat:
1. Abracadabra
2. Anana's
3. Casona de Don Roberto II
4. Chifa Jardín
5. El Alamo
6. Eli's Pizzería
7. El Viejo Tonel 3
8. Los Patos
9. México
10. Pueblo Viejo
11. Puerto del Sol
12. Rancho de la Abuela
13. Trattoria Tiberius

pizza, very popular (also at Comercio 914); opposite is *Unicornio*, great ice cream, slice of pizza and soft drink for US$1.25, lunch buffet upstairs, good; *Patito Pekín* (1687), good Chinese, reasonably priced; *California Donuts II* (1695), American-style food, expensive, US$2-10, opens at 1230 (*Número I* is at Avenida Camacho 1248, *Número III* is on Avenida Arce); *Utama*, in *Plaza* hotel (1789) excellent salad bar, great value lunch, excellent view, highly recommended; *Tokio* (1832), good, also has tea room and patisserie and good for *salteñas*, but look out for high prices not written on menus, expensive; *Super 10* (1991 y Villazón), very good, *almuerzo* US$4, open Sunday evenings.

On Plaza Estudiante: *Pizza l'Passo II*, good but expensive; *Il Fiore*, snacks, ice cream, pizza; *Café Ciudad*, 24-hour coffee shop, full menu, good, expensive; *Mary's Tee*, near Plaza Estudiante, for excellent pies and cakes.

South of Plaza del Estudiante: *Kranky*, Avenida Villazón 1987, good, cheap sandwiches, burgers, ice cream. On Avenida Arce are: *Andromeda*, No 2116, T354723, European-style and vegetarian, excellent US$3 lunch, recommended; *Pizzeria Morello*, No 2132, very good but very expensive; *Jalapeños*, No 2549, excellent Mexican food for around US$5-8 per main dish. Excellent buffet Monday and Wednesday, 2000-2300, at *Radisson Plaza Hotel*, US$5.50, delicious, friendly to backpackers; *Mongo's*, Hermanos Manchego 2444, near Plaza Isabela la Católica, T353914, popular with expats, cable TV for sports, Budweiser, open Monday-Sunday, US$4 lunch Monday-Friday 1130-1500, evening meals Monday-Sunday 1730-0100, good fish and chips; *El Batau*, Landaeta 402, T 342518, German owner, Bolivian and international cuisine, recommended; *Chifa Emy*, Cordero 257, best Chinese in town, very good service, takes credit cards, US$12.50 per person with drinks; *Rigo's*, Plaza Organo, near Museo Semisubterráneo, pleasant and good set lunch; *Vienna*, Federico Zuazo 1905, T 391660, excellent German, Austrian and local food, excellent service, lunch US$12 for two, very fashionable with Bolivians and popular with foreigners, too; *La Bodeguita Cubana*, Federico Zuazo 1653, Cuban favourites such as *ropa vieja*, excellent *mojito* cocktails, strictly meat so vegetarians will have to concentrate on the drinks.

In the Sopocachi district: *Pronto*, Jauregui 2248, T 355869, Monday-Saturday 1830-2230, below Imprenta Quipus behind 6 de Agosto between Guachalla and Rosendo Gutiérrez,

beautiful decor, up-market Italian cuisine, about US$7 per person, serves three different types of pasta; regular, integral and de quinoa, 'must be unique in South America', popular, good service; *Montesano*, Sánchez Lima 2329, near Plaza Abaroa, excellent Italian, US$35 for two, also fish and steaks.

On Avenida 6 de Agosto: *El Arriero* (Número 2535, Casa Argentina), best barbecue with large portions, but quite expensive; *Mocambo*, 6 de Agosto y Rosendo Gutiérrez 319, good Spanish food and service, US$15 per person; *Sergiu's Pizza*, No 2036, good.

On Avenida 20 de Octubre: *Mamma Mia*, buffet lunch, art gallery by day, good Italian restaurant at night, expensive but good pizzas; *La Quebecoise*, near Plaza Abaroa, French Canadian, good value, pleasant atmosphere; *El Gaucho*, No 2041, steakhouse, good, about US$20 per person. *Ipanema*, Avenida Ecuador 2139, between Aspiazu and F Guachalla, T 372306, Brazilian *feijoada* on Saturday and Sunday, closed Monday, recommended; *Gringo Limón*, Plaza Abaroa, delicious, not too expensive; *La Caldera Mágica*, JJ Pérez 322 y 20 de Octubre, nice atmosphere, good lunches, bar.

On Avenida Mariscal Santa Cruz (Prado): *Los Escudos* (Edificio Club de La Paz, T 322028/350586), Munich-type bierkeller with fixed four-course lunch, good *peña* on Friday and Saturday nights (2100-0100), US$5 cover charge; *Restaurant Verona*, on the corner with Colón, for good economical *plato del día*, very popular in the evenings; *La Fiesta*, No 1066, excellent, good lunches, recommended; *Tambo Colonial*, in *Residencial Rosario* (see **Accommodation**), excellent local and international cuisine, expensive but recommended, peña at weekend. On Plaza Velasco, at the top of Santa Cruz, is *Kory Punku*, which serves excellent *parrilladas*, cheap and popular, live music some evenings.

On Calle México, running parallel to the Prado: *La Estancia*, No 1553, good *almuerzo*, recommended; *Capullito*, No 1490, pleasant café and *confitería*. México continues west as Murillo: at No 1040 is **Casa del Corregidor**, T 353633, centrally heated, behind Correo, Spanish colonial restaurant with Bolivian and European dishes, excellent food which is not too expensive, bar; *El Horno*, open Monday-Saturday, lunches from US$2.50 including vegetarian, free *peña* at nights (see **Entertainment** below); *Crístal*, No 726, outdoor, quite cheap, good.

On Calle Sagárnaga: *Naira* (No 161 downstairs), serves good food, especially beef; above is *Resolana*, often confused with the *Naira* restaurant, very good pizzas and puddings but not cheap, live jazz most evenings, recommended; *El Montañés* (No 323), opposite *Hotel Sagárnaga*, good, clean, family-run, opens at 0700, very good American breakfast for US$2.50, also good omelettes, soups and hot chocolate. In the same area are: *El Lobo*, Santa Cruz 441 esq Illampu, good, huge portions, clean, Israeli dishes, good meeting place, noticeboard, limited menu, very popular, not cheap but recommended; *Los Laureles*, on Evaristo Valle, good four-course lunch for US$1.50, recommended; *Clávida*, opposite the train station, excellent set lunch including potatoes and cheese in peanut curry sauce.

In the shopping and business district north of the Prado there are numerous snack bars and cheap restaurants: *Club de la Prensa*, Calle Campero, set in a pleasant garden, the limited menu is typical Bolivian – meat only, in copious quantities – and the company is lively; *Chifa Jardín*, Socabaya 461, next to *Hotel Torino*, good Chinese, cheap lunch US$1.20, poor service; *Confitería California*, Potosí 1008, Centro Comercial Cristal, does good set lunches for US$2.75. Also on Calle Potosí: *La Kantuta*, in *Hotel Presidente*, No 920, excellent food, good service; *Subterráneo*, No 1120, cheap and OK; *Chez Pierre*, No 1320, good lunches; *Dumbo*, Camacho y Loayza, large portions, good; *Burger Center*, Ayacucho y Camacho, excellent American-style burgers, not cheap but recommended; *Wall Street Café*, Camacho 1363 entre Loayza y Colón, good food and coffee, not cheap, owner speaks English and French and is very helpful; *La Fregata*, Yanacocha 525, good value; *Casa Chang*, Juan de la Riva y Bueno, good set course Chinese meals, highly recommended; *Los Pinochos*, Genardo Sanjines 553 entre Comercio y Ingavi, excellent cheese *empanadas* and steaks, good food in large portions, popular; *La Casa de los Paceños*, Sucre 856, very good Bolivian food, especially its *fritanga*; *Confitería Rivoli*, Colón 415, small and pleasant snack bar, good and cheap hotel; *Internacional*, Avenida Ayacucho 206, a lunch-time favourite of local businessmen and has good shows Friday and Saturday nights. There are many other snack bars and Chinese restaurants on Calle Comercio, eg *La Diligencia Churrascaría*, No 803, good grill and set meals, recommended; *Taiwan*, opposite Mercado Camacho, large portions, excellent; and North

Americans longing for a taste of home should try the food at No 914.

Zona Sur: The **Calacoto** district situated in The Valley 15 minutes south of the city (US$0.40 by *trufi* or minibus), is home of the resident foreign community. Calacoto has recently developed into an important area in its own right. It has international shopping centres, supermarkets stocked with imported items and some of the best restaurants and bars in La Paz. The area begins after the bridge at La Florida where there is an attractive park, Plaza Humboldt, which has exhibitions of local art work on Sunday and a collection of kiosks selling cheap snacks. The main road, Avenida Ballivián begins here at Calle 8 and continues up the hill to the shopping district of San Miguel on Calle 21 (about a 20-minute walk).

On the main avenue, between Calle 8 y 9 is *El Viejo Tonel 3*, a lively Mexican/Brazilian *rodizio* restaurant with bar and disco which attracts a young crowd. *Puerto del Sol* is a good Chinese restaurant on the left on the corner of Calle 11. Opposite, still on the main road, is an excellent arts and handicrafts shop with weavings, ceramics, silver etc. Continuing up the hill on Avenida Ballivián, at esquina Calle 14, is *Los Patos*, which serves traditional Bolivian food. Next door to *The Britannia* (see **Bars** below) on the main avenue is US-owned *Abracadabra*, open 7 days for lunch and dinner, it boasts great ribs and the best hamburgers and pizza in La Paz. On Calle 16 is the upmarket Italian, *Trattoria Tiberius*. *Chifa Jardín*, at Calle 18, is an upmarket Chinese. Between Calle 19 y 20 is *Casona de Don Roberto II*, a meat and mariscos *rodizio* which is good but very expensive.

Five minutes' walk further up the hill on the right is Calle 21 in the district of **San Miguel**, which has a huge variety of shops, fast-food cafés, banks and a post office. Recommended places to eat are: *Pueblo Viejo*, a small Mexican bar/restaurant. Beside the church of San Miguel, a useful landmark, is *Anana's* deli, café and bar. On Avenida Mariscal de Montenegro are: *Rancho de la Abuela*, with a traditional Bolivian meat-dominated menu; *Eli's*, pizzas, submarines, burgers and sandwiches, the same as on the Prado except they also sell Chilean wine; *Restaurant México*, small but bigger than *Pueblo Viejo*. A recommended Mexican place is *Tacos Teru K*, Ignacio Cordero 1294, San Miguel (behind Loreto College) T 794513.

Back on the main avenue and continuing up the hill between Calle 24 y 25 is *The Chalet Suisse*, which is expensive but highly recommended, with excellent fondue and steaks, booking is essential on Friday evenings. Almost next door is *The Galeon* for some of the city's best seafood. Another Zona Sur restaurant worth making the effort to visit, if you have the money, is *Zur Mönchsklause*, Calle 13 y Ovanda Candia, Irpavi, German, open Friday-Sunday and holidays, garden, meat dishes and some fish.

Vegetarian restaurants: *Hotel Gloria*, Potosí 909, excellent buffet lunch for US$3.50, very popular, be there by 1200 for a table, also buffet breakfast and dinner after 1900, closed Sunday, good coffee next door at *Café Pierrot*; *Natur Center*, Sagárnaga 233, set lunch US$1.50, open lunchtime only, closed Saturday; *Lila Vatty*, Santa Cruz 266, 1st floor, good value; *Palacio del Buen Gusto*, 16 de Julio 1698, closed weekends, not cheap; *Imperial*, Sagárnaga 213 y Murillo, 2nd floor, no sign, international dishes, good and inexpensive, clean, balcony tables, US$1.50 *almuerzo*, frequently recommended.

Increasingly popular with Paceños are *cevicherias*, which serve only spicy raw fish dishes. Don't try this until your stomach has adjusted to South America, but after that, it's great. Normally, you get a bowl of marinaded raw fish and then a very spicy soup. The nearest thing you get to the Indian curry effect and great for hangovers. Try *Acuario* at the bottom of Calle Rodríguez, above Murillo behind the central post office.

Comedor Popular, often referred to as *Comedor Familiar*, is for strictly limited budgets. Every big market has a **Comedor Popular**. Don't try this until your stomach has adjusted to South America. After that, it's the cheapest way to eat – you cannot buy the ingredients for less yourself. The biggest Comedor Popular is in Mercado San Francisco above the plaza of the same name between Calle Figueroa and Avenida Montes. Also available at Camacho and Lanza markets. A US$1 *almuerzo* involves a big soup, often containing some identifiable part of a chicken's anatomy (claws or head, normally), and then an unidentifiable piece of meat with rice, potato and salad. Fried chicken, fried rice and other types of meat are available but cost more than the basic *almuerzo*.

The foodstalls at the top of Jiménez sell good T-bone steak cheaply. Stalls in the market district sell hamburgers for US$0.75 each including chips, egg and tomato, have 2 for a filling meal, but don't have *aji*, mayonnaise or mustard if worried about hygiene and watch your burger being cooked. Bread from street vendors and Cochabamba wholemeal bread (*pan integral*) is sold at the main markets. Marraquetas are crusty white bread rolls. Fresh dairy produce can be found at *Pil* on Bueno y Cárdenas. *Kremrik* is a chain of good ice-cream parlours, with outlets at Plaza Murillo 542, and on Avenida Villazón, just off Plaza del Estudiante.

Cafés: *Café es Art*, Avenida Arce 2895, one block down from the US embassy, this is the most stylish café in La Paz, art exhibitions, open fire, try their excellent bagels with smoked trout and cream cheese, set lunch costs US$5, live music on Friday, open Monday-Friday 1100-2100; *Kuchen Stube*, Rosendo Gutiérrez, Edificio Guadalquivir, closed Monday, excellent cakes, coffee and German specialities, also at Mercado 1328, Monday-Friday 0930-1230, 1500-1900; *Confitería Club de la Paz*, Camacho 1202, on the corner where Ayacucho joins Avenida Mariscal Santa Cruz, good tea room, traditional, meeting place for businessmen and politicians, great coffee and cakes, expensive; *Café París*, in *Gran Hotel París*, Plaza Murillo esq Bolívar, good food, quite expensive; *Solo Café*, Calle Potosí 1108, excellent coffee and cappucino; *Confitería Arabesque*, Mercado y Loayza, excellent *café con crema*.

● **Airline offices**
Lloyd Aéreo Boliviano (LAB), Camacho 1460, T 367701/7/367718/371020; Aero Sur, 16 de Julio 1607, T 371834, F 390457; Transportes Aéreo Militar, Avenida Montes 738 esquina Serrano, T 379286/5, open Monday-Friday 0830-1200 and 1430-1830; British Airways, at Batallón Colorados 40, one block from Plaza del Estudiante (in same building as Aero México), T 373857/371270, F 362697; KLM, Plaza del Estudiante 1931, T 323965/322903; American Airlines, Avenida 16 de Julio 1440, Edificio Herman, T 372009; AeroPerú, Edificio Avenida, 16 de Julio 1490, 2nd floor, T 370002-4; Aerolíneas Argentinas, Edificio Banco de la Nación Argentina, Avenida 16 de Julio 1486, T 351711/351624; Varig, Avenida Mariscal Santa Cruz 1392, Edificio Cámara de Comercio, T 314040, F 391131; Ecuatoriana, T 0800-3001; LanChile, Avenida 16 de Julio 1566, 1st floor, T 358377.

● **Banks & money changers**
There is an endemic shortage of change in Bolivia. The biggest note, the Bs 200 (about US$40) is virtually unusable unless you are paying for an expensive meal for two or three, flight tickets or an expensive hotel. Do not accept it. The Bs 100 is difficult to break in La Paz and impossible in the countryside.

If arriving on Friday night, bring bolivianos or US dollars cash as it is difficult to change travellers' cheques at the weekend, especially on Sunday. Try *El Lobo* restaurant, which usually changes travellers' cheques at any time at good rates, or *Hotel Gloria* which gives good rates for most western currencies. If you leave Bolivia with bolivianos you may not be able to change them in neighbouring countries. Watch out for forged currency, especially dollars and Chilean pesos.

Banks: Citibank, Multicentro, Calle Rosendo Gutienez 146, T 430099, cashes its own travellers' cheques for a very high commission and will receive money sent from any US bank, but will not advance cash to holders of Citibank Mastercard. **Banco Industrial**, Avenida Gral Camacho 1333, open 0830-1700, Saturday 1000-1300, good service, changes cash and travellers' cheques. Cash advance (in bolivianos) on Visa and Mastercard at: **Banco de La Paz** on Prado (limit of US$300 per day, no commission); **Banco Santa Cruz de la Sierra** (branch in Shopping Norte is open Saturday pm); Banco Mercantil, Mercado 1124 (good, quick service); Banco Popular; Banco Nacional and Banco Boliviano Americano, Camacho (good, quick service). Visa has an office on Avenida Camacho 1448, eleventh and twelvth floors, T 369975/357014, F 354066, for cancelling lost or stolen credit cards. Automatic cash dispensers for Visa and Mastercard can be found at several sites in the city including Avenida Camacho 1223, the airport and Shopping Norte shopping centre (look for the sign Enlace – Visa at branches of ATC). Enlace ATMs accept bank cards on Cirrus system. When using Visa/Mastercard to get money from a bank it is possible to get the money in dollars, bolivianos or a mixture. **Amex**, Avenida 16 de Julio 1490, piso 5, T 323954/341201.

Exchange houses: *Casas de cambio* are generally faster for money changing than the banks and money is changed in hotels or *casas de cambio* rather than in banks. **Sudamer**, Colón 256, good rates, also for currencies other than US dollars, no commission on travellers' cheques into bolivianos, 1.5% commission into dollars, frequently recommended; **Unitours**, Mercado 1300, 1% commission on travellers' cheques. **Casa de Cambio Silver**, Mercado 979, charges 1% commission to change travellers' cheques into dollars, good rates; several others around Mercado y Colón. Very few deal in Argentine and Chilean pesos.

Money changers can be found on street corners around Plaza del Estudiante, Camacho,

Colón and Prado. There is no black market rate but outside banking hours money changers give a worse rate. Always count your money immediately in front of the money changer.

● **Embassies & consulates**
Argentine Consulate, Sánchez Lima 2103, T 353089/343516, 24 hours for visa; **Brazilian Consulate**, Avenida 20 de Octubre, 20-38 Edificio Fonconain, Embassy 11th floor, visa office, 9th floor, T 352108, 0900-1300, Monday-Friday (visas take 2 days). **Chilean Consulate**, H Siles 5843, corner of Calle 13, Obrajes district, T 785269, open Monday-Friday 0830-1130, visa same day if requested in the morning, take microbus N, A or L from Avenida 16 de Julio. **Ecuador** 16 de Julio 1440, 14th floor, T 321208. **Paraguayan Consulate**, Edificio Illimani, Avenida 6 de Agosto, T 322018, very good visa service; **Peruvian Consulate and Embassy**, 6 de Agosto 2190 y Calle F Guachalla, Edificio Alianza, T 353550, 0930-1300, visa costs US$10 in US$ bills and is issued on the same day if you go early; **Venezuelan Embassy and Consulate**, Avenida Arce 2678, Edificio Illimani, 4th floor, T 375023, consulate open Monday, Wednesday, Friday 0900-1200 – visas are only given to Bolivian residents, if you need one, get it in your home country.

United States Embassy and Consulate, Avenida Arce 2780, opposite Edificio Illimani, T 350120/430251, F 359875, Casilla 425; **Canadian Consulate**, Avenida 20 de Octubre 2475, Plaza Avaroa, T 375224, Monday-Friday, 0900-1200; **Japanese Embassy**, Rosendo Gutiérrez 497, esq Sánchez Lima, PO Box 2725, T 373151.

Austrian Consulate, Edificio Petrolero, seventh floor, Oficina 1, Avenida 16 de Julio 1616, T 326601, 1600-1800; **British Embassy and Consulate**, Avenida Arce 2732-2754, T 357424, F 391063, Casilla 694, Monday-Thursday 0900-1200, 1400-1600, Friday 0900-1300, has a list of travel hints for Bolivia, doctors, etc; **Danish Consulate**, Avenida 6 de Agosto 2577, Edificio Las Dos Torres, 12th floor, T 430046, F 430064, open 0930-1230; **Finnish Consulate**, Mercado 1004, c/o Sibo SA, T 350900/367227; **French Consulate**, Avenida Hernando Siles 5390, esq Calle 08, Obrajes, T 786114, take bus Número 11 or microbus N, A or L down Avenida 16 de Julio; **Belgian Embassy** is one block from French at Número 5290, T 784925; **German Embassy**, Avenida Arce 2395, T 390850, slow service, Monday-Friday 0900-1200; **Italian Embassy**, 6 de Agosto 2575, PO Box 626, T 323597, F 391075; **Netherlands Consulate**, Avenida 6 de Agosto, Edificio Hilda, 7th floor, T 432020, F 431004, Casilla 10509; **Norwegian Consulate**, Avenida 6 de Agosto 2410, T 322528; **Spanish Consulate**, Avenida Arce y Calle Cordero, T 343518; **Swedish Consulate**, Avenida Arce 2856, Casilla de Correo 852, T 327535, open 0900-1200; **Swiss Embassy**, Avenida 16 de Julio 1616, 6th floor, T 353091, F 391462, Casilla 9356, open 0900-1200, 1400-1500; **Israeli Embassy**, Avenida Mariscal Santa Cruz, Edificio Esperanza, 10th floor, T 358676/ 371287, Casilla 1309/1320.

● **Entertainment**

The best entertainment for visitors are the folk shows (*peñas*). Various restaurants also have shows worth seeing. At these, visitors will be able to listen to the wide variety of local musical instruments (for a full description see page 51). Enquire at the *Rumillajta* shop (in the *galería* close to San Francisco church) about future performances by the famous folk group of that name. There's a good *peña* at *Casa del Corregidor*, Calle Murillo 1040 (T 363633), dinner show Monday-Thursday, no cover charge, Friday and Saturday *peña* US$4, colonial atmosphere, traditional music and dance (see also under **Places to eat**). See also under **Places to eat** for *Los Escudos*. Another *peña* is *Marko Tambo* on Calle Jaén, US$7 all inclusive, repeatedly recommended (also sells woven goods). Indigenous dance halls, for example on Max Paredes, should only be visited in the company of Bolivians. If you wish to learn a local indstrument, contact *Academia 'Walisuma'*, Avenida Apumalla 512 (old Cemetery District between José M Asin and José M Aliaga): Pedro March teaches bi-lingual courses, English/Spanish, for *quena*, *zampoña* and *charango*.

La Paz has a resident ballet and symphony orchestra and several theatre companies. **Teatro Municipal** has a regular schedule of plays, opera, ballet and classical concerts, at Sanjines y Indaburo. Next door is the new **Teatro Municipal de Cámara**, a small studio-theatre which shows small-scale productions of dance, drama, music and poetry.

There are some good **cinemas**, films being mainly in English. Best are: *Cine 16 de Julio* on the Prado by Plaza del Estudiante; *Monje Campero*, on the Prado next to *Eli's Pizzeria*; and *6 de Agosto* (on 6 de Agosto, would you believe). Expect to pay around US$2.50. The rest of La Paz's cinemas are flea pits showing Kick Boxer equivalents or flesh flicks. Films are advertised in all the papers every day. For film buffs there is the excellent *Cinemateca Boliviana*, Pichincha

y Indaburo, La Paz's art film centre with festivals, courses, etc; entry is US$1.20, students US$0.60.

Casa Municipal de la Cultura 'Franz Tamayo', almost opposite Plaza San Francisco, hosts a variety of exhibitions, paintings, sculpture, photography, videos, etc, most of which are free. The **Palacio Chico**, at Ayacucho y Potosí, in the old Correo, is operated by the Secretaría Nacional de Cultura, it has exhibitions (good for modern art), concerts and ballet. The SNC is also in charge of many regional museums. Listings are available in Palacio Chico.

There are clown and mime shows in Parque del Ejército on Sunday, which are colourful and popular. The Parque Central has a children's amusement park, US$0.20.

● **Bars & clubs**

Friday night is Big Night Out in La Paz. Thursday and Saturday are quieter and the rest of the week is very quiet. The two most popular drinks are beer (in volume) and Singani, a spirit which gives you a hangover from hell. Singani is traditionally drunk mixed 50-50 with Sprite or 7-Up while playing dice. The game appears to be over when one of the players falls unconscious face down on the table thereby preventing further play. If the player falls over backwards or sideways there appears to be some confusion as to whether the game should go on. If you want to see Bolivians in action on Friday night, pop into any of the small bars on the Prado or the streets off the Prado. Note, the toilets in these establishments are usually indescribable. The best bar in the centre of town is *La Luna*, at Calle Oruro 197 y Murillo, it opens at 2200 and is good value, try their cocktails, the owner speaks English and German and is very friendly.

Between the centre and Sopocachi: *Vía Libre*, Avenida Villazón 1972, opposite UMSA, is a bar/restaurant/*salteñería* and music venue which is open 24 hours; *Pig and Whistle*, Goitia 155, serves pints of lager, popular and architecturally one of the most interesting places to drink. Also on Goitia is *La Bodega*, with live music and a good atmosphere.

In Sopocachi: *Café Montmarte*, Fernando Guachalla 399, off Avenida 6 de Agosto, next to Alliance Française, good atmosphere, very popular bar with live music Thursday, Friday, Saturday, also good French menu, set lunch US$4. Calle Belisario Salinas is full of bars starting just below Plaza Abaroa and continuing all the way up to Avenida Ecuador. Turn left onto Avenida Ecuador to reach the *Tequila Bar*, esquina Salazar, which also does food, and *Juan*

Sebastian Bar and *Planet – the Funky Nachos Bar*, Prol Ecuador 2638 (Montículo), Wednesday-Saturday from 2100, rock and grunge, Mexican food. Continue along Ecuador and past Plaza España to arrive at the *Forum*, at Sanjines 2908, La Paz's biggest night club and disco, open until 0600 Friday, Saturday and Sunday mornings, US$5 cover includes a drink, it's very popular (I should know, I used to live next door – Ed).

For live music there's *Equinoccio*, on Calle Belisario Salinas, just below Plaza Abaroa, which has music nearly every Thursday, Friday and Saturday, as does the hot and sweaty *Socavón*, Aspiazu y Avenida 20 de Octubre 2172. Many bars have music reasonably regularly, eg *Café Montmartre*, *Mongo's* (see under **Places to eat**), *Matheus*, *Vía Libre* and *La Luna* – check flyposters for details. There's excellent jazz at *Marius Club*, Presbítero Medina y Salazar (near Plaza Abaroa). The local radio station, *Radio Fides*, Calle Sanjines y Sucre, has Andean music on Thursday, when it is open to the public (2000, US$0.75), but not all year round, check in advance, T 359191.

Those few Westerners who can successfully wiggle their hips will find good salsa at *El Loro en su Salsa*, on Rosendo Gutiérrez, on the corner of Avenida 6 de Agosto, open Thursday, Friday and Saturday pm; but please note that once you hit the dancefloor there will be no respite until you're carted off on a stretcher suffering from exhaustion. It's probably a good idea to take a few lessons first; try *Gym Cec*, Illampu 868, 1st floor, T 310158, US$4 per hour.

Zona Sur: over the last few years a vibrant and classy night life has been developing along Avenida Ballivián and through San Miguel. Calle 21 appears to have been brought to Bolivia directly from some town in the US and reflects the fact that many rich Bolivians are US-educated. Everything you need is here: bowling alley, shops, supermarkets, bars, restaurants, banks and a post office. There are no hotels as it is a suburban area, and no cinema. There's no point as everyone has a video at home. Prices tend to be higher than in the centre, but so is the quality. Transport is easy from the centre of La Paz: take any minibus marked Calacoto, San Miguel, Achumani or Chasquipampa.

On Avenida Ballivián between Calle 9 y 10 is *Rumors*, an American/Mexican bar and restaurant with excellent music, a popular late night place, the biggest and possibly the best of the Zona Sur bars, US-style and drinks, Bud, JD, etc. Opposite is *El Alamo*, the newest of the bars; you can't miss it – it looks like a Wild West

wooden fort. Between Calle 15 y 16 on the left is *The Britannia*, opened as an authentic English pub by an Englishman, open Tuesday-Sunday from 1700, Friday night is the main night, popular with ex-pats and diplomats. Next door is *Abracadabra* (see **Places to eat** above) and then the *Ronería*, which is very popular and held by many to be the Zona Sur's best bar. **In San Miguel**, *Vic's Place* is the best place around, and often has live music, Thursday-Saturday.

● **Hospitals & medical services**
Contact your embassy or the Tourist Office for a recommended doctor who speaks your language. Check that any medical equipment used is sterilized. The following clinics have been recommended as efficient and not too expensive: *Clínica del Accidentado*, Plaza Uyuni 1351, T 328632/321888, which offers first aid; *Clínica Americana* Avenida 14 de Septiembre 78, T 783509; *Clínica Alemana*, 6 de Agosto 2821, T 323023/327521/373676, has English-speaking doctors; *Clínica Bustillos*, Héroes del Acre 1793, T 321553/372084, US$20 for consultation; *Clínica Rengel*, T 390792/8; *Clínica Santa María*, Avenida 6 de Agosto 2487, English-speaking doctors, consultation costs US$16, simple analysis US$24, course of antibiotics US$8; *Clínica del Sur*, Avenida Hernando Siles y Calle Siete, Obrajes. *Red Cross*, opposite Mercado Camacho, will give inoculations if required, T 323642. *The Methodist Hospital*, twelfth block of Obrajes, T 783809 (take *micro* 'A' from the Prado) runs a clinic, US$5 for a consultation, telephone for appointment. Travellers with insurance can try *Hospital Obrero*. For those without insurance there is *Hospital General*.

Dentists: Dr Remy Zegarra at *Hostal Austria*, Yanacocha 531, T 212083 (home). Dr Horacio M Rosso, Avenida 20 de Octubre, Edificio Guadalquivir, T 354754, his wife speaks German. Also recommended: Dr Benjamín Calvo Paz, Edificio Illimani, Avenida Arce esq Campos, T 343706, and Dra Esperanza Aid, Edificio Mercurio 3rd floor, 6 de Agosto 2809, opposite US Embassy, T 431081, both speak English.

Doctors: *Dr Ricardo Udler*, Edificio Mariscal de Ayacucho, Calle Loayza, T 360393/327046, speaks very good German. *Dr César H Moreno*, Pinilla 274, Edificio Pinilla, T 433805/792665 (home). *Dr Eduardo Fernández*, Edificio Avenida, Avenida 16 de Julio, 9th floor, oficina 3, T 370385 (surgery)/795164 (home), speaks English, US$30 for consultation. *Dr Mauricio Gutfronjd*, Terapia del Color, Avenida Arce

2630, consultario 207, T 431133 (emergency T 390222) specialist in acupuncture, speaks English and Hebrew. A recommended gynaecologist is *Dr Marcelo Koziner*, oficina 313, 3rd floor, Edificio Mariscal Ayacucho, Calle Loayza esquina Camacho, T 377283, speaks English and German.

Health and hygiene: *Unidad Sanitaria La Paz*, on Ravelo behind *Hotel Radisson Plaza*, gives yellow fever shot and certificate for US$12. *Ministerio de Desarrollo Humano, Sectretario Nacional de Salud*, on Avenida Arce to the right of *Hotel Radisson Plaza*, vaccination for yellow fever plus certificate, also rabies and cholera shots and malaria pills, bring your own syringe which costs US$0.20 from any pharmacy. Malaria pills are available at *Centro Piloto de Salva*, Avenida Montes y Basces, T 369141, about 10 minutes' walk from Plaza San Francisco, north of the main bus station, recommended as helpful and friendly. *Laboratorio Inti*, Socabaya 266, has been recommended, also for vaccines (human immunoglobulin, cholera, typhoid, rabies vaccine – but make sure you know precisely how it should be administered).

There are lots of pharmacies and prescriptions are unnecessary. The newspapers print every day a list of those that will be open that night and the police Radio Patrulla 110 have a list. Tampons may be bought at most *farmacias* and supermarkets; others say they are impossible to find, especially outside La Paz. For contact lenses, *Optaluis*, Comercio 1089, has a stock of 5,000 lenses, including 'semiduros'.

● **Language schools**

Centro Boliviano Americano (CBA, address under **Libraries** below) US$140 for 2 months, 1½ hours tuition each afternoon. *Alliance Française* (see also below). *Instituto de La Lengua Española*, Calle 14 esq Aviador No 180, Achumani, T 796074, US$7 per hour for one-to-one classes, recommended, will arrange accommodation with local families. Private Spanish lessons from: Alice, T 783064; William, T 340676/812341 and Cecilia T 365428. *María Isabel Daza*, Murillo 1046, 3rd floor, T 360769, US$3 per hour, individual or group lessons, speaks English and Danish, recommended. For English language teaching try *Pan American English Centre*, Edificio Avenida, 7th floor, Avenida 16 de Julio 1490, T 340 796, Casilla 5244, native speakers only, minimum stay 3 months; similarly Goethe-Institut, Alliance Française, CBA and foreign schools.

● **Laundromats**

Wash and dry, 6-hour service, at *Gelmi-Lava-Sec*, 20 de Octubre 2019, suite 9, T 352930, helpful service, US$1.40 for 1 kilo; *Lavandería Cinco Estrellas*, 20 de Octubre 1714, US$3 for 3 kilos. *Limpieza Rosario*, Avenida Manco Kapac, near *Hotel Andes*, US$1 per kilo, quick and highly recommended; *Lavandería Bandel*, Avenida Mariscal Santa Cruz 1032, local 10, T 353563; *Lavandería Select*, Avenida Arce, down from *Hotel La Paz*, 3-hour service, recommended; *Limpieza Finesse*, Illampu 865, good but closed Saturday afternoon. The usual charge is US$1 per kilo and you normally leave laundry early morning and collect the same evening.

● **Libraries**

Centro Boliviano Americano (CBA), Parque Zenón Iturralde 121, T 351627/342582 (see map on page 80), has public library and recent US papers, open Monday-Wednesday 0900-1230, 1500-1930, till 2000 Thursday and Friday; *USIS* has lending library and second-hand paperbacks; *Alliance Française*, F Guachalla 399 y Avenida 20 de Octubre, T 324075, open Monday-Friday 1000-1200, 1500-1930, good for French newspapers and magazines; *Goethe-Institut*, Avenida 6 de Agosto 2118, T 374453, open Monday and Wednesday, 0900-1200, 1500-2000, Tuesday and Thursday 1500-2000, Friday 0900-1200, 1500-1900, excellent library, recent papers in German, CDs, cassettes and videos free on loan.

● **Places of worship**

Protestant Community Church (inter-denominational), in English, American Co-operative School, Calle 10 Calacoto (T 795639 or 792052). Sunday service at 1100, but there are 'lots of activities during the week'. Anglican-Episcopalian services are held at the Community Church on the third Sunday of each month.

Synagogues: Calle Landaeta 330 (Saturday am services only); Colegio Boliviano Israëlito, Cañada Strongest 1846 for Friday service – it looks like a private house.

● **Post & telecommunications**

Post Office: Correo Central is at Avenida Mariscal Santa Cruz y Oruro, open Monday-Saturday 0800-2200, Sunday 0900-1200. Stamps are sold only at the post office (there's a good philately section on the first floor). There are a number of shops selling good postcards, gifts and stationery. The Poste Restante keeps letters for 3 months and offers a good service at no charge. Check the letters filed under your surname and first name.

To send parcels the procedure is as follows: all is arranged downstairs (office hours only, Monday-Friday 0800-1200, 1430-1830); have contents inspected by customs, then seal parcel with glue, US$1 for each parcel (for mailing prices see page 325). Don't forget moth balls for textile items. These are difficult to buy – try Calle Sagárnaga. To collect parcels costs at least US$0.50. Express postal service (top floor) is expensive. **DHL**, Avenida Mariscal Santa Cruz 1297; **Federal Express**, Calle Jorge Sáenz 1333, Miraflores.

Telecommunications: **Entel** (T 367474) office for telephone calls and fax is at Ayacucho 267 (the only one open on Sunday), and in Edificio Libertad, Calle Potosí. There's a long wait for incoming calls. There are also many small Entel offices throughout the city, with a quicker service. For international and national calls, rather than wait for a booth, buy a phonecard (Bs 5, 10, 20 or 100) and use it in the phones to the left in the main Entel office, also in the Entel offices or phone boxes springing up throughout the city, eg Prado. Cotel red or orange phone booths are used for local calls. Buy a *ficha* (US$0.10) from the person selling them next to the booth. Or use a phone in any shop or stall with 'teléfono' (US$0.20).

E-mail: *WaraNet Cyber Café*, Office 115, ground floor, Edificio Cristal, Calle Yanacocha 372, T 375690, cybercafe@waranet.com. Open Monday-Friday 0900-1300 and 1430-2000, Saturday 1500-1800. E-mail, WWW, telnet, post restante (put full name as subject), scanner for sending those holiday snaps to your mates (US$4 per scan). Terminal time US$2 for 15 minutes, US$3 for 30 minutes, US$6 for 1 hour. Printouts US$0.40 a page. Free account opening. Manager Richard Melgarejo speaks fluent English. *Proyecto Net Internet Café*, Calle Mercado 273, proyectonet@hotmail.com. Open Monday-Saturday 0900-2000. E-mail, WWW, post restante (put full name as subject). Terminal time US$4 for 30 minutes, US$6 for 1 hour. Page charge for printouts.

● **Shopping**
You need never go into a shop in La Paz – everything is available on the street from computers, cellular phones to tummy trimmers, and a few useful things like food and handicrafts.

Handicrafts: look around and bargain first. Most shops close Saturday afternoon and Sunday. There are good jewellery stores throughout the city: eg *Joyería Cosmos*, Handal Center, Local 13, Socabaya y Avenida 16 de Julio, Inca and Bolivian designs in gold and silver, colonial objects; *Joyería Kings*, Loayza 261, T 328178, F 324147, relocated in 1997 to larger premises, specializing in fine silver. Visit the gold factories for lower prices and special orders. There is inexpensive silver and jewellery in the little cabinets outside Lanza market on Avenida Santa Cruz.

On Calle Sagárnaga, by the side of San Francisco church (behind which are many handicraft stalls in the Mercado Artesanal), are booths and small stores with interesting local items of all sorts, especially textiles, leather and silverware. It's best to go on Sunday morning when prices are reduced. At Sagárnaga 177 is an entire gallery of handicraft shops. Upstairs is *Artesanía Sajama*, recommended for woollens. *Millma*, Sagárnaga 225, and in *Hotel Radisson*, for alpaca sweaters (made in their own factory) and antique and rare textiles. *Wari* on Sagárnaga will make to measure very quickly, English spoken, prices reasonable; also *Toshy* on Sagárnaga for top quality knitwear. *Artesanía Sorata*, Linares 862, and Sagárnaga 311, 0900-1930, Monday-Saturday, specializes in dolls, sweaters and weavings made by a women's cooperative and handmade textiles. *Artículos Regionales* in Plaza del Estudiante is recommended. *Suma Ampara*, Avenida Villazón 1958, has a wide variety of woven goods, but prices are not as low as in street markets. The recommended *Casa Fisher* (see Cochabamba **Shopping** page 247) has an outlet in Handal Center, Store No 2, Calles Mariscal Santa Cruz y Socabaya, T/F 392948. Alpaca goods are about 50% more expensive than in Puno. Sweaters are much more expensive than Peru (beware of moths in woollen goods). Handmade clothing for children is good value. For more information on textiles, see also page 102. Angora, high quality rabbit wool products, are for sale at *Angora Sport* on Avenida 16 de Julio next to *Eli's Pizza*.

For musical instruments visit *Rumillajta*, one of the Galería shops adjacent to the San Francisco church entrance. There are also many shops on Sagárnaga/Linares, eg *Sumaj Supay*, No 851, and *Coral* at No 852. But shop around as prices vary greatly.

You'll find good antiques at Javier Núñez de Arco, Avenida 6 de Agosto 2255 downstairs, his father is upstairs, nice items, very expensive, also old photographs. Try also *La Casa de Pino*, Hermanos Manchego near Avenida Arce; *Tradicional*, Calle Pinilla entre Ascarrunz y Presbitero Medina; and *Da Vinci*, Salinas 345. The lower end of Sagárnaga is good for antiques.

The markets are a good place for ponchos and local handicrafts (see page 83). Many local objects are sold near Avenida Buenos Aires, and musical instruments can be found much cheaper than in the shops on Calle Granier, near the main cemetery. At Gallardo 1080, one block above Buenos Aires, there is the small workshop of the late master mask-maker, Antonio Viscarra, now run by his daughter and son-in-law. Costume, mask and trinket shops for Gran Poder abound above Buenos Aires.

Shopping Norte, Potosí y Socabaya, is a modern mall with restaurants and expensive merchandise. Also try San Miguel in Zona Sur. Calle Evaristo Valle is good for South American CDs. La Paz is a good place to buy cheap, good quality spectacles. Mercado Rodríguez street market is good for fresh food. Saturday and Sunday mornings are the main days but the market is open every day. Calle Isaac Tamayo and Tumusla sells chocolate, biscuits and all packaged food. There is a chain selling wholemeal bread, cheese, etc, *Irupana*, eg Calle Zoilo Flores 1226 (near Rodríguez market) and at Calle F Guachalla 505 (just below Sopocachi market). *Zatt* supermarket chain: the closest to the centre is Calle Sánchez Lima esquina Plaza Avaroa, Sopocachi. *Ketal* in Calle 21, San Miguel, has a better range and the *Ketal* being built on Avenida Ballivián esquina Calle 15 will be the biggest supermarket in the city.

Bookshops: you'll find a large stock of English, French and German books, and US magazines at *Los Amigos del Libro*, Mercado 1315, also Edificio Alameda, Avenida 16 de Julio (one block from *Plaza Hotel*) and El Alto airport, they also sell a few tourist maps of the region from Puno to the Yungas, and walking-tour guides; they will ship books. Also recommended is *Gisbert*, Comercio 1270, books, maps, stationery, will ship overseas. *Multi-Libro*, Loayza 233, T 391996, small, good for maps, politics, religion, psychology etc, open till 2100 Monday-Friday, and am Saturday and Sunday. *Librería La Paz*, Colón y Ballivián, has a wide selection of maps. *Librería Plural*, Pedro Salazar 489, on Plaza Avaroa, good selection of hard-to-find books on culture, sociology and ecology. Historian Antonio Paredes-Candia has a kiosk selling rare historical works on Villazón, opposite San Andrés University. There are second-hand stalls on Avenida Ismael Montes and occasional book fairs on the Prado. German books are available at the Goethe Institut (see above).

Cycle spares: try the shop at the Velódromo in Alto Irpavi, about 10 km out of town.

Films: any film can be developed at a decent developer. It is normal to get a free film, album or 15 x 21 cm print. *Foto Visión*, 6 de Agosto 2044 and other branches, cheap, good prints. *Foto Linares*, Mercado y Loayza, expensive but best for anything out of the ordinary. *Linares* and *Kavlin*, Potosí 1130, develop black and white. *Agfa Centre*, Loayza 250, for slide film, US$4. Fuji and Kodak slide film is more expensive. All slide film should be developed 'sólo revelado', ie without mounts, because they tend to get scratched, about US$2 per film. Cheap Fuji, Kodak or Agfa at street stalls, US$2 for 36. Check the date on film and take care buying film at street stalls – it may be old cinema reel taped to the leader section; pull the film out a little way to check. **Repairs** at Avenida Sánchez Lima 2178 by Rolando Calla C, recommended, just ring the bell (1400-1700), there is no sign.

Maps: Instituto Geográfico Militar head office is at Estado Mayor General, Avenida Saavedra Final, Miraflores, open 0900-1100, 1500-1700, take passport to purchase maps immediately; or go to Oficina 5, Juan XXIII 100, cul-de-sac off Rodríguez between Murillo y Linares, Monday-Thursday 0800-1200 and 1430-1800, Friday 0800-1400. IGM map prices: 1:50,000 topographical sheet US$6.70 (photocopy US$4.80); 1:250,000 sheet US$7.65 (copy US$5.75); national communications map (roads and towns) US$6.70; four-sheet Bolivia physical 1:1,000,000, US$16.25; four-sheet political 1:1,500,000 US$10.50. Liam P O'Brien has produced a 1:135,000, full colour, shaded relief topographic map of the Cordillera Real, US$10 per copy, from 28 Turner Terrace, Newtonville, MA02160, USA (add US$2 for shipping), or from map distributors (Bradt, Stanfords, etc). Walter Guzmán Córdova colour maps of Choro-Takesi-Yunga Cruz, Mururata-Illimani, Huayna Potosí and Sajama, available from bookshops. The German Alpine Club (Deutscher Alpenverien) produces two good maps of Sorata-Anchohuma-Illampu and Illimani, best bought before arrival. Senac (the national road service) publishes a Red Vial 1989 map, which is probably the best, but is still inaccurate, about US$4.50 from the office on eighth floor of Ministerio de Transporte y Comunicaciones, Avenida Mariscal Santa Cruz, it's the tall building behind the Correo, open till 1800, you have to show passport. Also reported as inaccurate are the maps of the Automóvil Club Boliviano. Maps are generally hard to find. They are sold at *Ichthus* bookshop on the Prado, No 1800; also at *Librería La Paz* and *Amigos del Libro* (see

Bookshops above). A map and guide of La Paz, in English, is published by Editorial Quipus, Casilla 1696, Calle Jaúregui 2248, T 340062; also Tiwanaku, Sucre and Cochabamba guides. Quipus is also the Poste Restante for South American Explorer Club members.

● **Sports**

Football: is popular and played on Wednesday and Sunday at the national Hernando Siles Stadium in Miraflores (Micro A), which is shared by both main La Paz teams, Bolívar and The Strongest. Any national soccer match is marked by lots of flag-waving, driving around with horns beeping, face painting – and that's before kick-off. Most match days are de facto half holidays depending on the time the match starts. During the game all Bolivian goals are marked by fireworks and if the team wins its party, party, party.

Golf: Mallasilla is the world's highest golf course, and there's also one at Pinos. Non-members can play at Mallasilla on weekdays. Club hire, green free, balls, and caddie costs US$37, the course is empty on weekdays, so there's no need to book; it is in good condition and beautiful.

Swimming: there is an Olympic-sized swimming pool in Alto Obrajes which sometimes has water.

Jogging: those who would like to go running with the Hash House Harriers should ask at The *Britannia* pub in Calacoto (see **Bars** above).

Snooker/pool: *San Luis*, Edificio México, segundo Sótano, Calle México 1411; *Picco's*, Edificio 16 de Julio, Avenida 16 de Julio 1566, both have good tables and friendly atmosphere.

Tennis: La Paz Tennis and Sucre Tennis.

YMCA sportsground and **gymnasium**: opposite the University of San Andrés, Avenida Villazón, and clubhouse open to the public, Avenida 20 de Octubre 1839 (table tennis, billiards, etc). There are regular meetings on Tuesday and Thursdays at 1930 of a mountaineering group which runs weekend excursions (see also page 18).

● **Tour companies & travel agents**

Crillon Tours, Avenida Camacho 1223, Casilla 4785, T 374566, F 391039, e-mail: titicaca @wara.bolnet.bo, Web http://www.titicaca .com,with 24-hour ATM for cash on credit cards; in USA, 1450 South Bayshore Dr, suite 815, Miami, FL 33131, T (305) 358-5353, F (305) 372-0054, joint scheduled tours with Lima arranged; *Transturin*, Camacho 1321 esq Colón, T 328560/ 363654, F 391162, Tx 2301 TRTURIN BV, and Mariscal Santa Cruz 1295, 3rd floor, T 342164.

Both these agencies offer full travel services, with tours ranging from La Paz to the whole country; for full details of their Lake Titicaca services see under **Lake Titicaca**, page 132).

Turismo Balsa, Capitán Ravelo 2104, T 360189/357817, F 391310, and Avenida 16 de Julio 1650, T 354049, PO Box 5889, city and local tours are recommended (see also under **Puerto Pérez**, page 130); *Turisbus*, Illampu 702, Casilla 442, T 369542, F 375532, helpful, trekking equipment rented, agent for Peruvian railways, ENAFER, tickets to Puno and Cusco (US$12 and US$31), also local and Bolivian tours, recommended; *Exprinter*, Edificio Herrman, Plaza Venezuela (exchange facilities, helpful) to Cusco, US$28, 21 hours, three times a week, via Desaguadero with a stop in Puno; *Magri Turismo*, Avenida 16 de Julio 1490, 5th floor, T 323954/341201, F 366309, e-mail: Magri_emete@megalink.com. Amex representative, gives travellers' cheques against American Express card, but cannot give cash or exchange travellers' cheques, offers all other Amex emergency services and clients' mail, recommended for tours in Bolivia, travel services; *Pachamama Tours*, Avenida Mariscal Santa Cruz y Colón, Galería Edificio Litoral, subsuelo, oficina 17, T 322311, recommended for tours of La Paz, Tiwanaku, Titicaca, etc, also arranges tours throughout Bolivia; *Diana Tours*, Sagárnaga 328, T 340356/375374/350252, F 360831, some English spoken, tour to Coroico and Tiwanaku, bus to Puno US$12; *Titikaka Tours*, Loayza between Riva and Camacho, good for flights; *Tawa Tours*, Sagárnaga 161 and Rosendo Gutiérrez 701, T 325796, French-run, run jungle tours to their own camp as well as the Salt Lake areas, friendly, good guides (also charter flights to Europe and USA); *Shima Tours*, Potosí 1310, very helpful, good for flight tickets; *Combi*, on Illampu next to *Residencial Copacabana*, classical tours and transport to Copacabana; *Fremen*, Calle Pedro Salazar 537, Plaza Avaroa, T 416336, F 417327, Casilla 9682, e-mail: vtfremen@wara.bolnet.bo, they own Flotel in Trinidad for jungle cruises in the Beni and Hotel El Puente in the Chapare, and run tours throughout the country, eg Salar de Uyuni and Che Guevara Trail, Michel Livet is helpful and speaks English, French and Spanish, also have offices in Santa Cruz, Cochabamba and Trinidad; *Paititi*, Avenida 6 de Agosto y Aspiazu, and *Aparthotel Camino Real*, Capitán Ravelo 2123, 0900-1900, T 340108/ 341018/ 353558, F 329625, organizes adventure tours, recommended, Javier Palza is helpful and speaks English,

German, French, Italian; *Peru Bolivian Tours*, Loayza, Edificio Mariscal de Ayacucho, planta baja, oficina 8, T 363720, F 365845; *America Tours*, Avenida 16 de Julio 1490, T 328584, F 374204, Casilla 2568, Swiss-Bolivian owned, cultural and ecotourism trips to many parts of the country, English, German, French spoken; *Carmoar Tours*, Calle Bueno 159, T/F 340633, headed by Günther Ruttger, has information and maps for the Inca Trail to Coroico, rents trekking gear; *Reinaldo Pou Munt*, Capitán Ravelo 2401, T 327226, Casilla 13632, expensive, offers excellent tours of the city and environs, speaks English and German; *Nuevo Continente*, at *Hotel Alem*, recommended for trip to Zongo, Clemente is a good driver, cheap service to airport, very friendly and helpful; *Tauro Tours*, oficina 4, planta baja, Edificio Mariscal Ballivián, Calle Mercado 1328, T 361877, F 392549, Casilla 11142, top end adventure tourism agency, jeep tours anywhere in the country, organized by the very experienced and German Mountain Guides Association-trained Carlos Aguilar. For information on and arrangement of climbing and adventure tours see also **Mountaineering** section on page 18; eg *Colibrí*, Sagárnaga 309, T 371936.

Many agencies arrange excursions or travel to Peru (Puno, Cusco, Arequipa), as well as local tours. *Bracha*, T 327472, has details of and sells tickets for trains from Santa Cruz. **NB** Flight tickets can be bought more reliably from airlines than through agencies.

● **Tourist offices**
The information office, at the bottom end of Avenida 16 de Julio (Prado) on Plaza del Estudiante on the corner with Calle México, is helpful; English and French spoken, ask here for information on train services, free leaflets, map of La Paz US$2.50. **Secretaria Nacional de Turismo**

(Senatur) is at Edificio Ballivián, 18th floor, Calle Mercado, T 367463/64, F 374630, Casilla 1868. Telephone directories in La Paz have economic and tourist information in English on all the provinces.

● **Useful addresses**
Asociación Boliviana de Agencias de Viajes y Turismo, Edificio Litoral, Mariscal Santa Cruz 1351, Casilla 3967. **Instituto Nacional de Arqueología de Bolivia**, Calle Tiwanaku 93.

Immigration: to renew a visa go to Migración Bolivia, Avenida Camacho 1433 (opposite Banco de Santa Cruz), T 379385/370475, open Monday-Friday 0900-1200, 1600-1800, fast and efficient service.

Tourist Police: Plaza del Estadio, Miraflores, next to *Love City* disco, T 225016, for insurance claims after theft, English spoken, helpful.

YMCA: 20 de Octubre 1839, Casilla 963.

● **Transport**
Local Bus: there are three types of city bus: large Fiat buses run by the city corporation, on fairly limited routes; *micros* (Bluebird-type buses), which charge US$0.18 in the centre, US$0.24 from outside the centre; and *kombis* (minivans), US$0.20/0.34, which are quicker than *micros*. Don't expect to get anywhere fast in the centre as *micros* and *kombis* often have to stop every few metres to let passengers on and off. If you can't keep your backpack on your lap, you will be charged extra in *kombis*.

Car hire: cars may be hired direct from Localiza, F (591) 2415188, E-mail: localiza@3millenium.com.bol; Imbex, Avenida Montes 522, T 316895, F 379884, well maintained Suzuki jeeps from US$50 per day, including 100 km free for four-person 4WD, highly recommended; National, F Zuazo 1935, T/F 376581, recommended; Rent-a-Car International, F Suazo 1942, T 357061; Kolla Motors, Rosendo Gutiérrez

502, T 341660/351701, have well-maintained six-seater 4WD Toyota jeeps, insurance and gasoline extra. Petita Rent-a-car, Cañada Strongest 1857-A, T 379182, F 322596, Swiss owners Ernesto Hug and Aldo Rezzonico, recommended for well-maintained VW 'beetles' and 4WD jeeps, etc, they also offer recommended adventure tours, Jeeping Bolivia, German, French and English spoken. Ernesto also has a garage for VW and other makes at Avenida Jaimes Freyre 2326, T 342279, highly recommended. Those needing a **Car Park** can find a safe and central one on the corner of Ingavi and Sanjines, US$1.75 for 24 hours.

Motorcycle rental: Moto Rent, Avenida Busch 1255, Miraflores Norte, T 357289, 650 Kawasaki endurance type, US$50 per day unlimited mileage, US$250 per week. Motorcycle spares: J Landivar, Avenida Saavedra 1235, T 329774, F 392427, recommended for Honda and other Japanese makes.

Taxis: normal taxis charge US$0.40 per person for short trips within city limits. *Trufis* are fixed route collective taxis with a little flag on the front which charge US$0.28-0.40 per person within city limits. Taxi drivers are not tipped. Don't let the driver turn the lights out at night. Radio taxis (eg Alfa T 322427, La Rápida 392323) charge US$1.45 in the centre and US$2.80 to the suburbs. They are also good value for tours for three or more people, but negotiate price. Eduardo Figueroa, T 786281, taxi driver and travel agent, has been recommended. Adolfo Monje Palacios, in front of *Hotel El Dorado* or T 354384, is recommended for short or long trips. Oscar Vera, Simón Aguirre 2158, Villa Copacabana, La Paz, T 230453, specializes in trips to the Salar de Uyuni and the Western Cordillera, he speaks English and is also recommended.

Air El Alto, above La Paz, the highest commercial airport in the world (4,058m) connected to the city by motorway, T 810122/3. A taxi between the centre and airport takes about 30 minutes, US$6 up to the airport, US$5 down to the centre. Current prices, including luggage, should be on display at the airport exit. Enquire at the tourist office in town, or at the airport. Cotranstur minibuses, white with 'Cotranstur' and 'Aeropuerto' written on the side and back, go from Plaza Isabel La Católica, anywhere on the Prado and Avenida Mariscal Santa Cruz to the airport between 0800-0830 to 1900-2000, US$0.55 per person, allow about 1 hour and best to have little luggage. They leave from the airport every 5 minutes or so. Colectivos from Plaza Isabel La Católica charge US$3.45 per person, carrying four passengers.

Airport: the bank in the international departures hall will change cash at OK rates. To change money when the bank is closed, ask at the departure tax window near information. The international departures hall is the main concourse, with all check-in desks and is the hall for all domestic arrivals and departures. There's a small tourist office at the airport with some maps available, English spoken, helpful (when staffed). There's an expensive bar/restaurant and a cheaper café/*comedor* upstairs. Also a duty-free shop.

Services: LAB and Aero Sur fly to the main cities and towns and TAM (Transportes Aéreo Militar) flies to destinations in the eastern and northern lowlands (see **Airline offices**, page 97 for addresses and telephone numbers). Fares are comparatively low for internal flights. For details, see under destinations. Note that TAM uses the nearby military airport.

Trains The rate of terminal decline of Bolivian railways has accelerated since privatization. Trains are more expensive, slower, and harder to catch than buses and the timetable could be described variously as outrageously antisocial or

pure fantasy. According to reports in September 1997, there were no trains running from La Paz. La Paz-Oruro and Oruro-La Paz services have been suspended indefinitely, as have services between Potosí and Sucre. For information T 353510/352510/ 373069. Micros which go to the station are A, M, N, P, 130, 131, C. The ticket office, at the rear of the building at the north end of the main station, opens Monday-Wednesday 0700, and Friday 0830-1200, but get there at least 2 hours beforehand.

To **Villazón** for Argentina, see under Uyuni **trains** (page 190).

La Paz-Arica International Railway travels for 447 km west across the Andes to Chile. In the Bolivian section the line climbs to El Alto and then runs southwest to Viacha (Km 32) the junction of lines to Antofagasta, Guaqui (freight only) and Villazón. It coninues to Corocoro, the copper mining town, crosses the Río Desaguadero at Calacoto (Km 98) and then runs southwest to the border at Charaña (Km 208), a very cold place to change trains or wait for a bus. The mountain peaks visible en route include Illimani, Huayna-Potosí, Mururata, and many others. **NB** Chilean pesos can be bought in La Paz at good rates.

There is a Bolivian *ferrobus* service straight through to Arica, on Monday and Friday at 0715, arriving on Tuesday and Saturday at 1940; US$52 pullman, US$96 *especial*, includes breakfast and lunch, max 20 kilograms baggage is free, extra charge for excess. The trip is worth it for the spectacular scenery. Book your ticket 1-2 weeks in advance at Estación Central, especially the in high season, when extra trains are added. **NB** This service was suspended in 1997 after flooding. It is not clear if the La Paz-Arica service is included in the September 1997 suspension of rail services. We include the above details in the expectation that it will be restored. Alternatively take a train to **Charaña** on Wednesday from Viacha at 0300 (US$3 pullman), then change to a colectivo to Arica. On the second and fourth Wednesday of each month a train leaves Charaña at 0930, arriving in Arica at 1800 (every Wednesday January-March). The return from Charaña to Viacha departs at 1600.

La Paz-Antofagasta in Chile by Antofagasta and Bolivia Railway. This trip is 1,173 km and definitely for the adventurous who are impervious to cold at night, or blazing sunshine at tedious daytime border changes. The train is full of contrabandistas, impromptu folk music, and the ride is very rough and subject to long delays. The train starts at Uyuni, running as far as

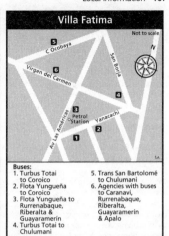

Villa Fatima

Not to scale

Buses:
1. Turbus Totaí to Coroico
2. Flota Yungueña to Coroico
3. Flota Yungueña to Rurrenabaque, Riberalta & Guayaramerín
4. Turbus Totaí to Chulumani
5. Trans San Bartolomé to Chulumani
6. Agencies with buses to Caranavi, Rurrenabaque, Riberalta, Guayaramerín & Apalo

Calama in Chile, then by bus (240 km) to Antofagasta. This route passes through magnificent scenery. For details see under Uyuni **trains** (page 190).

Buses For information, T 367275/367274. Buses to **Oruro, Potosí, Sucre, Cochabamba, Santa Cruz, Tarija, Villazón** and all points south of La Paz leave from the main terminal at Plaza Antofagasta (micros 2, M, CH or 130), as do international buses. See under each destination for details. The terminal (open 0700-2300) has a post office, ENTEL, restaurant, luggage store. Agencies to Peru, such as Turisbus, Diana and Vicuña are cheaper here than their offices in town. Touts find passengers the most convenient bus and are paid commission by the bus company.

Buses to **Sorata, Copacabana, Tiahuanaco** and destinations north of La Paz leave from various streets around the Cemetery district (see Cemetery district map). Companies include Flota Copacabana, Manco Kapac, 2 de Febrero, Ingavi, Trans Perla Andina. To get to the Cemetery district, take any bus or *kombi* marked 'Cementerio' going up Calle Santa Cruz (US$0.17); the route is Santa Cruz, Max Paredes, Garita de Lima, Mariano Bautista, Plaza Félix Reyes Ortiz/Tomás Katari. Look out for the cemetery arch on your left. On Plaza Reyes Ortiz are Manco Kapac, recommended (T 350033) and 2 de Febrero (T 377181) for Copacabana and Tiquina. Several micros (20, J, 10) and *kombis* (223, 252, 270, 7) go up Kollasuyo; look for 'Kollasuyo' on the windscreen in most, but not all, cases.

Buses to **Coroico and the Yungas** leave from Villa Fátima, which is 25 minutes by micros B,V,X,K, 131, 135, or 136, or *trufis* 2 or 9, which pass Pérez Velasco coming down from Plaza Mendoza, and get off at the service station (see La Paz orientation map).

International buses: to **Buenos Aires**, daily at 1630 (San Roque, T 329769), via Yacuiba, or at 1700 with San Lorenzo (T 328911), both take 2½ days; also Atahualpa via Yacuiba or La Quiaca/Villazón. Alternatively, go to Villazón and change buses in Argentina.

To **Arica** via the frontier at Tambo Quemado and Chungará, the road is completely paved, except for a 20 km stretch and in good condition. The journey takes 11 hours. Litoral leave at 0530 Tuesday, Friday and Sunday, US$29, T 358603 (office No 19 bus terminal), buses reported as old. Géminis use better buses but only leave on Saturday, US$29; also Trans Salvador three a week, also US$29, and Transportes Cali, US$22. There is no direct service to Arica via the frontier at Charaña and Visviri; the trip must be done in stages. Senobus (Calle Hujutri, 400m from train station in direction of Cementerio), departs Tuesday, Friday and Saturday evenings, US$11; also El Cariñoso, which is cheaper. In Charaña take a taxi to Visviri (US$0.65), then a bus on Tuesday and Friday, US$7, or colectivo taxi to Arica. It is a beautiful, exhausting trip, but doing it in stages, rather than straight through, involves extra waiting at the border. All companies involve several changes of bus; the entire trip takes 18 dusty hours. Military checks can be expected on both sides of the frontier.

To **Iquique**, Tuesday, Saturday and Sunday 1700, US$32, 22 hours, with Litoral. To **Tacna**, also with Litoral, Thursday and Saturday, 0700, US$20, 10 hours. There are no Bolivian customs or immigration at the border for exit stamp, Peruvian entry is given in Tacna. To **Cusco**, Cruz del Sur, three a week, US$20, 20 hours, 'not luxurious', stops in Puno. Colectivos and agency buses leave daily to **Puno** with different companies and are most easily booked through travel agencies, US$12-15.50, 10 hours. **NB** Of the various La Paz-Puno services, only Transturin does not make you change to a Peruvian bus once over the border. Exprinter/Cruz del Sur, T 362708, go via Desaguadero Tuesday, Thursday, Saturday 0800, US$7.20. For transport to Peru see under **Lake Titicaca** (page 133).

There are two routes. The shortest and most widely used is the road from La Paz to Arica via the border towns of Tambo Quemado (Bolivia) and Chungará (Chile). The majority of Bolivia's imports, including foreign cars, jeeps and large vehicles from Chile's Pacific seaports, Arica and Iquique, are brought to La Paz by truck via this route.

From La Paz take the main highway south towards Oruro to **Patacamaya**. The town is 104 km from central La Paz – about 1½ hours on a good paved road – and 130 km north of Oruro. There is a Sunday market with no tourist items. **G** *Los Angeles*, is a basic hotel, and there's other cheap accommodation and restaurants. At Patacamaya turn right (west towards the Cordillera) at the green road sign to Puerto Japonés on the Río Desaguadero – the sign is only visible coming from La Paz – and from there to Tambo Quemado. Take extra petrol as there is none available after the Chilean border until Arica, and food and water. The journey is worthwhile for the breathtaking views.

Midway between Patacamaya and Tambo Quemado is the town of **Curahuara de Carangas**. Accommodation on the plaza in an *Alojamiento*, which is **G**, dirty, no electricity. Watch for speed restrictions upon entering town past the military school. There's a possible overnight stop in Sajama Village (4,200m) 22 km east of Tambo Quemado at the foot of Mount Sajama (see **Sajama National Park**, page 186).

FRONTIER WITH CHILE: TAMBO QUEMADO

● **Bolivian customs**
Bolivian customs is at Lagunas, 12 km further on from Sajama Village. It's a popular 'truck-stop', where petrol is available.

● **Bolivian immigration**
The Bolivian border control at **Tambo Quemado**, 10 km from Lagunas, consists of *tránsito*

(highway police), immigration, and international police. It closes for lunch. It is worth double checking all documents including visa requirements with the Consulate of Chile in La Paz before travelling.

● **Crossing with a private vehicle**
The normal road user fee for a '*particular*' (private non-commercial vehicle) is approximately US$4.50. Check with the Autómovil Club Boliviano in La Paz for any special documents which may be required, depending on the registration of your vehicle. Bolivian vehicles require a Temporary Export Certificate in order to leave Bolivia. This has to be obtained in La Paz prior to travel. Temporary Import/Export Certificates are normally valid 90 days.

● **Chilean immigration**
From Tambo Quemado there is a stretch of about 7 km of 'no-man's land' before you reach the Chilean frontier at Chungará. Here the border crossing, which is set against the most spectacular scenic backdrop of Lake Chungará and Volcán Parinacota is strictly controlled. The border is open 0800-2100. A Temporary Import Certificate, which costs US$2, must be obtained from customs at Chungará on entering Chile. Expect a long wait behind lines of lorries. It's best to travel midweek; avoid Sunday. Drivers must fill in '*Relaciones de Pasajeros*', US$0.25 from the kiosk at the border, giving details of driver, vehicle and passengers. Border control consists of immigration, Customs and Police and Ministry of Agriculture and Livestock (SAG) – control of animals entering Chile is rigidly enforced; do not take any fruit, vegetables, or dairy products into Chile.

● **Exchange**
It's best to change a small amount of currency into Chilean pesos in La Paz.

● **Transport**
For details of buses between La Paz and Arica see **International buses** above.

● **Accommodation**
In Lagunas the restaurant/bar *Lagunas* offers a cheap set menu, and is helpful and friendly. The owner can usually find accommodation somewhere in the village for around US$1; you'll need your own sleeping bag, extra blankets and warm clothing. Facilities are at best very basic; you may well be sleeping on a straw mattress on a dirt floor. There's no water or electricity, gas lamps or candles are usual. It may be possible for men to sleep at the Puesto Militar, beside the new road, 100m from the village. Nights here can be bitterly cold and very windy. In the daytime there are spectacular views of nearby snowcapped Mount Sajama.

● **Into Chile**
From Chungará the first 50 km section to Putre goes through the spectacular Lauca National Park. There are some treacherous bends as the road descends dramatically to sea-level where it meets the Pan Amerian Highway (Route 5) 12 km north of Arica. There are several *carabinero* road checks on the road to Arica as this is a major drug and contraband route. Searches are very thorough and professional.

FRONTIER WITH CHILE: CHARAÑA

An alternative route into Chile, on which there are no trucks, is to go by a good road from La Paz via Viacha to **Santiago de Machaco** (130 km), where petrol is available. Then it's a further 120 km on a very poor road to the border at **Charaña**.

● **Immigration**
Immigration is behind the railway station. Only a 30-day permit is given on entry.

● **Accommodation**
In Charaña at **G** *Alojamiento Aranda*.

● **Into Chile**
Chilean border formalities are in **Visviri**. There is no fuel, accommodation, bath or electricity here; ask for a restaurant and bargain a price. Immigration is open 0800-2400. There is a US$2 charge for private vehicles. From Visviri a regular road runs to Putre. There are buses and colectivos to Arica.

A variation from Viacha is to take the roads which more-or-less follow the railway to Charaña (4WD essential). On this scenic route you pass **Comanche** (see **Excursions From La Paz** below) and **General Campero** in the Ciudad de Piedra. Near the football field in General Campero is a house which lets a room and has water. From General Campero roads go to General Pérez, Abarao and on to Charaña. From this route treks can be made south to the mountains towards Sajama and, from Charaña, to Sajama itself.

EXCURSIONS FROM LA PAZ

VALLE DE LA LUNA

The best nearby excursion is to Río Abajo and the Mallasilla golf course. The route passes through the rich suburbs of Calacoto and La Florida, following the river road past lovely picnic spots and through some weird rock formations, known as the **Valle de la Luna**, 'Moon Valley'. Just before the Valle are the Aranjuez Forest, the Aniceto Arce cactus gardens (which are badly eroded) and the *Playa de Aranjuez*, a bathing spot popular for lunch at weekends. About 3 km from the bridge at Calacoto the road forks; sharp right leads to the Caza y Pesca Club and Mallasilla golf course. Get out of the minibus at the turning and walk a few minutes east to the Valle entrance, or get out at the football field which is by the entrance. Take good shoes and water.

● **Accommodation & places to eat** Just past the Valle de la Luna and the Mallasilla Golf Course is Mallasa where several small roadside restaurants and cafés have opened: **B** *Oberland*, T 745040, F 745389, E-mail: wschmid @wara.bolnet.bo, is a Swiss-owned, chalet-style restaurant and hotel resort, popular at weekends, especially with the expat community, cabañas, sauna, swimming pool, racket ball, tennis, it has been recommended for superb fondue, raclette, pasta and salads, book in advance; also *Los Lobos*, highly recommended for *churrasco* steaks, US$4.50.

● **Transport** *Kombi* A, numbers 231 and 273 pass the Valle de la Luna en route to the Mallasa

recreation area, a large weekend excursion area near Mallasa village. If you do not want to walk in the valley, stay on the bus to the end of the line and take a return bus, 2 hours in all. Alternatively take Micro 11, a small bus marked 'Aranjuez', from Calle Sagárnaga, near Plaza San Francisco, US$0.65, and ask the driver where to get off. Most of the local travel agents organize tours to the Valle de la Luna. These are very brief, 5 minutes stop for photos in a US$15 tour of La Paz and surroundings. A taxi will cost US$6.

ZOO

The Zoo is on the road to Río Abajo; the entrance is just past Mallasa. It has well-housed animals in a beautiful, wide open park-like setting. The climate in this valley is always much warmer than in the city, where the zoo previously was. Open daily 0900-1700, US$0.40 adults, US$0.20 children.

TO ACHUMANI

Beyond Valle de la Luna is Achumani which offers good views of the valley and a glimpse of the palatial mansions of the wealthy. To reach it go up Avenida Ballivián through Calacoto and turn left at Calle 17. Further beyond Calacoto and Cota Cota is the new residential zone of Chasquipampa on the Palca road, near which is the **Valle de las Animas**. Here the eroded landscape is similar to, but much larger than, the Valle de la Luna and is good for walking and picnics.

To Chasquipampa take any *kombi* or micro marked 'Ovejuno' or 'Chasquipampa' from the Prado. On the way back

there are good views of the southern districts and the city above.

LA MUELA DEL DIABLO

This is a gigantic, tooth-shaped rock which can be seen from the Valle de la Luna road. Take Micro 'Ñ' from Murillo y Sagárnaga or from the University (last stop Cota Cota), *kombi* 213 to Rosales, or *trufi* 288 from Plaza Isabel La Católica to Urbanización Pedregal (ask the driver where to get off). Cross the river and climb through the village to the cemetery; from there it is 1½ hours easy climb to the rock which is 'more impressive, especially if the wind is blowing, than Moon Valley'. The road continues to Ventilla, the start of the Inca trail.

ZONGO VALLEY

Global warming has completely destroyed the ice cave, which used to be the Zongo Valley's main attraction. The Valley lies at the end of a steep but scenic ride down past several of La Paz's electric power plants. From the dam, the road drops almost 3,000m in less than 40 km and is popular with mountain bikers.

It is quite safe to drive yourself (in a suitable vehicle) and hike. The road passes a series of lakes and an aqueduct on the left. Keep left at each junction en route. Twenty minutes past the abandoned Milluni tin mine, its large roadside cemetery (which is also on the left) and the colourful but polluted Lago Milluni, you come to the last hydroelectric dam and on the right, a white guard house (4,750m), where you get off. Walk up and over the small hill on the righthand side of the road until you meet the aqueduct again. Follow it for 45 minutes, taking special care as it is cut into the side of a sheer cliff in places with some spectacular drops, then cross it and walk up to reach the base of the Charquini glacier. Do not go onto the glacier unless you have crampons and are roped. At the end of the bridge, turn right uphill to a marker of rocks piled one on top of the other.

Continue over the hill, cross a stream and go straight up the next hill at a similar rock marker. From the top of the hill, it is only a few minutes down to the site of the former ice cave. It's about 1¼ hours' walk in all.

● **Transport** Either arrange a jeep through a tourist agency for US$70, or go to Plaza Ballivián in El Alto to catch a *camión* at midday on Monday, Wednesday and Friday for US$1; or haggle with the drivers of empty minibuses for around US$10. You can also hire a taxi for US$30 for the return trip; or contact *Refugio Huayna Potosí* which organizes regular transport. If driving, make sure you have your passport and driving documents as there is a police checkpoint immediately before the mine. To get back from the dam if you haven't arranged transport, the truck returns passing the Zongo dam at about midday on Tuesday, Thursday and Saturday. There are La Paz-bound jeeps and minibuses at irregular intervals during the season.

URMIRI

Take the asphalted road from La Paz south to Oruro to Km 75 where a sign points left to Urmiri. A steep scenic descent leads to two pools filled by mineral springs, a sauna, a hot waterfall and a pleasant though basic hotel with a very good restaurant. The thermal baths are completely isolated in a beautiful mountain setting and definitely worth a visit. There's a good walk down to the village of Sapahuaqui, in a fruit-growing region, and you can hitch back up to the hotel.

The best time to visit the thermal baths is Tuesday-Friday. At weekends it's full of locals and their children. The main pool is closed Monday for cleaning, refilling and cooling (the water comes out of the ground at 72°C; it takes 2-3 minutes to boil an egg). Daytrippers pay US$3pp for use of the pools and the sauna.

● **Accommodation D** for room with a private pool for two or four people or with a thermal bath tub; rooms with shared private pool, **E**. Breakfast is included, other meals are available. Discount 10% for groups of five or more staying for 2 nights and having all meals. Reservations necessary. Shiatsu US$10 per hour and massage US$6 for 30 minutes.

• **Transport** New owners, *Hotel Gloria* (see La Paz **Hotels** above) runs transport 0800 Tuesday, Thursday and Sunday US$6 per person return, 2½ hours. Return to La Paz same days at 1600. Alternatively, take any bus going to Oruro and get off at Km 75. Lifts from the crossroads are few and far between.

PALCA CANYON

Possible there and back in 1 day from La Paz, the **Palca Canyon** is an amazing eroded mud valley surrounded by steep mud walls and pinnacles. The river runs into the Río Abajo which cuts through the Andes to split the Cordillera Real from the Cordillera Quimza Cruz. The route follows the bed of the Quebrada Chua Kheri and should not be attempted in the wet season.

In Huni look out for a broad road leading down right and follow it down, past the school and on. The path becomes prehispanic stone paving and leads down to the canyon floor. Walk through the canyon for 2 hours until it opens out. Follow the path up and left to Palca which takes another 30 minutes.

Palca is a pleasant village, often full at weekends with visiting Paceños but quiet the rest of the week with limited accommodation and many shops. There are regular buses back to La Paz especially at weekends, US$1. Or arrange to be picked up by jeep, US$35. From Palca, you could walk 30 minutes up the road to Ventilla and then up the valley of the Río Choquekhota to Choquekhota and continue up the valley to Mina San Francisco at the top of the valley for Takesi, Alto Takesi, and Reconquistada trails. Map: IGM Palca 6044 III covers the trail but is not really necessary.

• **Transport** Take the bus to Palca and get off at Huni. The bus leaves from outside the *Comedor Popular* in Calle Max Paredes above the junction with Calle Rodríguez at 0530 every day, US$1. Alternatively, get the micro Ñ or minibus 385 from central La Paz to Chasquipampa or Ovejuyo and then it takes 30 minutes to walk along the road to reach a pass area near a lake with great views of Illimani and Mururata. From here its 25 minutes down to Huni where the trek starts.

A climb to **Corazón de Jesús** is worth it for the views over the city and the Altiplano, but is for the acclimatized only. The statue at the top of the hill is reached via the steps at the north end of Calle Washington, then left and right and follow the stations of the cross. Watch out where you put your feet. Do not go alone as there is a risk of robbery and beware of dogs. Take a bus to Ceja El Alto (eg Número 20 or 22) to save yourself some of the walk.

To see Puya Raimondii flowers, go to the village of **Comanche**, 2½ hours from La Paz. Micros leave from the railway station to Viacha 1 hour away, from where it's a rough, dusty and cold truck ride to Comanche. Trains leave Tuesday 2200, and return on Wednesday only at 1500, US$1.50 each way. Some travel agencies arrange tours.

There is also trout fishing in the many glacial lakes and streams near La Paz.

TIAHUANACO

By far the most popular excursion from La Paz is the remarkable site of Tiahuanaco, 72 km west of the city on the road to Desaguadero on the Peruvian border.

At first sight, there's not much to recommend the Pampa Koani, a cold, bleak, windswept valley on Lake Titicaca's southeastern edge. But only a few kilometres west is the site of the ruins of an ancient culture of the same name, Tiahuanaco (or Tiwanaku), one of the world's greatest and longest running empires.

History

Archaeologists had long believed that Tiahuanaco was a relatively unimportant era in the history of Andean civilization. Until, that is, Alan Kolata, an anthropologist from the University of Illinois in Chicago, led an archaeological expedition to the site in 1986. Kolata came up with some amazing finds, not least of which was evidence that the Pampa Koani, now barely able to sustain a population of 7,000 in dire poverty, was 1,500 years ago a vast agricultural area that produced enough to support 125,000 people.

Kolata's expedition showed that the Pampa Koani was just one Lake Titicaca valley among many that produced great harvests every year for a 1,000 years. This was due to an immense system of raised fields (*Sukakollu*) built by the Tiahuanaco empire more than 2,000 years ago. These harvests fed the equivalent of the entire population of Bolivia today and even allowed for surpluses to be stored for poor years. The raised fields proved that, far from being a minor period in Andean civilization, Tiahuanaco was a great imperial capital and the inspiration for the better-known Inca empire that followed it.

Learning from the past

Of all the accomplishments of the Tiahuanaco culture, including its trade routes, architecture and artistry, the single greatest feat has to be its system of raised fields. The many, many years of empirical study that went into perfecting them, the sheer effort of building them and the amazing levels of production that came out of them are all unparalleled in history, according to US anthropologist, Alan Kolata.

The ancient people of Tiahuanaco had to overcome the many problems that bedevil local farmers today – floods, droughts, soil exhaustion and salinization from Lake Titicaca's slightly salty waters. Even international aid agencies have failed to improve conditions. At such extreme altitude the climate seems too harsh and the soil too poor to succeed in making a difference.

The system of raised fields developed by the Tiahuanaco people was so carefully engineered and built that many of them remain intact today. They are massive constructions, over 1m high, with planting surfaces sometimes as large as 15m wide and 200m long. Each is a carefully layered structure with a thick cobblestone base which is covered with a layer of impermeable clay. Over the clay is a layer of coarse gravel and then another layer of finer gravel. Over all that sits the topsoil.

The raised fields lie parallel to one another, separated by deep irrigation channels running in straight lines or graceful curves which form precise geometric patterns. The irrigation ditches provided water in times of drought and the elevated fields protected crops in times of flooding. These fields and ditches cover nearly 50 square km of the Pampa Koani. To achieve this, the ancient engineers straightened the Catari river and moved it 1½ km to the east.

The layer of clay at the base of the fields prevented the brackish water of nearby Lake Titicaca from seeping up from below ground and into the topsoil. The exact positioning of the fields and ditches was designed to take advantage of the fierce Andean sun. By efficiently exposing the ditches to the sun, the water in them gets enough heat by day to protect the fields from frost damage during the bitterly cold nights. The heated water in the ditches also promoted the rapid growth of algae that fed the fish. Furthermore, it attracted a resident population of ducks which also entered the local diet as meat and eggs. Duck droppings, decayed algae and fish remains then formed a rich sludge that was scraped off the bottom of the ditches to be used as fertilizer for the topsoil.

The idea of using this ancient, long-forgotten agricultural technology to increase output on the barren Altiplano is currently under discussion, spurred on by the efforts of Alan Kolata. If the Tiahuanaco people could grow what they needed to eat and more, using these same fields and without the benefit of tractors, water pumps and chemical fertilizers, surely it could be done again. Rural Bolivians today could yet reap what their ancestors sowed.

Fashion victims

Physical appearance and beauty were regarded very highly in the culture of Tiahuanaco. Costume and jewellery played a very important part in daily life. But the most striking physical characteristic of the 50,000 inhabitants of the city of Tiahuanaco was the shape of their heads. One of the few things that the elite and their subjects had in common was the practice of skull deformation, on their children; a popular trend in many Andean cultures.

Shortly after the birth of a baby, its head was clamped between two boards to force the soft skull into a more pointed shape. The boards stayed on the child's head until about the age of five, by which time the pointed shape was permanent, leaving them with no brow and a forehead that sloped back dramatically from the eyebrows to a point at the back of the skull. This pointed skull was regarded as a mark of cultural distinction. Or perhaps it was just a way of keeping 'ahead' in the fashion stakes.

The Tiahuanaco empire comprised nearly half of present-day Bolivia, southern parts of Peru, the northwest section of Argentina and nearly half of Chile. It was built on the vast produce of its agricultural systems. The continual surplus crops gave Tiahuanaco the time and energy to raise armies that then went on to conquer the Andes. This empire continued to expand after AD 1,000, establishing huge agricultural colonies across the Andes based on its own system of raised fields. Its armies reigned supreme over many different cultures and its engineers built a vast system of paved highways over mountains and through jungles and deserts, which enabled it to maintain a constant flow of goods throughout the empire. All these roads led to one place – to the nondescript little market town which was once the site of a mighty imperial capital of 50,000 inhabitants.

The ancient city of Tiahuanaco must have been an impressive sight to visitors with its skyline dominated by great pyramids, temples and palaces. The two largest edifices, the Kalasasaya Temple and the Akapana Pyramid, were 200m long and over 20m high. They were constructed from massive blocks of andesite weighing more than 150 tons that were ferried on reed boats from quarries across Lake Titicaca. The exterior of the buildings was decorated with intricately-carved stone friezes and bas-relief work, much of it covered with thin plates of gold or painted in hues of blue, red, gold and black. The overall effect must have been dazzling.

Life in Tiahuanaco

Life in the capital city 1,500 years ago would have revolved around the comings and goings of the emperor-priest, who was both leader and god to his people. He and his family conducted both the affairs of state and the culture's most sacred religious rituals. The empire's rulers inherited their positions and were raised to lead their people in spiritual and temporal matters. They married the daughters of families of equally high status, sometimes even their own sisters.

The city was also populated by the most skilled artisans in the empire; sculptors, jewellers, weavers and potters. They were patronized by the elite in order that they might further develop their skills and produce the finest possible examples of their crafts.

Life in the royal household was sumptuous and lived on a scale of barely conceivable wealth and power. Much of their time was taken up with the observance of religious ceremonies. Powerful hallucinogenic drugs, imported from the low-lying coastal desert regions, played an integral part in these ceremonies.

All the great temples were decorated with elaborately carved sacred monoliths up to 5m high which depicted idols in stylized human form. They were positioned to remind the priests of the passage of important ritual days. One of these, the Bennett Stele – named after Wendell Bennet, a US archaeologist who found it in the Kalasasaya Temple area in the 1930s – shows complex markings that have been deciphered as a solar and lunar calendar more accurate than our own.

The calendar was of vital importance as an agricultural guide. It also kept track of the religious rituals, including animal and human sacrifices, that had to be observed with the arrival of the planting season. This was a time of great celebration in the imperial city when members of the nobility would congregate from all parts of the empire. The great avenues leading to the temple and the lanes running through the adobe houses of the commoners were full of drunken revellers and crowds gathered to watch the specially-trained young virgins offered as human sacrifices to the gods.

Life for the commoners and colonial subjects of Tiahuanaco was rather less sumptuous than that enjoyed by the ruling elite, but it was not without its benefits. For a start, the empire offered them security. It also ensured freedom from hunger. Furthermore, with its vast armies, there was protection from the hostile kingdoms and savage tribes that lurked on its frontiers.

Survival through conquest

Besides their advanced agricultural techniques, the Tihuanaco culture also relied on the conquest of rival kingdoms as a form of insurance. This allowed access to regular supplies of foods that could be grown at the extreme altitude of the Altiplano as well as precious minerals and medicinal and psychedelic drugs.

The imperial armies were well-armed, well-organized and evidence shows that the soldiers were particularly ferocious in battle, beheading anyone who dared to oppose them. Ritual trophy head-taking was an important part of Tihuanaco art.

The style of conquest was to lay siege to the enemy. Supplied from their base by a secured route of llama caravans, the army would surround an enemy town, wait until its people began to starve, and then move in for the deciding battle. Each time a kingdom or territory was conquered an administrative army of up to 5,000 was sent to start the business of running things. At the extreme edges of the empire, groups of traders and soldiers established frontier posts to protect the empire's interests.

The maintenance and protection of these far-flung outposts was one of the emperor-priest's biggest headaches. Taxes had to be levied, armies maintained and communications kept open with distant administrators. To this end, huge llama caravans of up to 500 beasts were used to provide transportation of goods coming in from the deserts of Chile and Peru and the tropical regions of Bolivia and to export highland products and, most importantly, agricultural knowledge.

By 100 BC Tiahuanaco was emerging as the most important urban centre on Lake Titicaca. The products from its raised fields fed the growing trade routes to neighbouring kingdoms and trade became the impetus for empire-building. But like most Andean cultures, the rulers of Tiahuanaco did not want to rely simply on trade to get what they needed from other regions. They wanted direct access, so they colonized the areas that produced what they needed rather than rely on uncertain trade partners.

Tiahuanaco was more successful in this respect than any predecessor. By AD 100 it ruled all of its neighbouring kingdoms at the southern end of the lake. By AD 400 it had defeated its main rivals, the Pukara people of Peru and ruled the entire lake basin.

The fall of empire

Tiahuanaco was the longest-running empire of all the Andean civilizations. But

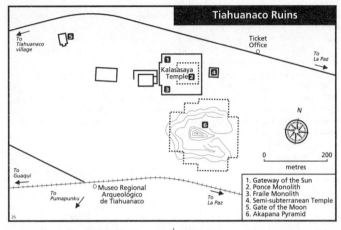

Tiahuanaco Ruins

To Tiahuanaco village

Ticket Office

To La Paz

Kalasasaya Temple **2**

1

3

4

6

5

N

0   200
metres

To Guaqui

Museo Regional Arqueológico de Tiahuanaco

To Pumapunku

To La Paz

1. Gateway of the Sun
2. Ponce Monolith
3. Fraile Monolith
4. Semi-subterranean Temple
5. Gate of the Moon
6. Akapana Pyramid

sometime after AD 1,000 it all ended. The empire collapsed, the raised fields were abandoned and no one really knows why.

In a 50-year period Tiahuanaco disappeared rapidly and completely. One of the earliest theories was that it was destroyed by a massive earthquake, but there is no geological or archaeological evidence of such a cataclysmic event. Another theory was that the empire was invaded. But again, there is no evidence to support this idea. Except for the looting by the Spanish invaders, Tiahuanaco's temples and religious icons have largely remained as its people left them.

Yet another theory holds that the Tiahuanaco empire was ended by a prolonged drought. This is perhaps the most credible proposal, given that a drought ended the great Pueblo civilization in the United States around the same time. Whatever the cause, the empire collapsed between AD 1150 and 1200 and was supplanted by smaller kingdoms made up of Tiahuanaco's former subjects. These smaller kingdoms were constantly at war with each other for more than two centuries until the armies of the newly emerged Inca empire marched down from Cusco and conquered them all in the 1430s.

Tiahuanaco today bears little relation to its former magnificence. The gold-crazed Spanish had a lot to do with this. It did not take them long to tear apart every one of its temples and palaces. But not only were the Spanish to blame. Indeed, until the middle of this century, vast quantities of stonework from the imperial city were used as building material for local churches and houses. Shamefully, too, a British construction company in the 1890s dynamited temple stoneworks and icons, turning them into gravel for the train tracks of a railroad from La Paz to Peru.

Fortunately, the ancient Tiahuanaco empire was so vast in size that many of its greatest works still survive in other sites. There are other, greater sites that have never been examined closely. One of these, at Khonko Wankané, a day's walk from the imperial city of Tiahuanaco, is believed to contain even larger temples and palaces.

THE SITE

The main structure is the **Kalasasaya Temple**, which was the holiest part of the site and the burial place of the ruling elite. The name means 'standing stones', referring to the statues found in that part. Two of them, the Ponce monolith (in the centre of inner patio) and the Fraile monolith (in the southwest corner), have been re-erected.

In the northwest corner of the Kalasasaya is the **Puerta del Sol**, or Gateway of the Sun, which was originally at Pumapunku. The split in the top probably occurred in the move. This massive carved portal was hewn from a single block of stone 3m high, nearly 4m wide and weighing 10 tons. The central motif is a figure common throughout the empire. It displays many of the typical Tiahuanaco features: puma faces looking downwards, condor faces, two left hands and the snake with a human face. This is thought to represent the principal deity of Tiahuanaco. As mentioned above, the complex markings are thought to be part of an elaborate calendar.

The Gate of the Sun

In front of the Kalasasaya is a large sunken courtyard, the **Templo Semisub-terráneo**. 1,500 years ago this was filled with the sacred monolithic icons of the kingdoms conquered by Tiahuanaco. They were positioned there for all to see that Tiahuanaco's gods were more powerful than any others. According to some theories, though, the faces on the walls depicted states of health, the temple being a house of healing.

The **Akapana**, next to the Kalasasaya, originally a pyramid, was the largest structure, but is now no more than a hill. A little way from the main site, on the other side of the railway is **Pumapunku**, a mysterious collection of massive fallen stones, some of which weigh up to 100 tonnes. The widespread confusion of fallen stones has led some to suggest a natural disaster putting a sudden end to the construction before it was finished.

Central figure from the Gate of the Sun

The entrance ticket to Tiahuanaco costs US$2.50 for foreigners, including entry to the museums. The site opens at 0900. There is a small museum at the ticket office and the Museo Regional Arqueológico de Tiahuanaco, near the Pumapunku on the other side of the railway from the main site. The latter contains a

A face in the Templo Semisubterráneo

well-illustrated explanation of the raised field system of agriculture. It also has clean toilets. Most of the best statues are in the Museo Tiahuanaco or the Museo Semisubterráneo in La Paz. Locals trade arrowheads and bronze figures (almost all fakes). You should allow 4 hours to see the ruins and the village.

THE ROAD TO TIAHUANACO

The road from El Alto is now completely paved. It passes through the village of **Laja** (Laxa), the first site of La Paz, at the junction of the roads between Potosí and Lima and Potosí and Arica. Because there was no water, La Paz was moved to its present site on the Río Choquepayu.

Laja's church was the first cathedral of the region. On its mestizo baroque façade, note the fruits and plants, the monkey (an indigenous symbol of reconstruction), the double-headed Habsburg eagle (the Spanish king, Charles I, was also Habsburg Emperor), and the faces of King Ferdinand and Queen Isabella as natives on the left bell tower. The right bell tower was built in 1903. The church has a solid silver altar, but is closed to visitors. Simple meals can be found for US$0.80 in the village. At the highest point on the road between Laja and Tiahuanaco are wide views of the Cordillera and a site where offerings to Pachamama are made.

TIAHUANACO VILLAGE

Tiahuanaco, the present-day village, has arches at the four corners of its plaza, dating from the time of independence. The church, built 1580-1612, used precolumbian masonry.

Local festivals On **21 June** the winter solstice is celebrated at the site before sunrise with colourful dances, llama sacrifices, etc. In Tiahuanaco village, on the eighth day of carnival (Sunday) is a colourful local carnival when souvenirs are for sale. Bargain hard and do not take photographs. Market day in Tiahuanaco is Sunday; do not take photos then either.

● **Accommodation & places to eat G** pp *Hostal-Restaurant El Puerto del Sol*, is the on road out of the village to La Paz, clean, friendly, meals US$0.50-1.00, the owner is very knowledgeable about the ruins. There are three restaurants along the main street serving *almuerzo* and *comida familiar*.

● **Transport** Transportes Ingavi, José María Azin y Eyzaguirre (take any Micro marked 'Cementerio'); US$0.90, 1½ hours (see map of La Paz cemetery district on page 107). They leave almost hourly, first one at 0700; the frequency may change according to demand, so the earlier you go the better. They are usually full but tickets can be bought in advance. Some buses go on from Tiahuanaco to Desaguadero and virtually all Desaguadero buses stop at Tiahuanaco. Return buses leave from the plaza in the village. The last one back is at 1730-1800. A taxi for 2 costs about US$20 for the return trip with unlimited time at site. A trip including El Valle de la Luna costs US$30-40.

Most tours from La Paz cost US$15 return; they stop at Laja and the highest point on the road before Tiahuanaco. Some tours include El Valle de la Luna.

Guidebooks in English *Tiwanaku*, by Mariano Baptista, Plata Publishing Ltd, Chur, Switzerland, or *Discovering Tiwanaku* by Hugo Boero Rojo. They are obtainable from Los Amigos del Libro (or second-hand from stalls in Avenida Ismael Montes). *Guía Especial de Arqueología Tiwanaku*, by Edgar Hernández Leonardini, is a recommended guide on the site. By far the most comprehensive book on the site is that by Alan Kolata. An excellent map and historical explanation (US$2.50) published by Quipus is available at the site, or at La Paz bookshops, or at their offices (see La Paz **Maps**, page 104). Hiring a good guide at the site costs US$10.

TREKKING NEAR LA PAZ

● **Maps** Walter Guzmán *Los Caminos de los Incas* covers all four treks described at a scale of about 1:166,666 as does Liam O'Brien at 1:135,000 in his *A New Map of the Cordillera Real*. IGM sheets are listed with each trek.

● **Guidebooks** *Trekking in Bolivia* by Yossi Brain (The Mountaineers 1997), *Backpacking* *and Trekking in Peru and Bolivia* by Hilary Bradt (Bradt 1995).

The so-called 'Inca' trails (Takesi, Choro, Reconquistada and Yunga Cruz) link the Altiplano with the Yungas and each have excellent sections of stonework that might or might not have been built by the Incas. Route finding on the Takesi and Choro trails is easy and only marginally more difficult on the Yunga Cruz. La Reconquistada trek is unusual in that it passes through a 200m abandoned mining tunnel (take a torch). The differences in weather, temperature, and vegetation from the start to the finish of all these treks are extreme, taking you from the high Andes to the sub-tropics; so be prepared.

If you need a trekking (or climbing) partner, put a notice up in the *Hostal Austria*, *Hotel Torino* and/or *Club Andino*. These are also the best places to advertise buying or selling kit.

TAKESI TRAIL

Mina San Francisco to Yanacachi; 1-3 days.

Maps IGM Chojlla 6044 IV (and if you want the section from Ventilla to Mina San Francisco, Palca 6044 III).

Due to accessibility, beauty, and shortness (a little over 30 km), the Takesi trail is extremely popular with gringos and Bolivians. As a result there is a lot of litter along the trail (by Bolivian standards). The trail is especially popular with Bolivians on holiday weekends. At Easter up to 2,000 people have been known to do the trek.

● **Transport** To **Ventilla**: there are regular buses to Ventilla and Palca leaving from outside the *Comedor Popular* in Calle Max Paredes above the junction with Calle Rodríguez at 0530 every day, cost US$1. Alternatively, get any bus going to Bolsa Negra, Tres Ríos, or Pariguaya (see Yunga Cruz below). Or get a micro or minibus to Chasquipampa or Ovejuyo and try hitching a lift with anything heading out of La Paz. If there isn't any transport, haggle with drivers of empty minibuses in Ovejuyo; you should be able to get one to go to Ventilla for about US$10. To **Mina San Francisco**: there is

no public or regular transport, it is necessary to hire a jeep from La Paz for US$60, less than 2 hours.

The trek

From Ventilla (3,200m) head up the valley taking the left hand road just outside the village. After 1½ hours following the road gently uphill on the left hand side of the valley you will reach the traditional village of **Choquekhota** where it is necessary to ford the ankle-deep Río Quela Jahuira. Above Choquekhota on the right hand side of the road is a cemetery. Higher up a track goes off right. Do not follow it unless you want to get really close to Mururata.

Shortly after a river crossing 3 hours out of Ventilla you reach a falling down wall with a map of the trail painted on it. The road continues left to **Mina San Francisco** and the start of the Reconquistada trail. Do not follow it. Follow the broad path on the right for 1 hour over excellent prehispanic paving up to the large *apacheta* at the 4,630m pass.

The excellent stonework continues below the *apacheta* down to **Estancia Takesi** which is reached in another hour. Camping is possible above Estancia Takesi and also near the small lakes just below the pass.

Below Estancia Takesi the vegetation becomes ever-more dense and the path rises right and above the Río Takesi (fill water bottles before leaving the river) to reach in 2 hours the rather incongruous 'CGI' café (where the path up from **Estancia Chima** joins the Takesi trail) and 'Don Pepe's' cafe in the village of **Kakapi** in another 30 minutes where it is possible to camp. You may also be able to stay in the schoolhouse. Ask for Señor Genaro Mamani, a very helpful local expert and guide who has a basic but pleasant *refugio*.

Better camping is found 15 minutes below Kakapi after crossing the Río Quimsa Chata where the Alto Takesi rejoins the Takesi trail. While half the built bridge has long since been washed away,

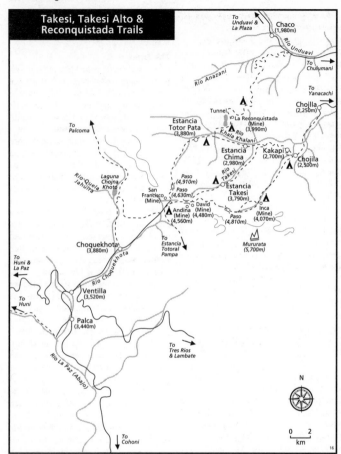

Takesi, Takesi Alto & Reconquistada Trails

there is a dodgy-looking and flexible-feeling three log bridge over the river. If you don't like the look of that it is quite easy to boulder hop slightly higher up.

From here it is uphill for 20 minutes along a clear cut and paved path to another cafe in what is **Chojila**. After 40 minutes of descent over mainly paved path you reach a bridge back over the Río Takesi. Cross the bridge and follow the path right to reach the start of an aqueduct in 40 minutes. There are a

couple of clearings between the path and the river where it is possible to camp if you don't feel like finishing the trek in the dark. When you feel concrete under foot and can see telephone wires overhead you are close to the rather unpleasant mining village of **Chojlla**, where you can sleep at the schoolhouse for US$0.80, or the rather grandly named but basic *Sheraton Inn* for US$1. A colectivo leaves Chojlla for La Paz daily at 0600/0700 and 1200; US$2.

At the point where the aqueduct ends, follow the road around and at the junction head up and left and go through some mine workings. Stick with the road as it rises up to the right of Chojlla and then starts the descent to **Yanacachi** which is reached in 2 hours from the end of the aqueduct. Shortly before Yanacachi there is a 4m high gate across the road to control access to the mining settlement of Chojlla. The gate keeper often asks tourists to register. Do not pay anything for this privilege. At night the gate is locked and it is necessary to wake up the gatekeeper (who is armed with a rifle) and ask him politely to open the gate.

There are a number of hotels and *alojamientos* in Yanacachi around the end of the trail at the top of the village. The centre and lower parts of the village are completely colonial and very attractive. There are a number of shops, a Cotel telephone office, and some places to eat which are sometimes open and sometimes have food.

From Yanacachi there are regular minibuses to La Paz at 0600 but they are often full. Buy your ticket the day before departure; US$2.85, 4 hours. It is possible to continue down to the Chulumani road in 1 hour from Yanacachi and hitch a lift. To get to the Chulumani road do not follow the road out of Yanacachi at the top of the village but walk down to the plaza. With your back to the Cotel office, leave the plaza by the downhill left hand cobbled street. A track wide enough for vehicles zigzags down but takes forever. There is a direct path which cuts off the zigzags, repeatedly crossing the track which will get you down from Yanacachi to the Chulumani road in under 1 hour passing through citrus orchards. Head up and left to go to La Paz. Alternatively, jump a bus or truck going down and right to Chulumani (see **Yungas** section page 167).

TAKESI ALTO

This trail is higher and harder than the Takesi – it takes 2-3 days – but is rarely done so it is litter-free and you can enjoy complete solitude. (For maps and transport, see Takesi above).

The trek

Follow the Takesi route until 35 minutes below the *apacheta* when you reach the abandoned camp of **Mina David**. At Mina David do not follow the good paving down but continue along the broad but unpaved path that starts climbing right.

After 1 hour there is a lake and camping possibilities among more derelict miners' houses.

Follow the path up to the *apacheta* in 1¾ hours. Cross the valley to reach the right hand side and follow the path down to the abandoned mining camp of **Mina Inca**, which takes 1½ hours. Camping is possible or continue down the valley for another 35 minutes to reach some more derelict houses and your first views of Chojlla, more than 1,700m below.

Unfortunately, the path is missing for the next section. The páramo grass has retaken what is its own since the mine was abandoned. It is necessary to descend steeply on the left hand side of the valley and then work a way back to the stream. The effort is compensated for by a beautiful waterfall from where it is basically flat and the path magically reappears at the other side of the flat section to the right of the stream. To reach this path can take up to 2 hours depending on the line you follow and your grass-descending abilities.

The difficulty of path-following then varies from easy to virtually impossible when it goes through a series of abandoned terraces but stay on the right hand side of the valley, gradually moving farther and farther away from the stream. After 2 hours you arrive at some houses to the side of a group of mature trees. Relax – path finding is straightforward from now on and you can in fact see the next section below.

Follow the path right, cross the pipe-fed stream to arrive at a fence across the path designed to stop animals attempting the airy descent on the other side. Climb over the fence and do not slip off the path. About 25 minutes below the houses you arrive at an ideal camping spot near the stream. At this point the Alto Takesi finishes, rejoining the Takesi trail (see above).

LA RECONQUISTADA

Mina San Francisco to El Castillo; 2-3 days. For maps and transport to the start see Takesi above. The path from Mina San Francisco to Totor Pata was rebuilt in 1995 with money from Conservation International showing what is possible with regards to path regeneration in Bolivia.

The trek

The first 3 hours from Ventilla are the same as for the Takesi trail above. When you reach the disintegrating plastered wall with map stay on the road and follow it to its end 30 minutes later among abandoned mining buildings.

The newly rebuilt path continues from where the road stops. After 1 hour there is a lake where it is possible to camp and where it is advisable to fill water bottles. It takes another 40 minutes to reach the *apacheta*.

Camping is possible from 20 minutes below the *apacheta* and it takes another hour to reach the bridge at **Totor Pata** and the end of the rebuilt path. Stay close to the stream on its right hand side to reach a pampa with good camping at the far end 45 minutes from the village.

From the end of the pampa, pick up the increasingly clear path to descend towards the Río Khala Khalani. As you descend, check out the path rising up in zigzags on the other side of the valley. While it looks very clear it is difficult to find the start so remember where it is.

After 45 minutes of descent there is a wood and mud bridge. Cross it and then leave the path and make your way down left to the river. It is possible to find the remains of the bridge and boulder hop to the other side. However, early in the season or after a heavy rain crossing the Río

Khala Khalani can be a serious business involving fast flowing waist-deep water.

With the remains of the bridge behind you, head up right aiming roughly northwest to meet up with the path which is very unclear near the river but becomes clearer and clearer the higher you get, being cut and paved.

From the bridge remains it is 1¾ hours to reach an *apacheta* and then some deserted mine buildings on the side of Laguna Khellhuani where camping is possible with great views of Mururata. Follow the path along the right hand side of the lake to reach the abandoned **Mina La Reconquistada** buildings in 45 minutes. The area is perfectly flat for camping but there is very little, if any, water.

It takes 20 minutes to head directly up from the mine on a zigzag path that takes you to the tunnel entrance. The tunnel is 200m long but it is not possible to see the other end because of bends and a 15m descent. Immediately before the descent there is a shaft on the left dropping steeply down. The descent is very roughly stepped but extreme caution should be excercised while descending. From the bottom of the descent you can see the light at the end of the tunnel.

It is possible but extremely dangerous to avoid the tunnel by going around the mountain, but this cannot be recommended as it involves scrambling followed by a very narrow path along a very steep hillside with a very large drop and then scrambling up steep loose scree. The tunnel is the safer, and by far the quicker, option.

From the tunnel exit, follow the broad road to reach an excellent wide path skirting around the valley head before arriving at a narrow pass, *apacheta*, and deserted mining buildings in 1¼ hours.

The descent is easy but long and takes you from the mountains at 4,080m to the heart of the Yungas at 1,950m. From scrubby high altitude grass, the vegetation rapidly increases to dense sub-tropical forest. After 35 minutes you can see the Chulumani-La Paz road way down to the right, 5 minutes later you can see the Coroico-La Paz road way off to the left at about the same height. It is possible to camp here, near a lake. Another 15 minutes later on is another lake with the last camping and water possibilities.

From the lake it is 3 hours down to the Sud Yungas road. The path becomes narrow as the vegetation has grown back. You can feel below your feet that the road is level and gravel-covered but you are still pushing your way through vegetation. There is water only 1½ hours below the last lake and 30 minutes below that from small streams flowing across the path.

Come out on the road and flag down anything going up and left towards La Paz, which is reached in about 3 hours, or flag down anything going down and right if you want to visit Chulumani which is reached in 2 hours (see page 167). While the La Paz-Chulumani road is statistically a lot safer than the La Paz-Coroico road, it is just as impressive and drivers avoid driving it at night. There is little transport in the afternoons and none once it gets dark.

If you can't get a lift or just want to relax, walk up to the striking stone-towered *El Castillo* hotel in the village of Chaco. The distinctive, stone, round-towered building was built by prisoners of the 1932-35 Chaco War with Paraguay and is now a relaxing hotel with its own swimming pool, river, and waterfall (see also page 167).

CHORO TRAIL

La Cumbre to Coroico; 3-4 days. Prehispanic paving and a spectacuar but savage descent plus easy route finding – once you've found the start – make the Choro trail a popular choice for trekkers.

● **Maps** IGM Milluni 5945 II and Unduavi 6045 III.

● **Transport** To La Cumbre: take a bus or *camión* from Villa Fátima in La Paz, US$1. It takes less than 1 hour to climb the 22 km, but make sure the driver knows you want to get off at La

Cumbre. Alternatively, get a radio taxi from central La Paz for about US$12 or hire a jeep for US$40. (For details of transport see under Corioco **Buses** page 174).

The trek

Immediately before the paved Yungas road drops down from **La Cumbre** there is a falling down plastered brick wall on the left which marks the start of the trail. However, there is nothing to help get you across the 3 km of featureless moonscape to the **Apacheta Chucura** (1 hour) where the trail starts properly.

Follow the jeep track. When you reach a lake, look up for a path that rises up right to the *apacheta*. Cloud and bad weather are normal at the 4,660m La Cumbre. Follow the left hand of the statue of Christ, take a map and compass to get you to the start of the trail which is then well (and pointlessly) marked with lots of paint splashed around.

The descent is spectacular following a well-built prehispanic road down the left hand side of the valley. The gradient slackens off once you hit **Samaña Pampa**, 4 km farther on and 1,300m farther down. It takes 4 hours to get to **Achura** (also known as Chucura) and then another 1¼ hours to get to **Challapampa** (also known as Achapalla Pampa) where it is possible to camp, though the locals will ask for money or food. Doña Juana lets rooms, **G**. It is possible to camp in Achura but this would just extend what is a long second day. There is little to buy in Achura and nothing in Challapampa.

The sub-tropical vegetation begins and in 2 hours and 8 km below Challapampa you will reach the Choro bridge. Fill your water bottles as the next 2 hours and 7 km are dry until you cross the Río Jacu-Manini which is a nice spot for lunch with constricted camping space. It is another dry 3 hours to **Sandillani** where it is possible to camp in the carefully-tended garden of Tamiji Hanamura, a Japanese immigrant who has lived in Bolivia for many years. He keeps a book with the names of every passing traveller and

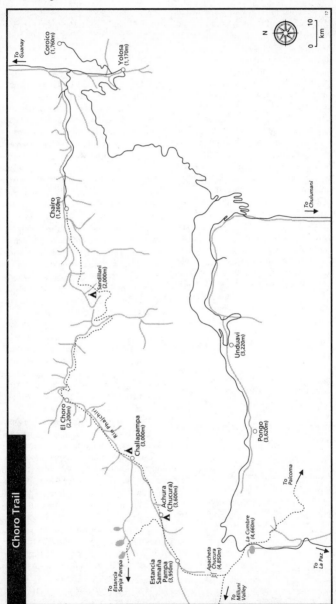

Choro Trail

he likes to see postcards and pictures from other countries. Another family in the village sells food and drinks.

From Sandillani there is good pre-his-panic paving down to Villa Esmeralda and then continue for 2 hours to **Chairo**, where there are limited supplies for sale, such as bread and tinned food. If you've got the money, stay at the five star *Hotel Río Selva*. There is also cheaper accom-modation, or sleep under the eaves of the schoolhouse. The friendly Paredes de la Tienda family will provide food.

From Chairo it is 17 km, 4 hours, to Yolosa; 'an awful walk'. The trudge along the road is alleviated by the views of orange, grapefruit, lemon, banana, and coffee plantations, but it is hot. Early in the season the river crossing can be tricky; take care. Allegedly, there is a truck at 0600, but you are unlikely to get there on time. A truck will run if there are enough people willing to pay US$2.25 each, which makes it one of the most expensive truck trips in Bolivia given the distance, but it is well worth it. From Yolosa it is 8 km uphill to Coroico with regular trans-port for US$0.60 per person.

YUNGA CRUZ

Lambate or Chuñavi to Chulumani; 3-7 days of hard walking, depending on your level of fitness. This is the best but hardest of the three so-called 'Inca' trails and therefore less popular. A major advantage of this is that there is less litter and begging than on the other treks and more wildlife, such as condors, hawks, and humming-birds. Water is a major consideration. Once you get below Cerro Khala Ciudad fill water bottles where you can. Each per-son should have containers to carry at least 2 litres each and preferably more.

● **Maps** IGM Lambate 6044 II and Chulumani 6044 1.

● **Transport** Take the bus going to Pariguaya at 0900, Monday-Saturday, from the corner of Calle General Luis Lara and Venacio Burgoa, San Pedro, US$2, 6 hours to Chuñavi, US$2.25; 6¼ hours to Lambate which is 3 km farther on.

Buses to Tres Ríos and Bolsa Negra also leave at the same time but stop well before Chuñavi or Lambate. It is not possible to buy tickets in advance as there is no ticket office, so send someone up at 0700-0800 on the day to ensure a ticket. The bus stops at 1000 for an hour in the outskirts of La Paz for lunch.

The trek

From Chuñavi: follow the path left (east) from the La Paz road contouring gently up. You pass some small lakes after 50 minutes and reach the deserted shell of a building after another 30 minutes. Camp-ing is possible down to the right. Continue staying on the left hand side of the ridge to reach a stream and camping after 1½ hours below **Cerro Khala Ciudad** (liter-ally, 'Stone City Mountain' – you will see why). A good paved stone path continues along and up. After 50 minutes you reach a junction where the path from Quircoma comes up from the right to join the Chuñavi path. Camping is possible down to the right. There is also accommodation in Chuñavi at the school or in the garden, but ask for permission.

From Lambate: from the village, drop down almost 1,000m to the Río Kheluluni and follow the path alongside the right hand side of the river. The river changes its name to Río Chunga Mayu and just before the confluence with the Río Colani, cross the Río Chunga Mayu, then the Río Colani and start the climb to **Quircoma**. In Quir-coma, start the unrelenting 5-hour climb towards Cerro Khala Ciudad staying at first to the left of the Río Kasiri and then con-touring right to join it. Camp near Laguna Kasiri and then go around it to the right and up and over a 4,200m pass to the right (east) of the mountain and descend to join the path from Chuñavi. This option nor-mally takes 2 days from Lambate, involving a hot and sweaty haul up from the Río Chunga Mayu.

From the junction, continue north to Cerro Cuchillatuca and then onto Cerro Yunga Cruz in 1½ hours, where there is water and it is possible to camp. The next water and camping is possible in

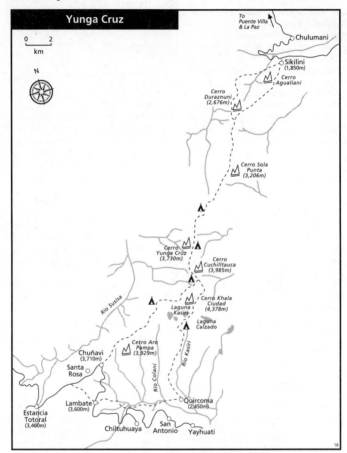

Yunga Cruz

0   2
km

N

To
Puente Villa
& La Paz

Chulumani

Sikilini
(1,850m)

Cerro
Agualiani

Cerro
Duraznuni
(2,676m)

Cerro Sola
Punta
(3,206m)

Cerro
Yunga Cruz
(3,730m)

Cerro
Cuchilltauca
(3,985m)

Cerro Khala
Ciudad
(4,378m)

Laguna
Kasiri

Laguna
Calzado

Río Susisa

Cerro Aro
Pampa
(3,929m)

Río Kasiri

Chuñavi

Santa
Rosa

Río Colani

Quircoma
(2,450m)

Lambate
(3,600m)

Estancia
Totoral
(3,460m)

Chiltuhuaya

San
Antonio

Yayhuati

18

30 minutes just before the start of the descent to the Yungas.

The path deteriorates as it goes down before going left around a ridge and dropping, improving before making two stream crossings, the first in cloud forest, the second in the open, in 15 minutes. The quality of the path then deteriorates again. There are three streams (the last water) within the next 30 minutes with camping possible just before the third stream. Camp or fill up at least 2 litres as there is no more water for a very long time. There are a number of clearances on the way down, but no place for camping with water until you reach **Chulumani**.

The whole way down from this point is tiring. The vegetation increases often obstructing the way, forcing you to duck under bamboo and other plants which form tunnels. This is tremendous fun with a full rucksack. A machete is useful, especially early in the season when not many other people have passed through.

After 1½ hours there is a fork in dense vegetation. Take the right fork and come out into the open on the side of a ridge 5 minutes later. After another 30 minutes you come to what was a clearing where Bolivians regularly camp and leave their litter.

At the end of the clearing the trail goes to the right of Cerro Duraznuni in front. Go up and then drop down. From the shoulder of Cerro Duraznuni descend on the other side to reach a road which is followed into the village of **Sikilini**. Just before a tennis court on the right, there is a good path leading off to the left to a viewpoint giving a good view to the left of Huancane. Follow the path down which soon turns into a track which leads down to Chulumani in 1¾ hours.

From Chulumani there are buses and minibuses to La Paz every couple of hours through the mornings, US$2.50, 4-5 hours. (For further details on Chulumani see page 118).

Lake Titicaca

N O VISIT to Bolivia would be complete without witnessing the sapphire-blue expanse of mystical Lake Titicaca. This gigantic inland sea covers 8,000 square kilometres and is the highest navigable lake in the world, at 3,856m above sea level. It straddles Bolivia and Peru and lies only a few hours from La Paz. With the towering peaks of the Cordillera Real as a backdrop, you can wander along its shores, passing through traditional villages where Spanish is a second language and where the ancient myths and beliefs still hold true.

Lake Titicaca is actually two lakes joined by the Straits of Tiquina. The larger, northern lake – Lago Mayor, or Chucuito – contains the Islas del Sol and de la Luna at its southern end. The smaller lake – Lago Menor, or Huiñamarca – has several small islands. The waters are a beautiful blue, reflecting the hills and the distant cordillera in the shallows of Huiñamarca, mirroring the sky in the rarified air and changing colour when it is cloudy or raining.

Periodically the water level rises, inundating low-lying land, but its size is much reduced from prehispanic times. The trout fished in the lake and served in many restaurants is not native, but delicious nevertheless. The local catch is *pejerrey* and *karachi*. Also beginning to be farmed are the Lake's giant frogs, whose legs are served, fried, with chips, in several places.

The traditional totora-reed boats are still around but just for the tourists. A reed boat takes 3 days to build and last

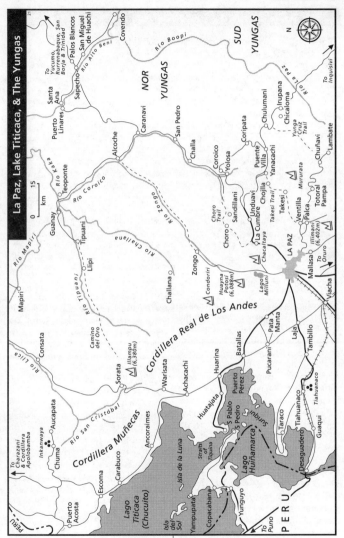

La Paz, Lake Titicaca, & The Yungas

7-8 months, while a wooden boat takes longer to build but lasts 7-8 years. If someone falls into the lake, like a fisherman, it is traditional not to rescue them, but to let them drown as an offering to the Earth Goddess Pachamama. Storms do blow up on the lake, which is the size of a sea, so Pachamama is given offerings every year, averaging four fishermen normally. But don't let that put you off taking a trip on the lake. It really is a must if you're in the area. Boat services are given below.

The sacred lake

Lake Titicaca has played a dominant role in Andean beliefs for over 2 millenia. This, the highest navigable body of water in the world, is the most sacred lake in the Andes.

Near Titicaca arose the population and ceremonial centre of Tiahuanaco, capital of one of the most important civilizations of South America. Tiahuanaco ceremonial sites were built along its shores, indicating that the lake was considered sacred at least 2,000 years ago.

At the time of the Spanish conquest, one of the most important religious sites of the Inca empire was located on the Isla del Sol. From its profound, icy depths emerged the Inca creator deity, Viracocha. Legend has it that the sun god had his children, Manco Capac and his sister, Mama Ocllo, spring from the lake's azure waters to found Cusco and the Inca dynasty. Legends about the lake abound. Among them are several which describe underwater cities, roads and treasures.

Titicaca was perceived by its ancient cultures to be an island sea connected to the ocean, mother of all waters. Today, people still believe that the lake is involved in bringing rain and that, closely associated with mountain deities, it distributes the water sent by them. The people who utilize the lake's resources still make offerings to her, to ensure sufficient totora reeds for the boats, for successful fishing, for safe passage across its waters and for a mild climate.

LA PAZ TO COPACABANA

A paved road runs northwest from La Paz across the Altiplano for 114 km to the village of San Pablo on the eastern shore of the **Straits of Tiquina**. It then continues from San Pedro, on the opposite side of the straits, for a further 44 km to Copacabana, a convenient and worthwhile stopping-off point on the way to or from Peru. The road to Copacabana, though, is not without its own interesting diversions. If you have the time, it's worth breaking the journey somewhere along the way.

PUERTO PEREZ

Puerto Pérez is the closest point to La Paz on Lake Titicaca; only 72 km and less than 1 hour by car. The views of the lake and mountains from Puerto Pérez are superb and the sunsets are spectacular, too. The massive Mount Illampu provides a backdrop, seeming very close in the thin Altiplano air. Because of the winds off the lake, the town enjoys almost permanent sunshine. It is very hot during the day, but bitterly cold at night.

The port was the original harbour for La Paz, founded in the nineteenth century by British navigators as a harbour for the first steam boat on the Lake. The vessel was assembled piece-by-piece in Puno.

The town has appeared to benefit from the influx of tourists who come to the *Hotel Las Balsas* (see below). The large plaza is fronted by brightly-painted houses and local people work on new water projects, building wells to irrigate what was once dry, ungiving soil.

Colourful fiestas are held at New Year, Carnival (Monday and Tuesday before Ash Wednesday), 3 May and 16 July.

● **Accommodation & places to eat A3** *Hotel Las Balsas*, owned and operated by Turismo Balsa (see La Paz **Travel Agents**), T (02) 357817, F 391310, T/F 813226, in a beautiful lakeside setting with views of the Cordillera, all rooms have a balcony overlooking the lake, it's advertised as a five-star, they are willing to negotiate out of season; fitness facilities include massage, jacuzzi, sauna and racket ball and a swimming pool is currently under construction (mid-1997); the restaurant is expensive, but the fixed price lunch or dinner is good value at US$12, they use a very good camembert cheese

Totora reed boat on Lake Titicaca

produced locally by a German priest. Nearby on the Plaza is **D** *Hostería Las Islas*, also owned by *Hotel Las Balsas'* Jacques Valletón and his wife Hortensia, shared bath, hot water, comfortable heated rooms, *Blue Note* jazz bar is next door, also seminar rooms and there are plans to open a small cinema showing art-house movies. Turismo Balsa operate boat trips to Suriqui and Kalahuta as well as services to Puno and Cusco. There are some small restaurants in town which serve trout.

● **Buses** There is a regular minibus service from La Paz Cementerio district (see La Paz **buses**, page 107); US$0.75. There is no public transport from Batallas to Puerto Pérez.

The road to Puerto Pérez turns off the main La Paz-Copacabana road at **Batallas**, a typical Altiplano market town so named because of the final battles between the Spanish commanders Almagro and Pizarro. The road to Puerto Pérez is a fascinating insight into life on the Altiplano and makes a pleasant, if lengthy, walk. Tiny adobe houses, some with tin roofs, dot the parched brown plain.

Women and children tend cattle, sheep and pigs and the banks of streams are a blaze of colour with clothes spread out to dry. The people you meet on the road going about their daily business are extremely friendly and courteous.

HUARINA AND HUATAJATA

At **Huarina**, 42 km before the Straits of Tiquina, a road turns off to Achacachi, Sorata and the road along the eastern shore of Titicaca to Puerto Acosta (see page 107). The next town is **Huatajata**, which is home to the *Yacht Club Boliviano*. Its restaurant is open to non-members, but is open Saturday and Sunday for lunch only; sailing is for members only. Also here is Crillon Tours' International Hydroharbour and *Inca Utama Hotel* (see below).

Beyond Huatajata is **Chúa**, where there is fishing, sailing and Transturin's catamaran dock (see below). The public telephone office, Cotel, is on the plaza just off the main road.

● **Accommodation & places to eat** In Huatajata: next to Crillón's *Inca Utama*, is *Restaurant Huatajata Utama*, which is highly recommended; then there's *Inti Raymi*, which offers boat trips, and there are several others. The restaurants are of varying standard. Most are lively at weekends and in the high season. On the waterfront is **F** per person *Inti Karka*, T 813212, a basic, three-storey hotel run by Máximo Catari, breakfast is extra, with shower, water is unreliable, some rooms have a lake view, ask for extra blankets, the restaurant is on the main road with a full menu, open 7 days, average prices, good fish. **Between Huatajata and Huarina** (at Km 65 from La Paz): **B** *Hotel Titicaca*, T (02) 374877, F 391225, with beautiful views of the lake, also sauna, pool and a good restaurant, it's very quiet during the week; their address in La Paz is Potosí y Ayacucho 1220, second floor. **About 2 km before Chúa** is a turning to the right to *La Posada del Inca*, a restaurant in a beautiful colonial *hacienda* which is open Saturday, Sunday and holidays for lunch only, good trout, average prices.

● **Transport** La Paz-Huatajata/Tiquina, US$0.85, Transportes Titikaka, daily from 0400, returning between 0700 and 1800 (see La Paz **buses**, page 107).

TOURS ON LAKE TITICACA

Crillon Tours (address under La Paz **Travel Agents**, page 104), run a hydrofoil service on Lake Titicaca with excellent bilingual guides. Crillon's tours stop at the Andean Roots cultural complex at the **A1** *Inca Utama Hotel*, reservations through Crillon Tours, T (02) 374566/ 350363; the sixty rooms in this five-star hotel are comfortable, with heating, electric blankets and good service; there is a bar, and the restaurant serves good food. Part of the complex is the Bolivian History Museum which includes a 20-minute recorded commentary in all languages; a 15-minute video precedes the evening visit to the fascinating *Kallawaya* museum, where you can have your fortune told by a *Kallawaya* using coca leaves. The *Inca Utama* also has a health spa based on natural remedies. Also at *Inca Utama* is an observatory (*Alajpacha*) with retractable thatched roof for viewing the night sky, a floating restaurant and bar on the lake (*La Choza Náutica*), a new colonial-style tower with fifteen de-luxe suites, panoramic elevator and two conference rooms. Health,

astronomical, mystic and ecological programmes are offered. The hydrofoil trips include visits to the Andean Roots complex, Copacabana, Isla del Sol and Isla de la Luna, the Straits of Tiquina and past totora reed fishing boats. You can stay on Isla del Sol at *La Posada del Inca* (see below). Trips can be arranged to/from Cusco and Machu Picchu: hydrofoil and train one way and flight the other. Other combinations of hydrofoil and land-based excursions can be arranged (also jungle and adventure tours). The cost is US$173 from La Paz to Puno and US$145 for a day excursion from La Paz, which is fascinating, not least for the magnificent views of the Cordillera on a clear day. All facilities and modes of transport are connected by radio.

Transturin (see also La Paz **Travel Agents**, page 104) run catamarans on Lake Titicaca, either for sightseeing or on the La Paz-Puno route. La Paz-Copacabana costs US$129; overnight at *Hotel Titicaca* and tour costs US$168. From their dock at Chúa, 3-hour trips go to Copacabana, with a bar, video, sun deck and music on board. One-night tours to

A swimming feline

The name Titicaca derives from the word *titi*, an Aymara mountain cat and the Quechua word *caca* meaning rock. The rock refers to the Sacred Rock at Chincana on the Isla del Sol which was worshipped by the pre-Incan people on the island. The mountain cat inhabited the shores of the lake and is said to have visited the Isla del Sol occasionally. Presumably this cat was able to swim, as there is no record of tourist boats leaving Copacabana in precolumbian times.

The link between the rock and the cat comes from the legend that the ancient indigenous people saw the eyes of a mountain cat gleaming in the Sacred Rock and so named it *Titicaca*, or Rock of the Mountain Cat.

The *titi* has characteristics – such as its swimming ability and the brilliance of its eyes – that conceptually link it with a mythological flying feline called *ccoa*. The role of the *ccoa* was (and in some parts still is) important throughout the Andes. It is believed to have thrown lightning from its eyes, urinated rain (hence the expression), spit hail and roared thunder. It was generally associated with the gods that controlled the weather.

Among the Quechua people today the *ccoa* is believed to be one of the mountain god's servants and lives in the mountains. It is closely involved in the daily life of the Quechuas and is considered the most feared of the spirits as it uses lightning and hail.

Copacabana are also available. The cata-marans are slower than the hydrofoils of Crillon so there is more room and time for on-board entertainment. Transturin runs through services to Puno without a change of bus, and without many of the usual formalities at the border. Transturin has offices in Puno, Jirón Libertad, T (054) 352771/351316, and Cusco, Avenida Portal de Panes 109, oficina 1, T (084) 222332.

ISLANDS OF LAKE HUIÑAMARCA

On **Suriqui**, 1½ hours from Huatajata, you can visit the museum/craft shops of the Limachi brothers – who now live at the *Inca Utama* cultural complex – and Paulino Esteban, who helped in the construction, out of totora reeds, of Thor Hey-erdahl's *Ra II*, which sailed from Morocco to Barbados in 1970. Heyerdahl's *Tigris* reed boat, and the balloon gondola for the Nasca flight experiment in Peru (see *Peru Handbook* or *South Amercican Handbook*), were also constructed by the craftsmen of Suriqui. Reed boats are still made on Suri-qui, probably the last place where the art survives. On **Kalahuta** there are *chullpas* (burial towers), old buildings and the un-inhabited town of Kewaya. On **Pariti** there is Inca terracing and very good examples of weaving.

● **Boat trips** Máximo Catari (see above) arranges boats to the islands in Lago Huiñamarca: Pariti, Kalahuta and Suriqui. Prices are as follows: to Suriqui US$22 for four-five people; to all three islands US$40; 1 hour boat trip US$7.50; sailing boat for three US$16 for a day. The boat trips are recommended. Paulino Esteban (see above) is also recommended; contact through Servitur, PO Box 8045, La Paz, T (02) 340060, F 391373. Boats can also be hired from San Pablo or San Pedro (see below) for trips to Suriqui; they cost US$3 per person in a group.

From Chúa the main road reaches the east side of the Straits at **San Pablo**, which has a clean restaurant in a blue building, with good toilets. On the west side of the Straits is **San Pedro**, the main Bolivian naval base, from where a paved road goes to Copacabana. Vehicles are transported

across on barges, US$4. Passengers on buses to or from Copacabana get off here and pay US$0.20 to ride in a launch to the other side where you rejoin the bus which has been taken across by pontoon. Pass-ports are checked. Expect delays during rough weather, when it can get very cold.

COPACABANA

158 km from La Paz is this attractive little town with red-tiled roofs, nestled between two hills on the shores on Lake Titicaca. Copacabana, capital of the province of Manco Kapac, is a popular stopping-off point on the way to or from Peru and definitely worth a brief visit.

Its main plaza is dominated by the impressive and heavily restored Moorish-style cathedral. Every Sunday in front of the cathedral a line of cars, trucks, buses and minibuses, all decorated with gar-lands of flowers, waits to be blessed, as a spiritual form of accident insurance.

NB Copacabana's water supply can be in-termittent. Beware of sunburn especially on the lake, even when it does not feel hot. **NB also** New arrivals may also be pressur-ized into paying for 'entry' to the town; the fee is in fact for the sanctuary.

Places of interest

The cathedral was built between 1610 and 1620 to accommodate the huge numbers of pilgrims who flocked to the town when miracles began happening in the Sanctuary

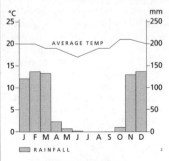

Climate: Cochabamba

Copacabana Cathedral

of Copacabana after the presentation of a black wooden statue of the Virgin Mary, carved in the late 1570s by Francisco Yupanqui, grandson of the Inca Tupac Yupanqui. The Virgin is known both as the Dark Virgin of the Lake, or the *Virgen de la Candelaria*, the patron saint of Bolivia. It is encased in glass and never moved from the cathedral (except during the festival, see below) as the townsfolk believe that its disturbance would cause a devastating flood from Lake Titicaca.

Architecturally speaking, the cathedral is notable for its spacious atrium with four small chapels. The main chapel has one of the finest gilt altars in Bolivia. The basilica is clean and white, with coloured tiles decorating the exterior arches, cupolas and chapels. An *hospicio* (serving now as an almshouse) with two arcaded patios is worth a visit; ask permission before entering. There are 17th and 18th century paintings and statues in the sanctuary. Entrance is by the side of the Basilica opposite the Entel office; US$0.60, open Monday-Friday, 1100-1200, 1400-1800, Saturday and Sunday, 0800-1200, 1400-1800, only groups of eight or more can visit.

On the main plaza, on the corner of Ballivián, is the **Museum of Miniatures**. Opposite the cemetery, on the road to La Paz, is the Intinkalla or **Asiento del Inca**.

Excursions

A pleasant, if tiring, walk is up a long series of steps to the top of **Cerro Calvario**, the headland which overlooks the town and port. On Sundays you can buy little miniature items (cars, suitcases, money etc) and have them blessed.

On **Cerro Sancollani**, the hill behind the town overlooking the lake, is the **Horca del Inca**, two pillars of rock with another laid across them. It is probably a sun clock rather than a gallows, and is now covered in graffiti. The hill is roughly southeast of the Basilica. With the church entrance behind you, turn right up Calle Murillo towards the green house at the end of the street. At the green house turn right and immediately left up a rocky hill. There is a path marked by white stones. Boys will offer to guide you, but fix a price in advance if you want their help. Above the Horca, on the other side of the ridge, is the **Flecha del Inca**, an arrow-shaped hole in a rock.

A few kilometres to the north is **Cusijata** with its **El Baño del Inca**. There is also a small archaeological museum, entrance US$0.60. To get there, follow Calle Junín out of town for 1½ km, then head for a large group of eucalyptus trees on a hillside 500m away.

Local festivals

Festivals in Copacabana are frequent and frantic affairs and to be heartily recommended, especially to those who like drinking, dancing and eating. See also **Festivals**, page 55.

24 January, *Alacitas*, held on Cerro Calvario and Plaza Kolquepata, similar to La Paz when miniature houses, cars etc are sold and blessed. **1-3 February**, *Virgen de la Candelaria*, a massive procession of the Dark Virgen takes place, this is a real

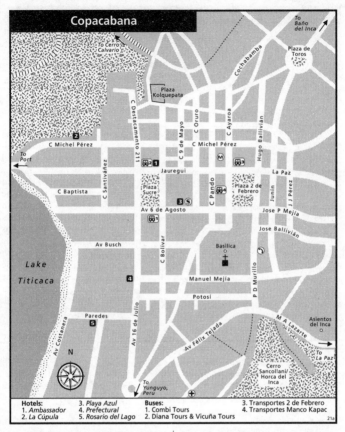

Copacabana

To Baño
del Inca

Plaza de
Toros

To Cerro
Calvario

Plaza
Kolquepata

C Destacamento 211

C Michel Pérez

C 9 de Mayo

C Oruro

C Ayaroa

Hugo Balliván

To
Port

C Michel Pérez

Jauregui

La Paz

C Santiváñez

C Baptista

Plaza
Sucre

C Pando

Plaza 2 de
Febrero

Junin

J J Pérez

Av 6 de Agosto

Jose P Mejia

Jose Balliván

Av Busch

C Bolivar

Basilica

Lake
Titicaca

Manuel Mejia

P D Murillo

Potosí

Av Costanera

Paredes

Av 16 de Julio

Av Félix Tejada

M A Lazarte

Asientos
del Inca

N

To
La Paz

To Yunguyo,
Peru

Cerro
Sancollani/
Horca del
Inca

Hotels: 3. *Playa Azul*   **Buses:**   3. Transportes 2 de Febrero
1. *Ambassador*   4. *Prefectural*   1. Combi Tours   4. Transportes Manco Kapac
2. *La Cúpula*   5. *Rosario del Lago*   2. Diana Tours & Vicuña Tours   21a

highlight with much music, dancing, fireworks and bullfights. **End February/beginning March**, Carnival. **Semana Santa**, at Easter there is a huge pilgrimage to the town. **2-5 May**, *Fiesta del Señor de la Cruz*, this is very colourful with dances in typical costumes. **5 June**, the anniversary of the province of Manco Kapac. **12-13 June**, *San Antonio*, procession and fireworks. **23 June**, *San Juan*, this is also celebrated throughout the region and on Isla del Sol. **15-17 July**, anniversary of La Paz department, a chance to share drinks and coca leaves with the locals, also marches and bull-

fights. **24-25 July**, *Fiesta del Señor Santiago*, dancing in typical costumes. **4-6 August**, *La Virgen de Copacabana*, the plaza becomes a huge market and there are dancing and fireworks.

During festivals the town gets very full and hotel prices treble.

Local information
● Accommodation

C-B *Playa Azul*, 6 de Agosto, T 320068, full board, rooms OK, but chilly, half-board is also a possibility, tepid electric showers, water supply and toilets poor, good food; **C** *Residencial Rosario del Lago*, Rigoberto Paredes between Avenida Costanera and Avenida 16 de Julio,

An answer to your prayers

In Copacabana all your dreams will come true. At least that's what the local people believe. And when you see them fervently blessing all manner of material goods on the Cerro Calvario perhaps you will start to believe it, too.

On Sunday, a procession of the faithful makes its way up the steps to the summit of the Calvario to perform this ritual – a strange mix of the spiritual and the material. The many believers, old and young alike, climb the steep stairs past the fourteen stations of the cross, pausing at each station to bless themselves and to enjoy a brief respite from the lung-bursting ascent. Once at the top, they find an array of stalls offering a veritable multitude of miniature items to pray for: cars, trucks, minibuses, houses (for the more optimistic), bricks and sacks of cement, cookers, wheelbarrows, tiny bags of pasta, suitcases stuffed with dollar bills, even mini certificates to ensure a successful graduation from University.

The devout take their pick before descending to a series of little altars where, for a small fee, they get a bag of incense to burn during the blessing of their desired object. Cars and money seem to be the favourite choices. These are carefully arranged before a miniature version of Copacabana's famous Virgen de la Candelaria.

The ceremony then begins, in either Latin or Aymara. Those electing the latter definitely get more value for money, with much chanting, dancing, histrionics and even flames emitting from a large cup. The alternative ceremony is an altogether more sedate affair. Only smoke instead of flames, a few lines of Latin, a song and some sprinkled flower petals. At a signal from the priest a *cholita* then dutifully rushes over with a few bottles of beer which are shaken up and sprayed over the altar.

The ceremony over, the priest and his small congregation drink a toast to good fortune before the weekend pilgrims depart, happy in the belief that their heavenly benefactor will deliver the goods before the year is out.

same ownership as *Residencial Rosario* in La Paz and similar colonial style building, price includes breakfast, hot water (solar power), Turisbus office, all rooms with lake view, beautifully furnished, recommended.

D-C *Ambassador*, Bolívar y Jauregui on Plaza Sucre, rooms with balcony, heater US$2 per day, cheaper without bath, water shortages, rooftop restaurant, great beds, reduction for more than one night or with YHA card, luggage stored for US$2; **D-E** *La Cúpula*, Calle Michel Pérez 1-3, T 0862-2029, six rooms, **F** per person without bath, bright and comfortable rooms, sitting room with TV and video, fully-equipped kitchen, library, hot water, book exchange, vegetarian restaurant, great breakfast, offer local tours, run by Amanda and Martin Strätker whose *Centro Cultural Arco y Hamaca* offers painting and sculpting classes and courses in Spanish and English, nice atmosphere, highly recommended; **D** pp *Prefectural*, Avenida 16 de Julio, full board, now owned by *Hotel Gloria* in La Paz, fully refurbished in 1996.

E *Boston*, Conde de Lemos, near the Basilica, T 0862-2231, **F** without bath, clean, helpful, good, quiet; **E** *Residencial Sucre*, Murillo 228, T 2080, hot water, with bath, clean and friendly, good beds, filthy shared bathrooms, parking, quiet, good cheap breakfast, laundry US$3, offers tours of lake.

F *Alojamiento Aransaya*, Avenida 6 de Agosto 121, T 229, basic but clean, hot shower but water problems, good trout in restaurant; **F** *Alojamiento Aroma*, Avenida Jauregui, towards beach, hot showers, helpful and informative owner; **F** *Alojamiento Oasis*, Pando 222, with bath, clean, safe, great view from top rooms, arrange boat trips to Isla del Sol; **F** *El Turista*, Pando 378, inadequate shower facilities, otherwise recommended; **F** *Kota Kahuaña*, Avenida Busch 15, blue house, hot showers on request, cheap, quiet, some rooms with lake view, recommended; **F** *Residencial Porteña*, by market on Jauregui, safe, good value.

G *Emperador*, Calle Murillo, behind the Basilica, very popular, breakfast served in room for

US$2, order it the previous night, laundry service and facilities, shared hot showers but not enough of them, helpful for trips to Isla del Sol, cheap and friendly, repeatedly recommended as great value; **G** *Hostal La Luna*, Calle José P Mejía, T 2051, hot showers, very comfortable, laundry, breakfast brought to room on request, changes travellers' cheques, can arrange discounts on trips to Isla del Sol, owner Walther can also arrange discount on accommodation on Isla del Sol, kayaks and motor boats for rent, excellent value, highly recommended. There are many other *residenciales* in our **F** and **G** categories.

● **Places to eat**
On Plaza 2 de Febrero are the following restaurants: *Napolés*, reasonable prices, does vegetarian tortilla, changes money; *Colonial*, decent lunch and good trout. On 6 de Agosto are: *Snack 6 de Agosto*, good trout, big portions, some vegetarian dishes, serves breakfast; *Puerta del Sol*, good, excellent trout for around US$4; *Bolivia*, near Plaza Sucre, good trout and vegetarian noodles; *Sujna Wasi*, Calle Jauregui 127, T 2091, open Wednesday-Monday from breakfast to dinner, excellent food and atmosphere in the café/restaurant plus a very good collection of books on Bolivia in the Sala Cultural. *Bar Milagros* is on Murillo next to Entel, it's run by German Andreas and serves pizzas and drinks in a nice atmosphere. Many other restaurants offer decent cheap meals and good trout. Good breakfasts and other meals, especially fish, can be found in the market on Calle Abaroa. Very few places open before 0800.

● **Banks & money changers**
Bidesa, in the same building as *Hotel Playa Azul*, open Wednesday-Friday 0830-1200, 1430-1700, Saturday-Sunday 0830-1430, changes dollar bills and travellers' cheques, pesos and bolivianos, no credit cards and no soles. Several *artesanías* on Avenida 6 de Agosto buy and sell dollar bills and soles. The bank is closed on Monday and Tuesday, as are many shops.

● **Entertainment**
There is a video cinema in the Municipality on the main plaza.

● **Post & telecommunications**
Entel: open every day; Sunday-Tuesday 0800-2000, Wednesday-Saturday 0800-2100; national and international phone and fax. They also accept dollars at a good rate. **Post Office**: open Monday-Saturday 0900-1200, 1400-1800, Sunday 0900-1300, but they are very flexible about opening. Also *Poste Restante* service.

● **Hospitals & medical services**
Hospital: see map of town for location. Offers medical and dental treatment and a 24-hour pharmacy, but if you're seriously ill you should go to La Paz.

Pharmacies: opposite Entel (open Tuesday-Sunday 0900-1200, 1400-1800).

● **Tourist offices**
The Tourist Information kiosk on Plaza 2 de Febrero is helpful when open. Motorcycles and bicycles can be hired on the beach, but bargain. You can also hire a kayak or rowing boat in Copacabana for US$4.50 per hour.

● **Transport**
Road By car from La Paz to Copacabana takes about 4 hours. Take the exit to 'Río Seco' in El Alto. The road is paved all the way.

Agency buses: several agency buses go from La Paz to Puno in Peru and vice-versa, stopping at Copacabana for lunch. They charge US$12-15 and leave La Paz at 0800. They leave Copacabana at 1330. The journey from La Paz to

Copacabana takes 4 hours. Companies are: *Diana Tours* at *Hotel Ambassador*, Plaza Sucre, Copacabana; *Combi Tours*, on the main plaza in Copacabana, T 2110, office open 0930-1400, 1530-2000; *Vicuña Tours*, Calle 6 de Agosto, two blocks from the main plaza, Copacabana, T 2155, open 0900-1400, 1630-2030; *Turisbus*, Calle 6 de Agosto, Copacabana. These agencies continue to the Peruvian border at Yunguyo and on to Puno, stopping for immigration formalities and to change money in Yunguyo. It takes 3½ hours to Puno and costs US$3.30-US$4.25 depending on the season. They leave around 1200-1400. *Diana Tours* have been recommended; they leave at 1300. It is also possible to catch a tour bus to Cusco, usually departing around 1400; tickets cost US$17-20. You change bus in Puno; the tour company arranges the connection. For public transport to Peru, see **Frontier via Copacabana** below.

Public buses to/from La Paz: a ticket costs US$2.35 plus US$0.20 for the Tiquina crossing. There are several departures daily between 0700-1700 (1730 on Saturday-Sunday) with Manco Capac, T 2234 (or 350033 in La Paz) and 2 de Febrero, T 2233 (or 377181, La Paz). Both have offices on Copacabana's main plaza and in La Paz at Plaza Reyes Ortíz, opposite the entrance to the cemetery (see La Paz **buses**, page 107). If you travel to Copacabana on Friday buy a ticket in advance as buses fill up quickly, similarly if coming back to La Paz on a Sunday. Conversely, during the week, buses are often cancelled because there are not enough passengers. 1-day trips from La Paz are not recommended as they allow only 1½-2 hours in Copacabana. A bus to **Huatajata** is US$2.10 and to **Huarina**, US$2.50.

TREKKING NEAR COPACABANA

This is a beautiful location for some easy trekking. The most worthwhile walk is to the end of the peninsula, to the fishing village of **Yampupata**. It's a bizarre experience stopping to fill your water bottle while going along a sandy beach – the water is fresh. A map which covers the trek described below can be obtained from IGM Copacabana 5745 I.

You can start this trek from the Straits of Tiquina and follow a prehispanic road through Parquipujio, Chisi (which has some ancient ruins), the stone village of Sampaya and other villages to reach Yampupata. This particular version of the trek gives fantastic views of the Cordillera Real across the lake.

Most people, though, set out from Copacabana. It is 17 km along the side of the peninsula from Copacabana to Yampupata and takes about 5 hours. Walk out of Copacabana along the rarely used lakeside road. After 2½ hours you cross the stream below a grotto and then follow a short paved section of prehispanic path which rejoins the road. In another 30 minutes you get to the very strung out village of **Sicuani**. Here you can ask for a rowing boat to Isla del Sol, or José Quispe Mamani who provides a motor launch, plus meals and accommodation. Camping is possible on the other side of Sicuani an hour later where there is an *alojamiento*. Alternatively, continue to the fishing village of Yampupata in another hour.

ISLA DEL SOL

This is the site of the Inca creation legend. A sacred rock at its northwestern end is worshipped as the birthplace of Manco Kapac and Mama Oclló, son and daughter of Viracocha and the first Incas. Though only a short distance by boat from Copacabana, Isla del Sol has an altogether different feel to it. It has a quiet, almost serene beauty and makes the perfect place to relax for a few days.

It is worthwhile staying overnight on the Isla del Sol for the many beautiful walks through villages and Inca terraces, some of which are still in use. Isla del Sol is, by Bolivian standards, intensively inhabited (an estimated 5,000 people live there) and cultivated and so is covered in trails. The west side is far less cultivated and inhabited and has the highest point on the island.

The most impressive ruins are at the far north at Chincana and the Labyrinth. It is possible to arrange a motor launch to take you there and then walk back across the island to be picked up at the Inca Steps at the other end, where there are a second set of ruins (much more visited) at Pilcocaina and the Inca Spring. Walking from one end of the island to the other takes 5 hours, so it's not really possible to see all the sites on the island and return to Copacabana in one day.

Starting at the north end of the island is the village of **Challapampa** near the sacred rock of *titicaca* (after which the lake is named) and the ruins of **Chincana**; an Inca temple and nunnery which have been restored by the National Institute of

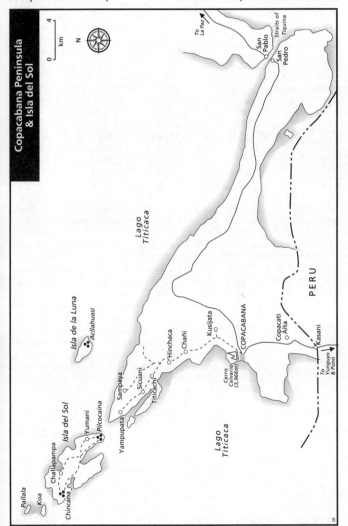

Copacabana Peninsula & Isla del Sol

Underwater mystery

Among the many legends that abound about Lake Titicaca is the existence of an underwater city lying between the islands of Koa and Pallala, near the Isla del Sol.

This city was said to exist before there was a lake. In the city was a temple which could only be entered by women dedicated to the sun. Each day these women would go to fill their water jars at a spring located in the ruins of Chincana, near the Sacred Rock. One day two men followed the women and surprised one of them who dropped her water jar, breaking it. Due to the power of Viracocha, the Inca creator god, the water continued to flow, thus creating Lake Titicaca.

Despite numerous diving expeditions, including one led by the late Frenchman, Jacques Cousteau, no evidence of an underwater city have yet been discovered. However, investigations near the island of Koa have uncovered many ancient artifacts lying around a natural ridge. Among the artifacts are stone boxes which are thought to have been used for ritual sacrifice offerings. It is believed, therefore, that the underwater ridge at Koa could have been a ceremonial site.

Of further significance is the name Koa, which is thought to derive from ccoa, the powerful feline deity that controlled the weather around Lake Titicaca. It has even been suggested that human sacrifices may have been carried out by a water/weather cult at the underwater site as offerings to the feline god. Local people today still call the ridge the 'altar of Viracocha' and fishermen refuse to pass over it in their boats. The ridge could also appear and disappear, depending on the level of the lake waters, thus adding to the eerie reverence that surrounds it. For an in-depth description of the underwater archaeological investigations at Koa see *An Insider's Guide to Bolivia* by Peter McFarren (Quipus Cultural Foundation).

Culture. There is a museum in Challapampa containing artifacts from archaeological excavations at the nearby island of Koa, plus maps and pictures. It costs US$1 to visit the ruins and museum on the same ticket; the entry fee goes towards the restoration of the ruins and therefore benefits the local community. There is basic accommodation in the village (see below).

One hour from Challapampa, on the east side of the island in a small bay, is the friendly village of **Challa**, which is very nice and worth a stay. From Challa it's about 2 hours southeast to **Yumani**, where there are a number of places to stay. Below Yumani is the jetty for Crillon Tours' hydrofoils and other boats. A series of steep Inca steps leads up from the jetty to the **Fuente del Inca**, three natural springs which help in matters of love, health and eternal youth. A 2 km walk from the spring takes you to the main ruins of **Pilcocaina**, a two-storey building with false domes and superb views. The Sun Gate from the ruins is now kept in the main plaza in Copacabana. Entry to the ruins is US$1.20. There is accommodation by the ruins.

Apart from places to stay in Challapampa, Challa and Yumani there are plenty of places to camp, especially on the western side of the island where it is possible to camp in a secluded bay. As dusk falls the lake stops lapping and you can listen to the silence. If camping take all food and water (or water sterilizers).

NB Begging – especially by children – on the Isla del Sol is widespread, persistent, unwarranted, and annoying. The only reason you get pestered by the children is because gringos before you have given sweets/money/ballpoint pens, etc.

Southeast of the Isla del Sol is the **Isla de la Luna** (or Coati), which can also be visited as part of a day tour, though this doesn't leave you enough time on Isla del

Sol. The best ruins on Isla de la Luna are an Inca temple and nunnery, both sadly neglected.

Local information
● Accommodation
Most of the accommodation is at **Yumani**. By far the nicest place to stay is Crillon Tour's *La Posada del Inca*, a restored colonial hacienda which was once the home the writer Franz Tamayo (see page 58), it is perched on the spur of a hill overlooking the southern part of the island, it has solar-powered electricity and hot water, the rooms are heated, one room has private bath, the others have shared bathrooms, the dining room serves good food, the *posada* is quaint and rustic but very comfortable, you can only stay here as part of a tour (see La Paz **Tours companies**, page 58).

There is more modest accommodation available in Yumani, all **G** per person and all offering basic meals. Up the hill from *La Posada del Inca* is *Inti Huayra*, basic but clean, no electricity or hot water, meals provided for US$1-2. Slightly further up the hill is *Mirador del Inca*, slightly cheaper and more comfortable, clean, friendly, no shower, breakfast US$0.75, meals US$1.50-2. Nearby is the Entel office. Uphill from the school on the right is *El Imperio del Sol*, which is very comfortable, friendly and recommended, breakfast US$1.50-2, other meals US$1.50-2, pasta, eggs, fish etc. At the top of the hill in an orange building is *Posada de las Ñustas*, with great views all around, nine rooms, solar-heated shower, breakfast US$1, also snacks and meals for US$1.50-2.

Next to the ruins of Pilcocaina is **G** pp *Albergue Inca Sama*, sleeps twenty on mattresses on the floor, continental breakfast US$1.50, lunch and dinner US$4, good food, also camping in typical tents called *chujlla*, to arrange transport and accommodation contact *Hotel Playa Azul* in Copacabana, or La Paz T 356566/357817, or the Entel office in Yumani (T 0811-5006), Sr Gonzalo Pusari, who runs the place and looks after the ruins, also offers boat tours to the north of the island for US$20 per boat (6-8 people) and to Isla de la Luna, and from there to Kalaka on the other side of the lake, from where you can take a truck to Achacachi and then a bus to Sorata.

In Challapampa: there are several *alojamientos* around the plaza straight up from the landing jetty, near the church. Ask for Lucio Arias or his mother Antonia, they will find a room, cook for you and are friendly.

In Challa: G per person *Posada del Inca*, situated right on the beach, only has 2 rooms but more are being built, owned by Juan Mamani Ramos, contact through Entel office (T 0811-5006), food is provided and beer or *refrescos* are for sale.

● Boats to the island
Inca Tours and *Titicaca Tours* run motor boats to Isla del Sol and Isla de la Luna; both have offices on 6 de Agosto in Copacabana. A full-day tour leaves Copacabana at 0815 and returns from the island at 1600, arriving back at 1730. A half-day tour returns at 1100, arriving back at 1230. With the same ticket you can stay on the island and return another day. Half-day tours, or full-day tours which include the north and south of Isla del Sol and Isla de La Luna are not recommended as too much time is spent on the water and not enough on dry land.

A half-day tour which goes to the southern part costs US$3 per person and is described as a waste of time as you only get 1 hour on the island. A full-day tour drops you off at Challapampa at around 1000, gives you enough time to visit the ruins, then takes you to the ruins at the southern end. Or you can be dropped off at Challapampa and picked up at Yumani at 1600, leaving you just enough time to visit the ruins in the north and hike south to Yumani. Alternatively, you can stay on the boat and visit Isla de la Luna instead. A full-day tour costs US$4-5 per person, depending on the season. Tickets can be bought at the agency offices, or through your hotel.

Note that boats stop only briefly at the jetty by the Fuente del Inca, leaving punctually at 1600. Make sure the boat is equipped with life-jackets; some are not. Conditions on the lake can change very quickly and you don't want to end up as the next offering to the gods.

You can also take a boat to the island from Yampupata. Motor launches from Yampupata to Fuente del Inca on the southern end of the Isla del Sol cost US$8. A rowing boat costs US$3 (or US$1 per person) and takes 40 minutes. Arrange the time and day of your return.

FRONTIER WITH PERU

There are two principal routes into Peru from La Paz, both of which skirt the shores of Lake Titicaca. The less used one takes the road to Tiahuanco and goes along the west side of the lake to Guaqui, then onto Desaguadero on the border. The more common route goes via Copacabana and on to Yunguyo and then Puno. **NB** Peruvian time is 1 hour behind Bolivian time.

Along the west side of Lake Titicaca

The road heads west from La Paz 91 km to **Guaqui**, formerly the port for the Titicaca passenger boats. The road crosses the border at **Desaguadero**, a cold and miserable place 22 km further west, and runs along the shore of the lake to Puno. In Guaqui is *Residencial Guaqui*, near the port, which is basic but good value and friendly. A tiny restaurant on the Plaza de Armas has been recommended.

● **Bolivian immigration**

Just before the bridge. Open 0830-1230 and 1400-2030. Thirty days are normally given on entering Bolivia, so ask for more if you need it. Get your exit stamp, walk 100m across the bridge, then get an entrance stamp on the other side. Both offices may also close for dinner around 1830-1900. Get a visa in La Paz if you need one. Peruvian immigration opens same hours (Peruvian time).

● **Accommodation & places to eat**

G pp *Residencial San Francisco*, looks OK; also **G** pp *Hotel Bolivia* and *Alojamiento Avaroa II*, plus a couple of very dodgy-looking places to stay on the Peruvian side. There are several restaurants on both sides of bridge.

● **Exchange**

Money changers just over the bridge on the Peruvian side give reasonable rates for bolivianos or dollars.

● **Transport**

The road is paved as far as Tiahuanco and pretty bumpy thereafter to Desaguadero. Buses from La Paz to Guaqui and Desaguadero depart from Transportes Ingavi office in the Cementerio district in La Paz (see La Paz **buses**, page 107) at 0745 and 1000, US$1.40, 3½ hours. They are usually full but tickets can be bought in advance. If entering Bolivia here, the last bus from Desaguadero to La Paz departs at 1700, 4 hours, US$2-3, though buses may leave later if there enough passengers, but will charge a lot more. There are frequent buses from the Peruvian side to Puno until 1930, US$2, 2½ hours.

Via Copacabana

The most popular route into Peru is from Copacabana. An unpaved road leads to the Bolivian frontier at Kasani, 20 minutes away, then on to Yunguyo. Do not photograph the border area.

● **Immigration**

The border is open till 1900 (Bolivian time). Buses/colectivos stop at Kasani and on the Peruvian side; or you can walk, 400m, between the two posts. There should be a statutory 72 hours period outside Bolivia before renewing a visa but 24 hours is usually acceptable. Ask for 90 days on return. Thirty days is often given on entering Bolivia, but there are no problems extending in La Paz. Ninety days is normally given on entering Peru. If crossing into Bolivia with a motorcycle, do not be fooled into paying any unnecessary charges to police or immigration.

● **Exchange**

Money can be changed in Yunguyo at better rates than at the border. Soles can be changed in Copacabana (see above).

● **Transport**

Transport to Puno does not start till Yunguyo, a further 600m from Peruvian immigration. A colectivo Copacabana-Kasani costs US$0.50 per person; Kasani-Yunguyo US$0.60 per person. Colectivos leave from Plaza Sucre in Copacabana. Agency buses will take you from La Paz or Copacabana to Puno and stop for border formalities and to change money in Yunguyo. For details of these buses see under Copacabana **Transport** (see page 137), La Paz **International buses** (page 108) or La Paz **Tour companies** (page 104). Note the common complaint that through services La Paz-Puno (or vice versa) deteriorate once the border has been crossed, eg smaller buses are used, extra passengers taken on, passengers left stranded if the onward bus is already full or drivers won't drop you where the company says they will. Generally, though these services are fine.

● **Entering Peru**

There is accommodation in Yunguyo. By far the best is **E** *Hostal Isabel*, San Francisco 110 near Plaza de Armas, T 350233, shared bath, hot water, clean, pleasant. There are a few others on the plaza which are very basic, to say the least. There are also a few places to eat. The Bolivian Consulate is near the main plaza and is open Monday-Friday 0830-1500, for those who need a visa. There is no consulate in Puno. The *Casas de Cambio* offer good rates for dollars cash, but rates for travellers' cheques are poor. The road to Puno is paved. There are buses and colectivos all day which leave from the plaza; US$1.50, 2½ hours.

North of La Paz

I N THE NORTH of the La Paz Department are some of Bolivia's most stunning and least-visited attractions. The mountain town of Sorata is easily reached from La Paz and quite rightly included on many itineraries. But further north lies a wild, remote and untamed land of incomparable beauty, home to the famed *Kallawayas*, Bolivia's ancient and wise medicine men. This is trekking paradise (or hell, depending on your point of view) and a must for the adventurous, the reckless and the downright crazy.

LA PAZ TO SORATA

The road from the capital heads northwest to the shores of Lake Titicaca before branching off at Huarina towards the village of Achacachi, where there is a military checkpoint, so remember your passport. All foreigners must get off the bus and register here; don't leave anything on the bus while registering.

ACHACACHI

It's not easy to think of a good reason to linger here, although there are good views of Lake Titicaca from the church up the hill from the left side of the plaza. It is possible to walk to the lake in 1½ hours. There is also an 'interesting' Sunday market behind the main plaza and a local *fiesta* is celebrated on 14 September.

● **Accommodation & places to eat** None of the three *alojamientos* is clean or welcoming, so it's better stay somewhere else. There are two restaurants.

North of La Paz

● **Buses** Plenty of buses leave for La Paz in the morning, US$1.30. From La Paz to Achacachi buses depart every 15 minutes from the Cemetery district (see La Paz **Buses**, page 107). Achacachi is a good place for connections if coming from Peru to Sorata. From Copacabana take a bus to Huarina and change there for a bus direct to Sorata. From Sorata to Peru: take a La Paz bus and get out at Huarina; from there take a bus to Copacabana. This is best done in the morning. See also under Sorata **Buses** below.

From Achacachi the road continues north to **Warisata**, passing through a tremendous marsh, with sheets of water, dykes, farms, cattle, people working the fields and many birds. In the distance snow-capped peaks can be seen. It then reaches the wide open spaces of the Altiplano and climbs to a pass in fields with stone walls and boulders before beginning its descent in a landscape of huge valleys and ridges. It continues to descend the side of a valley, then crosses a bridge and climbs up from the river to Sorata.

SORATA

(*Altitude* 2,695; *Population* 2,500; *Phone code* 0811) Local people insist that Sorata is the real Garden of Eden. Whether or not you accept this rather outrageous claim, it is difficult to deny that this old colonial town enjoys one of the most beautiful settings in the whole country, nestled at the foot of Mount Illampu with panoramic views over lush, green alpine-like valleys.

The town has been a centre for coca, quinine, and rubber growing and is currently enjoying something of a renaissance as a popular tourist destination. This is not surprising as it's a great place to wander around, hang out and relax. It has a lovely atmosphere with chickens and children playing in the narrow cobbled streets, but it was not always so laid back. In 1781 during the great Peru-Bolivia Indian revolt of 1780-82, Andrés, nephew of the Peruvian rebel leader Túpac Amaru, killed all the Spanish in the town after a 3 month siege.

Sorata is 1,000m lower than La Paz and so is noticeably warmer. It is 1,000m higher than the Yungas towns and so is cooler and has fewer swimming pools, but the setting is more spectacular and there is better hiking and trekking.

Places of interest

The main plaza is named after General Enrique Peñaranda who was born in the nearby village of Chuchulaya in 1892 and was president 1940-43. On a clear day, from among the giant palms you can see Illampu (on the left) and Ancohuma (on the right). The view of the mountains is better from the smaller Plaza Obispo Bosque. The bishop lived 1829-90 and also had a village on the Consata road named after him.

The **Residencial Sorata** on the main plaza was built by a series of 19th century German quinine and rubber barons. It has only been a hotel since 1968 when the then mayor threatened to expropriate the buildings due to under-use. *The Spectator* Diary (London, 1997) described it thus: "Vast rooms, high ceilings, sepia tinted photographs of turn-of-the-century German matrons – all surrounding a glorious hummingbird-packed garden".

There is a one-room museum upstairs at the **Alcaldía** with a collection of locally found ceramics from the Tiahuanaco and Mollu cultures. It is open 0800-1200 and 1400-1700 Monday-Friday, 0800-1300 Saturday.

Local festivals

Sorata's biggest bash is on 14 September, **Fiesta Patronal del Señor de la Exaltación**. The **Fiesta Pascua** or San Pedro, held 7 days after Easter, is also well-supported.

Local information
● **Accommodation**

C pp *Ex-Prefectural*, Avenida Samuel Tejerina, T/F 5201, at the entrance to the village, immediately above the police checkpoint (tranca), spacious, newly-decorated following privatization, large garden with great views, swimming pool, restaurant, prices include continental breakfast and set lunch and dinner, cheaper Monday-Friday and with shared bathroom, accepts Visa, Mastercard and AmEx but with 13% surcharge.

Win two Iberia flights to Latin America

We want to hear your ideas for further improvements as well as a few details about yourself so that we can better serve your needs as a traveller.

We are offering you the chance to win two Iberia flights to Latin America, currently flying to 25 destinations. Every reader who sends in the completed questionnaire will be entered in the Footprint Prize Draw. 10 runners up will each receive a Handbook of their choice.

Fill in this form using a ball-point pen and return to us as soon as possible.

Mr ☐ Mrs ☐ Miss ☐ Ms ☐ Age

First name

Surname

Permanent Address

Postcode/Zip

Country

Email

Occupation

Title of Handbook

Which region do you intend visiting next?

North America ☐	India/S.Asia ☐	Africa ☐
Latin America ☐	S.E. Asia ☐	Europe ☐
Australia ☐		

How did you hear about us?

Recommended ☐	Bookshop	☐
Used before ☐	Media/press article	☐
Library ☐	Internet	☐

There is a complete list of Footprint Handbooks at the back of this book. Which other countries would you like to see us cover?

Offer ends 30 November 1998. Prize winners will be notified by 30 January 1999 and flights are subject to availability.

If you do not wish to receive information from other reputable businesses, please tick box ☐

Footprint Handbooks

...step inside a world other travel guides miss

Footprint Handbooks
6 Riverside Court
Lower Bristol Road
Bath BA2 3DZ
T 01225 469141
F 01225 469461
handbooks@footprint.cix.co.uk
www.footprint-handbooks.co.uk

Affix Stamp Here

Footprint Handbooks
6 Riverside Court
Lower Bristol Road
Bath
BA2 3DZ
England

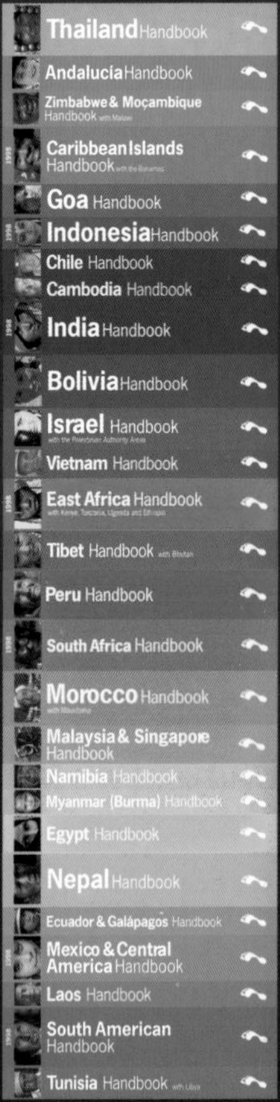

Win two Iberia flights to Latin America

IBERIA

E pp *Copacabana*, Avenida 9 de Abril, below the soccer pitch, T/F 5042, e-mail: agsorta@wara.bolnet.bo, **F** pp with shared bathroom, clean, modern, German-run, good restaurant 0700-2300, videos, jacuzzi US$10 per 30 minutes, Club Sorata agency (see Travel Agencies below).

F pp *Paraíso*, Calle Villavicencio, T 5043, clean, modern, all rooms with private bathroom, restaurant, American breakfast US$1.80; **F** pp *Residencial Sorata*, on the corner of the main plaza and Villavicencio, T/F 5044, e-mail: resorta@ceibo.entelnet.bo, **G** pp with shared bathroom at the back, 'best value in the Americas',

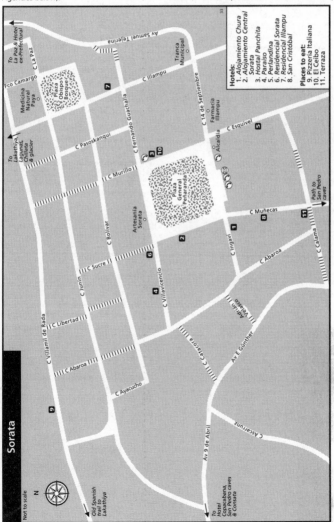

Sorata

Not to scale

N

To La Paz & Hotel ex-Prefectural
La Paz
Fco Camargo
Av Samuel Tejerina
C Illampu
Tranca Municipal
Medicina Natural Paya
Plaza Obispo Bosque
C Pasoskangui
To Lakathiya, Laguna Chillata & glacier
C Fernando Guachalla
14 de Septiembre
C Esquivel
Farmacia Illampu
C Murillo
Alcaldía
Artesanía Sorata
C Bolívar
Plaza General Peñaranda
C Muñecas
Path to San Pedro caves
C Sucre
C Ingavi
C Abaroa
C Calama
C Junín
C Villavicencio
C Villamil de Rada
C Libertad
Av J Ortín
Av Peñaranda
Av E Gunther
C Ayacucho
C Ascarrunz
To Hotel Copacabana, San Pedro caves & Consata
Av 9 de Abril
Old Spanish trail to Lakathiya

Hotels:
1. Alojamiento Chura
2. Alojamiento Central Sorata
3. Hostal Panchita
4. Paraíso
5. Perlandina
6. Residencial Sorata
7. Residencial Illampu
8. San Cristóbal

Places to eat:
9. Pizzería Italiana
10. El Ceibo
11. Terraza

the best rooms overlook the garden, the rooms at the back are half the price, a rambling place with original fixtures, fittings and drawing room, hummingbirds, dragon flies, snake skins, three-wheel Heinkl bubble car. According to the Australian Gourmet Traveller magazine, 'the best breakfasts in Bolivia', US$2, 0700-1200. Restaurant, videos, machine washing US$1.60 per 4 kilos, e-mail and fax service, bike hire US$1.20 per hour/US$5 per day, book exchange for beer, food and lodging as well as other books.

G pp *Alojamiento Central Sorata*, on the corner of the main plaza and Villavicencio, friendly, spartan courtyard; **G** pp *Alojamiento Chura*, Calle Ingavi corner Muñecas, first and second floors, clean and light, hot showers; **G** pp *Hostal Panchita*, on the corner of the main plaza and Guachalla, T 5038, clean and modern; **G** pp *Residencial Illampu*, Calle Illampu esquina Guachalla, basic; **G** pp *San Cristóbal*, Muñecas 350, near the market, basic, friendly, shared bath, no single rooms, has a small restaurant; **G** pp *Perlandina*, Calle Esquivel, enter through the garage doors, for poor locals only.

● **Places to eat**
Without doubt the best place to eat is the *Restaurante Pizzeria Italiana*, Calle Villamil de Rada between Junín and Abaroa (follow the signs), the food is as good as the service is slow but you can use the time to watch the sun go down over the Río San Cristobal valley from the terrace, serves pizza, pasta and ice cream, believe it or not, open 0900-2130; *Residencial Sorata*, full breakfast US$2, almuerzo US$2.75, cena US$2.80 (vegetarian also available); *Hotel Copacabana* does a set cena for US$3 and à la carte all day, 0700-2300. There are a number of small restaurants around the plaza, the best is *El Ceibo* below *Hostal Panchita*. *Restaurant Terraza*, just below

the market, serves almuerzo and cena as does *Hotel San Cristóbal* which also does api and empanadas.

The cheapest place to eat is the comedor popular in the market.

● **Banks & money changers**
There are no official outlets. Try *Artesanía Sorata*, *Residencial Sorata* and *Hotel Copacabana*.

● **Entertainment**
Videos are shown every day for guests at *Residencial Sorata* and *Hotel Copacabana* (non-guests can watch videos at the *Copacabana* for US$1). There is a one-table pool hall on the main plaza on the same side as the Transportes Unificado office, entrance through number 138. There is a one-room video-game arcade on Calle Fernando Guachalla just above the corner with Pasoskanqui.

● **Post & telecommunications**
Post Office: on the main plaza next to Cotel.

Telecommunications: (all on the main plaza) **Cotel** for local calls including to La Paz, 0830-1230 and 1400-2030 every day. **Entel** for local, long distance and international calls 0800-1300 and 1400-2100 every day. Entel booth underneath *Hostal Panchita* 0800-1200 and 1330-2100 every day. Calls to La Paz cost the same, whichever office you use. There are also a number of card phones, including in the *Residencial Sorata* which sells phonecards.

● **Shopping**
There are small shops all over the town. The stalls and shops in Calles Ingavi and Muñecas cover just about everything available in Sorata: packaged food, films, photocopying, machetes, gold buyers. The market is just off the plaza, half a block down Muñecas on the right. There are stalls selling fresh fruit and vegetables every day but market days are Thursday, Saturday and

Sunday, the latter being the biggest.

Artesanía Sorata, on the main plaza near the Transportes Unificado office, sells postcards, handicrafts, jumpers, gloves, wall hangings and the English language weekly newspaper of the *Bolivian Times*, it cashes travellers' cheques and accepts them as payment, open 0900-2000 Monday-Saturday, 0900-1600 Sunday.

The only chemist in Sorata is *Farmacia Illampu* on Calle 14 de Septiembre near the corner with Esquivel, open 0830-1230 and 1400-2100 Monday-Friday, 0830-2230 Saturday-Sunday. The *Centro de Medicina Natural Paya*, Plaza Obispo Bosque, sells natural foods and medicines.

● **Tour companies & travel agents**
Club Sorata (see *Hotel Copacabana* for contact details) has more information about climbing than anywhere else in town. They also organize mules and guides for trekking. It is also possible to get guides and mules through the *Residencial Sorata*, US$5 per day, for treks and to reach basecamps. There are maps up on the walls and the French-Canadian manager Louis Demers is the best source of information on local treks.

● **Transport**
Buses Buses to Sorata leave from Calle Manuel Bustillos, corner Avenida Kollasuyo, two blocks up from Cementerio, La Paz (see La Paz **buses**, page 107) 0600-1400 every day, US$2, 4½ hours; booking recommended on Friday. Sit on the right for the best views of the Cordillera Real.

Buses to La Paz leave from the main plaza in Sorata every hour or two from 0500 to 1400; later on Friday and Sunday. **NB** Remember your passport. There is a military checkpoint at Achacachi. If you are continuing to Peru you can get off the bus at Huarina, US$1.80, 2½ hours, and then flag down a bus to Copacabana (see also Copacabana **buses**, page 138).

There are pick ups to Ancoma most mornings from the main plaza, and to Santa Rosa most afternoons. Check with Louis Demers at the *Residencial Sorata*.

EXCURSIONS FROM SORATA

San Pedro Caves

One of the most popular walks near Sorata is to the **San Pedro Caves** beyond the village of San Pedro where the road splits take the lower road and look for the white building above. It is also possible to walk to the cave along the Río Cristóbal. The caves are not much in themselves and said to be in poor condition but the walk there and back (3-4 hours each way) is well worth it. Take a torch; it's best not to go alone. The lake is at 21°C and can be swum in. Entrance is US$1; there are toilets at the entrance. Continue past the cave for 30 minutes to reach a point on the ridge which gives great views over the surrounding valleys. Get clear directions before setting out. Take water, at least 1 litre per person, or else take sterilizing tablets and fill up at the tap in San Pedro. Ask for the house selling refrescos in San Pedro.

Cerro Istipata

A good 1-day walk is to **Cerro Istipata**. Either take a La Paz-bound bus to below the cross on Cerro Ulluni Tijja (US$0.40), and then follow the ridge up and over Cerro Lorockasini and on to Cerro Istipata, or walk the whole way from Sorata. Follow the La Paz road until just before the YPFB garage opposite the *Hotel Ex-Prefectural*. Drop down right, cross the Río San Cristobal and head up through the spread out village of Atahuallani and then up to join the ridge between Cerro Lorockasini (on the right) and Cerro Istipata.

Lakathiya

This is another 1 day walk. Follow the old Spanish stone trail up starting at the cemetery and following the ridge and then descend the broad and well-used path back to Sorata. It takes 4-6 hours to get to Lakathiya which is at 4,000m, and 2-3 hours to descend to Sorata.

Yani

Yani is a 400-year-old stone-built village in a beautiful setting. From Yani it is possible to follow the ancient Mapiri trail from Hulaya through vegetation tunnels for 8 hours to Ucumani (literally, 'the place of the bears') and then to a *garita*, an abandoned stone-built toll-house. The trail continues to the abandoned village of Chiñijo and then joins the Mapiri trail proper.

Below Yani is **Ingenio** which has two *alojamientos*: US$1 (with bed) and US$0.60 (floorspace only). On the other side of the Río Yani is a set of ruins called Pueblo

Antiguo. You can also walk to Tacacoma which has a hotel. Ingenio is the start of the Mapiri trail (see below).

● **Transport** To Yani leaves from the main plaza in Sorata every couple of days, US$6. To walk from Sorata takes 2 days. *Residencial Sorata* can arrange guides for a 4-5 day trip to Tacacoma and Yani.

TREKKING NEAR SORATA

All routes out of Sorata are difficult to follow owing to the number of paths in the area, which makes it difficult to pick the right one. Another downer is that all routes climb very steeply out. To overcome these two problems it makes sense to hire mules for the first day – ask at the *Residencial Sorata* or *Hotel Copacabana*. When trekking in this area avoid glacier melt water for drinking and treat with iodine all other water.

● **Maps** DAV Cordillera Real Nord (Illampu) or IGM Sorata 5846 I and Warizata 5846 II, Liam O'Brien. **NB** Nearly the whole of the Mapiri trail and the middle of the Camino del Oro are unmapped at any useful scale. Tacacoma 5847 II covers the start of the Mapiri trail and Tipuani 5947 I covers the end of the Camino del Oro.

● **Guidebooks** *Trekking in Bolivia* by Yossi Brain (The Mountaineers, 1997) covers all the treks described below. *Backpacking and Trekking in Peru and Bolivia* by Hilary Bradt (Bradt, 1995) has a description of the Camino del Oro.

LAGUNAS GLACIER AND CHILLATA

This trek is short, steep and beautiful on the way up. Laguna Glacier is high – 5,038m – and has small icebergs floating around, but there are also ducks and hummingbirds, amazing sunsets and fantastic views of Illampu and across the San Cristobal valley. Laguna Chillata is a sacred lake surrounded by legend and mystery, tales of gold and the deaths of those who have tried to extract it. Local witches ('brujos') communicate with the lake to cure people of diseases and afflictions. There are also the ruins of Inca Marka, dating back to the precolumbian Mollu culture. This is a burial place, and therefore a

sensitive area. Do not touch anything, not even bits of paper, bottles, etc, which may be offerings.

The trek

Day 1 to Titisani; day 2 to Laguna Glaciar; day 3 to Laguna Chillata; day 4 down to Sorata.

To give yourself a good idea of the route, wander up to Plaza Obispo Bosque in Sorata from where you can see Illampu, Ancohuma and the ground joining them. Laguna Glaciar is immediately below the lowest point between the two massifs (see **Illampu Circuit: North**).

From the main plaza in Sorata head up and aim to leave the village heading southeast and into the left hand (northern) side of the Río Lakathiya valley. After 45 minutes, head down right towards the Río Tucsa Jahuira which is crossed to the right 1¼ hours out of Sorata. Follow paths up and over the ridge above in another hour. Cross the fairly flat section but do not follow the road because it takes too long to get to where you are going. Follow a gently rising southerly traverse and then turn left and up following the first decent stream to reach an excellent spot for lunch in 30 minutes with full-on views of Illampu on the left and Ancohuma on the right.

Continue southwards and upwards following any of the numerous paths heading for the gap between Illampu and Ancohuma. A notch at 4,400m is reached in 1½ hours overlooking the moraine, rock, and glacier below Pico Schulze. Mules cannot make the short, steep descent so you will have to carry your packs down and then up to reach the abandoned mine and camping at **Titisani** in 25 minutes.

From the camp, head up the right hand side of the stream that runs through the camp and then follow a rising traverse with views of Sorata 1,700m below, Titicaca and, to the north, the glaciated peaks of the Cordillera Apolobamba. The path is normally clear and there are spray paint marks on the rocks which sometimes help when needed. Two hours later cross a series of streams flowing from the glacial tongue and then head up on to the right hand side moraine ridge to arrive at **Laguna Glaciar** and camping in another hour. The main stream from the lake is full of sediment, but there are a number of clear ponds within a few minutes of the camping area.

The descent is the same to the notch above the abandoned Titisani mine. Fifteen minutes from the notch at about 4,300m head off right following a series of faint paths to reach **Laguna Chillata** (4,204m) in 45 minutes where it is possible to camp. The ruins are to the north of the lake.

From Laguna Chillata you can head straight down until you meet up with the path again or head off cross country following animal paths to reach the valley of Río Tucsa Jahuira above the confluence with the Río Lakathiya. Descend to the river, cross to the right and follow the good path back to Sorata in 4 hours.

ILLAMPU CIRCUIT

This is a tour around the entire Illampu-Ancohuma massif. It's hard work, with three passes over 4,000m and one over 5,000m. However, the effort is worth it with stunning mountain views and the chance to see condors, viscachas, and andean geese, amongst others.

The Illampu circuit is normally done in 7 days camping above Lakathiya, at Ancoma, before Cocoyo, above Chajolpaya, at Lago Kacha and at the top of the Millipaya valley.

The trek

The trek starts with a solid ascent from Sorata to **Abra Illampu** at 4,741m. This normally takes a day and a half but it is highly recommended to organize mules to **Lakathiya** at 4,000m. Hiring mules neatly solves the route finding problems of getting out of Sorata and onto the right path. There are a myriad of paths as the area is densely populated, by Bolivian standards, and intensively cultivated – mainly maize

and other cereals lower down and potatoes higher up. For the first section of the trek see Illampu circuit – North map on the following page.

From the main plaza in Sorata head up and aim to leave the village heading southeast and into the left hand (northern) side of the Río Lakathiya valley. There are many paths, if you're not sure keep asking for **Quilambaya** (3,200m) which is reached in 1¾ hours.

In Quilambaya go around the back of the church, up through a cacti avenue and continue. Cross the aqueduct and carry on up before turning right (east) to contour along to a bridge across the Río Lakathiya in 1¼ hours. From the bridge stay on the path on the right hand (eastern) side of the stream for 15 minutes and then head up right through once-cultivated terraces and reach the village of **Lakathiya** (4,000m) in another 35 minutes.

Locals (if they are not carrying a load) can get to Lakathiya from Sorata in 2½ hours; mule time is 4-5 hours depending on how obstinate the beasts are and how many rests are taken; gringos carrying their own packs take 6 hours or more.

In Lakathiya the bigger path drops down left to a stream crossing. Do not take it. Instead, continue along the narrow path contouring and right through the village and drop down to cross the stream at a small bridge below the obligatory soccer pitch. Do not follow the path up the broad valley of the soccer pitch but take the smaller valley to the left above the bridge. There is excellent camping 45 minutes after the bridge. If you have time and energy continue up the path on the left hand (northern then western) side of the valley until immediately before the stream crossing for camping at 4,200m in 1 hour.

Fill water bottles for the dry ascent to **Abra Illampu** which takes 1¼ hours. The pass gives fantastic views of Illampu and is marked by an *apacheta* (small pile of rocks).

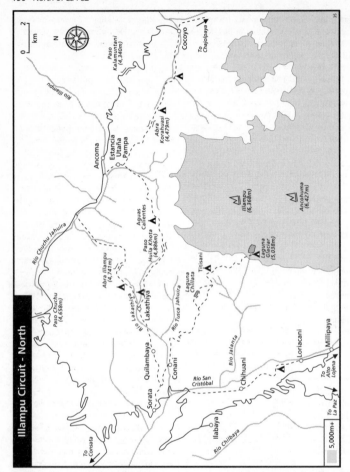

Illampu Circuit - North

The descent through Quebrada Illampu to the Sorata-Ancoma-Cocoyo road takes 1½ hours and passes plenty of camping possibilities. Join the road and turn right (southeast) and follow it down for 40 minutes to **Estancia Utaña Pampa** 3,877m. The Estancia, now a small village rather than a single farm, is also home to a trout farming co-operative.

From Estancia Utaña Pampa take the track down right immediately before the road bridges Río Chuchu Jahuria in Estancia Utaña Pampa to reach a one-stone bridge across Quebrada Ancohuma Jahutra and then head along the left hand side of the stream keeping a look out for a path heading up left (southeast). Camping is possible around Estancia Utaña Pampa but not recommended owing to the close proximity of the village. If you want to camp here head up the Quebrada Ancohuma Jahutra valley as far as possible – but not as far as the climbers who use this valley to Aguas Calientes as one of the approaches for Illampu – and then retrace your steps the next morning.

Head up and into the hanging valley and continue to **Abra Korahuasi** (4,479m) arriving after 2 hours of ascent. The descent passes plenty of camping possibilities before the path contours right and out of the valley giving impressive views down to the Cocoyo plain – wide, long and flat with steep sides. The path follows a series of zigzags to reach the head of the plain $1\frac{3}{4}$ hours after the pass, where excellent camping is possible.

It is 35 minutes to the village of **Cocoyo** 3,512m staying on the left hand (northern) side of the valley. There are two shops close to the bridge, one before and one after, where bread, tuna, tinned tomatoes and some other basics are normally available (though Sunday mornings and the mornings after a fiesta are not good times for shopping here as elsewhere). Cocoyo is mainly peopled by inquisitive children and dogs and their mining and llama herding parents and owners.

Cross the Cocoyo bridge and follow the track up and right (southeast) and out of the village. Go around the corner where there is a bridge across the Río Sarani. Do not cross the bridge. Continue up the right hand (western) side of the valley. Camping is possible 15 minutes above Cocoyo and then in many places the whole way up the Sarani valley.

After $1\frac{1}{2}$ hours a huge flat boulder forms a bridge across the Río Sarani taking the path onto the left hand (eastern) side of the valley. A couple of minutes later there is a group of houses on the left. Go towards the houses and then follow the path that rises up left immediately after them. There is camping on the flat and sometimes boggy valley floor, but better camping 15 minutes along the path up the left hand side of the valley near a couple of derelict houses. It takes another hour to Paso Sarani (4,600m).

Camping is possible 10 minutes below Paso Sarani, 15 minutes below the pass cross the stream to the right. Five minutes after the stream there is a a good path going off right (south) which reaches the valley bottom in 30 minutes.

The Illampu circuit continues up the right hand (northwest) side of the Río Chajolpaya. Initially the path is not clear as it crosses and goes around a boggy section, but after that it becomes a wide, roughly paved path, the Calzada road.

ILLAMPU CIRCUIT – SOUTH

It takes 5 hours to reach the **Calzada Pass** at 5,045m (see **Illampu Circuit: South**). It is a long way so it's best to try and get as far up the valley as possible before camping. There is excellent camping 35 minutes up the Calzada road and then $1\frac{1}{2}$ hours farther up with views of Calzada to the left and Kasiri to the right. The last good camping before the pass is immediately before the path climbs up left (southwest) from the valley floor, $4\frac{1}{4}$ hours after you join the Calzada road. The Río Chajolpaya is full of sediment, side streams are clear but spaced out.

The Calzada Pass is broad and barren but camping is possible near the numerous small lakes if you want to try sleeping at over 5,000m.

From the pass follow the broad path down to the right (west) of **Laguna Carizal** and on down to **Laguna Chojña Khota** in $1\frac{1}{4}$ hours. Camping is possible at the southern end of the lake. The path then crosses Quebrada de Kote to the left (east) and rises up on the other side. Either follow the path and then drop back down to **Laguna Cacha** or go cross country staying on the right hand side of the valley to Laguna Cacha. Either way, you should be at Laguna Cacha in another $1\frac{1}{4}$ hours.

From the northern end of Laguna Cacha there are two options:
1) Follow the path down and around to the right (west) and then up to **Laguna San Francisco**.

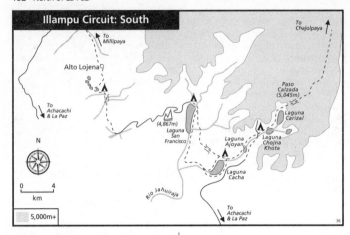

Illampu Circuit: South

2) Better, head straight up to the ridge to the northwest. The climb takes 50 minutes but is worth it for the views of Lake Titicaca, Ancohuma, Kasiri, Calzada, Chearoco, and Chachacomani. From the ridge, descend right (northwest) to the top (north) end of **Laguna San Francisco** in 1¼ hours where there is excellent camping.

From the lake head up to join the path which goes left (southwest) and then bears right (west) across a plain joining and then leaving the disused road to reach a pile of stones, Point 4,867, in 1½ hours. Kasiri, Calzada, Chearoco, and Chachacomani are all visible as is Lake Titicaca, 1,057m below. If you think that is a long way down remember that Sorata is 1,132m below the lake and that's where the trek is going.

Follow the disused road down for 1¼ hours from Point 4,867. As the valley flattens out to the right and you feel closer to civilization the road crosses a small disused aqueduct and a path which cuts back right (north) to a stream. Follow this path, cross the stream and then 5 minutes later look out for a path heading right (northwest). Head northnorthwest for Laguna Hualatani and then follow the path on the right hand (eastern) side. The path crosses an aqueduct shortly before

reaching an *apacheta* an hour after the stream crossing. From this point on the rest of the trail is basically down, down, down.

Camping is possible after the trail crosses a new road 20 minutes below the *apacheta*. The new rarely-used road is not marked on any available maps. The descent joins the road shortly before **Alto Lojena** which is reached 35 minutes after the road crossing. The road has been washed away at a number of points – no one built culverts for the streams – explaining its lack of use. It takes another 40 minutes to get to **Millipaya** at 3,475m (see **Illampu Circuit: North**).

Trucks to La Paz leave irregularly from Millipaya joining the La Paz-Sorata road above Umanata. If you want a lift back to Sorata take a ride to the junction and then get a lift with anything heading right (north) to Sorata. There is irregular transport to Sorata along the road on the right hand (northeastern) side of the valley. If you ask any locals the way to Sorata they will tell you to take the road – walking takes 3-4 hours to Sorata. Don't. You won't see Illampu, Ancohuma and the other snow peaks high above the right hand side of the valley.

From Millipaya go to **Loriacani**, the end of the driveable road, 25 minutes from Millipaya. Route finding for the next hour is difficult because of the vegetation and the numerous narrow paths linking fields, going up and over the ridge to the La Paz road and dropping down to small riverside mines. However, it is worth the effort for the views across the valley and down to Sorata. At Loriacani cross the stream and head down following the path through some houses, along a stream bed and out between some cultivated fields. Head up left to join a good but narrow path that takes you in and out of a series of *quebradas*. There is excellent camping 45 minutes after Loriacani up and left from the path.

From here the path gets clearer and broader, there are no more route finding problems and there are fantastic views across the valley of the glaciated massifs, Illampu on the left and Ancohuma on the right.

From Loriacani to **Chihuani** at 3,140m takes 1½ hours dropping down right (north) to the village, through the village and then the path drops more steeply. There are many paths. Avoid dropping too quickly to the Río San Cristóbal or going too high. It is possible to pick paths that will bring you out exactly at the point where the La Paz-Sorata road bridges the Río San Cristóbal at 2,665m in just over 1 hour. Cross the bridge to reach the right hand side of the Río San Cristóbal and follow the road to Sorata in 1 hour.

MAPIRI TRAIL

This is only for hardcore trekkers owing to the fact that the trail is covered in fallen trees in many places so you have to crawl under them. There are also very many insects, and problems with cows. On top of this it rains a lot or you are in cloud and there is a lack of water for much of the route – you need capacity to carry at least 4 litres of water per person for the lower part of the trail which is dry; the upper

part is wet. If you get into trouble you will have to get yourself out of it as there are very few if any people about.

Matthew Parris, author of *Inca Kola: a traveller's tale of Peru*, called Mapiri the 'trail of blood and tears'. He goes on: "When the Lord sent ten plagues down on the Egyptians, He was only testing. From the slopes of the Andes to the depths of the rainforest; through snow, sun, rain, mud and jungle; through blisters, toads, flies, bees, wasps, hornets, mosquitos and ants; through hummingbirds, butterflies and parrots; through such beauty and exhaustion as I never thought to see; it was an incredible journey, a week of fury and exhaltation". You get the picture.

The history of the Mapiri trail has been investigated by Louis Demers, the manager of the *Residencial Sorata*. The trail is not Inca or prehispanic – it was built to facilitate the transport of quinine out of the Mapiri area. Unfortunately, the trail was finished around 1879 in time for quinine to be industrially cultivated in other parts of the world where it was considerably cheaper to transport and the bottom fell out of the Bolivian quinine market.

However, rubber was then found and developed in the same area and the trail was used for that trade until the 1950s. Following the decline of the rubber trade, the Mapiri trail was used less and less and disappeared until reopened by miners looking for gold in 1989.

The trek

As long as the path has been used or cut recently, route finding is straightforward.

Mules cannot do this trek because of the sections where you have to crawl under fallen trees, but guides can be hired in Sorata. Start as early as possible each day as cloud normally comes in around 1200-1400 and it rains most days during the afternoon.

Day 1 Sorata to Ingenio by pick up from Sorata, 4 hours, US$6, and then trek to

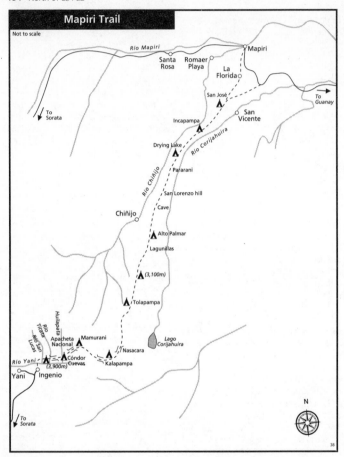

Mapiri Trail

Not to scale

Río Mapiri

Mapiri

Santa Rosa

Romaer Playa

La Florida

To Guanay

San José

To Sorata

San Vicente

Incapampa

Río Corijahuira

Drying Lake

Pararani

Río Chiñijo

San Lorenzo hill

Cave

Chiñijo

Alto Palmar

Lagunillas

(3,100m)

Tolapampa

Lago Corijahuira

Huilapata

Río Ticata

Río San Lucas

Apacheta Nacional

Mamurani

Nasacara

Cóndor Cuevas

Río Yani

(3,900m)

Kalapampa

Yani

Ingenio

To Sorata

N

38

the Río Ticata; day 2 to Mamurani; day 3 to before or after Nasacara; day 4 to ridge-top camp at 3,100m; day 5 to Altopalmar; day 6 to drying lake below Pararani; day 7 to San José; day 8 to Mapiri. From Mapiri it is possible to continue to Guanay by boat.

From Ingenio, walk 50m to the start of the trail running down the right hand side of the village. Follow the paving down to the **Río Yani**, cross to the other side and then cross the tributary **Río San Lucas**

and follow the trail, reaching camping at 3,550m after 1 hour just before the **Río Ticata**.

Cross the Río Ticata and carry on up past the last two inhabited houses to a pass in 1¼ hours at 3,900m. Drop down, cross a ridge, through **Huilapata** and cross a river which runs back to the Río Yani and camping.

Head up and over another ridge and up to a second ridge in 1¼ hours which marks the divide between the Río Yani and Río Chiñijo valleys. Below the **Cóndor Cuevas** at 3,850m there is excellent camping. There is a lake 100m up left from the trail and it is another 30 minutes to the **Apacheta 'Nacional'**, as it is painted.

A well-built staircase drops 120m down. After the bottom of the zigzags a path leads off left. Do not follow it, it is probably an attempt to reopen a very old path to Chiñijo but whoever tried it, gave up. In 45 minutes from the pass there is a another stream and immediately afterwards and good camping at **Mamurani** at 3,650m, but watch out for the cows.

From Mamurani it is 1¼ hours to a lake where it is also possible to camp. Another 1½ hours brings you through an area called **Kalapampa** and to the next river and possible camping, 15 minutes below the next pass. Thirty minutes on is another stream and camping and then stone steps up, cross the next stream and you will reach the top of a ridge at a point called **Nasacara** at 3,950m. Farther on it is possible to look back to the valley of the Río Yani.

From here the trail follows the top of the ridge where the cloud comes up from the jungle and condenses on the ridge. The river down to the right is the Río Corijahuira.

After 2 hours or so on the ridge there is a cave off to the right and camping before the next river. Thirty minutes further on is **Tolapampa** marked by an abandoned house (built in 1895 to shelter muledrivers), a stream and camping. Following the ridge, you drop into and rise out of bits of jungle, and after 3 hours reach excellent camping on top of the ridge at 3,100m. Enjoy it. After here it is jungle. If this area is dry and parched you should seriously consider abandoning the route and walk back to Ingenio because water will be very scarce – if you can find any at all – below this point.

Note that the water sources mentioned below exist during average years of rainfall. As you enter the jungle, keep a careful eye on the trail – it is visible – and tend

right. Two hours later there is a small clearing with water.

Landslides are quite common on the ridge and there is a big one here. **Do not attempt to cross the landslides**. It is quite easy to slip and slide 400m down the landslide – which is not too bad – but then be dumped 20m into rocks. It would take anyone with you a long time to get down safely and a very long time to get you out; on the off chance that you survived.

Beyond the landslide is a hilltop at 2,800m, 1½ hours from the clearing. Two more dry hilltops and 4 hours later you get to **Lagunillas** which is the last guaranteed water and a good place to camp, but leaves you with a very long waterless next day. Fifty years ago, when the trail was in regular use, mulateers would wade waist-deep across this section through a bog which was churned up by mule trains every day. A better alternative is to fill all water containers and carry on up for 1 hour to **Altopalmar** at 2,700m. This part is dry, but it is possible to camp and it shortens the dry section by 1 hour.

From here on it is down and dry all the way. You need to have enough water to get through the whole of the next day. After 4 hours when you reach the lowest point there is a cave to the right of the trail with a drip which would provide emergency water for a small group.

From the cave it is 45 minutes up to the dry **San Lorenzo hilltop** at 2,200m and the bees and flies start in earnest. Three hours down, 1½ hours below an area called **Pararani**, there is a drying lake which is the next source of water. This is 8 hours from Altopalmar and 9 hours from Lagunillas. Camp before the lake.

Exit the jungle and 4 hours later is **Incapampa** and a marsh, which can sometimes provide water in the middle if you dig a bit, and there is camping shortly afterwards. Three hours later there is better camping and water at a long-abandoned *hacienda* site called **San José** (watch out for cows). The water is 300m from the *hacienda* site following a trail to

San Carlos, a *hacienda* still in use, back up right.

This section is famed for its long grass which conceals snakes, ticks, bees, and horseflies. Cows are also a problem; they graze at night which can keep you awake and they are inquisitive and will push around, knocking down tents unintentionally or intentionally. They appear to be after the sodium in your sweat.

From San José, carry on down for an hour to reach a junction. You can make a run for the road off right which is 1½ hours away, but unless you get a lift it is a 4-6 hour road slog to Mapiri. It's a better idea to carry on through **La Florida** and you can reach Mapiri in 4 hours.

MAPIRI TO SORATA

Mapiri is an ugly mining town on the river of the same name. You can stay at **G** pp *Alojamiento Porvenir*, which is reported as the best accommodation in town.

From Mapiri get a pick up for the hour-long journey to **Santa Rosa** (*Residencial Judith* is nice with a pool, wait here for a lift to La Paz or Sorata). From Santa Rosa it is 11 hours to Sorata, US$12 per person. The scenery is superb, but the road is narrow, slippery and dangerous, especially in the rainy season. Try to sit in front with the driver; there is usually a carpet to protect passengers against rain, but there is also a lot of dust. Have warm clothing handy for the road crosses the pass at 4,700m before dropping to Sorata.

Alternatively, take a boat to Guanay, 3 hours, US$6, from where it is possible to get a bus back to La Paz or continue down by boat to Rurrenabaque, US$20 (see **Yungas** section, page 174).

CAMINO DEL ORO

This very hot and strenuous 7-8 day hike to Guanay may not be in existence for much longer. The road from Guanay has slowly been moving up the Tipuani valley, destroying the trail from below. There are now plans to drive the road down from Ancoma which will completely destroy the trail. So, do it now, while you can.

Either walk to **Ancoma** in 2 days (see **Illampu Circuit** above) or hire a jeep from the main plaza in Sorata, US$55, 3 hours. Locals like to charge US$2 per person to camp in Ancoma. There is no legal basis for this charge and you don't get anything for your money. Similarly, people in **Lambramani** try to collect a toll, but don't pay as it will only encourage them.

Camp in Ancoma or **Tusguaya** and then **Sumata**, **Quillapituni** and **Ticumbaya** and then stay in whichever village you get to before returning to La Paz.

Follow the valley of the Río Illampu down to where it becomes the Río

Camino del Oro

Tipuani. Continue downwards through the villages of **Sumata**, **Wainapata** and **Chusi** (18 hours from Ancoma). The An-coma-Llipi section is the most interesting, following the Río Tipuani, climbing Inca staircases, crossing rivers on precarious plank bridges and going through an Inca tunnel. Trail-finding is straightforward but there is not much flat ground for camping.

End the trek where the trail joins the road or continue down until you meet up with transport to **Llipi** (8 hours from Chusi), **Unutuluni** (2-3 hours from Llipi), or **Tipuani**. From Tipuani there is regular transport to Guanay (US$5) and on to Caranavi and La Paz.

MOUNTAINEERING NEAR SORATA

Sorata is dominated by views of the Illampu-Ancohuma massif which is made up of 30 or so peaks higher than 5,000m and marks the northwestern end of the Cordillera Real. Ancohuma is the highest mountain in the area at 6,427m. However, according to *The Times Atlas of the World*, Ancohuma is 7,012m which would make it the only mountain in the world higher than 7,000m outside the Himalayas. It also would make it the highest mountain in South America, an honour usually given to the 6,960m Aconcagua in Argentina.

The normal routes on Ancohuma are long but without technical difficulty. Access is traditionally via Cocoyo, 5 hours by jeep from Sorata, US$80, or a 2-day walk via Abra Illampu (see **Illampu Circuit** above). Once in Cocoyo arrange llamas – which only carry loads of 12 kilograms each – for the next day to basecamp at Laguna Jacha Leche Khota at 4,721m in 6 hours. It is cheaper to go in from the west following the route to Laguna Glaciar (see **Illampu Circuit** above). From the exit end of Laguna Glaciar, head up aiming for Point 5573. From here, rope up and pick a way across the heavily crevassed glacier, aiming to get as far across as possible and set up camp on the glacier at about 5,800m.

The easiest route on Illampu (6,368m) is difficult. This should not be attempted by inexperienced climbers with or without a guide. There are no mountain guides based in Sorata. If you want a mountain guide you will have to organize one in La Paz which is expensive. You have to pay the guide to get to Sorata and then go to the mountain.

● **Maps** See **Trekking Near Sorata** above.

● **Guidebooks** *Bolivia – a climbing guide* by Yossi Brain (The Mountaineers, 1997). *La Cordillera Real de los Andes* by Alain Mesili, in Spanish (Los Amigos del Libro, 1984, reprint 1996).

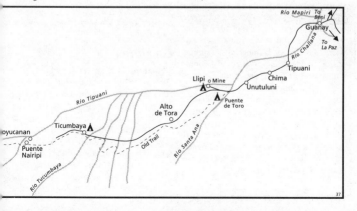

CORDILLERA APOLOBAMBA

The remote and beautiful Cordillera Apolobamba stretches from Charazani north to Pelechuco and then on into Peru. There is only one other sizeable village in the area, Ulla Ulla on the Altiplano, so the area is one of the best for spotting condors and torrent ducks while the extremely rare spectacled bear has been seen on the eastern slopes of the Cordillera.

● **Maps** None are published in Bolivia. The best available map is that done by the Boundary Commission of the Royal Geographic Society in 1911-13, updated by Paul Hudson 1993, and published by the RGS, London. There are mistakes and omissions but it is by far the best map available.

ACHACACHI TO CHARAZANI

The road to the Cordillera Apolobamba leaves Achacachi (see page 143) and follows the eastern shore of Lake Titicaca north and then west, passing through **Ancoraimes** (small Sunday market), **Carabuco** and **Escoma**, which has a large Aymara market every Sunday morning. At Escoma the road branches: northwest to Puerto Acosta (see below); and north to **Charazani** (see below). The road is very scenic, climbing to 4,500m. It ends at **Apolo**.

On the road north from Escoma to Charazani is a turn-off right. The road crosses a 5,000m pass before descending to **Aucapata**. Continue down a very poor jeep track then hike 1 hour down a cactus-filled canyon to the ruins of **Iskanwaya**, a major archaeological site on the eastern Andean slopes, at about 1,500m. The city stands on two built-up platforms, with delicate walls, plazas, narrow streets, storerooms, niches, pot shards, etc. Admission to the museum in Aucapata is by donation. Great care is needed not to damage this site. A recommended guidebook is *Iskanwaya: la ciudadela que sólo vivía de noche*, by Hugo Boero Rojo (Los Amigos del Libro, 1992).

● **Transport** To Aucapata there is a truck (and rumours of a bus) from the Cementerio district in La Paz, Friday 0200, 27 hours (see La Paz **buses**, page 107). Hire a jeep for US$400 round trip: one driver who knows the way is Oscar Vera, La Paz T 230453.

ESCOMA TO PUERTO ACOSTA

From Escoma a road runs northwest to **Puerto Acosta** just before the border with Peru. The Peruvian authorities, however, do not officially recognize the road as being a border crossing. Officially, you must get your entry stamp in the Department of Puno, but as this is next to impossible on this route, you will run into difficulties later on. There is an immigration office in Puerto Acosta, but it is advisable to get an exit stamp in La Paz first.

The area around Puerto Acosta is good walking country and the locals are friendly. From La Paz to Puerto Acosta the road is fine during the dry season (approximately May to October). North of Puerto Acosta towards Peru the road deteriorates rapidly and should not be attempted except in the dry season.

● **Accommodation** G *Alojamiento Espinosa*, basic but friendly. There are no restaurants.

● **Transport** Buses leave from La Paz (Cementerio district) to Puerto Acosta, US$3.25, Friday 1130, Saturday/Sunday 0630. Many trucks travel La Paz-Puerto Acosta on Tuesday and Friday afternoons. The only transport beyond Acosta is early on Wednesday and Saturday mornings when a couple of trucks go to the markets, some 25 km from Puerto Acosta on the border.

CHARAZANI

Charazani (official name Villa Juan J Pérez) is the biggest village in the region. At 3,200m it is noticeably warmer than La Paz and there are thermal baths (entrance US$1) 10 minutes below the village in which to cool off. Another local attraction is a 3-day fiesta around 16 July which is famous for having some of the best highland music and non-stop dancing (and drinking). The road to Apolo follows the left hand side of the valley dropping below Charazani.

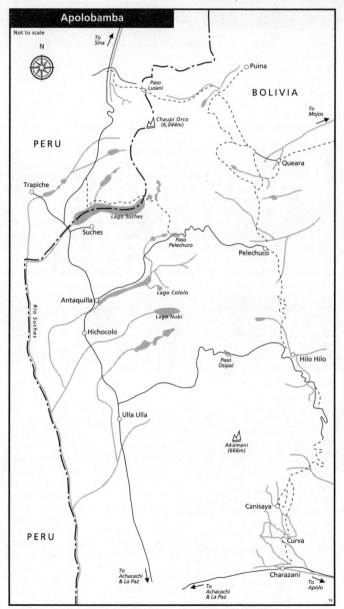

Apolobamba

Not to scale

N

To Sina

Paso Lusani

Chaupi Orco (6,044m)

BOLIVIA

Puina

To Mojos

PERU

Trapiche

Queara

Lago Suches

Suches

Paso Pelechuco

Pelechuco

Río Suches

Antaquilla

Lago Cololo

Lago Nubi

Hichocolo

Paso Osipal

Hilo Hilo

Ulla Ulla

Akamani (666m)

Canisaya

Curva

PERU

To Achacachi & La Paz

To Achacachi & La Paz

Charazani

To Apolo

19

A taste of their own medicine

🐾 When a Bolivian is ill, he or she is more likely to pay a visit to the local *curandero* (healer) than arrange an appointment with a doctor. In rural areas in particular Western medicine is seen only as a last resort. Every village or community in Bolivia has its own *curandero* who knows the medicinal properties of plants and herbs.

Traditional medicine is an integral part of Andean culture and, unlike Western practices, takes into account the patient's own perceptions of his or her illness and emotional condition. Healers believe that physical illnesses originate from the soul and are caused by the *ajaya* (life force) leaving the body. The healer's job is to coax the *ajaya* back into the body and restore the mind/body equilibrium. In this way, the healer instills confidence in the patient and lowers psychological resistance to the purification process.

The pop stars of Bolivian traditional medicine are the *Kallawayas*, the famous travelling healers of the Andes. With their bag of herbs, roots, ointments and amulets, the *Kallawayas* travel the length and breadth of the Andes from Ecuador to Argentina, dispensing spiritual wisdom and natural remedies.

Curiously, the *Kallawayas* all hail from the same region, a group of six small villages in the Apolobamba Mountains. Why this should be the case is something of a mystery, though one theory is that they are descendants of the Tiahuanaco culture. Something like a quarter of the residents of these villages are believed to possess considerable knowledge and healing powers. The *Kallawayas'* travels have given them access to and knowledge of as many as 1,000 plants and herbs.

The *Kallawayas* pass their knowledge on to their sons, or occasionally apprentices. Women are traditionally not allowed to become *Kallawayas*, though they play an essential role as midwives and as healers of the female reproductive system.

Renewed interest in natural medicine has helped preserve the *Kallawaya* tradition which was in danger of disappearing. Perhaps Western doctors will finally learn to accept herbal medicine as a valuable and well-researched science instead of dismissing it as some form of witchcraft.

● **Accommodation, places to eat & services** There are some small shops and eateries (which often serve trout for dinner) around the plaza and a number of *alojamientos*: the best is **G** *Hotel Kallawaya*. There is a medical post but no telephone and no electricity since 1994.

● **Transport** Buses from La Paz to Charazani from Calle Reyes Cardona, corner Avenida Kollasuyo above Cementerio, Friday, Saturday, Sunday, and Monday at 0600, US$4.40, 10 hours (see La Paz **buses**, page 107). The bus sometimes goes up to Curva to pick up passengers for the return trip to La Paz, 1½ hours, US$1.40. Return to La Paz from Charazani Friday, Sunday, Monday, and Wednesday at 0400, Monday at 1900. A La Paz-Charazani jeep costs US$250 and takes 6½ hours. For the Apolobamba South trek (see below) it is possible to continue by jeep to Curva in another 1½ hours. Arrive early enough to trek to the first camping at or below Jatunpampa.

APOLOBAMBA SOUTH TREK

This 5-day trek from Charazani or Curva to Pelechuco is probably the best mountain trek in Bolivia, passing through traditional villages and then up into the mountains of the southern Cordillera Apolobamba. There are more people around than in the northern half of the range, but after Curva you are unlikely to see more than a few people a day and no other gringos. For the few people there are, their first language is Quechua followed by Aymara and then Spanish.

Day 1 Charazani to beyond Curva; day 2 to Incachani; day 3 to Sunchuli; day 4 to above Hilo Hilo; day 5 to Pelechuco.

The trek

Starting in Charazani it takes 4 hours to walk to **Curva**. Do not follow the road to Curva – it takes forever. Instead, follow the road to Curva out of the village, drop down to the thermal baths, cross the river and follow paths up the other side to rejoin the road.

Follow the road until opposite the village and then look for a path heading up left to the church on the hill with white tower and yellow building. Down on the right you can see the village of **Niñocorin** where in 1970 the remains of a *Kallawaya* medicine man were found, carbon-dated to 800-1000 BC. From the church go down on the other side of the hill and turn left when you reach the better path which contours and drops through terraced wheat fields to a bridge. Cross the river and head up to Curva, arriving in the main plaza.

Curva is an attractive hilltop village at 3,900m. It is the capital village of the *Kallawayas*, the travelling witch doctors of the area, and is situated below their sacred mountain of Akamani. However, Curva has nothing to offer in terms of accommodation or food. Its fiesta is particularly well supported by the local population for most of the week around 29 June.

From the plaza in Curva it is possible to see a cross on the hill to the north overlooking the village. Contour around the hill keeping the cross on the left and descend to a stream crossing in 1 hour.

Move up towards the first valley on the right through walled fields. Stay to the right of the stream and continue upwards. There are a number of possible camping sites, but if there is time continue up until you cross the stream above some small cultivated walled fields and join a well-defined path coming into the valley from the left. Follow this to reach an excellent camping spot in a narrow but flat pampa with a stream in another 1¼ hours called locally **Jatunpampa** (4,200m).

Continue up the valley and across a second pampa to reach a col in 1 hour. It takes another 20 minutes to reach the pass at 4,700m which gives fantastic views of Akamani to the left. At the col cairn head off downhill to the right to reach a camping spot near the waterfall

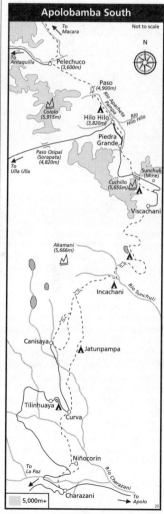

Apolobamba South

To Macara

Not to scale

N

To Antaquilla

Pelechuco (3,600m)

Paso (4,900m)

Cololo (5,915m)

Hilo Hilo (3,820m)

Rio Apacheta Pampa

Rio Hilo Hilo

Piedra Grande

Paso Osipal (Sorapata) (4,820m)

To Ulla Ulla

Cuchillo (5,655m)

Sunchuli (Mine)

Viscachani

Akamani (5,666m)

Rio Sunchuli

Incachani

Canisaya

Jatunpampa

Tilinhuaya

Curva

To La Paz

Niñocorin

Rio Charazani

5,000m+

Charazani

To Apolo

20

of **Incachani** at 4,100m in 1¼ hours. There are plenty of places to stop for lunch on the way down. An early camp gives plenty of time to wash in the cold, fast-moving stream, to spot wild horses and viscachas and to examine the ascent which faces you first thing next morning.

Cross the stream at the bridge below the waterfall and follow the zigzag path up into a scree gully which is often frozen together and remains in the shade until 1000. It takes 1¼ hours to get to the col from where it is possible to see Ancohuma and Illampu to the south before reaching the pass at 4,800m in another 15 minutes.

Contour left and gently up until you join the ridge in 20 minutes which gives views of Ancohuma, Illampu and the Cordillera Real to the south and Sunchuli mountain to the north. Follow the path down, pass a small lake before arriving at a second larger lake in 30 minutes which gives fantastic views of Akamani and where it is possible to camp.

From the lake, rise up to another ridge before descending left to the small mining settlement of **Viscachani** in 30 minutes where the dirt road to Hilo Hilo (Illo Illo) starts. Follow the road to the pass at 4,900m which takes 45 minutes from where it is possible to see the Cordillera Real stretching away to the south and Sunchuli mountain and the other mountains surrounding the Sunchuli valley to the north and west.

As the road drops down into the valley and bears right, look out for a path that leads off to the left. The path drops quite quickly towards the goldmine of **Sunchuli** – which reopened in 1992 and is worked by up to 100 miners – and then contour along the side of the valley staying above the aqueduct until you arrive at an ideal camping spot at 4,600m in 1 hour below Cuchillo.

The next section is possibly the best of the trek but it is north all the way (equivalent to south in the northern hemisphere) so the sun is in your face all day. From

here on there is a good path all the way used by Inca gold miners and campesinos ever since.

From camp, head up to the road which reaches the pass via a series of switchbacks. The plod uphill can be shortened and made more exciting by cutting off the corners. It takes 1¼ hours to reach the pass which is the highest of the trek at 5,100m and gives excellent views. It is possible to scramble up to a cairn above the road for even better views dominated by Cololo, the highest mountain in the southern Cordillera Apolobamba at 5,915m.

Follow the road down from the pass for a couple of minutes and then head off right down a steep path which crosses a good stream after 15 minutes opposite the glacier lake below Sunchuli mountain. Continue down to the bottom of the valley which takes 1 hour. Turn right and join the road a couple of minutes above the small, traditional, and picturesque stone and thatch village of **Piedra Grande** which is reached in 15 minutes.

Stay on the road until a prehispanic paved path leads off downhill to the right after 1 hour. Cross a bridge and follow the path up right to reach the village of **Hilo Hilo** in 1 hour. There are a couple of small shops selling crackers, pasta, tuna, soft drinks, beer, candles, matches, and batteries but not much else and rarely anything fresh.

Be careful when leaving Hilo Hilo not to follow the path up to the left which leads west to Ulla Ulla and the Altiplano. It is necessary to walk out of the village between the *baño* and the cemetery. Note that the newer and richer graves are roofed with corrugated iron.

Follow the path above the new school and then pick a route through walled fields and llama pastures before the path becomes clear again, crosses a bridge and heads up the valley with a pointed rock peak at its head. It takes 2 hours passing through two flat areas, called *pampas*, to reach a bend in the valley with large fallen stones where there is ideal camping. It is also possible to camp in either of the other pampas.

Continue up the valley to reach a bridge across the stream after 30 minutes and then start to climb up to the final pass at 4,900m which takes 1 hour.

From here it is downhill all the way via a lake after 20 minutes, through llama and alpaca pastures and some prehispanic paving before arriving in Pelechuco in 1½ hours.

PELECHUCO

Pelechuco is at 3,600m, set in the steep valley of the river of the same name on the eastern side of the Cordillera Apolobamba bordered to the north by the snow-capped peaks of the Katantica and Matchu Suchi Cuchu groups. The village's name comes from the Quechua *puyu kuchu* which means 'cloudy corner'. While the main economic activity of the area is gold mining, Pelechuco is old enough to have many

fine stone and colonial buildings; it was founded in 1560.

The village is basic. There is no phone, no electricity, and no latrine system, but there is a medical post which is often manned. Shops and cafes selling and serving the basics are found on all four sides of the plaza. The single table Pelechuco pool hall is a few balls short of a rack.

The biggest fiesta is held on the week around 25 July to celebrate the foundation of the village but there are fiestas every month. The locals are proud of this and support each one with enthusiasm and a lot of drinking.

● **Accommodation** There are a number of basic *alojamientos*: **G** pp *Rumillajta*, behind the church; **G** pp *Pensión México*, and *Chujlla Wasi*, both on the main plaza.

● **Transport** La Paz-Pelechuco bus from Calle Reyes Cardona corner Avenida Kollasuyo, three blocks up from Cementerio, Wednesday 1100. US$6, 18-24 hours (see La Paz **buses**, page 107). Return from Pelechuco Friday 2000, Saturday

High in fibre

🦙 The vicuña is the smallest representative of the South American camelids. It resembles the guanaco but is smaller and more slender and has a relatively long neck. They are strictly territorial, living in small herds of 8-12, led by a single male. Young males are expelled from the breeding herd by their mothers when 8-10 months old and live together in groups often 100 strong. Their territorial boundaries are aggressively defended by the dominant male which attacks intruders by biting, or by spitting regurgitated food.

Vicuña wool is probably the finest and lightest in the world. During Inca times only royalty were allowed to wear vicuña robes. They refuse to breed in captivity and so have never been domesticated. As a result, they are hunted. Estimates suggest there were more than 1 million vicuñas in Bolivia during pre-Inca times. The first laws to protect vicuñas in Bolivia were passed in 1918, but by the 1950s numbers were down to 400,000 and in 1965 6,000 were left. In 1965 there were 97 vicuñas in the area now covered by the reserve. There are now more than 5,700. It is illegal to kill vicuñas but illicit hunting goes on. Hunters using rifles with silencers have killed vicuñas in sight of the Ulla Ulla reserve headquarters.

Baby Vicuña

1600. Outward tickets from La Paz can and should be bought in advance from the small office in Calle Reyes Cardona, corner Avenida Kollasuyo, or from the buses themselves which park in the afternoon before departure in Calle Reyes Cardona. Return tickets should be organized when you get to Pelechuco. To or from Pelechuco by jeep costs US$300 and takes 10 hours or more.

ROUTES Buses to and from Pelechuco pass through the Ulla Ulla National Park (see below).

The journey through the Río Pelechuco valley is well-worth doing in daylight. Those who choose to travel by night should note that overnight journeys across the Altiplano in less than state-of-the-art transport are extremely cold, so take your sleeping bag onto the bus with you. If you're returning from Pelechuco by jeep, a visit to the Putina thermal baths, 2 hours by jeep from Pelechuco near **Antaquilla** is a must, followed by a daylight trip through the vicuña reserve of Ulla Ulla. If you have time on the way out or back, try and visit some of the first colonial churches built in Bolivia in the villages of Carabuco and Escoma.

RESERVA NACIONAL DE FAUNA ULLA ULLA

The Reserve was set up in 1972 to protect the vicuña, the antelope-looking smaller relative of the llama and alpaca. It covers a roughly defined area of just over 200,000 hectares from the Peruvian border to the Cordillera Apolobamba, from Pelechuco in the north to Charazani in the south.

There is much to see and do in the park. If you have your own transport, the wild vicuña herds can be observed at close range and followed cross country. During the day, especially in the dry season, the vicuñas graze in the marshy areas, mixed in with the alpacas, but towards evening, when their domesticated cousins return home to their stone-walled corrals, the vicuñas wander off to more isolated pastures. It's a particularly beautiful sight to see these graceful animals grazing on the plains at dawn against a backdrop of snowy peaks.

The reserve headquarters are at La Cabaña, 5 km outside the village of Ulla Ulla. There is basic but clean accommodation and food and visitors are very welcome. Orphaned vicuñas which would otherwise die are reared at La Cabaña. This allows you to get closer to them than anywhere else.

For more information contact the Centro Canadiense de Estudios y Cooperación Internacional, Calle Jaimes Freyre 2907, La Paz, T 411767.

The Yungas

ONLY A FEW hours from La Paz lie the warm, sub-tropical valleys known as the Yungas. These lush, forested slopes sit between the high Cordillera and the vast green carpet of jungle that stretches east, providing a convenient break for jungle-bound tourists travelling overland.

The Yungas are the main production area of citrus, bananas, coffee and coca leaves for the capital. This is also a popular tourist attraction. Coroico, in the Nor Yungas, is a favourite retreat for those escaping the Andean chill, while Chulumani, in the Sud Yungas, offers an equally attractive alternative.

The Yungas

LA PAZ TO THE YUNGAS

The most commonly used route to the Yungas goes via La Cumbre, northeast of La Paz. The road heads out of La Paz and climbs up and over La Cumbre pass at 4,725m, reaching its highest point in an hour. All around are towering snow-capped peaks. The roads to Chulumani and Coroico divide just after Unduavi, where there is a *garita* (check point), the only petrol station and dozens of food

The Kantuta,
national flower of Bolivia

A way of life

Coca has always played an important role in Bolivian society. As casual as a coffee-break and as sacred as Communion, coca chewing is an ancient ritual in the Andes. Coca can be bought anywhere and most Bolivians use it regularly; from *campesinos* in the highlands to non-Indian urban middle classes. Coca is chewed with a piece of *cal*, or lime, which activates with the saliva to produce a slight numbing of cheek and tongue. The desired effect is to numb the senses, which helps stave off hunger pangs and exhaustion, and to help people live at high altitude with no ill-effects.

As well as being a prerequisite for manual workers, such as miners, coca is also taken in a social context. The native population used to deny this because, in the eyes of the bosses and clergy, an increase in labour productivity was the only permissible reason for tolerating consumption of 'the devil's leaf'. The only places where coca is not chewed is in church and in the marital bed. The masticated leaves are spat out at the bedside.

Coca is also used in various rituals, such as in offerings to Pachamama, or Mother Earth, to feed her when she gets hungry. Various items such as flowers and sweets, along with the ubiquitous coca leaves, are put together in bundles called *pagos* and burned on the mountains at midnight. In countless Andean markets different *pagos* are sold for different purposes – to put into the foundation of a new house; for help in matters of health, business or love; or for magic, white or black.

Coca also has numerous medicinal qualities and possesses healthy constituents such as protein, minerals, salts and vitamins. This was discovered in 1989 after Jaime Paz Zamora, then president of Bolivia, asked foreign researchers to make an objective analysis of the effects of coca consumption in an attempt to have coca removed from the international register of prohibited substances.

Despite the findings coca remains a banned substance on the international market. Even *mate de coca*, an infusion of coca leaves, cannot be sold overseas, despite its outstanding curative qualities, not least of which is to limit the symptoms of altitude sickness. Just imagine, you could be arrested at customs for smuggling teabags into the country!

stalls. Soon after Unduavi the road becomes 'all-weather' and drops over 3,400m in spectacular fashion to the green semitropical forest in 80 km.

NB If travelling by truck from La Paz to the Yungas via La Cumbre, the best views can be seen in May and June, when there is least chance of fog and rain on the heights. It is very cold at La Cumbre and, further down, there are waterfalls at San Juan that baptise open vehicles – be prepared.

SUD YUNGAS

The Sud Yungas is largely neglected by foreign travellers who choose instead to head north to Coroico. Those with enough

time, though, should make this worthwhile diversion and get off the beaten track. The economy of the Sud Yungas is dominated by coca, but the leaves grown here are used for traditional purposes and not for cocaine production as in the Chapare region near Cochabamba. This is also a fruit-growing region; bananas, mangoes, papayas, oranges, pineapples and strawberries are all grown locally, as well as excellent coffee.

The road to the Sud Yungas branches east just beyond Unduavi. Though less nerve-wracking than the road to Coroico, this is nevertheless a scenically rewarding trip as the road follows the steep-sided valley of the Río Unduavi.

Offering of Coca leaves and alcohol to Pachamama

The first settlement you pass after Unduavi is Chaco, where you can stop at the *Hotel El Castillo*, 1 km before the end of **La Reconquistada** trek (see **Trekking near La Paz**, page 122). A few kilometres further on is Florida, where a dirt road turns off to the right to the attractive colonial village of Yanacachi, where the **Takesi Trail** ends (see **Trekking near La Paz**, page 119).

The main road continues to **Puente Villa**, 25 km before Chulumani. Just outside the village in a beautiful setting is the recommended **C** *Hotel Tamapaya*, which has good rooms with shower and swimming pool.

ROUTES An alternative and rarely travelled route to Chulumani is possible if you have your own transport. The road starts 10 km before **Panduro** on the La Paz-Oruro road. From the turn-off, it's 88 km to **Quime** on a good gravel road. There is basic and clean accommodation, **F**, in Quime. From Quime it's a 7-hour drive to Chulumani (200 km) passing through pristine cloud forest before reaching the village of Irupana (see **Excursions from Chulumani** below). There is no public transport on this route between **Inquisivi** and **Circuata**.

CHULUMANI

Chulumani (*Altitude* 1,700m; *Phone code* 0811) is the capital of Sud Yungas. It's an attractive, peaceful, relaxed and friendly little town perched on the slopes of a hill with magnificent views across the valley to Apa Apa and the villages of Chicaloma and Irupana.

Chulumani gets its name from two Aymara words meaning 'puma that drinks water', referring to a time before colonization when wild animals would drink from the stream above the town. Its neat little streets are a mix of colonial-style houses and modern buildings. Running off the lovely plaza is Calle Lanza, lined with stalls selling fruit and vegetables, piles of green bananas and several cheap eating places. The town holds a *Fiesta* on 24 August.

Near Chulumani is the village of **Sikilini**, which is at the end of the **Yunga Cruz** trek (see **Trekking near La Paz**, page 118). There are plenty of interesting walks in the area – to ancient villages, down to Apa Apa Ecological Park, up to Inca terraces at Pastogrande or simply take any path leading out of town (see **Excursions from Chulumani** below).

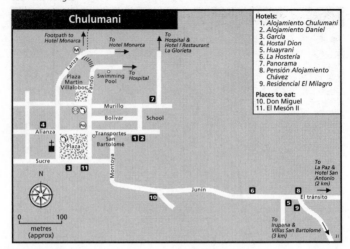

Chulumani

Hotels:
1. Alojamiento Chulumani
2. Alojamiento Daniel
3. García
4. Hostal Dion
5. Huayrani
6. La Hostería
7. Panorama
8. Pensión Alojamiento Chávez
9. Residencial El Milagro

Places to eat:
10. Don Miguel
11. El Mesón II

Local information

● Accommodation

A3 *Villas San Bartolomé*, 2 km from *tránsito* down the road to Irupana, arrange hotel transport beforehand if arriving by bus, there are no taxis, pleasant cabins in a superb setting with fabulous views of the surrounding valleys, swimming pool, can be booked through the *Hotel Plaza*, La Paz, T 378311, Ext 1221 (or Plaza Tours in La Paz).

C *San Antonio*, 3 km out of town back along the road to La Paz, pleasant cabins with pool.

D pp *La Glorieta*, 30-40 minutes walk beyond *Hotel Panorama*, near the top of Loma Linda with spectacular views, accommodation for twelve in comfortable, peaceful surroundings, shared bath, tastefully furnished rooms, the restaurant will prepare vegetarian meals on request, book through Sra Aida de Carrasco at *Hotel Panorama*; **D** *La Hostería*, Junín, near *tránsito*, T 6108, **E** without bath, includes breakfast, bar, pool table, good restaurant, run by Saturnino who is very friendly and helpful, great value and highly recommended; **D** *Monarca*, on the outskirts of town below Calle Lanza (see map), with pool, open to non-residents for a small fee; **D** *Panorama*, at top of the hill on Murillo, T 6109, comfortable and friendly with garden, restaurant and small pool; **D-E** *Residencial El Milagro*, at the entrance to town by the *tránsito*, clean rooms and a lovely garden with great views and barbecue facilities.

E *García*, on Plaza Libertad, cheaper without bath, basic but clean, the restaurant has a nice terrace with great views across to Apa Apa, noisy at weekends from disco; **E** pp *Huayrani*, near the *tránsito* just off Junín, T 6117, five cabins for four-six people, nice garden, pool, more expensive at weekends.

G pp *Alojamiento Chávez*, by the *tránsito*, shared bath, basic but clean, restaurant. On Bolívar is **G** pp *Alojamiento Chulumani*, basic and clean with shared bath; next door is **G** pp *Alojamiento Daniel*, which is similar but more modern.

● Places to eat

Don Miguel, just off Junín, on the left heading towards the Plaza, German-owned, good, fondue speciality, rents comfortable rooms **D** pp full board, with bath and TV; *El Mesón*, on the Plaza, good cheap meals. There are many cheap places to eat on Calle Lanza and around the *tránsito*.

● Post & telecommunications

Post office and **Cotel** are beside the Prefectura building just off the main plaza. There is an **Entel** booth on the plaza.

● Transport

Buses from La Paz: Trans San Bartolomé, Calle Ocabaya 435, Villa Fátima, T 211674, daily at 0800 and 1230, 4 hours, US$2.50. Turbus Totai, at the top of Calle Yanacachi, Villa Fátima, T 210607, daily at 0730, 0900, 1100 and 1400; they also go to Irupana (see below) on Thursday

From Africa to the Yungas

One of the more incongruous sights in the tropical Yungas are the black *cholas*, women of African origin wearing the traditional Aymara bowler hat and voluminous skirts.

17,000 blacks, descendants of African slaves, were brought from Peru and Argentina to work in the silver mines of Potosí, 4,000m up on the Altiplano. But they could not adapt to the harsh climate and were moved to the Yungas to work on coca plantations. Slaves that spoke the same language were separated to prevent them conspiring against their owners. But they learned Spanish and developed a dialect based on Spanish that could not be understood by the colonial rulers or the indigenous people. Bolivian blacks still speak these dialects, which include African words, but many of them also speak Aymara.

Africans were first brought to South America in the 16th century by European slave traders. By the 17th century half a million blacks lived on the continent. The vast majority live in rural areas with little or no access to economic or political power, but their influence has been felt in the music and dance of the country. In *La Morenada*, one of the most famous of Bolivia's folkloric dances, performed at the Oruro carnival, figures wearing masks to represent black slaves and to caricature their bosses play a prominent role (see Oruro **Carnival**, page 185).

at 0730. For the location of bus offices in Villa Fátima see Villa Fátima section on **La Paz orientation** map, page 107. Buses return to La Paz from the Plaza daily at 0600 and 1200, buy your ticket at the office. Other buses depart from the *tránsito* but have no fixed times; ask around.

EXCURSIONS FROM CHULUMANI

From Chulumani it is 1½ hours to the old colonial village of **Irupana**, which hosts a *Fiesta* on 5 August. There are several cheap and basic places to stay in Irupana; a recommended place is **F** *Hotel Casablanca*, with pool. A bus from Chulumani departs at around 1100 from the *tránsito*, US$1, or take any passing truck at the *tránsito*. It can be difficult finding transport back to Chulumani.

Beyond Irupana are the Inca ruins and terraces of **Pastogrande**. To get there you head down to the Río La Paz where there are lots of mango trees, then walk up through a dry area until you reach the perfectly preserved Inca terraces which are still in use. Ask for directions in Irupana.

Another road to Irupana goes via the ancient village of **Ocabaya**, where the 1952 revolution began, and passes through **Chicaloma**. This road is less direct and used

less often. Transport from the *tránsito* in Chulumani is infrequent; ask around.

Apa Apa Ecological Park

The main road to Irupana passes the turnoff to Apa Apa, a protected forest area of over 100 hectares, 8 km from Chulumani. This is the last area of original sub-tropical Yungas forest with plenty of interesting wildlife; small deer, agoutis, hoachi, nocturnal monkeys, many species of birds including parrots and lots of hummingbirds, porcupines, wildcats, pumas and even the Andean spectacled bear are among those sighted.

The flora includes the giant *leche-leche* trees which have a small 'cave' in the trunk. A recent study done in the park revealed seven new types of tree and many new ferns. At the moment one trail is open for tourists; a 3-hour hike through the lower part of the forest.

The park is managed by Ramón Portugal and his US-born wife Tildi. Ramón was born locally and knows the area well, he also speaks English. Their home is an 18th century *hacienda* which runs as a working farm. Near the house is a campsite with bathrooms (there are plans to

The highs and lows of bus travel

The journey to Coroico must be the most impressive in all Bolivia. It's an absolute must for adrenalin junkies but a definite no-no for those of a more nervous disposition. It could easily carry a government health warning. Whether you love it or loathe it will depend to a large extent on three things: 1) the weather; 2) how much alcohol your driver has consumed; and 3) the condition of the vehicle.

The first time I did the trip was in a *kombi* with dodgy brakes and an alcoholic driver with a death wish. I got off in Coroico, stumbling slightly on shaking legs, and vowed never to return. But several visits later, I'd still recommend it.

Some claim that this is one of the most dangerous roads in the world. That may or may not be true, but the biggest single vehicle accident in history apparently happened here in the 1980s, when a lorry packed with almost one hundred *campesinos* plunged over the edge. There are no accurate statistics on how many people actually die on this road. The police don't know if an accident occurs unless someone tells them. That's because the vegetation swallows up those unfortunate cars, trucks and buses that plunge over the edge. Whatever the real figures, the accident rate can't be helped by the fact that, according to Bolivian road law (yes, there are some), the vehicle going downhill should keep to the outside of the road, closest to the drop.

Bear this in mind when you board the bus in La Paz and insist on a left-sided seat for the best views. For a few hours later you will view this decision as a foolish act of bravado, which you now regret deeply. This is the scenario: your driver rounds yet another bend to come face to face with yet another massive timber truck. He reverses back uphill, getting ever closer to the edge of the precipice until you look out the window and can see no part of the road, only the tops of the trees far below. This gets to you after a while.

But the dangers of the road to Coroico are far outweighed by the thrill of the journey. The views are magnificent as you descend from the snows of the *cordillera* to the humid sub-tropics on a narrow strip of gravel cut into the sheer cliff-face, in places passing under waterfalls. Not forgetting the considerable delights of Coroico itself, of course. After a couple of days relaxing by the pool, enjoying a cold beer and the magnificent scenery, this trip won't seem so bad.

build barbecue grills and a pool). You can buy food from the farm.

There is a US$10 park entry fee which includes transport from Chulumani and a hiking guide. To get there ask in Chulumani for transport and ask to get off at the turn-off, then walk 15 minutes up to the *hacienda*. You can also phone 0811-6106 to arrange transport from town, or T (La Paz) 790381; or write to Casilla 10109, Miraflores, La Paz.

NOR YUNGAS

The preferred option for most travellers is to head for the northern part of the Yungas and the beautiful little town of Coroico. From Unduavi the steep, twisting road clings to the side of sheer cliffs on its way down to **Yolosa**, the junction 8 km from Coroico. Drivers should note that uphill vehicles must keep to the cliff side, be it left or right, and downhill vehicles keep on the outside.

Another road branches off at Yolosa to the village of **Chairo**, which marks the end of the **Choro Trail** (see page 123), and the five-star *Hotel Río Selva Resort* (reservations in La Paz at Calle Romecín Campos 696, Sopocachi, T 02-327561/362281), with cabins or bedrooms, pools, gym, sports complex, sauna, etc.

An alternative route to Coroico is from
Sorata via Guanay. There are various
ways to get to Guanay. You can take a truck
from Sorata to the mining town of **Mapiri**
via Santa Rosa (see Sorata **transport**, page
147), or hike the tortuous **Mapiri Trail** to
Mapiri (see page 153) and get a boat from
there to Guanay (see below). Alternatively, you can hike the **Camino del Oro**
to Tipuani and catch a bus from there to
Guanay (see page 156). From Guanay the
road goes to Caranavi and back to Coroico
(see below).

COROICO

Coroico (*Phone code* 0811) is perched on a
hill at 1,760m amid orange and banana
groves and coffee plantations. The town
enjoys stupendous views, particularly to
the southwest where you can see the distant snowy peaks of the Cordillera Real.

This place is not for the hyperactive.
There's not a huge amount to do here
except eat, drink and lay by the pool
soaking up the sun. Sounds great, doesn't
it?

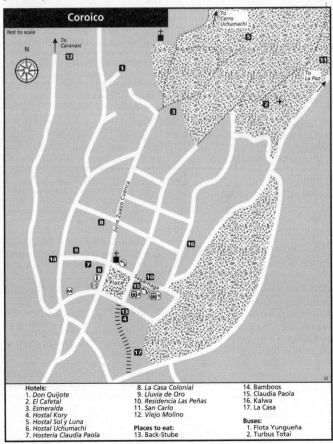

Hotels:
1. Don Quijote
2. El Cafetal
3. Esmeralda
4. Hostal Kory
5. Hostal Sol y Luna
6. Hostal Uchumachi
7. Hostería Claudia Paola
8. La Casa Colonial
9. Lluvia de Oro
10. Residencia Las Peñas
11. San Carlo
12. Viejo Molino

Places to eat:
13. Back-Stube

14. Bamboos
15. Claudia Paola
16. Kalwa
17. La Casa

Buses:
1. Flota Yungueña
2. Turbus Totai

Excursions

For those who can manage to tear themselves away from the pool-side, there are a number of good walks around Coroico. One is down to the pools at the **Río Vagante**, 7 km away off the road to Coripata. It takes about 3 hours to get there. Ask Fernando at *Hotel Esmeralda* for directions.

Another good walk is up to the waterfalls, starting from **El Calvario**. Follow the Stations of the Cross by the cemetery, off Calle Julio Zuazo Cuenca which leads uphill from the plaza. Facing the chapel at El Calvario, with your back to the town, look for a path on the left, which soon becomes well-defined. It leads in 1 hour to the **Cascada y Toma de Agua de Coroico**, the source of the town's water supply. Walk beyond this to a couple of waterfalls further on which are better for swimming.

The best walk is up **Cerro Uchumachi**, the mountain behind El Calvario. It is considered sacred and witchcraft is practised at various sites. Look for the red and white antenna behind the church at El Calvario. From there it's about 2 hours uphill. At the top of the mountain another trail continues to the right for about 1 hour to a campsite. The views from Uchumachi in the morning are spectacular. There's no water en route, so take your own and watch out for biting insects.

A good local guide for hiking and jeep tours is Don César Argandoña; ask for him in the main plaza in Coroico.

Local festivals

There is a colourful 4-day festival on **19-22 October**, when accommodation is hard to find. It is great fun, but it might be an idea to wait a day or two before returning to La Paz, in order to give your driver time to recover. On **2 November**, All Souls' Day, the local cemetery is festooned with black ribbons.

Local information

● Accommodation

For such a small town Coroico has a large variety of accommodation. Due to its popularity, however, the best hotels are booked up during holidays and are often full at weekends.

1 km out of town on the road to Caranavi is *El Viejo Molino*, four-star, with pool, T 0811-6004 (in La Paz, *Valmar Tours*, T 361076, F 352279). Also 1 km out of town, but on the road to La Paz is *San Carlo*, T 0811-3266 (La Paz 372380), with restaurant, pool and sports facilities, modern and recommended. 500m out of town, on the road to Coripata, is **D** *Don Quijote*, with pool and restaurant.

E pp *Esmeralda*, T 0811-6017, 5 minutes uphill from the plaza, Casilla 9225, La Paz, **F** pp in rooms without bath or view, free pick-up service (ring from *Totai Tours*), the owner Fernando speaks English, German and Spanish, great pool and lovely garden, hikes can be arranged, Visa, Mastercard taken, changes travellers' cheques at a decent rate, credit card phones, great views, fantastic hot showers, videos, excellent restaurant with terrace, laundry service, usually full so it's best to book ahead, highly recommended; **E** *Hostal Kory*, at the top of the steps leading down from the plaza, pool, cheaper without bath, weekly rates are available, there's not always hot water, lovely terrace, restaurant, laundry, good beds; **E** *La Casa*, downhill from *Hostal Kory*, hot water, pool, clean, quiet, excellent restaurant (see below); **E** *Lluvia de Oro*, one block from the church, T 6005, shared bath, good value, good food, cheap, pool, top floor rooms are best; **E-F** *Sol y Luna*, 15-20 minutes beyond *Hotel Esmeralda*, dormitory accommodation **G** pp, meals available, try their superb Indonesian banquet, also two *cabañas* for rent with kitchen, **D**, camping US$1 per person, small pool, garden, laundry service, highly recommended, reserve through *Chuquiago Turismo*, Planta Baja, Edificio La Primera, Avenida Santa Cruz 1364, Casilla 4443, La Paz, T 362099/359227.

F pp *La Casa Colonial*, on the next street uphill from the church running parallel, shared bath, comfortable, good value.

G pp *El Cafetal*, a long walk from town beside the hospital, French-run, excellent French cuisine, hammocks, excellent value; **G** pp *Hostería Claudia Paola*, opposite *Lluvia de Oro*, clean, basic; **G** pp *Las Peñas*, opposite the Entel office, shared bath, good, cheap, clean and friendly, good value lunch in their restaurant; **G** pp *Hostal Peregrino*, on Julio Zuazo Cuenca, cold water only, restaurant (good soups), good breakfast, nice terrace; on the same street is **G** pp *Residencial de la Torre*, with a nice garden; **G** pp *Hostal Uchumachi*, on the plaza, shared bath, restaurant. There's also a campsite by the small church on the hill overlooking the town (see **Excursions** above).

● **Places to eat**

La Casa, German-run, good food and setting, excellent salads, vegetarian dishes, fondue US$4, and raclette, reserve in advance, wonderful views, recommended. The convent opposite sells biscuits, peanut butter, wine and coffee liqueurs. *Confitería Claudia Paola*, next to Turbus Totai on the plaza, good pizza one. Around the corner is *Balneario-Restaurant Claudia Paola*, swimming pool with restaurant, open for breakfast and lunch; *Back-Stube*, next to *Hostal Kory*, good cakes, muesli, delicious vegetarian lunch and dinner for US$3.20, but not on Tuesday, friendly atmosphere; *Bamboos*, good Mexican food, US$4-5 per main dish, live music some nights with a small cover charge; *Kalwa*, just off the plaza on the road to the hospital, lunch US$1.50, hires bikes for US$1.50 per hour, also raquetball US$2 per hour. Cheap meals can be found at the market, near the plaza on the street beside the post office. Honey is sold in various places throughout the town.

● **Banks & money changers**

There are no banks in town. Change travellers' cheques at Turbus Totai, but the rates are poor. Better rates at *Hostal Kory* or *Hotel Esmeralda*.

● **Entertainment**

On Calle Julio Zuazo Cuenca are *Wiskería Taurus*, which is good for a beer, and *Safari*, restaurant-*peña* and disco at weekends. The open-air cinema is worth a visit for its rustic charm, entry US$0.40.

● **Post & telecommunications**

Post Office is on the plaza. **Entel**, on Sagárnaga next to Flota Yungueña, is for international and local calls; **Cotel** is next to the church; it also has a public TV.

● **Tourist information**

Next to the post office on the plaza.

● **Transport**

In La Paz all companies are on Calle Yanacachi, beside the YPFB station in Villa Fátima (see Villa Fátima inset on **La Paz orientation** map, page 107): Turbus Totai (T 212391), US$2.50, 3 hours, six daily to La Paz from 0830-1730; Coroico to La Paz at 0400 and hourly 0700-1730 daily except Sunday. Flota

Yungueña (T 212344), five daily to La Paz from 0800-1600. It's worth booking in advance. Extra services run on Sunday. It can be difficult to book journeys to La Paz on holidays and on Sunday evenings/Monday mornings, though these are good times for hitching. Trucks and pick-ups from La Paz may drop you at Yolosa, 8 km from Coroico, but there is usually transport Yolosa-Coroico, US$1. Or you can walk for 2 hours uphill all the way. In Coroico trucks leave from the market.

Buses, trucks and pick-ups run from Yolosa to **Caranavi**, 3-4 hours, US$3.25, **Guanay**, 7-8 hours, US$5.20 and **Rurrenabaque**, 13-15 hours, US$8.75. Flota Yungueña run daily at 1500 from Yolosa (they will take you down to Yolosa to catch the bus from La Paz). Turbus Totai run daily except Sunday at 1730, leaving from the plaza.

Frustratingly, a road runs between Coroico and Chulumani but there is no public transport. This means you have to return to La Paz if you want to visit both towns, or get off at Unduavi and hope for a seat on a passing bus. **Coripata** is about halfway between the two towns (accommodation in **F** *Hotel Florida*). This road joins the Unduavi-Chulumani road at Puente Villa (see **Sud Yungas** above).

CARANAVI

From the road junction at Yolosa the lower fork follows the river northeast to **Caranavi**, a very ugly town 164 km from La Paz and 75 km from Yolosa. From here the road continues towards the settled area of the Alto Beni, at times following a picturesque gorge. Market day in Caranavi is Saturday.

● **Accommodation** Most hotels are along Avenida Mariscal Santa Cruz, the main street: **E** *Landiva*, T (0811) 6234, nice pool, unhelpful staff; **F** *Caranavi*, recommended; **F** *Residencial Avenida*, basic and cheap; **F** *Alojamiento Capitol*, basic; **G** *Hostal La Paz*, clean, basic.

● **Places to eat** *Paradiso*, cheap; *Tropical*, good set menu and cheap.

● **Transport Buses** From Villa Fátima in **La Paz**: Flota Yungueña daily at 1300; Turbus Totai (T 212526), at 1530, 6-7 hours. Buses continue to **Rurrenabaque**. A direct bus **Coroico-Caranavi** leaves on Sunday, or you can take a

truck, US$2.15. If you want to continue into the Beni Lowlands without going into Caranavi, wait at the checkpoint before the town where all transport has to stop and ask for a ride there.

GUANAY

Some 70 km northwest of Caranavi is the gold mining town of **Guanay**, an interesting, friendly place at the junction of the Tipuani and Mapiri rivers. You can change cash with shopkeepers or gold dealers.

● **Accommodation E** *Panamericana*, helpful, popular with tour groups; **F** pp *Perla Andina*, cold water, rooms on the street are less hot than those on the courtyard, there are fans in the rooms but electricity 1800-2400 only; **F** *Hotel Ritzy*, on the main plaza, with mosquito nets; **G** pp *Alojamiento Los Pinos*, opposite the football pitch, cold water, basic, may arrange exchange of travellers' cheques with commission; **G** pp *Estrella Azul*, basic; **G** pp *Pahuichi*, nice restaurant. Camping is possible next to the football field.

● **Places to eat** *Restaurant La Bamba*, opposite *Panamericana*, good value, English spoken. There are many other eating places on the main street which have fixed-price meals; one, with courtyard, monkey and parrot, serves excellent value breakfast. Electricity is rationed – every 10 minutes or so – and water is available before 1200 only.

● **Transport Road** There are direct buses from La Paz: Flota Yungueña and Estrella Azul, about US$8; also trucks, which make frequent stops and diversions. There is also frequent transport to Caranavi. **River To Mapiri**: from Guanay dock, three blocks from the plaza, boats leave at 0700 daily, or when full, US$5. Do not rely on cargo boats at other times. En route mines can be seen among the tropical vegetation. Boats go down the Río Beni to Rurrenabaque (see page 292), 8-12 hours, it will cost US$11-18 depending on how successfully you negotiate and the availability of vessels. Cargo is now carried by road so you have to wait till the boat is full, which can take several days. 'Expreso' boats can be hired from Flota Fluvial, opposite *Perla Andina*, costs US$150-300, depending on size and your ability to bargain. The journey goes through gold mining settlements, then narrow, fertile river banks.

The Southern Altiplano

THIS REMOTE corner of Bolivia stretches from the mining centre of Oruro south to the borders of Chile and Argentina. There would appear to be little to attract the tourist to this barren plateau sitting on the roof of the world. It's a bleak, windswept terrain of parched scrub, with the occasional tiny adobe settlement blending into the uniform brown landscape. But tourists do come to this starkly beautiful corner of Bolivia and are rewarded with some of the greatest visual delights that this country has to offer. In the far south is a Salvador Dalí landscape of bizarre rock formations, white-capped volcanoes, shimmering kaleidoscope lakes filled with pink flamingoes, steaming geysers and inconceivably vast expanses of blinding white salt flats.

There appears to be no visible means of support for the people who live here. But these hardy, redoubtable Aymaras manage to eke out a meagre existence, sustained by traditional customs and beliefs that have remained unchanged for centuries. They herd llamas and grow a huge variety of tubers, the only crop that will grow in such a harsh environment. These are freeze-dried and then carried by llama down to the warmer valleys where they are exchanged for crops such as maize, which can be used to complement the diet or to make *chicha*, the fermented corn beer which is an integral part of festivals.

This vast region is rich in mineral deposits. Oruro and Llallagua are centres of tin production, while in the more remote southern parts concentrations of antimony, bismuth, copper, salt, sulphur and magnesium among others remain relatively unexploited owing to a lack of capital and expertise.

ORURO

ROUTES Oruro is 230 km southeast of La Paz by an asphalted road. At Km 104 it reaches Patacamaya, the turn-off for the road west to the Chilean frontier (see under La Paz, **By Road to Chile** page 108). It then passes Sica Sica and, 10 km before Panduro, a turn-off which eventually leads to Chulumani in the Sud Yungas (see page 167).

(*Population* 183,422; *Altitude* 3,706m; *Phone code* 052) Oruro is the biggest settlement

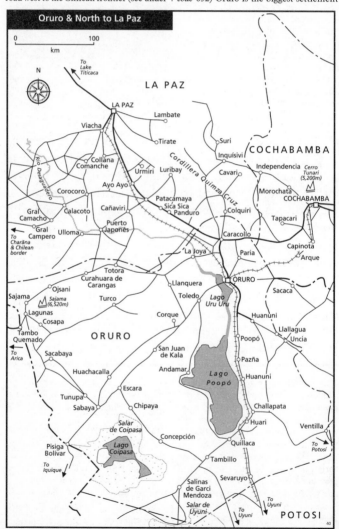

Oruro & North to La Paz

on the Altiplano. It began in the 16th century as a mining community extracting silver, tin, antimony and lead from the hills to the west of the city and was formally founded in 1606 as the Villa Real de San Felipe de Austria de Oruro. It became the second largest city in the Americas after Potosí and later the centre of the Bolivian rail network. It is now the commercial and administrative centre of the southern Altiplano though nearby gold mines, such as Inti Raymi (the largest and most profitable mine in Bolivia) and the Vinto tin smelter (the biggest in the country) are important economically.

Arriving at the bus terminal, you are faced with a ten block journey up the broad, windy and desolate Avenida 6 de Agosto to reach the city centre. This is not a good introduction to Oruro – the centre has many fine buildings and churches revealing the city's former wealth. The other immediately obvious feeling is the cold: 18°C to minus 10°C, with an average temperature of 10°C. However, this is forgotten for carnival in February when Oruro explodes with colour and life in the biggest and best celebration outside Rio de Janeiro. Carnival has made Oruro the official folklore capital of Bolivia.

Places of interest

The central square, Plaza 10 de Febrero, is named after the anti-Spanish revolt of

The Southern Altiplano

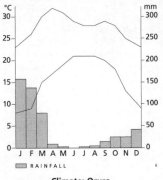

Climate: Oruro

1781 and is surrounded by grand colonial buildings, notably the **baroque concert hall**, which is now a cinema. There is a statue of Aniceto Arce, former president and founder of the Bolivian railways. The Correo at Calle Montes 1456 is 19th century with lots of wrought ironwork.

There is a good view of the city from the **Cerro Corazón de Jesus**, near the church of the **Virgen del Socavón**, five blocks west of Plaza 10 de Febrero at the end of Calle Mier. Worship of the Virgen del Socavón – the central point of miners' Christian worship – began at this site in the 16th century and the first church was built in 1781. The present church was built in the 19th century. The baroque entrance was built in the 16th century by the Jesuits and was part of the old cathedral until it was demolished in 1979. It was rebuilt at the Santuario in 1994. In front there is a monument of an armed miner.

Iglesia de San Miguel, presently hidden inside the Penny children's home in Calle Soria Galvarro, is the oldest church in the city. Built to convert the local people, it contains much original colonial art; ask at the tourist office for details of how to visit. **San Francisco** in Calle Bolívar near Soria Galvarro has an 18th century façade. **Santo Domingo**, in Calle Ayacucho next to Mercado Fermín López, was started in

1602 but was subsequently remodelled in the 18th and early 20th centuries.

The **Casa de la Cultura** was built by French architects 1900-13 for tin baron Simón Patiño (see Museums below). It was finished a year after he emigrated to Hamburg in Germany.

The baroque stone **Portada de Beaterio Madre Nazaria**, Calle Soria Galvarro between Sucre and Murguia, is worth a look, as is the Colegio Nacional Simón Bolívar which was built in 1827 and is impressively grand and colonial; Calle Murguia between Montes and La Plata.

The **Faro de Conchupata** at the end of Calle Montes is easily seen at night; it's torch-like glass structure atop a column is illuminated. It marks the first place where the present Bolivian tricoleur was raised in 1851 and gives a good view over the flat city below. The flag was not formally adopted until 1888: the red represents the courage of the Bolivian army, yellow (gold) the country's mineral wealth and green the fertility of its soil.

The disused **San José mine**, worked for over 450 years for silver, tin and other minerals, lies 5 km west of the city. It can be visited with a permit from Comibol, the state mining company. Ask at the Tourist Office about visiting; the *Intendencia* of the mine will provide a guide. A 20,000 tonnes-a-year tin smelter nearby at **Vinto** is open to visitors with a permit; apply 24 hours in advance in Oruro.

Museums

Museo Etnográfico Minero is inside the Santuario del Socavón (see above). From the back of the church you descend through some of Oruro's oldest preserved mining tunnels past displays showing mining techniques to reach a representation of *Tío*, the god of the underworld. The museum is open Monday-Saturday 0900-1200 and 1500-1800, Sunday 0800-1200 and 1600-1800; entrance US$0.60, permission to take photos US$0.60.

Casa de la Cultura Museo Patiño, Soria Galvarro 5755, is now run by the Universidad Técnica de Oruro. It was built as a palace by French architects for the "King of Tin", Simón Patiño, the museum contains colonial art, French furniture in the style of Louis XV and XVI and other displays. Open Monday-Friday 0900-1200, 1430-1800, US$1.45.

Museo Mineralógico y Geológico is part of the University; take any micro south to the Ciudad Universitaria. There are 5,500 examples of rocks - one of the largest collections in South America. Open Monday-Friday 0800-1200 and 1430-1700, entrance US$0.60.

Museo del Beaterio Madre Nazaria, on Calle Soria Galvarro between Sucre and Murguia, has a display of masques; entrance US$0.40. For opening times check with the tourist office.

Museo Antropológico Eduardo López Rivas, is south of the centre on Avenida España esquina Urquidi, T 60020. It has a unique collection of stone llama heads, prehispanic mummies, artefacts from the Uru, Wankarani and Chipaya peoples and carnival masks and costumes. It also has a good selection of postcards and an *artesanía* shop. Open Monday-Friday 0900-1200, 1400-1800; Saturday/Sunday 1000-200, 1500-1800, US$0.75. To get there, take micro A heading south or any *trufi* going south.

Parks and zoos

One block away at the north end of Calle Urquidi is the Parque Zoológico, open Monday-Sunday 0800-1200 and 1400-1730, entrance US$0.20. It is better than it was and gives you the chance to see condors, eagles, alpacas, quirquinchos (armadillos) and other Altiplano species in cages. The quirquincho's body was used to make charangos, the small, guitar-like instruments, and as a result it is nearly extinct in the wild.

Excursions

There are thermal baths at **Capachos**, which is 12 km from Oruro, and **Obrajes**, 25 km away. Both have long been visited for the medicinal properties of the thermal

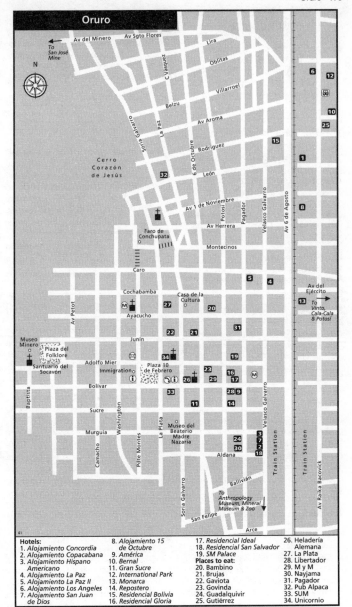

Oruro

To San José Mine

Av del Minero
Av Sgto Flores
Lira
C Vásquez
Oblitas
Villarroel
Belzu
La Paz
Soria Galvarro
Av Aroma
6 de Octubre
Rodríguez
15
32
León
1
8
Cerro
Corazón
de Jesús
Potosí
Pagador
Velasco Galvarro
Av 6 de Agosto
Av 1 de Noviembre
Av Herrera
Faro de
Conchupata
Montecinos
Caro
5
4
Av del
Ejército
Av Petot
Cochabamba
Casa de la
Cultura
13
To Vinto, Cala-Cala & Potosí
27
20
Ayacucho
Junín
22
21
31
34
19
Museo Minero
Plaza del Folklore
Santuario del Socavón
Adolfo Mier
Immigration
Plaza 10 de Febrero
23
16
Bolívar
26
29
17
Baptista
33
28 **9**
11
14
Sucre
Washington
Pte Montes
La Plata
Murguía
Camacho
Museo del Beaterio Madre Nazaria
24
3
7
Aldana
30
2
18
Velasco Galvarro
Train Station
Train Station
Av Raika Bacovick
Ballivián
To Anthropology Museum, Mineral Museum & Zoo
Soria Galvarro
San Felipe
Arce
6
12
10
25

Hotels:
1. *Alojamiento Concordia*
2. *Alojamiento Copacabana*
3. *Alojamiento Híspano Americano*
4. *Alojamiento La Paz*
5. *Alojamiento La Paz II*
6. *Alojamiento Los Angeles*
7. *Alojamiento San Juan de Dios*
8. *Alojamiento 15 de Octubre*
9. *América*
10. *Bernal*
11. *Gran Sucre*
12. *International Park*
13. *Monarca*
14. *Repostero*
15. *Residencial Bolivia*
16. *Residencial Gloria*
17. *Residencial Ideal*
18. *Residencial San Salvador*
19. *SM Palace*

Places to eat:
20. *Bambino*
21. *Brujas*
22. *Gaviota*
23. *Govinda*
24. *Guadalquivir*
25. *Gutiérrez*
26. *Heladería Alemana*
27. *La Plata*
28. *Libertador*
29. *M y M*
30. *Nayjama*
31. *Pagador*
32. *Pub Alpaca*
33. *SUM*
34. *Unicornio*

waters and have covered swimming pools, but Obrajes is better. Capachos is free and entrance to Obrajes is US$1.20, with the choice of private baths or swimming pool.

Buses leave from Calle Caro either side of 6 de Agosto, 0700-1700, US$0.40 to Capachos, US$0.80 to Obrajes. Go early as return transport is difficult after 1600. Taxis sometimes make the run. Avoid Sunday, when it is very crowded.

The **Qala Qala (Cala Cala) cave paintings** are 20 km to the southeast of Oruro.

The pictures and carvings are mainly of llamas and are thought to date from the Wankarani period, 800 BC-400 AD. Trucks and buses leave 0700-1100 from Calle Brasil esquina Ejército. A taxi there, plus wait and return is about US$16. Find the guardian, Francisco León, and pay the US$1 entrance.

Local information
● Accommodation

Near the bus terminal: **B** *International Park*, above the bus terminal, T 53209, F 53187, Oruro's best hotel, price includes continental breakfast, every room has phone, TV and private bathroom, parking facilities.

C-D *Terminal*, above the bus terminal, T 53797, modern, heating, good views, expensive restaurant, dirty, noisy.

D-E *Lipton*, Avenida 6 de Agosto 225, T 41538, **F** pp without bath, secure, parking extra, open 24 hours, good value; **D-E** *Residencial Verano*, 200m from the bus terminal, T 41742, without bath, modern, clean, open 24 hours; **E** *Bernal*, Calle Brasil 701, opposite the terminal, T 42468, clean, modern, good value, excellent hot showers.

F pp *Residencial El Turista*, 6 de Agosto 466, T 41888, without bath, unhelpful, safe parking.

G pp *Alojamiento Los Angeles*, Calle Bakovic 432 opposite the terminal, T 41183, basic and noisy.

Between bus terminal and centre: **C** *Monarca*, Avenida 6 de Agosto esquina Ejército, T 54300, F 50006, comfortable hotel, shame about the location.

F pp *Residencial Bolivia*, Calle Rodríguez 131, T 41047, open 24 hours, it's the cheapest place to take Visa/Mastercard (which adds 13% to your bill), without bath, hot water, good value but poor restaurant.

G pp *Alojamiento 15 de Octubre*, Avenida 6 de Agosto 890, T 40012, first floor, go up the stairs on the left, without bath, hot showers, safe, good value, friendly; **G** pp *Alojamiento La Paz*, Calle V Galvarro 180, T 60882, cheap and basic; **G** pp *Alojamiento La Paz II*, Calle Cochabamba 266, around the corner, from the people who brought you *Alojamiento La Paz*; **G** pp *Alojamiento Concordia*, Calle León 110, T 31376, cheap, basic, friendly.

In the centre: **B** *S M Palace*, Calle Mier 392, T/F 55132, not as interesting as the name suggests but modern, all rooms with phone, TV and private bathroom, price includes continental breakfast.

C *Gran Sucre*, Sucre 510 esquina 6 de Octubre, T 53838, F 50744, cheaper with shared bathroom, all rooms with phone and TV, it has more character than most Oruro hotels, heater on request, recommended.

D *Repostero*, Sucre 370 y Pagador, T 50505, with private bath, **E** without, ageing but clean, friendly, hot water, parking; **D** *América*, Bolívar 351 y Pagador, T 60707, F 60707, ring the bell to get in, **E** without bath, all rooms with TV, restaurant.

F pp *Gloria*, Potosí 6059, T 52250, interesting 19th century building, private bathrooms available, basic, hot water, open 24 hours; **F** pp *Residencial Ideal*, Bolívar 386, T 52863, not as good as the name suggests, basic but central, poor beds.

Near the railway station: **F** *Residencial San Salvador*, Calle V Galvarro 6325, hot water, the best of the group.

G pp *Alojamiento Hispano-Americano*, Calle V Galvarro 6392, T 61117, despite what the street numbering would suggest this is next door to the others, it's the cheapest of the four hotels on this street and bigger and older than its neighbours; **G** pp *Alojamiento Copacabana*, Calle V Galvarro 1856, T 54184, possibly slightly cleaner than its neighbours, luggage storage; **G** pp *Alojamiento San Juan de Dios*, Calle V Galvarro 1846, T 53083, surrounds a large courtyard. The three *alojamientos* each have a standard and cheap restaurant attached.

● Places to eat
There are lots of cheap eats in Oruro including the *comedor popular* in the centre of Mercado Campero (*api* and *pasteles* are the best breakfast available for warming up, from 0800). Unlike La Paz, Oruro is reasonably lively on Sundays until 2100 with many restaurants and cafés open. A

traditional dish is *charquekan*, which sounds like a well-known soul/funk singer but is actually grilled sun-dried llama meat served with maize, potato, egg and cheese.

Nayjama, Calle Aldana esquina Pagador, the best restaurant in Oruro, very popular for lunch, huge servings, main dishes US$4-6; *La Cabaña*, Junín 609, comfortable, smart, good international food, bar, reasonable prices, closed Monday; *Club Social Croata*, Junín 729 y Presidente Montes, good value lunches; *Govinda*, 6 de Octubre 6071, excellent vegetarian restaurant, *almuerzo* US$1.40 from 1300, Monday-Friday. Another vegetarian is *El Huerto*, Bolívar 359, good cheap food. *SUM Confitería*, Bolívar esquina S Galvarro, *salteñas*, good coffee, cakes, popular at lunch, open late. Diagonally opposite is *Heladería Alemana*, good ice cream, including chirimoya. *Mateos*, Bolívar y 6 de Octubre, good, reasonable prices, also sells ice cream.

Other *confiterías* are: *Unicornio*, on Calle La Plata esquina Mier, one block from the main plaza, open evenings only, smart, good service, good menu, main dishes around US$4; *Capri*, Bolívar 749, on the plaza, excellent breakfast, bar café, open late; and *M y M*, Calle Bolívar 490. A good *pizzería* is *La Casona*, Presidente Montes 5970, opposite the Post Office. Good traditional places to eat include: *Gaviota*, Calle Junín 676; *Guadalquivir*, Calle Pagador 6320; *Restaurant Pagador*, Calle Pagador 1430; *Restaurant La Plata*, Calle La Plata 5759; *Libertador*, Calle Bolívar 347, excellent set lunch for US$1.50; and *Bambino*, Calle Ayacucho 445. The best place to eat near the bus terminal is *Restaurant Gutiérrez*, Calle Bakovic 580, meat and fish main courses US$3-4.

● **Banks & money changers**

Oruro has one of the worst exchange rates in Bolivia – up to 5% below the official rate. If possible take enough bolivianos and Enlace-compatible plastic to avoid changing money or travellers' cheques. There are Enlace ATMs in Calle La Plata 6153 opposite **Banco Nacional de Bolivia** and Calle Bolívar esquina Montes outside **Banco de La Paz**, where you can get a cash advance, but there is a US$3.75 authorization charge. If you have to change travellers' cheques try **Banco Boliviano Americano**, Calle Bolívar esquina S Galvarro, 5% commission; and at **Banco Santa Cruz**, Calle Bolívar 470 and Pagador y Caro, open Saturday 0900-1200. Other banks: **Banco Mercantil**, Calle Bolívar, Plaza 10 de Febrero; and **Banco de Crédito**, Calle Ayacucho esquina S Galvarro.

If you desperately need to change dollars there are many shops in the centre and around Mercado Campero displaying signs saying "Compro Dolares". It is quite also easy to change dollars on the street.

● **Entertainment**

Brujas, Junín y 6 de Octubre, café, bar and gig venue, Friday and Saturday, mainly rock music, open 2100 till late for snacks; *Pub Alpaca*, Calle La Paz 690, Finnish-owned, lively Friday and Saturday.

Cinemas: (make sure you dress warmly). **Palais**, Plaza 10 de Febrero; and **Gran Rex**, Calle Mier between 6 de Octubre and S Galvarro. Farther out from the centre: **Imperio**, Avenida 6 de Octubre esquina 1 de Noviembre; and **Elisa**, Calle Pagador 5344.

Alliance Francaise, Calle Mier 844, gives charango lessons. Target shooting is possible at the military bases of Cuartel Camacho and Cuartel Vinto, you pay per bullet. For more information ask at the tourist officice. Horse riding is possible at US$3 per hour from the military Grupo Braun, 8 de Cabellería at the end of Avenida del Ejército on the way to Vinto.

● **Laundry**

Alemania, Aldana 280.

● **Post & telecommunications**

Post Office: Calle Montes 1456, half a block from Plaza 10 de Febrero. **DHL** is at Edificio Santa Teresa, Calle Montes esquina Sucre.

Entel: Calle Bolívar esquina S Galvarro.

● **Shopping**

Markets: Mercado Campero, Calle V Galvarro esquina Bolívar, for film, clothes, food, hardware, stationery, cosmetics, hats, cloth, junk and *comedor popular*, it also has an interesting *brujería* section where you can find *curanderos*' magical concoctions. **Mercado Fermín López**, Calle Ayacucho and Montes, food and hardware with big covered *comedor popular*. Calle Bolívar is the main shopping street in Oruro. **Compañía Importadora Escandinavia**, Calle S Galvarro near Plaza 10 de Febrero, sells Swiss Army penknives.

There's a musical instrument shop at Avenida 6 de Octubre 6187. **Artesanía Oruro**, Calle Ayacucho 856, sells ponchos, wall-hangings, rugs, jumpers and bags. Also **Multi Artes La Tradición**, Calle La Paz 4916. **Reguerín**, 6 de Octubre 6001 esquina Mier, good Diablada dolls and masks. On Avenida La Paz the blocks between León and Rodríguez are largely given over to workshops producing masks and costumes for Carnival.

● **Tour companies & travel agents**
There are three travel agents in Oruro, none of whom cater for incoming foreigners. However, there are plans to open an agency aimed at *turismo receptivo* – ask at the tourist office. A recommended driver and tour guide is *Juan Carlos Vargas*, T 40333, contact via the tourist office.

● **Tourist offices**
Probably the most helpful and informative in Bolivia is at Montes 6072, Plaza 10 de Febrero, T/F 50144, 0800-1200 and 1400-1830 Monday-Friday. Kiosk outside Entel in Calle Bolívar, open 1000-1200 and 1430-1730 Monday-Friday, 1000-1200 Saturday. They have a colour map and guide (Spanish only) US$1. Also available is a colour guide to Parque Nacional Sajama US$1. Other maps and guides: Oruro city map and guide in English (Quipus) US$2.50. For a detailed explanation of the Oruro Carnival and its dances and dancers see the booklet *Carnaval Oruro 97* by the *Asociación de Conjuntos del Folklore de Oruro* (Spanish).

● **Useful addresses**
Immigration: Calle Montes 6006 (Plaza 10 de Febrero).

● **Transport**
Local Within city: minibus US$0.15, taxi US$0.40 per person; taxi to Ciudad Universitaria US$0.70 per person, to Vinto US$1 per person.

Trains Check in advance which services are running, T 60605. To Uyuni on Wednesday and Sunday 1930, US$2.50, 6 hours. Change at Uyuni (see below) for trains to Villazón and Calama (Chile). There are no trains to La Paz, Potosí or Cochabamba. Ticket office opens at 0700, best to be there early. See also Uyuni **trains** (page 190).

Buses The bus terminal is ten blocks north of the town centre at Calle Bakovic and Aroma, T 53535. US$0.20 terminal tax to get on any bus. Buses leave daily, times of first and last departures are: to **La Paz** at least every hour 0400-2200, US$2, 3 hours. To **Cochabamba** 0430-2200, US$3, 4½ hours. To **Potosí** 0800-1900, US$4, 8 hours. To **Sucre** 0900 and 1900, US$6, 12 hours. To **Uyuni** 1900, US$5-7, 9-10 hours. To **Santa Cruz** 0600-1530, US$7, 12 hours. To **Pisiga** (Chilean frontier) 2100-2300, US$6, 5 hours. To **Challapata** 0700-1830, US$1.40, 2 hours. To **Llallagua** 0630-1900, US$2, 3 hours.

International buses (US$2 to cross border) To **Iquique** via Pisiga, with Trans Jímenez on Tuesday, Thursday and Saturday 2200, US$28; Trans Delta on Monday and Wednesday 2230, US$23. To **Arica** via Tambo Quemado, with Trans Salvador on Monday, Tuesday, Wednesday and Sunday 1000, US$34; Trans Litoral on Tuesday, Saturday and Sunday 2200, US$34.

THE ORURO CARNIVAL

The normally cold, austere city of Oruro undergoes a complete transformation during its carnival. Over the week or so of celebrations the townsfolk go wild, so you can get hopelessly drunk with the locals, dance until you drop and in the process get soaked to the skin from a million water bombs. This is a rare opportunity to get involved in some serious partying with the indigenous people and not stand out like a sore thumb. You would be well advised not to miss it. For culture vultures this is also a fascinating insight into Aymara folk legends and a chance to enjoy some of the finest Bolivian music and dance.

Devil dancer

The origins of Carnival

🦶 The origins of the Carnival go back to the late 18th century and the worship of the *Virgen del Socavón*. Legend has it that an outlaw who lived in the area was mortally wounded, but was saved at the last moment by an unknown woman of great beauty. She turned out to be the *Virgen de la Candelaria*, whom the outlaw had worshipped in the cave where he lived. A century later, the church of the *Virgen del Socavón* was built on the very spot where he was saved. This was how the *Virgen de la Candelaria* became the *Mamita del Socavón* (Beloved Mother of the Mineshaft) and her feast was changed to Carnival Saturday, as it was on that day that she saved the outlaw.

The cult of the *Virgen del Socavón* has gradually merged over the years with the worship of the devil or *Supay Tío* as he is known in these parts. Coincidentally, it was around the end of the 18th century that a company of *Diablos* first took part in Carnival and the association of *Supay Tío* with the Carnival began.

In the early 19th century, in an attempt to counter these indigenous myths and deities, a Spanish priest introduced the *relato*, the depiction of the struggle of the Seven Deadly Sins against the Archangel Michael. Like so many expressions of Bolivian culture, therefore, the Oruro Carnival is a mix of indigenous elements and those of Catholic Church.

Carnival is a moveable feast, usually held around the middle of February. When it was first held only the miners danced, but several other guilds have taken up the custom and now traders, business people and professionals take part. The working-class Oruro district known as La Ranchería is particularly famous for the excellence of its costumes.

The Entrada

The most impressive part of the Oruro Carnival is the *Entrada*, or entry procession, which starts its 5 km route through the town at 0700 on the morning of the Saturday before Ash Wednesday. Over fifty dance companies take part, not just from Oruro but from all over the country. The most important are the *Diablos* (Devils) and *Morenos* (Blacks). The size of the companies ranges from around fifty dancers up to 200-300 – so you can imagine the massive scale of the *Entrada*.

Leading off the procession are the *cargamentos*, a motorcade of vehicles covered with fine embroidery, jewels, gold and silverware, old coins and banknotes. These are to recall the treasures once offered up in worship of the sun on *Inti Raymi* (the ancient Inca feast day), or the wealth of *El Tío* (Uncle) who lives in the mineshafts.

Next comes **La Diablada**, the central part of the *Entrada*. The procession is led by a condor and a pack of frolicking apes and bears. Then follows a procession of masked dancers, led by two luxuriously costumed masqueraders representing Lucifer and Satan. The Archangel Michael urges on hundreds of leaping, gesticulating dancers in ferocious diabolical costumes. Prancing seductively at the head of columns of demons, a band of female dancers, wearing red wigs and

Devil mask

La Diablada

🐾 The most important part of the *Entrada* is *La Diablada*, the Dance of the Devils. It dates back to the 12th century, in the region of Catalonia in Spain, where they performed the Dance of the Devils as well as the Dance of the Seven Deadly Sins. It has since been adopted by the miners of Oruro as part of their own faith and mythical ancestry.

La Diablada is a religious/pagan dance which incorporates the forces of evil, as represented by Lucifer, Satan and *China Supay*, the seven deadly sins and the forces of good, represented by the Archangel Michael. The condor and the bear, ancient Andean symbols, also take part. During Carnival the Devil fights with the Archangel Michael, who is the only celestial figure capable of overcoming the forces of evil.

The main symbol of Carnival is the Devil (known as *Supay* or *El Tío*), who must be honoured to avoid incurring his wrath and to receive his protection. According to tradition, the Devil lives in the shadows and caves of the mines, only appearing on the Sunday of Temptation.

The Devil plays an important part in Andean mythology. In mining centres such as Oruro he is the lord and master of the rich mineral seams running through the *cordillera*. He lives in the mines, giving minerals if he wants to show kindness, or hiding them at will, and causing the tunnels to, or preventing them from, collapse. The miners are careful not to invoke any other gods, so as not to offend *Supay*. They offer him coca, cigarettes, alcohol and light candles in his honour next to a crude image of him.

masks, represent *China Supay*, Lucifer's consort, who plays the role of carnal temptress. A mighty brass band in the rear drives on the first great team of devils.

The costumes always feature the heavy, gruesome mask modelled in plaster, with a toad or snake on top; huge glass eyes; triangular glass teeth; a horsehair wig; and pointed, vibrating ears. Tied around the neck is a large, silk shawl embroidered with dragons or other figures, and the dancer also has a jewelled, fringed breastplate. Over his white shirt and tights he wears a sash trimmed with coins and from it hang the four flaps of his native skirt, embroidered in gold and silver thread and loaded with precious stones. Special boots equipped with spurs complete the elaborate outfit. Satan and Lucifer wear scarlet cloaks and carry a serpent twisted around one arm and a trident.

Behind the *Diablada* follow at least fifty other groups, including more *Diabladas*, each with its own band. Among the following groups is the company of the Incas, representing important figures from the time of the conquest, such as the Inca Huáscar, and the *conquistadores* Francisco Pizarro and Diego de Almagro. The jungle tribes conquered by the Inca Yupanqui during the empire's expansion are portrayed by the *Tobas*, who perform war dances with large tropical feathers on their heads and carrying lances. Other companies taking part in the *Entrada* are the *Llameros* (llama drivers) and the *Kallawayas*, the ancient medicine men who dance with their bags of herbs.

One of the most important of the dancing groups are the *Morenos*, or blacks, who perform the famous *Morenada*, led by the *Rey Moreno* (Black King) and the *Caporal* (chief). According to tradition this dance represents the black slaves brought to South America and led off in chains to work in the mines of Potosí. The richly decorated costumes of the participants represents the wealth of the slave owners, while the protruding eyes and tongue of the masks conveys the fatigue of the slaves

Devil and Angel in La Diablada

and their suffering from altitude sickness. The dance of the *Caporales*, which satirizes the Spanish slave bosses, has its origins in the African culture of the Yungas.

The parade ends at 0400 on Sunday when it reaches the Sanctuary of the *Virgen del Socavón*, where the dancers invoke her blessing and ask for pardon. The company then proceeds to the Avenida Cívica amphitheatre, where the Angel and Devils perform two masques: the first is a contest between good and evil, in which Saint Michael defeats the Devils. In the second, the *relato de los diablos*, seven devils are forced to confess to the Seven Deadly Sins. After the performance the dancers all enter the sactuary, chant a hymn in Quechua and pray for pardon.

Before and after the Entrada

The preparations begin 4 months before the actual event, on the first Sunday of November, with the 'First Invitation' and a mass in honour of the *Virgen del Socavón*. Rehearsals are held every Sunday until 1 week before carnival, when the 'Second Invitation' takes place, preceded by a communion mass for the participants.

The Friday before *Entrada* is the *Anata Andina*, when peasants come to the city from all over the surrounding area to celebrate the harvest in Plaza 10 de Febrero. Traditional miners' *cha'llas* are also held at mines, including the sacrifice of a llama. Visitors may only attend with a guide and permission from Comibol, via the tourist office.

The *Entrada* is followed the next day (Sunday) by the *Gran Corso del Carnaval*, a very spectacular display.

On Monday is *El Día del Diablo y del Moreno* in which the Diablos and Morenos, with their bands, compete against each other on Avenida Cívica in demonstrations of dancing. Every group seems to join in, in 'total marvellous chaos'. The action usually parades out of the amphitheatre, ending up at the Plaza de Armas. In the afternoon is the *Despedida de la Virgen* (Farewell to the Virgin). At dusk dancers and musicians go their separate ways, serenading until the early hours.

By Tuesday the main touristic events have ended. The *Carnaval del Sur* takes place, with *ch'alla* rituals to invoke ancestors, unite with Pachamama and bless

Respect to the Gods

The *cha'lla* is not only an important part of carnival but of Andean customs and beliefs in general. It consists of sprinkling alcohol on all things, fixed or moving, and in adorning them with confetti and streamers so that abundance will come, or that it will continue or even increase. This is how the protection of the gods of plenty is invoked and respect shown to them.

personal possessions. This is also the *día del agua* on which everyone throws water and sprays foam at everyone else (though how they distinguish this from the other days remains a mystery).

On Wednesday, Thursday, Friday and Saturday more *cha'llas* are held, this time for the condor, the toad and the viper, followed by huge parties on Avenida Cívica. The following day is *Temptation Sunday*, when a ceremony is held in the southern part of the city to "bury" the carnival until next year. Paradoxically, while this going on, a celebration of the birth of the next carnival takes place, ending in a week of more partying!

● **Seating** Around the Plaza de Armas, along Avenida 6 de Agosto and on Avenida Cívica, seats cost US$3 a day, bought from the Alcaldía in the plaza, or whichever business has erected stands outside its building. Seats on Avenida Bolívar, etc, cost US$2 a day from the shops who built stands. To wander among the dancers you are officially supposed to purchase a professional photographer's ticket for US$15, but amateurs can pay only US$1.50 by showing a small camera and insisting.

● **Accommodation** Accommodation costs five times more than normal during carnival and must be booked in advance. Hotel prices range from US$15 per person without bath, to US$20 per person with, to US$100 per person per day in the better places. The tourist office has a list of all householders willing to let rooms. Host and guest arrange the price, but expect to pay at least US$10 per person.

● **Transport** Prices from La Paz triple. Organized day trips from La Paz cost US$50, including transport, food and a seat in the main plaza. They depart at 1900, missing the last 8-9 hours.

SAJAMA NATIONAL PARK

A 1-day drive to the west of Oruro is the **Parque Nacional Sajama**, established in 1945 and covering 60,000 hectares. The park contains the world's highest forest, consisting mainly of the rare Kenua tree (Polylepis Tarapana) which survives up to 5,200m. The scenery is wonderful and includes views of three volcanoes: **Sajama**, Bolivia's highest peak at 6,530m; Parinacota and Pomerape. The Sajama area is a major centre of alpaca wool production.

This area has become more accessible since the completion of the new asphalted La Paz-Arica highway. There are restaurants in the park but no fresh food, so take your own. Once you move away from the Río Sajama or its major tributaries, the lack of water is a serious problem. In Sajama village (*Population* 500; *Altitude* 4,200m), Peter Brunnhart (Señor Pedro) and Telmo Nina have a book with descriptions of the various routes to the summit (Telmo Nina keeps the visitors book). There's good bathing in the hot springs 5 km north of the village. 6 km to the west of village is an interesting geothermic area.

The Park entry fee is US$1 and basic accommodation is available. It can be very windy and cold at night, so a good sleeping bag is essential. Crampons, ice axe and rope are needed for climbing the volcanoes. Mules can be hired for US$6 per day. An informative colour leaflet-guide to the park (in Spanish) is available from the tourist office in Oruro for US$1.

● **Buses** Take the Litoral La Paz-Arica bus, ask for Sajama and pay the full fare. The bus leaves La Paz at 0530 Tuesday, Friday and Sunday; it returns from Arica on Monday and Thursday at 2400. If continuing into Chile (same buses) remember that no meat, dairy products, fruit or vegetables may be taken across the border.

SOUTH FROM ORURO

A road and railway line run south from Oruro, through Río Mulato, the junction for trains to Potosí, to Uyuni (323 km), which is the usual starting point for tours of the Salar and Lagunas Colorada and Verde (see below). The road is bad to Pazña (between Oruro and Challapata) and asphalt thereafter. The unpaved parts are sandy and very difficult after rain, especially south of Río Mulato.

LAGO POOPO

About 65 km south on the road to Uyuni is the **Santuario de Aves Lago Poopó**, an excellent bird reserve on the lake of the same name. The lake dries up completely in winter.

The Sanctuary can be visited from **Challapata**, 120 km south of Oruro on a fairly good gravel road. There is a gas station in the village and basic lodging at the main crossing opposite the **G** pp *Hotel Potosí*, with good beds and a basic restaurant. There is a *fiesta* 15-17 July. Buses leave Oruro at 0800 and 1430, 2½ hours, US$1, they are always full.

SOUTHEAST FROM ORURO

Branching off the road to Uyuni, at Km 27, is a road that runs southeast to Sucre. 95 km from Oruro on this road is the mining town of **Llallagua** (*Altitude* 3,881m). Nearby is the famous Siglo Veinte, once the largest tin mine (ex-Patiño) in the country. It is now closed, but being worked by small cooperatives; visitors are welcome. There is an acute water shortage.

Further on at **Uncia**, Km 102, there are more former Patiño mines. There are good hot springs which can be reached by *trufi*. In town is a small *alojamiento* near the prison, **G**, which is clean, safe and basic. The restaurants are poor so it's best to eat at the market.

● **Accommodation In Llallagua**: **F** *Hotel Bustillo*; and *Santa María*. Also **G** *Hotel Llallagua*, small beds, no bath, seldom has water, perhaps the best, but not really recommended. There are few restaurants in Llallagua.

● **Buses** Llallagua can be reached by bus from Oruro; seven a day with Bustillos, Enta at 0900 and 1700 daily, 3 hours, US$2.50. Also at 1900 from La Paz.

SOUTHWEST FROM ORURO

A road also runs southwest from Oruro to the Chilean frontier at **Pisiga** (for transport to Pisiga see under Oruro **buses**).

The first town on this road is **Toledo**, at Km 38, where there is a colonial church. Further southwest is **Escara**, a lovely village with a beautiful plaza. It is a friendly place and you can rent bikes. The road continues 30 km southwest to **Sabaya** and from there for 52 km to the Chilean frontier. At Escara the road branches south to **Chipaya**, 25 km away, and 190 km from Oruro. Chipaya is the main settlement of the most interesting indigenous people of the Altiplano. They are the living remnants of a 4,000-year-old culture, probably the most ancient surviving in America. The Chipayas speak their own language unrelated to Aymara or Quechua, and thought to be closely related to the almost extinct Uru. Their distinctive dress and unique conical houses are beginning to disappear, however, as the community changes.

The Chipayas are well aware of the value of tourism and demand US$50 per person to visit. They can get nasty if you don't pay up. Also bear in mind that there is very little for the visitor to do and it is very cold, so it's possibly a better idea just to check out the display at the anthropological museum in Oruro.

From Chipaya with your own transport or an organized tour it is possible to head south through the Salar de Coipasa and on to the Salar de Uyuni.

This part of the country can be difficult to explore without your own transport (4WD recommended), but there is a daily bus from Oruro to Sabaya, southwest of Escara, via Huachacalla; it departs at 2100, 5 hours, US$4.50; there is also transport once a week in either direction from Huachacalla to Chipaya.

UYUNI

(*Population* 11,320; *Altitude* 3,665m; *Phone code* 0693) Hot in the sun, cold in the shade and bitterly cold in the wind and at night, Uyuni is a railway junction founded in 1889 and starting point for trips to Bolivia's most amazing scenery – the salt lake of the same name in the far southwest.

Once described as "a diamond encrusted in the shores of the Great Salar," Uyuni is also noted as the first place where a plane took off and landed on Bolivian soil in 1921 and possibly has the honour of being soccer's point of entry into the country, introduced by British railway engineers. The city was officially declared "Hija Predilecta de Bolivia" ("Bolivia's favourite daughter") in 1983 for the help given to returning soldiers from the disastrous and bloody Chaco War with Paraguay 1932-35.

Incoming (and outgoing) buses stop in Avenida Ferroviaria, between Arce and Bolívar. It is possible to spend your entire time in Uyuni within 100m of this point. The majority of tour operators, hotels and restaurants, the station and all the bus companies are in this area. A giant statue of an armed railway worker, erected after the 1952 Revolution, dominates Avenida Ferroviaria. Market days are Thursday, Friday and Sunday; *Fiesta* 11 July.

Places of interest

Once you've sorted out your tour (see below) there's not much to do in Uyuni, but if you have some time check out the train cemetery just over 1 km from the centre following Avenida Ferroviaria and then the railway line. Note that some agencies throw in a swift visit at the end of a tour, thereby saving you the walk. There is also a small museum, the **Museo Arqueológico y Antropológico de los Andes Meridionales** (open Monday-Friday 0830-1200 and 1400-1830, Saturday 0830-1200, entrance US$0.20), which has a well-labelled collection of deformed skulls, mummies, cloth and ceramics.

Excursions

Pulcayo is a small mining village 22km northeast of Uyuni on the road to Potosí. The train cemetery contains the first locomotive to enter Bolivia and a train robbed by Butch Cassidy and the Sundance Kid shortly before the end of their career (see **San Vicente** below). The name is best known in Bolivia for the Thesis of Pulcayo, a Trotskyist declaration made in 1946 which would have been forgotten, except that tin baron Simón Patiño had it reprinted in full in his newspaper *El Diario* as a warning. It remains important to miners and is still seen in graffiti. There is a small mining museum which allows you to go underground. Check opening times with Tito Ponce in Uyuni.

● **Accommodation G** *Hotel Rancho*, without bath, large old rooms, hot water, good meals.

Local information
● **Accommodation**
Hotel prices have doubled in the last 2 years without any apparent improvement in service. Apart from Hotels *Avenida* and *Mágia de Uyuni*, showers cost US$0.60-0.70 extra. All showers depend on the town's water and electricity supplies. Water is frequently cut off and may only be available between 0600 and midday. It can be difficult to find a bed in the better hotels if you're arriving around 0500-0600 in the high season.

D *Mágia de Uyuni*, Avenida Colón between Sucre and Camacho, T 2541, new and the best hotel in Uyuni, all rooms with private bathroom, price includes breakfast, recommended.

E pp *Avenida*, Avenida Ferroviaria 11, opposite the train station, T 2078, with private bathroom, **F** pp with shared bathroom, the most popular hotel in Uyuni with exactly four blankets per bed (according to the notice in reception) which are not to be "borrowed", good hot showers 0800-2000, washing facilities.

G *Residencial Sucre*, Calle Sucre 132, T 2047, clean and friendly though the three stars on the sign is a little optimistic; **G** pp *Residencial Urkupiña*, Plaza Arce, small (14 beds), basic, friendly and quite clean, hot shower US$0.50; **G** pp *Residencial Copacabana*, Plaza Arce, small and not particularly friendly.

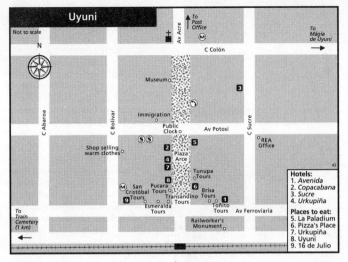

● Places to eat

16 de Julio, Avenida Ferroviaria, opens 0700, traditional dishes, overpriced, limited options for vegetarians; *Restaurant Uyuni*, Plaza Arce, good breakfasts, seemingly ever-open, nicely decorated with two armadillos nailed to the wall; *Urkupiña*, Plaza Arce, open for breakfast, good standard stuff; *Pizza's Palace*, Plaza Arce, good pizza for US$1.20 a slice, US$8 for a whole pizza; *La Paladium*, Plaza Arce, would be good if they could supply 50% of what their menu offers.

Avoid eating in the market. There have been incidences of cholera and Uyuni wouldn't be a good place to get ill, and worse still if you got ill on a tour.

● Banks & money changers

Bidesa, Avenida Potosí, which changes travellers' cheques in bolivianos or dollars cash (2% commission). Outside banking hours, try the photographer's shop on Avenida Potosí, which changes dollars or Chilean pesos. *Hotel Avenida* changes dollars cash. Some shops will change cash dollars for bolivianos. *Toñito* (see Tour operators below) change travellers' cheques with a 3% commission. All agencies accept cash dollars for payment for tours.

● Post & telecommunications

Post Office: at Avenida Arce esquina Calle Cabrera. **Entel**: Avenida Arce above Avenida Potosí.

● Shopping

The market at Avenida Arce esquina Calle Colón sells the basics. There is also a smaller indoor market on Calle Bolívar above Ferroviaria. Fleece jackets, scarves, long wool socks and other warm clothes are available from a shop on Calle Bolívar below Potosí.

● Useful addresses

The **Immigration Office** is at Avenida Potosí 10, open Monday-Friday 0830-1200 and 1430-1800, for exit stamps to leave Bolivia via Laguna Verde and Hito Cajón. Your agency can sort this out for you. Exit stamps are valid for up to 3 days.

Reserva Eduardo Avaroa (REA) office Avenida Potosí esquina Sucre has an excellent full colour map and guide to the reserve for US$2 and full-colour bird guide *Aves de la Reserva Nacional de Fauna Andina Eduardo Avaroa* by Omar Rocha and Carmen Quiroga (Museo Nacional de Historia Natural, La Paz 1996) (both in Spanish). This is also available from the tourist office and the REA headquarters at Laguna Colorada.

● Tourist offices

The underfunded tourist office is at Avenida Potosí 13, open Monday-Friday 0830-1200 and 1400-1830, Saturday-Sunday 0830-1200 (T/F 0693 2098, emergencies 2259). Sr Tito Ponce, a former guide, is very knowledgeable and helpful when he isn't out searching for lost jeeps on the Salar.

● **Transport**

Trains: check services on arrival at the office on the platform of the new but normally deserted station.

To **Oruro** Monday, Tuesday, Thursday and Friday, 0200 US$2.50, 8 hours. To **Villazón** Monday, Tuesday, Thursday and Friday 0130, US$3/US$3.85, 12 hours. To **Avaroa** on the Chilean border for connection with train to Calama and then bus to Antofagasta; Monday 0500, US$4, 12 hours.

By train to Chile: there is no through train from Uyuni to Calama. Buy the Ollagüe-Calama section after passing the border; pay only in pesos (US$5) which you can buy at the small shop opposite the water tower in Ollagüe. There are no money changers on the Bolivian side. It takes 1 hour to change trains at Avaroa, then it's 40 minutes to Ollagüe, where Chilean customs take 4-12 hours. After that it is an uncomfortable 6 hours to Calama.

In Bolivia, seats can be reserved as far as the border, but only 30 minutes before the train arrives. There is a restaurant car and waiter service. If you take your own food, eat fresh things first as the Chileans do not allow dairy produce, teabags (of any description), fruit or vegetables to be brought in. All passports are collected and stamped in the rear carriage and should be ready for collection after 1-2 hours; queue for your passport, no names are called out.

Buses All the bus offices are along Avenida Ferroviaria either side of Plaza Arce. Departures are daily unless otherwise stated.

To **La Paz** with Panasur Wednesday and Sunday 1800, US$9, 13 hours (Panasur from La Paz bus terminal opposite 31-A, Tuesday and Friday at 1730). To **Oruro** 1900, US$5, 8 hours. To **Potosí** 1000, US$4, 6 hours; it's a spectacular journey, sit on the right to avoid being in the sun the whole way. To **Sucre** 1000, US$7, 8 hours. To **Tupiza** Wednesday and Sunday 1000, US$5, 10 hours. To **Camargo** 1000, US$7, 11 hours. To **Tarija** 1000, US$12, 14 hours. To **Challapata** (change for buses to Oruro and La Paz or Potosí), Saturday 0530, US$4. To get to Chile by road transport, see below.

SALAR DE UYUNI

This is the highest and largest salt lake in the world at an altitude of 3,650m and covering 9,000-12,000 square km (depending on who you believe), and twice as big as the Great Salt Lake in the United States. Driving across it is one of the weirdest and most fantastic experiences anywhere on the continent, especially during June and July when the bright blue skies contrast with the blinding-white salt crust. Sunglasses are essential to avoid snowblindness. A 4-day tour across the Salar and down to Laguna Colorada and Laguna Verde on the Chilean border is not to be missed (see below for Lagunas Colorada and Verde).

The depth of the salt varies from 2-20m. During the last Ice Age most of the Altiplano was under a lake called Lago Minchín, of which the Salar was the deepest point. Until the Spanish arrived it was known as Paichichuta. This is a region of harsh extremes of climate. Temperatures have been recorded of 30°C at midday and minus 25°C the following midnight.

After particularly wet rainy seasons the lake is covered in water which adds to the surreal experience. It feels like you should be digging holes in the ice to fish while keeping a look out for penguins, seals and polar bears. Many agencies will not send jeeps out when the Salar has reverted to a wet lake because the salt water destroys the engines; but shop around, someone will want your money.

TOURS OF THE SALAR

20 km north of Uyuni is the tiny settlement of **Colchani**. A couple of minutes out of the village and you are on the salt. Workers from the village dig out piles of salt which are then loaded onto trucks and taken back to the village to be ground and iodised before being sold. Iodine deficiency leads to thyroid problems and goitre and it is now illegal to sell non-iodised salt.

Next is **D** pp *Hotel de la Playa*, 34 km from Uyuni, which apart from the roof is completely made of salt. It is run by Teodoro Colque and you can stay the night.

As you cross the Salar you pass *ojos de sal*, which are not eyes but breathing spaces for subterranean rivers flowing under the Salar. Approach these with caution as the

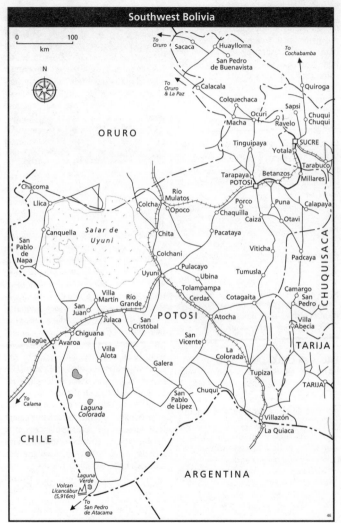

Southwest Bolivia

0   100
km

N

To Oruro — Sacaca — Huaylloma — *To Cochabamba*

San Pedro de Buenavista

Calacala — Colquechaca — Quiroga

To Oruro & La Paz

Ocuri — Sapsi — Chuqui Chuqui

Macha — Ravelo

Tinguipaya — Yotala — **SUCRE**

ORURO

Tarapaya — Betanzos — Tarabuco

POTOSI — Millares

Río Mulatos — Porco — Puna — Calapaya

Chacoma — Colcha — Opoco — Chaquilla — Otavi

Llica — Chita — Pacataya — Caiza

Salar de Uyuni — Canquella — Colchani — Viticha

San Pablo de Napa — Uyuni — Pulacayo — Ubina — Tumusla — Padcaya

Villa Martín — Río Grande — Tolampampa — Cerdas — Cotagaita — Camargo — San Pedro

San Juan — Julaca — San Cristóbal — Atocha — Villa Abecia

Chiguana — Avaroa — San Vicente — La Colorada — TARIJA

Ollagüe — Villa Alota — Galera — Tupiza — **TARIJA**

To Calama

San Pablo de Lípez — Chuqui — Villazón — La Quiaca

Laguna Colorada

CHILE

POTOSI

CHUQUISACA

ARGENTINA

Laguna Verde

Volcán Licancábur (5,916m)

To San Pedro de Atacama

46

salt near a hole might not bear your weight. The Salar is covered in pentagonal and hexagonal shapes which appear to have been carved by someone. The views north are dominated by the snow-capped Volcán Tunupa, 5,400m.

It takes 1-2 hours from *Hotel de la Playa* (depending on the state of the Salar and your vehicle) to go the 80 km to **Isla Pescado**, so-called because it allegedly looks like a fish. The 10-hectare island was originally known as *Incahuasi* (Inca

House) and is the most impressive of the 60-odd islands in the Salar. From among the giant cacti (some more than 10m high) there are stunning views across the huge white expanse of salt to mountains shimmering on the horizon.

In the dry season, tours then head south across the Salar to the Colcha K military post (also known as Villa Martín) and on to **San Juan** to spend the night (simple lodging, US$3 per person, electricity 1900-2100, running water). If the Salar is under water, tours normally head back to Uyuni and then continue south on not so much terra firma but certainly terra drier.

On the western side of the Salar, 5 hours from Uyuni, is **Llica**, capital of Daniel Campos province. The village is good for llama and other wool handicrafts, but there are no shops or electricity. Accommodation is available at the basic **F** *Alojamiento Municipal*. Angel Quispe in the plaza also has three beds, and meals are available in private houses. A bus leaves from Uyuni at 1200 daily, and a truck at 1100. There are delays and problems in the wet season.

LAGUNA COLORADA AND LAGUNA VERDE

A trip to this remote corner of Bolivia would not be complete without continuing to **Laguna Colorada** and **Laguna Verde**, 350 km southwest of Uyuni, over unmarked, rugged truck tracks. This region is one of Bolivia's most spectacular and most isolated marvels.

NB The diurnal temperature variation is minus 25°C to plus 25°C, though a wind develops during the afternoon which makes it feel even colder than it is.

The lagunas are situated in the **Reserva Eduardo Avaroa**, created in 1973 and extended in 1981 to protect flamingoes (Chilean, Andean and James), vicuñas and the ostrich-like *suri*. There are 80 species of bird in the area (64% of those found in the entire Altiplano). Other notables include the horned coot (*soca cornuda*), Andean

Flamingoes, Laguna Colorada

goose (*huallata*) and the Andean hillstar (*jurunkuta*), which lives up to altitudes of 4,500m.

The birdlife is best seen during the southern summer which is November-January; many birds migrate to avoid the cold winter, June-August, but some always remain. See the full-colour illustrated guide (in Spanish) *Aves de la Reserva Nacional de Fauna Andina Eduardo Avaroa* by Omar Rocha and Carmen Quiroga (Museo Nacional de Historia Natural, La Paz 1996). Animals (rarely seen) include pumas (*gato andino*), Andean foxes (*zorro andino*) and the rabbit-like *viscacha*. Vegetation to look out for includes *thola* (which after the wet season has an edible tuber called *sicha*), yareta grass (which looks like a green pillow, but feels like a rock), quinoa plants (which produce the high altitude Andean grain) and the kenua bush/tree which grows at altitudes up to 5,000m.

Tours to Lagunas Colorada and Verde

Tours continue south from **San Juan** (see above), via Chiguana (rail station and military post) to Laguna Hedionda. Or from Uyuni they head south, crossing the 50cm-deep Río Grande to **Alota**, a military checkpoint 5 hours away, with a number of **G** *alojamientos*. Then on through collections of eroded rocks surrounded by snow-capped mountains (including the active

Volcán Ollagüe) to Laguna Hedionda in another 2 hours.

Laguna Hedionda (literally, Stinking Lake due to the sulphur) is popular with flamingoes which are mainly white as the algae which create the pink colour are not so numerous in this lake.

Continuing south, the piles of light coloured gravel are *caliche*, which is heated up on yareta grass fires to extract sulphur. The route climbs up through a red-brown rock and sand landscape to reach the Siloli desert at 4,600m before dropping down to enter the **Reserva Eduardo Avaroa** (REA) and then the bizarre Arbol de Piedra (Rock Tree), an improbably balanced piece of wind-eroded rock. It continues down and south to reach Laguna Colorada in around 3 hours from Laguna Hedionda.

Laguna Colorada (Coloured Lake), 4,278m high and 60 square km, gets its name from the effect of wind and sun on the micro-organisms that live in it. The shores of the lake are encrusted with borax, used for soap and acid, which provides an arctic-white counterpoint to the flaming red waters. Up to midday, though, the lake is pretty normal coloured. The pink algae provide food for the rare James flamingoes, along with the more common Chilean and Andean flamingoes, which breed and live here and also gives them their pink colour. Some forty other bird species can also be seen here. The lake is less than 1m deep but the mud is very soft. Flamingoes can walk across it, but tourists – not even very skinny ones – can't. Nights are extremely cold here. The REA, which has its headquarters at the lake, recorded the record low of minus 30°C in 1996.

● **Accommodation** There are two places to stay at Laguna Colorada. The REA runs a modern, clean, comfortable, warmish 34-bed refuge with kitchen and friendly guardian, Oswaldo Rudzinski, for US$3 per person. Reservations can be made through the REA office in Uyuni. There is also a dirty waterless shack for US$3 per person, which remains popular with Uyuni agencies for some reason. The proprietor is Eustaquio Berna. Be careful with water – there's not much of it about.

An unpleasantly cold and early start on day three gets you to the **Sol de Mañana** 50m-high steam geyser for dawn. Do not step over this. Putting your hand in may seem a good idea until there's a change in geothermal activity and you will have the flesh removed from your hand by boiling, high-pressure steam. There are boiling mud holes and a strong stench of sulphur which, when combined with the 4,800m altitude, can make some people feel ill. Borax processors use the heat of the geysers to make acid and there is a geothermal electricity generation project.

You then continue to the 30°C thermal waters at the edge of **Laguna Chalviri**, 30 minutes from the geysers. It's a pleasant spot and the first (and last) chance of a wash.

You continue for an hour through the barren, surreal landscape of the Pampa de Chalviri at 4,800m, via a pass at 5,000m, to the wind-lashed jade waters of **Laguna Verde** (Green Lake) at 4,400m, the southern-most point of the tour. The stated causes of the lake's impressive colour range from magnesium, calcium carbonate, lead and arsenic. It covers 17 square km and is at the foot of Volcán Licancabur (5,868m) which is on the border between Bolivia and Chile. There is a small *Refugio* at Laguna Verde; it costs US$2, has mattresses, running water and a view of the lake.

It is possible to get dropped off at **Hito Cajón** and cross into Chile, but you must have previously got a Bolivian exit stamp from immigration in Uyuni. Transport is scarce to San Pedro de Atacama which is a waterless and cold 35 km or so away. Death through hypothermia is a possibility if there is no transport. Arrange with an Uyuni agency to be picked up on the Chilean side and taken to San Pedro; this will cost US$10pp (see also **Crossing into Chile** below).

Tours then start the 400 km plus journey back to Uyuni. There are a number of options for routes back; check out what your agency is offering. It is possible to go through the village of Quetana, Laguna Celeste and the *bofedales* (wet grassy areas popular with wildlife), or the bizarre and impressive Valle de las Rocas near Alota. All the eastern routes give views of huge glaciated mountains including Uturuncu, at 6,020m, the highest in the area and the only one to exceed 6,000m.

TOUR OPERATORS

Organization of tours from Uyuni is on the whole appalling. Luckily, the staggering scenery makes it worth the effort. Demand a written contract which states a full day-by-day itinerary, a full meal-by-meal menu (vegetarians should be prepared for an egg-based diet), what is included in the price and what is not. **NB** Accommodation is normally not included – add US$3 per person per night.

If the tour doesn't match the contract, go back to the operator and demand a refund. If this fails to satisfy, complain to

Sajama Volcano

Tito Ponce at the tourism office in Uyuni and then to the Director Regional de Turismo, La Prefectura del Departamento de Potosí, Calle La Paz, Potosí (T 062-27477). The Prefectura recognizes that there is a problem with Uyuni agencies and needs specific information to be able to act.

Trip prices are based on a six-person group. It is easy to find other travellers in Uyuni to join up with during the high season in April-September. Outside this period, it can be worth getting a group together before arriving. If there are fewer than six you each pay more, there is no discount for having seven people and it is less comfortable.

The standard 4-day trip (Salar de Uyuni, Lagunas Colorada and Verde) costs US$60-220 per person depending on the agency and season. There is no refund for leaving to Chile after Laguna Verde. Shorter trips are possible depending on what you are prepared to miss, and so are longer trips (eg including an ascent of Volcán Tunupa), but 4 days in a jeep is as much as most people's bottoms will stand. Take a good sleeping bag, sunglasses, sun hat, sun protection, lots of warm clothing, water bottle, water purification tablets or iodine tincture, lots of film and your own tapes to avoid 4 days of aural torture at the hands of your driver's musical taste.

Of the 24 agencies in Uyuni (a 50% increase in 2 years), very few can be recommended and even those that can are by no means perfect. Speak to travellers who have just returned from a tour and try the following agencies, all of which are within 50m of each other along Avenida Ferroviaria and in Plaza Arce. (Note, most agencies are open until at least 2000 so it is possible to arrive, organize a tour and leave the next day.)

● **Recommended agencies in Uyuni:** **Tunupa**, Plaza Arce 15 (T 2099); **Brisa**, Avenida Ferroviaria 320 (T 2096); **Toñito**, Avenida Ferroviaria 152 (T/F 2094); **Transandino**, Plaza Arce 2 (T 2132); **Pucara**, Plaza Arce 4 (T 2055);

Esmeralda, Avenida Ferroviaria esq Arce (T 2130); **San Cristóbal**, Avenida Ferroviaria (T 2223).

If you can afford it, go with one of the reputable La Paz agencies, eg *Colibrí* or *TransAmazonas*. Agencies in Potosí also organize tours, but this mainly involves putting you on a bus to Uyuni where you meet up with one of the Uyuni agencies and get the same quality tour for a higher price. There can be communication problems between agencies (eg you turn up and the subcontractor has no booking for you) and getting a refund out of a subcontractor is difficult. Either go directly to Uyuni or book, pay and go with an agency from elsewhere.

CROSSING INTO CHILE

If you plan to enter Chile via one of the unattended border crossings in the southwest region, you must get an exit stamp at the Bolivian immigration office in Uyuni (Monday-Friday only). The stamp is valid for 3 days, but more than 72 hours may be permitted if you state the exact date you intend to leave Bolivia. Most agencies will arrange transport from the border to San Pedro for US$10 per person and also take care of passport formalities on the morning you are leaving. Buy Chilean pesos in Uyuni.

TO CHILE VIA OLLAGÜE

From Colchani it is about 60 km across to the west shore of the Salar. There are two or three parallel tracks about 100m apart and every few kilometres stones mark the way. The salt is soft and wet for about 2 km around the edges of the Salar. You can get directions from the *Hotel Playa Blanca* near Colchani. There is no real danger of getting lost, especially in the high season, but it is a hard trip and the road is impassable after rain. There is no gasoline between Uyuni and Calama (Chile).

It is 20 km from the western shore to 'Colcha K', the military checkpoint. From there a poor gravel road leads 28 km to San Juan, where tour groups spend the night. Then the road enters the Salar de Chiguana, a mix of salt and mud which is often wet and soft with deep tracks which are easy to follow. 35 km away is Chiguana, another military post. It's 45 km to the end of the Salar, a few kilometres before the border. This latter part is the most dangerous; it's very slippery and there's very little traffic.

To hitch to Chile via Ollagüe, trucks first go north, then across the Salar de Ollagüe. The scenery on this route is amazing and, once in Chile, you will see lakes similar to Lagunas Colorada and Verde. There is nowhere to stay in Ollagüe, but police and border officials will help find lodging and transport for hitchers. Change bolivianos into pesos at the small shop in a blue house opposite the water tower.

TO CHILE FROM LAGUNA VERDE

From Laguna Verde it is 7 km to Hito Cajón, the frontier post with Chile. A further 8 km is La Cruz, the junction with the east-west road between the borax and sulphur mines and San Pedro. There are reports of a daily bus Hito Cajón-San Pedro, but it is much safer (and easier) to get a tour agency in Uyuni to arrange transport from Hito Cajón to **San Pedro de Atacama (Chile)**. The meteorological station at Laguna Verde will radio for a pick-up from San Pedro. This service costs US$10 per person Hito Cajón-San Pedro. The chance of finding other transport is remote. Adequate, food, water and clothing is essential. You can get a good rate for Chilean pesos from the lady who runs the little shop at the Bolivian border post. **Do not underestimate the dangers of getting stuck without transport or lodging at this altitude**. **Do not travel alone**.

TUPIZA

200 km southeast of Uyuni is **Tupiza** (*Population* 20,000; *Altitude* 2,990m; *Phone code* 0694), capital of Sud Chichas, a province of the Potosí Department. It's a very pleasant place to visit and enjoys a mild

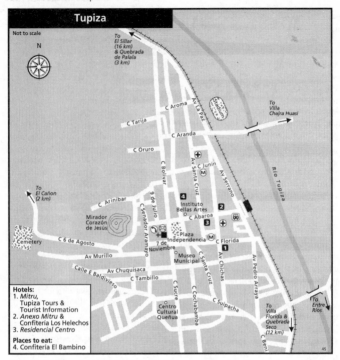

Tupiza

Not to scale

N

To
El Sillar
(16 km)
& Quebrada
de Palala
(3 km)

To
Villa
Chajra Huasi

To
El Cañon
(2 km)

Río Tupiza

C Aroma

C Tarija

C Aranda

C Oruro

C Arinibar

9 de Julio

C Senador Aramayo

C Bolívar

Av Santa Cruz

Av La Paz

Av Serrano

C Junín

C Abaroa

Instituto
Bellas Artes

Mirador
Corazón
de Jesús

Cemetery

C 6 de Agosto

7 de
Noviembre

Plaza
Independencia

C Florida

Av Murillo

Museo
Municipal

C Santa Cruz

C Chichas

Av Pedro Araya

Calle E Baldivieso

Av Chuquisaca

C Tambillo

C Sucre

C Cochabamba

C Suipacha

To
Villa
Florida &
Quebrada
Seco
(12 km)

To
Entre
Ríos

Centro
Cultural
Queñua

C Beni

Hotels:
1. *Mitru*,
   Tupiza Tours &
   Tourist Information
2. *Anexo Mitru* &
   Confitería Los Helechos
3. *Residencial Centro*

Places to eat:
4. Confitería El Bambino

45

climate. Tupiza lies in the narrow, fertile valley of the Río Tupiza, a beautiful and dramatic desert landscape of red, brown, grey, green and violet hills. Beautiful sunsets over the valley can be seen from the foot of a statue of Christ on a hill behind the plaza.

The town is a centre of the silver, tin, lead, and bismuth mining industries. The statue in the main plaza is to Victor Carlos Aramayo, the founding member of the Aramayo mining dynasty, which was pre-eminent in the late 19th and early 20th centuries. An Aramayo company payroll was held up by two certain US bandits going by the names of Butch Cassidy and the Sundance Kid (see **San Vicente** below).

Places of interest

Chajra Huasi, the palazzo-style and now abandoned home of the Aramayo family lies just out of town across the Río Tupiza and can be visited.

The local history museum is on the second floor of the **Casa Municipal de Cultura**, just off the plaza; free entry.

Excursions

The eroded desert landscape around Tupiza offers endless hiking possibilities. Make sure to take enough water and, if camping, keep away from the dried-up river beds as flash flooding is always a danger.

The **Quebrada de Palala** is a tributary of the Río Tupiza in the wet season, but in the dry season it is used by public transport as a route into the wilderness. Follow the gravel road up the steep mountain to reach **El Sillar**, a saddle between two mountains. Here you'll see the "stone forest", an area of eroded pinnacles of rock.

From Tupiza take a micro north to Palala and catch a bus there to El Sillar.

To the south of town is **Quebrada Seca**, an area of spectacular scenery. Take a Villa Florida bus to the outskirts of town. The quebrada is immediately before the YPFB plant. Follow the gravel road to the Río San Rafael. In the wet season it's impossible to follow the river left to Entre Ríos without wading through it several times.

Another interesting excursion is to **El Cañon** described by Wendy Chilcott and Steve Newman of Sussex, England: "Follow the road to the left of the cathedral out of town between the cemetery and the barracks. Continue as the road curves right until you reach a dry river bed. Follow this to the left towards the hills. After 200m take the right fork in the river bed. Here are some superb rock formations – huge pinnacles of rock and soil, only a few inches thick, which seem to defy gravity. The valley narrows rapidly but the path follows a stream bed for several hundred metres to a picturesque waterfall". The whole walk takes 2 hours; take water and food.

Sebastian Kruisselbrink and Lieneke Onderwater of the Netherlands recommend a hike from Tupiza to Escoriana. There are many little villages along the way and the scenery is spectacular.

Local information
● **Accommodation**

F Alojamiento Centro, two blocks from the train station, clean, nice patio, warm water; **F** Mitru, Avenida Chichas, run down but still the best, private shower and bath, water unreliable, downstairs rooms preferable, laundry can take 3 days, restaurant has good almuerzo, but no dinner; **F** pp Mitru Anexo, hot shower, clean, good value, snack shop and restaurant, both open for dinner; **F** Residencial Valle Hermoso, Avenida Pedro Arraya, hot showers, good value, friendly, will let you park motorbikes in their expensive restaurant; **F** Residencial My Home, Abaroa 288, shared bath, hot water, recommended.

G pp Residencial Monterrey, opposite railway station, clean, hot water, good beds but dirty toilets.

● **Places to eat**

Picantería Las Brisas, on the opposite side of the river, open Saturday and Sunday only, large helpings. Los Helechos and Il Bambino, are both recommended. Good ice cream at Cremelin, on the plaza; El Flamingo, good cheap meals; Snack López, Calle Abaroa near the plaza, good and cheap. For a good breakfast try the Mercado Negro.

● **Banks & money changers**

Travellers' cheques can be changed at Empresa Bernall Hermanos, but only in the presence of the owner, good rates. Many shops will also change dollars at better rates than in Villazón.

● **Sports**

Tennis players should look in on the Tenis Club Ferrovaria opposite the rail station. They're very welcoming and will be glad to give you a game. Also good meals at the club.

● **Tour companies & travel agents**

Tupiza Tours, in Hotel Mitru, Avenida Chichas 187, T/F 3001, Casilla 67, they offer 2-day tours which follow Butch and Sundance's movements in 1908, US$80-100 per person, including transport, guide, meals and lodging, run by Fabiola Mitru; they also offer horseriding tours for US$4-5 per hour and hikes to the local quebradas; Spanish-speaking guides only. The Butch and Sundance tour can also be booked through Potosí Tours, Galería Chuquiago, Calle Sagárnaga 213, T/F 350870, La Paz, Casilla 11034. Dr Félix Chalar Miranda, president of the local historical society, offers jeep tours to the hold-up site near Salo, the escape route and San Vicente; or contact via Inquietud newspaper office at Avenida Pedro Arraya 205.

● **Useful addresses**

Hospital Ferroviário (near Hotel Mitru), Dr Rolando Llano Navarro and staff are very helpful. The IGM office, for maps, is in the Municipal building.

● **Transport**

Trains To **Villazón**, arrive from Oruro and Uyuni on Monday, Tuesday, Thursday and Friday around 0700-0900; 3 hours to Villazón. To **Uyuni** and **Oruro** leave Monday, Tuesday, Thursday and Friday.

Buses To **Villazón** 3 hours, US$2.50, 1000 and 1500; to **Potosí**, US$5.40, O'Globo at 1000, 8 hours, Expreso Tupiza daily 2030, US$7.75; to **Uyuni**, US$5.20, 8-10 hours on a poor road. There is no direct bus to La Paz, only via Potosí. A new road is being built from Uyuni to Atocha, halfway between Uyuni and Tupiza. The road

A tale of two outlaws

👣 One of the most enduring of screen images is Paul Newman as Butch Cassidy fooling around on a bicycle with schoolteacher Etta Place to the music of Burt Bacharach in the movie *Butch Cassidy and the Sundance Kid*.

The movie is based on a true story, which began in the 1860s. The outlaw known as Butch Cassidy, born Robert LeRoy Parker on 13 April 1866, was the eldest of thirteen children in a Mormon family in Utah. His admiration for a young cowboy named Mike Cassidy and a stint as a butcher inspired his *nom de crime*.

The Sundance Kid, born Harry Alonzo Longabaugh in the spring of 1867, was the youngest of five children in a Baptist family in Pennsylvania. He earned his nickname by serving 18 months in jail at Sundance, Wyoming, for stealing a horse. Sundance's female companion is something of an enigma. Described as a prostitute, a teacher, or both, no one knows her true origin or fate. She was called Etta Place in the movie, but she was also known as Ethel.

Butch and Sundance belonged to a loose-knit gang dubbed the Train Robber's Syndicate, the Hole-in-the-Wall Gang and the Wild Bunch. They held up trains, banks and mine payrolls in the Rocky Mountain West. With US$1,000 rewards on their heads and the Pinkerton Detective Agency (later to become the FBI) on their tail, Butch and Sundance fled to South America with Ethel in 1901, settling finally in Patagonia in Argentina, where they peacefully homesteaded a ranch in the Cholila Valley in Chubut Province, raising sheep, cattle and horses.

The peaceful life didn't last, however. Their names were linked to a bank robbery in Río Gallegos and the Buenos Aires police chief issued an order for their arrest. But Butch and Sundance were tipped off and headed for Chile. Later that year the outlaws returned to Argentina where they heisted US$100,000 from a bank in Villa Mercedes. A few months later, Ethel returned to the United States for good.

In 1906, they found work at the Concordia Tin Mine in the central Bolivian Andes, but Butch still wanted to settle down as a respectable rancher. In 1907, he and Sundance travelled to Santa Cruz, which Butch described as the perfect place to realize his dream. The bandits quit their jobs in 1908, soon after turning up in the mining centre of Tupiza, where they intended robbing a local bank, perhaps to finance their retirement in Santa Cruz.

They soon turned their attention to the Aramayo mining company, after Butch had learned that the local manager would be taking an unguarded payroll worth

from Potosí which goes on south to Villazón is bad and is often closed in the rainy season because the road fords the Río Suipacha. Book in advance.

SAN VICENTE

Tupiza is a good base from which to explore Butch Cassidy and the Sundance Kid country. The outlaws were supposed to have been killed here in **San Vicente** (*Population* 400; *Altitude* 4,500m), 103 km northwest of Tupiza on a good dirt road (4-6 hours). It's a typically bleak Altiplano village, described by one

correspondent as "a very sad place to die". The famous shootout site is off the main street – ask the locals.

Butch and Sundance are buried in an unmarked grave in the cemetery, but the grave has yet to be found. An investigation of the supposed grave, by the Nova project in 1991, proved negative, but see *Digging Up Butch and Sundance*, by Anne Meadows (New York: St Martin's Press, 1994). The Aramayo *hacienda* in Salo, 1 hour north of Tupiza, where they held up an Aramayo company payroll, still stands.

half a million dollars from the Tupiza office to the operational headquarters at Quechisla, 3 days' journey to the northwest. So, on 3 November, the manager set off with his young son, a *peón*, several mules and the money, trailed discretely by Butch and Sundance. As they made their way up Huaca Huañusca (Dead Cow Hill), near Salo, they were held up by the two bandits. But instead of the expected half a million, the motley group had only US$90,000 in their possession, the larger payroll having been scheduled for the following week.

Once the bandits had departed, the manager alerted his bosses and the alarm went out to local authorities, as well as to Argentine and Chilean border officials. With military patrols and armed miners (whose pay had been stolen) in pursuit, the pair headed north towards Uyuni. They followed the long, rugged trail to San Vicente, a tiny mining village set in an utterly barren landscape 4,000m up in the Cordillera Occidental.

At sundown on 6 November 1908, they rode into town and stopped at the home of Bonifacio Casasola, where they were given a room for the night. There they met Cleto Bellot, the chief administrative officer, with whom they discussed their plans to head north to Uyuni. Bellot took his leave and went straight to the home of a neighbour, where a four-man posse from Uyuni was staying. The posse had galloped in that afternoon and told Bellot to be on the lookout for two Yankees with an Aramayo mule.

Accompanied by Bellot, they went to Casasola's home, where Butch and Sundance were ready and waiting. A brief gunbattle ensued, then all went quiet. The posse waited until dawn before entering the house. There they found the two bandits stretched out on the floor, dead, both with bullet holes in the head. Butch had shot his partner and then turned the gun on himself.

The outlaws were buried in the local cemetery that afternoon in anonymous graves, but their deaths were not widely reported in the United States until 1930. In the meantime, wild stories of their demise circulated. These rumours had them being killed on numerous occasions, everywhere from the slums of Paris in the early 1900s to Las Vegas in the 1940s. And the mystery continues. An exhumation at the San Vicente cemetery in 1991, sponsored by the PBS science programme NOVA, failed to settle this long-running controversy. (Adapted from *Death in the Andes: The Last Days of Butch Cassidy & The Sundance Kid* by Daniel Buck and Anne Meadows, Washington DC.)

● **Accommodation** There's a basic *alojamiento* on the main street marked 'Hotel'; restaurant 'El Rancho' is next-door. Several *tiendas* sell beer, soda, canned goods, etc.

● **Transport** Trucks from Tupiza on Thursday early in the morning from Avenida Chichas near *Hotel Mitru*. Alternatively hire a vehicle: Fermín Ortega at Taller Nardini, or Barrio Lourdes is recommended. Don Manuel at *Hotel Mitru* can suggest others; US$30 to US$80 one-way. San Vicente is also accessible and a bit closer from Atocha, but there are fewer vehicles for hire there.

ROUTES From Tupiza a paved road heads south for 91 km to the town of Villazón on the Argentine border.

VILLAZON

Villazón is a dusty frontier town (*Population* 13,000; *Altitude* 3,443m) tucked away at the southernmost edge of Potosí Department. It lies along the Río Villazón which separates it from the vastly more attractive Argentine town of La Quiaca. It has little of interest for the visitor other than the fact that it is one of Bolivia's most important official border crossings into and out of Argentina.

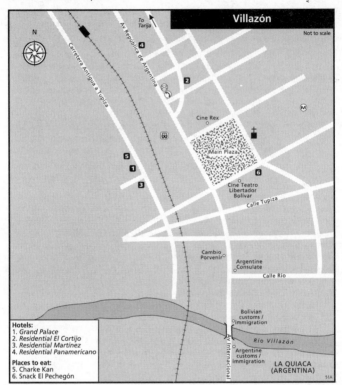

Villazón

Not to scale

To Tarija

Av República de Argentina

Carretera Antigua a Tupiza

Cine Rex

Main Plaza

Cine Teatro Libertador Bolívar

Calle Tupiza

Cambio Porvenir

Argentine Consulate

Calle Río

Bolivian customs / immigration

Río Villazón

Av Internacional

Argentine customs / immigration

LA QUIACA (ARGENTINA)

Hotels:
1. *Grand Palace*
2. *Residential El Cortijo*
3. *Residential Martínez*
4. *Residential Panamericano*

Places to eat:
5. Charke Kan
6. Snack El Pechegón

Settled in the mid-19th century, it exists primarily because of the thriving contraband trade carried on with its neighbour. Indeed, it is no exaggeration to say that fully three-quarters or more of the populace are involved in some way with illicit commercial activities, rivalling even Puerto Suárez in the Eastern Lowlands, in this *comercio de hormigas* (ant trade).

This retail smuggling endeavour is so named because at any time you will see long queues of people patiently awaiting (illegal) entry into Villazón from La Quiaca with all manner of goods bulging from overstuffed bags or strapped to their backs. The Bolivian customs officials do nothing to discourage this

trafficking, and to be fair, neither do the Argentine authorities. In fact, this trade has become so institutionalized that more conventional travellers entering Villazón from (or departing to) Argentina are advised to bypass the lengthy queues and simply proceed along to the respective immigration stations.

Local information
● Accommodation

Villazón has a surprising number of lodgings for the traveller who has to spend the weekend before passing into Argentina. All are very cheap and offer little beyond the basic amenities. Dollars, bolivianos or pesos are accepted, but not credit cards.

D *Residencial El Cortijo*, 20 de Mayo 338, across from the post office one block north of the plaza,

T 696209, the best of the lot, intermittent hot water, restaurant.

F pp *Grand Palace*, behind the bus terminal, safe; **F** *Hotel Bolivia*, one block from border, small rooms, run down, good value breakfast, hot showers extra; **F** *Residencial Martínez*, half block from the bus station opposite the *Grand Palace*, well signed, T 696562, hot water when town's supply is on, recommended; next door is **F** *Residencial 10 de Febrero*, very basic; **F** *Residencial Panamericano*, on the other side of the bus terminal from the *Grand Palace* across Avenida República de Argentina, laundry facilities, recommended.

● **Places to eat**

The town's culinary offerings are limited. The only bona fide restaurant is *Charke Kan*, next door to the *Hotel Grand Palace*. Off the plaza is *Snack El Pechegón*. There are also a handful of dubious-looking food stalls near the bus station, all of which are equally unappetizing. Most travellers suggest crossing the border in La Quiaca to eat.

● **Banks & money changers**

There is no bank in town. It's best to change money at one of the four *casas de cambio* on Avenida República de Argentina approaching the border: **Cambio Porvenir** is rumoured to be the best, but rates vary. Hotels and shops will probably not change anything other than small amounts. Travellers' cheques are virtually impossible to change and the rates are terrible anyway. Credit cards are not accepted anywhere in Villazón.

● **Entertainment**

Cultural options are non-existant, although there are two cinemas, *Cine Rex* and *Cine Teatro Libertador Bolívar*, both off the plaza. These show US movies with Spanish subtitles.

● **Post & telecommunications**

Post Office and **Entel** are in the same building, on Avenida República de Argentina across from the bus station. Both are open weekdays 0700-1800 (Entel sometimes until 2100) and Saturday 0800-1200.

● **Transport**

Road An improved road goes to Tarija. The road linking Potosí with Villazón via Camargo is in poor condition and about 100 km longer than the better road via Tupiza.

Buses To **Potosí**, several between 0830 and 1830, 10-15 hours, US$7-8 (the road is terrible in the wet and the journey can take 24 hours); to **Tupiza**, 0700 and 1500, US$2.50; to **Tarija**,

a beautiful journey but most buses go overnight only, daily at 1900/2000, US$6.50, 6 hours, it's very cold on arrival but passengers can sleep on the bus until daybreak. From **La Paz**, several companies, 25 hours, US$17.25, depart La Paz 1830, arrive Potosí 0700, depart Potosí 0830, arrive Villazón 1930; even though the buses are called 'direct', you may have to change in Potosí, perhaps to another company. It's the same procedure from Villazón to La Paz. The bus terminal is near the plaza, five blocks from the border. A taxi to the border is US$0.35, or hire a porter, US$1, and walk across.

Trains The rail station is about 1 km north of the frontier on the main road; a taxi costs US$2.35. To **Oruro** (a very dusty and cold journey), Monday and Thursday at 1630, US$5.60; Tuesday and Friday at 1600, US$7.50. Trains stop at Tupiza, Atocha and Uyuni. Latest reports suggest that trains go no further than Uyuni. The ticket office opens at 0800; expect long queues.

FRONTIER WITH ARGENTINA

● **Bolivian immigration**

The Bolivian office is on Avenida República de Argentina immediately before the bridge over the Río Villazón. It is open from 0700 to 1900, Monday-Saturday. They will issue an exit stamp, but note that immigration procedures are rather haphazard. Visitors may or may not have to pass through customs on either or both sides.

NB Contrary to popular belief, there is no fee to cross the border either way, and any attempts to levy a surcharge or tax are illegal. This does not prevent some officials (especially on the Bolivian side) attempting to extort money from unknowing visitors. You should be on your guard at all times at this border crossing; stories of illegal practices are rife.

● **Argentine consulate**

Three blocks south of the main plaza at the intersection of Avenida República de Argentina and Calle Río. Open weekdays 1000-1200 and 1400-1700, closed weekends and holidays.

● **Time difference**

Bolivian time is 1 hour behind Argentine time from October to April. From May to September Argentina loses an hour and keeps Bolivian time.

● **Entering Argentina**

Visitors entering Argentina from Villazón will encounter no difficulties in La Quiaca, though there are more checkpoints 20 and 100 km further south along the road to Jujuy. The Argentine authorities do take a dim view of suspect items such as packets of coca leaves or similar derivatives of the plant. Travellers are also advised to dress reasonably smartly and not wear anything that will arouse suspicion.

Bolivian consulate: in La Quiaca is one block south and west of the plaza, at the corners of Calle República Arabe Siria and San Juan; open 0830-1100 and 1400-1700 weekdays, Saturday 0900-1200 (in theory).

Exchange: the exchange situation in La Quiaca is similar to Villazón. Tavellers should note that the Argentine Province of Jujuy also issues it own paper currency (which is valid only in that province), so be sure to ask for *pesos nacionales*.

Potosí and Sucre

T HESE TWO small cities are the finest examples of Bolivia's colonial heritage. They lie only three hours apart – on one the country's few paved roads – but couldn't be more different. While Sucre exudes the confident charm of the young professional looking forward to a bright future, Potosí has the air of a dignified, but destitute old man showing the signs of a decadent past. Translated into tourist terms, this means that Sucre may enjoy a warmer climate, a healthier economy and a more attractive appearance, but Potosí is a more interesting place to visit.

POTOSI

This is not only the highest city in the world (together with the somewhat smaller Lhasa), but also one of the most beautiful. Silver from the 4,824m **Cerro Rico** (Rich Mountain) made Potosí the biggest city in the Americas and this wealth is reflected in the city's architecture which led it to be declared Patrimony of Mankind by Unesco in 1987. The Spanish still have a saying "vale un Potosí" ("worth a Potosí") for something incredibly lucrative.

Bring warm clothes – the average temperature is 9°C and there are 130 sub-zero nights a year. Take it easy on arrival; it's higher up than La Paz. To get an idea of the city's looks and layout you could ride the minibuses to avoid the high altitude walking. Potosí is the administrative

centre of the department of Potosí (*Population* 112,000; *Altitude* 3977m; *Phone code* 062; 533 km southeast of La Paz).

Potosí & Sucre

HISTORY

According to legend, the Inca Huayna Capac was on the point of mining silver in 1462 when a voice from above told him that he should leave it where it was because it was for someone else. The Inca then referred to the area as *Ppotojsi*, Quechua for ruin or spoil. According to another version, he described the voice as '*photoj nin*' ('a great din'). Another story says the name comes from the Aymara-Quechua word *Ppotoj*, meaning spring, from the numerous springs in and around the city. And yet another that it is from '*Potocchi*' ('source of silver').

Further legend says the silver was discovered in 1544 by Diego Huallpa who had lost some llamas and climbed Sumaj Orcko, as the Cerro Rico was then called. It got late, he got cold and made a fire which by morning had smelted a vein of silver. Huallpa told his mate Chalco or Guanca about the silver and they started mining. However, Chalco/Guanca told the Spanish who turned up and took possession of the mountain and founded the city in 1545 as the *Villa Imperial de Carlos V*. The official shield of the city carries the words "Soy el rico Potosí, del mundo soy el tesoro; soy el rey de los montes, envidia soy de los reyes" (I am rich Potosí, the treasure of the world; the king of mountains, the envy of kings).

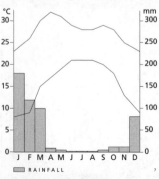

Climate: Potosí

The rise of Potosí

Within 18 months of the Spanish learning about the silver, the city had grown to 14,000; 25 years later the population numbered 120,000 making it the biggest city in the Americas. Potosí became the biggest single source of silver in the world despite the fact that it was being extracted by precolumbian methods. Within 20 years the surface deposits had been used up and people started going underground. The percentage of silver in the ore fell, increasing the costs of extracting it and Potosí entered the first of many crises.

The Viceroy of Lima, **Francisco de Toledo**, arrived in 1572, after pacifying Peru, to improve mining efficiency. He introduced the use of mercury to extract the silver (and a royal monopoly on mercury supplies), set up the **Casa Real de Moneda** to turn into ingots all silver mined so it could be taxed (20% went direct to the Spanish Crown) and reintroduced the *mita*, a pre-Incan forced collective labour scheme.

The most expensive part of mining was the manual labour needed to build and maintain a gallery – equal to the cost of a cathedral. The source of power to grind the ore was water, but this required a system of artificial lakes and aqueducts for which there was simply not the capital to pay someone to build.

Toledo dealt with this by dividing up what was then Alto Perú from Cusco to Potosí into sixteen provinces from which one-seventh of the adult male population had to work in Potosí for 1 year at a time, 3 weeks on, 3 weeks off. This provided 13,500 men (*mitayuqkuna*) a year, between a half and two thirds of the Potosí mining force. They were paid a nominal salary which did not cover living costs and so they were supported by their communities.

The boom years

Toledo's reforms turned Potosí into a boom city again. By 1585 there were 612 registered mines in Cerro Rico and a census in 1611 found there were 150,000 people living in the city including 6,000 black

Casa Real de Moneda

slaves. John Hemming, in his *Conquest of the Incas*, describes how, by the turn of the 16th century, Potosí had become one of the largest cities in Christendom, rivalled only by London, Paris and Seville. He states: "By the end of the sixteenth century the boom city of Potosí had all the trappings of a Klondike or Las Vegas: fourteen dance halls, thirty-six gambling houses, seven or eight hundred professional gamblers, a theatre, a hundred and twenty prostitutes and dozens of baroque churches."

Between 1570 and 1650, Potosí was the source of more than half the silver produced in the Americas, enough to pave a road all the way to Spain. This fuelled long term inflation and growth in Europe and paid for the import of goods from Asia. The city and local area could not support such a large population itself so all other areas supplied it: wheat and maize from Cochabamba, coca from the Yungas, mules, wine and sugar from northeast Argentina, cereals from Tarija and llamas from the northern Altiplano to transport the goods.

The silver was carried out to the coast by mule train. It took 25 days to cover the 885 km to Cobija on the Pacific coast, though Toledo also studied the geography and ordered the building of Arica, further north and a mere 750 km from Potosí. When what is now Bolivia was under the control of the Viceroy of Buenos Aires the silver had to be carried for 2,500 km to reach the Atlantic, a 52-day walk.

Decline

Silver production peaked in 1650 and then went into a century-long decline while Mexico took over as the biggest source. By 1690 the *mitayuqkuna* were down to 2,000. An outbreak of typhoid in 1719 killed an estimated 22,000 people in less than a year and by 1750 the population of Potosí was 70,000. By the 1780s it had fallen to 35,000. All Bolivian cities except La Paz stagnated or shrank during this period as a result of Potosí's contraction.

From 1730 silver production picked up, slowly, but never reached earlier levels nor had such a great impact on the rest of the country. However, at the start of the 19th century Potosí was still a prize worth fighting for during Bolivia's 16-year long struggle for independence from the Spanish, Lima and Buenos Aries. Potosí suffered badly and by the time independence was won, the city was down to 8,000 inhabitants and fifty working mines.

The demand for tin – a metal the Spaniards ignored – saved the city from absolute poverty in the first half of the 20th century, until the price slumped due to over supply. But mining continues in the treacherous tunnels that riddle the Cerro Rico – mainly tin, zinc, lead, antinomy and wolfram. The fabulous riches of Potosí's past have long gone. Now only the baroque churches remain to pay homage to the many hundreds of thousands who sacrificed their lives for the greed of their colonial rulers.

Places of interest

Just wandering around the centre of Potosí will take you past many colonial buildings. While Viceroy Toledo tried to bring order to the city's layout in 1574, the boom had

Cerro Rico

led to fast and unplanned development which has left Potosí with a less-than-grid-iron plan full of small streets with unexpected twists and turns – including the **Pasaje de las Siete Vueltas** (Seven Turn Passage), off Junín – which adds to the city's charm. There are lots of beautiful and ornate religious buildings well-worth seeing – during the colonial period there were thirty two churches in the city.

An active restoration project is permanently going on, organized by the city council and the Spanish Cooperation Agency, but there is a lot of work to do – the city boasts more than 2,000 colonial buildings. **NB** Restoration work means buildings can be closed to visitors for months, so check with the tourist office if there is anywhere you particularly want to visit.

Those who are into colonial architecture could do worse than begin in Calle Quijarro, one of Potosí's best-preserved streets. In colonial times it was known as Calle Ollería – potmakers – and Calle de los Sombreros (hats). At Quijarro and Omiste is the **Esquina de las Cuatro Portadas** (four houses with double doors), or Balcón de Llamancha. There is a fine stone doorway (house of the Marqués de

Otavi) in Junín between Matos and Bolívar. At Lanza 8 was the house of José de Quiroz and of Antonio López de Quiroga (now a school). Turn up Chuquisaca from Lanza and after three blocks right into Millares; here on the left is a sculpted stone doorway and on the right a doorway with two rampant lions in low relief on the lintel. Turning left up Nogales you come to an old mansion in a little plaza. Turn left along La Paz and one block along there is another stone doorway with suns in relief. At La Paz y Bolívar is the **Casa del Balcón de la Horca**.

Around the centre

Most visitors would begin in the central **Plaza 10 de Noviembre**, which used to be used for bull running. It's surrounded by some of the best buildings including the Alcaldía, court, Prefectura and the **Cathedral**, more impressive for its size than for its internal baroque decoration. The cathedral is open Monday-Friday, 0930-1000, 1300-1500, Saturday 0930-1000, guided tour only, US$1.

Half a block above the plaza is the imposing façade of the **Teatro Omiste**, finished in 1753 as the Belén church which has since been a hospital, royalist

Fighting for tradition

🐾 A tradition peculiar to the Potosí Department is the *tinku* ritual fight. Basically, what happens is that two neighbouring communities meet up and beat the living daylights out of one another – literally. For death, though much less common these days, is always a possibility.

The *tinku* may look like a drunken Saturday night pub brawl, but it is loaded with symbolism and carries a deep spiritual significance. It is a meeting of equals and is not about winning, but of recognizing your rivals, respecting them and defining your territory. It symbolizes the need to co-exist with other people. It is also a celebration of forgiveness of family or personal enemies. In the *tinku* any problem is solved and all debts are paid.

Before the fight, the combatants meet and drink *chicha* and stronger alcohol. The alcohol is to give them courage for the impending battle. The fight begins with fists; each fighter wears rings of bronze adorned with claws to ensure the opponents guts are ripped out. For protection, the pugilists wear a leather helmet, treated so that it is hard as steel, and a leather groin protector. Fighting is hand-to-hand and reaches a fever pitch of noisy violence. The losers begin to retreat and then stones rain down on both groups.

The winner of each fight then enjoys 1 year of dominance over his defeated opponent. The injured, though, are respected for standing their ground and fighting bravely. The corpses, meanwhile, are buried as an offering to *Pachamama*, to ensure a good harvest.

There is no sexual discrimination here. Women also fight in the *tinku*. It is said that they fight more cruelly and with more honour. During the *tinku*, bands play continuously and those who are too scared, ill, old, or sensible to fight dance around in a circle.

Tourists are a relatively new phenomenom, so be discreet. Things can get ugly after a couple of days' hard drinking and fighting, so it's wise to get out before the end. Some agencies, eg Koala, organize trips to the Macha *tinku* on 3 May and the Uncía *tinku* on 2 August, among others.

headquarters in 1823 during the wars of independence (the royalists knocked down the twin towers of the church in order to improve their cannon emplacements), a theatre from 1862 and then a cinema in the 20th century, before returning to life as a theatre.

Opposite is **Plaza 6 de Agosto** which was occupied by a church until the aforementioned royalists decided it was in the way. The bizarre white four-arch construction is a reminder of a forty-four-arch construction that was demolished earlier this century. Another block up Calle Hoyos is **La Merced church**, finished in 1687, which shows the Renaissance influence brought over by friars from Andalucía in Spain.

Two long blocks up, just below Calle Pizarro, is the **San Martín church** which was built by indigenous people forced to come and work in Potosí. It has an uninviting exterior, but has one of the most ornately decorated interiors of any church in Bolivia, with oil paintings and giltwork. It is normally closed for fear of theft. Ask the German Redemptorist Fathers to show you around; their office is just to the left of their church. On Calle Bolívar, below La Paz, is the highly decorated **Casa de las Tres Portadas**.

Below the main plaza on Calle Ayacucho is the **Casa de Moneda** (see **Museums** below) which fills a double block. Further down Calle Ayacucho below Bustillos is

Typical Potosí street

the ornate mestizo style tower of the Jesuit **Compañía de Jesus church** finished in 1707, with an impressive bell-gable. At the bottom of Calle Ayacucho is the convent, church and museum of **Santa Teresa** (see **Museums** below).

Outside the central market on Calle Héroes del Chaco is the extremely ornate 18th century mestizo-baroque façade of the **San Lorenzo church** (1728-1744), with a rich portal and fine views from the tower. The first church on this site, La Anunciación, was one of the first built in the city, but collapsed in 1557 after a heavy snowfall. The outside of San Bernardo, off Plaza Bolívar (also known as Plaza del Estudiante), is also impressive – it appears to be cobbled. The **San Francisco convent** is on Calle Tarija esquina Nogales (see **Museums** below) and provides one of the best viewpoints over the city.

Other churches worth checking out include **Jerusalén**, close to the *Hotel Centenario*, and **San Agustín** on Bolívar y Quijarro, with crypts and catacombs (the whole city was interconnected by tunnels in colonial times). The latter can only be visited by prior arrangement with the tourist office; the tour starts at 1700, US$0.10 admission. From **San Cristóbal church**, at Pacheco y Cañete, you can get a good view over the whole city.

The outskirts
Head south from the centre of the city, drop down and you cross the **Ingenios de la Rivera** area where the ore mined from Cerro Rico was processed. This was the biggest industrial area in the world at the start of the 17th century. Continue up on the other side and you enter what was the Indian part of the city during the colonial period, linked to the centre by eleven bridges. The streets are narrow and cobbled, the houses are roofed with terracota tiles. Two of the *ingenios* are particularly well-preserved: **San Marcos**, Calle Betazanos esquina La Paz (see **Museums** below) and **Ingenio Dolores**, on Calle Mejillones just down from Nicolás Benino.

Farther down Calle Mejillones is the adobe tower of the long-gone **Santa Bárbara church** which was built 1548-52 and was one of the first churches in the city. Other churches worth checking out on this side of the city include **San Pedro**, Calle San Pedro just above Vitoria, which has a wooden roof and an ornate gilded pulpit, and **San Juan Bautista** in Calle Hernández esquina Chuquisaca, which has a Collin clock from Paris. One and a half blocks further up Chuquisaca is the 1775 **Casa del Agua**.

Plaza **El Minero** is at the top of Calle San Pedro and has a monument of a miner with a drill in one hand and a rifle in the other, marking the role miners have played in Bolivian political history. Mine massacres are not a thing of the past, however. In December 1996 twelve miners, wives and children were shot dead by the army at Amayapampa in Potosí department during a mining dispute.

Museums
Casa Nacional de Moneda at Calle Ayacucho and Quijarro, T 23986, open Monday-Friday 0900-1200 and 1400-1730, Saturday 0900-1200 and 1400-1600, entrance for foreigners US$2, photo permission US$2, video permission US$4, 2-hour tour with guide (Spanish only) at 0900, 1000, 1400 and 1500.

All silver mined in Potosí had to be brought to the Casa (or Mint) to be turned into ingots so the Spanish Crown could tax it. Founded in 1572, rebuilt 1759-1773, it is one of the chief monuments of civil building in Hispanic America. It has 160 rooms and the walls are fortress-thick. You cannot fail to notice the huge, grinning Bacchus (mask) over an archway between two principal courtyards. This was put up in 1865 and, according to some, the smile is said to be ironic and aimed at the departing Spanish.

The fifty-odd room museum has a good collection of paintings including works by the best of the Bolivian colonial painters. One section is dedicated to the works of the acclaimed 17th-18th century religious painter Melchor Pérez de Holguín. Also featured are Gamarra, Berrio and Cruz. Displays cover the precolonial, colonial and republican periods and there is a collection of indigenous costumes from the Potosí Department.

Elsewhere are coin dies and huge wooden presses which made the silver strip from which coins were cut. The smelting houses have carved altar pieces from Potosí's ruined churches. There are also various collections of religious architecture, swords, guns and bombs and minerals. Wear warm clothes, as it is cold inside.

Museo del Ingenio San Marcos, Calle Betanzos esquina La Paz, is the only well-preserved piece of industrial architecture in the city. It has a 6m diameter water wheel which was used to power the machinery for grinding down silver ore before mercury was added to extract the metal. The Ingenio had a capacity to produce 119 kilograms of silver a month when it was working. Also café and restaurant.

Museo de San Francisco, Calle Tarija esquina Nogales, T 22539, open Monday-Saturday 1000-1200 and 1430-1630; entrance US$1.45, US$2 to take photos. This was the first church built in the city, started in 1547. The current building was begun in 1707 and has the oldest surviving cloisters in Bolivia. There are more than 200 paintings including one of Melchor Pérez de Holguín's best works, 'The

Erection of the Cross'. Don't miss the view from the roof.

Museo de Santa Teresa, Calle Ayacucho esquina Chichas, T 23847; entry US$2, plus US$2 to take photos; open Monday-Friday 0900-1200, 1300-1800, Saturday 0900-1200, but check at Tourist Office (tour in Spanish). The building was started in 1685 and has an impressive amount of giltwork inside. There is an interesting but shocking collection of flagellation tools (a must for sado-masochists), colonial paintings, religious architecture and furniture. At the end of a visit you can buy *quesitos*, sweets made by the nuns according to a 300-year-old tradition.

Museo Universitario, Calle Bolívar between Sucre and Junín, T 27310, open Monday-Friday 0900-1200 and 1400-1800, entrance US$1. The museum has some good modern Bolivian painting, as well as sculptures, costumes, musical instruments, fossils and minerals, ceramics and colonial furniture.

Museo Etno-indumentario, Avenida Serrudo 148, T 23258, open Monday-Friday 0900-1200 and 1430-1800, Saturday 0900-1200. A thorough display of the different dress and customs of Potosí department's sixteen provinces.

Local festivals

February-March, *Miners' Carnival*: The images venerated by the miners are taken out of the mines once a year on this date and carried to Plaza El Minero. Another miners' festival is *Fiesta de los Compadres* in **February**, for decorating the miners' god *El Tío* and the workplace.

8-10 March: *San Juan de Dios*, with music, dancing, parades etc.

Last Sunday in May, *Fiesta de Manquiri*: A pagan-based festival when vehicles and miniatures are blessed in the village 26 km northeast of the city. (Transport from Plaza Chuquimia.)

In **May** there is a market on Calle Gumiel every Sunday, with lotteries and lots of fun things for sale. On three consecutive Saturdays at the end of May,

The legend of Chutillos

🐾 Legends abound surrounding the origins of the festival of *Chutillos*, one of Potosí's greatest annual celebrations, which runs from 24-26 of August. *Chutillo* is the traditional name for a miner on muleback and is given to the main participants in the festival – the jockeys who wear white capes. On the first day of the festival, the *Chutillos* ride on mules or donkeys to the chapel of San Bartolomé, also known as *Cueva del Diablo* (the Devil's Cave), near the village of La Puerta.

According to one legend, an evil spirit called *Umphurruna* was banished from the House of Light and sent down to earth. On the way, he saw *Sapallay*, the sun, and instantly fell in love with her. He carried her off to La Puerta, to hide from the prying eyes of men. With his mysterious power, he cut into two the huge cliffs, opening up a narrow winding passage through the middle. *Umphurruna* took *Sapallay* to a dark cave in the ravine with sharp points like teeth. This became known as the devil's cave and *Unphurruna* was given the name *Chutillo*, or genie who harms and then escapes.

If anyone threatened to discover the devil's cave, the *Chutillo* would cause the cliffs to close, thereby crushing them to death. This finally ended when the Jesuits of the Compañía de Jesús church in the newly-founded Villa Imperial de Carlos V took an image of the Apostle San Bartolomé and put it in a smaller cave near the Devil's residence. This caused the evil spirit to rush out screaming and smash into the cliff walls, leaving a greenish black mark which is still visible today.

Ever since then the people of Potosí have celebrated San Bartolomé by visiting the site of the cave each year. This is how the *Chutillos* festival began.

beginning of June llama sacrifices are made at the cooperative mines in honour of *Pachamama*.

1 August, *Ritual del Espíritu*: More llama sacrifices.

24-26 August, *Chutillos (Fiesta de San Bartolomé)*: On the first day, *Chutillo*, people walk to the village of La Puerta, 5 km from the centre on the Oruro road, to the church of San Bartolomé (see **Excursions** below) to pray and then climb the nearby hill. On day 2, *Majtillo*, indigenous people in costume from all over the department make their entrance into the city. Day 3 is *Thapuquillo*, when people from the city and invited groups from other parts of the country and abroad parade through the streets.

First and second Sunday in October, *Virgen de La Merced* and *Virgen del Rosario*: Processions through decorated streets. People throw flower petals on passing religious images.

In **October/November**, *Festival Internacional de la Cultura*: Cultural events take place over 2 weeks in Potosí and Sucre.

10 November, *Fiesta Aniversario de Potosí*: Foundation celebrations.

Potosí is sometimes called the 'Ciudad de las Costumbres', especially at Corpus Cristi, Todos Santos and Carnaval, when special cakes are baked, families go visiting friends, etc.

Local information
● Accommodation

Unless otherwise stated hotels have no heating in rooms.

B *Hostal Colonial*, Hoyos 8, a pretty colonial house near the main plaza, T 24809, F 27146, popular, nicely designed, with heating, has names and phone numbers of guides, even if you're not staying they're very helpful, very expensive for long-distance phone calls, the best hotel in the centre.

C *Claudia*, Avenida Maestro 322, three-star, T 22242, F 25677, out of the centre, helpful, modern, highly recommended; **C** *Hostal Libertador*, Millares 58, T 27877, F 24629, Casilla 324, colonial building, heaters in rooms, quiet, helpful, comfortable, parking, highly recommended though not four-star; **C** *Jerusalem*, Oruro 143, T/F 22600, with private bathroom,

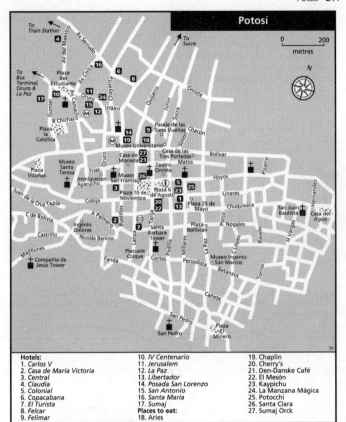

Potosí

0   200
metres

N

To
Train Station

Av Serrudo

To
Sucre

Av del Maestro

Av Cívica

Chayanta

Omiste

Quijarro

To
Bus
Terminal,
Oruro &
La Paz

Plaza
del
Estudiante

Oruro

Gumiel

R Chichas

Camacho

Ingavi

Junín

Sucre

Chacón

Pasaje de las
Siete Vueltas

Simón Bolívar

Plaza
la
Católica

Museo
Santa
Teresa

Museo
Vicuñas

Juan de la Cruz Tapia

Plaza
Vicuñas

Museo Universitario

Casa de la
Tres Portadas

Bolívar

Matos

Frías

Immigration
Ayacucho

Casa de
Moneda

Teatro
Omiste

Museo
San Francisco

Hoyos

Cobija

A Palmero

Bustillos

Plaza 10 de
Noviembre

Plaza 6
de Agosto

Linares

Pizarro

Hernández

C de Bolivia

Lanza

Tarija

Santa
Barbara
Tower

Plaza 25 de
Mayo

Chuquisaca

Porco

San Juan
Bautista

Casa del
Agua

Castrillo

Nicolás Benino

Ingenio
Dolores

Plaza
Ballivián

Nogales

La Paz

Ravelo

H Vargas

Mejillones

Compañía de
Jesús Tower

Fanda

Plazuela
Colque

Cortes

Pedilla

Millares

Periodista

Museo Ingenio
San Marcos

Betanzos

López

Torres

Cañete

San Pedro

San
Pedro

Plaza
El
Minero

Hotels:
1. *Carlos V*
2. *Casa de María Victoria*
3. *Central*
4. *Claudia*
5. *Colonial*
6. *Copacabana*
7. *El Turista*
8. *Felcar*
9. *Felimar*
10. *IV Centenario*
11. *Jerusalem*
12. *La Paz*
13. *Libertador*
14. *Posada San Lorenzo*
15. *San Antonio*
16. *Santa Maria*
17. *Sumaj*

Places to eat:
18. *Aries*
19. *Chaplin*
20. *Cherry's*
21. *Den-Danske Café*
22. *El Mesón*
23. *Kaypichu*
24. *La Manzana Mágica*
25. *Potocchi*
26. *Santa Clara*
27. *Sumaj Orck*

F pp without, pleasant, helpful, *comedor*, garage parking, laundry, good value, clean, comfortable, friendly, lots of light, travel agency next door, *Sumaj Tours*, T 24633, is part of the hotel.

D *Carlos V*, Linares 42 on Plaza 6 de Agosto, T 25151, with private bathroom, **E** without, breakfast, occasional hot water, luggage store, late night curfew, covered courtyard makes the inside a bit gloomy but very friendly; **D** *El Turista*, Lanza 19, T 22492, F 22517, friendly, helpful, hot showers, lots of light, breakfast for US$1, excellent view of the city from rooms 33, 34 and 35 on the top floor, good value, recommended; **D** *Hostal Felimar*, Junín 14, T 24357, hot water, price includes breakfast, only marginally cheaper to share a bathroom, two roof-top suites, solar-powered

(so no hot water early morning), first floor rooms have no exterior windows but are warm, quiet; *Hostal Santa María*, Avenida Serrudo 244, T 23255, hot water, comfortable, good cafeteria, popular though not particularly friendly; **D** *IV Centenario*, Plaza Bolívar/del Estudiante, T 22751, huge and empty with squeaky floors, a plaque says it was refurbished in 1996, but it looks like it's time for another one; **D** pp *San Antonio*, Oruro 136, T 23566, with private bathroom, **E** pp without, US$0.40 discount with valid youth hostel card if sharing a room with four other people, noisy.

F *Alojamiento El Barquito*, Oruro 7, T 22600, not obviously spotted, good, rustic but recommended; **F** *Casa de María Victoria*, Chuquisaca

148, T 22132, built in the 17th century as accommodation for friars from Santo Domingo, all rooms open on to a stone courtyard, clean, stores luggage, popular, laundry facilities, good travel agency, breakfast in courtyard, cheap mine tours, owner speaks English, recommended; **F pp** *Central*, Bustillos 1230 y Linares, T 22207, poor showers, breakfast, basic, surrounds a courtyard which is the main source of light; **F pp** *Felcar*, Serrudo 345 y Bustillos, T 24966, hot water, 0800-1200, clean, basic, friendly, popular; **F** *Residencial 10 de Noviembre*, Avenida Serrudo 181, clean, hot shower, ask for a room with a window, good lunch in the restaurant; **F pp** *Residencial Sumaj*, Gumiel 12, T 23336, small rooms, double room on top floor with good views, hot water 0800-1800, shared bathrooms only, mixed reports, still popular with travellers, friendly and helpful but it's a dark place apart from the central courtyard.

G *Alojamiento Ferrocarril*, Avenida E Villazón 159, T 24294, basic, hot showers US$0.55, close to the railway station; **G pp** *Alojamiento La Paz*, Oruro 262, T 22632, central, basic, big courtyard; **G pp** *Posada San Lorenzo*, Calle Bustillos 967, cheapest place in the centre, colonial building, nice courtyard; **G pp** *Residencial Copacabana*, Avenida Serrudo 319, T 22712, individual or shared rooms, restaurant, separate hot showers, will change dollars cash, safe car park (owner, Dr Hugo Linares Fuentes will give medical assistance), popular.

5 km from Potosí in the village of San Antonio is *El Tambo*, Km 5 Carretera a Oruro, T 25597, F 22985, three-star, the best hotel in the area, colonial/rustic architecture, three restaurants, Bodega Bar, all details from *Hidalgo Tours* (see below).

● **Places to eat**
Lots of places display Visa/Mastercard notices. Check 1) that they do and 2) the additional charge which is often 13 per cent.

Sumaj Orcko, Quijarro 46, excellent, but even better when they have what's offered, large portions, cheap set lunch, reasonably priced, very popular with travellers, heating, slow service; *El Mesón*, Calle Linares esquina Tarija on the corner of Plaza 10 de Noviembre, smart, possibly the best restaurant in town; *Plaza*, Quijarro 38, cheap set lunch, good; *The Sky Room*, Bolívar 701, good views of the town and the Cerro, good, slow service; *La Carreta*, Gumiel sin número, excellent, pleasant service, mid-price range; *La Manzana Mágica*, Oruro

239, small but excellent vegetarian, open 0700-2130, lunch US$2; *Kaypichu*, Millares 24, stylish and excellent vegetarian, open 0700-1300 and 1600-2100, stages cultural events; *Kivo's*, Quijarro 12, good Italian food, small, cosy, friendly; *Aries*, Calle Bolívar esquina Junín, second floor, meat-dominated menu, good value; *Coffee Snack El Farol*, Tarija 28, opposite San Francisco, high kitsch decor, bohemian atmosphere, popular with artists, open late.

Confiterías: *Confitería Cherry's*, Padilla 8 y Linares, good cakes and coffee, burgers, very popular, good breakfast, cheap, recommended, open 0800. *Den-Danske Café*, Calle Quijarro esquina Matos, opens 1300, Potosí's first gringo hangout, friendly, good food and music, foreign language games and magazines; *UMI Confitería Victoria*, Ayacucho y Bustillos, cheap breakfast, good coffee, owner Benjamín speaks English and German and changes money. *Santa Clara*, Plaza 10 de Noviembre esquina Quijarro, nice view onto the main plaza with Cerro Rico behind, breakfast, ice cream, burgers, pizza, empanadas with meat and excellent *llauchas* (spicy cheese-filled pasties), open Monday-Saturday 0800-1300 and 1430-2200, Sunday 1430-2200; *Chaplin*, Calle Bustillos 979, friendly, good value burgers (including vegetarian), excellent chips, good music, shut for lunch.

Comedor Popular in Mercado Central, between Oruro, Bustillos, Héroes del Chaco and Bolívar, breakfast from 0700, fresh bread from 0600, *api* and *pasteles* US$0.55, possibly the best thing to warm you up in the morning.

● **Banks & money changers**
You can find enlace ATMs outside **Banco Mercantil**, Calle Sucre between Matos and Hoyos and at Calle Junín near Sucre. **Banco Nacional**, Calle Bolívar y Junín 4-6, changes dollar travellers' cheques and cash. **Banco Popular**, Bolívar y Sucre, cash withdrawals on Visa. Other banks are **Banco de La Paz**, Plaza 10 de Noviembre esquina Plaza 6 de Agosto; **Banco de Crédito**, Calle Bolívar esquina Sucre. Many shops on Plaza Alonso de Ibáñez and on Bolívar, Sucre and Padilla display signs stating they change dollars and Argentinian pesos. Dollar travellers' cheques can be changed at *Distribuidora Cultural Sud*, Matos 19, 3% commission.

● **Entertainment**
Cinema at Padilla 31. *Potocchi*, Millares 13, T 28349, *peña* on Friday and Saturday, entrance US$1.40, good cafe/restaurant the rest of the week.

Public baths: *Sauna Florida*, Plaza Chuquimina, near bus station, open Friday, Saturday, Sunday, US$1.50 (also has racquetball).

● **Hospitals & medical services**
Clinics: *Clínica Británica*, on Oruro near *Alojamiento La Paz*, clinics mornings and afternoons, English spoken.

● **Language schools**
Open Door School of English, Cobija 12, T 25983, F 25556, teaches Spanish, they are often looking for TEFL-qualified native English speakers.

● **Laundry**
Limpieza la Veloz, Calle Quijarro, corner of Matos, Edificio Cademin, and at Camacho 258, US$1.30 per kilo.

● **Post & telecommunications**
Post Office: Calle Lanza 3 esquina Chuquisaca, open Saturday till 1900, Sunday 0900-1200; unreliable for overseas mail. **Entel**: on Plaza Arce at the end of Calle Camacho between Frías and Bolívar, T 43496; also at Avenida Universitaria near the bus terminal, and on Padilla 5, opposite *Confitería Cherry's*.

● **Shopping**
Mercado Central (see address above) sells mainly food and produce, but silver is sold near the Calle Oruro entrance. *Mercado Gremial*, between Avenida Camacho and Oruro, only sells household goods. There is an informal swap market every Friday night at the Plazuela, at Bolívar and Quijarro. *Mercado Artesanal*, at Sucre y Omiste, sells jumpers, rugs, wall-hangings, bags, good musical instruments. Some Fridays the merchants organize music, food and drink (*ponche*), not to be missed. Almost opposite is *Andina*, Sucre 94, for handicrafts and antiques. For musical instruments try Arnaud Gerard (Belgian), his workshop *Killay* at the back of Mercado Artesanal makes beautifully made and tuned pieces, designed to be played, will make to order, open Monday-Friday, 1700-1930. There are also *artesanía* shops along Calle Sucre between Omiste and Bolívar. Also *Artesanías El Cisne*, Padilla 17; and if you are desperate or an insomniac, *El Chasqui*, Calle La Paz esquina Linares, claims to be open 24 hours a day. The main shopping streets are Calle Bolívar and Calle Sucre which is pedestrianized between Bolívar and Plaza 6 de Agosto.

Bookshops: the best bookshop is at the University, open Monday-Friday, 1000-1200, 1500-1700. Postcards and gifts can be bought from the gift shop at the entrance to the Post Office.

● **Useful addresses**
Migración: at Calle Oruro esquina Frías.
Police station: on Plaza 10 de Noviembre.

● **Tourist offices**
Plaza 6 de Agosto half a block above the main Plaza 10 de Noviembre, allegedly open Monday-Friday 0800-1200 and 1400-1800. Town maps cost US$0.40 (English, French, German and Spanish editions) and are better than the glossy US$0.60 map (Spanish only). Also good is the colour Spanish *Guía Turística de Potosí* published by the Plan de Rehabilitación de las Areas Históricas de Potosí, US$5. Another guide is Potosí map and guide (Quipus), US$2.50. It's possible to buy maps at **Instituto Geográfico Militar**, Calle La Paz, 0900-1200, 1400-1800.

● **Tour companies & travel agents**
All guides must have an identity card issued by the Prefectura and must work through an agency. If you go with a guide who is not working through an agency and something goes wrong there is no insurance cover. If you want to book a Salar and Lagunas tour with a Potosí agency, check they operate the service themselves – many of them subcontract and just put you on a bus to Uyuni. If you pay in Potosí and then have problems in Uyuni refunds can be difficult.

It is difficult to differentiate between the agencies. They all offer (unless noted below) similar services including daily mine visits, city tours, trips to the thermal baths near Potosí and trips to the Salar de Uyuni and Lagunas.

The list of agencies in alphabetical order: *Cerro Rico Travel*, Quijarro 8, T/F 25552, organizes trips to village *artesanía* markets north of the city and to colonial *haciendas*, horse and mountain bike hire, treks in Kari Kari and Talacocha, trips to Toro Toro including cave visits; *Ecological Expeditions*, Calle Bustillos 1092, T 26183; *Hidalgo Tours*, Junín y Bolívar 19, T 28293, F 22985, Casilla 310, upmarket and specialized services within the city and to Salar de Uyuni; *Koala Tours*, Calle Ayacucho 5, T 24708, T 22092 (so named because koalas chew eucalyptus leaves in a similar way to miners chewing coca leaves, allegedly), they offer the best mine visits, guide and owner Eduardo Garnica is a former miner, excellent English, frequently recommended, optional traditional breakfast or lunch including high protein, low fat llama meat, *tinku* trips; *Potosí Tours*, Plaza Alonso de Ibáñez, T 25786, good tours of the city; *Transamazonas*, Calle Bustillos 1078, T 27175, F 24796, trekking in Kari Kari, probably the best

Salar de Uyuni tours but not cheap at US$220 per person; *Altiplano Tours*, Ayacucho 19, T 25353/27299; *Transandino Tours*, Bustillos 1078, T 26787 (see below), also changes travellers' cheques at reasonable rates; *Turismo Balsa*, Plaza Alonso de Ibáñez, T 26272, English spoken, daily city tours, upmarket (see also La Paz **Travel Agents**); *Victoria Tours* (see *Casa de María Victoria* in Accommodation for contact details), friendly and knowledgeable, have the recommended English-speaking guides Julio César Morales, Marco Mamani and Santos Mamani.

● **Transport**
Local Bus: within the city, *micros* US$0.12.
Taxi: within city limits US$0.50; approx US$1.30 per kilometre for longer journeys.

Air Aerosur, Calle Hoyos 10 (T 22088), flies Potosí to La Paz 0800 Monday-Saturday, US$87, 1 hour (La Paz to Potosí 0630 Monday-Saturday). A return ticket costs US$138. The airport is 5 km out of the city on the Sucre road. LAB does not fly from Potosí.

Trains Services to Sucre, Oruro and La Paz are suspended indefinitely. For more information, T 23101.

Buses The terminal, on Avenida Universitaria below the train station, is 20 minutes' downhill (30 minutes uphill) walk, or a short taxi or micro ride from the centre of town, T 27354. It's not that steep but you are starting at over 3,900m. Entel, Correo, police, US$0.10 terminal tax. When you buy your ticket you check your luggage into the operator's office and it is then loaded directly onto your bus.
　Daily services: to **La Paz** 0700 and 1830-1930, US$4-6, 11 hours, *buscama* from Flota Copacabana US$10. To **Oruro** 0630 and 1900, US$4, 7 hours. To **Cochabamba** 1830, US$6, 12 hours. To **Sucre** 0630, 0800, 1300, 1700 and 1800, US$3, 3 hours. To **Santa Cruz** 1900, US$12, 18 hours. To **Villazón** 0730, 0830, 1800 and 1900, US$4, 11 hours. To **Tarija** 0700, 1400, 1600 and 1700, US$6, 12 hours.
　Buses to **Uyuni** leave from either side of the railway line (uphill the road is called Avenida Antofagasta or 9 de Abril, downhill it is Avenida Universitaria), daily 1130 and 1200, US$5, 6 hours. (Trans 11 de Julio also run daily buses to Argentina.)
　Buses to the thermal baths at **Tarapaya** leave from outside the Chuquimia market on Avenida Universitaria and from one block higher every 30 minutes or so 0700-1700, US$0.50, 30 minutes.

EXCURSIONS FROM POTOSI

Tarapaya
Tarapaya is a volcanic crater lake almost 100m across with medicinal properties and a temperature of 30°C. It is also known as Baño del Inca (the Inca's Bath). It's a beautiful spot and ideal for freshening up after spending the morning crawling around in mine tunnels. You should take sun protection. On the other side of the river from the lake are thermal baths (public, US$0.30, private, US$0.60); the private baths, higher up, may be cleaner. There is also an Olympic-sized swimming pool. Tarapaya is 25 km outside the city on the road to Oruro; get off at the bridge and then follow the dirt road going left, or climb staright uphill for about 15 minutes to the lake. Nearby is **Balneario Miraflores** which also has swimming pools. The altitude, 3,300m, makes it noticeably lower and warmer than in Potosí.
　Buses to Tarapaya and Miraflores leave from outside the Chuquimia market on Avenida Universitaria and from one block higher every half hour or so 0700-1700, US$0.50, 30 minutes. A taxi costs US$7.50 for a group. The last bus back from Miraflores leaves at 1800.

There are also thermal waters at **Don Diego**, 24 km from Potosí on the road to Sucre, at **Chaqui**, 37 km from the city (pleasant, clean, closed Wednesday; take a truck or bus from Plaza Uyuni) and **Rosario**, 25 km from Potosí on the road to Uyuni.

Trekking in Kari Kari
Following Viceroy Toledo's reforms in the early 1570s, thirty-two artificial lakes were built to the east of the city to supply the *ingenios* with a steady supply of water to grind down the ore before adding mercury to extract the silver. About 20,000 Indians were used to build the dams over a 50 year period. On the afternoon of 15 March 1626 one dam wall broke sending a tidal wave through the city killing between 2,500 and 10,000 people, depending on who you believe. It was said that the ghosts of the dead

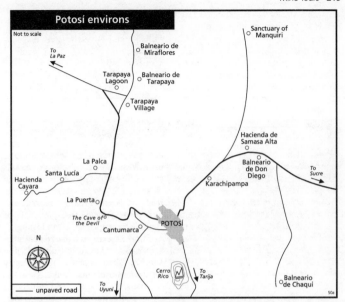

Potosí environs

Not to scale

To La Paz

Balneario de
Miraflores

Tarapaya
Lagoon

Balneario de
Tarapaya

Tarapaya
Village

Sanctuary of
Manquiri

Hacienda de
Samasa Alta

Balneario
de Don
Diego

To
Sucre

Karachipampa

La Palca

Santa Lucía

Hacienda
Cayara

La Puerta

The Cave of
the Devil

Cantumarca

POTOSÍ

N

Cerro
Rico

To
Tarija

To
Uyuni

Balneario
de Chaqui

—— unpaved road

inhabited the dam until the survivors said enough prayers to placate them. The lakes proved useful in the drought of 1983, having enough water to supply domestic and industrial needs in Potosí.

The series of lakes makes a pleasant trekking area, though for the acclimatized only. The average altitude is 4,600m. 1 and 2 day tours are organized by some of the agencies (see above).

La Puerta is a village 6 km from town on the road to Oruro and site of the **Chapel of San Bartolomé** which is visited by the people of Potosí during the Festival of San Bartolomé, or *Chutillos*. Nearby is the legendary **Devil's Cave**. Transport is the same as for Tarapaya.

Hacienda Cayara is the best-preserved *hacienda* in the area, 25 km west of the city, with colonial paintings and furniture.

Caiza

About 2 hours from Potosí, on a road which forks off the Tarija road at Ingenio Cucho, is Caiza, at a much lower altitude than Potosí, so it is hotter and can provide relief from *soroche*. Cooperatives produce handicrafts in tin and some silver. On 4 August, the entry of the Virgin of Copacabana is celebrated with dancing and traditional costumes. For information go to the tourist office in Potosí. There's accommodation at *Hotel San Martín de Porres*, near the plaza, clean, restaurant. Two daily buses leave from Plaza del Minero, Potosí, at 1330.

MINE TOURS

Most people come to Potosí for the unique experience of visiting one of the myriad mine workings of the infamous Cerro Rico, the pink conical mountain that towers 700m above the city.

Cerro Rico was described by one Spanish chronicler in the mid-16th century as 'the mouth of hell', and visitors should be aware that descending into its bowels is both physically and emotionally draining. The tour, as Koala Tours proclaim, is 'not for wimps or woosies'. The mine entrances are above 4,000m and you will be walking, or rather crouching, around breathing in noxious gases and seeing people working in appalling conditions in temperatures up to 40°C. You should be acclimatized, fit and not have any heart or breathing problems, such as asthma. Miners get first degree silicosis within 5 years of entering the mines, after 10 years it is second degree and after 15 is untreatable.

The standard price of a tour is US$10 per person. Make sure you are getting a helmet, lamp and protective clothing (but wear old clothes anyway). Tours follow a set itinerary. **NB** A full tour lasts 4-5 hours and does not give you time to join a tour of the Casa de Moneda afterwards. A trip to the thermal baths to clean up is a better option.

The mouth of hell

One of the mines visited by the tour groups in Potosí is La Candelaria. It is one of over 5,000 mineshafts which snake their way into the Cerro Rico and is part of the *Unificada Cooperativa* which leases 17 mines from the state. There are thirty cooperatives working the Cerro Rico and they account for the vast majority of the mines with over 6,000 miners. The state agency Comibol has two mines and 300 employees and in addition there are a handful of private operations.

Despite the fact that the cooperatives account for over 65% of the mining workforce in Bolivia, with over 35,000 affiliates, they have always been treated as a subsidiary sector by the state. Only Comibol and private mines receive credit from the Banco Minero and, as a result, there is no money for investment or savings for reinvestment. Without access to such finance the cooperatives continue their daily struggle for survival.

The cooperatives enjoy none of the privileges of the state workers such as a fixed salary, free housing and benefits; if they don't work they don't eat. But they do have one precious asset – freedom. As one miner explained: "why would I want to work for the state? They have to start on time. We can work when we like and everything we take out is ours." This is the law of the cooperative mines. The miners work alone or in pairs and sell what they extract to the cooperative at the market price. They use their own experience first to find and then tap the rich veins of tin, zinc or, amazingly, silver, still plentiful even after 500 years of mining.

The life of the cooperative miner is one huge gamble. They risk their lives in search of the jackpot. They can either strike it lucky or die penniless, most by the age of forty-two from silicosis. One legendary tale is of a miner, famous in the city, who made so much money in 1 week that he bought nine buses and started up his own transport company. But he lost everything through bad administration and is now back working in the mines. Apocryphal or not, such stories act as a spur to the thousands of miners who daily endure conditions unchanged since the 16th century.

Indeed, conditions are, if anything, even more dangerous than in colonial times. The Spaniards introduced the use of *socavones*, horizontal galleries to intersect workings, allowing simpler access, ventilation and drainage and much deeper mines. But at the lowest depths of La Candelaria there is no ventilation. Built after the Spaniards departed, there are no cut stone archways. The tunnels narrow, the ceiling drops and the miners (and visitors) have to stoop very low.

So, as you leave these gloomy depths, gulping down lungfuls of fresh air and stretching cramped backs, spare a thought for these miners burrowing on far below as they offer up their lungs and lives, and pray that their *tío* will not abandon them and they will not be eaten by the silver mountain.

Devil worship

👣 On your tour of the mine, you will come face to face with a tiny, grinning devil, cigarette in mouth, coca leaves spread around his feet and festooned in paper streamers. This is *El Tío*, whom the miners worship when working underground. They believe in Pachamama and Viracocha outside the mine, but inside the mine they pray to the devil for their safety and prosperity. This makes a lot of sense in a place which is as close to our vision of hell as anyone can imagine.

The miners believe that the devil owns the minerals in the earth and, in order to appease him, every mine has its own statue of *El Tío* where the miners make offerings of cigarettes, coca or alcohol.

'El Tío', the miners' protector

The tour begins with a visit to **Mercado Calvario** where you are expected to buy presents for the miners such as dynamite, coca leaves, meths, ammonium nitrate, cigarettes, etc. Then it's up to the mine where you kit up and enter one of the tunnels. A tour will usually go down all the way to the fourth level, meeting and talking to working miners on the way. You will see how dynamite is used and also meet *El Tío*, the god of the underworld (Friday afternoon is the main day for making offerings to *El Tío*). A good guide will be able to explain mining practices, customs and traditions little changed since the Spanish left and enable you to communicate with the miners. There is no problem with women visiting the mines. Women worked the mines during the Chaco War 1932-35.

A contribution to the miners' cooperative is appreciated as are medicines for the new health centre (*Posta Sanitaria*) on Cerro Rico. New projects (a radio, drinking water) have been, or will shortly be realized.

Recommended mine guides

By law all guides have to work with a travel agency and carry an ID card issued by the Prefectura. The following is a list of guides for which we have received positive reports, but this is not to say that those excluded are in any way less than professional.

Eduardo Garnica Fajardo, Hernández 1035, T 22092 (Koala Tours), he speaks English, French and some Hebrew; Koala Tours offer breakfast at 0600, 'plato típico' with llama meat; they also donate 15% of their fee to support on-site healthcare facilities (donations can be sent to Eduardo Garnica). **Julio César Morales** (Victoria Tours, see *Hotel Casa de María Victoria*), speaks English, takes small groups. **Raul Braulio**, Millares 147 (Transamazonas Tours), T 25304, experienced, speaks some English, takes only one or two people. **Santos Mamani**, Millares 147, T 28212. **Marco Mamani**, Pacheco 60, T 27299. **Geronimo Fuentes** and **Maria-Esther** (Transandino Tours), speak English and take small groups. **Salustio Gallardo**, Calle Betanzos 231, near Plaza Minero. **Juan Carlos González**, Avenida Japón 10, T 26349 (Turismo Balsa), Spanish spoken only. **Efraín Huanca** (Hidalgo Tours), friendly and very informative. **NB** The size of tour groups varies – some are as large as twenty people, which is excessive.

POTOSI TO SUCRE

The road from Potosí, 164 km northeast to Sucre, is fully paved. It passes Don Diego and Chaqui and goes through **Betanzos**.

There are a few *alojamientos* in Betanzos, **G**, also a hotel, **E**. Frequent buses leave from Plaza Uyuni and the cemetery

A man's gotta chew

Apart from the dream of striking it rich, it is coca that keeps the miners going. The only real break they get down in the bowels of the earth is *El Aculli*, when they chew coca.

The sacred leaves are masticated with *lejía*, a paste moulded from plant ashes which activates with saliva to produce the desired effect from the coca. This numbs the senses and staves off hunger pangs and exhaustion. It is only by chewing coca that the miners can work at all. "No coca, no work", as one miner put it.

They spend several hours chewing the leaves every morning before entering the mine. Not only does the coca give the miners the energy to carry on working without food, they also believe that it acts as a filter of dust and toxic gases.

Although coca is also taken in a social context, workers used to deny this because, in the eyes of the priests and bosses, an increase in labour productivity was the only permissible reason for tolerating consumption of 'the devil's leaf'.

in Potosí, US$0.70, 1 hour. The town holds its *Feria de Papas* within the first 2 weeks of May with folk dances, music and costumes. There is also a good market. A few kilometres away are the famous Umajalanta caves with well-preserved rock paintings.

SUCRE

Founded in 1538 by the Spaniard Pedro de Anzúres as the city of La Plata, it became capital of the audiencia of Charcas in 1559. Its name was later changed to Chuquisaca. The present name, Sucre, was adopted in 1825 in honour of the first president of the new republic. As if three names weren't enough, the city has also been known as Charcas. In fact, one of its unofficial titles is 'the city of four names'. But that should probably be 'the city of five names', because another of its nicknames is 'La Ciudad Blanca' (the White City), owing to the fact that, by tradition, all the buildings in its centre are whitewashed every year.

This is the official capital of Bolivia and though La Paz has long since overtaken it in political and administrative importance, Sucre still remains the country's legal centre. Long isolation has helped the city to preserve its courtly charm and given its citizens a certain air of self-importance. Despite being at a

relatively low 2,790m (practically at sea-level by Bolivian standards), Sucre has a high opinion of itself, which is not unjustified. Ask most Bolivians where you should go and they will almost unanimously answer 'Sucre'.

In 1992 Unesco declared the city a 'Patrimonio Histórico y Cultural de la Humanidad' and it's easy to see why. It's an absolute must for enthusiasts of colonial religious architecture, with many beautiful churches, all painted white except San Felipe Neri which is faced in brick. Sucre is not just a colonial museum, though, but a thriving university city. It is known as the student capital of Bolivia (make that the city of six names), which is evident from the thousands of young students filling every street, plaza,

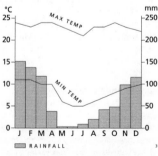

Climate: Sucre

bar and café. At times you may feel as if you're the only person here over the age of twenty-one.

There are two universities, the oldest, **Universidad de San Francisco Xavier**, dates from 1624, making it 24 years older than Harvard. This was the main source of libertarian thought and gave birth to the very first cry of independence heard on the continent on the 25 May, 1809.

Sucre (*Population* 131,769; *Altitude* 2,790m; *Phone code* 064) is a small, compact city which is easy to explore on foot. Its busy narrow streets generally run uphill from the plaza eastwards and downhill west towards the train station. It enjoys a mild climate with a mean temperature of 12°C; 24°C in November-December and 7°C in June.

Places of interest

The city's heart is the spacious and elegant **Plaza 25 de Mayo**. Here, the local residents, or Sucrenses as they are called, sit and chat, shaded from the midday sun by palm and ceibo trees. The plaza is surrounded by elegant buildings. Among these are the **Casa de la Libertad**, formerly the Assembly Hall of the Jesuit University, where the country's Declaration of Independence was signed on 6 August 1825. The actual document is on display. Also among its treasures is a famous portrait of Simón Bolívar by the Peruvian artist Gil de Castro '... hecho en Lima, con la más grande exactitud y semejanza' – the greatest likeness. The Casa de la Libertad is open Monday-Friday 0900-1130 and 1430-1830, Saturday, 0930-1130; entrance US$1, US$0.40 to take photographs, US$2.65 to use video.

Also on the Plaza is the beautiful 17th century **Cathedral**. A look inside is recommended, especially to see the famous jewel-encrusted Virgen de Guadalupe (1601), as well as works by the Italian Bernardo Bitti, the first great painter of the New World, who studied under Raphael, and other church treasures. Entrance to the cathedral is through the museum in Calle Ortiz. It is open Monday-Friday

Virgen de Guadalupe,
Patron of Sucre

1000-1200, 1500-1700, Saturday 1000-1200; entrance US$2. If the door is locked wait for the guide.

Four blocks northwest of Plaza 25 de Mayo is the modern **Corte Suprema de Justicia**, the seat of Bolivia's judiciary. Entry is free but you must be smartly dressed; leave your passport with the guard; a guide can be found in the library.

The nearby **Parque Bolívar** contains a monument and a miniature of the Eiffel tower in honour of Bolivia's richest 20th century tin baron, Francisco Arcandona, who created much of Sucre's latter-day splendour.

The column opposite the **Teatro Gran Mariscal**, in the nearby **Plaza Libertad**, was erected with the dough raised by fining bakers who cheated on the size and weight of their bread. Also on this plaza is the **Hospital Santa Bárbara**.

Southeast of the city, at the top of Calle Dalence, lies the Franciscan monastery of **La Recoleta** (see **Museums**) with good views over the city. Behind the monastery

Reviving the past

🦥 The textile traditions of the Chuquisaca area might have vanished into obscurity had it not been for the dedication and hard work of two anthropologists, Spanish-born Gabriel Martínez and his Chilean wife Verónica Cereceda. They set out to trace the origins of a number of weavings which, years before, had been passed off as antiques in tourist shops in La Paz and other Bolivian cities.

Little was known about the creators of these textiles. Collectors and merchants referred to them as 'Potolo pieces', after the largest town (of some 600 families) in the area of their origin, 50 km northeast of Sucre. This area was inhabited by an impoverished group of nearly 25,000 people who called themselves *Jalq'a*.

Martínez and Cereceda, along with Bolivian ethnologist Ramiro Molina, were pleased to see most villagers still wearing traditional dress, but the women's *axsus*, or overskirts, were a pale reflection of the weavings that had inspired their search. Gone were the subtle colours and exotic animal motifs, replaced by repetitive rows of geometric designs.

The reason for this was economic necessity. In the 1960s and 70s a ready source of much-needed income became available. A growing market for Andean textiles among tourists and overseas dealers spawned many itinerant traders who scoured the countryside for ponchos, shawls, *axsus*, belts and bags to sell on. The *Jalq'a* motifs were particularly sought after, but the people never learned the true market value of their finest textiles.

When the boom was over the *Jalq'a* found the core of their weaving inheritance – their ritual costumes, wedding garments and family heirlooms – gone. With no models to inspire the next generation of weavers, the tradition seemed to have vanished for ever.

But Martínez and Cereceda were determined to revive the ancient weaving traditions in this area. They started a grassroots support organization (GSO) called Antropólogos del Sur Andino (ASUR), whose centre can be visited in Sucre (see **Museums**, page 222). ASUR encouraged the ritual life among the *Jalq'a* communities. They also wanted to recover traditional songs and dances which had been

a road flanked by Stations of the Cross climbs the attractive, eucalyptus-covered **Cerro Churuquella**, to a statue of Christ at the top. The cemetery is worth visiting to see the mausoleums of presidents and other famous people; boys give guided tours. To get to the Cerro Churuquella take Calle Junín south to its end, seven or eight blocks from the main plaza.

Churches

Note that church opening times seem to change frequently, or are simply not observed.

The church of **San Miguel**, completed in 1628, has been restored and is very beautiful with Moorish-style carved and painted ceilings, pure-white walls and a gold and silver altar. In the Sacristy some early sculpture can be seen. It was from San Miguel that Jesuit missionaries went south to convert Argentina, Uruguay and Paraguay. The church is open 1130-1200; no shorts, short skirts or short sleeves.

Two blocks from the main plaza, on Calle Nicolás Ortiz, is the massive 17th century **San Felipe Neri** church and monastery, built in the neoclassical style with an attractive courtyard with cloisters. The monastery is now used as a school and the church is closed, except for the roof which offers fantastic views over the entire city. Access to the roof is only possible for an hour between 1600 and 1800 (times change); US$1 entrance fading from community life and encourage the wearing of traditional costumes at festivals.

The main problem in reviving the weaving traditon was that women still knew how to weave, but they could not recall the many strange animals, called *khurus*, which had been the hallmark of the distinctive *Jalq'a* designs. The solution was to contact the dealers and collectors in Bolivia and overseas and get them to send photographs of their weavings. Eventually enough photographs had been assembled to be circulated throughout the local communities, inspiring a renewed enthusiasm in their precious tradition and provoking the textile revival.

But that was not enough. Martínez and Cereceda wanted to let the outside world know what was going on. They collected the best of the new textiles and began to showcase them throughout Bolivia. This created a new respect among city dwellers not only for the neglected *Jalq'a* but also for other ethnic groups in the region. The effects of this exposure were great. The average price of the textiles began to rise along with the quality of weaving and women began to create their own designs, proving that the *Jalq'a* were at last back in touch with the same cultural sources that inspired their ancestors. The difference this time being that the *Jalq'a* now understood the value of what they were producing and could meet outside demand without selling off their inheritance. (Adapted from an article by Kevin Healy in *Grassroots Development*, 1992).

Jalq'a textile

with a free guide from Universidad de Turismo office, opposite the convent, at Nicolás Ortiz 182 (ask the guide nicely to see inside the church).

The church of **Santa Mónica**, at the corner of Arenales y Junín, is perhaps one of the finest gems of Spanish architecture in the Americas, but has been closed to visitors since 1995. Another church, **San Francisco** in Calle Ravelo, has altars coated in gold leaf and 17th century ceilings. The bell is the one that summoned the people of Sucre to fight for independence. The church is open 0700-0930, 1600-1930.

San Lázaro, Calvo y Padilla, built in 1538, is regarded as the first cathedral of

La Plata (Sucre). On the nave walls are six paintings attributed to Zurbarán. It also has fine silverwork and alabaster in the Baptistery. It is open daily for mass 0700-0745.

Museums

These include the University's anthropological, archaeological, folkloric, and colonial collections at the **Museo Universitario Charcas** and its presidential and modern-art galleries. The museum is at Bolívar 698; open Monday-Friday 0830-1200, 1500-1800, Saturday 0830-1200; entrance US$1, photos US$1.50.

The **Museo de Santa Clara** is next to the convent of the same name, founded in 1639. Amongst its displays is a valuable

San Felipe Neri Church

collection of works by Melchor Pérez Holguin, and his teacher, the Italian Bernardo Bitti. They also have exhibits of books, vestments, some silver and musical instruments (including a 1664 organ). There is a window to view the church and small items made by the nuns are on sale. At Calle Calvo 212; open Monday-Saturday 1000-1130, 1430-1700; entry US$0.65.

The **Museo de la Recoleta** is at the Recoleta Monastery, which was founded in 1601 by the Franciscans. The monastery is notable for the beauty of its cloisters and gardens. An adjoining chapel still contains the intricately carved wooden choirstalls above the nave. See also the martyrs transfixed by lances. In the grounds is the Cedro Milenario, a 1,000-year-old cedar. The monastery is on Plaza Pedro de Anzúres at the top of Calle Dalence. It is open Monday-Friday 0900-1130, 1500-1630; US$2 for entrance to all collections, guided tours only.

Also recommended is **Museo de Historia Natural**, on Calle San Alberto 156. It is open Monday-Friday 0830-1200, 1400-1800; entry US$0.50.

The **Caserón de la Capellanía** houses the textile museum run by Antropológicas del Sur Andino (ASUR). This is highly recommended for its explanations of local indigenous groups and their distinctive textiles. Their *Jalq'a* exhibit is perhaps the finest display of Bolivian ethnography now available. It includes superb examples of contemporary daily dress, as well as ritual costumes, photographs of earlier weavings, explanations of their history and descriptions of the iconography of the textiles. The exhibition has travelled to Paris, Geneva and to the Smithsonian Institute in Washington DC. The Caserón, which also houses the tourist office, is at San Alberto 413; open Monday-Friday 0830-1200, 1500-1800, Saturday 0930-1200; entry US$1, with English and French-speaking guide.

Excursions

5 km south of Sucre on the Potosí road is the grandiose **Castillo de la Glorieta**. The former mansion of the wealthy industrialist, Don Francisco Argandoña, was built at the end of the 19th century in a miniature estate with Venetian-style canals, beautiful gardens and fountains. The residential palace is an exotic mixture of Moorish, Spanish and French architectural styles.

Don Francisco's wife became known as '*La Princesa de la Glorieta*', a title bestowed on her by the Pope in recognition of her work with local orphans. Today, the house and gardens are run down, but restoration is under way after years of military use and neglect.

La Recoleta

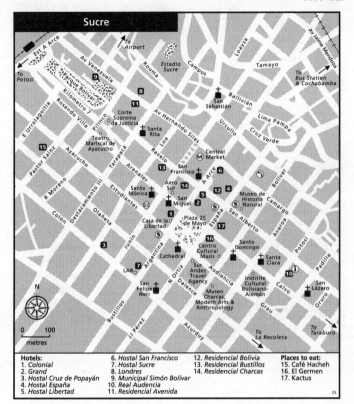

Sucre

Hotels:
1. Colonial
2. Grand
3. Hostal Cruz de Popayán
4. Hostal España
5. Hostal Libertad
6. Hostal San Francisco
7. Hostal Sucre
8. Londres
9. Municipal Simón Bolívar
10. Real Audencia
11. Residencial Avenida
12. Residencial Bolivia
13. Residencial Bustillos
14. Residencial Charcas

Places to eat:
15. Café Hacheh
16. El Germen
17. Kactus

The former mansion stands in the military compound; open daily 0900-1200, 1500-1700; entry is US$1 and includes a free guide, you may need your passport. To get there take *trufi* 4 or east from the corner of Arce y Siles.

Local festivals

February (movable), *Jueves de Compadres y Comadres*: held 10 days and 3 days respectively before carnival. **March**, *Pujllay*: in Tarabuco (see below). **April**, *Domingo de Ramos*: also in Tarabuco. **25 May** celebrates the first move towards independence, most services, museums and restaurants are closed. **16 July**, *Fiesta de la Virgen del Carmen*: similar to Alasitas in La Paz (see page 87). **25 July**, *Fiesta de Santiago Apostol*: Mass and processions and traditional music. **16 August**, *San Roque*. **8 September**, *Virgen de Guadalupe*: 2-day fiesta. **21 September**, *Día del Estudiante*: music and dancing around the main plaza. **October/November**: *Festival Internacional de la Cultura*, also held in Potosí, 2 weeks of cultural events. See also **Festival calendar** on page 55.

Local information

● **Accommodation**

A3 *Real Audiencia*, Potosí 142, T 52809, F 50823, excellent restaurant, modern, recommended.

B *Hostal Cruz de Popayán*, Loa 881, T 55156/51706, a beautiful colonial house with an interior courtyard, no heating, excellent breakfast served in room or in patio, recommended; **B-C** *Colonial*, Plaza 25 de Mayo 3, T 54709/55487, F 51912, expensive, good breakfast some rooms are noisy, but it's generally recommended.

C-D *Hostal Libertad*, Arce y San Alberto, first floor, T 53101/2, clean, friendly, hot water, spacious comfortable rooms with TV, heating, breakfast and snacks in restaurant, highly recommended; **C** *Hostal Sucre*, Bustillos 113, T 51411/51928, the rooms on the patio are noisy and those on the street are a bit dark, great American breakfast for US$2; **C** *Municipal Simón Bolívar*, Avenida Venezuela 1052, T 51216, with restaurant, very comfortable.

D *Grand*, Arce 61, T 52104, F 52461, comfortable rooms, hot showers, TV, including breakfast in room, good value lunch in *Arcos* restaurant, laundry, safe, helpful, recommended; **D** *Hostal Los Piños*, Colón 502, T 54403, comfortable, hot showers, nice garden, quiet, peaceful, friendly, including breakfast, a long way from the centre; **D** *Hostal San Francisco*, Avenida Arce 191 y Camargo, T 52117, **E** without bath, pleasant, meals available, includes breakfast, quiet, comfortable, safe motorcycle parking, large patio, laundry, recommended; **D** *Residencial Charcas*, Ravelo 62, T 53972, **E** without bath, good value breakfast, hot showers, friendly and cosy, helpful but the parrot in the courtyard cries like a baby all day, laundry facilities, will arrange bus to Tarabuco, highly recommended; **D-E** *Residencial Bolivia*, San Alberto 42, T 54346, cheaper without bath, spacious rooms, hot water, breakfast included, clothes washing not allowed, arranges transport to Tarabuco, very nice and clean, recommended.

Near the bus station on Avenida Ostria Gutiérrez are: **E** *Alojamiento Austria*, No 518, T 54202, hot showers, good value, restaurant; **F** *Alojamiento Chuquisaca*, No 33, T 54459, shared bathrooms, safe car parking (US$0.50 per day); **E** *Residecial Avenida*, Avenida H Siles 942, T 51245, hot showers, breakfast extra, laundry, helpful, recommended, good Argentine restaurant next door; **E** *Residencial Bustillos*, Ravelo 158, T 51560, **F** without bath, tiny rooms, hot water, stores luggage, an OK place.

F *Alojamiento Avaroa*, Loa 419, hot showers, uncomfortable beds, basic but clean and friendly, recommended; **F** *Alojamiento La Plata*, Ravelo 26, T 52102, without bath, limited shower facilities, basic, quiet and friendly, helpful, nice courtyard, good beds, recommended;

F *Alojamiento El Turista*, Ravelo 118, T 53172, hot showers 0700-1200 only, safe, basic but good, cheap meals, terrace, doors closed at 2300; **F** *Residential Oriental*, San Alberto 43, T 51644, with bath, clean, a bit run down but good value, unlockable interior windows, hot water, motorcycle parking.

● **Places to eat**

Many places are closed at the weekends.

General and local styles: *Las Vegas* on the southeast side of the Plaza, Nos 36-37, main restaurant and annex (less grand), good, main dishes about US$4, set lunch US$2.35; *La Plaza*, on the Plaza at No 33, with balcony, good food and pisco sours, good live music on Friday nights, very popular with locals, set lunch US$2.35; *Kactus*, Calle España 5, just off the main plaza, nice bar and restaurant, pizzas, expensive but highly recommended; *El Huerto*, Ladislao Cabrera 86, set in a beautiful garden, dishes from US$3, highly recommended; *Made in Brasil*, San Alberto 242, set lunch and dinner for US$2.50, good; *La Parrilla Argentina*, Bustillos 101 y Olañeta, huge portions, excellent beef, not expensive; *Chorizería Los Bajos*, Loa 759, serves typical local sausages (*chorizo chuquisaqueño*), good, daytime only; *Snack Miriam*, España 136, good *salteñas*; also on España, No 140 is *Snack Lucy*, recommended; *La Casona*, Ostria Guitiérrez 401, near the bus terminal, stylish, *platos típicos*, good value. There are good chicken and chips cafés on Camargo between Arce and Loa and on Loa and Hernando Siles. Also many fruit juice and snack stalls in the central market. The stalls here also sell cheap meals (US$0.75-1.40). The local sausages are delicious.

European styles: *Pizzería Napolitano*, on Plaza 25 de Mayo 30, excellent pizzas, and good home-made ice cream, not cheap, open evenings and some lunchtimes; *La Taverne* of the *Alliance Française*, Aniceto Arce 35, half a block from the plaza, closed Sunday, good value French food, also regular films and cultural events, good meeting place; *Piccolíssimo*, San Alberto 237, very good Italian food, not expensive, popular; *Bibliocafé*, Nicolás Ortiz 30, near the plaza, good pasta and light meals, music, opens 1800, closed Monday; *Suizo*, Nicolás Ortiz 42, good service, expensive but good, *peña* on Saturday, excellent *roesti*, live music some nights; *Kultur-Café Berlin*, Avaroa 326, open 1500-2400, good food but limited selection and small portions, German newspapers, *peña* every other Friday, closed Sunday (in same building as Instituto Cultural Boliviano Alemán

– ICBA), popular meeting place; *Le Repizza*, Calvo 70, very good value lunches, small but good pizzas in evening, recommended.

Oriental: *New Hong Kong II*, 25 de Mayo 30, expensive but good, authentic Chinese.

Vegetarian: *El Germen*, Calvo 7, 2nd floor, very good, good set lunches for US1.60, attractive, elegant with balcony overlooking main plaza, excellent breakfast, US$0.80-1.60, open Monday-Saturday 0800-2100, book exchange, German magazines, warmly recommended; *Nirvana*, Loa 777, near Olañeta, open daily for lunch, set lunch US$1.25, good food and atmosphere.

Cafés, etc: *Confitería Palet*, Plaza 25 de Mayo 8, good coffee; *Amanecer*, Pasaje Junín 810-B, German *pastelería*, run by social project supporting disabled children, excellent, opens 1530; *Bunkers*, Ravelo 38, good breakfasts, bar, open 0800 till late; *Café Hacheh*, Pastor Sainz 233, coffee bar, open 1100-2400, art gallery, tasty sandwiches and fresh fruit juices, highly recommended; *Salon de Té Las Delicias*, Estudiantes 50, great cakes and snacks, favourite student hangout. There are other good cafés on Estudiantes.

● **Banks & money changers**
Banco Nacional, Calle España esquina San Alberto, cash given on Visa card, US$4 commission, good rates for dollars, travellers' cheques changed, 2% commission; diagonally opposite is **Banco Santa Cruz**, 1% commission for cash on Visa and Mastercard, good rates for cash, ATM outside. **BIDESA**, on España and the plaza, changes travellers' cheques into dollars cash at no commission. Most banks have ATM for cash withdrawal. Travel agencies' rates are good and at *El Arca*, España 134, T 50189, good rates for travellers' cheques. **Casa de Cambio Ambar**, San Alberto 7, T 51339, poor rates for travellers' cheques. The stalls at the corner of Camargo and Arce buy and sell dollars cash as well as Argentine, Chilean and Brazilian currency at good rates. Many shops and street changers on Hernando Siles/Camargo buy and sell dollars cash.

● **Cultural centres**
The **Instituto Cultural Boliviano Alemán** (ICBA – Goethe Institute), Avaroa 326, Casilla 304, T 52091, shows films, has German newspapers and books to borrow (0930-1230 and 1500-2100), runs Spanish, German, Portuguese and Quechua courses and it has the *Kulturcafé Berlín* (see above). Spanish lessons cost from US$3.50 for 45 minutes for one person, with reductions the more students there are in the class. The ICBA also runs a folk music *peña* on Friday. **Alianza Francesa**, Aniceto Arce 35, T 53599, the noticeboard on Plaza 25 de Mayo (Casa de Libertad side) announces events. **Centro Boliviano Americano**, Calvo 437, T 51982, library open Monday-Friday 1500-2000, recommended for reference works, also for language courses. The **Centro Cultural Hacheh** (see address for *Café Hacheh* above), run by Felix Arciénega, a Bolivian artist who organizes folk and jazz concerts, conferences, exhibitions and discussions, and is the editor of an art and poetry journal *Hacheh*. **Casa de la Cultura**, Argentina 65, housed in a beautiful colonial building, presents art exhibitions, concerts, folk dancing etc, open Monday-Saturday 0900-1200, 1430-2000.

● **Embassies & consulates**
Germany, Arenales 215, T 54415; **Spain**, Pasaje Argandoña, T 51435; **Italy**, Vice Consul, Dalence 19, T 54280; **Perú**, Avaroa 472, T 55592.

● **Entertainment**
Folklore: **Centro Cultural Masis**, Bolívar 561, T 53403, Casilla 463, promotes the traditional Yampara culture through textiles, ceramics, figurines and music. It offers instruction in Quechua, traditional Bolivian music (3 hours a week for US$12 a month, recommended) and handicrafts. Also stages musical events and exhibitions; they will arrange *peñas* for groups at 24 hours' notice. Items for sale include musical instruments made to the highest professional standard and a very good CD of local traditional music. Open 1530-2130; contact the director, Roberto Sahonero at the centre Monday, Wednesday and Friday.

The Tanga-Tanga Children's Museum has been built in La Recoleta district by the Quipus Cultural Foundation. For more details contact Quipus in La Paz, T (02) 226371, F 390700, Casilla 1696.

● **Hospitals & medical services**
Doctor: *Dr Gaston Delgadillo Lora*, Colón 33, T 51692, speaks English, French, German, highly recommended.

Hospital: *Hospital Gastroenterológico Boliviano-Japonés*, for stomach problems.

● **Laundry**
Laverap, Bolívar 617, quick, US$5 wash and dry. *Lavandería Paola*, Bolívar 543, T 52477, charges per kilo, recommended.

● **Post & telecommunications**
Post Office: Ayacucho 100 y Junín, open till

2000. *Pòste Restante* is organized separately for men and women. **Entel**: España 271, open till 2245.

● **Shopping**

The central market is clean and colourful, with a wide variety of goods and many stalls selling *artesanía*. There are also lots of *artesanía* shops on the pedestrianized part of Calle Junín between Ravelo and Hernando Siles. A bus from the central market will take you to the *campesino* market on the outsirts of town. *Artesanías Calcha*, Arce 103, opposite San Francisco church, is recommended and the owner is very knowledgeable. *ASUR*, Antropológicos del Sur Andino, San Alberto 413, T 23841 (see **Museums** above), sells weavings from around Tarabuco and from the Jalq'a; their weavings are more expensive, but of higher quality than elsewhere. *Charcas*, Camargo 481 y España, high quality hats; *Artesanía Bolivia*, Argentina 31, has a variety of arts and crafts from Tarabuco. Camping gas can be bought at San Alberto 25. Chocaholics should note that Sucre is the chocolate capital of Bolivia.

● **Sports**

Swimming: the pool is on Avenida Venezuela, US$1 per person.

Tennis: Sucre Tennis Club, Avenida Venezuela, good clay courts, US$5 per person including equipment hire.

● **Tour companies & travel agents**

Sur Andes, Nicolás Ortiz 6, T 51983, F 42561, PO Box 736, organizes trekking from half a day to 5 days, including to precolumbian sites such as Pumamachay and the Camino Prehispánico. You must take a sleeping bag and good shoes, everything else is provided. *Seatur*, Plaza 25 de Mayo 25, T/F 32425, local tours, English, German, French spoken. Lucho Laredo and his son at Calle Panamá final 127, esquina Calle Comarapa, Barrio Petrolero, organize treks in the surrounding area and have been recommended.

● **Tourist offices**

Housed in the Caserón de la Capellanía/ASUR, Calle Potosí 102 esquina San Alberto, T 55983 (but has a different entrance), good map and guide for sale, US$2. Check church and museum opening hours. A sub-office at the airport is helpful. A tourist information office opposite the San Felipe Neri, at Nicolás Ortiz 182 (open 0800-1200, 1400-1800 Monday-Friday), is run by students who will show you around tourist sites for free. All offices are closed at the weekend. For country maps try Instituto Geográfico

Militar, Dalence 2, 1st floor, T 25514, open 0830-1200, 1430-1800, Monday-Friday.

● **Useful addresses**

Immigration: Plaza 25 de Mayo, in *Palacio de Gobierno*.

Car mechanic: at Camargo 450, recommended for Toyotas.

Motorcycle mechanic: Sr Jaime Medina, Motorservi Honda, Calle René Calvo Arana, T 25484. Will service all makes of machine. Also Gonzalo Arce at *Hi-store Motos*, Avenida Hernando Siles 916, T/F 561627, speaks excellent German and some English, for Honda, Kawasaki and Yamaha, and Cannondale, Haro and Raleigh pushbikes.

Police radio patrol: T 110 if in doubt about police or security matters.

● **Transport**

Local Taxi: US$0.55 per person within city limits.

Air LAB and/or Aero Sur fly to La Paz, Cochabamba, Santa Cruz and Tarija, all direct daily. Aero Sur, Arenales 204A, T (064) 54895 (Toll free 0800 3030). LAB, Bustillos 127, T 51140/51943 (Toll free 0800 3001). Tucsupaya Airport is 5 km northwest of town (T 54445). The airport minibus goes from the entrance and will drop you off on Hernando Siles y Junín, and returns from here, 1½ hours before flight (but not always); US$0.70, 20-30 minutes. A taxi from the centre is US$2-3. *Trufis* Número 1 and F go from the entrance to Hernando Siles y Loa, one block from the main plaza, US$0.55, 25 minutes.

Trains Enfe information, T 31115; the station is on Plaza Aniceto Arce. There were no trains to Potosí in 1997.

Buses The terminal is on the northern outskirts of town, 3 km from centre on Ostria Gutiérrez, T 52029. A taxi to/from the centre is US$0.65, or take Micro Calle or *trufi* Número 3.

Departures daily to/from: **La Paz** via Cochabamba (19 hours, US$14), many companies leave frequently between 0700 and 1700, 3 hours wait at Cochabamba (very cold at night); recommended companies are Illimani and Flota Copacabana (*bus-cama*); the first part of the road is very rough. La Paz via Potosí, US$13 (20-24 hours) at least four companies leave in the morning. To **Cochabamba** several companies depart daily from 1800-1830, 10-12 hours, US$9.75. To **Potosí**, 3 hours on a good paved road; with Andesbus daily at 0700 and 1700, US$6.50 (office at Bolívar 621, T 54251/30751);

also with Transtur (office on Loa but tickets etc from Sur Andes Travel Agency); Bustillos depart at 1100, US$4; Trans O'Globo goes daily at 0800 to Potosí, continuing to Tupiza (US$12.35) and Villazón (US$13). All buses to Potosí leave from the bus terminal. To Potosí daily with Emperador at 0715 and Andesbus at 0700. To **Uyuni**, Americana and Emperador, 0700, 10 hours, US$9, change buses in Potosí. To **Santa Cruz**, with Bolívar direct Tuesday, Friday, Sunday, at 1230, 17 hours; or via Cochabamba, Flota Unificada (highly recommended with video), Tuesday and Friday, 1700, also Mopar, Tuesday, Friday, Sunday (recommended) and others, US$13-17; most departures 1130-1300. To **Tarija**, Andesbus' service to Potosí on Monday, Thursday and Saturday at 0700 continues to Tarija, US$20, 19-20 hours, daily with Emperador via Potosí at 0715.

TARABUCO

One of the most interesting trips from Sucre is to the village of **Tarabuco** (3,295m), 64 km southeast on a good road. It is famous for its very colourful market on Sunday. The local people still wear their traditional dress of conquistador-style helmets, multi-coloured ponchos, *chuspas* (bags for carrying coca leaves) and the

Tarabuqueño

elaborate *axsu*, an overskirt worn by women. (See also the **Textiles** section on page 46).

The market starts around 0930-1000 and has been described as a bit of a tourist trap, but many still find it an enjoyable experience. Those in search of a bargain should have an idea about the quality on offer before buying. Many of the sellers come to Sucre through the week. **NB** The market is not held at Carnival (when all Tarabuco is dancing in Sucre), Easter Sunday or on a holiday weekend in November.

Local festivals In **March** thousands of *campesinos* from the area join tourists and Sucrenses in the celebration of *Pujllay*, one of the best traditional festivals in the country. It is held in celebration of the Battle of Jumbate when the local people defeated the Spaniards on 12 March 1816. It is a very colourful and lively affair with great music, local food and the obligatory *chicha*. No one sleeps during this fiesta so there are no accommodation problems.

On the first Sunday in **October** is *Virgen del Rosario*.

● **Accommodation & places to eat** There are at least two budget hotels, including **G** *Residencial Florida*, basic, cold and dirty, but serves a good *almuerzo* in the garden, with music and dancing, which is good fun. There are three other decent restaurants on the plaza and lots of food stalls in the market offering tasty local dishes.

● **Transport** Buses (US$2) and trucks (US$1.30) leave from 0630 or when full from Plaza Huallparimachi (take micro B or C from opposite the Mercado), 2½ hours journey. A taxi costs US$45. Shared *trufi* taxis can be arranged by hotels, with a pick-up service, starting at 0700, US$3.25 return. The first bus back is at 1300. AndesBus run a tourist service which departs at 0800, and returns at 1530, US$6, book at their office (address above). Transport is more difficult on weekdays; take an early bus and return by truck.

A good guide to Tarabuco is Alberto from the Sucre tourist office, US$45 for a full day in a car for four people.

The weavers' villages nearby include **Candelaria** (2 hours by truck from

Tarabuco), **Macha** (8 hours from Sucre), **Pocata** (1 hour from Macha), or **Ravelo** (59 km northwest of Sucre). At **Punilla**, on the road to Ravelo, there is a 2½ hours walk to **Incamachay** where there are precolumbian drawings. Punilla is also where you leave the truck for Challanaca and from there to **Potolo**, with its distinctive textile designs of red zoomorphic figures on a black or brown background. You can buy direct from the weavers – there are no stores – but it can be difficult to find them (see tinted box, page 220).

● **Transport** To **Ravelo** trucks leave between 0900-1000 from a departure point near the airport, 3 hours; trucks back to Sucre are invariably full. A *micro* does the trip, in theory, leaving at 0900, and returning at 1600, US$1.65, but check at the shop at Hernando Siles 843 if it's running. Trucks to **Potolo** (Thursday and Friday in the dry season) go direct from near Sucre airport. In the wet season you can only get to Challanaca and you walk for 3 hours from there.

ROUTES From Sucre it is 366 km to Cochabamba, via Epizana on the old Santa Cruz-Cochabamba road (see page 264). The first hour out of Sucre is OK, then it is terrible to Epizana. Thereafter the road is paved to Cochabamba.

SOUTHEAST FROM SUCRE

The main road southeast from Tarabuco continues towards ever greener valleys and mountains that signal the proximity of the tropical eastern lowlands. The road winds through **Monteagudo** (see below), **Camiri** and **Boyuibe** to the frontier with Paraguay at **Hito Villazón** (see **Eastern Lowlands** section, page 284). Hito Villazón is not to be confused with the other Villazón on the frontier with Argentina (see page 199).

At **Padilla** (Km 190, *Altitude* 2,080m, hotels on the plaza), a turn-off heads north 20 km to **Villa Serrano**, where the musician Mauro Núñez lived. A music festival is held on 28-29 December. The journey is beautiful through wild mountains. This road continues towards the tiny settlement of **La Higuera**, famous as the scene of Ché Guevara's fatal last battle (see page 267).

8 hours from Sucre, at Km 323, is **Monteagudo** lying in the sub-tropics at 1,138m. There are several basic hotels: **F** *Alojamiento los Naranjos* behind the plaza, with hot showers; *Alojamiento las Tablitas*, and *Alojamiento Oriental*, both on the main road. There are direct buses to Santa Cruz, twice a week, US$8, 14 hours.

The Southern Highlands

DEEP IN the south of Bolivia, snuggling up against the Argentine and Paraguayan borders, lies the department of Tarija, a part of the country seldom visited by Bolivians and still less by tourists. Those that do come here are usually drawn by Tarija's greatest claim to fame – its wine.

This is a region very different from any other in Bolivia. For a start, its inhabitants historically have more in common with neighbouring Argentina than the rest of their country. Their musical and culinary heritage, their accent and appearance and their attitudes are very distinct. It's easy to see why part of this isolated region actually declared independence from Spain and briefly operated under a sovereign government.

Visiting this southern pocket of Bolivia is getting off the beaten track without even trying. That's because, on the surface, there's little to attract the tourist – apart from a great climate, great food, great wine, great festivals and great hospitality. If that sounds appealing then you'll pretty much have it all to yourself.

ROUTES A road runs south from Potosí, passing through **Otavi**, **Padcaya**, **Camargo**, **Villa Abecia**, **El Puente** and on to **Iscayachi**. Here the road forks, southwest to the Argentine border at Villazón (see page 199), and east to the region's capital, Tarija.

CAMARGO

The neat, clean little town of **Camargo** (*Altitude* 2,406m; *Phone code* 0629) is 186 km south of Potosí. The vineyards around Camargo are said to produce the country's best singani, cognac and dessert wines. For a taste of these renowned wines and singanis, take a taxi to *Bar La*

Southern Highlands

Viña at Patapampa, set among vineyards 7 km away. Also see **accommodation** below. There is a branch of Bidesa bank at Ayacucho 250.

The town holds a *Feria Artesanal* on 25 May, when the arts and crafts of the region's rural communities are displayed. Another festival, on 23 September, is the *Feria del Vino de Singani y de la Canción Cinteña*, with songs and dancing to celebrate the local wines.

A driveable side road goes 45 km east from Camargo to Culpina and on to **Incahuasi**, near where a number of important fossils have been found, as well as rare varieties of cacti. *Micros* leave from the market area in Calle Chuquisaca.

● **Accommodation D** *Hostal Cruz Huasa*, on Plazuela Estudiantes, T 2092, with private bathroom, **E** without, comfortable, modern, cable TV, includes breakfast, nice garden, garage, cafeteria, the owner also owns the region's main vineyards 20 km away where new cabins and pool are planned for mid-1997, transport provided; **E** *Hostal Las Cañitas*, near the *tránsito* up a side street, T 2126, shared bathroom, **F** for single room, very friendly and comfortable, family atmosphere, TV lounge, cafeteria, nice garden, garage, owner also has an old bodega called *La Compañía Baja*, 3 km out of town, which produces singani and a singani and wine mixture; **G** pp *Media Luz*, Ayacucho 282, basic; **G** pp *Romay*, Bolívar 101, very basic but slightly better than **G** pp *Okay*, Chuquisaca 9, which doesn't even live up to its name.

● **Places to eat** The best restaurant is *Media Luz* on Plaza Abaroa, good value lunch, it's often filled with bus passengers taking their meal break. There are also two clean *comedores populares*; one is in the Mercado Central (entrance on Calle Litoral), the other is at the back of Calle Chuquisaca, both serve a good breakfast and lunch.

TARIJA

With approximately 109,000 inhabitants, **Tarija** (*Phone code* 066) is the capital and largest city of the department of the same name. Situated along the banks of the Río Guadalquivir, this tranquil agricultural and wine centre is linguistically and visually reminiscent of Spanish Andalucia, besides being culturally closer to Argentina than to the rest of Bolivia, qualities which the native Tarijeños (or Chapacos as they are also known) point to with pride. At 1,840m and blessed with plenty of sun and a spring-like climate almost year-round, Tarija rivals Cochabamba for the title of most pleasant spot in Bolivia. This is also where Bolivia's best-known wines are produced. The best time to visit is from January onwards, when the fruits are in season.

The city has a justly deserved reputation not only for its wonderful climate, but also for the easy-going nature of its inhabitants. Compared to the bleak Altiplano or the barren Chaco that flank it to the west and east respectively, Tarija can seem like paradise. The city, although growing at a fairly rapid rate, retains a small-town feeling and suffers few of the ills that plague other urban areas.

Of all Bolivian cities, perhaps Tarija comes closest to capturing the ambience of a 'typical' post-colonial settlement, with its date and orange tree-lined plaza, wide streets and prominent churches. As with most South American towns, the main **Plaza Luis de Fuentes y Vargas** is where most of the action is. Most of the city's restaurants, shops and offices are within easy walking distance of it, and at its centre it features the obligatory statue to the city's founder.

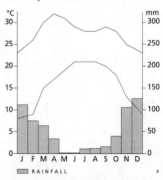

Climate: Tarija

Street numbering: all blocks west of Calle Colón have a small O before the number (oeste), and all blocks east have an E before the number (este); blocks are numbered from Colón outwards. All streets north of Avenida Las Américas are preceded by N.

History

Founded on 4 July 1574 by the Spanish colonizer Luis de Fuentes y Vargas, Tarija boasts a long history of autonomous rule. Never thoroughly subjugated by the Spanish, the inhabitants declared their independence from Spain as early as 1807, in the process becoming the first region in all of Latin America to do so. A decade later, on 15 April 1817, at the Battle of La Tablada on the outskirts of the city, a local militia under José Eustaquio Méndez defeated a superior Spanish force and made good its declaration of independence. Although coveted by Argentina, Tarija and its environs opted to join the newly-declared Republic of Bolivia in 1825, ending the area's short but vibrant period of independence.

Places of interest

Those seeking cultural and historical sites will not be worth seeing disappointed by Tarija's offerings. There are four churches worth seeing, including the city cathedral, on Calle La Madrid. The **Cathedral** itelf, built in 1611, contains a mortuary holding the remains of many prominent Chapacos, among them the city's founding father. It is open in the morning and from 1700.

Far more interesting, however, is the **Basílica de San Francisco**, on the corner of Avenida Daniel Campos and La Madrid. This is the oldest church in the city (built in 1606) and it is beautifully painted inside, with praying angels depicted on the ceiling. Note the four evangelists at the four corners below the dome. Besides the stunning artwork, it contains two libraries, the old one containing some 15,000 volumes, and the new one a further 5,000. A small museum boasts an outstanding collection of colonial books, including

a 1501 edition of *The Iliad*, as well as numerous modern reference works and 19th century photograph albums on Bolivia.

To visit the libraries, which requires permission from the Franciscan priests who maintain them, ask for either Father Lorenzo or Maldini at the rectory, at Calle Ingavi 0137. The Basílica is open 0830-1130, 1530-1730, Saturday 0830-1130.

Five blocks north of the cathedral on Avenida General Bernardo Trigo is the **Church of San Roque**, built in 1887 and dedicated to the town's patron saint. Although a minor church in ecclesiastical terms, the building is architecturally the most interesting, and serves as the city's most easily identifiable landmark.

The **Church of San Juan**, four blocks west of the cathedral, at the end of Avenida Bolívar, was built in 1632 and marks the site where the Spaniards officially surrendered after the Battle of La Tablada. It is a picturesque spot from which to view the city and its environs.

A good view can be had from **La Loma de San Juan**, a park due north of the church of San Juan. Follow Calle Domingo Paz to the top of the rise where the buses gather, turn right on the cobbled street, then right through the gate and follow the Stations of the Cross to the top (124 steps up). An equestrian statue of Moto Méndez is at the top (see **Excursions** below).

On the modern Avenida Las Américas (Víctor Paz Estenssoro, or Costanera), which flanks the river, is a pleasant children's park, with open-air theatre, nice gardens, swimming pools and small zoo, US$0.20.

Museums

The **Museo de Arqueología y Paleontología**, on the corner of Avenida General Trigo y Calle Virginio Lema, one block south of the main plaza, it is part of Tarija's university and contains a palaeontological collection (dinosaur bones, fossils, remains of an Andean elephant), as well as smaller mineralogical, ethnographic and anthropological collections. It is

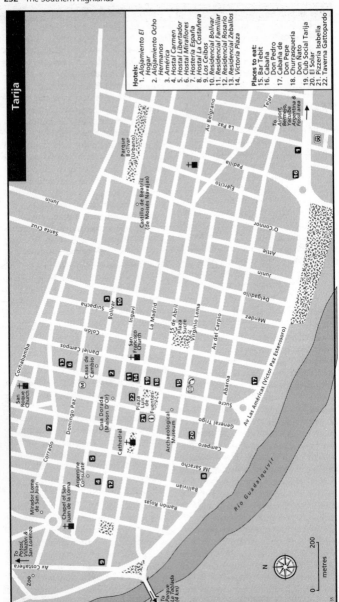

Tarija

Hotels:
1. Alojamiento El Hogar
2. Alojamiento Ocho Hermanos
3. América
4. Hostal Carmen
5. Hostal Libertador
6. Hostal Miraflores
7. Hostería España
8. Hostal La Costañera
9. Los Ceibos
10. Residencial Bolívar
11. Residencial Familiar
12. Residencial Rosario
13. Residencial Zeballos
14. Victoria Plaza

Places to eat:
15. Bar Tebit
16. Cabaña
17. Cabaña de Don Pedro
18. Churrasquería Don Pepe
19. Club Social Tarija
20. El Solar Don Nato
21. Pizzería Isabella
22. Taverna Gattopardo

Grape expectations

Tarijeños have been growing grapes and making wine since Franciscan missionaries brought cuttings to the region over 350 years ago. They found conditions perfect for vineyards. The grapes were harvested and then pressed by foot, fermented, bottled and then enjoyed by the friars over dinner.

Today, the old traditions of pressing wine by foot, known as *vino patero*, or 'foot wine', still persist. But modern enterprises like Concepción, Kohlberg and Aranjuez have made the region's wine much more widely available. Nearly 2½ million litres are now produced in the valleys that surround Bolivia's most southerly state capital and can be bought at very reasonable prices. The Castellanos family, for example, who run the Aranjuez bodega, produce a delicious, full-bodied Cabernet Sauvignon at around US$3.50 a bottle, as well as cheap but drinkable table wine at US$1 a bottle.

As well as producing white and red wines, Aranjuez is on the point of launching Bolivian champagne onto the market. But any plans for expansion face the threat of unfair competition from Bolivia's neighbours. Wine from the much larger producers Argentina and Chile pours across the border as contraband, giving them a huge competitive advantage over their Bolivian counterparts. It is hoped that the planned privatization of the customs service will make a difference.

theoretically open Monday-Friday 0830-1200 and 1430-1800; free entry, the brochure costs US$0.65.

Whilst neither strictly qualifies as a museum, two houses of the 19th century merchant Moisés Navajas, one of Tarija's most prominent citizens, are also worth a visit. The **Casa Dorada**, also known as Maison d'Or, at the intersection of Avenida General Trigo and Calle Ingavi (entrance on Ingavi), is the city's official Casa de Cultura. It is open weekdays 0830-1200 and 1430-1800, and Saturday 0900-1200; US$1 entry, guided tours in Spanish. Begun in 1886, the house has been repainted in original colours, silver and ochre on the outside, cerise, green and dark blue, with white trim, inside. The interior has Italian murals, art nouveau copies on ceiling panels and much gold in the rooms (the photography room contains pictures of Tarijan history and the restoration of the house). It has been described as a superb example of Kitsch decorative art.

For those who crave more of the same, it is possible to have a guided tour from the owner of Navajas' other town house, the **Castillo de Beatriz** (also known as

the Catillo de Moisés Navajas), which is on Calle Bolívar, just after the intersection with Calle Junín, a few blocks east of the plaza. The house is privately owned, but a knock on the front door during office hours is usually enough to gain entry.

Excursions

The area around the city, and especially the banks of the river, is home to numerous fossils and dinosaur bones, several of which are on display in the university museum. Take a micro or taxi in the direction of the airport. 5 km out of town, before the police control (*garita*), you see lovely structures of sand looking like a small canyon (*barrancos*). Here have been found bones, teeth, parts of saurian spines, etc, which come to the surface each year after the rains. Amateur paleontologists can roam around to their hearts' content, but any unusual findings should be left there and reported to the university.

A short 4 km across the Río Guadalquivir is the **Parque de la Tablada**, the site of Méndez's victory over the Spanish in 1817. The park is a nice spot to enjoy the river. During Tarija's Independence

Week celebrations (see below), you can see an increasingly rare gaucho rodeo (*rodeo chapaco*) here.

At **San Jacinto**, 8 km away, is a tourist complex beside the lake formed by a dam completed in 1991. At the dam there is a café, several shacks selling food and drink and boats for hire. There is a pleasant, level lakeside walk. Cross the dam, go past the food stalls and follow the clear track to the head of the lake. The track passes animals in fields. It takes about an hour until climbing a shoulder and then descending to more houses. Either return the same way (in which case you miss the best part), or climb the up the hill to the left (a bit of a scramble to the top) for a good, all-round view. Walk back along the ridge path which descends directly back to the steep ravine which is blocked by the dam. Take care on the final descent, in particular do not walk over the cliff where the dam is, and keep to the left, on the lake side. Take a *trufi* from Ingavi y Daniel Campos, by Palacio de Justicia, they leave every 30 minutes; 35 minutes journey, US$0.45.

A worthwhile trip is to **San Lorenzo**, 15 km from Tarija. The plaza is very pleasant, with palms, oranges and flowers, and the church is huge and unadorned. Just off the plaza is the Museo Méndez, the house of the independence hero Eustaquio Méndez, 'El Moto', who lost his right hand. There are many stories as to how it happened. The small museum exhibits his weapons, his bed and his 'testimonio'; entry US$0.30, open Monday-Friday 0900-1230, Saturday 0900-1200, 1500-1700, Sunday 1000-1200. Around the town the land is agricultural. You can walk down to the river (head north and turn right) and ask directions in the fields for the way up the eroded cliffs (45 minutes, fine views). To get there trufis leave from La Loma, at the top of Domingo Paz; they return from San Lorenzo plaza, 45 minutes, US$0.40.

The road to San Lorenzo passes **Tomatitas** river bathing (5 km), and the Parque Nacional Los Barrancos, an area of erosion.

Beyond San Lorenzo, 22 km from Tarija, are **Los Chorros de Jurina** with natural rock pools. You need a guide to walk there; check first if there is water in the falls.

Bodegas

If you're in Tarija then you really should not miss a visit to a local bodega to sample some of the excellent local wines and to see how they are produced. To visit the Aranjuez bodega, at Avenida Los Sauces 1976, ask Sr Milton Castellanos at the Agrochemical shop at Trigo 789.

Another local bodega is the Rugero Singani bodega at **El Valle de Concepción**, 36 km south of Tarija. To visit an appointment must be made in Tarija with Inginiero Sergio Prudencio Navarro, *Bodegas y Viñedos de la Concepción*, La Madrid y Suipacha sin número, T 25040, Casilla 99. Inginiero Prudencio will show visitors round the vineyards and the bodega. You should try their highly recommended 1994 Cabernet Sauvignon Reserve or their Muscat.

To get to Concepción, take a *trufi* from Plazuela Sucre every 20-30 minutes, US$0.55; they return from the plaza in Concepción. The route takes the road past the airport. At the *garita* the road forks left to Yacuiba/Pocitos and right to Bermejo. Take the latter and after a while take an unmade road to the right. This area is called Santa Ana. Look on your left for the signposted ex-Russian observatory (a good place to go at night to see the stars). Then you pass the Colonial winery, the Santa Ana bridge and Santa Ana Grande vineyards and the *Centro Vitivinícola, Cooperación Española*, before reaching Concepción and its plaza filled with bitter orange and ceibo trees.

Local festivals

15 April San Lorenzo celebrates the victory of Moto Méndez over the Spanish. Also in San Lorenzo, on the Saturday of

Easter week, is *La Pascua Florida*, on the eve of the Resurrection, which is named *Domingo de Pascua*. The town 'dresses up' to receive visitors from Tarija and elsewhere and there is a colourful procession.

15 August, *La Virgen de Chaguaya*: people walk all the way from the city to the Santuario Chaguaya, south of El Valle, beyond Padcaya by road, and 60 km south of Tarija. The pilgrimage route is 45 km. To get to Padcaya take a Línea P *trufi* from Plaza Sucre in Tarija, US$1; a bus to Chaguaya and Padcaya leaves from the terminal daily at 0700 and returns at 1700; US$1.35.

The most famous *fiesta* in Tarija is the *Fiesta de San Roque*, held during the first week in **September**. A procession on the first Sunday takes the richly dressed saint's statue around the various churches, ending in the church of San Roque. People dance before it as it goes, wearing lively colours, feather turbans and transparent veils, and women throw flowers from the balconies. The festivities last all week, with lots of music and dancing. Named after the town's patron saint, the festival also takes place on his feast day **16 August**, when the townsfolk decorate their dogs with ribbons for the day.

On the second Sunday in **October** is the *Fiesta de las Flores*, which commemorates the *Virgen del Rosario*. The procession sets out from the church of San Juan and winds its way through the town as onlookers shower the participants with flowers. The celebrations in San Lorenzo and Padcaya are particularly recommended, with colourful costumes, dancing and good food, carrying on till the next day. Also in **October**, on two weekends mid-month, there is a *beer festival* on Avenida de las Américas.

Local information
● **Accommodation**
A3-B *Victoria Plaza*, on Plaza Luis de Fuentes, T 22600, F 42700, hot water, phone, includes buffet breakfast, laundry service, accepts Visa and Mastercard, recommended.

B *Grand Hotel Tarija*, Sucre N-0770, T 42684, F 44777, modernized, comfortable, central, accepts major credit cards; **B** *Hostal La Costañera*, on the corner of Avenida Víctor Paz Estenssoro (Las Américas) and Calle J M Saracho, T 42851, F 32640; **B** *Los Ceibos*, Avenida Víctor Paz Estenssoro y La Madrid, T 34430, F 42461 (formerly *Prefectural*), includes excellent buffet breakfast, large rooms, phone, minibar, good restaurant, outdoor pool and cocktail bar, accepts major credit cards, recommended.

D *Gran Hotel Max*, Junín E-0930, 20 minutes walk from main plaza, with private bathroom, **E** without, cheaper still in shared rooms, includes breakfast; **D** *Hostal Bolívar*, Bolívar E-0265, T 42741, comfortable, hot water, poor breakfast, laundry; **D** *Hostal Carmen*, Ingavi O-0784 y Ramón Rojas, T 43372/44342, shower, good value, some ground floor rooms without exterior windows, good breakfast, provides transport to/from airport, organizes tours of the area, recommended; **D** *Hostal Libertador*, Bolívar O-0649, T 44231, phone, sporadic hot water, excellent breakfast extra, family-run, recommended.

E *América*, Bolívar E-0257, T 22627, hot showers, good, run down but quiet, includes small breakfast, good restaurant attached; **E-F** *El Turista*, Bolívar E-0138, basic, friendly, informative owner, recommended.

The following four hotels are all on Calle Sucre. All are passable but the best is; **F** *Alojamiento Ocho Hermanos*, No 782, T 42111, near the main plaza, clean, shared rooms only. The others are; **F** pp *Residencial Familiar*, No 656, T 42798, cheaper without bath, most downstairs rooms without windows; **F** *Hostal Miraflores*, at No 920, T 43355, the only one to accept credit cards; **F** pp *Residencial Zeballos*, No 908. **F** *Hostería España*, Alejandro Corrado 0-0546, T 43304, hot showers, pleasant, recommended; **F** pp *Residencial Rosario*, Ingavi O-0777, **F** without bath, good value, recommended. Opposite the bus terminal is **F** *Alojamiento El Hogar*, Avenida Las Américas, T 43964, clean, recommended.

● **Places to eat**
Culinary appetites will find a strong preference for meat-based dishes, a reflection of the area's Argentine influence. Tarija is also the headquarters of Bolivia's wineries, the two best known of which are Kohlberg and Aranjuez. Others worth trying are La Concepción and Santa Ana de Casa Real. These bodegas produce both whites and reds, as well as *singani*, the local grape-based

brandy (San Pedro de Oro and Rugero are recommended labels). Naturally, all Tarijeño restaurants stock these wines, which can also be bought at their respective bodegas (see above). **NB** Many restaurants (and much else in town) close between 1400 and 1600.

The majority of the better restaurants are found around the main plaza: *La Taverna Gattopardo*, pizza, *parrillada* with Argentine beef, hot dogs, snacks, excellent salads, local wines, Swiss owner, good value, lively atmosphere; *Pizzeria Isabella* and *Fechorias* are both on the west side next to the Prefectura and have good *salteñas* in the morning; *Club Social Tarija*, on the east side of the plaza, it's pleasant, old-fashioned, and a real haunt for Tarija's business community, excellent *almuerzo* for US$2, recommended; *Viejo Bar*, at Madrid 0358, on the plaza, good *confitería*, pizzas, ice cream, popular meeting place, bar atmosphere in the evening, good food, recommended.

The best in town is *Milano*, in an elegant white house at the west end of Bolívar where it meets Avenida Victor Paz (Las Américas), T 34093, home-made pastas and pizzas around US$2.50, fondue and raclette more expensive, excellent meat, good wine list, recommended, the annex which houses the *Churrasquería* is good value. *La Cabaña de Don Pepe*, Campos N-0136, near Avenida Las Américas, some way from the centre, has excellent steaks at reasonable prices, becomes a *peña* at weekends, one of the few places you can hear local folk music; *Cabaña Don Pedro*, in a lane off Avenida Victor Paz (Las Américas), one block west of the bus terminal, good typical food, outdoor patio, moderate prices; *Don Ñato*, 15 de Abril O-0844, typical *chapaco* dishes, good food and service; *El Solar*, Campero y V Lema, vegetarian, set lunch, closes 1400; *Chifa Hong Kong*, Ingavi y General Trigo, excellent, US$6 per person, good service; *Bar Tebit*, on Calle V Lema, Chinese dishes; *Pizzería Italia*, Calle A del Carpo O-0360, good pasta, reasonable prices, evenings only; *Tommy*, Calle Ingavi E-0178, cheap fish, excellent *chicha de uva*, recommended. For a cheap breakfast try the market.

● **Banks & money changers**
Banco Mercantil de Bolivia, Sucre y 15 de Abril, exchanges cash and gives cash against Visa and Mastercard (US$5 authorization charge). **Bidesa**, Sucre N-0651, offer the best rates for cash, 2% commission on travellers' cheques. Travellers' cheques can also be changed at *Café Irupana*, Avenida Domingo Paz

351, charges 3% commission; or at *Ferretería El Lorito*, also on Avenida Domingo Paz, two blocks further east. Dollars and Argentine pesos can be changed at similar rates in any of the five *casas de cambio* on Bolívar between Campos and Sucre.

● **Embassies & consulates**
Germany Campero N-0295, helpful; **Argentina** Ballivián N-0699 y Bolívar, T 442273, open Monday-Friday, 0830-1230; **Spain** Ingavi y Méndez.

● **Entertainment**
There are cinemas at Vema y D Campos and on Colón.

● **Hospitals & medical services**
Dr Martha Bass-Werner is an English and German-speaking dentist at Avenida General Bernardo Trigo near the Casa Dorada.

● **Language classes**
Julia Gutiérrez Márquez, T 32857, charges US$1 per hour and is recommended.

● **Post & telecommunications**
Post Office: at V Lema y Sucre. Entel: V Lema y D Campos, T 42676, F 23402, open 0800-2400 Monday-Saturday, 0800-2100 on Sunday. Both also have branches at the bus terminal.

● **Shopping**
The market is in the block between Domingo Paz, Sucre, Bolívar and Trigo; you can find good basketwork here. *Artesanía Juan Gabriel*, Avenida Domingo Paz y Suipacha, has a good selection of hand-woven bags, painted wooden toys and hand-embroidered garments.

● **Sports**
Swimming: at Tomatitas, 5 km from town, which is a popular picnic area (see **Excursions** above). At lunchtime on Sunday in Tomatitas, many courtyards serve very cheap meals.

● **Tour companies & travel agents**
Internacional Tarija, Sucre 721, T 44446/7, helpful; *Mara Tours*, General Trigo 739, T/F 43490, also helpful. See also *Hostal Carmen* above. As Tarija is a compact city and most tours are 1 day affairs, travellers may find it more economical to hire a taxi or walk.

● **Tourist offices**
Local Senatur office is on the main plaza in the Prefectura, T 31000, very helpful, city map and guide for US$0.20 each; closed from 1200-1500 and at weekends.

● **Useful addresses**

Immigration: on Calle V Lema. If you're crossing into Argentina at the weekend the office at the border in Bermejo is closed, so get your entry stamp here, or at the Argentine Consulate (see above), or at the airport or bus terminal.

● **Transport**

Air LAB flies to Santa Cruz, La Paz, Cochabamba, Sucre, Jujuy and Salta. Aero Sur flies daily except Sunday to La Paz. Check schedules as they change frequently; also flights are frequently cancelled and/or delayed. TAM fly to/from Tarija. LAB office: Plaza Luis de Fuentes, on the south side next to the *alcaldía*, T 45706. TAM office: La Madrid O-0470, T 45899. Aero Sur office: Ingavi O-0339, T 45820. Taxi to airport, US$1.30 per person, or *micro* drops you two blocks away. Some hotels have free transport to town, but you may have to call them. On arrival at Tarija, reconfirm your return flight immediately. Airport information T 43135.

Buses There are departures daily on the 935-km route **Potosí-Oruro-La Paz**; at 0700 and 1700, 26 hours, US$23.25 (check which company operates the best buses, eg San Lorenzo has heating). To **Potosí** (386 km), daily at 1630, US$13.65 with San Lorenzo, San Jorge, Andes-Bus and Emperador. To **Sucre**, via Potosí, check if you have to change buses in Potosí. To **Villazón**, Gran Chaco at 1930, Veloz del Sur at 1900, several other companies leave daily in the morning and afternoon, 7 hours, beautiful scenery. To **Santa Cruz**, US$19.50, 32 hours over rough roads, though the last 140 km from Abapó is paved; the road goes via Villamontes, Boyuibe and Camiri; with San Lorenzo and Expreso Tarija on Monday and Thursday at 0730, Saturday at 1730, Gran Chaco Thursday at 1800; the section between Entre Ríos and Villamontes is truly spectacular. The new bus station is in the outskirts on Avenida Las Américas (30 minutes walk from centre, 7-8 minutes from the airport). Trucks to all destinations depart from Barrio La Loma, ten blocks west of the market.

TO ARGENTINA

There are three possible routes into Argentina from Tarija; via Villazón, Bermejo or Yacuiba. **NB** Crossing to Argentina, expect up to 4 hours to pass through customs and immigration. Electronic goods must be entered in your passport for later checks. Also note Bolivia is 1 hour behind Argentina.

Via Villazón

The road to Villazón, 189 km, is the shortest route to Argentina, it takes 7 hours. The first 75 km out of Tarija is paved but the rest should be paved by the end of 1997. (For full details on this border crossing see page 199.)

Via Bermejo

An alternative route to Argentina via Bermejo is the most easily reached from Tarija, 210 km. The views are spectacular (sit on right). This route is not recommended in the rainy season or a month or so after. The road is quite rough apart from 50 km which are paved. Do not try to cycle. Many buses leave daily, usually at night, some early in the morning, 4-5 hours, US$7.75; or by truck, US$4.50.

At **Bermejo** (*Population* 13,000; *Altitude* 415m) there are at least three hotels, and two *casas de cambio* on the main street. Customs searches are very thorough. Cross the river by ferry to Aguas Blancas in Argentina, then take a colectivo to Orán.

Via Yacuiba

From Tarija to the Yacuiba/Pocitos border is 290 km. There are daily buses in the morning and at night to Yacuiba; from there a daily service runs to Buenos Aires, Salta etc with La Internacional, ticket includes free meals and drinks. Buses leave from Yacuiba to Santa Cruz from around 1700-1900. It can take a long time to cross here, depending on the availability of officials. During holidays and weekends the office is rarely open.

EAST FROM TARIJA

A road runs east from Tarija, passing through Entre Ríos to Villamontes, where it branches north to Santa Cruz, south to Argentina and continues east to Paraguay. The road from Villamontes to Tarija is good all-weather gravel surface all the way, but there are a few bad patches in the mountains out of Entre Ríos due to landslides and rockfalls. The last 30 km into Tarija is paved, part of the new Tarija-Bermejo highway. The section from Entre

Ríos to Villamontes is truly spectacular. The road is carved into the rockface high above the gorge of the Río Pilcomayo as it snakes its way down through densely forested slopes of the Eastern Cordillera.

ENTRE RIOS

This charming little colonial town, with cobbled streets and a pretty plaza full of roses, lies halfway between Tarija and Villamontes. A giant statue of Christ towers over the town from a summit on the outskirts. There are great views from the top of the steps leading up to it. Also there's good walking in the surrounding hills. It's 30 minutes to Santa Ana where you can swim; ask directions. You can also hire horses; ask around.

51 km south of Entre Ríos, 6 km beyond the town of **Salinas**, is the village of **La Misión**, where the original wooden portal and porch of the Jesuit mission church survives. The road is not driveable beyond La Misión.

● **Accommodation & services** There are several basic but clean *residenciales* all in our **F** range: *Plaza*; *San Jorge*; and *Reyes*. *Plaza* has the best location and a restaurant and *San Jorge* has the best plumbing. There are several restaurants around the plaza. Breakfast is available in the *comedores* in the market as well as cheap lunches. There is a branch of Bidesa bank, a hospital and an Entel office.

● **Transport** Minibuses leave for Tarija daily at 0900 with Flota Entrerriana, returning at 1700 from Plazuela Sucre in Tarija; 5 hours. San Lorenzo, Expreso Tarija and Trans Chaco buses all pass through on their way to Tarija, Yacuiba or Villamontes.

VILLAMONTES

Villamontes (*Phone code* 0684), 280 km east of Tarija, is renowned for fishing and holds a *Fiesta del Pescado* in August. It is a friendly town on the edge of the Gran Chaco and is on the road and rail route from Santa Cruz to the Argentine border at Yacuiba. The local Guaraníes make fine basketwork and cane furniture which is sold in shops outside the central market.

● **Accommodation & services D-C** pp *El Rancho*, T 2059, F 2579, lovely rooms with private bath, air conditioning, cable TV, includes a great breakfast, comfortable budget accommodation in their annexe **F** per person, rooms with fan and shared bathrooms, superb restaurant, five course lunch for US$3, parking in courtyard, highly recommended; **D** pp *Gran Hotel Avenida*, T 2297, F 2412, on the main street, very clean, air conditioning, includes breakfast served in your room, comfortable, all rooms with private bath, cable TV, helpful owner, parking; **D-E** *Residencial Roldes*, two blocks from the plaza, T 2086, with private bathroom, **E** with fan and shared bathroom, clean, neat rooms, pleasant shaded patio; **F** *Residencial Miraflores*, on the main street to the railway station, clean, helpful. Good, cheap meals at *La Pascana* and *Chifa Chino*, both on the plaza; the *comedor popular* in the market serves cheap lunches and is the only place to get breakfast coffee. Entel and TAM offices are on the plaza. Bidesa bank is one block from the plaza.

● **Transport Air** TAM flies to Tarija and Santa Cruz on Saturday (T 2135). **Buses** To Tarija via Entre Ríos, 8 hours, on Thursday at 0500 and 0600, Sunday 0600; via Yacuiba daily at 1700 with Gran Chaco; Expreso Cochabamba daily to Santa Cruz, Sucre, La Paz at 1830; also to Camiri, Tupiza, Villazón.

ROAD TO PARAGUAY

Two roads run east to Paraguay, both of which are only passable in the dry season in high clearance vehicles. One follows the Río Pilcomayo southeast to **Hito Esmeralda**.

The other road runs east to **Ibibobo**. The first 80 km is an all-weather gravel surface. From Ibibobo to the Bolivian frontier at Picada Sucre is 75 km. The first 25 km is gravel; the last 50 km is still under construction and is very rough going. From Picada Sucre to the border is 15 km, and from there to the Paraguayan frontier at Fortín Infante Rivarola is 8 km. There are no police or immigration officials at the border. Get an exit stamp in Tarija. There are a few small shops on either side of the border but take plenty of water.

Cochabamba

THIS IS A part of the country which is economically of vital importance to Bolivia. Not only is the Cochabamba valley the agricultural heart of the country, but the tropical lowlands of Chapare to the east produces Bolivia's fastest-growing export earner – cocaine.

The department of Cochabamba, however, is overlooked by most tourists, who see the city and its environs merely as a convenient stopping-off point between the Altiplano and the tropical lowlands of eastern Bolivia. We can't, of course, recommend the white stuff, but this region produces much else of value. This is where you'll find the country's best *chicha*, the fermented corn beer brewed by the Incas. Just look for a white flag outside the houses and you'll know you've found it. The third 'c' that attracts people here is Cochabamba's wonderful Mediterranean climate.

COCHABAMBA

(*Phone code* 042) Bolivia's third largest city deserves its unofficial title of 'City of Eternal Spring'. Set in a bowl of rolling hills at 2,570m, its inhabitants enjoy a wonderfully warm, dry and sunny climate, with an average temperature of 18°C. Its parks and plazas are a riot of colour; from the striking purple of the bougainvillaea to the subtler tones of jasmin, magnolia and jacaranda.

The name Cochabamba is derived from joining the Quechua words 'cocha' and 'pampa', which together mean swampy plain. The city was founded in 1574 by Sebastián de Padilla and named Villa de Oropeza in honour of the Count and Countess of Oropeza, parents of the Viceroy Francisco de Toledo who chartered and promoted the settlement of the place. During the heyday of Potosí's silver boom, the Cochabamba valley developed into the primary source of food for the population of that agriculturally unproductive area. Cochabamba came to be known as the

Cochabamba Department

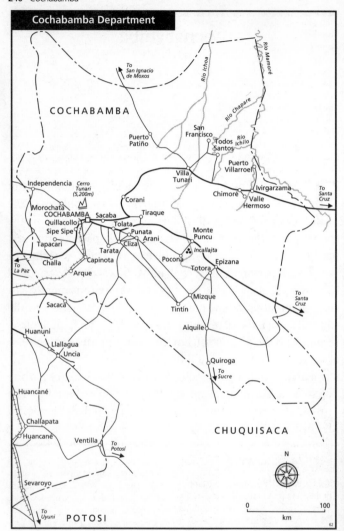

'breadbasket of Bolivia' because of its high volume of maize and wheat production.

Today, the valley is still an important agricultural centre, its rich soil yielding abundant crops of maize, barley, wheat, alfalfa and orchard and citrus fruits, as well as accounting for the bulk of the country's dairy products. Such a level of economic activity has seen Cochabamba grow to its present population of 594,790.

Though much new building is taking place throughout the city, especially in the shape of shiny new high-rise blocks of offices and apartments in the north, the centre retains much of its colonial character. There are many fine churches and streets lined with old colonial houses with overhanging eaves, balconies, wrought-iron windows and cool patios behind huge carved wooden doors. To the south of the main plaza, towards the disused rail station, are a wide range of bustling, colourful markets, which only add to the feeling that Cochabamba is more of an overgrown village than a modern urban centre.

Places of interest

At the heart of the old city is the attractive arcaded **Plaza 14 de Septiembre**. Facing the plaza is the neoclassical **Cathedral**, dating from 1571, but much added to since (it is open mornings only). Nearby are several colonial churches, including **Santo Domingo**, at Santiváñez y Ayacucho, which was begun in 1778 but is still unfinished. **San**

Cristo de la Concordia

Francisco church, is at 25 de Mayo y Bolívar. It was built in 1581, making it the second oldest in the city, but was heavily modernized in 1926. Also in the centre is the **Convent of Santa Teresa** at Baptista y Ecuador, and perhaps Cochabamba's finest religious building. Begun in 1753, the interior is quite beautiful and the floor is one of the most original in the Americas. Just off the main plaza at Baptista y Achá, is the church of **La Compañía,** whose white-washed interior is completely innocent of the usual riot of late Baroque decoration.

From the beautiful **Plaza Colón**, at the north end of the old town, the wide, palm-lined Avenida Ballivián runs northwest to the Río Rocha and beyond to the wealthy modern residential areas. Also known as **El Prado**, Avenida Ballivián is fronted by many fashionable cafés and restaurants.

To the south of the old town lie the bus and train stations and some of the best produce markets in Bolivia. Overlooking the bus station is the **San Sebastián hill**, offering grand views of the city. From here you can walk to the adjoining **La Coronilla hill**, topped by an imposing monument commemorating the defence of Cochabamba by its womenfolk from Spanish troops in 1812 (beware of robbery). At the east end of Avenida Heroínas is another hill, the **Cerro de San Pedro**, at the top of which stands an enormous statue of Cristo de la Concordia.

Cochabamba was the birth-place of Simón Patiño, the tin baron, who amassed one of the world's largest private fortunes. He built two houses in the city. One of these, in the centre, is now part of the **Universidad San Simón**. Next door to it, on the corner of Calama and Aguirre, is his bank, the Banco Mercantil, with an impressive domed interior of the main banking hall.

His other house, to the north of Plaza Colón at Avenida Potosí 1450, is the **Palacio de Portales**. This sumptuous mansion, which was built in 1927 but never occupied, sits in 10 hectares of extravagantly beautiful gardens designed by Japanese experts in the classic style of Versailles. The architectural style is predominantly French Renaissance. The great halls are filled with Napoleonic and Louis XV furniture. On the upper floor are chambers containing reproductions of the Sistine Chapel; the walls are covered in brocaded silk and it is decorated

Palacio de Portales

throughout in Carrara marble and paintings by Velásquez. There's even a copy of the Alhambra in Granada. Everything imported from Europe and no expense spared, the Palacio Portales bears testament to inconceivable opulence.

Now it is an educational and cultural centre and better known as the *Centro Cultural Pedagógico Simón J Patiño* (T 43137). The centre is open Monday-Friday 1700 and 1730, and Saturday at 1100 for guided tours in Spanish, entrance US$1, don't be late. It has a useful library and an excellent art gallery in the basement (open Monday-Friday 1430-1830, Saturday 0900-1200, Sunday 1000-1200). To get there take micro G from Avenida San Martín.

Museums

Among the city's museums, the most important is the excellent **Museo Arqueológico**, part of the Universidad de San Simón, at 25 de Mayo y Heroínas. It is one of the most complete in the country and displays artefacts dating from 15,000 BC up to the colonial period, including an interesting collection of prehistoric pieces, amerindian heiroglyphic scripts and pre-Inca textiles. It is open Monday-Friday 0900-1200, 1500-1900, Saturday 0900-1300; entry US$1.50 which includes a free student guide (Spanish, English or French).

Museo de la Casa de la Cultura, at 25 de Mayo y Heroínas, has exhibitions of paintings and occasionally shows films. It is open Monday-Friday 0900-1200, 1400-1800; entry free.

Local festivals

Carnival is celebrated 15 days before Lent. Rival groups (*comparsas*) compete in music, dancing, and fancy dress, culminating in El Corso on the last Saturday of the Carnival. *Mascaritas* balls also take place in the carnival season, when the young women wear long hooded satin masks. **14 September**: *Day of Cochabamba*. (See also **Festival calendar**, page 55). The Luzmilla Patiño festival of music takes place every

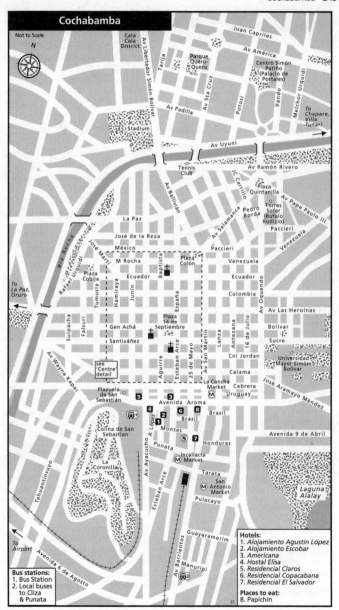

Cochabamba

Not to Scale

N

Caja Cala Cala District

Juan Capriles

Av América

Centro Simón Patiño (Palacio de Portales)

Tarija

Av Sta Cruz

Parque Queru-Queru

Potosí

Pando

Melchor Urquidi

To Chapare, Villa Tunari

Av Padilla

Av Libertador Simón Bolívar

Stadium

Av Uyuni

Tennis Club

Av Ramón Rivero

Av Ballivián

JC Carrillo

Plaza Quintanilla

Av Papa Paulo III

Pedro Borda

Torres Sofer (Bufalo Rodízio)

Av Salamanca

La Paz

Río Rocha

José de la Reza

México

Paccieri

Paccieri

Venezuela

Av Aniceto Arce

Rafael Urquidi

José Martí

M Rocha

Baptista

Plaza Colón

Venezuela

To La Paz, Oruro

Plaza Cobija

Ecuador

España

Ecuador

Av Oquendo

Colombia

Hamiraya

Junín

Tumusla

Falsuri

Suipacha

Gen Achá

Plaza 14 de Septiembre

Av Las Heroínas

Santiváñez

Aguirre

Esteban Arce

25 de Mayo

Av San Martín

Lanza

Antezana

16 de Julio

Bolívar

Sucre

see 'Centre detail'

Cni Jordan

Calama

Universidad Mayor Simón Bolívar

Av Wayna Kapac

Plazuela de San Sebastián

La Cancha Market

Cabrera

Uruguay

José Aramayo Méndez

5

Avenida 3 Aroma

4 **2** **6** **8** Brasil

1 Montes Brasil

Colina de San Sebastián

Av Ayacucho A López

Punata

S **7** Honduras

Avenida 9 de Abril

La Coronilla

Incallacta Market

Tarata

San Antonio Market

Laguna Alalay

Tahuantinsuyo

Esteban Arce

Pulacayo

Guayaramerim

To Airport

Avenida 6 de Agosto

Av Manuripi

Bus stations:
1. Bus Station
2. Local buses to Cliza & Punata

Hotels:
1. Alojamiento Agustín López
2. Alojamiento Escobar
3. Americana
4. Hostal Elisa
5. Residencial Claros
6. Residencial Copacabana
7. Residencial El Salvador

Places to eat:
8. Papichín

23

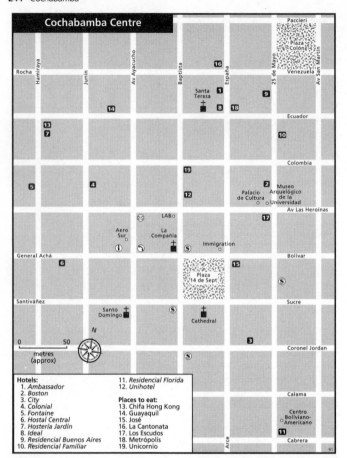

Cochabamba Centre

Hotels:
1. *Ambassador*
2. *Boston*
3. *City*
4. *Colonial*
5. *Fontaine*
6. *Hostal Central*
7. *Hostería Jardín*
8. *Ideal*
9. *Residencial Buenos Aires*
10. *Residencial Familiar*
11. *Residencial Florida*
12. *Unihotel*

Places to eat:
13. *Chifa Hong Kong*
14. Guayaquil
15. José
16. La Cantonata
17. Los Escudos
18. Metrópolis
19. Unicornio

2 years, usually around September/October; for details of the 1998 festival, T (042) 43137.

Local information

Street numbering: the city is divided into four quadrants based on the intersection of Avenida Las Heroínas running west to east, and Avenida Ayacucho/Avenida Libertador Simón Bolívar running north to south. In all longitudinal streets north of Heroínas the letter N precedes the four numbers. South of Heroínas the numbers are preceded by S. In all transversal streets west of Ayacucho the letter O (Oeste) precedes the numbers and all streets running east are preceded by E (Este). The first two numbers refer to the block, 01 being closest to Ayacucho or Heroínas; the last two refer to the building's number.

● **Accommodation**

L3 *Portales*, Avenida Pando 1271, T 48700, F 42071, five-star, swimming pool, a long way from the centre.

A1 *Aranjuez*, Avenida Buenos Aires E-0563, T 41935, F 40158, Casilla 3056, four-star, two blocks from Los Portales, small, colonial style, good restaurant, jazz in the bar on Friday and

Saturday night, recommended; **A2** *Gran Hotel Cochabamba*, Plaza Ubaldo Anze, T 82551, F 42823, beautifully set in the north part of the city (two blocks from Los Portales at La Recoleta), with garden, swimming pool (guests only) and tennis courts, popular with tour groups, recommended; **A3** *Ambassador*, Calle España N-0349, T 48777, F 28778, modern, central and reasonable, good restaurant.

B *Americana*, Avenida Aroma y Esteban Arce, T 50554, F 50484, fan, helpful, lift, laundry, parking, *rodizio* grill next door, good service.

C *Boston*, Calle 25 de Mayo 0167, T 28530, clean, restaurant, luggage deposit, quiet rooms at back, safe parking, recommended; **C** *Ideal*, España N-0329, T 35175, T/F 57930, includes breakfast, restaurant, comfortable, good value; **C** *La Fontaine*, Hamiraya N-0181, T 52838/30386, includes breakfast, with private bathroom, TV, phone, parking, bar and restaurant, café open at 0700 for breakfast, reasonable value; **C** *Las Vegas*, Calle Arce S-0352, just off the plaza, T 29217/29976, includes breakfast, has seen better days; **C** *Unihotel*, T 35065, Baptista S-0111 esquina Avenida Heroínas, includes breakfast, pleasant, helpful, modern, lift, central.

D *City Hotel*, Jordán E-0341, T 22993, central, includes breakfast, cheaper rooms on upper floors, noisy but modern; **D** *Colonial*, Junín N-0134 entre Colombia y Heroínas, T 21791, with garden and terrace, rooms with big balcony, peaceful, secure, laundry facilities, breakfast served on terrace, highly recommended; **D** *Hostal Elisa*, Agustín López, S-0834, T 27846, **E** without bath, good breakfast US$1.25, modern, garden, two blocks from the bus station, laundry service, unlimited hot water, very popular with travellers, best value, highly recommended; **D** *Hostería Jardín*, Hamiraya N-0248 (entre Colombia y Ecuador), T 47844, **E** without bath, garden, safe car-park, breakfast US$1 extra, comfortable; **D** *Residencial Buenos Aires*, 25 de Mayo N-0329, T 29518, **E** without bath, pleasant, clean communal bathrooms.

E *Alojamiento Escobar*, Aguirre S-0749, good value, but not to be confused with *Residencial Escobar* at Uruguay E-0213, which is not; **E** *Residencial Copacabana*, Avenida Arce S-0875 y Brasil, T 27929, near the bus station, hot showers, motorcycle parking, clean and friendly, recommended; **E** *Residencial El Salvador* Montes E-0420, T 27307, with bath, will store luggage, near market area, recommended; **E** *Residencial Familiar*, Sucre E-0554,

T 27988, with annex at 25 de Mayo S-0234, T 27986, pleasant, secure, good showers; **E-F** *Hostal Florida*, 25 de Mayo S-0583, T 57911, hot water, noisy, clean, friendly, popular, laundry service, safe deposit box, breakfast, recommended.

F *Residencial Agustín López*, Agustín López S-0859, T 27250, basic, hot water; **F** *Residencial Claros*, Avenida Aroma y Ayacucho, opposite the bus station, T 24732, hot water only at certain times, small rooms, laundry facilities, OK but not too clean; **F** *Residencial Urkupiña*, Avenida Arce S-0750, T 23502, basic, hot water, shared bath. There are many more cheap and basic places to stay near the bus station.

Youth hostel: ABAJ affiliate, **D** *Residencial Jordán*, Calle Antesana S-0671, modern, clean, basic. For long-term accommodation try Sra Nora de Durán, Ecuador E-0479, entre 25 de Mayo y San Martín, full board available, good value. Also near the bus station is *Hostal Masegal* at Calle Junín S-0671, T 59485, run by the director of tourism.

● **Places to eat**

Local and Latin American: *Miraflores*, Avenida Tarija N-0314, Bolivian food, large, popular, weekend speciality roast pig; *El Caminante*, Arce S-0628, pleasant patio, excellent food including duck with salad and vegetables; *La Estancia* Anecito Padilla block 7, in a side street off Plaza Recoleta, best steak in town, also grilled fish and chicken, a salad bar, recommended; *Los Troncos*, Junín 0-0942, barbecued meats, stylish, good; *Bufalo*, Torres Sofer, 2nd floor, Avenida Oquendo N-0654, Brazilian *rodizio* grill, all-you-can-eat buffet for US$6, great service, a must for carnivores, highly recommended; *Las Palmeras*, Lanza N-0248, very good food; *Papichín*, Aroma y 25 de Mayo, cheap and friendly, very good chicken and *churrasco*; *Cevichería Arriba Alianza*, Avenida Oquenda S-06 sin número, highly recommended for lovers of Peruvian *ceviche*, inexpensive; *Acuario Pub*, Ecuador y Hamiraya, superb four-course self-service meal for US$1.20; *Guayaquil*, Ecuador 0152 entre Ayacucho y Junín, seating in patio, excellent value lunch for US$1.10. You can find decent food in the Incallacta market for under US$1.

International and European styles: *Suiza*, Avenida Ballivián 820, T 45485, popular, recommended for international cuisine, good value; *BJ*, Avenida Libertador Bolívar 1580, T 48629, international cuisine, recommended; *La Cantonata*, España y Mayor Rocha, Italian, highly recommended, though expensive; *Pizzería Don Corleone*, España N-0350, expensive but great pizzas; *Metropolis*, España N-0299, good pasta dishes, huge portions, great salads, good value, gets very busy in late afternoon with students; *Carajillo*, España N-0386, Spanish-style, snacks and drinks, highly recommended; *Eli's Pizza Express*, 25 de Mayo N-0254, the one and only, great pizzas.

Chinese: *José*, Plaza 14 de Setiembre 0209, popular, not expensive; *Lai-Lai*, Aniceto Padilla 729, recommended, also takeaway service; *Chifa Hong Kong*, Hamiraya N-0260, excellent, huge portions, very friendly, main dishes about US$3.

Vegetarian: *Gopal*, Calle España 250, Galeria Olimpia, hare-krishna, excellent vegetarian lunch, US$1.60, good spiced bread, and Italian in the evenings, pleasant garden, English spoken; *Comedor Naturista*, Ecuador 0-0172, popular and cheap, be there by 1200 for lunch; *Tulasi*, Avenida Heroínas N-0254, open 0800-2200 daily, lunch US$1.35, highly recommended; *Snack Uno*, Avenida Heroínas E-0562, good lunches and dinners including vegetarian.

Cafés etc: excellent pastries and ice cream at the *Zurich Tea Room*, Avenida San Martín N-0143, open 1500-2000. There are some good ice-cream parlours on Avenida Heroínas: *Dumbo* 0440, popular eating and meeting spot, also does cheap meals; *Cristal*, three doors away, similar but smaller and quieter; *Unicornio*, Heroínas y Baptista, large, attractive, popular gringo hangout, expensive; *Café Bolívar*, on Bolívar between San Martín and 25 de Mayo, great coffee.

● **Banks & money changers**
You can get cash advances on Visa or Mastercard from many banks; no commission on bolivianos. You can also use Visa and Mastercard at 'Enlace' cash dispensers at **Banco Boliviano Americano**, Aguirre y Jordán; **Banco Santa Cruz**, 25 de Mayo S-0265; **Banco de La Paz**, Baptista y General Achá on main plaza. **Bidesa**, Jordán E-0224, best rates for travellers' cheques, 1% commission for cash dollars or bolivianos, good rates. **Exprint-Bol**, Plaza 14 de Septiembre 252, will change travellers' cheques into dollars at 2% commission. Money changers congregate at most major intersections, especially outside Entel, and offer good rates.

● **Cultural centres**
Centro de Cultura El Umbral, España N-0261, video-cinema with good films, theatre with resident company, concerts, dance, art gallery, café with traditional music, library and reading room. **Centro Boliviano Americano**, 25 de Mayo N-0567, T 21288, library of English-language books, open 0900-1200 and 1500-1900, also offers language classes. **Alianza Francesa**, Santiváñez O-0187. **Institut Cultural Boliviano-Alemán**, Sucre E-0693.

● **Embassies & consulates**
Argentina, F Blanco E-0929, T 55859, visa applications 0900-1300; **Brazil**, Edificio Los Tiempos Dos, Avenida Oquendo, 9th floor, T 55860, open 1400-1800; **Chile**, Heroínas y Lanza; **Netherlands**, Heroínas 473, *Gitano Tours*, T 28836/29409; **USA**, Avenida Libertador Bolívar 1724, T 43216, 0900-1200, they will also attend to Britons and Canadians.

● **Entertainment**
Cinemas: on 25 de Mayo opposite *Dumbo*; 25 de Mayo y Colombia; 25 de Mayo y Bolívar; and 25 de Mayo y Sucre.

There are frequent **concerts** and **plays** at the elegant *Teatro Achá*. More popular stage productions (stand-up comedy, music and dance) can be seen at *Tra La La*, Plazuela 4 de Noviembre, opposite the Chilean consulate, or *Champagne*, Calle Ballivián 0658.

Discos: *Arlequín*, Uyuni between Plaza Recoleta and the stadium; and *Reflejos*, Libertador y América; both are popular.

Nightlife: is moving to the northern area on América between Libertador and Pando. *Wunderbar* is in the centre, at Antesana two blocks from Plaza Colón, good music, darts upstairs.

● **Hospitals & medical services**
Health: a doctor recommended by the Tourist Office is *James Koller*, Calle Baptista N-0386, T 24191, call between 1700-1800.

● **Language classes**
There has been an explosion in the number of qualified language teachers. The following have all been recommended: *Sra Blanca de La Rosa Villareal*, Avenida Libertador Simón Bolívar 1108, esquina Oblitas, Casilla 2707 (T 44298) US$5 per 45 minutes lesson. *Runawasi*, J Hinojosa, Barrio Juan XXIII sin número, Casilla 4034, T/F 48923, Spanish and Quechua, also arranges accommodation. *Sra Alicia Ferrufino*, JQ Mendoza N-0349, T 81006, US$10 per hour. *Patricia Jiménez*, T 92455, Casilla 3968. *Elizabeth Siles Salas*, Avenida Guillermo Urquidi esquina Armando Méndez 1100, T 32278, Casilla 4659. *Professor Reginaldo Rojo*, T 423222, also teaches Quechua. *Ernestina Loma*, T 84615. *Centro de Apoyo Lingüístico*, T 86142, F 50373,

Casilla 5572, contact Carmen. *Carmen Galinda Benavides*, T 47072, Casilla 222. *Marycruz Almanza Bedoya*, T 27923/87201. *Haydee Lobo*, T 41447.

● **Laundry**
Superclean, 16 de Julio y Jordán, US$1 per kilo; *Limpieza Económico*, 16 de Julio entre Venezuela y Paccieri, safe, fast service; also at the Women's Prison, Plazuela San Sebastián, good and cheap (it's also possible to visit if you ask the guards).

● **Post & telecommunications**
Post Office: Avenida Heroínas y Ayacucho, next to LAB office (main entrance on Ayacucho); Monday-Saturday 0800-1900, Sunday 0800-1200. **Entel**: Bolívar y Ayacucho, international phone and fax (not possible to make AT&T credit card calls), open till 2300, T 25210.

● **Shopping**
Artesanías Casa Fisher, Calle Ramón Rivero E-0204, opposite the Tennis Club, PO Box 3782, T/F 49846, beautiful woollen goods, prices about US$85 locally, US$225-265 in USA. *Fotrama* Cooperative for alpaca sweaters, stoles, rugs, etc, expensive, run by Maryknoll Mission, factory at Avenida Circunvalación 0413, T 25468. *Asarti*, Mayor Rocha E-0375, beautiful hand-made and machine-knitted sweaters, can make to order, expensive. For made-to-measure leather goods and alpaca, *Chenza*, 25 de Mayo N-0344, mostly modern designs, highly recommended. Also recommended is *Arizona*, Juan Capriles E-0133. Good quality musical instruments can be bought at *Gamboa*, Avenida Manco Kapac 541.

Markets: these are very good for tourist items and souvenirs. The main market is called **San Antonio**. **La Cancha** market, near the railway station, is packed on Wednesday and Saturday with *campesinos*, it is huge and well worth a visit. Woollen items are expensive but high quality, US$35-50 for an alpaca sweater. There is a Saturday market at Avenida América y Libertador, which is best before 0900. **Mercado Incallacta** is mainly for fruit and vegetables, but also sells tourist souvenirs.

A very good **bookshop** is *Los Amigos del Libro*, Avenida de Heroínas 311 y España, General Achá 110, in *Hotel Portales* and *Gran Hotel Cochabamba*, and in the new Torres Sofer shopping centre, it stocks US and English magazines as well as the *South American Handbook*, and a good city map and guide in colour for US$2.50 (published by Quipus).

Camera repairs: *Maxell* on Plaza 14 de Septiembre, reasonable prices and recommended. For developing film try *Foto Broadway*, España y Colombia, reasonable prices, including slide transparencies. *Germán Grunbaum*, 25 de Mayo N-0345, good quality, recommended.

Camping equipment: available at a shop on 25 de Mayo, just before Plaza Colón, they have a wide variety of goods, the very helpful owner speaks English. Also Heroínas 225, T 29711. Camping gas is available at several shops on Avenida San Martín.

● **Sports**
Swimming: Tourist complex *El Carmen*, on the road to Quillacollo, US$2, popular, catch a micro on Junín. The swimming pool at *Club Social*, Calle México y Plaza Colón (US$1.50), is open to the public. Pool and restaurant at *Estancia El Rosedal* at Tiquipaya; take bus 12 from Antesana y Cabrera to the end of line. Most are open only at weekends in the summer; check before going.

Tennis: Club de Tenis de Cochabamba admits non-members for US$5 per day.

● **Tour companies & travel agents**
Fremen, Tumusla N-0245, T 43827, F 47126, run city and local tours, including to Torotoro, Samaipata and the 'Ruta del Ché' (see **Eastern Lowlands** section), they specialize in travel in the Bolivian Amazonia, using the *Reina de Enin* floating hotel out of Puerto Varador near Trinidad and run the *Hotel El Puente* in Villa Tunari (see below), also have offices in Santa Cruz, Trinidad and La Paz; *Tai Tours*, Avenida Heroínas E-0620, T 51723/21267, adventure tourism. *Turismo Balsa*, Avenida Heroínas O-0184, T 27065, daily city tours, excursions to Quillacollo, Inca-Rakay, Samaipata, Torotoro, etc, airline reservations (see also under La Paz **Travel agents**). *South Tours*, Mayor Rocha 0460 (Plaza Cobija), T 42180/63560, F 62698, tours to Inkachaca and Incallajta.

● **Tourist offices**
At General Achá 142, 3rd floor; open Monday-Friday 0900-1200, 1430-1700, helpful, they sell a city map and guide for US1.25, good service. Also at Jorge Wilstermann airport.

● **Useful addresses**
Immigration Office: Plaza 14 de Septiembre E-0231.

● **Transport**
Local Micros and colectivos, US$0.15; *trufis*, US$0.17; anything marked 'San Antonio' goes to the market. Trufis 'C' and 10 go from the bus terminal to the city centre. Buses leave from

Avenida Barrientos y Avenida 6 de Agosto, near **La Coronilla** for **Tarata**, **Punata** and **Cliza**. Buses leave from Avenida Oquendo S-0985 (at the edge of Lake Alalay; be careful around this area) to: **Villa Tunari**, US$4.50, 4 hours, several daily; **Chimoré**, US$5.75; **Eterazama**, US$5.75; **Puerto Villarroel**, US$7.75, 6 hours (daily from 0800 when full); **Puerto San Francisco**, US$6.50. **Taxis**: about US$0.65 from anywhere in the city to the Plaza; double after dark.

Air The very small Jorge Wilstermann airport is close to the city centre. Airport bus is Micro B from Plaza 14 de Septiembre, US$0.40; taxis from the airport to centre US$1. Reconfirm all flights (and obtain reconfirmation number), and arrive early for international flights. Several flights daily to/from **La Paz** (35 minutes) and **Santa Cruz** (40 minutes) with LAB and Aero Sur (book early for morning flights); LAB also fly to **Sucre**, **Trinidad** and **Tarija**. See **Information for travellers** for international flights. LAB is at Heroínas, between Ayacucho and Baptista, open 0800 (at airport T 50750/50650, opens 0500). Aero Sur is at Avenida Ayacucho S-0170, T 28385.

Buses The main bus terminal is at Avenida Aroma y Ayacucho. Buses leave early morning and evening to **Santa Cruz**, 9-10 hours, US$9-15; buses take the Chapare route, as opposed to the old mountain road via Epizana (except Cinta de Plata, once a week). See page 250 below. To/from **La Paz**, many companies do this route, shop around for the best times, services and prices (about US$7.75), by night or day, 7 hours on a paved road. Bus to **Oruro**, US$5.15, 4½ hours, eg Flota Cometa, 14 a day. To **Potosí**, US$6.75-9.50 via Oruro, several companies. Daily to **Sucre**, US$9.75, 10 hours on a rough road, several companies between 1800 and 2015 (Flota Copacabana and Trans Copacabana recommended; the latter's *bus-cama* costs US$10.40). To travel to Sucre by day take a bus to Aiquile (see below), then a bus at midnight-0100 passing en route to Sucre. If you want to take a truck in daylight, wait till the next day. To **Iquique** (Chile) TEPP (Punata) on Monday and Wednesday at 1430, via Oruro.

EXCURSIONS FROM COCHABAMBA

To the north of the city, 63 km away on the road to Morochota, is **Cerro Tunari**, 5,180m, in the Parque Nacional Tunari (see also National Parks, page 74). A road runs to within 300m of the top, usually sprinkled with a little snow. There are beautiful views of the Cochabamba valley from the mountain road which goes into the Parque Tunari from Cala Cala, ending at the lake which supplies drinking water. The views are best in the afternoon. There's no public transport.

Only 45 minutes by *trufi* is the **Taquiña brewery**, which produces the excellent local beer of the same name. There's a restaurant at the brewery where you can eat duck, a local speciality, drink beer and enjoy the view over the city below.

Quillacollo

(*Population* 20,000), 13 km west of Cochabamba, Quillacollo has a good Sunday market which is completely geared towards the local *campesinos*. There are no tourist items for sale. The town is famous for its **Fiesta de la Virgen de Urkupiña** which lasts 4 days with much dancing and religious ceremony; its date varies each year between June and August. The first day is the most colourful with all the groups in costumes and masks, parading and dancing in the streets till late at night. Many groups have left by the second day and dancing stops earlier. The third day is dedicated to the pilgrimage.

Cochabamba gets very busy at this time. Hotels are all full throughout the festivities. Be there before 0900 to be sure of a seat, as you are not allowed to stand in the street. There's plenty of transport from Cochabamba; micros and *trufis* leave from Heroínas y Ayacucho, 20 minutes, US$0.30.

Villa Albina

2-3 km beyond Quillacollo is a road to the beautiful Pairumani *hacienda*, centre of the Patiño agricultural foundation. Known also as Villa Albina it was built in 1925-32, furnished from Europe and inhabited by Patiño's wife, Albina. The house and Patiño mausoleum can be visited by prior arrangement (T 60082), it is open Monday-Friday 1500-1600, Saturday 0900-1130; to get there take Bus 7 or 38, or *trufi* 211 from Cochabamba.

• **Accommodation D-E** *Complejo Planeta de Luz* (Hotel Ecológico), is at Marquina (US$0.65 by bus from Quillacollo, US$10.50 for a taxi from Cochabamba), PO Box 318, Cochabamba, T 61234, F 91031. It is an ecological Quechua hostal, part of the Movimiento Pachamama Universal, with kitchen, games, reading and dance rooms, vegetarian restaurant, solar heating, sauna, gardens, pool, and natural medicine clinic; also camping. The main activities are meditation and tai chi. Note that the centre imposes strict rules which may not be to everybody's tastes.

The Inka-Rakay ruins

27 km west of Cochabamba, near Sipe-Sipe, are the Inca ruins of Inka-Rakay. The main attraction is the fantastic view from the site of the Cochabamba valley and the mountains ringing the ruins.

From Sipe-Sipe to the ruins there is either a 6 km footpath, or a 12 km road with almost no traffic, taking 3 to 4 hours to walk. It is a beautiful trip, and reports indicate that it is slightly less terrifying on foot than in a vehicle. Start early for it is a full day. Leave the plaza in Sipe-Sipe going up the street past the church, then left at the top and then right when you come to the wider road. Follow this road out of town, and while doing so look upwards for the area of whitish rock which you should be heading for. When the road crosses the stream and makes a sharp left, continue on the path to the left for 150m and then take the path uphill to the right, cross country, to the white rock. (At the stream do not take the obvious trail to the right; it leads to the mountains on the right of the valley). At the rock, turn about 45 degrees to the right as you climb, then you need to stay close to the valley to pick up a distinct trail to the ruins. These will appear first as a rough outcrop of rocks. If you hit the road, then you have gone too far left; turn right and climb the road to an obvious sign, from where it's 5 minutes on a wide path downhill. It may, of course, be easier to walk there all the way by road and return on the path, which can be found from the road a few hundred metres from the ruins.

It may be possible to hitch; alternatively hire a guide; Norberto Rojas Mariscal, who runs a shop in the plaza, is recommended, he speaks English. **NB** Take food and plenty of water as there is none available and beware of theft on the footpath. It's also worth taking a hat and sun-block as there is no shade on the path or road. In Sipe-Sipe are *La Cabaña* thermal baths, open all year, with a good restaurant (book in advance). Bus 245 goes direct from Cochabamba to Sipe-Sipe; also *trufi* 145 which is more frequent than bus. From Quillacollo, buses for Sipe-Sipe wait until there are enough passengers.

Tarata

The sleepy village of **Tarata**, 33 km southeast of Cochabamba, is worth visiting for its crumbling, colonial architecture. It has a lovely old arcaded plaza on which stand the church, containing an 18th-century organ and other colonial artefacts (open 0800-1300 daily), the Casa Consistorial, and the Municipalidad. Inside the Franciscan Convent overlooking the town are the remains of the martyr, San Severino, patron saint of the town, more commonly known as the 'Saint of Rain'.

A lively and colourful festival is held in his honour on the last Sunday of November, attracting many thousands of people. There's also a large procession on 3 May, day of La Santa Cruz, with fireworks and a brass band. Market day is Thursday. Ask for Doña Prima Fernández who sells sweaters at 'amazing prices'; she lives opposite the monastery. Frequent buses leave for Tarata, US$0.65, 1 hour; the last returns at 1800 (see **Transport** above).

At **Cliza**, 6 km further southeast, there is a large Sunday market. There is accommodation in **G** *Alojamiento*, near the bus terminal (see also **Transport** above).

Punata, 48 km east of Cochabamba, is an important agricultural centre and is famous for the production of the region's delicious *chicha*. The local speciality is *garapiña*, a mixture of *chicha* and ice-cream. Punata has a very lively and colourful market on Tuesday. Behind the main church, new vehicles are lined up to be blessed by the priest. Beyond Punata, at **Villa Rivera**, woven wall hangings are produced (see the introductory section on **textiles**, page 46).

At **Arani**, 7 km east of Punata, there is an *artesanía* market on Thursday.

TOROTORO NATIONAL PARK

Set in a beautiful, arid rocky landscape is **Torotoro National Park**, an area of 16,570 hectares which was declared a National Park in 1989. Torotoro straddles the departments of Cochabamba and Potosí but is best reached from Cochabamba (120 km). This is an isolated and relatively unexplored area of rare beauty and is highly recommended for the adventurous traveller with time and energy.

Torotoro is actually a huge hanging valley at 2,700m surrounded by 3,500m high mountains and criss-crossed by deep ravines. This is an area of great scientific interest; geologists, paleontologists, archaeologists and botanists have all carried out studies here to investigate the discovery of dinosaur bones, fossils of turtles and sea shells, as well as archaeological ruins and pictographs. Other attractions include caves, canyons, waterfalls, and 80 million year-old dinosaur tracks, which can be seen by the stream just outside the village. The area also has its living attractions. Condors and red-fronted macaws can be seen quite easily and scattered throughout the valley are small traditional communities whose people are friendly and welcoming. The climate is temperate all year round and in winter nights are fresh and the days are not too hot; ideal in fact for walking or camping.

The village of **Torotoro** lies at the head of the valley and is actually in the province of Potosí. It serves as a convenient starting point for all the hikes in the area and its people are very

hospitable. Tourist information is available at the national park office in Torotoro. Ask at Santiago, the only shop, for the key to the **Umajalanta cave**, about 8 km northwest of the village; a guide is necessary for both the cave and the dinosaur tracks, and will cost US$2.50 per person for whole day. Only 30-minutes from the village is the smaller **Chilijusco cave**. A 2 hours' walk away are the **Pozas Bateas**, passing 1,000 year-old rock paintings. Three hours away is **El Vergel** or 'Nariz de Vaca' (Cow's Nose), where you can swim in crystal clear water.

● **Fiestas** On **24-27 July** is the *Fiesta de Santiago*, when people from surrounding communities congregate to sing, dance and drink.

● **Accommodation & services** Take your own food as only a limited range is sold at the shop in Torotoro. You can sleep in the *alojamiento* near the bus terminal in the village; **G**, friendly. Or ask the priest for other places to sleep. Also cheap rooms are available in locals' homes. The village has no electricity.

● **Transport** Trucks and *micros* go to Torotoro from Avenida República y Punata, near the market in Cochabamba, at 1800 Sunday and Thursday, US$4, 12 hours, or a truck also goes from the market at Cliza at about 0800, 10 hours. Trucks return to Cochabamba every Monday and Friday. Alternatively, hire a jeep, US$220 for 3 days including mileage and fuel, which is quite an adventure. **NB** Travel to Torotoro is all but impossible in the wet season (end November-May), as flooded rivers wash out roads. Check bus schedules in advance at all times of the year.

COCHABAMBA TO SANTA CRUZ

There are two routes east from Cochabamba to the thriving city of Santa Cruz in the eastern lowlands of Bolivia (see page 256). A 500-km mostly paved road goes via the mountains and Epizana to Santa Cruz. The new lowland route, which goes via Villa Tunari in the Chapare region, is preferred by most transport. (For a more detailed description of the condition of the old mountain road, see page 264.)

THE MOUNTAIN ROAD TO SANTA CRUZ

The road heads for 119 km to **Montepunco**, and 3 km further on is the turn-off for the road to **Pocona**. 15 km down this road is **Collpa**, which is the turn-off for the Inca ruins of Inkallajta.

INKALLAJTA

The ruins, on a flat spur of land at the mouth of a steep valley, are extensive and the main building of the fortress is said to have been the largest roofed Inca building.

Inkallajta is the most important archaeological site in the Cochabamba Department. A few decades before the Spanish conquest, the Inca empire had expanded to cover most of the Cochabamba valley, in an attempt to benefit from its enormous agricultural potential. To this end, the Incas built an extensive system of roads, market centres and forts. The Inca Topa Yupanqui ordered the construction of Inkallajta to protect the advancing Imperial army from the attacks of the fearsome local Chiriguano tribes. The fort was abandoned, however, in the aftermath of the internal strife that marked the beginning of the end of the Inca empire.

● **Accommodation & services** To get there without your own transport, take a micro to the checkpoint 10 km from Cochabamba, then a truck to Km 119. From there walk towards Pocona or take a truck for 15 km, to where a large yellow sign indicates the trail. After approximately 10 km the trail divides; take the downhill path and the ruins are a further 2 km. Take food and camping gear. There are several good camping sites. The Cochabamba Archaeological Museum has some huts where visitors can stay, free, but take sleeping bag and food. Water is available at a nearby waterfall.

Epizana, 13 km beyond Montepunco at Km 128, is the junction for the 237 km road south to Sucre (see page 218), a scenic drive of 6-7 hours; all but the last hour is rough and narrow in parts. There's accommodation in Epizana at the grim-looking *Hotel Urkupiña*, on the main road. There are several restaurants and service stations.

SOUTH TO SUCRE

Totora, 14 km south of Epizana on the Sucre road, is a beautiful, unspoiled little colonial town, at 2,789m. It has a charming arcaded plaza with fine 19th century mansions which are now crumbling, and a pretty fountain. There are pleasant walks in the wooded hills above the town from where you get good views of the jumble of red-tiled roofs below. Days are hot and the nights are cool.

● **Accommodation** The only place to stay is *Hotel Centenario*, with "two grubby rooms, very primitive toilets and a restaurant". Aiquile has better accommodation.

● **Buses** There are daily buses from Cochabamba: Pullman Totora (Avenida Barrientos S-2387, T 29144) at 1600, also at 1430 on Saturday; returning at 0500 Monday-Saturday and at 1100 on Sunday. A daily bus goes to Aiquile at 1600 and on to Sucre.

South of Totora is **Aiquile** (2,242m), 149 km from Sucre and 217 km from Cochabamba. It is famous for its fine hand-made *charangos*. The Museo Arqueológico Regional has extensive exhibits on Omereque and Yampara cultures. The town hosts the annual *Feria del charango* in early November; ask at the tourist office. Another festival is on 2 February in honour of the town's patron saint, *La Virgen de la Candelaria*, and involves 7 days of bull-running through the streets. There's also a weekend market.

● **Accommodation** F *Hostal Campero*, Bolívar 960, clean, good food; F *Hotel Escudo*, hot shower, comfortable, good food; F *Hotel Italia*, OK, good restaurant.

● **Buses** Daily buses from Cochabamba with Trans Campero (Avenida Barrientos S-2291; 100m past Avenida 6 de Agosto junction, *trufis* 1, 10, 14, 16, 20 pass in front), daily except Sunday at 1300 (Saturday 1400), 5 hours; Flota Aiquile (Avenida Barrientos S-2365) daily except Sunday at 1300.

From Epizana the road continues east to Santa Cruz. At Km 386 is Samaipata

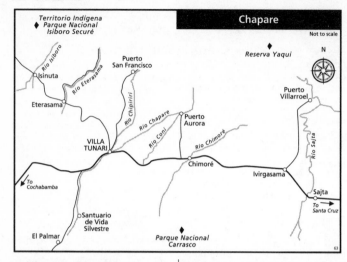

Chapare

Territorio Indígena
Parque Nacional
Isiboro Secure

Reserva Yaqui

Not to scale

N

Río Isiboro

Isinuta

Río Eterasama

Puerto
San Francisco

Puerto
Villarroel

Eterasama

Río Chipiriri

Río Chapare

Puerto
Aurora

VILLA
TUNARI

Río Coni

Río Chimoré

Río Sajta

Chimoré

To
Cochabamba

Ivirgasama

Sajta

To
Santa Cruz

Santuario
de Vida
Silvestre

El Palmar

Parque Nacional
Carrasco

(see page 264). 95 km before Samaipata is **Comarapa**. 20 km east of here is the Tambo Mission School, near which is excellent birdwatching. You can find shared accommodation at the school if it's not already in use; meals are at set times and there's strictly no alcohol. 2 km west is San Isidro with restaurant *El Turista* and a hotel.

THE LOWLAND ROUTE TO SANTA CRUZ

The lowland road from Cochabamba to Santa Cruz runs through Villa Tunari (166 km). The 465 km road is fully paved except for a 25 km stretch before Villa Tunari, almost at the end of the winding descent from the mountains, known as El Sillar. It's a beautiful trip, dropping from over 2,500m down to the lush, tropical lowland forests. Travellers should note that the road passes through the Chapare, Bolivia's prime cocaine-producing region. While it's safe in the main towns, you not stray too far off the beaten track.

VILLA TUNARI

The little town of **Villa Tunari** (*Population*

2,500; *Altitude* 300m; *Phone code* 0411), 4 hours from Cochabamba, is a relaxing place. Nestled between the San Mateo and Espíritu Santo rivers, it is Cochabamba's gateway to the tropics and the main tourist centre of the Chapare region. Among the many activities awaiting the eager traveller are white-water rafting and fishing. The town holds an annual Fish Fair on 5 and 6 August, with music, dancing and delicious food.

Villa Tunari enjoys a warm, humid climate and nights are comfortable. Average temperature is 24°C, reaching 40°C in the summer (December-February) and as low as 10°C with the arrival of the *surazos* in the winter. The heaviest rainfall comes in November-April.

Parque Ecoturístico Machía is just outside town and offers good trails through semi-tropical forest. The 36 hectare park includes a well-signposted 3 km interpretive trail which explains the park's ecology. There are also panoramic lookouts and picturesque waterfalls as well as a wide variety of wildlife. The park is on the left-hand side of the road after crossing the bridge towards Santa Cruz. Entry is free.

To visit the Yuqui Indian Reserve contact Marcelo Ondarza Vilaseca, T 4102 (Entel office).

● **Accommodation & services A3** *Country Club Los Tucanes*, opposite the turn-off for *El Puente*, includes breakfast, air conditioning, two swimming pools; **D** *Las Palmas*, T 47554, 1 km out of town, clean, friendly, with pool and good restaurant, recommended; **D** *El Puente*, Avenida de la Integración, accommodation from two people to family-size in cabins with private bathroom, the hotel has natural pools where you can swim (US$2 per person for non-guests), to get there continue on the highway through town, cross the second bridge, turn right on the first road to the right, then go 2 km, the turn is clearly marked, book in advance at *Fremen Tours* in Cochabamba (see **Travel agents**, page 247), or in La Paz or Santa Cruz; **E** *Los Araras*, across the bridge on the main road to Santa Cruz, T 4116, large rooms, nice

Coca and cocaine production

In recent years, the production of coca and cocaine has been one of Bolivia's most important sources of employment and income. It is estimated that about 10% of the working population are directly dependent on the coca industry for their livelihoods. Though no official statistics are available, it is an established fact that coca and cocaine production has now completely taken over from tin as Bolivia's most important export product. Bolivia is now the second largest producer of coca after Peru (and of cocaine after Colombia), generating some US$650-700 million a year, of which US$150-200 million stays in the country.

Until the 1952 revolution, coca cultivation had been concentrated in the tropical valleys of the Yungas, where the climate is warm and not too dry and the altitude ideal. Today, most of the coca grown for traditional uses and domestic consumption comes from the Yungas. The huge expansion of coca production in recent decades has largely been the result of the colonization of eastern Bolivia. This coca is less suitable for chewing but international demand is high enough to ensure a market for it.

Most of the coca is grown by small peasant farmers who moved from the Altiplano following the closure of the tin mines. They settled in the higher parts of the Beni and, above all, in the Chapare plain of Cochabamba and now own small parcels of land of between 1 and 2 hectares. Many are also attracted to these regions by the relatively high wages which they can earn as labourers: a *pisador* can earn US$10 a night for treading coca leaves.

Coca cultivation provides a much higher return for the small peasant farmer than any other crop. It can continue on the same land for at least 15 years and can be harvested 4 times a year, whereas other crops can exhaust the soil within as little as 3 years. It is for these reasons that peasant farmers in the Chapare are reluctant to abandon coca cultivation in favour of the proposed crop substitution programmes.

While Bolivia has been hailed by the US as a symbol of the triumph of the free-market economic model, the role played by coca and cocaine remains a thorn in the flesh of policy-makers. Alternative development programmes have been implemented in recent years to limit and eventually eradicate coca cultivation in the Chapare, but have proved to be of very limited effect, owing to the lack of financial incentive for the coca farmers. Furthermore, the financial and monetary success of the free-market model in Bolivia is largely based on a successful government policy which manages to keep a large part of the profits from the cocaine trade in the country. It is, therefore, not surprising that US-funded anti-drug campaigns are carried out with little enthusiasm in a country which depends so much on narco-trafficking.

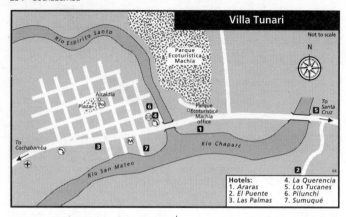

Hotels:
1. Araras
2. El Puente
3. Las Palmas
4. La Querencia
5. Los Tucanes
6. Pilunchi
7. Sumuqué

gardens, good breakfast; **F** *La Querencia*, pleasant terrace on river front, avoid noisy rooms at the front, good cheap food, clothes washing facilities. There are several other hotels and also restaurants. Try the freshly-caught *surubí* or *pacú* served with fried cassava. There's also an Entel office (T 4101/4102), Post office and bank.

● **Buses** There are lots of buses heading back to Cochabamba or onwards to Santa Cruz. It's also easy to flag down buses on the main road (see also Cochabamba **Buses**, page 248).

CARRASCO NATIONAL PARK

South of Villa Tunari lies the Carrasco National Park, covering 622,600 hectares. It lies between altitudes of 300 and 4,500m, includes eleven ecological life zones and offers superb birdwatching opportunities. 20 minutes by car from Villa Tunari in the park is the **Cavernas del Repechón Wildlife Sanctuary**. This consists of several caves inhabited by the rare *guácharo* or oilbird. These are nocturnal, fruit-eating birds that venture out of their cave only at night, in the process emitting a strange clicking sound that is used for navigation by echo location.

Access to the National Park is via El Palmar and the Wildlife Sanctuary, or Sajta.

ISIBORO-SECURE NATIONAL PARK

This 900,000 hectares protected area lies in the northwest corner of the Chapare region. Ranging from 200m to 1,600m in altitude, the park includes vast expanses of tropical rainforest and savannah lands and is home to the Trinitario and Yuracaré indigenous groups. Road access is difficult and there are no tourist facilities as yet. The park can be visited by river via the Río Chipiriri from **Puerto San Francisco**, which is about 1 hour from Villa Tunari. The park can also be visited from Trinidad

Cock of the Rock

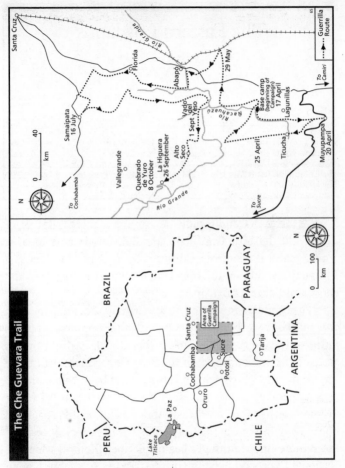

The Che Guevara Trail

(see page 303). **NB** Parts of Isiboro-Secure are strictly off limits to visitors. This is in the heart of cocaine territory. Check on local conditions before venturing too far.

The Santa Cruz road continues east from Villa Tunari to **Chimoré**. Before Chimoré is the turn-off for the river port of **Puerto Aurora**.

● **Accommodation & places to eat In Chimoré**: *Hotel Copacabana*, used maily by the military and prostitutes. Water cuts are common June-September. *Restaurants El Tamarindo*, on the right entering the village from Cochabamba, and *El Curichi*, on the left, both are mainly for bus passengers with a token system and limited menu, but OK.

Beyond Chimoré is **Ivirgarzama** (*Hotel El Torero*, very basic; *Restaurant Punata*, 100m from bus station, popular). This is the turn-off for the major river port of **Puerto Villaroel** (see page 302).

The Eastern Lowlands

THE VAST and rapidly developing plains to the east of the Eastern Cordillera are Bolivia's richest area in natural resources. Bordered by Brazil to the east and Paraguay to the south, this region comprises most of the enormous Santa Cruz Department.

The capital of the region, Santa Cruz, is a booming modern city, unlike any other in the country, and a stopping-off point for most travellers heading to or from Brazil. It also provides access to Trinidad, capital of the Beni Department. But more importantly for the tourist, it is the perfect base from which to visit some of Bolivia's best kept secrets: the beautiful Jesuit Mission towns to the northeast; Amboró National Park, only 3 hours away and one of the truly great wildlife experiences; and the remote but stunningly beautiful Noell Kempff Mercado National Park, said to be the inspiration for Sir Arthur Conan Doyle's famous *Lost World*.

SANTA CRUZ DE LA SIERRA

Santa Cruz de la Sierra, capital of the Department of Santa Cruz, is 851 km by road and 552 km by air from La Paz. Bolivia's second largest city, with a population of 730,000, is an incongruous mix of the old and the new. In the centre are low, red-tiled roofs with overhanging eaves giving pedestrians much needed shade from the fierce sun. The narrow streets, though, are jam-packed with flashy new 4WD vehicles and its shops are crammed with expensive imported electrical goods. On first impression, you may feel you've missed Bolivia and passed straight on to Brazil.

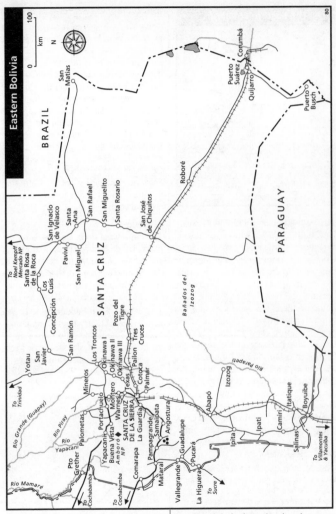

Eastern Bolivia

The people of Santa Cruz like to call themselves *Cambas* and are generally more open and laid-back than their Andean counterparts. This relaxed attitude could be attributed partly to the intense heat and humidity. It can get very hot and sticky, particularly around midday when Cruceños go home for lunch and their siesta, leaving the streets free from traffic and people, save for the occasional tourist or guidebook editor. This is a good time to frequent one of the city's many air-conditioned ice-cream parlours or sit in the shaded plaza and watch the world go by – a favourite local pastime.

The Eastern Lowlands

The city was founded in 1561 by the Spaniard Ñuflo de Chávez, who had come from Paraguay. As little as 40 years ago, Santa Cruz was nothing more than a remote backwater where horses were the usual mode of transport on streets of red earth. New rail and road links ended this isolation. Now there is an ever-increasing flow of immigrants from the highlands, as well as Mennonites, mostly from USA and Canada, and Japanese settlers, such as the Okinawan colony 50 km from Montero, who come to grow soya, maize, sugar, rice, coffee and other crops. As well as agriculture, cattle breeding and timber projects are also important. The exploitation of oil and gas in the Department of Santa Cruz, not to mention more dubious activities, have also greatly contributed to the city's rapid development.

BASICS *Altitude* 437m; *Phone code* 03. It is usually hot and windswept from May to August. When the cold *surazo* blows from the Argentine pampas during these months the temperature drops sharply. The rainy season is December-February.

Places of interest

The **Plaza 24 de Septiembre** is the city's main square with the impressive **Cathedral**, the Casa de Cultura (see **Museums** below) and the Prefectura set around it. Look for the sloths who live in the trees of the plaza. The Cathedral has some interesting hand-wrought colonial silver and its museum contains what is considered the smallest book in the world, only 7x7 mm; the museum is open Monday and Thursday, 1600-1800, and Sunday, 1800-2000; entry US$0.75. The heart of the city, with its arcaded streets, retains a colonial air, despite the variety of modern shops and the new building that surrounds it.

Five blocks north of the Plaza is **Parque El Arenal**. On an island in the middle of the lake is the Museo Etno-Folklórico (see below). At the lakeside is *Artesanías Salón de Exposición y Ventas*, a building housing various shops selling regional arts and crafts.

Museums

The city's **Casa de la Cultura** is on the plaza. It has occasional exhibitions, an archaeological display and plays, recitals, concerts and folk dancing. The **Museo de Historia Natural** is at Avenida Irala sin número, entre Velasco y Independencia.

The **Museo Etno-Folklórico** is in the Parque Arenal (entry free). It contains a small but interesting collection of musical instruments, masks, weapons, weavings etc of the various ethnic groups of the Eastern Lowlands. The exterior of the

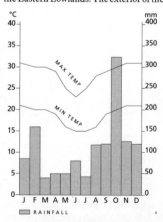

Climate: Santa Cruz

Santa Cruz

Not to Scale

To
Viru Viru Airport
& the North

Hotels:
1. *Alojamiento Santa Bárbara*
2. *Brasil*
3. *Copacabana*
4. *Cortez*
5. *España*
6. *Excelsior*
7. *Felimar*
8. *Gran Hotel Santa Cruz*
9. *Hostal Cañoto*
10. *House Inn*
11. *Internacional*
12. *Italia*
13. *Las Américas*
14. *Libertador Simón Bolívar*
15. *Mediterráneo*
16. *Posada El Turista*
17. *Residencial Ballivián*
18. *Residencial Bolívar*
19. *Residencial 26 de Enero*
20. *Roma*
21. *Viru-Viru*

Places to eat:
22. *La Pascana*

Av Cristóbal De Mendoza

Statue of Christ

Santa Fe

Platanillos
Cañada
Strongest

Fortín Toledo

Av Busch

Perú

P Rico

Fortín Corrales

Asunción

D'Orbigny

Moss Rivero

JR Coimbra

MJ Justiniano

Quijarro

Campero

Centro Cívico

Av Uruguay

Av Cañoto

Celso Castedo

Andrés Ibáñez

Primer Anillo

Rafael Peña

Vaca Díez

6 de Agosto

Cuellar

Fremen Tours

Seoane

Immigration

España

Santa Bárbara

Sara

Buenos Aires

Florida

Junín

Casa de Cultura

Plaza 24 de Septiembre

Ayacucho

Prefectura

Cathedral

Ingavi

Colón

Suárez De Figueroa

Camiri

SIETE CALLES

Pari

Mercado

Av Cañoto

Isabel la Católica

Valle Grande

Cordillera

José Callali

N

21 de Mayo

24 De Septiembre

Libertad

Parque El Arenal

Los Pozos Market

Suárez Arana

Caballero

Charcas

Arenales

Murillo

Aroma

Quijarro

Campero

Arenales

Bolivar

Sucre

Tarija

Ballivián

Beni

Chuquisaca

La Paz

Cochabamba

Potosí

Centro Boliviano-Americano

Independencia

Velasco

René Moreno

Ñuflo de Chávez

Warnes

LAB

Republiquetas

Moldes

Saavedra

Lemoine

Mons Salvatierra

Parapeti

La Riva

Taxis to Samaipata

Lemoine

Aero Sur

Av Irala

Primer Anillo

Av Irala

Picada

Cañada

Senda

Solís de Olguín

To Cochabamba

To El Trompillo Airport

H De Zalazar

Plaza Héroes del Chaco

Diego De Mendoza

Potosí

Av Argentina

La A Peña

To Train Station

26

museum is decorated with a mural by the celebrated painter, Lorgio Vaca, which depicts the city's history.

Excursions

Las Lomas de Arena del Palmar are huge sand-dunes, 20 km to the south of the city. In some parts are small lagoons where you can swim. You may be able to get there by taxi, but private transport is best. It may be possible to hitch at weekends, but a 4WD vehicle is normally required.

Los Espejillos (little mirrors) are a series of many little wwaterfalls, 40 km to the southwest. To the west, at the end of Avenida Roca Coronado, 10 minutes by bus from the town centre, you can swim in the Río Piray during the wet season, though at weekends it is very crowded. Some huts on the beach sell local delicacies.

20 km east of the city is **Cotoca** (20 minutes), whose church has a miraculous virgin, associated with which is a religious handicraft tradition. The town holds a *fiesta* on 8 December. Try the local *sonzos* in the market.

5 km out of town on the road to Cotoca are the new **Botanical Gardens**. Take a micro or colectivo from Calle Suárez Arana; 15 minutes.

Local festivals

Cruceños are famous as fun-lovers and their music, the *carnavalitos*, can be heard all over South America. Of the various festivals, the best is **Carnival**, celebrated for the 15 days before Lent. It's a wild and raucous time with music and dancing in the streets, fancy dress and the coronation of a queen. As with all Bolivian festivals at this time, you're almost certainly going to get very wet. The *mascaritas* balls also take place during the pre-Lent season, when girls wear satin masks covering their heads completely, thus ensuring anonymity. It's a good time to be in town, especially if you're male.

The rather more sedate **International Trade Fair** is held each September. 24 September is a local holiday.

Local information
● **Accommodation**

NB Accommodation is relatively expensive here and good value mid and lower-range hotels are hard to find.

L1-L3 *Yotaú*, Avenida San Martín y James Freyre, T 367799, suites, five-star, air conditioning, sauna, all services.

A1 *Cortez*, Avenida Cristóbal de Mendoza 280, on Segundo Anillo near the Cristo, T 331234, F 351186, pool, good, air conditioning, recommended for medium or long stays; **A1** *Los Tajibos*, the biggest, Avenida San Martín 455 in Barrio Equipetrol out of town in 15 acres of lush vegetation, five-star, T 421000, F 426994, air conditioning, *El Papagayo* restaurant is good (their *ceviche* is particularly recommended), business centre, Viva Club Spa has sauna etc, swimming pool for residents only; **A1-A2** *House Inn*, Colón 643, T/F 362323, Casilla 387, five-star suites, two pools, restaurant, air conditioning, parking, modern, recommended.

A2 *Gran Hotel Santa Cruz*, Pari 59, T 348811/348997, F 324194, pool, open to non-residents, fully restored to its 1930s glory, air conditioning, spacious, recommended; **A2** *Las Américas*, 21 de Mayo esquina Seoane, T 368778, F 336083, air conditioning, discount for longer stay, parking, arranges tours and car rental, restaurant, bar, five-star service, recommended.

B *Hostal Cañoto*, Florida 45-47, T 331052/3, includes breakfast, air conditioning, pool; **B** *Colonial*, Buenos Aires 57, T 333156, F 339223, air conditioning, restaurant, comfortable, recommended; **B** *Dallas*, has two entrances, one at Calle Pari 457, the other at Calle Camiri 168, T 371011, F 371331, suites with private bath, colour TV, air conditioning, elevator, includes breakfast, laundry, restaurant; **B-C** *Felimar*, Calle Ayacucho 445, T 351111, F 351112, breakfast included, air conditioning, elevator, TV, phone; **B-C** *Internacional*, Colón 437, T 330833/333592, F 326587, air conditioning, TV, laundry, parking, pool, restaurant; **B** *Libertador Simón Bolívar*, Buenos Aires 119 esquina Libertad, T 351235/351376, F 342696, air conditioning, colour TV, phone.

C *Bolivia*, Libertad 365, T 336292, modern, comfortable; **C** *Copacabana*, Junín 217, T 339937, **B** with air conditioning, cheap laundry service, includes breakfast, a bit overpriced; **C** *Mediterráneo*, Vallegrande y Camiri 71, T 338804, F 361344, air conditioning, fridge, includes breakfast, cheaper with fan.

Halfway between the city centre and the airport on Carretera al Norte is **D** *Cataluña*, with private bathroom, pool, clean, very friendly and helpful, quiet, recommended; **D** *Brasil*, Santa Bárbara 244, T 323530, with bathroom and breakfast, friendly; **D** *España*, at Cordillera 599, next to the bus terminal, no single rooms, with private bathroom, TV, phone, pool, parking, restaurant; **D** *Excelsior*, René Moreno 70, T 325924, includes breakfast, good rooms, good lunches; **D** pp *Italia*, Rene Morenó 167, T 323119, with private bathroom and breakfast, TV, phone; **D** *Residencial Cañada*, Cañada 145, near the bus terminal, T 345541, **E** without bath, good; **D** *Residencial 26 de Enero*, Camiri 32, T 321818, F 337518, **E** without bath, very clean; **D** *Roma*, 24 de Septiembre 530, T 338388, pleasant, good value, helpful; **D** *Viru-Viru* Junín 338, T 322687, includes breakfast, air conditioning, cheaper with fan, pool, pleasant, recommended.

E *Alojamiento San José*, Cañada 136, near the bus terminal, T 328024, hot showers, not great value; **E** *Alojamiento Santa Bárbara*, Santa Bárbara 151, T 321817, hot showers, helpful, will store luggage, very popular, recommended; **E** *Residencial Ballivián*, Ballivián 71, T 321960, basic, shared hot showers, nice patio, recommended; **E** *Residencial Bolívar*, Sucre 131, T 342500, hot showers, some rooms with bath, nice courtyard with hammocks, excellent breakfast US$1, repeatedly recommended.

F *Alojamiento Ferrocarril*, Avenida Capitán Arrien 131, near the train station, T 321061, stores luggage; **F** *Posada El Turista*, Junín 455, small basic room, shared bathrooms, central, quiet, friendly.

● **Places to eat**
La Castañuela, Velasco 308 esquina Pari, in a beautifully-restored colonial Casona, Spanish restaurant, fine wine list, expensive but good quality; *El Fogón*, Avenida Viedma 434 and *La Buena Mesa*, Avenida Cristóbal de Mendoza 538, are both excellent for *parrillada* and *churrasquería*; there are many other barbecue restaurants all around the Segundo Anillo; *Churrasquería El Palenque*, Avenida El Trompillo y Santos Dumont, good; *Michelangelo*, Chuquisaca 502, excellent Italian, not cheap; *Pizzería Mesón de René*, 24 de Septiembre 285, bright and clean, good; *El Boliche*, Arenales 135, open 1930 onwards, serves good crêpes, expensive. Chinese restaurants include: *El Patito Pekín*, 24 de Septiembre 307, basic cheap Chinese food, open on Sunday evening; *Shanghai*, Avenida 26 de Febrero 27; and *Mandarin 2*, Avenida Potosí 793, both excellent. *Naturcenter*, Arenales 638, vegetarian self-service, good value, also at Warnes 138; *Vegetarismo*, Ayacucho 491, piso 1, good set lunch. *Español*, Junín y España, popular, cheap, good meals; *Sirari*, Calle Junín 179, excellent food, reasonable prices, shame about the service; *Hawaii*, Sucre y Beni, open at 0700, good breakfasts and coffee; *La Pascana*, on the Plaza, very popular with tourists and locals, meals, ice-cream and snacks, expensive; *Dumbos*, Ayacucho 247, burgers, great ice-cream and full meals, recommended; *Heladería Pastelería Manolo*, 24 de Septiembre 170, good sandwiches, cakes and ice cream, reasonable prices; *Kivón*, Ayacucho 267, highly recommended for ice cream, also at Quijarro 409 in Mercado Los Pozos. *Salteñería San Andres*, Calle Charcas 64, cheap set lunch for US$1. For a takeaway pizza call *Eclipse Pizza Express*, at Canal Isuto y Radial 26, Tercer Anillo, T 420940.

There are many cheap restaurants near the bus terminal on Avenida Cañoto serving fried chicken. Also on the extension of Calle 6 de Agosto behind Los Pozos market (daytime).

Excellent *empanadas* are sold in the food section of Los Pozos market. The bakeries on Junín, Los Manzanos and España sell the local specialities: *empanadas de queso* (cheese pies), *cuñapés* (yucca buns), rice bread and *humitas* (maize pies). Try the local speciality *arroz con leche* in the markets; it's only available before 1100.

● **Airline offices**

LAB, Warnes y Chuquisaca, T 344411; **Aero Sur**, Irala/Colón, T 367400; **Varig**, Junín 284, T 391105, open till 1200 on Saturday; **AeroPerú**, Beni/Bolívar, T 365385; **American Airlines**, Arenales/Beni, T 341314; **Aerolíneas Argentinas**, Edificio Banco de la Nación Argentina, on main Plaza, T 339776; **Lan Chile**, Libertad 144, T 335951; **Iberia**, main Plaza, T 327448.

● **Banks & money changers**

Banks open 0830-1130, 1430-1730; they won't change travellers' cheques on Saturday afternoon. **Banco de La Paz**, René Moreno y Ballivián, Enlace cash dispenser; **Banco Mercantil**, René Moreno y Suárez de Figueroa, gives cash advance on Visa and changes cash and travellers' cheques; **Banco de Santa Cruz**, Junín 154, Enlace cash dispenser, bolivianos on Visa and Mastercard, no commission; **Banco Boliviano-Americano**, René Moreno 366 and Colón y Camiri (Siete Calles), Enlace cash dispenser for Visa and Mastercard; **Bidesa**, Calle Ñuflo de Chávez 150, good for cash and travellers' cheques.

Casas de cambio: **Mendicambio** on Plaza 24 de Septiembre will change travellers' cheques into dollars at 3% commission; also on the main plaza, **Alemana** (changes travellers' cheques at 2% commission for dollars or bolivianos) and **Sudamer**. **Cambios** can also be found on Libertad, eg **Latina** and **Oriente** on the first block. **Magri Turismo**, Ingavi 14, T 345663, two blocks from the main plaza, is the American Express agent, it doesn't change American Express travellers' cheques, but you may have to go there to have cheques certified before a *casa de cambio* will accept them. Street money changers are to be found on Plaza 24 de Septiembre and around the bus terminal.

● **Cultural centres**

Centro Boliviano Americano, Cochabamba 66, T 342299, has a library with US papers and magazines, also English classes and some cultural events; **Instituto Cultural Boliviano Alemán**, Junín 363, T 329906, library, films, language courses, etc; **Centro Iberoamericano de Formación**, Arenales 583, T 351311, F 322217, Casilla 875, concerts, films, art exhibitions, lectures, etc, worth a visit.

● **Embassies & consulates**

Brazil, Avenida Busch 330, near Plaza Estudiantes, T 336888, opens at 0830, it takes 24 hours to process visa applications, reported as unhelpful; **Argentina**, in Edificio Banco de la Nación Argentina, Plaza 24 de Septiembre, north side, T 347133; **Uruguay**, Moldes 436, T 329317, Monday-Friday 0900-1100; **Paraguay**, Chuquisaca y Ballivián, Edificio Oriente, T 36613, colour photo required for visa; **Peru**, Libertad 349, 2nd floor, oficina 213, T 368979; **USA**, Chuquisaca y Ballivián, Edificio Oriente, 3rd floor, oficina 313, T 330725; **Chile**, Calle de Mendoza 441, T 327907; **Britain**, Parapetí 28, 2nd floor, T 345682; **France**, Avaroa 70, T 334818; **Netherlands**, Ayacucho 284, 2nd floor, T 334485; **Italy**, Avenida El Trompillo 476, T 535873; **Switzerland**, Guatemala 245, T 349971; **Denmark**, Km 5½ Carretera al Norte, T 421816, Monday-Friday, 0830-1200, 1430-1800; **Germany**, Avenida Las Américas 241, T 324825; **Belgium**, Avenida Cristo Redentor, T 420662.

● **Entertainment**

Discotheques: *Doña Icha*, René Moreno 239, two blocks from the plaza, is a *Whiskería* with a 'pub atmosphere', recommended; also good are *Wall Street*, at Chuquisaca 113, and *Dalí Bar de Tapas*, at Beni 222, open 2000.

Check listings in the local press for discos and bars.

● **Hospitals & medical services**

Clínica Lourdes, René Moreno 352, T 25518. *Dr Pepe Arzabe Quiroga* has a clinic at Coronel Félix Romero 63, T 332970, he is a specialist in tropical diseases. *Dr Ronald Lee Firestone*, Rene Moreno 552, oficina C1, T 323091, the country's only chiropractor, very helpful and speaks English.

● **Laundry**

Lavaseco Universal, at Bolívar 426, T 327715, and Beni 747, T 327252, same day service; *Lave Rápido*, Pasaje Callejas 70, side street on Republiquetas, Plaza Callejas, self-service.

● **Post & telecommunications**

Post Office: Calle Junín 146. **Entel**: Warnes 83 (entre Moreno y Chuquisaca), T 325526, local and international calls and fax; open Monday-Friday 0730-2300, Saturday, Sunday and holidays 0800-2100; also small Entel office at Quijarro 267.

● **Shopping**

There are *artesanía* shops on Libertad and on Plaza 24 de Septiembre y Bolívar. *RC Antigüedades*, Bolívar 262, 2nd floor, has a small

Inca, Tiahuanaco and antiques collection, the manager also produces and sells good maps of Santa Cruz City and department. *Artecampo*, Salvatierra esquina Vallegrande, T 341843, run by a local NGO, sells handicrafts made in rural communities in the department, high quality, excellent value.

Los Pozos market, takes up the whole block between 6 de Agosto, Suárez Arana, Quijarro and Campero. It is clean and good for midday meals, the food aisles serve local and Chinese food, and is worth visiting in the summer for its exotic fruits. The market is open daily; beware of bag-snatching. There are plenty of smuggled Brazilian goods on sale, exchanged for Bolivian coca. *Bazar Siete Calles* sells mainly clothing, but food and fruit is sold outside. The main entrance is in 100 block of Isabel La Católica, also on Camiri and Vallegrande, past Ingavi. There is a fruit and vegetable market at Sucre y Cochabamba. *El Aventurero Caza y Pesca*, Florida 126-130, has absolutely everything you need for fishing, climbing, trekking, or arctic and tropical regions.

Books: *Los Amigos del Libro*, Velasco 37, sells foreign language books and magazines. International magazines and newspapers are often on sale in kiosks on the main Plaza, eg *Miami Herald*, after the arrival of the Miami flight.

Film: processing *ABC*, Junín 467 (and Casco Viejo local 5), top quality, 36 prints, plus new film, US$9.50. *Foto Relieve*, Ingavi 256, excellent processing, English spoken.

● **Sports**
Clubs: *Club Las Palmas*, 2½ km on the road to Cochabamba, has an 18-hole championship golf course and olympic-length pool. *Club de Caza y Pesca*, Avenida Argentina 317, T 35707, gives advice on fishing, hunting and safaris.

● **Tour companies & travel agents**
Exprinter, Avenida Busch 127, T 335133; *Magri Turismo*, address under **Banks & money changers**, helpful, recommended; *Fremen*, Avenida Cañoto esquina 21 de Mayo, T 338535, F 360265, run city and local tours to Amboró, Samaipata etc, also tours of the Jesuit Missions, jungle river cruises on the *Flotel Reina del Enin*, all inclusive packages covering the Che Guevara Trail and they run the *Hotel El Puente* in Villa Tunari (see also **Tour companies** in Trinidad, Cochabamba and La Paz for the addresses of their other offices); *Bracha*, at the train station, T 467795, open daily 0830-1230, 1430-1900, for rail tickets to Quijarro and Yacuiba and Empresa Yacyretá

buses to Asunción; *Anavin*, 21 de Mayo 208, T 352009; *Amazonas Adventure Tours*, Centro Comercial Cañoto, local 122, T 338350, F 337587, PO Box 2527, operates tours to Perseverancia, a centre for ecotourism and scientific research, in the **Ríos Blanco y Negro Wildlife Reserve**, in the far northwestern corner of Santa Cruz Department (see **National Parks**, page 72). Mario Berndt, *Kayara Tours*, Casilla 3132, home address Tapiosí 113 (near the zoo), T 420340, is highly recommended for tours in the high Andes and the lowlands; he is a professional photographer, is knowledgeable about culture, flora and fauna, and speaks English, German and Spanish. *Selva Tours*, Bolívar 262, T 332725, F 360471, for city and area tours, trips to Amboró, Samaipata, Jesuit Missions and gold prospecting, English and German spoken.

● **Tourist offices**
In Prefectura del Departamento, on the main Plaza, T 32770, ext 144, you need your passport for entry. They have a free city map; also a kiosk at the airport. *Guía de Santa Cruz*, published by Rede, is available in bookshops, it gives all details on the city.

● **Useful addresses**
Migración: España 383 esquina Seoane, T 36442/332136, Monday-Friday 0830-1200, 1430-1800, reported as friendly and efficient for a 90-day extension.

● **Transport**
Local Taxis: about US$1 inside the Primer Anillo, US$1.20 inside the Tercer Anillo, fix fare in advance.

Air LAB flies at least twice daily to La Paz and Cochabamba, also daily to Trinidad (book 48 hours in advance), and to Sucre, Tarija and Puerto Suárez. Aero Sur flies to La Paz (several daily), and daily to Cochabamba, Trinidad, Puerto Suárez and Sucre. For international flights see **Information for travellers**, page 312. Note that flying is the only straightforward way from Santa Cruz to Paraguay.

The international airport is at Viru-Viru, about 16 km from town. Information on 181; it has an Emigration/Immigration office, Entel office, luggage lockers, duty free shop, and an expensive restaurant. The bank is open 0830-1830 and changes cash and travellers' cheques, cash withdrawal on Visa and Mastercard. When the bank is closed try the AASANA desk, where you pay airport tax. There's a helpful Tourist Information kiosk in the Check-In hall, where English is spoken (free map). There's an airport bus which runs every 30 minutes to and from the bus terminal; 20 minutes (US$0.70). A taxi to town costs US$5-6.

From Trompillo airport in the southern part of the city, there are flights in small planes to local destinations.

Trains To Puerto Suárez, for Brazil see page 283; to Yacuiba, for Argentina see page 237.

Buses The bus terminal is on the corner of Avenida Cañoto and Avenida Irala, T 338391 or 340772 (taxi to centre US$1). Daily buses to **Cochabamba** (US$9-15, 10 hours, sit on the left for best views), many *flotas* leave between 0830 and 2030. The only Santa Cruz-Cochabamba bus not to take the lowland route is Cinta de Plata, via Epizana, leaving on Sunday at 1700. Direct to **Sucre** daily with Mopar, Unificado, Copacabana and Bolívar at 1700, 12 hours, US$13-17 (20% discount for students with Copacabana). To **Oruro** and **La Paz**, 16 hours, direct with Flota Copacabana, US$18.75, 8 a day (plus *bus-cama* at 1900, Monday, Thursday, Saturday, US$36, 19 hours). To **San Ignacio**, see under **The Chiquitano Jesuit Missions**. To **Trinidad**, several buses daily, 12 hours, US$5.80, all depart at 1800 or 1830. To **Camiri**(US$10-12), **Yacuiba** and **Tarija**, several companies daily; 26-32 hours to Tarija. To **Cotoca** and **Montero**, many colectivos and micros leave from outside *Hotel España*.

WEST FROM SANTA CRUZ

Two roads run west from Santa Cruz to **Cochabamba** (see page 250). The newer lowland route is the one used most frequently by buses to and from Santa Cruz. The other route, the old road, heads southwest to Samaipata and then across the mountains via Comarapa and Epizana (see page 251).

THE OLD MOUNTAIN ROAD

Though this road is shown as paved on maps, it is mostly dirt or gravel, with only the first 115 km out of Santa Cruz recently paved. The rest is full of pot holes with a washboard surface. There are occasional bits of the original paving scattered around, some about 100m long, others about 1m. Large sections have been swept away by mudslides and every 10 km or so there is a muddy gap of about 1 km, some of them on treacherously steep mountainsides. Nevertheless it is a spectacular trip leaving Santa Cruz along the Piray gorge and up into the highlands.

SAMAIPATA

Some 120 km along this road is **Samaipata** (*Altitude* 1,960m; *Phone code* 0944; median temperature 24°C). This peaceful little town has become a popular tourist resort, famous for its plant nurseries (*viveros*), experimental orchards, jams and sweet wines. Local *artesanías* include ceramics.

The **Museo Arqueológico Regional** has a collection of pots and vases with

---

Japanese settlers

Only 3 hours northeast from Santa Cruz you arrive in the heart of Japan – or so it seems – for the community of Okinawa is made up of Japanese immigrants who settled here in the aftermath of World War Two.

1 million Japanese left for South America, with financial assistance from the Japanese and US governments. Most settled in Brazil, Peru and Argentina but several thousand made their way to the eastern tropics of Bolivia.

The Bolivian government gave each family 50 hectares of land and the US provided machinery and equipment such as tractors, but life was very tough for the pioneer settlers of the community, now named after their original home. They literally carved an existence out of the inhospitable jungles. Wells had to be dug for drinking water and Santa Cruz was reachable only by a 2-day horseback ride over difficult terrain. But thanks to many years of hard work and help from the Japanese government, Okinawa is now a rich agricultural area producing poultry, eggs, wheat, soya and rice.

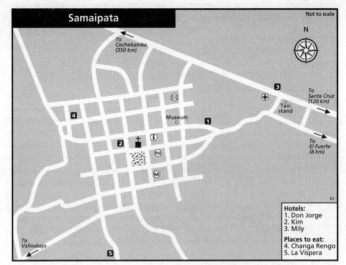

anthropomorphic designs, dating from 200 BC to 200 AD and, most importantly, provides information on the nearby, pre-Inca ceremonial site commonly called **El Fuerte**. The museum is open daily 0900-1200, 1430-1830; entry US$1.

El Fuerte is a sacred structure consisting of a complex system of channels, basins, high-relief sculptures, etc, carved out of one vast slab of rock. Latest research suggests that Amazonian people created it around 1500 BC. There is evidence of subsequent occupations and that it was the eastern outpost of Collasuyo, the Incas' Bolivian Empire. El Fuerte is 9 km from the town; 3 km along the highway, then 6 km up a signposted road. It's a 2 hour walk one way, or drive to the entrance; entry US$2. A round trip to the ruins by taxi from Santa Cruz will cost around US$40.

20 km from town, beyond El Fuerte, is the beautiful **Chorro de Cuevas**, marked by a wooden sign on the right hand side of the road. Head up a small stream along a path. After 15 minutes the path opens onto two waterfalls and lagoons bordered by sandy beaches and rock formations. It's a great spot for a swim.

● **Accommodation & places to eat** E *Don Jorge*, Bolívar, T 6086, shared baths, includes breakfast, clean, hot showers, good beds, large shaded patio, good set lunch; **F** *Mily*, T 6151, on the main road at the entrance to town, with bath, good value; **G** pp *Residencial Kim*, near the plaza, clean and friendly. *La Víspera* is a Dutch-owned organic farm with accommodation in three cabins, two of which sleep up to 2 for US$30 per night, the other sleeps up to 15 for US$70 per night, it's a very peaceful place to stay. There are several restaurants on and around the plaza, most of which are cheap. *Chancho Rengo* offers a wide selection but is more expensive. 7 km from town and 6 km from an access point for Amboró National Park (see below) is *Achira Sierra Resort*, cabins, camping, horse riding, sports facilities, restaurant, they can be contacted in Santa Cruz at Igmiri 506, Barrio Urbari, T 52256 Casilla 1020.

● **Transport** A 24-hour taxi service runs from Santa Cruz, at Calle Lemoine y Avenida Cañoto (T 335067), 2 hours, US$4 per person for four people; you can return by taxi or on any micro or bus passing Samaipata en route to Santa Cruz between 1600-1800. Many buses and micros leave Santa Cruz for Vallegrande, Sucre and other towns between 1600 and 1800, passing through Samaipata. Colectivos leave from Calle Tundy 70, near the bus terminal, 2 hours, US$3 per person.

A revolutionary life

One of the most enduring images of youthful revolutionary zeal is that of Che Guevara staring proud, implacable and defiant under that trademark black beret. It is an image that has graced many a student's wall. But how did this great 20th century icon come to die in a miserable little hamlet in the Bolivian wilderness?

Ernesto Guevara de la Serna, or Che as he became known, was born in Argentina on 14 June 1928 to wealthy middle-class parents. However, his eyes were soon opened to the plight of South America's poor during a journey around the continent on a beat-up old motorcycle (chronicled in *The Motorcycle Diaries*). He qualified as a doctor at the University of Buenos Aires but would dedicate the rest of his life to the fight for 'liberation of the American continent'.

He met Fidel Castro in Mexico in 1956 and together they planned the overthrow of the harshly repressive dictatorship of Fulgencio Batista in Cuba. This was finally achieved in January 1959, after an extraordinary and heroic 3-year campaign with a guerrilla force reduced at one point to twelve men.

Renowned for his strict discipline, Che worked tirelessly to create the ideal socialist model in Cuba as well as establish links with other, sympathetic nations. But his overriding ambition had always been to spread the revolutionary word and take the armed struggle to other parts. With this in mind he 'disappeared' from Cuba in 1965 to lead covertly guerrilla operations in the African Congo. Meanwhile, in Bolivia, conditions seemed propitious for a zealot such as Che to foment revolution there. In 1964 President Paz Estenssoro was overthrown by a military junta and in May 1965 the union leader, Juan Lechín, was exiled. This prompted a general strike and the military declared a state of siege.

Bolivia seemed the obvious choice for Fidel and Che to begin their mission to 'liberate South America', especially as it bordered Argentina. It had always been Che's dream to create a socialist state in his home country, but conditions were not right and would have to be prepared from neighbouring Bolivia. He left Cuba for Bolivia in November 1966, telling his small band of fighters "Bolivia must be sacrificed so that revolutions in neighbouring countries may begin. We have to create another Vietnam in the Americas with its centre in Bolivia."

After a brief stay in La Paz, at the *Hotel Copacabana*, Che travelled to the guerrilla base at Ñancahuazú, a farm 250 km south of Santa Cruz where they began their preparations. Things soon started to go wrong, however. Their constant movements aroused the suspicion of neighbours and the army were alerted.

VALLEGRANDE

At **Mataral**, where there is a gas station and restaurants, a dirt and gravel road heads south of the main Santa Cruz-Cochabamba road 55 km to **Vallegrande**, at 2,030m. The road is terrible in the wet and it can take up to 6 hours.

Vallegrande is a charming, unspoiled little colonial town in cattle-farming country. It has a Sunday handicraft market and several pleasant, basic places to stay. Here, in the hospital laundry, the body of

Che Guevara was laid out after his execution in nearby La Higuera. You can still visit the hospital laundry, now an abandoned shed behind the main building. It's an evocative place, the walls covered in signatures and slogans scratched into the peeling plaster. One of the most poignant is actually on the adobe wall of the public telephone office. It reads: "Che – alive as they never wanted you to be".

For information on Che, ask for Don Calixto Cárdenas, head of the civic

Knowledge of the guerrillas' presence became widespread and Che and his group were on the run from April 1967 when the army began looking for them. The government had outlawed the Bolivian Communist Party and its leaders had to go underground, so there was little hope of help from that direction. Furthermore, General Barrientos had waged a successful propaganda war against the insurgents, playing on the people's patriotism in the face of this 'foreign' invasion. There was, therefore, little sympathy from the Bolivian peasantry.

At the end of April Che wrote: "our isolation appears to be complete. Sicknesses have undermined the health of some comrades, forcing us to divide forces, which has greatly diminished out effectiveness". Che and his men were now very much on their own and worse was to come. One of his men had been captured and, under interrogation, confirmed Che's presence in the country, contrary to the CIA belief that he had been killed in the Congo. The USA immediately despatched a group of Special Forces to create a counterinsurgency battalion, the Bolivian Army Rangers, and stop Che gaining a foothold.

By August, Che was sick and exhausted, as were many of his dwindling force. On 31 August he lost one third of them in an army ambush. The army had enlisted the help of local peasants to inform them of the guerrillas' movements, so they were ready and waiting when Che and his men made their way slowly north towards Vallegrande, the Argentine now crippled by his chronic asthma and travelling by mule.

They reached the tiny village of La Higuera, where they faced the US-trained Army Rangers in what would be their final battle. On 8 October the surviving guerrilla's were trapped in a ravine. A prolonged gun battle ensued during which a wounded Che was caught while trying to escape. He was held prisoner in the village schoolhouse until 1230 the following day, 9 October, when the order came from Barrientos to execute him. Within the hour, Che Guevara was dead, at the age of 39. According to the CIA advisor who interviewed him before his execution, Che faced his impending death with courage and dignity, living up to his prophetic message to the Communist Tricontinental in which he said, "Wherever death may surprise us, let it be welcome".

A highly recommended account of Che's life is *Che Guevara: A Revolutionary Life* by Jon Lee Anderson (Bantam Press, 1997). Also recommended is a personal account of Che's travels in South America, *The Motorcycle Diaries: A Journey Around South America*.

committee. He saw Che's body in 1967 and is very helpful.

● **Accommodation, places to eat & services** F pp *Ganadero*, one block from the plaza, hot water all day, large rooms, tables and chairs, comfortable beds, great value. There are others, all **F** or **G**, on or around the plaza. There are two restaurants next door to each other on the plaza on the same street as *Hotel Ganadero* and several cheap places to eat near the market. There's also a branch of Bidesa bank.

● **Transport** Flota Bolívar has daily buses from Santa Cruz at 1730, 5 hours, returning most days at 0730 and/or 1300.

ROUTES There are two routes to Argentina from Vallegrande: one heads southeast, the other detours southwest through Pucará. The former requires the crossing of the Río Grande at the *Vado del Yeso* by boat. This is the scene of the ambush that killed part of Che Guevara's group. You have to arrange the crossing with the local fishermen. The latter route crosses the river by a bridge but is longer and the road is not as good.

LA HIGUERA

45 km south from Vallegrande is **Pucará**.

CHE GUEVARA

A daily bus leaves at 0800 from the market in Vallegrande. There is basic accommodation in Pucará and a market on Wednesday. From Pucará there is transport to the 'miserable little hamlet' of **La Higuera** 15 km away. Here, the Cuban revolutionary hero Che Guevara met his end on 9 October 1967. Che's universal appeal lives on, but the ultimate tribute is a new 'Che Guevara Trail', opened by the Bolivian tourist authority to commemorate the 30th anniversary of his death.

The trail follows the last movements of Che and his band as they tried to flee the pursuing Bolivian Army. The entire 815-kilometre circuit can be covered in 3 to 6 days. It winds its way along dirt roads in the sub-tropical area bordering the Santa Cruz and Chuquisaca departments. Tourists, whether Che pilgrims or curious backpackers, will be able to ride local buses to the battlegrounds where the Cuban-backed revolutionary brigade clashed with Bolivian forces.

The tourist trail ends near the airstrip at Vallegrande, where Che's body was dumped in a secret grave. The precise whereabouts of his final resting place had remained a mystery, until it was finally discovered in July, 1997. He now lies in peace in his beloved Cuba.

THE LOWLAND ROAD TO COCHABAMBA

The new road route to Cochabamba passes through the fertile lowlands to the north-west of Santa Cruz. It goes north through **Warnes**, where there is a statue of a man leading an ox-cart-load of bananas at the town entrance, then a further 37 km north to **Montero** (*Population* 30,000), where sugar and cotton are grown and processed. A non-stop shuttle minibus service leaves Santa Cruz bus station for Montero when full; US$1, 50 minutes. The town is named after the Independence hero, Marceliano Montero. The statue to him in the plaza is in the same style as the statue of Bolívar in Santa Cruz, the horse supported by broken cannon.

Just north of Montero the road branches west through Buena Vista (see below) and past the northern edge of Amboró National Park (see below) towards Villa Tunari (see page 252). Another branch runs east to the incongruously-named town of **Okinawa**. The name is not so strange when you realize that this is the main centre of Bolvia's Japanese immigrant community. The road then continues north to the first of the Jesuit Mission settlements at San Javier, though this is not the route used by buses (see below).

AMBORO NATIONAL PARK

Only 3 hours west of Santa Cruz is Amboró National Park, one of the last untouched wildernesses on earth and a place of special beauty. The 430,000 hectares park, situated at the extreme northwest edge of Santa Cruz's Ichilo province, lies in an amazingly lush and unique ecosystem area. The park encompasses at least three distinct major ecosystems: those of the Amazon River basin, the foothills of the Andes mountains, and the Chaco plain. Nowhere else in the world do three such vast environments converge, and nowhere else can you see so many diverse life systems.

It has been conservatively estimated that in Amboró there are more species of insect, bird, flora and fauna per hectare than anywhere else on earth, including numerous endangered species. Moreover, perhaps a third of Amboró's inhabitants have yet to be scientifically classified. Extensive botanical and zoological research in the area has repeatedly confirmed the park's unique biodiversity.

The area is one of Bolivia's first national parks, having been officially opened in 1973 as the Silvestre Germán Busch Wildlife Preserve. It is perhaps the best managed (albeit woefully understaffed) park in Bolivia, and should be at the top of every visitor's list. Whatever a traveller's appetite, it is likely to be sated by a trip to the park. Whether you want to see large game or whether your tastes run to rare tropical or Andean birds, Amboró has it all. Only patience and, if possible, an experienced guide is needed. More than a few first-time visitors to the park have discovered a new species!

The park is home to a huge number of birds, including the nearly extinct bluehorned currasow, the bird of paradise, the very rare quetzal and cock-of-the-rock and more common chestnut-fronted macaws, hoatzin and cuvier toucans. In total, 712 species of bird have been discovered. Most mammals native to Amazonia are also here. They include capybaras, peccaries, tapirs, several species of monkey such as howlers and capuchins, jungle cats like the jaguar, ocelot and margay, and the increasingly rare spectacled bear, the only bear found in South America.

Amboró will appeal mostly to those hardy souls who are at home in the great outdoors. There are numerous tributaries of the Yapacani and Surutú rivers to explore, as well as numerous waterfalls and cool green swimming pools, moss-ridden caves and the fragile yet awe-inspiring virgin rainforest. The best time of year to visit the park is during the May-October dry season.

Those wishing to visit Amboró should bear in mind that although access is relatively easy, penetration into the park's more remote areas should always be undertaken with an experienced guide or as part of an organized tour. Much of the park is very wet all year round and many

Paradise under threat

Parque Nacional de Amboró is both potentially Bolivia's greatest ecotourist attraction and ecological tragedy. Initially only covering 180,000 hectares, in 1984 the reserve was proclaimed a national park, and 6 years later was expanded to 630,000 hectares. However, intense settlement along its eastern borders led the government to establish the park's total area at its current size in 1995.

The government's action was seen by many observers as a concession to the illegal settlers, and led to vociferous opposition by conservation groups worldwide. Nonetheless, the 200,000 hectares abandoned to the colonists was designated a 'multiple use area', ostensibly free from rampant development and theoretically to be opened up only under strict guidelines.

The reality is far different however, and each year unchecked agricultural and mineral pursuits threaten the park's unique ecosystem. To make matters worse, Amboró lies between two of Bolivia's most heavily travelled roads, the old and the new Santa Cruz-Cochabamba highways, and is scarcely 25 km west of Santa Cruz itself. If encroachment is not halted soon, the entire area may one day fall prey to 'slash and burn' farming, its fragile ecosystem permanently damaged.

Hoatzin birds

of the routes are riverine or along poorly (if at all) marked trails. A good supply of food and water, insect repellent, a machete, good boots and long sleeved shirts and long trousers are a must.

The park's infrastructure is minimal: there are no hospitals, stores, telephones or any public facilities. Notwithstanding, a well-prepared 2-3 day trip into one or more of Amboró's ecosystems is an incredible experience. Keep in mind that most tours do not go beyond a week's stay and that great patience is needed actually to spot some of the more exotic creatures in the park. Particularly in the case of the larger game, nocturnal sightings are invariably more common than daylight ones.

Access to the Park

Access to the area is strictly by road. There are no trains or flights available, although there is a private airstrip nearby, with plans to fly visitors in late 1998. The vehicle of choice is a sturdy 4WD Jeep or similar model, although the routes to the main entrance are quite good. Despite its vast area the best entry to Amboró is almost always Buena Vista, to the northeast of the park along the new Santa Cruz-Cochabamba highway, which is asphalted.

BUENA VISTA

The peaceful little town of Buena Vista is where you can stock up on all supplies,

attempt to hire guides (which is not as easy as it seems, depending on the time of year) and/or join an organized tour group. You could also join a group expedition from La Paz, Santa Cruz or, occasionally, Cochabamba. There is a park information office in town (T 932-2054) which provides advice (but no maps), can hire guides for US$5-8 per day and issues a free permit. The town hosts a *fiesta* on 26 October.

● **Accommodation & places to eat** D *Hotel Amboró*, on Calle Celso Sandoval, just outside of town, T/F 932-2054, Casilla 2097, comfortable, horse riding, this is the meeting point for expeditions into the park, the owner Robin Clark runs guided tours of park. There are also a few cheaper *alojamientos* in Buena Vista and a couple of basic restaurants.

● **Transport** Buses leave Santa Cruz terminal (also minibuses from Montero) to Buena Vista (see Santa Cruz **buses** above).

Approach from Buena Vista

From Buena Vista there are three possible entrances to the park, all of which require crossing the Río Surutú first. As rainfall varies throughout the year, the crossing may be made on foot, in a vehicle, or by raft, depending on the season.

There is a daily morning bus out of Buena Vista whose route runs alongside the river for several kilometres (departure time varies so check in advance). The bus stops at all the entrances, but be sure to let the driver know at which entrance you want to get off if there are no other people going to the same place. The stops, in descending order going south from Buena Vista, are: **Santa Bárbara, Huantu, San Rafael de Amboró, Espejitos, Santa Rosa de Amboró** and **Las Cruces**. The third and fifth stops do not have entrances to the park. The most popular staging point seems to be from Las Cruces, as the trail leads directly to the settlement of Villa Amboró, just inside the park's perimeter.

There is an alternative entrance to Amboró from the north, via **Yapacani**, a town on the highway to Cochabamba. This entrance first crosses the Río Yapacani, then the Río Surutú and has a rough track that can be negotiated by a 4WD vehicle most of the year. It leads to one of the park's cabañas, **Mataracú** (free, take your own food). Buses leave from Buena Vista to Yapacani at 0800; then you can take a motorcycle taxi to the river, US$5, 1 hour. To return ask the park guard to radio for a motorcycle taxi.

Approach from the south

The park can also be approached from the south, via the resort town of **Samaipata**, off the old Santa Cruz-Cochabamba road (see page 264). But the going here is rough and a guide is highly recommended. Many travellers taking this route suggest first contacting the *Fundación Amigos de la Naturaleza* (FAN) office at the intersection of Calles Sucre and Murillo (T 944-6017) in Samaipata. They can offer accurate up-to-date information and will allow trekkers to use their radio telephone to contact the few park rangers in the area.

From Samaipata two approaches are feasible: from **Mairana**, 20 km west of town, and **Comarapa**, another 95 km west (see also page 252). There is a guest hut at the first site and access is somewhat easier. However, the Comarapa entrance leads to a more interesting, albeit hilly, section of Amboró.

Accommodation in or near the park

On the border of the park (in the multiple use area) accommodation is practically non-existent. There are a handful of cabañas, only one of which, **Mataracú** in the north (see above), can be reached by vehicle. All cost US$2 per person per night and are basically no more than rooms to sleep in, but they do offer privacy and relief from insects. Always enquire in advance at the information office in Buena Vista if they are available.

Cabañas Saguayo, **Agua Blanca**, **Macunucú** (reportedly the most popular) and **Semayo** are reached via trails from Santa Bárbara, Huaytu and Las Cruces repsectively. They are situated at various points along the park; none are actually in the park, except Mataracú. There is also a park rangers' campsite along the Río Isama that is usually open (US$2 per night) to campers. It has cooking facilities as well as rudimentary beds.

There are small settlements along the park's fringe in the area for development. These include **Villa Imperial** in the north, **El Carmen** in the northeast, and **Villa Amboró** and **San Juan del Colorado** in the southeast. No formal accommodation exists in these tiny settlements, but villagers often rent travellers a room for the night. Most of these settlers are at odds with conservationists and naturalists, so it is a good idea not to discuss the merits of the park's development.

THE CHIQUITANO JESUIT MISSIONS

East of Santa Cruz is the province of Chiquitos, a vast, sprawling, sparsely populated area mainly given over to cattle ranching and seemingly of little interest to the traveller, except perhaps those with a bovine fixation. But this is a part of Bolivia with a unique and fascinating history and a precious heritage.

Here lie the six surviving Jesuit Mission churches of San Javier, Concepción, Santa Ana, San Rafael, San Miguel and San José de Chiquitos, all of which are UNESCO World Heritage sites. The church at San Ignacio de Velasco was demolished in 1948 and is being rebuilt (see below). These are perhaps the finest examples of colonial religious art and craftsmanship in the country and will impress even those travellers who are not familiar with church interiors.

THE HISTORY OF THE JESUITS

The Jesuits first arrived in Lima in 1569 and were assigned to the religious instruction of the Aymaras on Lake Titicaca. Soon they had moved to Paraguay where they set up an autonomous religious state. It was from there that they expanded

Father Martin Schmidt

The majority of the Jesuits naturally came from Spain, but one of the factors in the efficiency of their methods was that many of the priests also came from the countries of northern and central Europe. One of these was Father Martin Schmidt, a Swiss musician and architect born in 1694.

Father Schmidt began his education with the Jesuits in Lucerne and in 1728 travelled from Cádiz to Buenos Aires. Later he travelled through Bolivia before settling in Santa Cruz. Despite having no formal training in making musical instruments, he made all kinds of instruments for the communities and even built organs for the churches. He also taught the Indians to play them and even wrote music, some of which is still played today on traditional instruments.

As if that wasn't enough, Father Schmidt also built the churches of San Rafael, San Javier and Concepción and the altars of some of the others. He even published a Spanish-Idioma Chiquitano dictionary based on his knowledge of all the dialects of the region. By the time of the expulsion of the Jesuits in 1767 he was 73 years old. He died in Lucerne in 1772.

northwards to the vast unexplored region of the eastern lowlands of Bolivia.

The Jesuits then set about the seemingly impossible task of converting the various indigenous communities to Christianity and persuading them to first build and then live together in self-sufficient settlements. These settlements of 2,000-4,000 inhabitants, known as *reducciones*, were organized into productive units, headed by two or three Jesuit priests. Architects, sculptors and musicians were enlisted to help construct the churches and communities. They also formed military units which, for a time, were the strongest and best trained on the continent. These armies provided a defence against the Portuguese in Brazil and the more aggressive native tribes.

Politically the settlements were ruled by the Audiencia de Charcas and ecclesiastically by the Bishop of Santa Cruz, but in reality, due to their isolation, they enjoyed a considerably degree of independence. The internal administration was the responsibility of a council of eight Indians, each of whom represented an ethnic group, and who met each day to receive the orders of the priests.

In 18th century terms the *reducciones* were run on remarkably democratic principles. The land and the workshops were the property of the community and work was obligatory for all able-bodied members. Nevertheless, the Jesuits' prime concern was to save the Indians' souls, therefore the indigenous customs and beliefs were suppressed. So effectively were Christian values imposed on the people that little is known today about the indigenous cultures of this region.

In saying that, however, the establishment of the *reducciones* brought economic advantages to this previously barren corner of Bolivia. Such was the success of the Jesuits' commercial network with the Quechuas and Aymaras of the highlands that a surplus was sent in the form of money to Europe as well as being used to enhance the splendour of the churches. These massive temples of ostentation were the biggest and most beautiful in the Americas, each one built by the Indians under the supervision of the priests.

The Jesuits also trained the Indians to become great craftsmen in wood and precious metals. They even taught them to make and play unfamiliar musical instruments such as violins and harps. Each settlement had its own orchestra which performed concerts and even Italian baroque operas. The orchestral music fascinated the indigenous peoples and was a factor in persuading them to partake in the Jesuit experiment. More important, though, in ensuring their full co-operation was the fact that those who formed part of the *reducciones* remained free from the system of *encomiendas*, whereby groups of labourers were sent to the mines of Potosí.

The Expulsion of the Jesuits

Despite the economic and religious success of the Jesuit settlements and the fact that they played a large part in limiting the territorial ambitions of neighbouring Brazil, in 1767 the missions were dismantled and the Jesuits expelled from the continent.

There were various reasons given for the Jesuits' expulsion, some of them less than credible. Basically, the Spanish Crown became aware of their influence and success in this part of South America and believed they had usurped too much power from the state. Furthermore, this was the age of enlightenment and the militant Jesuits were seen as a major obstacle to the progress of reason.

Whatever the real motivation, many of the settlements were abandoned and the inhabitants suffered the consequences. The priests who replaced the Jesuits treated the indigenous peoples badly, fomenting war and hatred among the disparate groups while prospering from the livestock that had been introduced to the region. Even after independence the exploitation of the local people continued during the years of the rubber boom.

The mission buildings survived this upheaval, partly due to the work of the Swiss architect Hans Roth, who has dedicated the last two decades or more to the restoration of the churches built by his fellow countryman, Father Martin Schmidt, over two centuries ago.

A TOUR OF THE MISSIONS

There are two possible routes to the Chiquitano missions. The first is by road from Santa Cruz east through **Cotoca** (see Santa Cruz **Excursions** above) to **Puerto** **Pailas** where it crosses the Río Grande and continues to **Pailón**. From there the road heads north, passing Mennonite farms, to **San Ramón**, 139 km from Santa Cruz, where the road branches northwest to **Trinidad** (see page 303) and northeast for 45 km to **San Javier**. Most of the road is paved but some of the unpaved parts are bumpy, because of the number of timber trucks.

The road then heads east, becoming increasingly more difficult, for 68 km to **Concepción** and on to **San Ignacio de Velasco**, 175 km and 4 hours from Concepción. Two roads head south to **San Rafael**; one via **San Miguel** and the other via **Santa Ana** (these three mission settlements are best visited as day trips from San Ignacio). A road continues east from San Rafael to San Matías and the Brazilian border. Another road heads south to **San José de Chiquitos**. From here you can complete the circuit by catching the Quijarro-Santa Cruz train back to Santa Cruz.

Alternatively, you could do the tour in reverse. Take the Santa Cruz-Quijarro train to San José and from there travel north by road to visit the other mission towns. There is an airstrip at San Ignacio, and there are flights once a week with TAM (see below).

You should spend at least 4 days on the mission route. The most interesting time to visit is Holy Week or at the end of July when many of the settlements celebrate their patron saint festivals. Tours can also be organized from Santa Cruz (see Santa Cruz **Tour companies**).

SAN JAVIER

(*Phone code* 0963) The small town of **San Javier** was the first Jesuit mission in Chiquitos, founded in 1692. Its church, one of the most striking in the region, was designed and built by Padre Schmidt between 1749 and 1752. The original wooden structure has survived more or less intact and restoration was undertaken between 1987 and 1993 by the Swiss architect Hans

Roth. Subtle designs and floral patterns cover the ceiling, walls and carved columns. One of the bas-relief paintings on the high altar depicts Martin Schmidt playing the piano for his Indian choir. The modern town prospers from extensive cattle ranching. There are many fine walks in the surrounding countryside, which is good for cycling with an all-terrain bike. A local *fiesta* is held 3 December.

● **Accommodation & places to eat** C *Gran Hotel El Reposo del Guerrero*, more expensive at the weekend, **E** pp with shared bath, includes breakfast, comfortable, T 0963-5022, or Santa Cruz 327830, restaurant, bar; **E** *Alojamiento San Javier*, including breakfast, hot water, garden, *artesanía* shop, good value, recommended; **F** *Posada Pinto*, clean, nice, one block from plaza. A few kilometres out of town on the road to Concepción are the luxurious *Cabañas Totaitú*, with pool, tennis court, and horse riding, they offer all inclusive packages from Santa Cruz, Sucre, Cochabamba or La Paz (3 days/2 nights from Santa Cruz costs from US$58 per person). The best restaurant is *Ganadero*, in Asociación de Ganaderos on the plaza, excellent steaks. There are others on the plaza.

● **Buses** Many buses pass through town late at night on the way to Santa Cruz and San Ignacio. There are also micros to Santa Cruz, 4-5 hours, US$4.85; several between 0700 and 1830.

CONCEPCION

(*Phone code* 0964) The hot, sleepy colonial town of **Concepción** is one of the loveliest and friendliest of the mission settlements. It boasts one of the region's most beautiful plazas, surrounded by covered sidewalks and buildings with red-tiled roofs. The buildings are ornately painted in the style of the beautiful church, which was completed by Padre Schmidt in 1756. It was totally restored between 1975 and 1982 by Hans Roth, whose team of European experts had to recreate the building from the crumbling original. The interior of this architectural gem is very fine, with an altar of laminated silver. In front of the church is a bell-cum-clock tower housing the original bells and behind it are well-restored cloisters. Hans Roth lives here and works with local artisans in the restoration of local churches. In the workshops near the church you can see the remains of the original church.

There is a lake nearby where you can swim and fish. Ask at the *Gran Hotel Concepción* for horse riding to one of the local *estancias*.

● **Accommodation, places to eat & services** B *Gran Hotel Concepción*, on the plaza,

Concepción Church

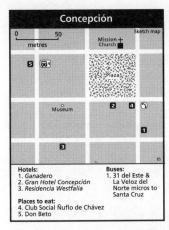

Concepción

Sketch map

0   50
metres

Mission
Church

Plaza

Museum

Hotels:
1. Ganadero
2. Gran Hotel Concepción
3. Residencia Westfalia

Buses:
1. 31 del Este &
La Veloz del
Norte micros to
Santa Cruz

Places to eat:
4. Club Social Ñuflo de Chávez
5. Don Beto

T 0964-3031, very comfortable, excellent service, includes buffet breakfast, pool, bar, highly recommended; **F** pp *Residencial Westfalia*, two blocks from the plaza on the same street as the Centro Médico, with private bathroom, cheaper without, German-owned, nice patio; **F-G** pp *Ganadero*, one block from the plaza, basic, clean, pleasant patio, shared bathrooms. *El Buen Gusto*, on the plaza, opens early, delicious *empanadas*, snacks, meals; *Club Social Ñuflo de Chávez*, on the plaza, excellent huge *almuerzos* for US$2.30, and breakfast US$1.15, seating in a pleasant patio with views of the church opposite, best value in the region. *Don Beto*, one block from the plaza, good *almuerzo*, popular. On the corner of the plaza is the Entel office. The private Centro Médico is one block away.

● **Buses** Many buses between Santa Cruz and San Ignacio pass through, about midnight. They drop you at the main road, several blocks from the plaza. Ask around at one of the restaurants here for transport to the centre; the locals are friendly and helpful so it shouldn't be a problem. Flota La Veloz del Norte and 31 del Este share an office opposite *Restaurant Don Beto*. Micros leave from here to San Javier (1½ hours, US$1) and Santa Cruz (US$5.80) at 0800, 1400 and 1800.

SAN IGNACIO DE VELASCO

San Ignacio (*Phone code* 0962) is a hot and dusty commercial centre lying on the main transport route east to Brazil. A series of wide streets of red earth runs from the busy market area down to a large plaza fronted by the church which is in the process of being restored. It was, in fact, a lack of funds for restoration which led to the demolition of San Ignacio's Jesuit church in 1948. The modern replacement contains the elaborate high altar, pulpit and paintings and statues of saints. A museum in the Casa de la Cultura on the plaza has a few musical instruments from the old church.

On the outskirts of town, down the road behind the church, is the artificial Laguna Guapomó, the source of the town's potable water. It is good for swimming, boating and fishing. The town hosts a *fiesta* on 31 July in the Casa de la Cultura on the plaza.

San Ignacio is the main starting off point for an overland visit to the **Noell Kempff Mercado National Park**. For a full description of the park see page 286 below. A mostly unpaved and very rough road runs 200 km to the north to **La Florida**, which is 25 km west of the park's only vehicular entrance at Los Fierros (see also **National Parks** page 72).

● **Accommodation D** *Apart-Hotel San Ignacio*, on 24 de Septiembre y Cochabamba, T 2157 (or Santa Cruz (03) 428613), with private bathroom, fan, includes breakfast, clean, comfortable, nice garden; **D** *Plaza*, with private bathroom, hot water, includes breakfast, fan, comfortable, clean, good value; **E** pp *Casa Suiza*, at the end of Calle Sucre, five blocks west of the plaza (taxi US$0.75), this small guesthouse run by Horst and Cristina Schultz is a real home from home, price includes all meals, very comfortable, twelve beds, German and French spoken, excellent food, they can hire out horses (US$3 per hour) and provide a packed lunch, Cristina is a former nurse and can help with medical problems, very warmly recommended; **D** *Palace*, on plaza, includes breakfast, fan, no single rooms; **E-F** *Guapamó*, Sucre, two blocks from the market and bus offices, pleasant, restaurant; **F** *31 de Julio*, on the plaza next to *Hotel Palace*, basic, clean. There are several other cheap lodgings.

● **Places to eat** There are several places to eat on the plaza, including *Pizzería Pauline*, good,

San Ignacio de Velasco

To San Miguel & Santa Ana

To San Miguel & Santa Ana

24 de Septiembre

To Lake

To La Casa Suiza (250m)

To Concepción

0 — 100 km

Santa Cruz

La Paz

Sucre

Cochabamba

Oruro

Hotels:
1. Alojamiento 31 de Julio
2. Apart-Hotel San Ignacio
3. Guapomó
4. Palace
5. Plaza

Places to eat:
6. Barquito
7. Cayoni's
8. Club Privado
9. Pizzería Pauline
10. Riabé
11. Snack Marcelito

Buses:
1. Flota Chiquitano buses
2. Trans Brasil
3. Trans Bolivia
4. Trans Velasco
5. Micros 31 del Este
6. Expreso San Ignacio
7. Micros to San Miguel, San Rafael & Santa Ana
8. Flota Universal (to San José)

US$4-5 per dish; **Snack Marcelito**, good salteñas, **Cayoni's Bar**, chicken and burgers; **Riabé**, on Sucre, is cheap and good. Also **Barquito**, on 24 de Setiembre opposite correos. There are plenty of cheap places to eat in the market (US$1) but think of your poor stomach. Entertainment seems to consist of karaoke night at **Club Privado**.

● **Useful services** Entel is two blocks from the plaza.

● **Transport Air** TAM fly on Wednesday from Santa Cruz, returning on Thursday; they also fly to San Matías on the Brazilian border. **Buses** From **Santa Cruz**, Flota Chiquitana leaves the terminal at 1900 daily, 10 hours, US$6.75. At least seven other companies leave, most from Calle Suárez Arana at the Avenida Uruguay end, en route to San Matías for Brazil; eg Trans Bolivia (at No 332), 2000, and Flota Veloz del Este (No 318), 1800. From San Ignacio: Flota Chiquitano daily at 1800; Trans Velasco at 1900; both from near the market; Trans Brasil at 2030 (office on plaza). A special tourist service is Expreso Misiones del Oriente which leaves from Avenida Virgen de Cotoca 235 (T 467878),

Santa Cruz, at 0800 and 2030; it stops in San Javier and Concepción for 1 hour to see the churches; it leaves San Ignacio for the return trip at 0800 and 2030, office on Calle La Paz near La Casa Suiza; there are also offices in San Javier (Avenida Padre José de Arce, T 5050) and Concepción (Calle Cabo Moreno sin número, T 3034). To **San Matías** for Brazil (see below), there are frequent buses Santa Cruz-San Ignacio-San Matías-Cáceres; Trans Velasco and Trans Bolivia leave San Ignacio at 0800 and 1800-2100, US$9.70 (the final 92 km of road from Las Petas is very poor). To **San José de Chiquitos**, Flota Universal, 1½ blocks from the plaza on the same street as Restaurant Pizzería Pauline (T 2198), leave Monday, Wednesday, Friday at 1100 and 1500, Sunday at 1000, US$6, 5 hours, goes via San Miguel and San Rafael. Micros to **Santa Ana** (1 hour, US$1.35) and **San Rafael** (1½ hours, US$1.95) leave from the market area at 1000 and 1700, returning from San Rafael around 1300-1400. To **San Miguel**, from the same place at 0800 and 0930-1000, 1 hour, US$1, returning at 1230-1300. There are no tickets on sale for micros to San Miguel and San Rafael, just turn up about 30 minutes before departure and hope to get a seat. A day trip by taxi from San Ignacio to San Miguel, Santa Ana and San Rafael US$35-40, but bargain hard.

SANTA ANA

The tiny, timeless village of **Santa Ana** has its unique original church on one side of a huge plaza where cattle and donkeys graze. Some of the houses still have palm thatch roofs. The church of **Santa Ana** was built in 1755 and is the only one in the region which has not been restored. Nevertheless, this lovely wooden building is in good condition. To see inside ask for Sr Luis Rocha who will also explain its history. Ask for his house at the shop on the plaza where the bus stops. In a sky-blue house on a corner of the plaza, the lady will prepare a meal for visitors and has a spare room for an overnight stay.

SAN RAFAEL

San Rafael was founded in 1696 and its church was completed by Padre Schmidt between 1740 and 1748. It is beautifully restored with frescoes in beige paint over the exterior. You can find accommodation at the pink house at the entrance to the village. There are two restaurants on the plaza and a public phone.

SAN MIGUEL

Founded in 1721, **San Miguel** is 40 minutes from San Rafael. Its church has been completely restored and, though it is similar in style to the other churches, its carved and gilded altar is unique. It is generally considered to be one of the most beautiful of the mission churches. The frescoes on the façade of the church, built in 1754, depict St Peter and St Paul and designs in brown and yellow cover all the interior and the exterior side walls. The pitched red-tiled roof blends in with the village architecture. The mission runs three schools and a workshop. The sisters are very welcoming and will gladly show tourists around. 4 km away is the Santuario de Cotoca, beside a lake where you can swim. Ask at *La Pascana* for transport.

San Miguel Church

● **Accommodation, places to eat & services**
You can spend the night here at **G** pp *Alojamiento y Restaurant La Pascana*, on the plaza, which is basic and serves cheap meals. Just up the hill, a few doors from the plaza is *Alojamiento Pardo*. Opposite is another *alojamiento*, and and a few doors up from there is the Entel office. There are a few other restaurants and you can throw a few shapes at the *Amadeus Disco*.

SAN JOSE DE CHIQUITOS

San José de Chiquitos (*Phone code* 0972), capital of Chiquitos province, lies roughly halfway between the departmental capital of Santa Cruz to the west and Puerto Suárez to the east. As the chief settlement between the two, this town of 12,000 people is the area's transportation hub, cattle-raising centre and oil exploration headquarters, as well as a convenient jumping-off point for tours of the Jesuit Missions circuit.

The town is in many ways reminiscent of Santa Cruz 50 or so years ago. Although it is served by both train and bus, with a partially-paved highway that connects it to the region's major towns, San José itself retains the feel of a dusty, frontier town, with its few unpaved streets, even fewer cars and no electricity between 0200-0600. This 'lights out' policy is set to end, however, with the coming of the Santa Cruz-São Paulo pipeline in 1999.

As with most South American towns, San José is centred around its main **Plaza 26 de Febrero**, with a statue of Ñuflo de Chávez, the founder of Santa Cruz. Scattered throughout the town are a number of concrete sculptures (some of which have to be seen to be believed), all of which appear to have been done by the same 'artist'. Clustered around the toboroche tree-lined plaza are the town's main enterprises and lodgings on one side and the Jesuit mission complex on the other. The other centres of activity are the town's railway depot, on the road to Santa Cruz, and the local market, a few metres up from the plaza on Avenida Monseñor Carlos Gericke. On Monday, members of the local Mennonite colony bring their produce to sell at the market and to buy provisions. The colonies are 50 km west and the Mennonites, who speak English, German, plattdeutsch and Spanish, are happy to talk about their way of life.

While hardly comfortable, the climate is at least bearable, and vastly preferable to the humid lowlands to the east. The influence of nearby Brazil is obvious, in everything from the bilingual signs in shops and restaurants to the items of food found inside, the vast majority of which arrive by train from Brazil.

The Mission Church Complex

Founded by the Spanish Jesuits Felipe Suárez and Dionisio de Avila on 19 May 1697, San José was the third of the seven main Jesuit missions to be established. The original church, erected in 1696, was replaced by the current one in 1748. This massive neo-baroque structure, although still incomplete at the time of the Jesuits' expulsion, was built entirely by hand by Chiquitano Indians with mostly wood and plaster.

The mission compound, with its unique exterior architecture and astonishing carvings, completely dominates the town centre, occupying the whole of one side of the plaza. It was declared a Patrimony of Humanity by the United Nations in 1992.

The stone buildings, in Baroque style, are connected by a wall and have a uniform façade, giving the compound an almost military appearance. The buildings are: the restored chapel (1750); the church, with its triangular façade; the four-storey bell-tower (1748); and the mortuary (*la bóveda* – 1754), with one central window but no entrance in its severe frontage. Weather and age have taken their toll and, as a result, restoration is an ongoing concern. At any given time portions of the compound may be closed to visitors. Nevertheless, even the more jaded sceptic or church-weary traveller will not fail to be impressed by the wealth of detail and superb collection of ecclesiastical paraphernalia. Those wishing to find out what's open and what isn't should call the rectory, T 972-2156.

Excursions

A worthwhile trip from San José is to the **Parque Nacional Histórico Santa Cruz la Vieja**, 4 km south of town on the old Santa Cruz highway. The park's heavily-forested hills contain much animal and bird life and interesting vegetation, including the aromatic guayacan and palo santo trees, as well as the ruins of the original site of Santa Cruz, dating from about 1540. It also contains a plethora of insects, so you are strongly urged to carry repellent. There's a *mirador* giving views over the jungle and, 5 km into the park, a sanctuary. Guides are available from the small village in the park to show you around the various trails. 2 km past the entrance, at the end of the road at the foot of high hills, is a pleasant waterfall – reputedly the source of much of the town's drinking water – that descends from a mountain stream, and a natural swimming hole fed by the waterfall's overflow.

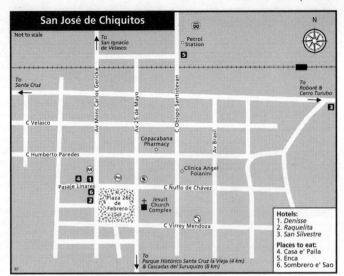

Entry to the park is US$2; open daily. The swimming 'pool' is free, but there are no facilities other than changing rooms. Take your own refreshments. The park and pool are best visited by car or taxi (roughly 1 hour) because it is a very hot, dusty walk there.

A second excursion is to **Cerro Turubo**, a forested peak east of town (the highest in the province) that affords an excellent view of San José and the surrounding area. Access is along the road to Puerto Suárez, although a guide is recommended as the trail is unmarked in several sections.

Perhaps San José's best kept secret are the **Cascadas del Suruquizo**, an easy 4 km south of Santa Cruz la Vieja National Park. Locals attribute invigorating and healing powers to these three waterfalls and their nearby springs.

Local information
● Accommodation
E *Hotel Raquelita*, on the plaza, T 2037, the best of the lot, laundry service, snack bar serves a good breakfast.

F *Denisse*, at the intersection of Monseñor Carlos Gericke and Pasaje Linares, T 2230, basic but

OK; **F** *San Silvestre*, opposite the train station, basic, good food.

● Places to eat
Restaurants offer a surprising selection of dishes, a benefit of San José's status as a ranching centre and its position along the rail line to Brazil. Prices, though, are as high as the standard of the food on offer. *Sombrero e' Sao*, next to *Hotel Raquilita*, with sidewalk seating under trees, highly recommended; *Casa e' Paila*, on Pasaje Linares, excellent food, also has *artesanías* for sale; *Enca*, along the road to San Ignacio near the bus station, also good. There are also several food stalls about the bus and rail terminals and a handful of dubious chicken-only spots near the plaza.

● Banks & money changers
The only bank in town is **Bidesa**, on Calle Ñuflo de Chávez (T 2130/2020), changes dollars, bolivianos or *reais* cash and travellers' cheques into dollars cash or bolivianos. Occasionally, stores or restaurants will change small amounts (US$30 or less), but it's best not to count on this. Dollars are accepted everywhere, but *reais* less so, and other foreign currencies not at all. Do not attempt to change money with anyone at either the bus or rail station, unless you really want to end up with less than you started out with.

Bolivia-Brazil border - Puerto Suárez, Quijarro & Corumbá

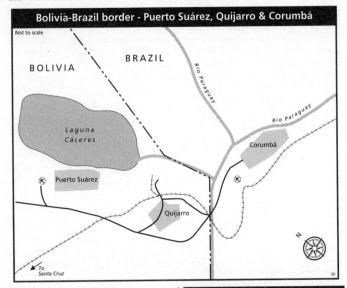

● **Hospitals & medical services**
Hospital Ferrocaja is across from the rail station, T 2091/2111. *Clínica Angel Foianini* is an eye clinic on Calle Obispo Santistevan, T 2094, it is run by a US-trained doctor, though he is more likely to be found at his Santa Cruz office. There is a pharmacy on Calle Jesus Chávez, T 2046.

● **Post & telecommunications**
National and international phone and fax at the local Cotas office on Calle Virrey Mendoza, one block east of the plaza, T 2000.

● **Transport**
Trains The times from Santa Cruz are as for Quijarro (see **Travel to Brazil**), 8 hours to San José, US$3.20 by Expreso del Oriente, US$7 by Tren Rápido first class, US$5 in second. San José-Santa Cruz trains leave about 8 hours after departure from Quijarro, but check the expected arrival time in advance. It is impossible to reserve seats on either service.

Buses To San Ignacio, Flota Universal, Monday and Friday at 1200, Tuesday and Saturday at 2000, from the station area. The route goes via San Rafael and San Miguel, 5 hours. Reserve your seat and check the time in advance at the company's terminal. The terminal is some distance from town; take a taxi.

TRAVEL TO BRAZIL

There are three possible routes to Brazil: one is by air to Puerto Suárez, near Quijarro; the second is by rail to Quijarro from Santa Cruz; and a third by road from Santa Cruz via San Matías (see below), with road links to Cáceres, Cuiabá and the northern Pantanal in Brazil.

On the Brazilian side of the border from Puerto Suárez/Quijarro is Corumbá and the southern Pantanal.

The populated area by the Brazilian border is made up of several towns which are gradually growing into each other: Puerto Suárez, Puerto Quijarro and Arroyo Concepción. Trade here grew because of increasing prices in Brazil during 1995-1996 and a *Zona Franca* (customs free zone) has been established in the area to encourage development.

PUERTO SUAREZ

Puerto Suárez (*Population* 15,000) on the shore of Laguna Cáceres, a large backwater of the Río Paraguay, was an important commercial port at the beginning of the 20th century, until a dam built by Brazil upriver reduced the water level of the lake and put an end to shipping and the town's prosperity. It is today a friendly, quiet, small town, with a shady main plaza. There is a nice view of the lake from the park at the north end of Avenida Bolívar. The area around the train station is known as *Paradero*.

Excursions

Fishing and photo tours to the Pantanal can be arranged more cheaply than on the Brazilian side, though tourism in general is still poorly organized on the Bolivian side. Stewart and Sandra Williams of *Tours Aguas Tranquilas* (enquire at *Hotel Frontera Verde*) offer air-boat trips along small tributaries of the Río Paraguay, which are not accessible with other types of water craft. You'll see lots of wildlife and there's good fishing; US$10 per person per hour (minimum US$40), US$150 to hire a boat for 4 hours, includes lunch and fishing gear, US$250 per 7 hours, maximum capacity nine, English spoken. Also contact Sr Roberto J Rodríguez, president of the Fishermen's Association of Puerto Suárez, Avenida América esquina Assis Abdalá, T 62778/62572; he has his own boats and offers fishing and wildlife watching tours at reasonable prices.

Local information
● **Accommodation**

Don't drink the water as it is straight from the river.

C *Bamby*, Santa Cruz 31 y 6 de Agosto, T 62015, air conditioning, **D** with fan, cheaper with shared bath, comfortable; **C** *Frontera Verde*, Vanguardia 24 y Simón Bolívar, T 62468, F 62470, best in town, air conditioning, **D** with fan, breakfast included, parking, helpful, English spoken; **C-D** *Sucre*, Bolívar 63 on the main plaza, T 62069, recently renovated, private bathroom, nice rooms with air conditioning, colour TV, includes breakfast, good restaurant.

D *Beby*, Avenida Bolívar 111, T 62270, air conditioning, **E** with shared bath and fan; **D** *Ejecutivo*, at the south end of Bolívar, T 62267, air conditioning, parking, cheaper with fan, comfortable; **D** *Roboré*, 6 de Agosto 78, T 62170, fan, **E** with shared bath, basic, restaurant next door.

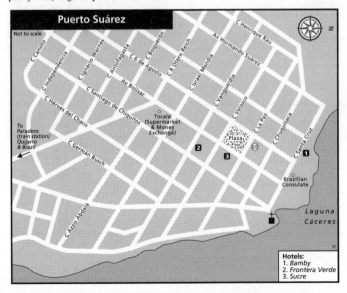

Puerto Suárez

Not to scale

To Paradero (train station) Quijarro & Brazil

Tocale (Supermarket & Money Exchange)

Plaza

Brazilian Consulate

Laguna Cáceres

Hotels:
1. Bamby
2. Frontera Verde
3. Sucre

E *Progreso*, Bolívar 21, shared bath, basic; **E** *Residencial Puerto Suárez*, Bolívar 105, shared bath, fans, showers, basic.

● **Places to eat**
Parillada Jenecherú, Bolívar near the plaza, grilled meats; opposite is *Al Paso*, Bolívar 43, very good value set meals and à la carte, popular; *Bolivia*, at *Balneario Los Delfines*, friendly, good regional food, also swimming pool; *El Mirador*, overlooks Laguna Cáceres, regional dishes including *piraña* soup and fried *jacaré*, fresh fish, very friendly owner; *El Taxista*, Bolívar 100 block, with several other small inexpensive restaurants nearby.

● **Airline offices**
LAB, La Paz 33, T 62241; *AeroSur*, Bolívar near the Plaza, T/F 62155; *TAM*, Calle del Chaco sin número, T 62205.

● **Banks & money changers**
Supermercado Tocale changes Bolivianos, reais and dollars, cash only. **Banco de la Unión** in Paradero is reported to change travellers' cheques.

● **Embassies & consulates**
Brazilian Consulate, Santa Cruz entre Bolívar y 6 de Agosto.

● **Post & telecommunications**
Post Office: on La Paz opposite the main plaza. **Entel**: on La Paz, three blocks from the plaza and in Paradero.

● **Shopping**
Supermercado Tocale, Bolívar next door to *Residencial Puerto Suárez*, has a wide selection of Brazilian, Bolivian and imported goods. There are several fishing and hunting supply shops.

● **Tour companies & travel agents**
Tours Aguas Tranquilas, see **Excursions** above; *R B Travel*, Bolívar 65 by the plaza, T62014, for airline tickets, helpful.

● **Transport**
Local Taxis: to Paradero US$1.65; to airport US$2; to Quijarro or the border, US$5 (day), US$6 (night) or US$0.80 per person in a colectivo.

Air The airport is 6 km north of town, T 62347; airport tax US$2. Daily flights to Santa Cruz with Aerosur and LAB. TAM flies to Santa Cruz, and continues to Trinidad and La Paz. **NB** Do not buy tickets for flights originating in Puerto Suárez in Corumbá, you will have to pay more. There is an airport immigration office where they will issue Bolivian exit/entry stamps.

Trains The station for Puerto Suárez is about 3 km from town. It is the first station west of Quijarro. Bracha agent, Bolívar 86, T/F 62577.

PUERTO QUIJARRO

The eastern terminus of the Bolivian railway is at **Puerto Quijarro** (*Population* 15,000), the gateway to Brazil, a town created around the railway station. To coincide with efforts to develop tourism in the Bolivian Pantanal, the town is struggling to improve its infrastructure and image. There have been reports of drug trafficking and related problems in this border area and caution is recommended.

● **Accommodation NB** The water supply in many hotels is frequently unreliable, so try the tap before checking in. Most people prefer to go on to Corumbá where hotels are better. **C** *Santa Cruz*, Avenida Brasil two blocks east of the station, T 82113, F 82044, air conditioning, cheaper with fan, **D** with shared bath, good rooms, nice courtyard, good restaurant, parking, highly recommended; **D** *La Frontera*, Rómulo Gómez sin número, five blocks from the station on the south side of the tracks, T 82010, fan, parking; **D** *Gran Hotel Colonial*, Avenida Brasil y Panamá, T/F 82037, air conditioning, cheaper with fan, **E** with shared bath, good restaurant; **D** *Oasis*, Avenida Argentina 20, T 82159, air conditioning, fridge, **E** with shared bath and fan, OK; **D** *Yoni*, Avenida Brasil opposite the station, T 82109, air conditioning, fridge, **E** with shared bath and fan, comfortable, mosquito netting on windows; **F** *Residencial Paratí*, Guatemala sin número, shared bath, fan, laundry facilities. On Avenida Brasil across from the station are: **F** *Alojamiento Urkupiña*, shared bath, basic, unfriendly; **F** *Residencial Ariane*, T 82122, shared bath, basic, new rooms with bath and air conditioning; **F** *Vasco de Gamma*, very basic, cheap.

● **Places to eat** The best restaurant in the area is in Arroyo Concepción (see below). Owing to poor hygienic conditions, the food stalls by the station and market are best avoided.

● **Banks & money changers** Bolivianos, reais and dollars cash are traded along Avenida Brasil opposite the station by changers with large purses sitting in lawn chairs. Rates are good, but beware of tricks.

● **Post & telecommunications Post Office**: in Puerto Suárez. **Entel**: at the south end of

Avenida Naval, for national and international calls, Monday-Saturday 0700-2300, Sunday 0700-2000. There's also a small office at Guatemala y Brasil near the station.

● **Shopping** A duty free zone is at Puerto Aguirre, 700m north of Quijarro. It's mostly electrical and luxury goods for Brazilian shoppers. Construction of a new, larger, duty free centre was started in 1996.

● **Tour companies & travel agents** *Santa Cruz*, in the hotel of the same name; sells Bracha and airline tickets, and organizes tours to Pantanal.

● **Transport Local Taxis**: to the border (Arroyo Concepción) US$0.40 per person; to Puerto Suárez US$0.80 per person or US$5 (day), US$6 (night). **Trains** See below.

BORDER WITH BRAZIL

The Municipality by the border is known as **Arroyo Concepción**.

Going to Brazil: you need not have your passport stamped if you visit Corumbá for the day. Otherwise get your exit stamp at Bolivian immigration (see below), formalities are straightforward. There are no formalities on the Brazilian side, you must get your entry stamp in Corumbá. There is also an office at the bus station which is usually closed. A Yellow Fever vaccination is compulsory to enter Brazil; have your certificate at hand when you go for your entry stamp, otherwise you will be sent to get revaccinated.

● **Bolivian immigration**
At the border at Arroyo Concepción. It's a blue building on the right just before the bridge; opens at 0700. Also at Puerto Suárez airport. Passports may be stamped at Santa Cruz station if you're leaving by train, which may avoid spurious exit charges at Quijarro. No money has to be paid to anyone at the border.

NB You can leave Bolivia at Quijarro when the border post is closed, but you have to return from Brazil for a Bolivian exit stamp.

● **Accommodation & places to eat**
The fanciest hotel on either side of the border is in Bolivia, 1½ km from the frontier: **L3** *El Pantanal Hotel Resort & Casino*, T 82089, F 82020, five-star luxury resort, air conditioning, buffet breakfast and airport transport included, restaurants, disco, pool, modern buildings on nice grounds, horseback riding, tours to the Pantanal and to the nearby caves. One of the better restaurants in the area is also here; *Pescadería Ceará*, 250m from the border, with excellent fish.

● **Brazilian consulate**
In Santa Cruz (see page 262) or Puerto Suárez (see above). A yellow fever certificate is required.

● **Banks & money changers**
Money can be exchanged at the Quijarro border; you will probably only be able to sell bolivianos in Bolivia.

● **Transport**
Air The simplest way to Brazil is to fly to Puerto Suárez then share a taxi to the border, US$7.50 per car. See **Puerto Suárez Transport** above.

Trains The station in Santa Cruz for the railway to Quijarro is on the eastern edge of the city on Calle Cochabamba at the Cuarto Anillo, T 348883. Take a Number 12 bus to/from the centre, or a taxi US$1. All trains go via San José de Chiquitos to Quijarro, from where travellers must go by colectivo to the border post (beware overcharging, fare should be US$1 per person), then by bus to Corumbá (US$0.50).

Expreso del Oriente Pullman (all first class, air conditioning, meals available) leaves Santa Cruz on Monday and Friday at 1415, returning from Quijarro on Tuesday and Saturday at 1700. Tren Rápido Pullman leaves Santa Cruz on Wednesday and Sunday at 1350, returning on Monday and Thursday at 1345. Tren Mixto leaves Santa Cruz on Monday and Friday at 1915. The journey is scheduled to take 22-24 hours. It is a mixed train with three classes: *Bracha* luxury coaches, air conditioning, US$22; first class – quite basic, US$8; second class – bench seats, US$6.50. Take food, drinking water, insect repellent and a torch, whichever class you are travelling in. From March-August take a sleeping bag for the cold. Be prepared for delays. Only men are allowed to ride on the roof. It is a monotonous journey through jungle, except for the frequent stops at towns, where the train's arrival is a major event, and for the company of your fellow passengers.

Tickets can be bought the day prior to travel; counter opens at 0800, but go early because queues form hours before and tickets sell fast. Take your passport. Tickets for *Bracha* (see Santa Cruz **Tour companies**, page 263), can be bought in advance at travel agencies. *Bracha* staff are very friendly and honest, they charge a 10% fee, but are highly recommended to avoid queues at the station. They also advise on transporting vehicles by rail. They have an office in Quijarro (T 0976-2325); and in La Paz (T 327472). At Quijarro station Willy Solís Cruz, T 2204, runs a left-luggage room, speaks English and is very helpful; he assists with ticket purchases for US$3 and has been known to let people sleep in the luggage room. The Quijarro ticket office sells tickets only on the day of departure; open 0700-1600, but queuing starts much earlier. It gets crowded, there's much pushing and shoving, and touts resell tickets at hugely inflated prices. Note that the times of departure from Quijarro are approximate as they depend on when trains arrive.

CORUMBA

Corumbá (*population* 89,585) is situated on the south bank by a broad bend in the Río Paraguay, 15 minutes from the border. It offers beautiful views of the river, with great photo opportunities, especially at sunset. Its climate is hot and humid (70%), the hottest months being September to January, the coolest June and July. It has millions of mosquitoes between December and February, but is a pleasant place nonetheless.

There is a spacious shady Praça da Independência and the port area is worth a visit. Avenida General Rondon between Frei Mariano and 7 de Setembro has a pleasant palm-lined promenade which comes alive in the evenings. The Forte Junqueira, the city's most historic building, which may be visited, was built in 1772.

Corumbá had thrived on tourism and trade until 1994, but high prices have limited both and much business is moving to the *Zona Franca* in Quijarro across the border. The combination of economic hard times and drug-running make the city unsafe at night.

There is a wide range of hotels and restaurants. All services are available, including money exchange, post and telecommunications, and there are frequent air and bus links with the rest of Brazil. The tourist office, *Emcotur*, is at Rua América 969, T 231-6996.

Corumbá is the best starting point for the southern part of the Brazilian Pantanal, with boat and jeep trips and access to the major hotels/farms. Many travel agencies offer tours, but visitors are advised to shop around and ask others who have been on tours for recommendations. The *South American Handbook* and *Brazil Handbook* give full details on trips to the Pantanal.

● **Brazilian immigration** Formalities are constantly changing so check procedures in advance. Passports are stamped by the Brazilian Policia Federal at their main office, Praça da República, next door to the Nossa Senhora da Candelária church, T 231-5848, open 0800-1730 (knock after hours).

● **Bolivian consulate** Rua Antônio Maria Coelho 852, Corumbá, Monday-Friday 0700-1100, 1500-1730.

BY ROAD TO BRAZIL

The road route from Santa Cruz is via San Ignacio de Velasco to San Matías, and from there to Cáceres and Cuiabá. See under San Ignacio (page 276) for bus information. **San Matías** is a busy little town with hotels, restaurants and a bank (Bidesa). TAM flies to/from Santa Cruz and San Igancio once a week; also Servicio Aéreo Pantanal daily from Santa Cruz (office at El Trompillo airport, T 531066).

SOUTH FROM SANTA CRUZ

A road south from Santa Cruz passes through Abapó, Camiri and Boyuibe. From Boyuibe a road runs east to **Paraguay** (see below) and another heads south to Villamontes (see page 237) and on to Yacuiba on the border with **Argentina** (see page 237). The road from Santa Cruz to Villamontes has been described as "a nightmare of churning clay and mud dug up by heavy truck traffic". (Patrick Symmes, New York). It is almost impassable on a bicycle.

CAMIRI

From **Camiri** (*Population* 20,000; *Altitude* 827m) you can head north to Santa Cruz, south to Boyuibe (see below) or northwest to Sucre (see page 228). The town is growing rapidly because of nearby oilfields.

- **Accommodation & services** As a garrison town it has several hotels, all **E/F** range, including: **E** *Gran Hotel Londres*, Avenida Busch 36, motorcycle parking; **F** pp *Res Chaqueña*, Calle Comercio, clean, good; also restaurants, bars (expensive) and a post office.

- **Transport** Emperador and Andesbus run from Sucre via Monteagudo daily in each direction, at least 20 hours, US$20. Several minibuses run from Santa Cruz to Camiri daily, US$10-12, 7-8 hours.

CROSSING INTO PARAGUAY

It is possible to drive from Camiri into Paraguay direct in a truck or 4WD high clearance vehicle. Make sure you are carrying insect repellent and enough food and water for a week. No help can be relied on in case of a breakdown. A winch is also advisable, especially after rain. There are some rivers to ford and although they are dry in the dry season they can be impassable if there is rain in the area.

- **Buses** Empresa Yacyretá run twice weekly Santa Cruz-Asunción; Tuesday and Friday at 1300. Their office in Santa Cruz is at Calle Cordillera 485, T 349315. Tickets can also be booked through the *Bracha* travel agency.

BOYUIBE

This is the last town in Bolivia before heading east to Paraguay (Km 519;*Altitude* 817m). It is on the regular bus route Tarija-Entre Ríos-Villamontes-Santa Cruz. Fuel and water are available here. It is also on the Yacuiba railway (see page 237). Rail fare Santa Cruz-Boyuibe: *ferrobus* US$13 and US$10; *rápido* US$5.50 and US$4.

- **Accommodation F** *Hotel Guadalquivir*, or **F** *Hotel Chaqueño* next door, both serve meals.

FRONTIER WITH PARAGUAY

It is about 115 km from Boyuibe to the Bolivian border post at **Hito Villazón** (manned by a Bolivian army unit). The road is very bad; it takes 3 hours by bus. You can camp at Hito Villazón, but no food is available, nor is there much water. Passports are stamped at the military

checkpoint here. If travelling by bus, passports are collected by the driver and returned on arrival at Mariscal Estigarribia, Paraguay, with Bolivian exit stamp and Paraguayan entry stamp.

750m after the military checkpoint turn left past a large water tower. From then on just follow the most used road. Accurate directions can be obtained from the army before leaving Boyuibe. If hitching, be at the customs post before 0600.

The frontier is 12 km east of Hito Villazón at Guaraní and the Paraguayan post is 10 km further east at Fortín General Eugenio A Garay. Camping is possible here and for a small contribution the troops may give you the use of showers and a kitchen. There is a military post, where water is available, at Fortín Mister Long, about 15 km, further on. "There are long stretches where the road disappears beneath ridges of soft dust; be prepared to spend many hours digging/pushing/pulling your bus out of the countless dust pits in 40° heat" (Simon Watson Taylor, London NW6).

Beyond Fortín Mister Long the road improves through Estancia La Patria, although even small amounts of rain can turn the highway to mud and cause long delays. Motorists should carry plenty of food and water. The airbase at Nueva Asunción, 95 km before Estancia La Patria, may give water, but papers may be inspected. At Estancia La Patria a Centro Urbano Rural has a motel (**E**), supermarket and fuel. Buses run to Filadelfia, which is the major town in the Paraguayan Chaco, via Mariscal Estigarribia, which has a large military base and where Paraguayan entry stamps are given (if you arrive after Friday 1700, you must wait until you get to Asunción, the capital, and report to immigration there). There is accommodation in Mariscal Estigarribia, but there is more in the way of services in Filadelfia, the largest of three important Mennonite colonies, 472 km from Asunción, 304 km from the border with Bolivia.

NOELL KEMPFF MERCADO NATIONAL PARK

In the far northeastern corner of Santa Cruz Department, Noell Kempff Mercado is reached by road from San Ignacio de Velasco. This is one of the world's most unique and diverse natural habitats, with a range of animal and plant species to match anywhere in the world. Its remoteness has not only helped to preserve this great biodiversity, but has also placed the park out of the reach of most travellers.

Among its wide variety of habitats is virgin rainforest, seasonally flooded savannah, Brazilian cerrado, gallery forest, thorn scrub, humid forests and marshes similar to the Pantanal. The wildlife count is staggering: so far over 620 bird species have been identified, which is approximately one quarter of all the birds in the neotropics. Blue and yellow, scarlet, golden-collared and chestnut-fronted macaws; over 20 species of parrots; crimson-bellied parakeet; red-necked aracari; Amazonian umbrellabird; pompadour cotinga; helmeted manakin; curl-crested jay; hoatzin and harpy eagle are just some of the species found within the park's boundaries.

Brown Capuchin monkey

The park is also abundant in fauna. Among the many large mammals frequently sighted are the tapir, grey and red brocket deer, silvery marmoset, and spider and black howler monkey. Giant otter and capybara are relatively common along the Iténez and Paucerna rivers, as are jabiru and maguari stork. giant anteaters, marsh deer and the rare maned wolf inhabit the western grasslands and the endangered pampas deer roam the dry twisted forest of the Huanchaca Plateau. Pink river dolphin can be seen in the rivers as well as the black and spectacled caiman.

Rising over 500m above the surrounding plain is the 3,000 square km Huanchaca Plateau, which is drained by numerous rivers and streams which merge to form the headwaters of the Verde and Paucerna rivers. Steep cliffs of 200 to 500m bound the plateau, creating spectacular waterfalls; Arco Iris and the Federico Ahlfeld Falls on the Río Paucerna are two of the finest on the continent. The narrow Río Paucerna winds its way through dense towering rainforest on its way to join the Río Iténez. Here you can see Jaguar and Giant Otter.

Since Colonel Fawcett's 'discovery', little further exploration was carried out in this area until 1979, when 541,000 hectares were set aside and decreed the Huanchaca National Park, largely as a result of the efforts of Noell Kempff Mercado, a pioneer of Bolivia's conservation movement. In February 1988, the Bolivian government changed the name of the park in honour of the notable scientist, who was killed there. In August of the same year, the park was expanded to 706,000 hectares. The park has recently been extended again to include all lands bordering the Paragua and Tarvo rivers. It now encompasses 1,600,000 hectares, an area the size of Massachusetts in the USA. For details on access see National Parks, page 72.

Those requiring more information should contact: *Fundación Amigos de la*

Naturaleza (FAN), Km 7 a Samaipata, Casilla 2241, Santa Cruz, T 591-3-524921/535426, F 533389, e-mail: fan@fan.rds.org.bo. For details on organized trips into the park contact: International Expeditions Incorporated, One Environs Park, Helena, AL 35080, USA, F (205) 428-1714, e-mail: intlexp@aol.com.

Discovering the Lost World

The first to discover the Huanchaca Plateau was the legendary British explorer Colonel Percy Fawcett. He discovered the plateau in 1910 while exploring the Río Verde and demarcating the national boundaries for the Bolivian government.

Colonel Fawcett was the archetypal early 20th century explorer. Disappearing into the heart of the Amazon on his last expedition in 1925, never to be seen again, he became almost as much of a legend as the lost city for which he tirelessly searched. His life of jungle exploration was an inspiration to many. It is claimed that Arthur Conan Doyle, who was a friend of the colonel's, wrote *The Lost World* as a result of a conversation about the flat-topped Huanchaca when he was shown photographs of the apparently unscaleable cliffs and imagined an isolated plateau inhabited by dinosaurs. (For a detailed account of Colonel Fawcett's adventures see *Exploration Fawcett*, published by Century, 1988.)

The Amazon Basin

BOLIVIA'S AMAZON BASIN accounts for about 70% of national territory and comprises the Beni and Pando departments. The northern parts of the region, near the border with Brazil, are covered by Amazon rainforest. But from the steamy jungles south to the Andes lies a huge, flat area of savannah, dotted with isolated patches of jungle. In the wet season, when the many rivers overflow, most of this region becomes a giant inland sea. In the dry season, however, it turns into a sun-scorched prairie interspersed with small lagoons bursting with all manner of wildlife.

This is pioneer country – home to missionaries, rubber tappers, loggers and cocaine refiners. It is also gaining a healthier reputation as a nature paradise. Thanks to improved roads to Rurrenabaque and Trinidad, the area is opening up to ecotourism and wildlife expeditions are becoming increasingly popular.

Beni department has 53% of the country's birds and 50% of its mammals, but destruction of forest and habitat is proceeding at an alarming rate. The Beni Biosphere Reserve was set up to protect the fragile environment but is one of only two preservation areas in the whole region. There are, however, plans to extend the country's protection of its precious tropical lowlands in the next decade and

The Amazon Basin

BRAZIL

PERU

Trinidad

La Paz

CHILE

PARAGUAY

ARGENTINA

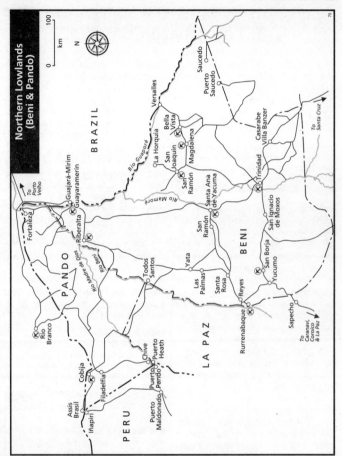

Northern Lowlands (Beni & Pando)

it is hoped that the influx of tourists will speed up the process.

ROUTES There are two main land routes into the Beni: one is from La Paz to Rurrenabaque via the Yungas and the other is from Santa Cruz to Trinidad.

CARANAVI TO RURRENABAQUE

From Caranavi in the Yungas a road runs north to **Sapecho**, where there is an interesting cocoa cooperative and a bridge over the Río Beni. Accommodation is available at **E-F** *Alojamiento Rodríguez*, which is very friendly and pleasant.

Beyond Sapecho, the road passes through Palos Blancos, 7 km from the bridge, with a Saturday market day and several cheap lodgings.

A good all-weather gravel road continues to **Yucumo**, 3 hours from the Sapecho *tránsito*. In Yucumo there are *hospedajes* (**F**) and restaurants. 550,000 hectares of jungle are under cultivation in this area, with rice, sugar, corn and fruit being planted. The local Chimane people are trying to survive the influx of settlers from the Altiplano. At Yucumo the road heads northwest to Rurrenabaque, fording rivers twenty-one times on its way. Another road heads east to San Borja, continuing to San Ignacio de Moxos and Trinidad (see page 306).

● **Buses** Yucumo is on the La Paz-Caranavi-Rurrenabaque or San Borja routes. Rurrenabaque-La Paz bus passes through about 1800. If you're travelling to Rurrenabaque by bus or truck take extra food in case there is a delay waiting for river levels to fall.

RURRENABAQUE

For many people, Rurrenabaque (or "Rurre", as the locals call it) is the jumping-off point for the many Amazon jungle and pampas tours now available in this once-remote area of northwest Bolivia, approximately 200 km northeast of La Paz. Situated on the banks of the Río Beni, with San Buenaventura on the opposite bank, Rurrenabaque is an important trading centre and transportation link for Beni Department. A rapidly growing town of 15,000, its status as a gateway to the Amazon has brought it some degree of prosperity, and many of its citizens are now involved in one way or another with the burgeoning ecotourist trade.

Rurre is an astonishingly beautiful place whatever your interests. Whether it is the lush Amazon jungle, the savannah-like pampas, or the sub-tropical lowlands, this is the logical starting point. In spite

Macaw

of the usually humid climate, the town has a charming quality, and even if your itinerary doesn't include one of the many tours around the area, just walking about the town itself is a unique experience. It is with good reason that the settlement is considered the most picturesque in the Beni. The only real drawback is the occasional flooding of the Río Beni, which rarely overflows its banks, but when it does the place becomes a real mess.

Unlike most Bolivian towns, the businesses, restaurants and offices in Rurre are not centred around the plaza (2 de Febrero), but instead are clustered together one or two blocks north along Calles Vaca Diez and Santa Cruz. Just north of Calle Santa Cruz a small branch of the river effectively divides the town in two. The vast majority of businesses, including the many tour operators, are south of the estuary. Both of the town's markets are above it: the main market, between Calle Avaroa and Anecito Arce; and the farmer's market, two blocks north and three blocks east.

Local information
● **Accommodation**

Most hotels in Rurrenabaque are safe, good and relatively inexpensive. Most offer laundry and breakfast, although only one takes credit cards and none has air conditioning (the better ones have ceiling fans). Travellers should be aware that the electricity suply is erratic, especially at night.

D pp *Taquara*, on the plaza, generally better than the others with more amenities, the only hotel which accepts credit cards.

E *El Porteño*, on Calle Vaca Díez, cheaper without bath, quite popular but charges more for what it offers than the others.

F pp *Oriental*, on the plaza, **G** without private bath, breakfast available, clean, friendly, recommended; **F** pp *Rurrenabaque*, one block east of the plaza, safe, cooking and laundry facilities, good; **F** pp *Santa Ana*, on Calle Vaca Díez, one block north of the plaza, cheaper without private bath, basic, cold water, laundry, pretty courtyard, recommended; **F** pp *Tuichi*, Calle Avaroa y Santa Cruz, **G** pp without private bathroom, kitchen and laundry facilities, fan, generally regarded as the best value, best place to make up tour groups, accepts travellers' cheques and may even change them. There is also *Hotel Berlín*, but the less said about it the better.

● Places to eat

For a town of its size, Rurre has a large number of places to eat. Though none is five-star or accepts credit cards, many have received favourable reports. The best known are *Illimani*, on Calle Comercio one block up from the plaza, serves excellent meals at reasonable prices; also good is *Heladería Bambi*, opposite the Flota Yungueña office at Avaroa y Santa Cruz, which is just as much a restaurant as an ice-cream parlour and a good meeting place; *Club Social Rurrenabaque*, one block north-west of the plaza, is also good and serves vegetarian dishes on request, its opening hours are erratic; *El*

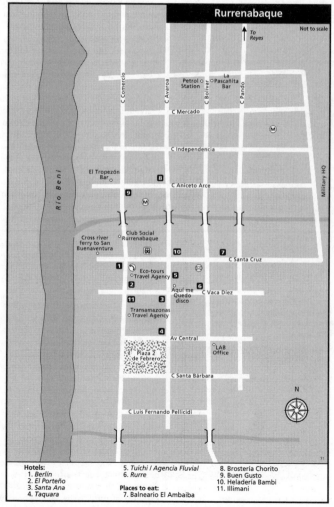

Rurrenabaque

Not to scale

To Reyes

Río Beni

C Comercio
C Avaroa
C Bolívar
C Pando

Petrol Station
La Pascañita Bar

C Mercado

C Independencia

El Tropezón Bar

C Aniceto Arce

Cross river ferry to San Buenaventura

Club Social Rurrenabaque

Eco-tours Travel Agency

Aquí me Quedo disco

Transamazonas Travel Agency

C Santa Cruz

C Vaca Díez

Av Central

LAB Office

Plaza 2 de Febrero

C Santa Bárbara

C Luis Fernando Pellicidi

Military HQ

N

71

Hotels:
1. *Berlín*
2. *El Porteño*
3. *Santa Ana*
4. *Taquara*

5. *Tuichi / Agencia Fluvial*
6. *Rurre*

Places to eat:
7. *Balneario El Ambaiba*

8. *Brostería Chorito*
9. *Buen Gusto*
10. *Heladería Bambi*
11. *Illimani*

Tacuara, next to *Ecotour*, is good. Other good places to eat are **Buen Gusto**, **Brostería Charito** and **Balneario El Ambaiba**. There are also plenty of places offering chicken and a handful of decent fish restaurants facing the canoe dock offer good cheap meals.

● **Banks & money changers**
There are no banks or *casas de cambio*. Hotels and some of the tour agencies may change small amounts of dollars. Travellers' cheques are difficult to cash anywhere, but try **Agencia Fluvial**, who charge 5% commission.

● **Post & telecommunications**
Entel: is on Calle Comercio two blocks north of the plaza, T 2205. **Post office**: is on Calle Bolívar. Both are open during lunch and on Saturday.

● **Shopping**
Apart from its picturesque setting, the town's main attractions are the excursions. Consequently, there's little to do except kit yourself out for these trips. There are plenty of stores selling all manner of highly-priced wilderness gear and trekking equipment along the river and in the main market. However, some of the more common items can be bought more cheaply than in La Paz: head gear, mosquito nets, hammocks and insect repellent.

● **Transport**
Air LAB has an office on Calle Bolívar. TAM also fly in and out of Rurre (US$40 one way); they have an office at the airport. Check flight times in advance as they change frequently, and expect delays and cancellations in the rainy season. Itemox Express flies from Trinidad to Reyes, 30 km to the north (lodging, restaurants), a useful alternative to the bus ride. A motorcycle taxi from town costs US$1.

Road To/from La Paz via Caranavi Monday-Saturday with Flota Yungueña and Totai, leaving at 0700, 1200, 1500 and 2100; 18-20 hours, US$9-11. Buses to Riberalta leave Tuesday, Thursday, Saturday and Sunday at 2330, 12 hours; they continue to Guayaramerín but it's difficult to guarantee a seat or to know when they will arrive from La Paz. Trucks also go to Riberalta. To **Trinidad**, Tuesday, Thursday, Saturday, Sunday at 2230 with Trans Guaya via Yucumo and San Borja; the road is often closed in the rainy season.

River Boats to Guanay cost US$16 per person; ask at *Agencia Fluvial* or other tour agencies. You need to take your own food.

TOURS FROM RURRENABAQUE

Visitors to the vast areas of Bolivia through which the many Amazon tributaries flow, and in particular to the middle and upper reaches of the Río Beni, will probably encounter the broadest spectrum of wildlife the country has to offer. Whilst other regions of Bolivia are also blessed with all manner of flora and fauna, it is the area around Rurrenabaque that offers the traveller the greatest opportunity to spot exotic and rare animal life. And unlike other, more remote regions of the country, the town is no more than 3 hours from the jungle, with easy access by river or horseback.

By the same token, it must be remembered that patience is a real virtue when it comes to sighting wildlife, especially in the Amazon with its elusive inhabitants. The traveller who allows only 15 minutes in the hope of seeing a jaguar or peccary in broad daylight will, inevitably, be disappointed. However, with a modicum of perseverance and luck, and a willingness to travel to the animals' natural habitat, you may be in for the experience of a lifetime. Some fortunate visitors to Rurrenabaque, including first-timers, have even made discoveries of species that were previously believed extinct or wholly unknown to science.

The fecundity of animal life outside Rurrenabaque beggars belief. In addition to the better-known varieties of caiman, fish, snakes, monkeys and turtles – all of which are easily spotted here – the observant visitor will not have much difficulty spotting their rarer tropical cousins, as well as a whole plethora of bird and insect life not found elsewhere. There are a vast number of armadillos, butterflies, deer, sloths, squirrels and tapirs that roam the area, as well as many lesser-known species: river otters and dolphins, ostrich-like rheas, giant anacondas and even the nearly-extinct spectacled bear.

Some of these creatures are nocturnal and are not likely to be sighted on day

Killer fish

The much-maligned piranha has a fearsome reputation as a frenzied flesh-eating monster who will tear any unsuspecting tourist to shreds within seconds of setting foot in a tropical river. But is this infamous fish really so bad? Or is it merely the unfortunate victim of some bad publicity?

There are over thirty types of piranha in South America but only one or two types are flesh eaters. Some feed on other fish and some are even vegetarians. The red-bellied piranhas, though, are real flesh eaters. These 20 cm long fish with razor-sharp teeth hunt in packs or schools in the many rivers that intersect the Beni floodplains.

They breed early in the wet season, when both sexes turn a black colour and the female is swollen with eggs. Then begins the courtship ritual, which can last several nights, as the female takes her time in deciding on her potential partner's suitability as a father. Once her mind is made up they mate and the female takes off, leaving the male to guard the eggs.

Although as many as 4,000 come from a single batch of eggs, only a handful survive the first few months. Their greatest test comes in the dry season when there is a danger of becoming isolated from the main rivers and food becomes scarce. The weaker piranhas then become victims as they fall prey to the stronger ones in a frenzy of cannibalism. Birds also join in, feeding on the dying fish. The fabled killer now has no defence against the elements. Those that are too large to be swallowed by the storks are picked off by vultures. Caiman also feed on dying piranhas, attracted by the birds. Piranhas are their favourite snack.

But when the rains come the savannah is turned into a huge inland sea and the tables are turned. The piranhas prey on the great white egrets which nest in the trees, attracted by the young egrets' constant pleading for food. In their desperate attempts to find more food than their parents can supply the clumsy chicks leave the nest and fall into the rivers where they are grabbed by the piranhas.

trips, such as the increasingly rare jaguar (or panther) and many varieties of deer. However, there are also numerous animals that keep normal office hours, such as the giant anteater, capybara, jochi, peccary and tapir. Flying overhead will be birds of paradise, parrots and toucans, while flying squirrels and monkeys flit from tree to tree. Into this dazzling array of fauna must be included the innumerable insects – over 200 species of butterfly alone – and rodents, as well as fish of every description, from the enormous Amazon sturgeon to the tiny needlefish. Outside Amboró National Park near Santa Cruz, and the Noell Kempff Mercado National Park, it is a safe bet that no other area of Bolivia harbours such a wide variety of wildlife.

Apart from the many trips offered from Rurrenabaque itself, two major parks are within a day's journey: **Alto Madidi National Park**, across the Río Beni; and the **Biosphere Reserve of the Beni**, less than 100 km east on the road to San Borja (see also **National Parks**, page 74). Both parks offer limitless opportunities to see wildlife in their native habitat and guides are usually available for hire in Rurrenabaque or San Buenaventura (for Alto Madidi) or San Borja (for the Biosphere Reserve). Another day's trip south along the Beni river will bring you to the isolated **Isiboro-Securé National Park** (see also **National Parks** and **Villa Tunari**, page 252). This would be an ideal spot for wildlife-watching were it not for the fact that it lies in the middle of an extremely

Wildlife of the Beni

The **tapir** is a shy, nocturnal animal which confines itself to an intricate network of trails in the forests of the marshy lowlands of Bolivia, Brazil, Colombia, Venezuela, Ecuador, Peru and the north of Argentina.

Water is essential for its survival; it drinks a great deal and is an excellent swimmer. It is herbivorous, eating water plants and the leaves and twigs of trees. Its only enemies are jaguars and alligators against which its only defence is to use its teeth.

Jaguars are the largest of the New World cats. Jaguars are great wanderers, roaming even further than pumas. Usually they haunt forests where they hunt for deer, agoutis and especially peccaries. They follow the herds of these South American swine and pounce on the stragglers. They also attack capybara. Unlike most cats, jaguars are often found beside rivers and frequently enter the water. It attacks the tapir as it comes down to drink and will even scoop fish from the water with its paws. It is referred to as the *tigre* to distinguish it from the ocelot, or *tigrillo*.

The **ocelot** is the next largest South American cat after the puma and jaguar. It inhabits forests and though its spotted buff-brown coat assists in hunting it has made it an attractive target for man. When left undisturbed it is diurnal, but becomes nocturnal in areas where it is hunted. Though it can climb it normally hunts on the forest floor, making good use of its acute sight and hearing. It preys on agoutis and pacas (which are large rodents), peccaries, brocket deer, birds and some reptiles. It has even been known to kill large boas.

The **giant otter** is found along the tributaries of the Amazon. It can measure up to 2m in length. They are active by day when they hunt for food, often in small groups. They are not rare but are rarely seen as they are shy and submerge quickly at the slightest hint of danger. They feed on fish, molluscs and crustaceans, also small mammals and birds. They can be tamed easily and are often raised as pets by some tribes.

The **capybara** is a large aquatic rodent that looks like a cross between a guinea pig and a hippopotamus. It is the largest of all the rodents at over 1m long and weighing over 50 kg. They live in large groups along the river banks, where they graze on the lush grasses. It comes out onto dry land to rest and bask in the sun, but at the first hint of danger the whole troop dashes into the water. Its greatest enemies are the jaguar and puma. They are rather vocal for rodents often emitting a series of strange clicks, squeaks and grunts.

Caiman are South American alligators. They are relatively small, usually growing to no more than 2.5m in length. They are found in areas of relatively still water, ranging form marshland to lakes and slow-flowing rivers. Youngsters feed mainly on aquatic invertebrates while adults also take larger prey, including wild pigs and small travellers. During the dry season when pools dry up caimans can stop feeding altogether and burrow into the mud at the bottom of a pool waiting for the return of the rains.

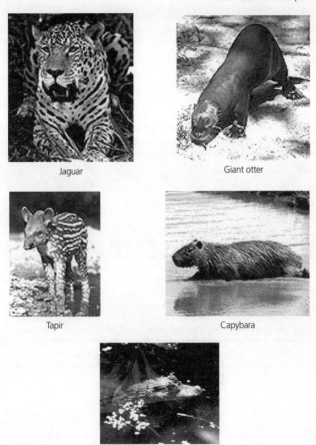

Jaguar

Giant otter

Tapir

Capybara

Caiman

dangerous battleground between anti-narcotics squads and narco-traffickers.

Viewing Rurrenabaque fauna need not be a solely river-based experience. Although many trips do start by canoe and travel the Río Beni, there are also horseback expeditions and even treks on foot. The roads around Rurrenabaque are not ideally suited for animal watching, though. A 4WD is needed at all times and with the exception of the more common types

of monkeys, rabbits, squirrels, snakes and the occasional badger or capybara, little wildlife will be found within eye or earshot of a road in any case.

The area around Rurrenabaque may sound like a tropical paradise, but certain precautions should always be taken. Travellers coming here should note that insect repellent is an absolute necessity at any time of year, and that the jungle during the rainy season (January-March) can be a miserable experience even under the best of conditions. Finally, patience and respect are the most valuable commodities to bring with you. Spotting elusive and rare animals takes time. Responsible ecotourism – in this case a healthy respect for the jungle and lowlands about the town, and their animal inhabitants – will ensure that future travellers have the opportunity to see one of the world's last great wilderness areas in a relatively intact state and possibly help to reverse the damaging direction in which many of Bolivia's pristine wildlife environments are headed.

NB The basic rules of thumb are to avoid trips during the rainy season; the humidity and insects will conspire to annoy even the most enthusiastic adventurer, and there are far fewer animals to be seen.

The debonnaire dolphin

One of the most bizarre examples of the wide diversity of flora and fauna in the Bolivian Amazon is a strange, prehistoric-looking mammal which can transform itself into a suave gentleman in a white linen suit.

Or so local legend would have it. But the Amazonian river dolphin is a strange creature indeed. Part myth, part real, this beast can change its skin colour from a pale grey to a bright, luminescent pink. The indigenous people of the Amazon rainforest have long revered what they call the *bufeo*, and even today, unwanted pregnancies within Indian communities are sometimes blamed on this magical animal with an impressive line in seduction techniques.

Stories about the *bufeo* have been passed down from generation to generation. One such tale is of an underwater city where the *bufeo* walk on pavements made from turtle shells and lie in hammocks strung from anacondas. While the more formal and elegant white suit is donned when in human form, underwater they prefer the casual look and lounge around in catfish shorts and stingray hats.

Another common belief serves to protect the dolphins from being hunted by local fishermen. This stems from the analogy between dolphins and witchdoctors. The *bufeo* can be a malevolent creature, if hunted, and will avenge the death of one of their own. To kill a dolphin, then, is the same as killing a powerful witchdoctor, with the same inevitable consequences.

These pink river dolphins were, until recently, a forgotten species, considered extinct. All that remained was the skeleton of one in Paris, brought back from South America as a gift to Napoleon, and a few vague scientific papers dating from the 19th century in the Natural History Museum in London. The *bufeo* was rediscovered by a British expedition in 1956, but then forgotten again. In 1987, however, Jacques Cousteau astounded TV viewers around the world with the first ever pictures of pink dolphins frolicking in the waters of the Amazon.

Now visitors to the Río Beni can see the *bufeo* in the flesh – be it grey or pink, or even dressed in a white suit. But women travellers should beware any charming, smartly-dressed gentlemen in these parts.

One-day trips are reportedly a waste of time as it takes 3 hours to reach the jungle. You see far more wildlife on a pampas tour and the weather and general conditions are far more pleasant. The best season is from July to October. Take swimming costume, insect repellent to ward off sandflies and mosquitoes and a camera.

TOUR AGENCIES

Many tour agencies have set up recently to take advantage of Rurrenabaque's growing popularity. Anyone wanting to join a tour should investigate carefully what the various companies are offering. The state of Bolivian ecotourism has improved dramatically over the past few years, but advance preparation is still necessary. Most agencies in Rurre have received good reports but you should still ask around and compare prices. Hotels often have good advice on which companies are best for particular tours.

Note also that not all trips offer English-speaking guides and that accommodation is spartan (bring plenty of insect repellent, mosquito netting, toilet paper etc). Finally, always set the price in advance and make sure it includes all expenses.

● Recommended agencies

Agencia Fluvial, at *Hotel Tuichi*, the longest running outfit, run by Tico Tudela whose wife Eli runs the hotel. They offer jungle tours on the Río Tuichi, normally 4 days, but shorter by arrangement, for a group of five or more, US$25 per person per day (payable in dollars) including food, transport and mosquito nets. 3 nights are spent in the jungle, learning about plants, survival and the foods of the region. Fluvial also run 3-day 'Pampas Tours' on a boat to Río Yacuma, US$30 per person per day. Fluvial tours can be arranged through *Hotel Tuichi*. Tico Tudela has opened *Hotel de la Pampa* near Lago Bravo, 2½ hours from Rurrenabaque. It's a base for visiting Lago Rogaguo (birds) and Río Yacuma (anacondas, monkeys, caiman, capybara, pink dolphins, etc). Fully inclusive tours (including meals and accommodation) cost US$40 per person per day.

Another recommended agency is Nahama Tours, at Avenida Santa Cruz y Avaroa, or through Hotel Santa Ana. Run by Leo Jancke, they charge US$30 per person per day for pampas tours and US$25 per person per day for jungle tours.

Pampas and jungle tours are also available with *Eco-tours*, opposite *Hotel Berlin* on Calle Comercio. It is run by the five Mamani brothers; they charge US$30 per person per day for the pampas and US$25 per person per day for the jungle. They also specialize in environmentally sound tours of 4 or more days, although 2 and 3-day tours can be arranged. Both the above agencies also run longer trips of up to 1 month for the more serious adventurer. **NB** in late 1997 we receieved reports of problems involving women travellers: check carefully with returning tourists and be especially careful if told the company has been temporarily closed down at any time in the past.

ROUTES From Rurrenabaque an all-weather road leads via **Santa Rosa** to **Riberalta**. In Santa Rosa there is accommodation at **F** *Hotel Oriental*, which will change dollars, and a good place to eat is the friendly and recommended *Restaurant and Confitería El Triángulo*.

RIBERALTA

The charming town of Riberalta (*Population* 60,000; *Altitude* 175m) is at the confluence of the Madre de Dios and Beni rivers, which together flow into the Mamoré north of Guayaramerín. It is in the very far northern reaches of the Beni and well off the beaten track. The town is also very laid back, a kind of Bolivian version of Gabriel García Márquez' Macondo. If you want to fit in with everyone else then you should hire a motorcycle from one of the agencies on the plaza.

The whole region attained temporary importance during the natural-rubber boom of the late 19th century. But this collapsed, as it did throughout South America, in the second decade of the 20th century when cheaper Asian rubber cornered the world market. It is now the centre for brazil nut production. An area encompassed by Riberalta, Tumi-Chucua (see below), Cachuela Esperanza 98 km to the northeast, and Villa Bella a further 32 km northeast, is in fact known as the *triángulo de la goma y castaña* (rubber and nut triangle). This is one of the least discovered parts of the Bolivia Amazon but as such has practically no tourist infrastructure and is only for the hardiest and most experienced of travellers.

Some 25 km away is **Tumi-Chucua** situated on a lovely lake where you can swim. Nearby are the Nature Gardens. You can also fish in the lake, and the area is good for birdwatching. They also have lots of information on the rainforest, the rubber boom and brazil nut production. For further information, contact Dr Willy Noack, T/F (591) 3 522497, e-mail: Tumi-Chucua@netmail.tfnet.org. Website: http://www.bolivianet.com/tumi-chucua.

Local information
● Accommodation
Ask for a fan and check the water supply.

C-D *Hostal Tahuamanu*, M Hanicke 75, T 8006, modern, smart, very comfortable, air conditioning, includes excellent breakfast, highly recommended.

E *Residencial Los Reyes*, near the airport, with fan, safe, pleasant but noisy disco nearby on Saturday and Sunday; **E-F** *Colonial*, Plácido Méndez 1, charming colonial casona, large, well-furnished rooms, nice gardens and courtyard, comfortable, good beds, helpful owners, highly recommended.

F pp *Comercial Lazo*, Calle NG Salvatierra, **D** with air conditioning, comfortable, laundry facilities, good value; **F-G** *Residencial El Pauro*, Salvatierra 157, basic, shared baths, good café.

Two recommended hotels, for which we don't have prices are *Bajio*, on the banks of the river, and *Las Palmeras*.

● Places to eat
Club Social Progreso, on the plaza, good value *almuerzo*, excellent fish; next door is *Tom Bowles*, good food and good meeting place; *Club Social Riberalta*, on Maldonado, good *almuerzo* US$3.50, smart dress only; *Quatro Ases*, Calle Arce, good; *Tucunare*, M Chávez Martínez, recommended; *Tropical*, nice atmosphere, good typical food. You can get a good lunch at the *comedor popular* in the market for US$1.50.

● Banks & money changers
Banco Internacional de Desarollo (Bidesa) on Maldonado, changes cash and travellers' cheques for dollars or bolivianos. You can also change cash in shops and on the street.

● Transport
Air Aero Sur, on the plaza (T 2798), flies six times weekly to Trinidad. Expect delays in the wet season. LAB fly to Guayaramerín, Trinidad, La Paz, Cobija and Cochabamba; their office is at M Chávez 77, T 2239. TAM flies to Cochabamba, Santa Cruz and La Paz (US$98 one way); their office is at Avenida Suárez Chuquisaca, T 2646. Check all flight details in advance.

Road Several companies (including Yungueña) go to La Paz, via Rurrenabaque and Caranavi Tuesday-Saturday at 1100, also Tuesday, Thursday and Saturday at 1000; US$19.50. To Trinidad with 8 de Diciembre on Monday, Wednesday, Thursday, Saturday and Sunday at 0830, also Trans Guaya daily at 0930, via Rurrenabaque. To Guayaramerín, twelve weekly services on Tuesday, Thursday, Saturday and Sunday at 0630, 1400 and 1700; daily with TransAmazonas at 0730 and 1630. To Cobija on Wednesday, Friday and Saturday at 0900 with 8 de Diciembre; Monday and Thursday at 1000 with TransAmazonas. Buses stop in Santa Rosa for meals.

River Cargo boats carry passengers along the Río Madre de Dios, but they are infrequent. There are not many boats to Rurrenabaque.

GUAYARAMERIN

From Riberalta the road continues east, crossing the Río Yata before reaching **Guayaramerín**, a cheerful, prosperous little town (*Population* 35,000; *Phone code* 0855) on the bank of the Río Mamoré, opposite the Brazilian town of Guajará-Mirim. It has an important *Zona Libre*. Passage between the two towns is unrestricted. The boat trip across the river costs US$1.65 (more at night).

Local information
● Accommodation
Outside Guayaramerín in nearby Cachuela Esperanza is the eco-friendly **B** *Esperanza*, Casilla 171, reserve through Aero Sur, T 2201, or in La Paz *American Tours*, T 374204, F 328584, price includes breakfast.

C *San Carlos*, 6 de Agosto, four blocks from port, T 2152/3, with air conditioning (**D** without), hot showers, changes dollars cash, travellers' cheques and reais, swimming pool, reasonable restaurant.

E *Santa Ana*, 25 de Mayo, **F** without bath, close to airport, recommended.

F pp *Litoral*, on 25 de Mayo, near the LAB office, cold water only, free coffee, recommended; **F** *Plaza Anexo*, on Plaza, good value, cold water only, ceiling fan.

● **Places to eat**

All on the plaza are: *Made in Brazil*, good coffee; *Gipssy*, good *almuerzo*; *Los Bibosis*, popular with visiting Brazilians. *Only*, at 25 de Mayo y Beni, serves a good *almuerzo* for US$2.50, plus Chinese. On the road to the airport is the excellent *Heladería Tutti-Frutti*.

● **Transport**

Air Aero Sur, on the plaza (T 2493) to Trinidad. LAB flies to Trinidad, Riberalta, La Paz, Cobija and Cochabamba; office on 25 de Mayo, T 2040. TAM flies to Cochabamba, Santa Cruz and La Paz; office at 16 de Julio on the road to the airport.

Buses To/from **La Paz**, Flota Yungueña, five a week, 36 hours, US$21.50. To **Riberalta**, 2 hours, US$5.75, seven departures daily 0700-1730. To **Trinidad**, on Friday, 30 hours, US$23. To **Rurrenabaque**, US$16. To **Cobija**, four a week. To **Santa Cruz** via Trinidad, one-two a week, 2½ days. Buses leave from General Federico Román. Roads to all destinations are very difficult in the wet season; the roads are generally appalling.

River Check the notice of boats leaving port on the Port Captain's board, prominently displayed near the immigration post on the river's bank. Boats up the Mamoré to Trinidad are fairly frequent – a 3-day wait at the most.

FRONTIER WITH BRAZIL

● **Bolivian immigration**

Avenida Costanera near the port; open 0800-1100, 1400-1800. Passports must be stamped here when leaving, or entering Bolivia.

Entering Bolivia: passports must be stamped at the Bolivian consulate in Guajará-Mirim.

● **Brazilian consulate**

On 24 de Septiembre, Guayaramerín, open 1100-1300; visas for entering Brazil are given here.

● **Banks & money changers**

Exchange money here as this is very difficult in the State of Rondônia in Brazil. Travellers' cheques can be changed at 2% commission in Bidesa bank on the plaza.

COBIJA

At the extreme northwest of Bolivia sits the hot, steamy and languid town of **Cobija**, capital of Pando, the country's newest department. Roughly 500 km northwest of La Paz, and until recently accessible only by air or river, Cobija is situated on a bend of the Río Acre which forms the frontier with Brazil. It is also only 40 km east of the border with Perú.

Founded in 1906 as Bahía, Cobija was settled during the rubber boom then sweeping the area. As production declined, however, so did town's importance. Although the largest town in Pando, it remains a quiet, humid outpost whose chief importance is as a transportation centre and processor of tropical fruits and nuts. Consequently, there is little to see or do here, although it can provide a decent stop-over for Amazon-bound travellers.

In spite of its general lacklustre aura, Cobija has received a disproportionate amount of national and even international aid over the past decade or so. In recent years, for instance, a modern brazil nut processing plant has been built on the outskirts, an impressive hospital has been built and the town boasts two airports, one of which has international status (though it is used only in the rainy season). Though Cobija has done little to exploit its natural draw as an ecotourism spot or its proximity to the Amazonian rivers, and the borders with Brazil and Peru, it should be remembered that the

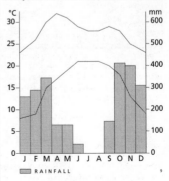

Climate: Cobija

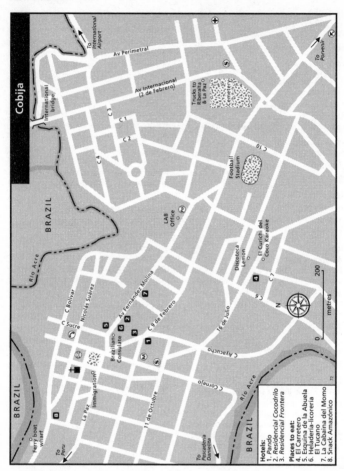

Cobija

Trucks to Riberalta & La Paz

Football Stadium

LAB Office

El Curichi del Coco Karaoke

Discoteca Lemon

Brazilian Consulate

Immigration

Ferry boat wharf

Hotels:
1. Pando
2. Residencial Cocodrilo
3. Residencial Frontera

Places to eat:
4. Carretero
5. Esquina de la Abuela
6. Heladería-licorería
7. El Tucano
8. La Cabaña del Momo
9. Snack Amazónico

city is the wettest place in all Bolivia. It receives more than 1,770 mm of rain annually, a statistic which does little to endear it to tourists.

Unlike most Bolivian towns, Cobija does not follow a standard street grid but has a number of roads that meander through the town. It does have a main plaza and most of the main buildings are located around it, such as the church which has interesting primitive artwork. Scattered around the centre are a few original wooden buildings, constructed during the rubber boom. Most have long since rotted away in the intense heat and humidity, but a few interesting ones remain. Also on the plaza is the virtually redundant tourist office, whose city plan is hopelessly out of date as many of its streets are now non-existent due to the gradual encroachment of the surrounding jungle.

One thing Cobija does have is its duty-free shopping offering a huge selection of imported consumer goods at bargain prices to the Brazilians and Peruvians who flock here to stock up. Natives, however, reap no savings on prices and, in fact, pay a lot more than the rest of the country for almost everything thanks to the town's relative isolation.

The rainy season is November to March; the rest of the year is dry and hot. Temperatures average 29°C but can reach 40°C, or fall to 15°C when the *surazo* blows. *Population* 12,000; *Altitude* 252m; *Phone code* 0842.

Local festivals
Last week of August is the *Feria de Muestras*, which showcases local crafts. Also 24 September.

Local information
● **Accommodation**
D-E *Prefectural Pando*, on Calle Ayacucho one block from the Brazilian consulate (see below), T 2230, including breakfast, *comedor* does good lunch, poor value, manager Sr Angel Gil is helpful; **E** *Residencial Cocodrilo*, Avenida Molina, T 2215, comfortable, good atmosphere, rooms with fan; **F** *Residencial Frontera*, behind the Brazilian consulate, T 2740, with private bathroom and breakfast, basic but adequate, clean, fan.

● **Places to eat**
Most food is a mixture of Brazilian and Yungas-inspired dishes. The overwhelming favourite place to eat is *La Esquina de la Abuela*, at Avenida Molina and Calle Sucre, excellent dishes and reasonable prices; opposite is *Heladería El Tucano*, which serves ice-cream and doubles as a liquor store. Just down the road a bit is *La Cabaina del Momo*, Cobija's only true *churrasquería* offering a unique mix of Brazilian-Argentine meat dishes, all for under US$4. At the far end of Calle Nicolás Suárez, near the ferry, is **Snack Amazónico**, which serves cheap meals, including fresh fish. Just outside town on the west end of Calle Cornejo, is *Pescadería Danielita*, which specializes in fish dishes. Good cheap meals can also be found in the *comedor popular* in the central market.

● **Embassies & consulates**
Brazil, on Calle Beni and Avenida Molina, one block east of the plaza, T 2188, open 0830-1230 weekdays.

● **Banks & money changers**
There are money changers in abundance here, especially along Avenida 2 de Febrero. **Bidesa Bank**, also on Avenida 2 de Febrero, changes travellers' cheques, the only bank in town which will do so. Brazilian reais are accepted by many places; Peruvian soles much less so. *Casa de Cambio Horacio* offers decent rates for dollars, bolivianos and reais; they have offices at Calle Cornejo and 11 de Octubre, and on Avenida Internacional opposite the cemetery on the east side of town.

● **Entertainment**
There are two good discos; *El Curichi del Coco Karaoke* and *Lemon*, on opposite sides of Calle 16 de Julio on the way to the old airport. The others are best avoided.

● **Hospitals & medical services**
There is an old hospital, a recently built one (Japanese-funded), and the Red Cross

● **Post & telecommunications**
Post Office: on the plaza. **Entel**: on Calle Sucre, for national and international telephone calls and fax, which are much cheaper than from Brazil.

● **Useful addresses**
Immigration: open weekdays only from 0900 to 1800, for entry or exit stamps.

● **Transport**
Local Taxis: are very expensive, charging according to time and distance, eg US$10 to the outskirts, US$12 over the international bridge to Brasileia. Besides taxis there are motorbike taxis (much cheaper).

Air Aero Sur, in *Hotel Pando*, T 2562, flies daily except Sunday to Trinidad and to La Paz three times a week. The LAB office is on Avenida Molina, T 2170; they fly to Riberalta, Guayaramerín, Trinidad and La Paz. TAM office is on 2 de Febrero; check their schedule as it changes frequently (US$98 to/from La Paz).

Buses Flota Yungueña goes to La Paz via Riberalta and Rurrenabaque on Saturday at 0700 (check times first, T 2318). To Riberalta with several bus companies and trucks, which leave from 2 de Febrero, most on Wednesday, Friday and Sunday at 0600. The road is a good all-weather surface, the journey involves five river crossings on pontoon rafts and takes 10-11 hours.

CROSSING TO BRAZIL AND PERU

Brazil: travellers going on to Brazil should note that there are now two official points of departure from Cobija, both of which lead to Brasileia on the opposite bank. One is by boat from the ferry boat wharf just off Calle Bolívar at the west end of town. The other is via the international bridge at the other end of town. The former is often quicker, and certainly cheaper (US$0.35), as taxis are expensive (US$12). Note that buses do not cross into Brazil. All visitors must carry a Yellow Fever certificate, which can be obtained at the hospital in Cobija, and go to the Policia Federal on arrival in Brasileia.

Peru: crossing into Peru is difficult but not impossible. But travellers should note that the Peruvian department of Madre de Dios is still considered dangerous from narco-terrorist activities. The crossing is best attempted by cargo boat from Porvenir, but only after securing all necessary papers. Travellers without all documents will be turned back at the border. There is no Peruvian consulate in Cobija.

TO TRINIDAD FROM PUERTO VILLAROEL

Another route into the Beni Department is via the lowland road between Cochabamba and Santa Cruz. At **Ivirgarzama**, east of Villa Tunari, the road passes the turn-off to **Puerto Villarroel**, 27 km further north (see also page 302).

NB As this is coca-growing territory the police advise not to stray from the main road, don't talk to strangers and don't guard or carry other people's luggage.

PUERTO VILLARROEL

From here cargo boats ply irregularly to Trinidad in about 4-10 days (see below). You can get information from the Capitanía del Puerto notice board, or ask at the docks.

● **Accommodation & services** *Hannover*, no fans, dirty toilets, facilities are shared with late night disco; *Alojamiento El Jazmín*, small, helpful, pleasant, meals served; also *Alojamiento Petrolero*. There are very few stores in Villarroel. Sr Arturo Linares at the Cede office organizes boat trips to the jungle, but is not cheap.

● **Transport** *Camionetas* go from the junction on the main road at Ivirgazama to Puerto Villarroel a few times a day, 1 hour, US$1.20. From Cochabamba you can get a bus to Puerto Villarroel (see Cochabamba **Buses**, page 248), Puerto San Francisco, or Todos Santos on the Río Chapare.

BY BOAT TO TRINIDAD

Puerto Villarroel is the main port for river transport to the north of Bolivia. The road network is being extended, but many roads can only be used in the dry season. Boats sail between Puerto Villarroel, Trinidad and Guayaramerín, taking passengers. This trip is only for the hardy traveller. In the rainy season when the river is high it takes about 3 to 5 days to Trinidad, which involves 45 hours actual sailing, but boats stop from sunrise to sunset. It costs US$15 for 3 days and nights including meals – prices and quality vary. In the dry season, ie between May or June and August-December, it may last 8 to 10 days. At this time the river is lower, cleaner and there may be more animals to see on the shore, but there may be no boats October-December. It is another 5 days to Guayaramerín.

If you are fussy about food in general, don't make the trip because the kitchen is beyond description and the toilet facilities, too. Take your own drinking water, or water sterilizing tablets as the water served is taken from the river. Supplement the diet with fruit and any other interesting food you can find beforehand. The countryside between Puerto Villarroel and Trinidad is more or less cultivated, with plantations of bananas and cattle ranches. Among the wildlife you can see *petas* – small turtles basking in the sun – capybara, river dolphin, jumping fish, the occasional monkey on the beach, and many types of birds. A mosquito net is a 'must', a hammock a good idea, and binoculars for watching the wildlife a useful extra. Bathing in the river is safe.

TRINIDAD

The capital of the lowland Beni Department (*Population* 60,000; *Altitude* 237m; *Phone code* 046) has the look and feel of Santa Cruz perhaps 30 or 40 years ago. A few blocks either side of the plaza the streets are paved, but thereafter earth, turning to mud in the rainy season. The road to the bus terminal is particularly bad. Avenida 6 de Agosto is paved for several blocks, as is the road to the airport. Work is also under way to pave the road to Laguna Suárez (see below).

The city was founded in 1686 as one of the earliest Jesuit settlements in the region by Father Cipriano Barace, a revered missionary who was later martyred by an indigenous tribe he was attempting to convert. There are no buildings in Trinidad that remain from the missionary era. The impressive cathedral was built at the beginning of this century on the site of the original Jesuit church.

Trinidad vies with Iquitos in Peru as the motorcycle and scooter capital of South America. The plaza resembles a race track at night. Sometimes you'll see improbable numbers on one small bike – entire families, including grandparents and distant cousins. In fact, the only people who walk here are tourists and the occasional impoverished guidebook editor. If you do manage to converse with the locals, on their way to or from their bikes, you'll find them open and friendly.

Trinidad has three types of weather: hot and sticky; very hot and sticky; and insufferably hot and sticky. So hot is the midday sun that those seen wandering the streets between midday and 1500 should probably be locked away as crazy or dangerous.

Excursions

You can hire a motorbike or jeep to go to the river, which offers good swimming on the opposite bank. Boat hire costs US$5.

5 km from town is the **Laguna Suárez**, with plenty of wildlife. The water is very warm, and the bathing safe where the locals swim, near the café with the jetty. Elsewhere there are stingrays and caimans. A motorbike taxi from Trinidad is US$1.30.

17 km north of town is **Chuchini**, a wildlife sanctuary, with the Madriguera del Tigre, an ecological and archaeological centre, accessible by road in the dry season and by canoe in the wet season. Contact Efrém Hinojoso at Calle Cochabamba 232 entre Bolívar y Sucre, T 21811; or Edwin Portugal in La Paz, T 341090, T/F 343930. A trip of 3 days/2 nights will cost US$210 per person, including accommodation and meals. Efrém will run tours with only one or two people for the same price. There is plenty of wildlife to be seen, including parrots, macaws, toucans, caiman, turtles, capybara, anacondas, monkeys and many birds. Also included in the trip is the **Museo Arqueológico del Beni**, containing human remains, ceramics and stone objects from the precolumbian Beni culture, said to be over 5,000 years old. Tours to Chuchini can also be booked through the tour agencies in town.

Local information
● Accommodation

A2-A3 *Gran Moxos*, Avenida 6 de Agosto y Santa Cruz, T 22240, price includes breakfast, air conditioning, fridge bar, cable TV, phone, good restaurant, accepts Visa and Mastercard; **A2-A3** *Mi Residencia*, Manuel Limpias 76,

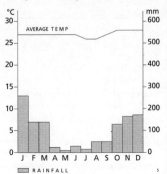

Climate: Trinidad

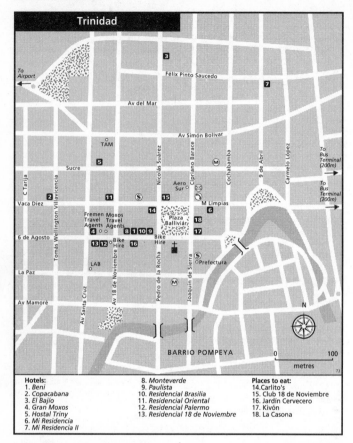

Trinidad

To Airport

Félix Pinto Saucedo

Av del Mar

Av Simón Bolívar

TAM

Sucre

Nicolás Suárez

Cipriano Barace

Cochabamba

9 de Abril

Carmelo López

To Bus Terminal (200m)

To Bus Terminal (200m)

C Tarija

Tomás Wellington Villavicencia

Vaca Díez

Aero Sur

M Limpias

Fremen Travel Agents

Moxos Travel Agents

Plaza Balliviár

6 de Agosto

Bike Hire

Bike Hire

LAB

Av 18 de Noviembre

Av Santa Cruz

Pedro de la Rocha

Joaquín de Sierra

Prefectura

La Paz

Av Mamoré

BARRIO POMPEYA

N

0   100
metres

Hotels:
1. Beni
2. Copacabana
3. El Bajío
4. Gran Moxos
5. Hostal Triny
6. Mi Residencia
7. Mi Residencia II

8. Monteverde
9. Paulista
10. Residencial Brasilia
11. Residencial Oriental
12. Residencial Palermo
13. Residencial 18 de Noviembre

Places to eat:
14. Carlito's
15. Club 18 de Noviembre
16. Jardín Cervecero
17. Kivón
18. La Casona

T 21529/21376, F 22464, air conditioning, including breakfast; **A2-A3** *Mi Residencia II*, Félix Pinto Sancedo y 9 de Abril, quieter and with pool.

B *El Bajío*, Avenida Nicolás Suárez 520, T 22400/20030, air conditioning, cheaper with fan, includes breakfast, pool (US$2 for non-residents).

C-D *Monteverde*, 6 de Agosto 76, T 22342/22738, with or without air conditioning, fridge bar, includes breakfast in your room, clean and comfortable, the owner speaks English, recommended.

D *Copacabana*, Tomás Villavicencio, three blocks from the plaza, T 22811, F 21978, good

value, **F** pp without bath; **D-E** *Hostal Triny*, Calle Sucre 353, T 22613, good value, fan; **D-E** *Paulista*, Avenida 6 de Agosto 36, T 20018, cheaper without bath, comfortable, good restaurant.

E *Residencial Oriental*, 18 de Noviembre near Vaca Díez, T 22534, with bath, good value.

F *Brasilia*, 6 de Agosto 46, T 21685, shared bath, fan, basic, not very clean; **F** *Residencial 18 de Noviembre*, Avenida 6 de Agosto 135, with private bathroom, clean, friendly, laundry facilties; next door is **F** *Residencial Palermo*, Avenida 6 de Agosto 123, T 20472, shared bath, basic, restaurant.

● Places to eat

Brasilia, Avenida 6 de Agosto, good dinner; *Carlito's*, on Plaza Ballivián, recommended; *Pescadería El Moro*, Bolívar and 25 Diciembre, excellent fish. There are also several good fish restaurants in Barrio Pompeya, south of the plaza across the river; try *Pescadería Don Pedrito*, on Calle Manuel Maraza. A good value lunch can be had for US$1.55 at *Jardín Cervecero*, opposite the *Hotel Monteverde* on Avenida 6 de Agosto; *Club Social 18 de Noviembre*, N Suárez y Vaca Díez on the plaza, good lunch for US$1.35; *La Casona*, on the main plaza, for good pizzas and set lunch, closed Tuesday; *La Estancia*, on Ibare entre Muibe y Velarde, excellent steaks. Burgers, ice cream and snacks at *Kivón*, a cafeteria on the main plaza; also on the plaza is *Heladería Oriental*, good coffee, ice-cream, cakes, popular with locals. Cheap meals, including breakfast, are served at the fruit and vegetable market. Try sugar cane juice with lemon – delicious.

Balneario Topacare is a restaurant and bathing resort 10 minutes out of town on Laguna Suárez, it offers delicious local specialities for lunch or dinner, it's set in a beautiful location, with excellent bird spotting and it's a favourite spot for locals at the weekends.

● Banks & money changers

Travellers' cheques can be changed at **Bidesa**, on Vaca Díez sin número, near the plaza, 2% commission for dollars or bolivianos; **Banco Mercantil**, Joaquín de Sierra, near the plaza, changes cash and travellers' cheques, cash advance on Visa. Street changers can be found on 6 de Agosto.

● Post & telecommunications

Entel and **Correos** are both open daily till 1930; they're in the same building at Avenida Barace, just off the plaza.

● Tour companies & travel agents

All on 6 de Agosto: *Tarope Tours*, No 81, T/F 21468, Casilla 351, their guide Papachu is recommended (US$35 per person per day). *Paraíso Travel*, No 138, T/F 20692, Casilla 261, does 'Conozca Trinidad' packages. *Moxos*, No 114, T 21141, Casilla 252, recommended. *Fremen*, No 140, F 21834, run speed boat trips along the Mamoré and Iboré rivers and to Isiboro-Securé National Park; their *Flotel Reina de Enin* offers tours of more than 1 day, US$70 per person per day, good food. *Jarajorechi* is an ecotourism centre which offers accommodation and snacks, also jungle trips, equipment and transport hire; for more information contact

Graciela Neira, Avenida 6 de Agosto esquina 27 de Mayo, T 21409, F 21716, Casilla 299, Trinidad.

Most agents offer excursions to local *estancias* and jungle tours down river to Amazonia. Most *estancias* can also be reached independently in 1 hour by hiring a motorbike. Note that the more distant parts of Isiboro are at present too dangerous owing to violent disputes between *cocaleros* and the authorities. Tours to Isiboro are very expensive because of the distances involved.

● Tourist offices

In the Prefectural building at Joaquín de Sierra y La Paz, ground floor, T 21722, very helpful, sells guide and city map, US$2.

● Transport

Local Motorcycle hire: rental on the plaza from US$2 per hour, US$8 per half day; also at the junction of Avenida 6 de Agosto and 18 de Noviembre, same prices. Take your passport. **Taxis**: a motorcycle taxi in the city costs US$0.40; to the airport is US$1.20. Motorbike taxis will take people with backpacks from the bus station to the centre for US$0.45.

Air LAB office is at Santa Cruz 324, 20595; flights to La Paz (daily direct), Cochabamba, Santa Cruz, Magdalena, San Joaquín, Cobija, Guayaramerín and Riberalta (check schedules). Aero Sur, Avenida Barace 51, T 20765/21117; flights daily to La Paz and Santa Cruz, daily except Sunday to Cobija, Guayaramerin, San Borja, and except Saturday to Riberalta. TAM, at the airport, T 20355, to Baures, Bella Vista, Magdalena and Huacaraje, Riberalta, Guayamerín, Santa Cruz and La Paz. Itemox Express, at Avenida 6 de Agosto 281, T 22306, has flights to Baures, Huacaraje, Bella Vista, Magdalena, Reyes (near Rurrenabaque) and Santa Rosa. Airport authority, AASANA, T 20678.

Buses The terminal is on Mendoza, between Beni and Pinto, nine blocks east of the main plaza. Several *flotas* daily to/from **La Paz** via San Borja and Caranavi, 20-21 hours, leaving at 1730, US$17.50 (see also under San Borja, **Transport**, page 307). A minibus goes daily to San Borja at 0900, US$11.50. To **Santa Cruz**, 12 hours in the dry season, US$5.80, and **Cochabamba**, US$11.60, with Copacabana, Mopar and Bolívar, leaving at 1700, 1730 and 1800. The Trinidad to Casarabe section of the road is paved as is Santa Cruz to El Puente, and all the sections of unpaved road have a good gravel surface. To **Rurrenabaque** (US$15.40), **Riberalta** (US$21.15) and **Guayaramerín**

(US$23), connecting with a bus to **Cobija**; with Guaya Tours daily at 1000. The road is often impassable in the wet season, and it can take at least 24 hours to Rurrenabaque.

River There are two ports, Almacén and Varador, check which one your boat is docking at. Puerto Varador is 13 km from town on the Río Mamoré on the road between Trinidad and San Borja. Cross the river by the main bridge by the market, walk down to the service station by the police checkpoint and take a truck, US$1.70. Almacén is 8 km from the city. Cargo boats down the Río Mamoré to Guayaramerín take passengers; 3-4 days, assuming no breakdowns. They are best organized from Puerto Varador (speak to the Port Captain). *Argos* is recommended as friendly, US$22 per person. Take water, fresh fruit and toilet paper; ear-plugs are also a good idea as hammocks are strung over the engine on small boats. This trip is only for the hardy traveller.

MAGDALENA

A road from Trinidad heads northeast to **San Ramón** and then turns east to **Magdalena**, a charming town (*Population* 5,000) on the banks of the Río Itonama. It was founded by Jesuit missionaries in 1720, made a city in 1911 and is now the capital of the province of Iténez. Beef is the main product of the region and the river is the means of transporting cattle and other agricultural produce. 7 km upriver is the **Laguna La Baíqui**, which is popular for fishing. There is an abundance of wildlife and birds in the surrounding area. The city's main festival is on 22 July, *Santa María Magdalena*, attracting many groups and visitors from all over Beni and beyond.

● **Accommodation & places to eat** F *San Carlos*, private toilet, fan, shower and water bed; also *Residencial Iténez* and F *Ganadero*, which are modest but clean. Restaurants: *El Gato*, on the road off the plaza beside the church, drinks and nightly dancing; *Heladería Laidi*, one block from the plaza, simple meals and good juices. Drinking water is available and electricity runs from 1800-2400.

● **Useful information** There is a bank, which changes travellers' cheques, and an Entel office and Correos on the plaza.

● **Transport Air** Itemox Express has daily flights to Trinidad (US$31, in five-seater). There are also flights to Bella Vista, Baures and Huacaraje. LAB flies from Trinidad. **Roads** An unpaved road goes to Trinidad via San Ramón, passable only in the dry season. A road to Bella Vista (see below), was due open in 1996.

BELLA VISTA

East of Magdalena on the Río Blanco, **Bella Vista** is considered by many to be one of the prettiest spots in northeast Bolivia. Lovely white sandbanks line the Río San Martín, 10 minutes paddling by canoe from the boat moorings below town. Local boatmen will take you, returning later by arrangement. The sandbanks are also accessible by motorcycle. Check that the sand is not covered by water after heavy rain. Other activities are swimming in the Río San Martín, canoeing, hunting and the countryside is good for cycling.

● **Accommodation, services & transport** F-G *Hotel Cazador*, shared bath, provides meals for guests (restaurant to be built), the owner Guillermo Esero Gómez is very helpful and knowledgeable about the area. There are three well-stocked shops on the plaza, but none sells mosquito repellent or spray/coils. Bring your own as there are many mosquitoes at the beginning of the wet season (apply repellent before leaving the plane). There is no bank or Entel office. There are flights to Bella Vista with Itemox Express, from Magdalena or Trinidad, but no fixed schedule.

WEST FROM TRINIDAD

A road heads west from Trinidad through San Ignacio de Moxos, to **San Borja** and then a further 50 km (1-2 hours) to **Yucumo**, where it joins the road from the Yungas to Rurrenanbaque (see also page 289). There are five-six river crossings and, in the wetlands, flamingoes, blue heron and a multitude of waterfowl. The section from Trinidad to San Ignacio is good, but from San Ignacio to San Borja is poor, with long stretches rutted and pot-holed. From San Borja to Yucumo is very good. The road passes through the north part of the Beni Biosphere Reserve (see **National**

Parks page 74). Gasoline is available at San Ignacio, San Borja and Yucumo.

SAN IGNACIO DE MOXOS

Lying 90 km west of Trinidad, **San Ignacio de Moxos** is known as the folklore capital of the Beni Department. The traditions of the Jesuit missions are still maintained with big *fiestas*, especially during Holy Week. 31 July is the town's patron saint's day, one of the country's most famous and colourful celebrations. 60% of the population are *Macheteros*, who speak their own language.

• **Accommodation** There are a few fairly cheap *residencias*: **E** *Plaza*, on the main plaza, with or without bath, fan, good value, restaurant, recommended; **E-F** *Don Joaquín*, on the main plaza, with bath, fan, family atmosphere. There are several other basic *alojamientos* on and around the plaza. Electricity is supplied in town only from 1200 to 2400.

• **Places to eat** Restaurants do not stay open late. *Isireri*, on the plaza, good and cheap set lunches and delicious fruit juices; *Casa Suiza*, good European food; *Donchanta*, recommended for tasty meat dishes.

• **Buses** The bus from Trinidad to San Borja stops at *Restaurant Donchanta* for lunch; otherwise it is difficult to find transport to San Borja. A minibus goes to Trinidad daily at 0730 from the plaza; there are also *camionetas*, but check times beforehand.

SAN BORJA

West of San Ignacio, San Borja is a small, dusty cattle-raising centre with hotels and restaurants clustered near the plaza. This is a coca-growing region and it is unwise for travellers to wander alone inside the Parque Nacional Isiboro in case they are mistaken for DEA agents by coca farmers.

• **Accommodation** **D-E** *Hostal Jatata*, T 3103, two blocks from plaza, modern, comfortable, fans, good snack bar, highly recommended; **F** *Trópico*, one block from the main plaza, clean, recommended; **E-F** *Residencial Manara*, just off the plaza, with private bathroom, clean, comfortable, some rooms with air conditioning; **G** *Jaropa*, clean, basic.

Fiesta at San Ignacio de Moxos

• **Places to eat** *Taurus*, good food, cheap; *Club Social*, two blocks from the plaza, covered open-air restaurant, good *almuerzos*.

• **Banks & money changers** Good rate for dollars at *Joyería San Borja* next to the entrance to the supermarket round the corner from the central market.

• **Transport Air** Aero Sur flies to Trinidad, daily except Saturday; also TAM flies to and from La Paz, but check schedules. **Buses** Flota Yungueña daily except Thursday at 1300 to La Paz (19 hours); also to Rurrenabaque, Santa Rosa, Riberalta and Guayaramerín on Thursday, Saturday and Sunday. Minibuses and *camionetas* run daily between San Borja and Trinidad throughout the year (US$15); it's about 7 hours including 20 minutes crossing of the Río Mamoré on a ferry barge. 1 de Mayo runs daily to San Ignacio (US$8), Trinidad and Santa Cruz at 0850. Trucks reportedly go to Yucumo at 0800, US$2.

Section 4

Information for travellers

BEFORE TRAVELLING

ENTRY REQUIREMENTS

● Documents

A passport only is needed for citizens of almost all Western European, North and South American countries, Australia and New Zealand. All are granted 30 or 90 days on entry. If you're only granted 30 you can easily extend to 90 at immigration. Among those countries whose nationals require a visa are the countries of Eastern Europe (except Poland and the Czech Republic), Middle East (except Israel), Africa (except South Africa) and South East Asia (except Japan and the Philippines), the former Soviet Union and the former Yugoslavia, India, Pakistan and Haiti. Authorization from the Bolivian Ministry of Foreign Affairs is required and can take 3-5 weeks. Those countries which require a visa but not authorization are; Croatia, Cuba, Hungary, South Korea, Malta, Mexico, Panama, Slovenia and Venezuela (takes 1-2 working days). The cost of a visa varies from nationality to nationality.

Visas (or permit to stay) can be renewed at any Migración office up to 90 days. After 3 months further renewal is at the discretion of the immigration officer. If refused, leave the country and return. On arrival ensure that visas and passports are stamped with the same, correct date of entry or this can lead to 'fines' later. Business visitors (unless passing through as tourists) are required to obtain a visa from a Bolivian consulate. This costs £35 (or equivalent); applicants should check all requirements and regulations on length of stay and extensions in advance.

If you are in full-time education you will be entitled to an International Student Identity Card, which is distributed by student travel offices and travel agencies in 77 countries. The ISIC gives you special prices on all forms of transport (air, sea, rail etc), and access to a variety of other concessions and services. If you need to find the location of your nearest ISIC office contact: The ISIC Association, Box 9048, 1000 Copenhagen, Denmark T (+45) 33 93 93 03. If you're planning to study in Latin America for a long period, make every effort to get a student visa in advance.

NB Latin Americans, especially officials, are very document-minded. You should always carry your passport in a safe place about your person, or if not going far, leave it in the hotel safe. If you're staying for several weeks, it is worthwhile registering at your Embassy or Consulate. Then, if your passport is stolen, the process of replacing it is simplified and speeded up. Keeping photocopies of essential documents, including your flight ticket, and some additional passport-sized photographs, is recommended.

It is your responsibility to ensure that your passport is stamped in and out when you cross frontiers. The absence of entry and exit stamps can cause serious difficulties: seek out the proper migration offices if the stamping process is not carried out as you cross. Also, do not lose your entry card; replacing one causes a lot of trouble, and possibly expense. Citizens of countries which oblige visitors to have a visa can expect more delays and problems at border crossings.

NB Membership cards of British, European and US motoring organizations can be useful for discounts off hotel charges, car rentals, maps, towing charges, etc. Student cards must carry a photograph if they are to be of any use in Latin America for discounts. Business people should carry a good supply of visiting cards, which are essential for good business relations in Latin America. Identity, membership or business cards in Spanish (or a translation) and an official letter of introduction in Spanish are also useful.

● **Tourist information**

Secretaria Nacional de Turismo (Senatur), Edificio Mariscal Ballivián, piso 18, Calle Mercado, La Paz, T 367463/64, F 374630, Casilla 1868. The addresses of tourist offices are given in the main text, in the Local information sections. See under **Useful addresses** (page 332) for a list of specialist tour operators operating from outside Bolivia.

MONEY

● **Cost of living**

Bolivia is cheaper than most neighbouring countries. Rents, appliances, some clothing, and especially toilet goods and medicines, are highly priced. Food, accommodation and transport are not expensive, however. Budget travellers can get by on US$25-30 a day for two travelling together. For a basic hotel expect to pay US$3 per person; breakfast US$1-2; *almuerzos* cost from US$2-3.

● **Currency**

The unit of currency is the boliviano (Bs), divided into 100 centavos. There are notes for 200, 100, 50, 20, 10, 5 and 2 (rare) bolivianos, and coins of 2 and 1 boliviano and 50, 20, 10 and 5 (rare) centavos. Bolivianos are often referred to as pesos. Expensive items, including hotel rooms, are often quoted in dollars. Change is often given in forms other than money: eg cigarette, sweet, or razor blade. It is almost impossible to buy dollars at points of exit when leaving or to change bolivianos in other countries.

The three main ways of keeping in funds while travelling are with US dollars cash, US dollars travellers' cheques or plastic.

● **Cash**

Sterling and other currencies are not recommended. Though the risk of loss is greater, the chief benefit of US dollar notes is that better rates and lower commissions can usually be obtained for them. As in many other South American countries, US dollar notes are only accepted if they are in excellent, if not perfect condition (likewise, do not accept local currency notes in poor condition). Low-value US dollar bills should be carried for changing into local currency if arriving in the country when banks or *casas de cambio* are closed (US$5 or US$10 bills). They are very useful for shopping: shopkeepers and exchange shops (*casas de cambio*) tend to give better exchange rates than hotels or banks (but see below). The better hotels will normally change travellers' cheques for their guests (often at a rather poor rate), but if you are travelling on the cheap it is essential to keep in funds; watch weekends and public holidays carefully and never run out of local currency. Take plenty of local currency, in small denominations, when making trips into the interior.

● **Travellers' cheques**

These are convenient but they attract thieves (though refunds can of course be arranged) and you will find that they are more difficult than dollar bills to change in small towns (denominations of US$50 and US$100 are preferable, though one does need a few of US$20). American Express, Visa or Thomas Cook US$ travellers' cheques are recommended, but less commission is often charged on Citibank or Bank of America travellers' cheques, if they are cashed at branches of those banks. These travellers' cheques are always accepted by banks, even though they may not be as well known outside banks as those of American Express, Visa or Thomas Cook. (It is also easier to obtain refunds for stolen travellers' cheques with the last three than with Citicorp cheques.) It is a good idea to take two kinds of cheque: if large numbers of one kind have recently been forged or stolen, making people suspicious, it is unlikely to have happened simultaneously with the other kind. Several banks charge a high fixed commission for changing travellers' cheques – sometimes as much as US$5-10 a cheque – because they don't really want to be bothered. Exchange houses (*casas de cambio*) are usually much better for this service. Some establishments may ask to see the customer's record of purchase before accepting. It can be impossible to change travellers' cheques outside the main cities.

● **Plastic**

It is straightforward to obtain a cash advance against a credit card and, in the text, we give the names of banks that do this.

There are two international ATM (automatic telling machine) acceptance systems, Plus and Cirrus. Many issuers of debit and credit cards are linked to one, or both (eg Visa is Plus, Mastercard is Cirrus). Look for the relevant symbol on an ATM and draw cash using your PIN.

In La Paz, Cochabamba, Sucre and Santa Cruz automatic cash dispensers displaying the 'Enlace' sign accept Visa (ATC outlets) and Mastercard. Frequently, the rates of exchange on ATM withdrawals are the best available. Find out before you leave what ATM coverage there is in Bolivia and what international 'functionality' your card has. Check if your bank or credit card company imposes handling charges. Obviously you must ensure that the account to which your debit card refers contains sufficient funds. With a credit card, obtain a credit limit sufficient for your needs, or pay money in to put the account in credit. If travelling for a long time, consider a direct debit to clear your account regularly. Do not rely on one card, in case of loss. If you do lose a card, immediately contact the 24-hour helpline of the issuer in your home country (keep this number in a safe place). (With thanks to Nigel Baker, Debit Card Manager, Natwest Bank plc, London.)

For purchases, credit cards of the Visa and Mastercard (Eurocard, Access) groups, American Express (Amex), Carte Blanche and Diners Club can be used. American Express is not as useful as Visa, or, to a lesser extent, Mastercard.

Make sure you know the correct procedure if cards are lost or stolen. Credit card transactions are normally at an officially recognized rate of exchange; they are often subject to tax. Many establishments charge a fee of 5-10% on credit card transactions; although forbidden by credit card company rules there is not a lot you can do about this, except get the charge itemized on the receipt and complain to the card company. For credit security, insist that imprints are made in your presence and that any imprints incorrectly completed should be torn into tiny pieces. Also destroy the carbon papers after the form is completed (signatures can be copied from them).

Money can be transferred between banks. A recommended method is, before leaving, to find out which local bank is correspondent to your bank at home, then when you need funds, telex your own bank and ask them to telex the money to the local bank (confirming by fax). Give the exact information to your bank of the routing number of the receiving bank. Funds can be received within 48 banking hours.

● **General tips**

Bolivia has freedom of exchange between US dollars and the local currency. When changing money on the street, if possible, do not do so alone. If entering Bolivia by land and you are unsure of the exchange rate and currency, check rates with more than one changer at the border, or ask locals or departing travellers.

Whenever you leave, sell any local currency before leaving, because the further away you get, the less the value of a country's money. **NB** If departing by air, do not leave yourself too little money to pay the airport departure tax, which is never waived.

Americans should know that if they run out of funds they can usually expect no help from the US Embassy or Consul other than a referral to some welfare organization. Find out before you go precisely what services and assistance your embassy or consulate can provide if you find yourself in difficulties.

WHAT TO TAKE

Everybody has his/her own list, but those most often mentioned include air cushions for slatted seats, inflatable travel pillow for neck support, strong shoes (and remember that footwear over 9½ English size, or 42 European size, is difficult to obtain in Bolivia); a small first-aid kit and handbook, fully waterproof top clothing, waterproof treatment for leather footwear, wax earplugs (which are almost impossible to find outside large cities) and airline-type eye mask to help you sleep in noisy and poorly curtained hotel rooms, sandals (rubber-thong Japanese-type or other – can be worn in showers to avoid athlete's foot), a polyethylene sheet 2m x 1m to cover possibly infested beds and shelter your luggage, polyethylene bags of varying sizes (up to heavy duty rubbish bag size) with ties, a toilet bag you can tie round your waist, if you use an electric shaver, take a rechargeable type, a sheet sleeping-bag and pillow-case or separate pillow-case – they may not be changed often in cheap hotels; a 1½-2m piece of 100% cotton can be used as a towel, a bedsheet, beach towel, makeshift curtain and wrap; a mosquito net (or a hammock with a fitted net), a straw hat which can be rolled or flattened and reconstituted after 15 minutes soaking in water, a clothes line, a nailbrush (useful for scrubbing dirt off clothes as well as off oneself), a vacuum flask, a water bottle, a small dual-voltage immersion heater, a small dual-voltage (or battery-driven) electric fan, a light nylon waterproof shopping bag, a universal bath- and basin-plug of the flanged type that will fit any waste-pipe (or improvise one from a sheet of thick rubber), string, velcro, electrical insulating tape, large penknife preferably with tin and bottle openers, scissors and corkscrew – the famous Swiss Army range has been repeatedly recommended (for knife sharpening, go to a butcher's shop), alarm clock or watch, candle, torch (flashlight) – especially one that will clip on to a pocket or belt, pocket mirror, pocket calculator, an adaptor and flex to enable you to take power from an electric-light socket (the Edison screw type is the most commonly used), a padlock (combination lock is best) for the doors of the cheapest and most casual hotels (or for tent zip if camping), spare chain-lengths and padlock for securing luggage to bed or bus/train seat. Remember not to throw away spent batteries containing mercury or cadmium; take them home to be disposed of, or recycled properly.

Useful medicaments are given at the end of the 'Health' section; to these might be added some lip salve with sun protection, and pre-moistened wipes (such as 'Wet Ones'). Always carry toilet paper. Natural fabric sticking plasters, as well as being long-lasting, are much appreciated as gifts. Dental floss can be used for backpack repairs, in addition to its original purpose. Never carry firearms. Their possession could land you in serious trouble.

A note for contact lens wearers: lens solution can be difficult to find in Bolivia. Ask for it in a chemist/pharmacy, rather than an optician's.

GETTING THERE

BY AIR
● **From Europe**
Either fly to Lima (see below), to Rio de Janeiro, São Paulo or Buenos Aires for connections, or via Miami.

● **From North America**
American and LAB fly from Miami daily to La Paz and Santa Cruz.

● **Within South America**
From Lima to La Paz, there are twelve flights a week by AeroPerú, or LAB whose flights also go to Cochabamba and Santa Cruz (three a week each). Aero Perú flies Cusco-La Paz daily except Sunday, LAB three times a week. LAB flies twice a week Quito-Lima-La Paz-Cochabamba. From Santiago, Iquique and Arica to La Paz, daily by Lan Chile and four a week by LAB (with continuations to Cochabamba and Santa Cruz). From Buenos Aires there are daily flights by Aerolíneas Argentinas and LAB to La Paz via Santa Cruz. LAB has one direct flight Buenos Aires-Cochabamba per week. LAB flies twice a week Tucumán-Jujuy (Argentina)-Santa Cruz, and three times a week from Salta. LAB also flies

four times a week Montevideo (Uruguay)-Santa Cruz-La Paz. From Asunción, Lapsa and LAB twice a week to Santa Cruz, LAB continuing once to La Paz. Varig flies daily São Paulo-Santa Cruz, six times a week Rio de Janeiro-São Paulo-Santa Cruz-La Paz; LAB flies São Paulo-Santa Cruz-Cochabamba six days a week, while Vasp flies this route twice a week. LAB flies also from Cuiabá and Manaus to Santa Cruz. LAB flies twice a week Bogotá-Santa Cruz, once Bogotá-La Paz, and five times a week Mexico City-Panama City-Santa Cruz. You can fly from Caracas once a week by LAB to La Paz, twice to Santa Cruz.

● **General tips**
Airlines will only allow a certain weight of luggage without a surcharge; this is normally 30 kg for first class and 20 kg for business and economy classes, but these limits are often not strictly enforced when it is known that the plane is not going to be full. On some flights from the UK special outbound concessions are offered (by Iberia, Air France, Avianca) of a two-piece allowance up to 32 kg, but you may need to request this. Passengers seeking a larger baggage allowance can route via USA, but with certain exceptions, the fares are slightly higher using this route. On the other hand, weight limits for internal flights are often lower; it's best to enquire beforehand.

● **Prices and discounts**
1 It is generally cheaper to fly from London rather than a point in Europe to Latin American destinations. Fares vary from airline to airline, destination to destination and according to time of year. Check with an agency for the best deal for when you wish to travel.

2 Most airlines offer discounted fares of one sort or another on scheduled flights. These are not offered by the airlines direct to the public, but through agencies who specialize in this type of fare. In the UK, these include: Journey Latin America, 14-16 Devonshire Road, Chiswick, London, W4 2HD (T 0181-747 8315) and 28-30 Barton Arcade, 51-63 Deansgate, Manchester, M3 2BH (T 0161 832 1441); Trailfinders, 194 Kensington High Street, London, W8 7RG (T 0171-938 3939); South American Experience, 47 Causton Street, Pimlico, London, SW1P 4AT (T 0171-976 5511); Last Frontiers, Swan House, High Street, Long Crendon, Buckinghamshire, HP18 9AF (T 01844 208405); Passage to South America, Fovant Mews, 12 Noyna Road, London, SW17 7PH (T 0181 767 8989); STA Travel, Priory House, 6 Wrights Lane, London, W8 6TA (T 0171-361 6166); Encounter Overland, 267 Old Brompton Road, London, SW5 9JA (T 0171 370 6845); Hayes & Jarvis, 152 King Street, London, W6 0QU (T 0181 222 7844); Cox & Kings Travel, St James Court, 45 Buckingham Gate, London (T 0171-873 5001).

The very busy seasons are 7 December – 15 January and 10 July – 10 September. If you intend travelling during those times, book as far ahead as possible. Between February-May and September-November special offers may be available.

3 Other fares fall into three groups, and are all on scheduled services:

● **Excursion (return) fares** with restricted validity eg 5-90 days. Carriers are introducing flexibility into these tickets, permitting a change of dates on payment of a fee.

● **Yearly fares**: these may be bought on a one-way or return basis. Some airlines require a specified return date, changeable upon payment of a fee. To leave the return completely open is possible for an extra fee. You must fix the route (some of the cheapest flexible fares now have 6 months validity).

● **Student (or Under 26) fares**: some airlines are flexible on the age limit, others strict. One way and returns available, or 'Open Jaws' (see below). Do not assume that student tickets are the cheapest; though they are often very flexible, they are usually more expensive than A or B above. On the other hand, there is a wider range of cheap one-way student fares originating in Latin America than can be bought outside the continent. **NB** If you foresee returning home at a busy time (eg Christmas-beginning of January, August), a booking is advisable on any type of open-return ticket.

4 For people intending to travel a linear route and return from a different point from that which they entered, there are 'Open Jaws' fares, which are available on student, yearly, or excursion fares.

5 Many of these fares require a change of plane at an intermediate point, and a stopover may be permitted, or even obligatory, depending on schedules. Simply because a flight stops at a given airport does not mean you can break your journey there – the airline must have traffic rights to pick up or set down passengers between points A and B before it will be permitted. This is where dealing with a specialized agency (like Journey Latin America) will really pay dividends. There are dozens of agencies that offer

the simple returns to Rio or Lima at roughly the same (discounted) fare. On multi-stop itineraries, the specialized agencies can often save clients hundreds of pounds.

6 Although it's a little more complicated, it's possible to sell tickets in London for travel originating in Latin America at substantially cheaper fares than those available locally. This is useful for the traveller who doesn't know where he will end up, or who plans to travel for more than a year. Because of high local taxes a one-way ticket from Latin America is more expensive than a one-way in the other direction, so it's always best to buy a return. Taxes are calculated as a percentage of the full IATA fare; on a discounted fare the tax can therefore make up as much as 30-50% of the price.

7 There are several cheap French charters to Colombia, Ecuador, Peru, Bolivia and the southern countries, but no-one in the UK sells them (though AOM tickets are available through Journey Latin America).

8 If you buy discounted air tickets always check the reservation with the airline concerned to make sure the flight still exists. Also remember the IATA airlines' schedules change in March and

October each year, so if you're going to be away a long time it's best to leave return flight coupons open.

In addition, check whether you are entitled to any refund or re-issued ticket if you lose, or have stolen, a discounted air ticket. Some airlines require the repurchase of a ticket before you can apply for a refund, which will not be given until after the validity of the original ticket has expired. The Iberia group and Air France, for example, operate this costly system. Travel insurance in some cases covers lost tickets.

9 Note that some South American carriers change departure times of short-haul or domestic flights at short notice and, in some instances, schedules shown in the computers of transatlantic carriers differ from those actually flown by smaller, local carriers. If you book, and reconfirm, both your transatlantic and onward sectors through your transatlantic carrier you may find that your travel plans have been based on out of date information. The surest solution is to reconfirm your outward flight in an office of the onward carrier itself.

SEA

Yes, we know, Bolivia is a land-locked country, but the coastal ports of southern Peru and northern Chile are easily reached from La Paz. Enquiries regarding passages should be made through agencies in your own country, or through John Alton of Strand Cruise and Travel Centre, Charing Cross Shopping Concourse, The Strand, London WC2N 4HZ, T 0171-836 6363, F 0171-497 0078. Strand Cruise and Travel are booking agents for all shipping companies, except Fyffes, whose booking agent is Cargo Ship Voyages Ltd, Hemley, Woodbridge, Suffolk, IP12 4QF, T/F 01473-736265 (who can also advise on the other sailings). In Europe, contact Wagner Frachtschiffreisen, Stadlerstrasse 48, CH-8404, Winterthur, Switzerland, T (052) 242-1442, F 242-1487. In the USA, contact Freighter World Cruises, 180 South Lake Avenue, Pasadena, CA 91101, T (818) 449-3106, or Travltips Cruise and Freighter Travel Association, 163-07 Depot Road, PO Box 188, Flushing, NY 11358, T (800) 872-8584.

CUSTOMS

● **Duty-free imports**
200 cigarettes, 50 cigars and 1 lb tobacco; one opened bottle of alcoholic drink.

ON ARRIVAL

● **Clothing**
Visitors to the Altiplano and the Puna should be prepared for the cold at night. The climate in the Eastern Lowlands is tropical. Oruro and Potosí are colder than La Paz and Cochabamba can be very warm.

Most Latin Americans, if they can afford it, devote great care to their clothes and appearance; it is appreciated if visitors do likewise. How you dress is mostly how people will judge you. Buying clothing locally can help you to look less like a tourist. It may be advantageous to carry a letter from someone in an official position testifying to one's good character, on official-looking notepaper. A medium weight shawl with some wool content is recommended for women: it can double as pillow, light blanket, bathrobe or sunscreen as required. For men, a smart jacket can be very useful.

● **Courtesy**
Remember that politeness – even a little ceremoniousness – is much appreciated. In this connection professional or business cards are useful. Men should always remove any headgear and say "con permiso" when entering offices, and be prepared to shake hands (this is much commoner in Latin America than in Europe or North America). Always say "Buenos días" (until midday) or "Buenas tardes" and wait for a reply before proceeding further. Always remember that the traveller from abroad has enjoyed greater advantages in life than most Latin American minor officials, and should be friendly and courteous in consequence. Never be impatient; do not criticize situations in public: the officials may know more English than you think and they can certainly interpret gestures and facial expressions. Be judicious about discussing politics with strangers. Politeness can be a liability, however, in some situations; most Latin Americans are disorderly queuers. In commercial transactions (buying a meal, goods in a shop, etc) politeness should be accompanied by firmness, and always ask the price first.

Politeness should also be extended to street traders; saying "No, gracias" with a smile is better than an arrogant dismissal. Whether you give money to beggars is a personal matter, but your decision should be influenced by whether a person is begging out of need or trying to cash in on the tourist trail. In the former case, local people giving may provide an indication. Giving money to children is a separate issue, upon which most agree: don't do it. There are occasions where giving food in a restaurant may be appropriate, but first inform yourself of local practice.

● **Hours of business**

Hours of business are normally 0900-1200 (sometimes 1130 in La Paz), and 1400-1800. Saturday is a half day. Opening and closing in the afternoon are several hours later in the provinces. Government offices are closed on Saturday. Banks 0900-1200, 1400-1630, but closed on Saturday.

● **Official time**

4 hours behind GMT.

● **Photography**

Always ask permission before photographing people. The price of film is relatively cheap in Bolivia in the markets of major cities. Pre-paid Kodak slide film cannot be developed in South America; it is also very hard to find. Kodachrome is almost impossible to buy. Some travellers (but not all) have advised against mailing exposed films home; either take them with you, or have them developed, but not printed, once you have checked the laboratory's quality. Note that postal authorities may use less sensitive equipment for X-ray screening than the airports do. Modern controlled X-ray machines are supposed to be safe for any speed of film, but it is worth trying to avoid X-rays as the doses are cumulative. Many airport officials will allow film to be passed outside X-ray arches; they may also hand-check a suitcase with a large quantity of film if asked politely.

Dan Buck and Anne Meadows write: A note on developing film in South America. Black and white is a problem. Often it is shoddily machine-processed and the negatives are ruined. Ask the store if you can see an example of their laboratory's work and if they hand-develop.

Jeremy Till and Sarah Wigglesworth suggest that exposed film can be protected in humid areas by putting it in a balloon and tying a knot. Similarly keeping your camera in a plastic bag may reduce the effects of humidity.

● **Police**

Whereas in Europe and North America we are accustomed to law enforcement on a systematic basis, in general, enforcement in Latin America is achieved by periodic campaigns. The most typical is a round-up of criminals in the cities just before Christmas. In December, therefore, you may well be asked for identification at any time, and if you cannot produce it, you will be jailed. If a visitor is jailed his/her friends should provide food every day. This is especially important for people on a diet, such as diabetics. In the event of a vehicle accident in which anyone is injured, all drivers involved are automatically detained until blame has been established, and this does not usually take less than 2 weeks.

Never offer a bribe unless you are fully conversant with the customs of the country. Wait until the official makes the suggestion, or offer money in some form which is apparently not bribery, eg 'In our country we have a system of on-the-spot fines (multas de inmediato). Is there a similar system here?' Do not assume that an official who accepts a bribe is prepared to do anything else that is illegal. You bribe him to persuade him to do his job, or to persuade him not to do it, or to do it more quickly, or more slowly. You do not bribe him to do something which is against the law. The mere suggestion would make him very upset. If an official suggests that a bribe must be paid before you can proceed on your way, be patient (assuming you have the time) and he may relent.

NB Bolivian law states that the police may only search bags at a police station, not on the street. Identity must be checked only by immigration officials; see their identity card and verify the date. Insist on going to the police station, or call the uniformed police if in doubt. If at all possible, insist on your right not to show your passport to anyone on the street. If you can get a witness, so much the better.

The procedure for reporting a robbery is to go to the Departamento de Criminalística, or the office for stolen property, in the town where the theft took place. Purchase official paper from the police for them to write the report, then, with patience and politeness, you may get a report costing between US$1.30 and US$5.25.

● **Safety**

Generally speaking, Bolivia is one of the safer countries to visit in Latin America. Nevertheless, in large cities (particularly in crowded places, eg bus stations, markets), crime exists, most of which is opportunistic.

General tips Keep all documents secure and hide your main cash supply in different places or under your clothes. Extra pockets sewn inside shirts and trousers, pockets closed with a zip or safety pin, moneybelts (best worn below the waist rather than outside or at it or around the neck), neck or leg pouches, a thin chain for attaching a purse to your bag or under your clothes and elasticated support bandages for keeping money and cheques above the elbow or below the knee have been repeatedly recommended (the last by John Hatt in *The Tropical Traveller*). Keep cameras in bags (preferably with a chain or wire in the strap to defeat the slasher) or briefcases; take spare spectacles (eyeglasses); don't wear wrist-watches or jewellery. If you wear a shoulder-bag in a market, carry it in front of you. Backpacks are vulnerable to slashers: a good idea is to cover the pack with a sack (a plastic one will also keep out rain and dust) with maybe a layer of wire netting between, or make an inner frame of chicken wire. Use a pack which is lockable at its base.

Ignore mustard smearers and paint or shampoo sprayers, and strangers' remarks like "what's that on your shoulder?" or "have you seen that dirt on your shoe?" Furthermore, don't bend over to pick up money or other items in the street. These are all ruses intended to distract your attention and make you easy for an accomplice to steal from. If someone follows you when you're in the street, let him catch up with you and 'give him the eye'. While you should take local advice about being out at night, do not assume that daytime is safer than nighttime. If walking after dark, walk in the road, not on the pavement/sidewalk.

Be wary of 'plainclothes policemen'; insist on seeing identification and on going to the police station by main roads. Do not hand over your identification (or money – which they should not need to see anyway) until you are at the station. On no account take them directly back to your lodgings. Be even more suspicious if a 'policeman' seeks confirmation of his status from a passer-by. If someone tries to bribe you, insist on a receipt. If attacked, remember your assailants may well be armed, and try not to resist.

It is best, if you can trust your hotel, to leave any valuables you don't need in safe-deposit there, when sightseeing locally. Always keep an inventory of what you have deposited. If you don't trust the hotel, lock everything in your pack and secure that in your room (some people take eyelet-screws for padlocking cupboards or drawers). If you lose valuables, always report to the police and note details of the report – for insurance purposes.

When you have all your luggage with you at a bus or railway station, be especially careful: don't get into arguments with any locals if you can help it, and lock all the items together with a chain or cable if you are waiting for some time. Take a taxi between airport/bus station/railway station and hotel, if you can possibly afford it. Keep your bags with you in the taxi and pay only when you and your luggage are safely out of the vehicle. Make sure the taxi has inner door handles, in case a quick exit is needed. Avoid night buses; never arrive at night; and watch your belongings whether they are stowed inside or outside the cabin. Roof top luggage racks create extra problems, which are sometimes unavoidable – make sure your bag is waterproof. Major bus lines often issue a luggage ticket when bags are stored in the bus' hold. When getting on a bus, keep your ticket handy; someone sitting in your seat may be a distraction for an accomplice to rob you while you are sorting out the problem. Finally, never accept food, drink, sweets or cigarettes from unknown fellow-travellers on buses or trains. They may be drugged, and you would wake up hours later without your belongings. In this connection, never accept a bar drink from an opened bottle (unless you can see that that bottle is in general use): always have it uncapped in front of you.

Rape This can happen anywhere in the world. If you are the victim of a sexual assault, you are advised in the first instance to contact a doctor (this can be your home doctor if you prefer). You will need tests to determine whether you have contracted any sexually-transmitted diseases; you may also need advice on post-coital contraception. You should also contact your embassy, where consular staff are very willing to help in cases of assault.

Drugs Users of drugs, even of soft ones, without medical prescription should be particularly careful, as some countries impose heavy penalties – up to 10 years' imprisonment – for even the simple possession of such substances. In this connection, the planting of drugs on travellers, by traffickers or the police, is not unknown. If offered drugs on the street, make no response at all and keep walking. Note that people who roll their own cigarettes are often suspected of carrying drugs and subjected to intensive searches. It's advisable to stick to commercial brands of cigarettes.

Travelling alone Many points of security, dress and language have been covered already. First time exposure to countries where sections of the population live in extreme poverty or squalor and may even be starving can cause odd psychological reactions in visitors. So can the exceptional curiosity extended to visitors, especially women. Simply be prepared for this and try not to over-react. These additional hints have mainly been supplied by women, but most apply to any single traveller. When you set out, err on the side of caution until your instincts have adjusted to the customs of a new culture. If, as a single woman, you can befriend a local woman, you will learn much more about the country you are visiting. Unless actively avoiding foreigners like yourself, don't go too far from the beaten track; there is a very definite 'gringo trail' which you can join, or follow, if seeking company. This can be helpful when looking for safe accommodation, especially if arriving after dark (which is best avoided). Remember that for a single woman a taxi at night can be as dangerous as wandering around on her own. At borders dress as smartly as possible. Travelling by train is a good way to meet locals, but buses are much easier for a person alone; on major routes your seat is often reserved and your luggage can usually be locked in the hold. It is easier for men to take the friendliness of locals at face value; women may be subject to much unwanted attention. To help minimize this, do not wear suggestive clothing and, advises Alex Rossi of Jawa Timur, Indonesia, do not flirt. By wearing a wedding ring, carrying a photograph of your 'husband' and 'children', and saying that your 'husband' is close at hand, you may dissuade an aspiring suitor. If politeness fails, do not feel bad about showing offence and departing. When accepting a social invitation, make sure that someone knows the address and the time you left. Ask if you can bring a friend (even if you do not intend to do so). A good rule is always to act with confidence, as though you know where you are going, even if you do not. Someone who looks lost is more likely to attract unwanted attention. Do not disclose to strangers where you are staying. (Much of this information was supplied by Alex Rossi, and by Deirdre Mortell of Carrigaline, Co Cork).

● **Shopping**
Best buys Llama-and alpaca-wool knitted and woven items are at least as good as those from Peru and much cheaper. Among the many items you can buy are ponchos, mantas, bags, chullos (bonnets), gold and silverware and musical instruments such as the charango (mandolin traditionally with armadillo-shell sound-box, now usually of wood) and the quena (Inca flute), and other assorted wooden items. Bargaining seems to be the general rule in most street markets, but don't make a fool of yourself by bargaining over what, to you, is a small amount of money.

If British travellers have no space in their luggage, they might like to remember *Tumi*, the Latin American Craft Centre, who specialize in Mexican and Andean products and who produce cultural and educational videos for schools: at 23/2A Chalk Farm Road, London NW1 8AG (F 0171-485 4152), 8/9 New Bond Street Place,

Bath BA1 1BH (T 01225 462367, F 01225 444870), 1/2 Little Clarendon Street, Oxford OX1 2HJ (T/F 01865-512307), 82 Park Street, Bristol BS1 5LA (T/F 0117 929 0391). Tumi (Music) Ltd specializes in different rhythms of Latin America. See *Arts and Crafts of South America*, by Lucy Davies and Mo Fini, published by Tumi (1994), for a fine introduction to the subject. There are similar shops in the USA.

● **Tipping**
Up to 10% in restaurants; in all other cases a tip is given in recognition of a service provided, eg to a taxi driver who has been helpful (an extra US$0.15-US$0.20), to someone who has looked after a car, carried bags, etc.

● **Voltage**
Varies considerably. Generally 110 volts, 50 cycles AC in La Paz, 220 volts 50 cycles AC elsewhere, but check before using any appliance. (You may even find 110 and 220 in the same room.) US-type plugs can be used in most hotels.

● **Working in Bolivia**
Getting a work visa is easy – just marry a Bolivian. Alternatively, you can get stuck in a bureaucratic maze. But be patient; it does actually work and there is far less bribery involved than you probably imagine. You will need to start a couple of weeks before your tourist visa runs out. There is a US$2 per day fine for exceeding your stay. Here is an easy-to-follow eleven-point guide to success:

1) Get a 3-month work contract signed by your employer and yourself. **2)** Go to a solicitor (*abogado*) and ask for legal requests with copies (*memoriales*) asking for the Policía Técnica Judicial (PTJ) for *registro domiciliario* (proof of where you live) and *antecedentes* (proof that you are not wanted by the police); these cost US$6 each. **3)** Return to the solicitor the next day to pick up the *memoriales*, take them to the ground floor of the PTJ and hand them in. **4)** Make a copy of the relevant page(s) of your passport, return to the PTJ the next day, buy the forms for *domiciliario* (US$1.40) and *antecedentes* (US$3) from the man with the briefcase on the ground floor, go up to the fourth floor, hand in the forms and your passport, get fingerprinted, and arrange to meet a policeman to take to your home. **5)** Meet the policeman at the PTJ either at lunchtime or after work, take him to your home, paying for whatever transport is required, give him copies of electricity, water and telephone bills plus a copy of your rent agreement. He will give you a form which needs the signatures of two Bolivians as guarantors plus photocopies of their identity cards. Once again, pay the policeman's transport costs, but nothing more. **6)** Go back to the PTJ a few days later to pick up the *domiciliario* and *antecedentes*. **7)** Buy an official medical certificate from the medical school in Calle Ballivián, between Bolívar and Colón (US$3), or from the tailor's shop next door or the photocopy shop displaying the sign '*Certificado Médico*'. Then go to the Institución Nacional de Salud Ocupacional in Calle Claudio Sanjines in Miraflores (open 0800-1100). Make sure you didn't drink too much the previous evening, don't eat breakfast and take a sample of urine (the first passed that morning), plus a copy of your passport. Then pay US$30 to be weighed and measured in the *enfermería*, hand in your urine sample and give a blood sample at the *laboratorio clínico*, where you are also given a thorough medical examination. Return the next day between 1000 and 1400 to collect your certificate. **8)** Return to the solicitor and get a *memorial* asking the Subsecretaría de Migración for a 3-month work visa (US$6). **9)** Go to Migración in Calle Camacho, below Loayza, Ventana 3 on the ground floor. Hand in the *memorial*, work contract, *domiciliario*, *antecedentes*, *certificado médico* and your passport. From Ventana 2 buy a folder (*carpeta*) to put everything in (US$1) and buy a work visa application form (US$100). Then you are given a form to buy stickers (*estampillas consulares*). **10)** Go to the tax office (*Renta Interna*) in Calle Ballivián between Colón and Loayza and buy the *estampillas consulares* (US$50), then take them back to Migración. **11)** Finally, return to Migración 48 hours later and pick up your passport with the 3 month work visa sticker stuck in and stamped. Congratualtions! You can now legally work for the next 3 months until you need to embark upon a similar, but lengthier and costlier process to get a 1 year work visa. Of course, you could always marry a Bolivian. (Thanks to Yossi Brain, La Paz.)

For more information on arranging work permits, visas and immigration in South America, send two x 25p stamps for information to Jobs Abroad, Worldwide House, Broad Street, Port Ramsgate, Kent, CT11 8NQ.

ON DEPARTURE

● **Departure taxes**
A tax of US$20, payable in dollars or bolivianos, cash only, is levied on leaving by air (US$30 extra if you have stayed over 3 months). On internal

flights a tax of US$1.95 is paid. Tax on airline tickets is 18%.

WHERE TO STAY

● **Hotels**
Outside the main cities, there are few higher-class hotels. These charge 20% tax and service. Even in La Paz, it is quite easy to find a clean, comfortable hotel room, without a private bathroom, for around US$4-5 per person. For those on a tight budget, a cheaper room can be found in a *hospedaje*, *pensión*, *casa familial* or *residencial*; they are normally to be found in abundance near bus and railway stations and markets. Note that there are often great seasonal variations in hotel prices in resorts and prices can rise substantially during public holidays and festivals.

Hotels must display prices by law. Throughout Bolivia the cheaper hotels impose their own curfews. In La Paz it tends to be midnight (check), but it can be as early as 2130 in Copacabana. These locking up times are strictly adhered to by hotel keepers. Ask for the hot water schedule; it changes with the season, water pressure, etc. Clothes washing is generally not allowed. Many mid-range hotels will keep money and valuables in the safe if there are no safety-deposit boxes. Cheaper hotels rarely have heating in the rooms. Youth Hostels are not necessarily cheaper: many middle range *residenciales* are affiliated to the IYHA.

Note that in the text 'with bath' usually means 'with shower and toilet', not 'with bath tub'. Remember, cheaper hotels don't always supply soap, towels and toilet paper; in colder (higher) regions they may not supply enough blankets, so take your own or a sleeping bag. In any class, hotel rooms facing the street may be noisy; always ask for the best, quietest room. Also note that hotel owners may try to let their less attractive rooms first, but are not insulted if you ask to see another room.

NB The electric showers used in innumerable hotels should be checked for obvious flaws in the wiring; try not to touch the rose while it is producing hot water.

● **Cockroaches**
These are ubiquitous and unpleasant, but not dangerous. Take some insecticide powder if staying in cheap hotels; Baygon (Bayer) has been recommended. Stuff toilet paper in any holes in walls that you may suspect of being parts of cockroach runs.

Hotel prices

Our hotel price ranges, including taxes and service charges but without meals unless stated, are as follows:

L1	Over US$200	**L2**	US$151-200	**L3**	US$101-150
A1	US$81-100	**A2**	US$61-80	**A3**	US$46-60
B	US$31-45	**C**	US$21-30	**D**	US$12-20
E	US$7-11	**F**	US$4-6	**G**	Up to US$3

NB Prices are for double rooms, except in **F** and **G** ranges where the price is almost always per person.

● **Toilets**

Many hotels, restaurants and bars have inadequate water supplies. Almost without exception used toilet paper should **not** be flushed down the pan, but placed in the receptacle provided. This applies even in quite expensive hotels. Failing to observe this custom will block the pan or drain, a considerable health risk. It is quite common for people to stand on the toilet seat (facing the wall – easier to balance).

● **Camping**

Warm sleeping gear is essential, even in the lowlands in the winter. Sleeping bags are also useful for getting some sleep on the buses or long distance trains, especially those crossing the Andes. Mosquito nets can be purchased in La Paz, but they are not cheap. Beware sandstorms south of Oruro.

Organized campsites are referred to in the text immediately below hotel lists, under each town. If there is no organized site in town, a football pitch or gravel pit might serve. Obey the following rules for 'wild' camping: (1) arrive in daylight and pitch your tent as it gets dark; (2) ask permission to camp from the parish priest, or the fire chief, or the police, or a farmer regarding his own property; (3) never ask a group of people – especially young people. If you can't get information from anyone, camp in a spot where you can't be seen from the nearest inhabited place, or road, and make sure no one saw you go there.

If taking a cooker, the most frequent recommendation is a multifuel stove (eg MSR International, Coleman Peak 1), which will burn unleaded petrol or, if that is not available, kerosene, *benzina blanca*, etc. Alcohol-burning stoves are simple, reliable, but slow and you have to carry a lot of fuel: for a methylated spirit-burning stove, the following fuels apply, *alcohol desnaturalizado, alcohol metílico, alcohol puro (de caña)* or *alcohol para quemar*. Ask for 95%, but 70% will suffice. In all countries fuel can usually be found in chemists/pharmacies. Gas cylinders and bottles are usually exchangeable, but if not can be recharged; specify whether you use butane or propane. Camping gas-style and Epigas cannisters are available in La Paz and all large cities; white gas for Coleman stoves is difficult to find. Kerosene is much easier to find outside La Paz, even in small towns. *Alcohol potable* (meths) is widely available.

GETTING AROUND

AIR TRANSPORT

Internal air services are run by Lloyd Aéreo Boliviano (LAB), Aero Sur and TAM between the main cities and towns. LAB and Aero Sur are generally reliable but TAM much less so. TAM also fly to many of the smaller settlements in the tropical lowlands. Note that TAM flights leave from the military airport, which is next to the main commercial one in El Alto.

Boarding passes are issued only at airports; after obtaining one, pay the airport tax (see above). LAB offers a 28-day unlimited domestic flight ticket for US$135 for international travellers using LAB (or a foreign carrier with whom LAB may have a pooling arrangement) and must be bought outside Bolivia. Only one stopover per city is allowed, except for connecting flights; note that many flights radiate from La Paz, Santa Cruz or Cochabamba. LAB have 20% discounts for family members if they travel together (take passport); LAB and Aero Sur also offer discounts of 20% to students and passengers over 60; and TAM offer 25% discount to students and over 60s. LAB can be contacted at 0800 3001 (toll free) and Aero Sur at 0800 3030 (toll free).

Note that a 'through' flight may require a change of plane, or be delayed waiting for a connecting flight coming from elsewhere. Only on international flights is overnight lodging provided

Main Air Routes

during delays. Insure your bags heavily as they tend to get left around.

NB If your internal flight is delayed keep your baggage with you and do not check it in until the flight is definitely announced. There have been robberies of prematurely checked-in baggage. Flights into and out of the tropical regions are badly affected in the wet season and may be cancelled at a moment's notice.

LAND TRANSPORT

● Trains

Bolivia has 3,774 km of railway. There are two private railways: Machacamarca-Uncia, owned by the Corporación Minera de Bolivia (108 km) and Uyuni-Pulacayo (52 km) owned by the Empresa Minera Pulacayo. The Empresa Nacional de Ferrocarriles (ENFE), was privatized in 1996 and the future of many services is in doubt. We have received reports that there is no service to or from La Paz as of August 1997. Even when

trains are running schedules change frequently. Always check departure times in advance. Tickets can be bought in advance. Trains tend to be a lot slower than buses; but there is the advantage of being able to see more of the scenery.

● Road

The national highway system at the end of 1993 totalled 42,438 km, of which only 4% were paved and under 25% gravel-surfaced. Descriptions of all major roads are given in the text, above. Nearly all Bolivian road surfaces, even the paved sections, are bad, and after flooding or rough weather they are even worse. Even main roads may be closed in the rainy season.

NB On election day no public transport runs whatsoever; only cars with a special permit may be on the road.

● Buses

Buses ply most of the roads (interurban buses are called *flotas*, urban ones *micros*, also minibuses and *trufis*). Reporting time is half an hour before the bus leaves. You should always try to reserve, and pay for, a seat as far as possible in advance and arrive in good time, but substantial savings can be made by buying tickets just before departure as there is fierce competition to fill seats. In the wet season, bus travel is subject to long delays and detours at extra cost. In the dry season journeys can be very dusty. On all journeys, take food and toilet wipes. Bus companies are responsible for any luggage packed on the roof. A small charge is made for use of major bus terminals; payment is before departure.

Many buses are comfortable but the difficulties of Andean terrain affect the quality of vehicles. In mountainous country do not expect buses to get to their destination after long journeys anywhere near on time. Do not turn up for a bus at the last minute; if it is full it may depart early. Tall travellers are advised to take aisle rather than window seats on long journeys as this allows more leg room. When the journey takes more than 3 or 4 hours, meal stops at country inns or bars, good and bad, are the rule. Usually, no announcement is made on the duration of a stop: follow the driver, if he eats, eat. See what the locals are eating – and buy likewise, or make sure you're stocked up well on food and drink at the start. For drinks, stick to bottled water or soft drinks or coffee (black). The food sold by vendors at bus stops may be all right: watch if locals are buying, though unpeeled fruit is of course reliable. So many buses now show video films that you can't see the countryside because the curtains are drawn. Complaining to the conductor that you cannot see the beautiful landscape may persuade him to give you his seat at the front.

● **Trucks**

Trucks congregate at all town markets, with destinations chalked on the sides. They are normally about half the cost when there is competition. Otherwise they charge what they judge the market will bear and can therefore seem expensive.

● **Motoring**

Road tolls vary from US$0.50 to US$2.50 for journeys up to 100 km. In theory, you need an International Driving Permit (and, since a driving licence number is requested, also your national driving licence, or some ingenuity). Just a national licence will do when hiring a car and the rental document usually suffices at police controls. Two authorization certificates are required

in La Paz: the first from the Automóvil Club Boliviano, corner of 6 de Agosto and Arce, T/F 372139, and the second from the traffic police at the Comando Departamental, Organismo Operativo de Tránsito, corner of Mariscal Santa Cruz and Plaza San Francisco.

Take great care when driving at night (it is best not to): cyclists do not usually have lights; truck drivers almost never dip their headlights (keep your own on full beam to make the truck dip his); some truck drivers are drunk, or fall asleep at the wheel; at the slightest sign of danger, pull out of the way. Day or night, watch out for people asleep at the roadside in lowland areas; they tend to lie with head and torso in the road where there are fewer mosquitoes.

Petrol (gasoline) two grades: 85 and 92 octane. 85 octane costs US$0.44, super US$0.56; diesel costs US$0.38 per litre. Costs are higher in Guayaramerín, Riberalta and Puerto Suárez. Around Lake Titicaca, there are no petrol stations as such, the only two that exist frequently run out. Petrol is sold from the drum in every small village.

The machine While a normal car will reach most places of interest, high ground clearance is useful for badly surfaced or unsurfaced roads and for fording rivers: 4WD is recommended for mountain terrain and unmade roads off the beaten track.

If you want to buy a second-hand car, check for corrosion and always check, if not change, the full set of tyres. Consider fitting wire guards for headlamps, and for windscreens too, if you don't mind peering out through a grill like a caged chimpanzee. Wherever you travel you should expect to find roads that are badly maintained, damaged or closed during the wet season, and delays because of floods, landslides and huge potholes. Don't plan your schedules too tightly.

Diesel cars are much cheaper to run than petrol ones, and the fuel is easily available. Most towns can supply a mechanic of sorts, and probably parts for Bosch fuel injection equipment. Watch the mechanics like a hawk, since there's always a brisk market in spares, and some of yours may be highly desirable. That apart, they enjoy a challenge, and can fix most things, eventually.

For prolonged motoring over 3,000 metres, you may need to fit high altitude jets on your carburettors. Some fuel injection engines need adjusting too, and ignition settings may have to be changed: check the manufacturer's recommendations. The electronic ignition and fuel metering systems on modern emission control-led cars are allergic to humidity, heat and dust, and cannot be repaired by bush mechanics. Standard European and Japanese cars run on fuel with a higher octane rating than is commonly available. A high compression fuel injection engine will not like this. The most easily maintained petrol engined cars, then, are the types manufactured in Latin American countries, ie pre-emission control models such as the VW Kombi with carburettors and conventional (non-electronic) ignition, or the old type Toyota Landcruisers. Older model American cars, especially Ford or GM pickups, are easily maintained, but high fuel consumption offsets this advantage.

Preparation Preparing the car for the journey is largely a matter of common sense: obviously any part that is not in first class condition should be replaced. It's well worth installing extra heavy-duty shock-absorbers (such as Spax or Koni) before starting out, because a long trip on rough roads in a heavily laden car will give heavy wear. Fit tubes on 'tubeless' tyres, since air plugs for tubeless tyres are hard to find, and if you bend the rim on a pothole, the tyre will not hold air. Take spare tubes, and an extra spare tyre. Also take spare plugs, fan-belts, radiator hoses and headlamp bulbs; even though local equivalents can easily be found in cities, it is wise to take spares for those occasions late at night or in remote areas when you might need them. You can also change the fanbelt after a stretch of long, hot driving to prevent wear (eg after 15,000 km per 10,000 miles). If your vehicle has more than one fanbelt, always replace them all at the same time (make sure you have the necessary tools if doing it yourself). If your car has sophisticated electrics, spare 'black boxes' for the ignition and fuel injection are advisable, plus a spare voltage regulator and the appropriate diodes for the alternator, and elements for the fuel, air and oil filters if these are not a common type. (Some drivers take a spare alternator of the correct amperage, especially if the regulator is incorporated into the alternator.)

Dirty fuel is a frequent problem, so be prepared to change filters more often than you would at home: in a diesel car you will need to check the sediment bowl often, too. An extra in-line fuel filter is a good idea if feasible (although harder to find, metal canister type is preferable to plastic), and for travel on dusty roads an oil bath air filter is best for a diesel car. It is wise to carry a spade, jumper cables, tow rope and an air pump. Fit tow hooks to both sides of the vehicle frame. A 12-volt neon light for camping and

repairs will be invaluable. Spare fuel containers should be steel and not plastic, and a siphon pipe is essential for those places where fuel is sold out of the drum. Take a 10 litre water container for self and vehicle. Note that in some areas gas stations are few and far between. Fill up when you see one: the next one may be out of fuel.

Security Apart from the mechanical aspects, spare no ingenuity in making your car secure. Your model should be the Brink's armoured van: anything less secure can be broken into by the determined and skilled thief. Use heavy chain and padlocks to chain doors shut, fit security catches on windows, remove interior window winders (so that a hand reaching in from a forced vent cannot open the window). All these will help, but none is foolproof. Anything on the outside – wing mirrors, spot lamps, motifs etc – is likely to be stolen too. So are wheels if not secured by locking nuts. Try never to leave the car unattended except in a locked garage or guarded parking space. Remove all belongings and leave the empty glove compartment open when the car is unattended. Also lock the clutch or accelerator to the steering wheel with a heavy, obvious chain or lock. Street children will generally protect your car fiercely in exchange for a tip. Be sure to note down key numbers and carry spares of the most important ones (but don't keep all spares inside the vehicle).

Documents Always carry your passport and driving licence. You also need the registration document in the name of the driver or, in the case of a car registered in someone else's name, a notarized letter of authorization.

According to the RAC in the UK only the *Libreta de Pasos por Aduana* issued by the Federación Interamericana de Touring y Automóvil Clubs (FITAC), is needed in Bolivia. The *libreta*, a ten-page book of three-part passes for customs, should be available from any South American automobile club member of FITAC. The cost is about US$350, but is more for those who are not members of automobile clubs; about a third of the cost is refundable.

Insurance for the vehicle against accident, damage or theft is best arranged in the country of origin, but it is getting increasingly difficult to find agencies who offer this service. It is very expensive to insure against accident and theft, especially as you should take into account the value of the car increased by duties calculated in real (ie non devaluing) terms. If the car is stolen or written off you will be required to pay very high import duty on its value. Get the legally required minimum cover, not expensive, as soon as you can, because if you should be involved in an accident and are uninsured, your car could be confiscated. If anyone is hurt, do not pick them up (you may become liable). Seek assistance from the nearest police station or hospital if you are able to do so.

● **Car Hire**

The minimum age for renting a car is 25. Car hire companies and rates are given in the text, but they do tend to be very expensive, reflecting the high costs and accident rates. Hotels and tourist agencies will tell you where to find cheaper rates, but you will need to check that you have such basics as spare wheel, toolkit and functioning lights etc.

Car Hire Insurance Check exactly what the hirer's insurance policy covers. In many cases it will only protect you against minor bumps and scrapes, not major accidents, nor 'natural' damage (eg flooding). Ask if extra cover is available. Also find out, if using a credit card, whether the card automatically includes insurance. Beware of being billed for scratches which were on the vehicle before you hired it.

● **Motorcycling**

People are generally very amicable to motorcyclists and you can make many friends by returning friendship to those who show an interest in you.

The Machine It should be off road capable for example: the BMW R80/100/GS, with its rugged and simple design and reliable shaft drive; a Kawasaki KLR 650s, Honda Transalp/Dominator, or the ubiquitous Yamaha XT600 Tenere would also be suitable. Buying a bike in the States and driving down works out cheaper than buying one in the UK. A road bike can go most places an off road bike can go at the cost of greater effort.

Preparations Many Bolivian roads are rough. Fit heavy duty front fork springs and the best quality rebuildable shock absorber you can afford (Ohlins, White Power). Fit lockable luggage such as Krausers (reinforce luggage frames) or make some detachable aluminium panniers. Fit a tank bag and tank panniers for better weight distribution. A large capacity fuel tank (Acerbis), +300 mile/480 km range is essential if going off the beaten track. A washable air filter is a good idea (K&N), also fuel filters, fueltap rubber seals and smaller jets for high altitude Andean motoring. A good set of trails-type tyres as well as a high mudguard are useful. Get to know the bike before you go, ask the dealers in your

country what goes wrong with it and arrange a link whereby you can get parts flown out to you. If riding a chain driven bike, a fully enclosed chaincase is useful. A hefty bash plate/sump guard is invaluable.

Spares Reduce service intervals by half if driving in severe conditions. A spare rear tyre is useful but you can buy modern tyres in most capital cities. Take oil filters, fork and shock seals, tubes, a good manual, spare cables (taped into position), a plug cap and spare plug lead. A spare electronic ignition is a good idea, try and buy a second hand one and make arrangements to have parts sent out to you. A first class tool kit is a must and if riding a bike with a chain then a spare set of sprockets and an 'o' ring chain should be carried. Spare brake and clutch levers should also be taken as these break easily in a fall. Parts are few and far between, but mechanics are skilled at making do and can usually repair things. Castrol oil can be bought everywhere and relied upon.

Take a puncture repair kit and tyre levers. Find out about any weak spots on the bike and improve them. Get the book for international dealer coverage from your manufacturer, but don't rely on it. They frequently have few or no parts for modern, large machinery.

Clothes and equipment A tough waterproof jacket, comfortable strong boots, gloves and a helmet with which you can use glass goggles (Halycon) which will not scratch and wear out like a plastic visor. The best quality tent and camping gear that you can afford and a petrol stove which runs on bike fuel is helpful.

Security Try not to leave a fully laden bike on its own. An Abus D or chain will keep the bike secure. A cheap alarm gives you peace of mind if you leave the bike outside a hotel at night. Most hotels will allow you to bring the bike inside. Look for hotels that have a courtyard or more secure parking and never leave luggage on the bike overnight or whilst unattended.

Documents Passport, International Driving Licence, bike registration document are necessary. Riders fare much better with a *libreta* than without it. Get your licence endorsed by police in Bolivia.

● **Cycling**

At first glance a bicycle may not appear to be the most obvious vehicle for a major journey, but given ample time and reasonable energy it most certainly is the best. It can be ridden, carried by almost every form of transport from an aeroplane to a canoe, and can even be lifted across one's shoulders over short distances. Cyclists can be the envy of travellers using more orthodox transport, since they can travel at their own pace, explore more remote regions and meet people who are not normally in contact with tourists.

Choosing a bicycle The choice of bicycle depends on the type and length of expedition being undertaken and on the terrain and road surfaces likely to be encountered. Unless you are planning a journey almost exclusively on paved roads – when a high quality touring bike such as a Dawes Super Galaxy would probably suffice – a mountain bike is strongly recommended. The good quality ones (and the cast iron rule is never to skimp on quality) are incredibly tough and rugged, with low gear ratios for difficult terrain, wide tyres with plenty of tread for good road-holding, cantilever brakes, and a low centre of gravity for improved stability. Although touring bikes, and to a lesser extent mountain bikes, and spares are available in the larger cities, remember that in the developing world most indigenous manufactured goods are shoddy and rarely last. Buy everything you possibly can before you leave home.

Bicycle equipment A small but comprehensive tool kit (to include chain rivet and crank removers, a spoke key and possibly a block remover), a spare tyre and inner tubes, a puncture repair kit with plenty of extra patches and glue, a set of brake blocks, brake and gear cables and all types of nuts and bolts, at least twelve spokes (best taped to the chain stay), a light oil for the chain (eg Finish-Line Teflon Dry-Lube), tube of waterproof grease, a pump secured by a pump lock, a Blackburn parking block (a most invaluable accessory, cheap and virtually weightless), a cyclometer, a loud bell, and a secure lock and chain. *Richard's Bicycle Book* makes useful reading for even the most mechanically minded.

Luggage and equipment Strong and waterproof front and back panniers are a must. When packed these are likely to be heavy and should be carried on the strongest racks available. Poor quality racks have ruined many a journey for they take incredible strain on unpaved roads. A top bag cum rucksack (eg Carradice) makes a good addition for use on and off the bike. A Cannondale front bag is good for maps, camera, compass, altimeter, notebook and small tape-recorder. (Other recommended panniers are Ortlieb – front and back – which is waterpoof and almost 'sandproof', Mac-Pac, Madden and Karimoor.) 'Gaffa' tape is excellent for

protecting vulnerable parts of panniers and for carrying out all manner of repairs.

All equipment and clothes should be packed in plastic bags to give extra protection against dust and rain. (Also protect all documents, etc carried close to the body from sweat.) Always take the minimum clothing. It's better to buy extra items en route when you find you need them. Naturally the choice will depend on whether you are planning a journey through tropical lowlands, deserts, high mountains or a combination, and whether rain is to be expected. Generally it is best to carry several layers of thin light clothes than fewer heavy, bulky ones. Always keep one set of dry clothes, including long trousers, to put on at the end of the day. The incredibly light, strong, waterproof and wind resistant goretex jacket and overtrousers are invaluable. Training shoes can be used for both cycling and walking.

Useful tips Wind, not hills is the enemy of the cyclist. Try to make the best use of the times of day when there is little; mornings tend to be best but there is no steadfast rule. Take care to avoid dehydration, by drinking regularly. In hot, dry areas with limited supplies of water, be sure to carry an ample supply. For food, carry the staples (sugar, salt, dried milk, tea, coffee, porridge oats, raisins, dried soups, etc) and supplemented these with whatever local foods can be found in the markets. Give your bicycle a thorough daily check for loose nuts or bolts or bearings. See that all parts run smoothly. A good chain should last 2,000 miles, 3,200 km or more, but be sure to keep it as clean as possible – an old toothbrush is good for this – and to oil it lightly from time to time. Always camp out of sight of a road. Remember that thieves are attracted to towns and cities, so when sight-seeing, try to leave your bicycle with someone such as a café owner or a priest. Country people tend to be more honest and are usually friendly and very inquisitive. However, don't take unnecessary risks; always see that your bicycle is secure (most hotels will allow bikes to be kept in rooms). In more remote regions dogs can be vicious; carry a stick or some small stones to frighten them off. Traffic on main roads can be a nightmare; it is usually far more rewarding to keep to the smaller roads or to paths if they exist. Most towns have a bicycle shop of some description, but it is best to do your own repairs and adjustments whenever possible.

The Expedition Advisory Centre, administered by the Royal Geographical Society, 1, Kensington Gore, London SW7 2AR has published a useful monograph entitled *Bicycle Expeditions*, by Paul Vickers. Published in March 1990, it is available direct from the Centre, price £6.50 (postage extra if outside the UK). (In the UK there is also the Cyclist's Touring Club, CTC, Cotterell House, 69 Meadrow, Godalming, Surrey, GU7 3HS, T 01483-417217, e-mail: cycling@ctc.org.uk, for touring, and technical information.)

Most cyclists agree that the main danger comes from other traffic. A rearview mirror has been frequently recommended to forewarn you of vehicles which are too close behind. You also need to watch out for oncoming, overtaking vehicles, unstable loads on trucks, protruding loads etc. Make yourself conspicuous by wearing bright clothing and a helmet.

COMMUNICATIONS

● Language
The official language is Spanish. Quechua, the language of the Inca empire, is spoken by many of the indigenous people of the highlands, as is Aymara, a pre-Inca language which has survived the passage of many centuries. Away from the main urban centres in the Altiplano, many indigenous people have no knowledge of Spanish.

● Media
In La Paz: morning papers – *Presencia*, daily, the largest circulation, largely Catholic; *La Razón*, *Primera Plana*, *Hoy* and *El Diario* (sensationalist). *Meridiano* (midday): *Ultima Hora*, and *Jornada* (evenings). In Cochabamba – *Los Tiempos*, *Extra*. In Oruro – *La Patria*, mornings (except Monday). *El Día*, *La Estrella del Oriente*, *El Mundo* and *El Deber* are the Santa Cruz daily papers; *Deber* also appears in La Paz and Trinidad. In Sucre, *El Correo*. *Presencia*, *El Diario*, *El Mundo*, *La Razón* all have good foreign coverage. Weekly: *Nueva Economía*. La Paz papers are on sale in other cities. The English language weekly *The Bolivian Times*, published Friday, US$1.50, is available in major cities, with many travel and cultural features and local news reports (details T 340062, F 390700, address Jauregui 2248, Sopocachi, La Paz, casilla 1696). International papers are available in La Paz. Also, there are about 85 radio stations, a commercial government TV station as well as a university TV service.

● Postal services
Post offices use the post box (casilla) system. Items sent by post should therefore bear, not the street address, but the casilla number and town. Hours are Monday-Saturday 0800-2000, Sunday 0800-1200. For security, send mail 'certificado'. There is a national and international express post system; special counters and envelopes provided. Air-mail letters to and from Europe take between 5 and 10 days. Letter/postcard up to 30g to Europe US$0.80, to North America US$0.70; letter over 30g to Europe US$2.50, to North America US$1.80. Parcels up to 2 kg can be sent airmail after inspection by customs; to Europe a 2 kg parcel costs US$37, to North America US$26. There is a choice of airmail (which takes 1 week) or APR/SAL (which takes a month). A 5 kg parcel to Europe airmail costs US$62, APR/SAL US$41; to North America airmail US$50, APR/SAL US$35. Parcels are checked by customs officers before being sealed. We have received several reports of customs officers attempting to charge for inspecting parcels: refuse to pay (politely).

NB Check before leaving home if your Embassy will hold mail, and for how long, in preference to the Poste Restante/General Delivery (Lista de Correos) department of the Post Office. (Cardholders can use American Express agencies.) If there seems to be no mail at the Lista under the initial letter of your surname, ask them to look under the initial of your forename or your middle name. Remember that there is no W in Spanish; look under V, or ask. For the smallest risk of misunderstanding, use title, initial and surname only. If having items sent to you by courier (eg DHL), do not use poste restante, but an address such as a hotel: a signature is required on receipt.

● Telephone services
The national telecommunications company is Entel, which handles all phone, telex and fax services. In the Department of La Paz, Cotel operates local services, alongside Entel. There is now direct satellite communication with Bolivia. Direct calls are possible from major cities to Europe, USA, Australia and elsewhere, clear lines, delays minimal; US$2.06 per minute to Europe and Mexico, US$1.76 to USA and South America, US$3.44 to Australia. BT Chargecard calls are available direct to UK. At the La Paz exchange you can pay by credit card and the phone shows the cost as you speak. Outside La Paz you may have to wait a while for an overseas connection, but otherwise there are no problems. Fax to Europe costs US$5 per page, to the USA US$3.80, to Australia, New Zealand US$6. Phone calls within city limits are free for private calls; for public phones, coins/*fichas* or phone cards are necessary. *Fichas* and phone cards only work in the city in which they are bought.

Direct collect-call numbers: US AT&T 0800 1111, MCI 0800 2222, Sprint 0800 3333, IDB (TRT) 0800 4444; UK BT 0800 0044; Spain

Telefónica 0800 0034; Brazil 0800 0055; Chile Entel 0800 0056; Canada Teleglobe 0800 0101; Japan KDD 0800 0081.

Communicating by fax is a convenient way of sending messages home. Many places with public fax machines (post offices, telephone companies or shops) will receive messages as well as send. Fax machines are often switched off; you may have to phone to confirm receipt.

● **E-mail**

E-mail is becoming more common and public access to the Internet is now possible with cybercafés opening in La Paz (see main text for details). There is usually a charge per page sent or received, which compares favourably with fax charges.

● **World Band Radio**

South America has more local and community radio stations than practically anywhere else in the world; a shortwave (world band) radio offers a practical means to brush up on the language, sample popular culture and absorb some of the richly varied regional music. International broadcasters such as the BBC World Service, the Voice of America, Boston (Mass)-based Monitor Radio International (operated by Christian Science Monitor) and the Quito-based Evangelical station, HCJB, keep the traveller abreast of news and events, in both English and Spanish.

Compact or miniature portables are recommended, with digital tuning and a full range of shortwave bands, as well as FM, long and medium wave. Detailed advice on radio models (£150 for a decent one) and wavelengths can be found in the annual publication, *Passport to*

World Band Radio (Box 300, Penn's Park, PA 18943, USA). Details of local stations is listed in *World TV and Radio Handbook* (WTRH), PO Box 9027, 1006 AA Amsterdam, The Netherlands, US$19.95. Both of these, free wavelength guides and selected radio sets are available from the BBC World Service Bookshop, Bush House Arcade, Bush House, Strand, London WC2B 4PH, UK, T 0171-257 2576.

SPORT

Bolivia offers many possibilities for hiking and climbing and various treks and climbs are outlined in the **Adventure Tourism** section at the beginning of the book. Skiing is also a possibility. Soccer is the main sport and is played in all the major cities. Rivalry between the two teams in La Paz is particularly fierce. You can play at the highest golf course in the world. Fishing, mountain biking and horse riding are also on offer to tourists. Volleyball and basketball are also popular.

HOLIDAYS AND FESTIVALS

● **Public holidays**

1 January, New Year's Day; Carnival Week, Monday, Shrove Tuesday, Ash Wednesday; Holy Week, Thursday, Friday and Saturday; 1 May, Labour Day; Corpus Christi (movable); 16 July, La Paz Municipal Holiday; 5-7 August, Independence; 12 October, Columbus Day; 2 November, Day of the Dead; Christmas Day. For a full list of local, regional and national festivals, see the **Festivals** section at the beginning of the book.

Section 5

Rounding up

ACKNOWLEDGEMENTS

For their help in the research and preparation of this Handbook and hospitality in Bolivia, I would like to thank the following: Yossi Brain, our resident drinking and climbing correspondent in La Paz, for his many contributions and valuable assistance. Also those who helped Yossi: Louis Demers (*Residencial Sorata*), Ulli Schatz, Oscar Vera, José Velasco, Omar Rocha, Jorge Echalar, Orustva Machado García and Tito Ponce. Thanks also to Geoffrey Groesbeck of Massachusetts for his considerable help. Thanks to Amanda and Martin Srätker of *La Cúpula*, Copacabana, for updates on Copacabana and Isla del Sol; Michel Livet of *Fremen Tours* in La Paz (also Mariel in Cochabamba, Mechy in Santa Cruz and Dora in Trinidad); Darius Morgan and Teresita Reyes of *Crillon Tours*; Jacques Valleton of *Turismo Balsa*; Ingrid Guttentag at *Los Amigos del Libro* in Cochabamba; Claudia Castellón Velarde, Marketing Director at the Secretaría Nacional de Turismo in La Paz; Victor Edmundo Salínas at *Sur Andes* in Sucre; Andy Jackson in Santa Cruz; Saturnino Machaca at *La Hostería* in Chulumani; Fernando at *Hotel Esmeralda* in Coroico; Peter McFarren, Quipus and *Bolivian Times*, La Paz; Dan Buck of Washington DC; Willi Noack at Tumi-Chucua in Riberalta; Claudia Villazón Pérez of La Paz; and Mo Fini and Lucy Davies at *Tumi*. Also thanks to all the specialist contributors mentioned at the start of the book and not forgetting Ben Box, editor of the *South American Handbook*.

Thanks are also due to all the travellers and correspondents who contributed to the 1998 edition of the *South American Handbook*.

Finally, special thanks to Beatriz Verástegui R for inspiration and encouragement.

FURTHER READING

An Insider's Guide to Bolivia, by Peter McFarren (Fundación Cultural Quipus, Casilla 1696, La Paz, 3rd edition, 1992, US$25), is available in many bookshops and larger hotels in La Paz, it gives a good historical background and includes an interesting article by Johann Reinhard about archaeological discoveries in Lake Titicaca (see page 140). Reinhard also contributed a chapter on 'Underwater Archaeological Research in Lake Titicaca' to *Ancient America, Contributions to New World Archaeology*, edited by Nicholas J Saunders (Oxford: Oxbow Monograph 24, 1992). Also published by Quipus is *La fe viva: las Misiones Jesuíticas en Bolivia*, a thorough history of the Jesuit Missions with many sumptuous photographs of the churches; and *Masks of the Bolivian Andes*. *Descubriendo Bolivia*, Hugo Boero Rojo (1989), is a tour through the departments of present-day Bolivia, with photographs and road routes (also available in English). *Bolivia in*

Focus, by Paul Van Lindent and Otto Verkaren (Latin American Bureau, London 1984) is a concise study of Bolivian politics, economy, culture and people.

For information on arts and crafts see *Arts and Crafts of South America*, by Lucy Davies and Mo Fini, published by Tumi, 1994.

In *The Incredible Voyage*, Tristan Jones (Futura Publications), the author describes over 8 months of cruising Lake Titicaca in his sailing cutter Sea Dart. An interesting insight into the lives of the Aymara is given in *Sons of the Moon*, by Henry Shukman (Fontana, 1991).

Jason Wilson's, *Traveller's Literary Companion*, South and Central America (Brighton, UK: In Print, 1993), has extracts from works by Latin American writers and by non-Latin Americans about the various countries and has very useful bibliographies. Those interested in birdwatching should see *Birds of the High Andes*, by N Krabbe and J Fjeldsa (Apollow Books, Denmark, 1990).

HISTORY

Many general books contain information on Bolivia: *The Cambridge Encyclopedia of Latin America and the Caribbean*, edited by Simon Collier, Thomas E Skidmore and Harold Blakemore, Second Edition 1992; *The Penguin History of Latin America*, Edwin Williamson, 1992. For a detailed history of the Inca people look no further than the excellent *The Conquest of the Incas*, John Hemming, 1972. A recommended study of Tiahuanaco civilization is by Alan Kolata. *We Eat the Mines and the Mines Eat Us*, June Nash, 1972, tells the history of mining in Bolivia and gives a detailed insight into the lives of the miners. For an account of the last days of Butch Cassidy and The Sundance Kid and the attempts to find their graves see *Digging Up Butch and Sundance*, by Anne Meadows (New York: St Martin's Press, 1994). Anyone interested in the life of Che Guevara and his time in Bolivia should read *Che Guevara: a Revolutionary Life* by Jon Lee Anderson (Bantam Press, 1997). An account of Che's travels around South America is given in the autobiographical *The Motorcycle Diaries: A jour-*

ney Around South America (1995). *Exploration Fawcett* (Century, 1988), tells of the famous British explorer's quest to discover El Dorado.

MAPS AND GUIDE BOOKS

Those from the Institutos Geográficos Militares in La Paz are often the only good maps available. It is therefore wise to get as many as possible in your home country before leaving, especially if travelling by land. A recommended series of general maps is that published by International Travel Maps (ITM), 345 West Broadway, Vancouver BC, V5Y 1P8, Canada, T (604) 879-3621, F (604) 879-4521, compiled with historical notes, by the late Kevin Healey: South America North West includes all of Bolivia (1:4M). Another map series that has been mentioned is that of New World Edition, Bertelsmann, Neumarkter Strasse 18, 81673 München, Germany (all 1:4M).

Backpacking and Trekking in Peru and Bolivia (1995), published by Bradt Publications, describes 3-9 day hikes in the Cordillera Real within easy reach of La Paz (Bradt Publications also publish *South America Ski Guide*). For information on Bradt Publications' Backpacking Guide Series and imported maps and guides, contact 41 Nortoft Road, Chalfont St Peter, Bucks, SL9 0LA, UK, T/F 01494 873478. *Bolivia – A Climbing Guide*, Yossi Brain (1998), published by The Mountaineers, Seattle, gives comprehensive coverage of Bolivia's mountains. Also by Yossi Brain is *Trekking in Bolivia* (1997). *Guía Boliviana de Transporte y Turismo* (GBT) published monthly at Plaza del Estudiante 1920, T 321027, F 391641, US$6 a month, US$65 a year, gives information on transport, accommodation, restaurants, useful data etc, with town plans, for the whole country. The local tourist office also produces leaflets with sketch maps on walks in the vicinity of La Paz. There are also some excellent guides available through local clubs. See also the maps and guide books section in **Adventure Tourism** at the beginning of the book (page 20) and also under **La Paz Maps** (page 103).

A very useful book, highly recommended,

aimed specifically at the budget traveller is *The Tropical Traveller*, by John Hatt (Penguin Books, 3rd edition, 1993).

Two books containing much practical information on South American motoring conditions and requirements are *Driving to Heaven*, by Derek Stansfield (available from the author, Ropley, Broad Oak, Sturminster Newton, Dorset DT10 2HG, T/F 01258-472534, £8.85 plus postage, if outside the UK), and the more recent *Central and South America by Road*, Pam Ascanio (Bradt Publications 1996).

The South American Explorers' Club has offices in Lima and Quito but not in Bolivia. However, books, maps and travel planning services are available at the US office: 126 Indian Creek Road, Ithaca, NY 14850, USA T (607) 277-0488, e-mail: explorer@samexplo.org. The Explorers Club is represented in the UK by Bradt Publications.

The *Latin American Travel Advisor* is a quarterly news bulletin with up-to-date detailed and reliable information on countries throughout South and Central America. The publication focuses on public safety, health, weather and natural phenomena, travel costs, economics and politics in each country. Annual airmail subscriptions cost US$39, a single current issue US$15, electronically transmitted information (fax or e-mail), US$10 per country. Payment by US$ cheque, MasterCard or Visa (no money orders, credit card payments by mail or fax with card number, expiry date, cardholder's name and signature). Free sample available. Contact PO Box 17-17-908, Quito, Ecuador, international F 593-2-562-566, USA and Canada toll free F (888) 215-9511, e-mail: LATA@pi.pro.ec, World Wide Web http://www.amerispan. com/latc/. Also many maps and guide books are available through the **Latin American Travel Consultants** at the same address.

Information on travel and language schools is available from Amerispan Unlimited, one of several language school brokers in the USA, PO Box 40007, Philadelphia, PA 19106-0513, T (USA and Canada) 800-879-6640, worldwide 215-985-4522, F 215-985-4524, e-mail: info@amerispan.com, website http://www. amerispan.com. See also the website http://www.planeta.com of Ron Mader's El Planeta Platica: Eco Travels in Latin America.

Useful addresses

EMBASSIES AND CONSULATES

Australia
210 Queen Street, 5th Floor, Penneys Building, Suite 517, Queensland.

Austria
Doblhoffgasse 316, A-1010 Vienna.

Belgium
Avenida Louse N 176 Boite 6, 1050 Brussels.

France
12 Avenue Du Président Kennedy, 75016 Paris 16.

Germany
Konstantinstrasse N 16, D-5300 Bonn-2.

Italy
Via Toscana 30 Int 28, 00187 Rome.

Netherlands
Hacquartraat 4, 1071 SH Amsterdam.

Sweden
Sveav General 31e TR 11134, Stockholm.

Switzerland
2 Rue Du Lyon D'Or 2/do Piso Gusa, CH 1003 Lausanne.

UK
106 Eaton Square, London, SW1 9AD, T 0171-235-4255.

USA
3014 Massachusetts Avenue NW, Washington DC.

TOURIST INFORMATION

It is not easy to obtain tourist information outside of Bolivia. The most reliable seems to be to contact Secretaría Nacional de Turismo (Senatur), Edificio Mariscal Ballivián, piso 18, Calle Mercado, T La Paz 367463/64, F 374630, Casilla 1868. Alternatively, consult the Bolivian embassy or consulate in your own country who may be able to advise (see above). Details of tourist information offices within Bolivia are given under local information under the respective towns and cities.

SPECIALIST TOUR COMPANIES

Journey Latin America
14-16 Devonshire Road, Chiswick, London, W4 2HD (T 0181-747 8315) and 28-30 Barton Arcade, 51-63 Deansgate, Manchester, M3 2BH (T 0161 832 1441). Long established company running escorted tours throughout the region. They also offer a wide range of flight options.

Trailfinders
194 Kensington High Street, London, W8 7RG (T 0171-938 3939).

South American Experience
47 Causton Street, Pimlico, London, SW1P 4AT (T 0171-976 5511).

Last Frontiers
Swan House, High Street, Long Crendon, Buckinghamshire, HP18 9AF (T 01844 208405, F 201400; E-mail: 100010.1225@compuserve.com).

Magic of Bolivia
182 Westbourne Grove, London, W11 2RH, (T 0171 221 7310, F 727 8756), a new company running specialist 3-week escorted tours.

Passage to South America
Fovant Mews, 12 Noyna Road, London, SW17 7PH (T 0181 767 8989).

STA Travel
Priory House, 6 Wrights Lane, London, W8 6TA (T 0171-361 6166).

Encounter Overland
267 Old Brompton Road, London, SW5 9JA (T 0171 370 6845).

Hayes & Jarvis
152 King Street, London, W6 0QU (T 0181 222 7844).

Cox & Kings Travel
St James Court, 45 Buckingham Gate, London (T 0171-873 5001).

Useful words and phrases

N O AMOUNT of dictionaries, phrase books or word lists will provide the same enjoyment as being able to communicate directly with the people of the country you are visiting. Learning Spanish is an important part of the preparation for any trip to Bolivia and you are encouraged to make an effort to grasp the basics before you go. As you travel you will pick up more of the language and the more you know, the more you will benefit from your stay. The following section is designed to be a simple point of departure.

General pronunciation

The stress in a Spanish word conforms to one of three rules: 1) if the word ends in a vowel, or in **n** or **s**, the accent falls on the penultimate syllable (*vent*a*na*, *vent*a*nas*); 2) if the word ends in a consonant other than **n** or **s**, the accent falls on the last syllable (*habl*a*r*); 3) if the word is to be stressed on a syllable contrary to either of the above rules, the acute accent on the relevant vowel indicates where the stress is to be placed (*pantal*ó*n*, *met*á*fora*). Note that adverbs such as *cuando*, 'when', take an accent when used interrogatively: *¿cuándo?*, 'when?'

Vowels

a not quite as short as in English 'cat'

e as in English 'pay', but shorter in a syllable ending in a consonant

i as in English 'seek'

o as in English 'shop', but more like 'pope' when the vowel ends a syllable

u as in English 'food'; after 'q' and in 'gue', 'gui', **u** is unpronounced; in 'güe' and 'güi' it is pronounced

y when a vowel, pronounced like 'i'; when a semiconsonant or consonant, it is pronounced like English 'yes'

ai, ay as in English 'ride'

ei, ey as in English 'they'

oi, oy as in English 'toy'

Unless listed below **consonants** can be pronounced in Spanish as they are in English.

b, v their sound is interchangeable and is a cross between the English 'b' and 'v', except at the beginning of a word or after 'm' or 'n' when it is like English 'b'

c like English 'k', except before 'e' or 'i' when it is as the 's' in English 'sip'

g before 'e' and 'i' it is the same as **j**

h when on its own, never pronounced

j as the 'ch' in the Scottish 'loch'

ll as the 'g' in English 'beige'; sometimes as the 'lli' in 'million'

ñ as the 'ni' in English 'onion'

rr trilled much more strongly than in English

x depending on its location, pronounced as in English 'fox', or 'sip', or like 'gs'

z as the 's' in English 'sip'

GREETINGS, COURTESIES

hello
hola

good morning
buenos días

good afternoon/evening/night
buenas tardes/noches

goodbye
adiós/chao

see you later
hasta luego

how are you?
¿cómo está?/¿cómo estás?

pleased to meet you
mucho gusto/encantado/encantada

please
por favor

thank you (very much)
(muchas) gracias

yes
sí

no
no

excuse me/I beg your pardon
permiso

I do not understand
no entiendo

please speak slowly
hable despacio por favor

what is your name
¿cómo se llama?

Go away!
¡Váyase!

BASIC QUESTIONS

where is_?
¿dónde está_?

how much does it cost?
¿cuánto cuesta?

how much is it?
¿cuánto es?

when?
¿cuándo?

when does the bus leave?
¿a qué hora sale el autobús?

– arrive?
– llega –

why?
¿por qué?

what for?
¿para qué?

what time is it?
¿qué hora es?

how do I get to_?
¿cómo llegar a_?

is this the way to the church?
¿la iglesia está por aquí?

BASICS

bathroom/toilet
el baño

police (policeman)
la policía (el policía)

hotel
el hotel (la pensión, el residencial, el alojamiento)

restaurant
el restaurante

post office
el correo

telephone office
el centro de llamadas

supermarket
el supermercado

bank
el banco

exchange house
la casa de cambio

exchange rate
la tasa de cambio

notes/coins
los billetes/las monedas

travellers' cheques
los travelers/los cheques de viajero

cash
el efectivo

breakfast
el desayuno

lunch
el almuerzo

dinner/supper
la cena

meal
la comida

drink
la bebida

mineral water
el agua mineral

soft fizzy drink
  la gaseosa/cola
beer
  la cerveza
without sugar
  sin azúcar
without meat
  sin carne

GETTING AROUND
on the left/right
  a la izquierda/derecha
straight on
  derecho
second street on the left
  la segunda calle a la izquierda
to walk
  caminar
bus station
  la terminal (terrestre)
train station
  la estación (de tren/ferrocarril)
bus
  el bus/el autobus/ la flota/el colectivo/ el micro etc
train
  el tren
airport
  el aeropuerto
aeroplane/airplane
  el avión
first/second class
  primera/segunda clase
ticket
  el boleto
ticket office
  la taquilla
bus stop
  la parada

ACCOMMODATION
room
  el cuarto/la habitación
single/double
  sencillo/doble
with two beds
  con dos camas
with private bathroom
  con baño
hot/cold water
  agua caliente/fría

noisy
  ruidoso
to make up/clean
  limpiar
sheets
  las sábanas
blankets
  las mantas
pillows
  las almohadas
clean/dirty towels
  toallas limpias/sucias
toilet paper
  el papel higiénico

HEALTH
Chemist
  farmacia
(for) pain
  (para) dolor
stomach
  el estómago
head
  la cabeza
fever/sweat
  la fiebre/el sudor
diarrhoea
  la diarrea
blood
  la sangre
altitude sickness
  el soroche
doctor
  el médico
condoms
  los preservativos
contraceptive (pill)
  anticonceptivo (la píldora anticonceptiva)
period/towels
  la regla/las toallas
contact lenses
  las lentes de contacto
aspirin
  la aspirina

TIME
at one o'clock
  a la una
at half past two/ two thirty
  a las dos y media
at a quarter to three

a cuarto para las tres/
a las tres menos quince
it's one o'clock
es la una
it's seven o'clock
son las siete
it's twenty past six/
six twenty
son las seis y veinte
it's five to nine
son cinco para las nueve/
son las nueve menos cinco
in ten minutes
en diez minutos
five hours
cinco horas
does it take long?
¿tarda mucho?
Monday lunes
Tuesday martes
Wednesday miercoles
Thursday jueves
Friday viernes
Saturday sábado
Sunday domingo
January enero
February febrero
March marzo
April abril
May mayo
June junio
July julio
August agosto
September septiembre
October octubre
November noviembre
December diciembre

NUMBERS

one uno/una
two dos
three tres
four cuatro
five cinco
six seis
seven siete
eight ocho
nine nueve
ten diez
eleven once
twelve doce

thirteen trece
fourteen catorce
fifteen quince
sixteen dieciseis
seventeen diecisiete
eighteen dieciocho
nineteen diecinueve
twenty veinte
twenty one, two veintiuno, veintidos etc
thirty treinta
forty cuarenta
fifty cincuenta
sixty sesenta
seventy setenta
eighty ochenta
ninety noventa
hundred cien or ciento
thousand mil

KEY VERBS

To Go
  ir
I go '*voy*'; you go (familiar singular) '*vas*'; he,
she, it goes, you (unfamiliar singular) go '*va*';
we go '*vamos*'; they, you (plural) go '*van*'.

To Have (possess)
  tener
tengo; tienes; tiene; tenemos; tienen (also
used as To Be, as in 'I am hungry' '*tengo
hambre*')
(**NB** haber also means to have, but is used
with other verbs, as in 'he has gone' '*ha ido*'.
he; has; ha; hemos; han.
'*Hay*' means 'there is'; perhaps more common is '*No hay*' meaning 'there isn't any')

To Be (in a permanent state)
  ser
soy (profesor – I am a teacher); eres; es;
somos; son
To Be (positional or temporary state)
  estar
estoy (en Londres – I am in London); estás;
está (contenta – she is happy); estamos;
están.

*This section has been compiled on the basis
of glossaries compiled by André de Men-
donça and David Gilmour of South American
Experience, London, and the Latin American
Travel Advisor, Number 9, March 1996.*

Health in Latin America

WITH the following advice and precautions you should keep as healthy as you do at home. Most visitors return home having experienced no problems at all apart from some travellers' diarrhoea. In Latin America the health risks, especially in the lowland tropical areas, are different from those encountered in Europe or the USA. It also depends on where and how you travel. There are clear health differences between the countries of Latin America and in risks for the business traveller, who stays in international class hotels in large cities, the backpacker trekking from country to country and the tourist who heads for the beach. There is huge variation in climate, vegetation and wildlife from the deserts of Chile to the rain forests of Amazonia and from the icy remoteness of Andean peaks, to the teeming capital cities. There are no hard and fast rules to follow; you will often have to make your own judgment on the healthiness or otherwise of your surroundings. There are English (or other foreign language) speaking doctors in most major cities who have particular experience in dealing with locally-occurring diseases. Your Embassy representative will often be able to give you the name of local reputable doctors and most of the better hotels have a doctor on standby. If you do fall ill and cannot find a recommended doctor, try the Outpatient Department of a hospital – private hospitals are usually less crowded and offer a more acceptable standard of care to foreigners.

BEFORE TRAVELLING

Take out medical insurance. Make sure it covers all eventualities especially evacuation to your home country by a medically equipped plane, if necessary. You should have a dental check up, obtain a spare glasses prescription, a spare oral contraceptive prescription (or enough pills to last) and, if you suffer from a chronic illness (such as diabetes, high blood pressure, ear or sinus troubles, cardio-pulmonary disease or nervous disorder) arrange for a check up with your doctor, who can at the same time provide you with a letter explaining the details of your disability in English and if possible Spanish and/or Portuguese. Check the current practice in countries you are visiting for malaria prophylaxis (prevention). If you are on regular medication, make sure you have enough to cover the period of your travel.

Children

More preparation is probably necessary for babies and children than for an adult and perhaps a little more care should be taken when travelling to remote areas where health services are primitive. This is because children can be become more rapidly ill than adults (on the other hand they often recover more quickly). Diarrhoea and vomiting are the most common problems, so take the usual precautions, but more intensively. Breastfeeding is best and most convenient for babies, but powdered milk is generally available and so are baby foods in most countries. Papaya, bananas and avocados are all nutritious and can be cleanly prepared. The treatment of diarrhoea is the same for adults, except that it should start earlier and be continued with more persistence. Children get dehydrated very quickly in hot countries and can become drowsy and uncooperative unless cajoled to drink water or juice plus salts. Upper respiratory infections, such as colds, catarrh and middle ear infections are also common and if your child suffers from these normally take some antibiotics against the possibility. Outer ear infections after swimming are also common and antibiotic eardrops will help. Wet wipes are always useful and sometimes difficult to find in South America, as, in some places are disposable nappies.

MEDICINES AND WHAT TO TAKE

There is very little control on the sale of drugs and medicines in South America. You can buy any and every drug in pharmacies without a prescription. Be wary of this because pharmacists can be poorly trained and might sell you drugs that are unsuitable, dangerous or old. Many drugs and medicines are manufactured under licence from American or European companies, so the trade names may be familiar to you. This means you do not have to carry a whole chest of medicines with you, but remember that the shelf life of some items, especially vaccines and antibiotics, is markedly reduced in hot conditions. Buy your supplies at the better outlets where there are refrigerators, even though they are more expensive and check the expiry date of all preparations you buy. Immigration officials occasionally confiscate scheduled drugs (Lomotil is an example) if they are not accompanied by a doctor's prescription.

Self-medication may be forced on you by circumstances so the following text contains the names of drugs and medicines which you may find useful in an emergency or in out-of-the-way places. You may like to take some of the following items with you from home:

Sunglasses
ones designed for intense sunlight

Earplugs
for sleeping on aeroplanes and in noisy hotels

Suntan cream
with a high protection factor

Insect repellent
containing DET for preference

Mosquito net
lightweight, permethrin-impregnated for choice

Tablets
for travel sickness

Tampons
can be expensive in some countries in Latin America

Condoms

340

Contraceptives

Water sterilising tablets

Antimalarial tablets

Anti-infective ointment eg Cetrimide

Dusting powder for feet etc containing fungicide

Antacid tablets
 for indigestion

Sachets of rehydration salts
 plus anti-diarrhoea preparations

Painkillers
 such as Paracetamol or Aspirin

Antibiotics
 for diarrhoea etc

First Aid kit
 Small pack containing a few sterile syringes and needles and disposable gloves. The risk of catching hepatitis etc from a dirty needle used for injection is now negligible in Latin America, but some may be reassured by carrying their own supplies – available from camping shops and airport shops.

Vaccination and immunisations

Smallpox vaccination is no longer required anywhere in the world. Neither is cholera vaccination recognized as necessary for international travel by the World Health Organisation – it is not very effective either. Nevertheless, some immigration officials are demanding proof of vaccination against cholera in Latin America and in some countries outside Latin America, following the outbreak of the disease which originated in Peru in 1990-91 and subsequently affected most surrounding countries. Although very unlikely to affect visitors to Latin America, the cholera epidemic continues making its greatest impact in poor areas where water supplies are polluted and food hygiene practices are insanitary.

Vaccination against the following diseases are recommended:

Yellow Fever This is a live vaccination not to be given to children under 9 months of age or persons allergic to eggs. Immunity lasts for 10 years, an International Certificate of Yellow Fever Vaccination will be given and should be kept because it is sometimes asked for. Yellow fever is very rare in Latin America,

but the vaccination is practically without side effects and almost totally protective.

Typhoid A disease spread by the insanitary preparation of food. A number of new vaccines against this condition are now available; the older TAB and monovalent typhoid vaccines are being phased out. The newer, eg Typhim Vi, cause less side effects, but are more expensive. For those who do not like injections, there are now oral vaccines.

Poliomyelitis Despite its decline in the world this remains a serious disease if caught and is easy to protect against. There are live oral vaccines and in some countries injected vaccines. Whichever one you choose it is a good idea to have booster every 3-5 years if visiting developing countries regularly.

Tetanus One dose should be given with a booster at 6 weeks and another at 6 months and ten yearly boosters thereafter are recommended. Children should already be properly protected against diphtheria, poliomyelitis and pertussis (whooping cough), measles and HIB all of which can be more serious infections in Latin America than at home. Measles, mumps and rubella vaccine is also given to children throughout the world, but those teenage girls who have not had rubella (german measles) should be tested and vaccinated. Hepatitis B vaccination for babies is now routine in some countries. Consult your doctor for advice on tuberculosis inoculation: the disease is still widespread in Latin America.

Infectious Hepatitis Is less of a problem for travellers than it used to be because of the development of two extremely effective vaccines against the A and B form of the disease. It remains common, however, in Latin America. A combined hepatitis A & B vaccine is now licensed and will be available in 1997 – one jab covers both diseases.

Other vaccinations:

Might be considered in the case of epidemics eg meningitis. There is an effective vaccination against rabies which should be considered by all travellers, especially those going through remote areas or if there is a particular occupational risk, eg for zoologists or veterinarians.

FURTHER INFORMATION

Further information on health risks abroad, vaccinations etc may be available from a local travel clinic. If you wish to take specific drugs with you such as antibiotics these are best prescribed by your own doctor. Beware, however, that not all doctors can be experts on the health problems of remote countries. More detailed or more up-to-date information than local doctors can provide are available from various sources. In the UK there are hospital departments specialising in tropical diseases in London, Liverpool, Birmingham and Glasgow and the Malaria Reference Laboratory at the London School of Hygiene and Tropical Medicine provides free advice about malaria, T 0891 600350. In the USA the local Public Health Services can give such information and information is available centrally from the Centre for Disease Control (CDC) in Atlanta, T (404) 3324559.

There are additional computerized databases which can be accessed for destination-specific up-to-the-minute information. In the UK there is MASTA (Medical Advisory Service to Travellers Abroad), T 0171 631 4408, F 0171 436 5389, Tx 8953473 and Travax (Glasgow, T 0141 946 7120, ext 247). Other information on medical problems overseas can be obtained from the book by Dawood, Richard (Editor) (1992) *Travellers' Health: How to stay healthy abroad*, Oxford University Press 1992, £7.99. We strongly recommend this revised and updated edition, especially to the intrepid traveller heading for the more out of the way places. General advice is also available in the UK in *Health Information for Overseas Travel* published by the Department of Health and available from HMSO, and *International Travel and Health* published by WHO, Geneva.

STAYING HEALTHY

INTESTINAL UPSETS

The thought of catching a stomach bug worries visitors to Latin America but there have been great improvements in food hygiene and most such infections are preventable. Travellers' diarrhoea and vomiting is due, most of the time, to food poisoning, usually passed on by the insanitary habits of food handlers. As a general rule the cleaner your surroundings and the smarter the restaurant, the less likely you are to suffer.

Foods to avoid: uncooked, undercooked, partially cooked or reheated meat, fish, eggs, raw vegetables and salads, especially when they have been left out exposed to flies. Stick to fresh food that has been cooked from raw just before eating and make sure you peel fruit yourself. Wash and dry your hands before eating – disposable wet-wipe tissues are useful for this.

Shellfish eaten raw are risky and at certain times of the year some fish and shellfish concentrate toxins from their environment and cause various kinds of food poisoning. The local authorities notify the public not to eat these foods. Do not ignore the warning. Heat treated milk (UHT) pasteurized or sterilized is becoming more available in Latin America as is pasteurized cheese. On the whole matured or processed cheeses are safer than the fresh varieties and fresh unpasteurized milk from whatever animal can be a source of food poisoning germs, tuberculosis and brucellosis. This applies equally to icecream, yoghurt and cheese made from unpasteurized milk, so avoid these homemade products – the factory made ones are probably safer.

Tap water is rarely safe outside the major cities, especially in the rainy season. Stream water, if you are in the countryside, is often contaminated by communities living surprisingly high in the mountains. Filtered or bottled water is usually available and safe, although you must make sure that somebody is not filling bottles from the tap and hammering on a new crown cap. If your hotel has a central hot water supply this water is safe to drink after cooling. Ice for drinks should be made from boiled water, but rarely is so stand your glass on the ice cubes, rather than putting them in the drink. The better hotels have water purifying systems.

TRAVELLERS' DIARRHOEA

This is usually caused by eating food which has been contaminated by food poisoning germs. Drinking water is rarely the culprit. Sea water or river water is more likely to be contaminated by sewage and so swimming in such dilute effluent can also be a cause.

Infection with various organisms can give rise to travellers' diarrhoea. They may be viruses, bacteria, eg Escherichia coli (probably the most common cause worldwide), protozoal (such as amoebas and giardia), salmonella and cholera. The diarrhoea may come on suddenly or rather slowly. It may or may not be accompanied by vomiting or by severe abdominal pain and the passage of blood or mucus when it is called dysentery.

How do you know which type you have caught and how to treat it?

If you can time the onset of the diarrhoea to the minute ('acute') then it is probably due to a virus or a bacterium and/or the onset of dysentery. The treatment in addition to rehydration is Ciprofloxacin 500 mg every 12 hours; the drug is now widely available and there are many similar ones.

If the diarrhoea comes on slowly or intermittently ('sub-acute') then it is more likely to be protozoal, ie caused by an amoeba or giardia. Antibiotics such a Ciprofloxacin will have little effect. These cases are best treated by a doctor as is any outbreak of diarrhoea continuing for more than 3 days. Sometimes blood is passed in ameobic dysentery and for this you should certainly seek medical help. If this is not available then the best treatment is probably Tinidazole (Fasigyn) one tablet four times a day for 3 days. If there are severe stomach cramps, the following drugs may help but are not very useful in the management of acute diarrhoea: Loperamide (Imodium) and Diphenoxylate with Atropine (Lomotil). They should not be given to children.

Any kind of diarrhoea, whether or not accompanied by vomiting, responds well to the replacement of water and salts, taken as frequent small sips, of some kind of rehydration solution. There are proprietary preparations consisting of sachets of powder which you dissolve in boiled water or you can make your own by adding half a teaspoonful of salt (3.5 gms) and four tablespoonsful of sugar (40 gms) to a litre of boiled water.

Thus the linchpins of treatment for diarrhoea are rest, fluid and salt replacement, antibiotics such as Ciprofloxacin for the bacterial types and special diagnostic tests and medical treatment for the amoeba and giardia infections. Salmonella infections and cholera, although rare, can be devastating diseases and it would be wise to get to a hospital as soon as possible if these were suspected.

Fasting, peculiar diets and the consumption of large quantities of yoghurt have not been found useful in calming travellers' diarrhoea or in rehabilitating inflamed bowels. Oral rehydration has on the other hand, especially in children, been a life saving technique and should always be practised, whatever other treatment you use. As there is some evidence that alcohol and milk might prolong diarrhoea they should be avoided during and immediately after an attack.

Diarrhoea occurring day after day for long periods of time (chronic diarrhoea) is notoriously resistent to amateur attempts at treatment and again warrants proper diagnostic tests (most towns with reasonable sized hospitals have laboratories for stool samples). There are ways of preventing travellers' diarrhoea for short periods of time by taking antibiotics, but this is not a foolproof technique and should not be used other than in exceptional circumstances. Doxycycline is possibly the best drug. Some preventatives such as Enterovioform can have serious side effects if taken for long periods.

Paradoxically constipation is also common, probably induced by dietary change, inadequate fluid intake in hot places and long bus journeys. Simple laxatives are useful in the short-term and bulky foods such as maize, beans and plenty of fruit are also useful.

HIGH ALTITUDE

Spending time at high altitude in South America, especially in the tropics, is usually a pleasure – it is not so hot, there are no insects

Nº 367 Carnaval Tarabuqueño
Indio Tocando su Tokuro
Carnival Tarabuqueño
Native Playing his Tokuro
Tarabuco - Chuquisaca - Bolivia

FOTO PACHECO COLOR.- SUCRE. Bolivia
Reproducción prohibida

and the air is clear and spring like. Travelling to high altitudes, however, can cause medical problems, all of which can be prevented if care is taken.

On reaching heights above about 3,000m, heart pounding and shortness of breath, especially on exertion are a normal response to the lack of oxygen in the air. A condition called acute mountain sickness (Soroche in South America) can also affect visitors. It is more likely to affect those who ascend rapidly, eg by plane and those who over-exert themselves (teenagers for example). Soroche takes a few hours or days to come on and presents with a bad headache, extreme tiredness, sometimes dizziness, loss of appetite and frequently nausea and vomiting. Insomnia is common and is often associated with a suffocating feeling when lying in bed. Keen observers may note their breathing tends to wax and wane at night and their face tends to be puffy in the mornings – this is all part of the syndrome. Anyone can get this condition and past experience is not always a good guide: the author, having spent years in Peru travelling constantly between sea level and very high altitude never suffered symptoms, then was severely affected whilst climbing Kilimanjaro in Tanzania.

The treatment of acute mountain sickness is simple – rest, painkillers (preferably not aspirin based) for the headache and anti-sickness pills for vomiting. Oxygen is actually not much help, except at very high altitude. Various local panaceas – Coramina glucosada, Effortil, Micoren are popular in Latin America and mate de coca (an infusion of coca leaves widely available and perfectly legal) will alleviate some of the symptoms.

To prevent the condition: on arrival at places over 3,000m have a few hours rest in a chair and avoid alcohol, cigarettes and heavy food. If the symptoms are severe and prolonged, it is best to descend to a lower altitude and to reascend slowly or in stages. If this is impossible because of shortage of time or if you are going so high that acute mountain sickness is very likely, then the drug Acetazo-

lamide (Diamox) can be used as a preventative and continued during the ascent. There is good evidence of the value of this drug in the prevention of soroche, but some people do experience peculiar side effects. The usual dose is 500 mg of the slow release preparation each night, starting the night before ascending above 3,000m.

Watch out for **sunburn** at high altitude. The ultraviolet rays are extremely powerful. The air is also excessively dry at high altitude and you might find that your skin dries out and the inside of your nose becomes crusted. Use a moisturiser for the skin and some vaseline wiped into the nostrils. Some people find contact lenses irritate because of the dry air. It is unwise to ascend to high altitude if you are pregnant, especially in the first 3 months, or if you have a history of heart, lung or blood disease, including sickle cell.

A more unusual condition can affect mountaineers who ascend rapidly to high altitude – acute pulmonary oedema. Residents at altitude sometimes experience this when returning to the mountains from time spent at the coast. This condition is often preceded by acute mountain sickness and comes on quite rapidly with severe breathlessness, noisy breathing, cough, blueness of the lips and frothing at the mouth. Anybody who develops this must be brought down as soon as possible, given oxygen and taken to hospital.

A rapid descent from high places will make sinus problems and middle ear infections worse and might make your teeth ache. Lastly, don't fly to altitude within 24 hours of Scuba diving. You might suffer from 'the bends'.

HEAT AND COLD

Full acclimatization to high temperatures takes about 2 weeks. During this period it is normal to feel a bit apathetic, especially if the relative humidity is high. Drink plenty of water (up to 15 litres a day are required when working physically hard in the tropics), use salt on your food and avoid extreme exertion. Tepid showers are more cooling than hot or

Water purification

There are a number of ways of purifying water in order to make it safe to drink. Dirty water should first be strained through a filter bag (camping shops) and then boiled or treated. Bringing water to a rolling boil at sea level is sufficient to make the water safe for drinking, but at higher altitudes you have to boil the water for longer to ensure that all the microbes are killed.

There are sterilising methods that can be used and there are proprietary preparations containing chlorine (eg Puritabs) or iodine (eg Pota Aqua) compounds. Chlorine compounds generally do not kill protozoa (eg giardia).

There are a number of water filters now on the market available in personal and expedition size. They work either on mechanical or chemical principles, or may do both. Make sure you take the spare parts or spare chemicals with you and do not believe *everything* the manufacturers say.

cold ones. Large hats do not cool you down, but do prevent sunburn. Remember that, especially in the highlands, there can be a large and sudden drop in temperature between sun and shade and between night and day, so dress accordingly. Warm jackets or woollens are essential after dark at high altitude. Loose cotton is still the best material when the weather is hot.

INSECTS

These are mostly more of a nuisance than a serious hazard and if you try, you can prevent yourself entirely from being bitten. Some, such as mosquitos are, of course, carriers of potentially serious diseases, so it is sensible to avoid being bitten as much as possible. Sleep off the ground and use a mosquito net or some kind of insecticide. Preparations containing Pyrethrum or synthetic pyrethroids are safe. They are available as aerosols or pumps and the best way to use these is to spray the room thoroughly in all areas (follow the instructions rather than the insects) and then shut the door for a while, re-entering when the smell has dispersed. Mosquito coils release insecticide as they burn slowly. They are widely available and useful out of doors. Tablets of insecticide which are placed on a heated mat plugged into a wall socket are probably the most effective. They fill the room with insecticidal fumes in the same way as aerosols or coils.

You can also use insect repellents, most of which are effective against a wide range of pests. The most common and effective is diethyl metatoluamide (DET). DET liquid is best for arms and face (care around eyes and with spectacles – DET dissolves plastic). Aerosol spray is good for clothes and ankles and liquid DET can be dissolved in water and used to impregnate cotton clothes and mosquito nets. Some repellents now contain DET and Permethrin, insecticide. Impregnated wrist and ankle bands can also be useful.

If you are bitten or stung, itching may be relieved by cool baths, antihistamine tablets (care with alcohol or driving) or mild corticosteroid creams, eg hydrocortisone (great care: never use if any hint of infection). Careful scratching of all your bites once a day can be surprisingly effective. Calamine lotion and cream have limited effectiveness and antihistamine creams are not recommended – they can cause allergies themselves.

Bites which become infected should be treated with a local antiseptic or antibiotic cream such as Cetrimide, as should any infected sores or scratches.

When living rough, skin infestations with body lice (crabs) and scabies are easy to pick up. Use whatever local commercial preparation is recommended for lice and scabies.

Crotamiton cream (Eurax) alleviates itching and also kills a number of skin parasites. Malathion lotion 5% (Prioderm) kills lice effectively, but avoid the use of the toxic agricultural preparation of Malathion, more often used to commit suicide.

345

TICKS

They attach themselves usually to the lower parts of the body often after walking in areas where cattle have grazed. They take a while to attach themselves strongly, but swell up as they start to suck blood. The important thing is to remove them gently, so that they do not leave their head parts in your skin because this can cause a nasty allergic reaction some days later. Do not use petrol, vaseline, lighted cigarettes etc to remove the tick, but, with a pair of tweezers remove the beast gently by gripping it at the attached (head) end and rock it out in very much the same way that a tooth is extracted. Certain tropical flies which lay their eggs under the skin of sheep and cattle also occasionally do the same thing to humans with the unpleasant result that a maggot grows under the skin and pops up as a boil or pimple. The best way to remove these is to cover the boil with oil, vaseline or nail varnish so as to stop the maggot breathing, then to squeeze it out gently the next day.

SUNBURN

The burning power of the tropical sun, especially at high altitude, is phenomenal.

Always wear a wide brimmed hat and use some form of suncream lotion on untanned skin. Normal temperate zone suntan lotions (protection factor up to seven) are not much good; you need to use the types designed specifically for the tropics or for mountaineers or skiers with protection factors up to fifteen or above. These are often not available in Latin America. Glare from the sun can cause conjunctivitis, so wear sunglasses especially on tropical beaches, where high protection factor sunscreen should also be used.

PRICKLY HEAT

A very common intensely itchy rash is avoided by frequent washing and by wearing loose clothing. Cured by allowing skin to dry off through use of powder and spending two nights in an airconditioned hotel!

ATHLETES FOOT

This and other fungal skin infections are best treated with Tolnaftate or Clotrimazole.

OTHER RISKS AND MORE SERIOUS DISEASES

Remember that rabies is endemic throughout Latin America, so avoid dogs that are behaving strangely and cover your toes at night from the vampire bats, which also carry the disease. If you are bitten by a domestic or wild animal, do not leave things to chance: scrub the wound with soap and water and/or disinfectant, try to have the animal captured (within limits) or at least determine its ownership, where possible, and seek medical assistance at once. The course of treatment depends on whether you have already been satisfactorily vaccinated against rabies. If you have (this is worthwile if you are spending lengths of time in developing countries) then some further doses of vaccine are all that is required. Human diploid vaccine is the best, but expensive: other, older kinds of vaccine, such as that derived from duck embryos may be the only types available. These are effective, much cheaper and interchangeable generally with the human derived types. If not already vaccinated then anti rabies serum (immunoglobulin) may be required in addition. It is important to finish the course of treatment whether the animal survives or not.

AIDS

In South America AIDS is increasing but is not wholly confined to the well known high risk sections of the population, ie homosexual men, intravenous drug abusers and children of infected mothers. Heterosexual transmission is now the dominant mode and so the main risk to travellers is from casual sex. The same precautions should be taken as with any sexually transmitted disease. The Aids virus (HIV) can be passed by unsterilized needles which have been previously used to inject an HIV positive patient, but the risk of this is negligible. It would, however, be sensible to check that needles have been properly sterilized or disposable needles have been used. If you wish to take your own disposable needles, be prepared to explain what they are for. The risk of receiving a blood transfusion with blood infected with the HIV virus is greater than from dirty needles because of the amount of fluid exchanged. Supplies of blood for transfusion should now be screened for HIV in all reputable hospitals, so again the risk is very small indeed. Catching the AIDS virus does not always produce an illness in itself (although it may do). The only way to be sure if you feel you have been put at risk is to have a blood test for HIV antibodies on your return to a place where there are reliable laboratory facilities. The test does not become positive for some weeks.

MALARIA

In South America malaria is theoretically confined to coastal and jungle zones, but is now on the increase again. Mosquitos do not thrive above 2,500m, so you are safe at altitude. There are different varieties of malaria, some resistant to the normal drugs. Make local enquiries if you intend to visit possibly infected zones and use a prophylactic regime. Start taking the tablets a few days before exposure and continue to take them for 6 weeks after leaving the malarial zone. Remember to give the drugs to babies and children also. Opinion varies on the precise drugs and dosage to be used for protection. All the drugs may have some side effects and it is important to balance the risk of catching the disease against the albeit rare side effects. The increasing complexity of the subject is such that as the malarial parasite becomes immune to the new generation of drugs it has made concentration on the physical prevention from being bitten by mosquitos more important. This involves the use of long sleeved shirts or blouses and long trousers, repellents and nets. Clothes are now available impregnated with the insecticide Permethrin or Deltamethrin or it is possible to impregnate the clothes yourself. Wide meshed nets impregnated with Permethrin are also available, are lighter to carry and less claustrophobic to sleep in.

Prophylaxis and treatment

If your itinerary takes you into a malarial area, seek expert advice before you go on a suitable prophylactic regime. This is especially true for pregnant women who are particularly prone to catch malaria. You can still catch the disease even when sticking to a proper regime, although it is unlikely. If you do develop symptoms (high fever, shivering, headache, sometimes diarrhoea), seek medical advice immediately. If this is not possible and there is a great likelihood of malaria, the treatment is:

Chloroquine, a single dose of four tablets (600 mg) followed by two tablets (300 mg) in 6 hours and 300 mg each day following.

Falciparum type of malaria or type in doubt: take local advice. Various combinations of drugs are being used such as Quinine, Tetracycline or Halofantrine. If falciparum type malaria is definitely diagnosed, it is wise to get to a good hospital as treatment can be complex and the illness very serious.

INFECTIOUS HEPATITIS (JAUNDICE)

The main symptoms are pains in the stomach, lack of appetite, lassitude and yellowness of the eyes and skin. Medically speaking there are two main types. The less serious, but more common is Hepatitis A for which the best protection is the careful preparation of food, the avoidance of contaminated drinking water and scrupulous attention to toilet hygiene. The other, more serious, version is Hepatitis B which is acquired usually as a sexually transmitted disease or by blood transfusions. It can less commonly be transmitted by injections with unclean needles and possibly by insect bites. The symptoms are the same as for Hepatitis A. The incubation period is much longer (up to 6 months compared with 6 weeks) and there are more likely to be complications.

Hepatitis A can be protected against with gamma globulin. It should be obtained from a reputable source and is certainly useful for travellers who intend to live rough. You should have a shot before leaving and have it repeated every 6 months. The dose of gamma globulin depends on the concentration of the particular preparation used, so the manufacturer's advice should be taken. The injection should be given as close as possible to your departure and as the dose depends on the likely time you are to spend in potentially affected areas, the manufacturer's instructions should be followed. Gamma globulin has really been superseded now by a proper vaccination against Hepatitis A (Havrix) which gives immunity lasting up to 10 years. After that boosters are required. Havrix monodose is now widely available as is Junior Havrix. The vaccination has negligible side effects and is extremely effective. Gamma globulin injections can be a bit painful, but it is much cheaper than Havrix and may be more available in some places.

Hepatitis B can be effectively prevented by a specific vaccine (Engerix) – three shots over 6 months before travelling. If you have had jaundice in the past it would be worthwhile having a blood test to see if you are immune to either of these two types, because this might avoid the necessity and costs of vaccination or gamma globulin. There are other kinds of viral hepatitis (C, E etc) which are fairly similar to A and B, but vaccines are not available as yet.

TYPHUS

Can still occur carried by ticks. There is usually a reaction at the site of the bite and a fever. Seek medical advice.

INTESTINAL WORMS

These are common and the more serious ones such as hookworm can be contracted from walking barefoot on infested earth or beaches.

Various other tropical diseases can be caught in jungle areas, usually transmitted by biting insects. They are often related to African diseases and were probably introduced by the slave labour trade. Onchocerciasis (river blindness) carried by black flies is found in parts of Mexico and Venezuela. Leishmaniasis (Espundia) is carried by sandflies and causes a sore that will not heal or a severe nasal infection. Wearing long trousers and a long sleeved shirt in infected areas protects against these flies. DET is also effective. Epidemics of meningitis occur from time-to-time. Be careful about swimmimg in piranha or caribe infested rivers. It is a good idea not to swim naked: the Candiru fish can follow urine currents and become lodged in body orifices. Swimwear offers some protection.

LEPTOSPIROSIS

Various forms of leptospirosis occur throughout Latin America, transmitted by a bacterium which is excreted in rodent urine. Fresh water and moist soil harbour the organisms which enter the body through cuts and scratches. If you suffer from any form of prolonged fever consult a doctor.

SNAKE BITE

This is a very rare event indeed for travellers. If you are unlucky (or careless) enough to be bitten by a venomous snake, spider, scorpion or sea creature, try to identify the creature, but do not put yourself in further danger. Snake bites in particular are very frightening, but in fact rarely poisonous – even venomous snakes bite without injecting venom. What you might expect if bitten are: fright, swelling, pain and bruising around the bite and soreness of the regional lymph glands, perhaps nausea, vomiting and a fever. Signs of serious poisoning would be the following symptoms: numbness and tingling of the face, muscular spasms, convulsions, shortness of breath and bleeding. Victims should be got to a hospital or a doctor without delay. Commercial snake bite and scorpion kits are available, but they will only be useful for the specific type of snake or scorpion for which they are designed. Most serum has to be given intravenously so it is not much good equipping yourself with it unless you are used to making injections into veins. It is best to rely on local practice in these cases, because the particular creatures will be known about locally and appropriate treatment can be given.

Treatment of snake bite Reassure and comfort the victim frequently. Immobilize the limb by a bandage or a splint or by getting the person to lie still. Do not slash the bite area and try to suck out the poison because this sort of heroism does more harm than good. If you know how to use a tourniquet in these circumstances, you will not need this advice. If you are not experienced do not apply a tourniquet.

Precautions

Avoid walking in snake territory in bare feet

or sandals – wear proper shoes or boots. If you encounter a snake stay put until it slithers away, and do not investigate a wounded snake. Spiders and scorpions may be found in the more basic hotels, especially in the Andean countries. If stung, rest and take plenty of fluids and call a doctor. The best precaution is to keep beds away from the walls and look inside your shoes and under the toilet seat every morning. Certain tropical sea fish when trodden upon inject venom into bathers' feet. This can be exceptionally painful. Wear plastic shoes when you go bathing if such creatures are reported. The pain can be relieved by immersing the foot in extremely hot water for as long as the pain persists.

DENGUE FEVER

This is increasing worldwide including in South and Central American countries and the Caribbean. It can be completely prevented by avoiding mosquito bites in the same way as malaria. No vaccine is available. Dengue is an unpleasant and painful disease, presenting with a high temperature and body pains, but at least visitors are spared the more serious forms (haemorrhagic types) which are more of a problem for local people who have been exposed to the disease more than once. There is no specific treatment for dengue – just pain killers and rest.

CHAGAS' DISEASE (SOUTH AMERICAN TRYPANOSOMIASIS)

This is a chronic disease, almost endemic in rural parts of Bolivia, and difficult to treat. It is, however, very rarely caught by travellers. It is transmitted by the simultaneous biting and excreting of the Reduvid bug, also known as the Vinchuca or Barbeiro. Somewhat resembling a small cockroach, this nocturnal bug lives in poor adobe houses with dirt floors often frequented by opossums. If you cannot avoid such accommodation, sleep off the floor with a candle lit, use a mosquito net, keep as much of your skin covered as possible, use DET repellent or a spray insecticide. If you are bitten overnight (the bites are painless) do not scratch them, but wash thoroughly with soap and water.

DANGEROUS ANIMALS

Apart from mosquitos the most dangerous animals are men, be they bandits or behind steering wheels. Think carefully about violent confrontations and wear a seat belt if you are lucky enough to have one available to you.

WHEN YOU RETURN HOME

Remember to take your antimalarial tablets for 6 weeks after leaving the malarial area. If you have had attacks of diarrhoea it is worth having a stool specimen tested in case you have picked up amoebas. If you have been living rough, blood tests may be worthwhile to detect worms and other parasites. If you have been exposed to bilharzia (schistosomiasis) by swimming in lakes etc, check by means of a blood test when you get home, but leave it for 6 weeks because the test is slow to become positive. Report any untoward symptoms to your doctor and tell the doctor exactly where you have been and, if you know, what the likelihood of disease is to which you were exposed.

The above information has been compiled for us by Dr David Snashall, who is presently Senior Lecturer in Occupational Health at the United Medical Schools of Guy's and St Thomas' Hospitals in London and Chief Medical Adviser to the British Foreign and Commonwealth Office. He has travelled extensively in Central and South America, worked in Peru and in East Africa and keeps in close touch with developments in preventative and tropical medicine.

Travelling with children

People contemplating overland travel in South America with children should remember that a lot of time can be spent waiting for buses, trains, and especially for aeroplanes. On bus journeys, if the children are good at amusing themselves, or can readily sleep while travelling, the problems can be considerably lessened. If your child is of an early reading age, take reading material with you as it is difficult, and expensive to find. A bag of, say 30 pieces, of Duplo or Lego can keep young children occupied for hours. Travel on trains, while not as fast or at times as comfortable as buses, allows more scope for moving about. Some trains provide tables between seats, so that games can be played. Beware of doors left open for ventilation especially if air-conditioning is not working.

Food

Food can be a problem if the children are not adaptable. It is easier to take biscuits, drinks, bread etc with you on longer trips than to rely on meal stops where the food may not be to taste. Avocados are safe, easy to eat and nutritious; they can be fed to babies as young as 6 months and most older children like them. A small immersion heater and jug for making hot drinks is invaluable, but remember that electric current varies. Try and get a dual-voltage one (110v and 220v).

Nappies Luggis are the best disposable nappies/diapers, other makes are useless.

Fares

On all long-distance buses you pay for each seat, and there are no half-fares if the children occupy a seat each. For shorter trips it is cheaper, if less comfortable, to seat small children on your knee. Often there are spare seats which children can occupy after tickets have been collected. In city and local excursion buses, small children generally do not pay a fare, but are not entitled to a seat when paying customers are standing. On sightseeing tours you should always bargain for a family rate – often children can go free. (In trains, reductions for children are general, but not universal.)

All civil airlines charge half for children under twelve, but some military services don't have half-fares, or have younger age limits. Children's fares on Lloyd Aéreo Boliviano are considerably more than half, and there is only a 7kg baggage allowance. (LAB also checks children's ages on passports.) Note that a child travelling free on a long excursion is not always covered by the operator's travel insurance; it is adviseable to pay a small premium to arrange cover.

Hotels

In all hotels, try to negotiate family rates. If charges are per person, always insist that two children will occupy one bed only, therefore counting as one tariff. If rates are per bed, the same applies. In either case you can almost always get a reduced rate at cheaper hotels. Occasionally when travelling with a child you will be refused a room in a hotel that is "unsuitable". On river boat trips, unless you have very large hammocks, it may be more comfortable and cost effective to hire a two-berth cabin for two adults and a child. (In restaurants, you can normally buy children's helpings, or divide one full-size helping between two children.)

Travel with children can bring you into closer contact with Latin American families and, generally, presents no special problems – in fact the path is often smoother for family groups. Officials tend to be more amenable where children are concerned and they are pleased if your child knows a little Spanish or Portuguese. Moreover, even thieves and pickpockets seem to have some of the traditional respect for families, and may leave you alone because of it!

Insurance tips

Insurance companies have tightened up considerably over recent years and it is now almost impossible to claim successfully if you have not followed procedures closely. The problem is that these often involve dealing with the country's red tape which can lead to some inconvenience at best and to some quite long delays at worst. There is no substitute for suitable precautions against petty crime.

The level of insurance that you carry is often dictated by the sums of medical insurance which you carry. It is inevitably the highest if you go through the USA. Also don't forget to obtain sports extensions if you are going to go diving, rafting, climbing etc. Most policies do not cover very high levels of baggage/cash. Don't forget to check whether you can claim on your household insurance. They often have worldwide all risks extensions. Most policies exclude manual work whilst away although working in bars or restaurants is usually alright.

Here are our tips: they apply to most types of policies but always check the details of your own policy before you leave.

1. Take the policy with you (a photocopy will do but make sure it is a complete one).

2. Do not travel against medical advice. It will invalidate the medical insurance part of the cover.

3. There is a 24 hour medical emergency service helpline associated with your insurance. You need to contact them if you require in-patient hospital treatment or you need to return home early. The telephone number is printed on the policy. Make sure you note the time of the call, the person you were talking to and get a reference number. Even better get a receipt from the telephone company showing the number you called. Should you need to be airlifted home, this is always arranged through the insurance company's representative and the hospital authorities. Ironically this can lead to quite intense discussions which you will not be aware of: the local hospital is often quite keen to keep you!

4. If you have to cancel your trip for whatever reason, contact your travel agent, tour operator or airline without delay.

5. If your property is damage by an airline, report it immediately and always within 3 days and get a "property irregularity report" from them.

6. Claims for baggage left unattended are very rarely settled unless they were left in a securely locked hotel room, apartment etc; locked in the boot of a car and there is evidence of a forced entry; cash is carried on your person or is in a locked safe or security box.

7. All loss must be reported to the police and/or hotel authorities within 24 hours of discovery and a written report obtained.

8. If medical attention is received for injury or sickness, a medical certificate showing its nature must be obtained, although some companies waive this if only out-patient treatment is required. Keep all receipts in a safe place as they will be needed to substantiate the claim.

9. Check your policy carefully to see if there is a date before which claims must be submitted. This is often within 30 days of returning home. It is now usual for companies to want your policy document, proof that you actually travelled (airline ticket or travel agent's confirmation of booking), receipts and written reports (in the event of loss). **NB** photocopies are not accepted.

Writing to us

Many people write to us - with corrections, new information, or simply comments. If you want to let us know something, we would be delighted to hear from you. Please give us as precise information as possible, quoting the edition and page number of the Handbook you are using and send as early in the year as you can. Your help will be greatly appreciated, especially by other travellers. In return we will send you details about our special guidebook offer.

For hotels and restaurants, please let us know:

- each establishment's name, address, phone and fax number
- number of rooms, whether a/c or air-cooled, attached (clean?) bathroom
- location - how far from the station or bus stand, or distance (walking time) from a prominent landmark
- if it's not already on one of our maps, can you place it?
- your comments - either good or bad - as to why it is distinctive
- tariff cards
- local transport used

For places of interest:

- location
- entry, camera charge
- access - by whatever means of transport is most approriate, eg time of main buses or trains to and from the site, journey time, fare
- facilities - nearby drinks stalls, restaurants, for the disabled
- any problems, eg steep climb, wildlife, unofficial guides
- opening hours
- site guides

TEMPERATURE CONVERSION TABLE

°C	°F	°C	°F
1	34	26	79
2	36	27	81
3	38	28	82
4	39	29	84
5	41	30	86
6	43	31	88
7	45	32	90
8	46	33	92
9	48	34	93
10	50	35	95
11	52	36	97
12	54	37	99
13	56	38	100
14	57	39	102
15	59	40	104
16	61	41	106
17	63	42	108
18	64	43	109
19	66	44	111
20	68	45	113
21	70	46	115
22	72	47	117
23	74	48	118
24	75	49	120
25	77	50	122

The formula for converting °C to °F is:
$$(°C \times 9 \div 5) + 32 = °F$$
and for converting °F to °C:
$$(°F - 32) \times 5 \div 9 = °C$$

WEIGHTS AND MEASURES

Metric

Weight
1 Kilogram (Kg) = 2.205 pounds
1 metric ton = 1.102 short tons

Length
1 millimetre (mm) = 0.03937 inch
1 metre = 3.281 feet
1 kilometre (km) = 0.621 mile

Area
1 heactare = 2.471 acres
1 square km = 0.386 sq mile

Capacity
1 litre = 0.220 imperial gallon
     = 0.264 US gallon

Volume
1 cubic metre (m³) = 35.31 cubic feet
          = 1.31 cubic yards

British and US

Weight
1 pound (lb) = 454 grams
1 short ton (2,000lbs) = 0.907 m ton
1 long ton (2,240lbs) = 1.016 m tons

Length
1 inch = 25.417 millimetres
1 foot (ft) = 0.305 metre
1 mile = 1.609 kilometres

Area
1 acre = 0.405 hectare
1 sq mile = 2.590 sq kilometre

Capacity
1 imperial gallon = 4.546 litres
1 US gallon = 3.785 litres

Volume
1 cubic foot (cu ft) = 0.028 m³
1 cubic yard (cu yd) = 0.765 m³

NB 5 imperial gallons are approximately equal to 6 US gallons

Year planner

1997

J	F	M	A	M	J	J	A	S	O	N	D
								1			1
			1			1		2			2
1			2			2		3	1		3
2			3	1		3		4	2		4
3			4	2		4	1	5	3		5
4	1	1	5	3		5	2	6	4	1	6
5	2	2	6	4	1	6	3	7	5	2	7
6	3	3	7	5	2	7	4	8	6	3	8
7	4	4	8	6	3	8	5	9	7	4	9
8	5	5	9	7	4	9	6	10	8	5	10
9	6	6	10	8	5	10	7	11	9	6	11
10	7	7	11	9	6	11	8	12	10	7	12
11	8	8	12	10	7	12	9	13	11	8	13
12	9	9	13	11	8	13	10	14	12	9	14
13	10	10	14	12	9	14	11	15	13	10	15
14	11	11	15	13	10	15	12	16	14	11	16
15	12	12	16	14	11	16	13	17	15	12	17
16	13	13	17	15	12	17	14	18	16	13	18
17	14	14	18	16	13	18	15	19	17	14	19
18	15	15	19	17	14	19	16	20	18	15	20
19	16	16	20	18	15	20	17	21	19	16	21
20	17	17	21	19	16	21	18	22	20	17	22
21	18	18	22	20	17	22	19	23	21	18	23
22	19	19	23	21	18	23	20	24	22	19	24
23	20	20	24	22	19	24	21	25	23	20	25
24	21	21	25	23	20	25	22	26	24	21	26
25	22	22	26	24	21	26	23	27	25	22	27
26	23	23	27	25	22	27	24	28	26	23	28
27	24	24	28	26	23	28	25	29	27	24	29
28	25	25	29	27	24	29	26	30	28	25	30
29	26	26	30	28	25	30	27		29	26	31
30	27	27		29	26	31	28		30	27	
31	28	28		30	27		29		31	28	
		29		31	28		30			29	
		30			29		31			30	
		31			30						

Year planner

1998

J	F	M	A	M	J	J	A	S	O	N	D
					1						
					2			1			1
			1		3	1		2			2
1			2		4	2		3	1		3
2			3	1	5	3		4	2		4
3			4	2	6	4	1	5	3		5
4	1	1	5	3	7	5	2	6	4	1	6
5	2	2	6	4	8	6	3	7	5	2	7
6	3	3	7	5	9	7	4	8	6	3	8
7	4	4	8	6	10	8	5	9	7	4	9
8	5	5	9	7	11	9	6	10	8	5	10
9	6	6	10	8	12	10	7	11	9	6	11
10	7	7	11	9	13	11	8	12	10	7	12
11	8	8	12	10	14	12	9	13	11	8	13
12	9	9	13	11	15	13	10	14	12	9	14
13	10	10	14	12	16	14	11	15	13	10	15
14	11	11	15	13	17	15	12	16	14	11	16
15	12	12	16	14	18	16	13	17	15	12	17
16	13	13	17	15	19	17	14	18	16	13	18
17	14	14	18	16	20	18	15	19	17	14	19
18	15	15	19	17	21	19	16	20	18	15	20
19	16	16	20	18	22	20	17	21	19	16	21
20	17	17	21	19	23	21	18	22	20	17	22
21	18	18	22	20	24	22	19	23	21	18	23
22	19	19	23	21	25	23	20	24	22	19	24
23	20	20	24	22	26	24	21	25	23	20	25
24	21	21	25	23	27	25	22	26	24	21	26
25	22	22	26	24	28	26	23	27	25	22	27
26	23	23	27	25	29	27	24	28	26	23	28
27	24	24	28	26	30	28	25	29	27	24	29
28	25	25	29	27		29	26	30	28	25	30
29	26	26	30	28		30	27		29	26	31
30	27	27		29		31	28		30	27	
31	28	28		30			29		31	28	
		29		31			30			29	
		30					31			30	
		31									

Year planner

1999

J	F	M	A	M	J	J	A	S	O	N	D
					1					1	
					2					2	
					3			1		3	1
			1		4	1		2		4	2
1			2			2		3	1	5	3
2			3	1	5	3		4	2	6	4
3			4	2	6	4	1	5	3	7	5
4	1	1	5	3	7	5	2	6	4	8	6
5	2	2	6	4	8	6	3	7	5	9	7
6	3	3	7	5	9	7	4	8	6	10	8
7	4	4	8	6	10	8	5	9	7	11	9
8	5	5	9	7	11	9	6	10	8	12	10
9	6	6	10	8	12	10	7	11	9	13	11
10	7	7	11	9	13	11	8	12	10	14	12
11	8	8	12	10	14	12	9	13	11	15	13
12	9	9	13	11	15	13	10	14	12	16	14
13	10	10	14	12	16	14	11	15	13	17	15
14	11	11	15	13	17	15	12	16	14	18	16
15	12	12	16	14	18	16	13	17	15	19	17
16	13	13	17	15	19	17	14	18	16	20	18
17	14	14	18	16	20	18	15	19	17	21	19
18	15	15	19	17	21	19	16	20	18	22	20
19	16	16	20	18	22	20	17	21	19	23	21
20	17	17	21	19	23	21	18	22	20	24	22
21	18	18	22	20	24	22	19	23	21	25	23
22	19	19	23	21	25	23	20	24	22	26	24
23	20	20	24	22	26	24	21	25	23	27	25
24	21	21	25	23	27	25	22	26	24	28	26
25	22	22	26	24	28	26	23	27	25	29	27
26	23	23	27	25	29	27	24	28	26	30	28
27	24	24	28	26	30	28	25	29	27		29
28	25	25	29	27		29	26	30	28		30
29	26	26	30	28		30	27		29		31
30	27	27		29		31	28		30		
31	28	28		30			29		31		
		29		31			30				
		30					31				
		31									

Tinted boxes

Illustrations

Advertisers

Index

364

Maps

Map Symbols

Administration

International Border
State / Province Border
Cease Fire Line

Neighbouring country
Neighbouring state

State Capitals □
Other Towns ○

Roads and travel

Main Roads
(National Highways)
Other Roads

Jeepable Roads, Tracks

Railways with station

Water features

River *Amazon*
Lakes, Reservoirs, Tanks
Seasonal Marshlands
Sand Banks, Beaches
Ocean
Waterfall
Ferry

Topographical features

Contours (approx),
Rock Outcrops
Mountains
Mountain Pass

Gorge
Escarpment
Palm trees

Cities and towns

Built Up Areas
One Way Street
National Parks, Gardens, Stadiums

Fortified Walls
Airport Ⓧ
Banks Ⓢ
Bus Stations (named in key) 🚌
Hospitals ⊕
Market Ⓜ
Police station Ⓟⁱ
Post Office ✉
Telegraphic Office Ⓣ
Tourist Office ⓘ

Key Numbers 1 2 3 4 5

Bridges
Cathedral, church

Guided routes

National parks, trekking areas

National Parks and
Bird Sanctuaries ♦
Hide
Camp site ⛺
Refuge
Motorable track
Walking track

Other symbols

Archaeological Sites ∴
Places of Interest ○
Viewing point

Footprint Handbooks

All of us at Footprint Handbooks hope you have enjoyed reading and travelling with this Handbook, one of the first published in the new Footprint series. Many of you will be familiar with us as Trade & Travel, a name that has served us well for years. For you and for those who have only just discovered the Handbooks, we thought it would be interesting to chronicle the story of our development from the early 1920's.

It all started 75 years ago in 1921, with the publication of the Anglo-South American Handbook. In 1924 the South American Handbook was created. This has been published each year for the last 73 years and is the longest running guidebook in the English language, immortalised by Graham Greene as "the best travel guide in existence".

One of the key strengths of the South American Handbook over the years, has been the extraordinary contact we have had with our readers through their hundreds of letters to us in Bath. From these letters we learnt that you wanted more Handbooks of the same quality to other parts of the world.

In 1989 my brother Patrick and I set about developing a series modelled on the South American Handbook. Our aim was to create the ultimate practical guidebook series for all travellers, providing expert knowledge of far flung places, explaining culture, places and people in a balanced,

lively and clear way. The whole idea hinged, of course, on finding writers who were in tune with our thinking. Serendipity stepped in at exactly the right moment: we were able to bring together a talented group of people who know the countries we cover inside out and whose enthusiasm for travelling in them needed to be communicated.

The series started to grow. We felt that the time was right to look again at the identity that had brought us all this way. After much searching we commissioned London designers Newell & Sorrell to look at all the issues. Their solution was a new identity for the Handbooks representing the books in all their aspects, looking after all the good things already achieved and taking us into the new millennium.

The result is Footprint Handbooks: a new name and mark, simple yet assertive, bold, stylish and instantly recognisable. The images we use conjure up the essence of real travel and communicate the qualities of the Handbooks in a straightforward and evocative way.

And for us here in Bath, it has been an extraordinary exercise working through this dramatic change. Already the 'new us' fits like our favourite travelling clothes and we cannot wait to get more and more Footprint Handbooks onto the book shelves and out onto the road.

The Footprint list

Andalucía Handbook
Cambodia Handbook
Caribbean Islands Handbook
Chile Handbook
East Africa Handbook
Ecuador Handbook
  with the Galápagos
Egypt Handbook
India Handbook
Indonesia Handbook
Laos Handbook
Malaysia & Singapore Handbook
Mexico & Central America
  Handbook
Morocco Handbook
  with Mauritania
Myanmar (Burma) Handbook
Namibia Handbook
Pakistan Handbook
Peru Handbook
South Africa Handbook
South American Handbook
Thailand Handbook
Tibet Handbook
Tunisia Handbook with Libya
Vietnam Handbook

New in Autumn 1997
Bolivia Handbook
Goa Handbook
Israel Handbook
Nepal Handbook
Zimbabwe & Moçambique
  Handbook with Malawi

New in Spring 1998
Argentina Handbook
Brazil Handbook
Colombia Handbook
Cuba Handbook
Jordan, Syria & Lebanon Handbook
Sri Lanka Handbook (new edition)
Venezuela Handbook

Web site
Our website is up and running. Take a look at http://www.footprint-handbooks.co.uk for the latest news, to order a book or to join our mailing list.

Mail Order
Footprint Handbooks are available worldwide in good bookstores. They can also be ordered directly from us in Bath either via the website or via the address below.

Footprint Handbooks
6 Riverside Court
Lower Bristol Road
Bath BA2 3DZ, England
T +44(0)1225 469141
F +44(0)1225 469461
E Mail handbooks@footprint.cix.co.uk